The Palgrave Handbook of International Communication and Sustainable Development

"Muhammad Jameel Yusha'u and Jan Servaes have edited a most significant collection of essays for scholars and practitioners interested in the intersection of communication, international development, and the sustainable development goals. Comprehensive in nature and insightful in breadth, depth, and scope, this diverse volume will appeal to both the expert and the layperson."
—Arvind Singhal, Ph.D., is the Samuel Shirley and Edna Holt Marston *Professor of Communication, The University of Texas at El Paso, USA*

"This new book makes an important addition to the field of international communication and sustainable development because of the wide range of salient and topical subjects covered, and the points of views represented. When we thought that interest in the field was ebbing because of deservedly increasing attention on information technology and artificial intelligence, this new collection comes along to show that communication and development are perennially relevant in our society."
—Professor Charles Okigbo, *North Dakota State University, USA*

"The scenario suggests a thriller. A global pandemic threatens humanity. Who will tackle it? How will it affect life as we know it? What will its consequences be for the future of humankind? Yet, not for the first time in history, it is real-life and no one knows the full extent of the havoc that has been wreaked. Despite advances in technology and research between the Spanish Flu in 1914–1918 and COVID-19 in 2020, the coronavirus still shocked the world. Worse still, the pandemic and its devastating impact has called into question whether the UN's Sustainable Development Goals (SDGs) can be achieved by 2030. This book represents a compilation by leading thinkers in the field of communication for development. It recounts the evolution of the SDGs and various well-established approaches to understanding communication for development, providing international perspectives on the SDGs in various countries.

The editors conclude with several key recommendations based on lessons learned. First, that funding the SDGs remains a huge challenge. Second, that journalism for sustainable development must be deepened. Third, that technology plays a crucial role in development. And fourth, that the timeline for the SDGs has to be reconsidered.

The Palgrave Handbook of International Communication and Sustainable Development calls for a profound rethink of how development takes place on the ground, what its true aims should be, and how genuine communication underlies every one of the Sustainable Development Goals."
—Philip Lee, Co-Editor, *Expanding Shrinking Communication Spaces* (2020)

Muhammad Jameel Yusha'u • Jan Servaes
Editors

The Palgrave Handbook of International Communication and Sustainable Development

palgrave
macmillan

Editors
Muhammad Jameel Yusha'u
Islamic Development Bank
Jeddah, Saudi Arabia

Jan Servaes
KU Leuven
Leuven, Belgium

ISBN 978-3-030-69769-3   ISBN 978-3-030-69770-9 (eBook)
https://doi.org/10.1007/978-3-030-69770-9

© The Editor(s) (if applicable) and The Author(s), under exclusive licence to Springer Nature Switzerland AG 2021
This work is subject to copyright. All rights are solely and exclusively licensed by the Publisher, whether the whole or part of the material is concerned, specifically the rights of translation, reprinting, reuse of illustrations, recitation, broadcasting, reproduction on microfilms or in any other physical way, and transmission or information storage and retrieval, electronic adaptation, computer software, or by similar or dissimilar methodology now known or hereafter developed.
The use of general descriptive names, registered names, trademarks, service marks, etc. in this publication does not imply, even in the absence of a specific statement, that such names are exempt from the relevant protective laws and regulations and therefore free for general use.
The publisher, the authors and the editors are safe to assume that the advice and information in this book are believed to be true and accurate at the date of publication. Neither the publisher nor the authors or the editors give a warranty, expressed or implied, with respect to the material contained herein or for any errors or omissions that may have been made. The publisher remains neutral with regard to jurisdictional claims in published maps and institutional affiliations.

Cover illustration: Daniel Grizelj / Getty images
Cover design: eStudioCalamar

This Palgrave Macmillan imprint is published by the registered company Springer Nature Switzerland AG.
The registered company address is: Gewerbestrasse 11, 6330 Cham, Switzerland

To my father, Shaykh Yusha'u Yusuf and mother, Hajiya Sa'adatu Anas Yusha'u, for being the best parents and for teaching me to respect and stand for other human beings; and in memory of my late uncle, Malam Idris Yusuf, late father in-law, Alhaji Ibrahim Sarkina, and late mother in-law, Hajiya Adama Sarkina.

To Fiona, Lisa, Patchanee, and the millions of people who strive for a sustainable future that is just and equitable, whilst living within the limits of supporting ecosystems.

Preface

The beauty about writing a book is that it evolves, grows, matures and then flourishes. You can see the trajectory of progress from the time it was just an idea, up to the time it lands in the hands of the reader, as it does right now.

This book is no different. The journey started in 2017 while following and attentively listening to a session on digital development on the sidelines of the World Bank Annual Meeting. The event itself was a good example of the power of communication, because it was transmitted live from Washington D.C., and people could watch from every part of the globe on their computers or mobile phones (https://live.worldbank.org/digital-economy-for-development). The session started with a brief discussion between then World Bank President Jim Kim and the co-founder of Airbnb, Joe Gebbia, where they discussed how the digital economy was making massive impact by lifting women out of poverty, helping reconstruct cities and improving lives in different parts of the world.

In the second part of the event on digital development was a panel discussion, and one of the guests was the founder and executive chairman of OneWeb, Greg Wyler. In his opening remarks during the panel discussion, Wyler made a very critical remark about the Sustainable Development Goals (SDGs). Wyler said almost none of the SDGs could be achieved without the internet, yet there was no independent goal in the SDGs about the internet. The comment by Wyler on this major omission to have a goal that addresses the importance of communication as signified by the internet inspired the writing of this book. Wyler was not alone; it is a point raised by many communication scholars and policymakers.

This is a major gap, not just from an industry perspective, but also in a pedagogical sense. There was an evident lack of appreciation on the role of communication in development. A total of 193 countries endorsed the 2030 agenda for development and forgot to make a provision for the oil that will help drive the engine of development. As you will find in the extended discussion in several chapters of this book, the COVID-19 pandemic strengthened our position, due to the role played by communication in managing the pandemic.

The thinking of writing this book got fruition in the summer of 2018 during the International Association of Media and Communication Research (IAMCR) conference in Oregon, United States. A meeting between Muhammad Jameel Yusha'u and Lucy Batrouney of Palgrave Macmillan led to the foundation of this book. It also set the process of the two of us coming together to work on this project for two years non-stop.

As human beings, what we did not and couldn't envisage while preparing this book was that a major historical phenomenon would occur in the middle of the work. It is called COVID-19 Pandemic. COVID-19 made an impact on this project in various ways. Some of the authors had to drop because the intensity of working from home while managing family life was too much to bear. Other contributors also sought for more extension in order to manage the work-life balance.

For us as editors, we had to incorporate the intrusion of COVID-19, and explore how its impact on the SDGs and how the role of communication for development and social change in the wider debate about the 2030 agenda for development will be transformed. We had to keep up to date with information emerging on COVID-19 and at the same time using the updates received to either rewrite or update chapters. It also meant some of the contributors had to make further revisions on their chapters to include information about COVID-19. We salute their resilience for keeping up to the pace of this project.

The reader will find in this book a discussion on why omitting a role for communication as an independent goal among the SDGs was a gigantic omission. A strong case is made in the book on why the SDGs should be revisited to address this oversight. The book contains chapters that provide a critical assessment of the successes recorded, gaps and omissions on several SDGs, financing the SDGs, impact of fake news on the SDGs and how COVID-19 changes the discourse on achieving the SDGs by 2030. An overview is provided on each of the SDGs. Without mincing words, the book has several proposals that are relevant to all stakeholders, including the need to be realistic and revisit the idea of maintaining 2030 as the year to achieve the global goals.

This book is an important resource for communication scholars, development experts, NGOs and civil societies, diplomats and graduate students interested in learning about the intersection between communication and the SDGs. They will find information about strategies for containing pandemics and why major social media firms should take responsibility by taking off fake news completely from their sites. Contributions are quite diverse with chapters about different topics/regions of the world.

We couldn't have done it alone. That is why we want to thank the team at Palgrave Macmillan, especially Lucy Batrouney, Shaun Vigil, Bryony Burns, Mala Sanghera-Warren and Emily Wood; and all the proof readers and revisers at Palgrave/Springer particularly NirmalKumar GnanaPrakasam, Kishor Kannan Ramesh, Shinko Mimura and Sylvia Anand for their support throughout the time it took to finish this book. Also the anonymous reviewers deserve commendation. Their critical input and suggestions made this book better. So also a big thank you to each of the contributors to the book.

Hauwa Sarkina Yusha'u helped a lot with media monitoring, and advice on the coverage of COVID-19 in major international media organisations. Habeeb Pindiga and Bashir Saad, apart from contributing a chapter, always shared an update on the ongoing debate about the SDGs.

Majority of the writing and revision of this book took place under the COVID-19 lockdown. So our families were "locked" in bearing with us throughout the process. Thank you Hauwa, Asma, Aishah, Lisa, Isaac, Fiona and Yai for your patience and support. We thank you for your understanding and unwavering support. This one is done; we just want to "reserve a seat" for the next book project.

We have done our best to present a book that is rich and useful to our readers. We will therefore welcome your feedback for improvement in the future. Views expressed in the book are those of the authors and does not represent the official position of the editors, their employers or the publisher.

We are glad that a vaccine for COVID-19 has been discovered. We remain optimistic about the SDGs despite the challenges of achieving them, and remain confident that COVID-19 too will soon become history.

Thank you

Jeddah, Saudi Arabia Muhammad Jameel Yusha'u
Leuven, Belgium Jan Servaes

Contents

Part I Introduction: Historical and Theoretical Perspectives 1

1 Communication for Sustainable Development in the Age of COVID-19 3
   Muhammad Jameel Yusha'u and Jan Servaes

2 The Sustainable Development Goals: A Major Reboot or Just Another Acronym? 31
   Jan Servaes

3 SDG18—The Missing Ventilator: An Introduction to the 2030 Agenda for Development 53
   Muhammad Jameel Yusha'u

4 Communication for Sustainable Development and Blue Growth: Towards New Theoretical and Empirical Directions 77
   Maria Touri, Fani Galatsopoulou, Clio Kenterelidou, and Ioanna Kostarella

5 A Buddhist Approach to Participatory Communication and Sustainable Development: A Case Study from Lao PDR 101
   Toung Eh. Synuanchanh and Evangelia Papoutsaki

6 Between Rights and Diversities: Can the Regulation of Communication Help Prevent Climate Change and Promote Sustainable Development? 127
   Anthony Löwstedt and Diana Igropoulou

7 Islamic Finance for SDGs: A Mirage? 149
   Hylmun Izhar and Rahmatina A. Kasri

Part II Communicating the Global Goals 169

8 **Community Learning Centre as a Promising Medium for Promoting Sustainable Development Goal 4: Lifelong Learning** 171
Gwadabe Kurawa

9 **Communicating Sustainable Development in Higher Education: Evaluation of Education Experiences and Proposals for Teachers' Orientation** 193
Noelia Santamaría-Cárdaba and Miguel Vicente-Mariño

10 **Media, Literacy and Education: Partners for Sustainable Development** 215
Carla Patrão, Dina Soeiro, and Sílvia Parreiral

11 **The Paradox in Discourse and Praxis of Gender Equality: A Communicative Framework for Sustainable Development** 235
Mohammad Ala-Uddin

12 **Achieving Sustainable Development Goals: An Analytical Overview of Indian Experience (2000–2019)** 259
C. S. H. N. Murthy

13 **Fostering Gender-Sensitive Programming and Practices Among Community Radios in India: The Road Ahead** 289
Kanchan K. Malik

14 **Miscommunication of Harms? A Critique of SDG 12: Responsible Consumption and Production Implementation in the Food Sector in Northern Ireland** 305
Ekaterina Gladkova

15 **Fake News and SDG16: The Situation in Ghana** 325
Kobby Mensah, Gideon Awini, and Gilbert Kofi Mensah

16 **Communication for Sustainable Social Change and the Pursuit of Zero Hunger: The Food Sovereignty Language Frame** 345
Joshua J. Frye and Samantha Stone

17 Internet Philanthropy as China's 'Digital Solution' to the 2030 Agenda for Sustainable Development: Policies, Practices, Politics and Critique   371
    Jian Xu, Dianlin Huang, and He Zhang

18 Facts Aren't Enough: Addressing Communication Challenges in the Pollinator Crisis and Beyond   393
    Lara Zwarun and Gerardo R. Camilo

Part III International Communication, Journalism and Sustainable Development   425

19 Egyptian TV Coverage of the Sustainable Development Strategy (SDS): Egypt Vision 2030   427
    Alamira Samah Saleh and Mahmoud Zaky

20 SDG #3: Communicating "Health for All" in German-Speaking Countries as Exemplified by HIV/AIDS Advertising Campaigns   449
    Isabell Koinig, Sandra Diehl, and Franzisca Weder

21 Global Communication and Sustainable Development: From the Earth Summit in Rio 1992 to the Olympic Games in Rio 2016   487
    Radoslaw Sajna-Kunowsky

22 A Comparative Analysis of American and Chinese News Media Coverage of Climate Change Issues over the Period 2007–2015   507
    Won Y. Jang, Edward Frederick, Eric Jamelske, Wontae Lee, and Youngju Kim

23 Running Ahead: Trump's Presidency and Climate Change Discourses. Has Trump's Presidency Changed Climate Change Discourses?: A Text Mining Analysis of Newspaper Contents in the United States   533
    Kenneth C. C. Yang and Yowei Kang

24 Communicating Development: News Coverage of the SDGs in the Nigerian Press   559
    Habeeb Idris Pindiga and Bashir Sa'ad Abdullahi

25 Selected Journalists' Role Perception Towards Achieving
    Agenda 2030 in Nigeria   585
    Taye C. Obateru

Part IV   Conclusion   603

26 Beyond the SDGs: From 2030 to 2050 Agenda for
    Development   605
    Muhammad Jameel Yusha'u and Jan Servaes

Index   621

Notes on Contributors

Mohammad Ala-Uddin is a lecturer in the School of Communication Studies at James Madison University, USA, and a PhD candidate in the School of Media and Communication at Bowling Green State University, USA. He investigates the intersection of global communication, digital media and social change. Ala-Uddin is particularly interested in understanding the role of digital technology in expanding the democratic capabilities of citizens and communities. His research, well rooted in communication, also takes on a multidisciplinary approach, looking to media and cultural studies, political economy, feminist theory, subaltern studies, critical ethnography, critical data studies and digital humanities. Ala-Uddin's research has been published in the journal of *Asia Pacific Media Educator* while he also serves as an ad hoc reviewer for a variety of journals, including *New Media and Society*, *Journal of Creative Communication* and *Society and Media in South Asia*. A former NORAD (The Norwegian Agency for Development Cooperation) fellow, journalist and community organiser, Ala-Uddin commits his works towards achieving the broad goals of social justice and empowerment.

Gideon Awini is a PhD student in Marketing at the University of Ghana Business School, Ghana. He holds a Bachelor of Science degree in Administration and a Master of Philosophy degree in Marketing from the University of Ghana Business School. His research interests are in the areas of sports marketing, consumer behaviour and communication. He has over ten years' experience in public relations, brand management and banking.

Gerardo R. Camilo holds a PhD from Texas Tech University, USA. He is Professor of Biology at Saint Louis University, USA, where he researches the ecology and conservation of native bees in urban environments. His research also addresses how aspects of socio-economic and cultural norms can influence bee diversity. Camilo is a senior conservation fellow of the St. Louis Zoo.

Sandra Diehl obtained her PhD from Saarland University, Germany. She is an associate professor and head of the Department of Media and Communications at the University of Klagenfurt, Austria. Her research interests include CSR and health communication, international and intercultural advertising, as well as media and convergence management. Diehl has written in journals such as the *International Journal of Advertising*, *Journal of Business Research*, *Media and Psychology*, *Advances in International Marketing*, *Advances in Consumer Research*, *International Marketing Review* and *European Advances in Consumer Research*. She has authored and edited several books, among them the *Advances in Advertising Research* and the *Handbook of Integrated CSR Communication*. She is a board member of the European Advertising Academy and conference manager.

Edward Frederick is Professor of Communication with an emphasis in public relations at the University of Wisconsin-Whitewater, USA. He is the co-author on several articles that applied the "Spiral of Silence" to explore the impact of news coverage and social media on the public expression of opinions about controversial political issues. He has also co-authored several articles about third-person and first-person effects studies that argued for the addition of a third concept, the second-person effect. His current research is examining opinion expression about controversial gender issues in online and offline communication settings in the Arab Gulf states. Frederick teaches courses in strategic planning and research and mass media and public opinion.

Joshua J. Frye has been working in grassroots community development and transforming food systems for over two decades. He served as a Sustainable Agriculture Extension Agent with the U.S. Peace Corps from 1997 to 1999 in Honduras. When he returned from Honduras he worked for three years in Madison, Wisconsin, on anti-hunger and food security programming in the non-profit sector. In 2007 he received a PhD from Purdue University, USA, where he secured a university-wide dissertation fellowship to work on the transnational framing of the organic agriculture movement. From 2007 to 2015 he was an associate professor in the SUNY system in upstate New York where he served on the Board of Directors for the Center for Agricultural Development and Entrepreneurship and developed sustainability education workshops for SUNY faculty across New York state. He is Professor of Communication at Humboldt State University where he has held an appointment with the Arcata City Council Committee on Agriculture and Open Spaces and collaborated on an applied community research project to develop a PBS documentary—*Locally Grown*—on the sustainable food system of the Northern California coast. When he is not in contract with the state of California, he works with a non-profit environmental education organisation leading programmes at Dartmouth College and in Ecuador and Costa Rica dedicated to creating the next generation of environmental leaders.

Fani Galatsopoulou is a senior teaching fellow and researcher at the School of Journalism and Mass Communications, Aristotle University of Thessaloniki,

Greece. She is an education specialist in the fields of lifelong continuing education and adult professional training. Her main research interests lie in the fields of formal and informal education and vocational training, digital media and communication, sustainable tourism and travel, ocean literacy and blue growth. She designs training syllabi and develops educational material for e-learning courses, open courses, seminars, semester courses and summer schools. She is a certified trainer for adult education and has participated in several research projects, collaborations, conferences and conventions about media literacy, tourism and communication, lifelong continuing training in travel and tourism. Her latest research and publications focus on nautical tourism, university-business collaboration for blue growth, travel journalism & environmental communication, and special forms of sustainable tourism.

Ekaterina Gladkova is Doctoral Researcher in Green Criminology in the Department of Social Sciences (Criminology) at the Northumbria University in Newcastle upon Tyne, UK. Gladkova's doctoral project focuses on the links between intensive food production financing and environmental injustice. It turns to strategies adopted by the local community in their struggle to resist environmental and social harms associated with intensive farming, and considers institutional assemblages behind intensive farming projects. Her previous research concentrated on environmental governance and climate change governance in the Chilean Antarctic.

Dianlin Huang is an associate professor at Communication University of China, China. He received two PhDs in Communications Studies from Communication University of China and Macquarie University. His academic research areas include Chinese media and social transformation, media and underprivileged groups and critical communication studies, with a particular interest on cultural practices and power relations in the context of contemporary China. His main publications include *The Construction of Citizenship: News Discourses and Migrant Workers in China* (2017), *China Review of Journalism and Communication Studies* (2014) and two translated books (Vincent Mosco's *Digital Sublime*, 2010 and Hall et al.'s *Policing the Crisis*, Eastern China Normal University Press). Other major publications include journal papers and book chapters published in China and overseas. He is also a columnist for *Guangming Daily*, one of the most important national newspapers in China.

Diana Igropoulou is with the Department of Media Communications at Webster Vienna Private University, Austria. Her areas of research interest include transnational media/tech policies and international development. She is enrolled in MA, Media Communications, in the Department of Social Sciences at City University London, UK.

Hylmun Izhar, Ph.D. is an internationally renowned Islamic finance expert, strategist and financial economist with over 17 years of experience in Islamic finance, strategy development and capacity building across Europe, Middle East, Africa and Asia. He possesses a sound understanding of economic issues and challenges, familiarity with industry players/stakeholders and has an in-depth experience of working with Shari'ah-compliant financial institutions, government bodies and infrastructure-enabling organisations. Izhar is a Senior Economist at Islamic Research and Training Institute, Islamic Development Bank Group. Previously, he was a lecturer at the Markfield Institute of Higher Education (MIHE), Leicester, UK, following a fellowship at the Oxford Centre for Islamic Studies (OXCIS), Oxford, UK. He was honoured with the "2017 Upcoming Personality in Global Islamic Finance" at the annual Global Islamic Finance Awards. His works have appeared in numerous reputable publications and journals including Palgrave and the *Journal of Risk*. He is the co-author of *I for Impact: Blending Islamic Finance and Impact Investing for the Global Goals* and textbook titled *Islamic Capital Markets: Principles and Practices*. He has also contributed to prominent events such as the Harvard Islamic Finance Forum and Durham Islamic Finance Summer School. He holds a PhD in Islamic Finance from Durham University, UK, and an MA (*with distinction*) in Islamic Finance from Loughborough University, UK.

Eric Jamelske is Professor of Economics at the University of Wisconsin, Eau Claire, USA. His writings about climate change issues and policy have appeared in the *Journal of Environmental Studies and Sciences, Climatic Change, International Journal of Climate Change Impacts and Responses, Environmental Economics & Policy Studies* and *Climate Policy*. His current research interests include investigating international climate change views focusing on China and the USA as well as examining health and nutrition issues for children and low-income households regarding fruit and vegetable intake. He teaches courses in microeconomics, environmental economics and health economics.

Won Y. Jang is Professor of Integrated Strategic Communication at the University of Wisconsin, Eau Claire, USA. His writings about communications have appeared in *Communication Theory, Journal of International Communication, Handbook of International and Intercultural Communication, Sage Handbook of Propaganda, International Communication Gazette, Media International Australia* and *Journal of Environmental Studies and Science*, among others. His current research interests include global communication issues, relationships between media and society in East Asian societies, health communication across borders and political communication. He teaches courses on research methodology, strategic communication, international communication and media law.

Yowei Kang is an assistant professor with Bachelor Degree Programme in Oceanic Cultural Creative Design Industries at National Taiwan Ocean University, Taiwan. Kang's research interests focus on digital game technologies and rhetorical analysis. He has written and presented papers that examine digital discourses in MMORPGs (massive multiplayer online role-playing games), digital in-game literacy, persuasion in advertising, rhetoric of technology and consumer behaviours.

Rahmatina A. Kasri is the Director of Islamic Economics and Business Center (PEBS) at the Faculty of Economics and Business, Universitas Indonesia (FEB UI), Indonesia. Previously, she was the Director of Islamic Economics Undergraduate Programme at the same institution. In addition, she serves as the Regional Head of Indonesian Association of Islamic Economists (IAEI) of DKI Jakarta Province and is a member of Central Board of Islamic Economic Society (DPP-MES). She also acts as an associate editor at the *International Journal of Islamic and Middle Eastern Finance and Management* (Scopus-indexed journal) as well as being a reviewer in a number of national and international journals. She specialises in Islamic economics and finance as well as development economics in general, with experience in academic and practical fields. In the academic field, she taught various courses and executive trainings particularly related to the basics of Islamic economics and finance, Islamic public finance, history of Islamic economic thoughts as well as fundamentals of Islamic social finance (zakat, waqf and Islamic microfinance). Her works has also been published in a number of book chapters, various national/international conferences and several reputable journals including SCOPUS-indexed international journals. Aside from the academic works, she is also involved in a number of research projects, policy assessments and advocacies with national and international institutions. Due to her contributions, in 2019, she was chosen as the top 40 most influential women in Islamic business and finance by Cambridge IFA, UK. She holds a PhD in Islamic Economics and Finance from Durham University, UK (2015), and an MBA in Islamic Banking and Finance from International Islamic University Malaysia (2008), in which she also received an award as the best student from the reputable university. Prior to that, she also obtained her MA in International and Development Economics from the Australian National University (2005) and BA in Economics from Faculty of Economics and Business Universitas, Indonesia (2002).

Clio Kenterelidou, Economist and Communications Specialist, is a tenured senior teaching instructor and research scientist at the School of Journalism and Mass Communications, Aristotle University of Thessaloniki, Greece. She has significant academic and professional experience as head of communications and freelance journalist in public and political communication, communications strategy, participation-development-public relations, strategic planning and on-site education. She has participated in international research initiatives; has written in journals, conference proceedings and books; and has co-edited collective volumes—all in the fields of communication, journalism and the media. She is also professionally involved as an accredited-certified expert in adult education/training at strategic institutions for executives of public administration and local self-government and in election observation for

EU, UN and Organization for Security and Cooperation in Europe (OSCE)/ Office for Democratic Institutions and Human Rights (ODIHR). She is an expert of the European Commission for Research and Innovation, for Communication, of the Hellenic General Secretariat of Research and Technology and of the European Communication Monitor (EUPRERA & European Association of Communication Directors).

Youngju Kim received her PhD from Sogang University, South Korea. She is a senior researcher and director of media research centre at Korea Press Foundation. Her research interests include change of audience behaviours, business strategies of news media in the digital media ecosystem.

Isabell Koinig received her PhD from the University of Klagenfurt, Austria. She is a postdoctoral researcher in the Department of Media and Communications at the Alpen-Adria University of Klagenfurt, Austria. She just finished her dissertation investigating how different pharmaceutical advertising appeals were received in a cross-cultural context. Her research interests predominantly concern the areas of health communication (pharmaceutical advertising, health campaigns, mHealth/eHealth), intercultural advertising, organisational health as well as media and convergence management.

Ioanna Kostarella is an assistant professor at the School of Journalism and Mass Communications, Aristotle University of Thessaloniki, Greece. She has had a long professional experience as a press officer for the local government. She was involved in media monitoring, crisis management and public relations with stakeholders. She has also worked as a journalist for local and national media. Kostarella has contributed to various research papers in journals, refereed conference proceedings and authored chapters in books. She has participated in several international scientific conferences, meetings, collaborations and research programmes in the field of communication and journalism. She speaks English, German and Italian and her research interests include journalism and new media, the interaction between media and foreign policy, European media and environmental communication.

Gwadabe Kurawa is an independent researcher and a member of Inclusive Education Task Team: Inter-agency Network for Education in Emergencies (INEE). He has extensive experience working in mainstream and challenging schools, colleges and universities in the UK and Nigeria. His teaching experience includes undergraduate and postgraduate supervision levels. He is now with University of Bristol and his research interests are in the areas of inclusive education, conflict and development. His programmes, at the Centre for Comparative and International Research in Education, focus on identifying and removing the barriers faced by all children, including the most vulnerable groups, not only in terms of their access, but their participation and achievement in education in alignment with Sustainable Development Goal (SDG) 4. His experience extends across all levels of the system from policy development, through curriculum development to service delivery. He is published widely, including authoring and co-authoring chapters in books and a series of articles in journals.

Wontae Lee is a research fellow at KISDI (Korea Information Society Development Institute), where he studies, develops and supports ICT policies for the Korean Government. He received a Doctorate in Political Science from Sogang University, Korea. Since then he has written a number of papers and books on Internet political participation, artificial intelligence ethics and algorithm regulation.

Anthony Löwstedt is Assistant Professor of Media Communications at Webster Vienna Private University, Austria. He has written extensively on media ethics, media and globalisation, the development of communication and media regulation. He has also worked for human rights organisations, as a media consultant to the United Nations Development Programme, and also taught at Webster University Geneva, the Austrian Media Academy in Salzburg and Birzeit University in Palestine.

Kanchan K. Malik is a professor in the Department of Communication at the University of Hyderabad, India, where she also served as the head from January 2017 to 2020. She is also a faculty fellow with the UNESCO Chair on Community Media since 2011 and editor of the newsletter—*CR News*. She is teaching postgraduate Journalism and Mass Communication courses for over 23 years now. She obtained her PhD in Communication from the University of Hyderabad in 2006. Her widely cited co-authored book with Prof. Vinod Pavarala, *Other Voices: The Struggle for Community Radio in India* (2007), documents the civil society endeavours for the third tier of broadcasting in India and freeing of the airwaves. The global edition of her recently published co-edited book *Community Radio in South Asia: Reclaiming the Airwaves* (2020) is now available and the South Asia edition will be out in October, 2020. With dual Masters in Economics and Mass Communication, she worked as a journalist with *The Economic Times*, New Delhi, for two years before settling for a career in academics. She has worked on several research projects and written research papers on media interventions by non-governmental organisations for empowerment at the grassroots level. Her research has also contributed to policy advocacy efforts for community radio in India. She has also authored reports and scholarly articles on, among others, the gender dimension of community radio as well as on the codes of practice for community media, in leading publications. She worked on the research *Religions, Ethics and Attitudes Towards Corruption* as part of the Religions and Development project of the University of Birmingham. She was awarded the United States federal grant by the U.S. Consulate General Hyderabad to develop an academic curriculum on Media Ethics in collaboration SUNY Plattsburgh Department of Communication Studies. Her scholastic and research interests include community radio, women in community communications, journalism studies, media laws & ethics and communication for social change.

Gilbert Kofi Mensah is a teaching assistant and a researcher at the University of Ghana Business School, Ghana. He holds a Master of Philosophy degree in Marketing and a member of the Chartered Institute of Administrators and Management Consultants—Ghana (CIAMC). His research interests are in social media analytics, political branding and marketing communications. He also has acquired industry knowledge from diverse fields within the marketing domain.

Kobby Mensah is a senior lecturer at the University of Ghana Business School, Ghana. Mensah believes in evidence-led, hands-on and collaborative teaching and research. His current edited book *Political Marketing and Management in Ghana: A New Architecture* was published by Palgrave Macmillan, UK. His teaching and research interests are in political marketing, political communication, advocacy and business-government relationship and social media. Mensah is a leading expert in political marketing in Africa and has been responsible for the growing interest in the field in Ghana. He is a prominent voice globally on creating awareness of Africa's emergence in the political marketing space. His opinion is engaged by local and international media such as the BBC, *Financial Times* (*FT*), Deutsche Welle (DW) and SABC amongst other news brands. Mensah obtained his PhD in Journalism from the University of Sheffield, UK, and an MSc in International Marketing from the Sheffield Hallam University, UK. He is a Chartered Marketer (CIM, UK). Mensah is a member of Political Marketing Specialist Group (PMSG) of the Political Studies Association (PSA). He is also a member of Palgrave Macmillan Board on Political Marketing Management Book Series.

C. S. H. N. Murthy, Ph.D. is Professor of Media and Film Studies. He has served as an assistant professor and media expert for the Ministry of Education, Government of Eritrea, sub-Saharan Africa, during 2003–2005. He has taught in several private and government universities in India and abroad. He has written more than 25 papers in peer-reviewed international journals on different areas of media studies. He was an associate of Singapore Internet Research Centre, Wee Kim Wee School of Communication, Nanyang Technological University (NTU), Singapore, during 2011–2014. He is also on the editorial board of *Asia Pacific Media Educator* (Sage) and *Communication Studies* (Taylor and Francis during 2011–2014) and *Mediterranean Journal of Social Sciences* (published from Italy).

Taye C. Obateru is a senior lecturer in the Department of Mass Communication, University of Jos, Nigeria, where he has taught since 2000. He obtained his PhD from the University of Salford, UK, and holds two Master's degrees: one in International Journalism from Edinburgh Napier University, Scotland, and the other in Law and Diplomacy from the University of Jos, Nigeria. He has over 25 years' experience as a journalist serving as

Regional Editor for *Vanguard*, one of Nigeria's top newspapers for many years. He has over 15 chapters/articles in books and journals. He had served as an editorial consultant to *GTZ* in Nigeria and the National Centre for Remote Sensing, Jos. His research interests cover media and journalism studies, mass media law and ethics and political communication.

Evangelia Papoutsaki, Ph.D. is an associate professor at the University of Central Asia, Kyrgyzstan, and editor-in-chief of *Unitec ePress*. She specialises in communication for development and social change with international development experience in the former Soviet Union and Asia Pacific regions. She has an extensive publication and research record, including three volumes on Pacific development communication issues and involvement in regional and international research projects employing indigenous and participatory research methodologies.

Sílvia Parreiral is a sociologist with a Master's and Doctorate in Education Sciences. He is a researcher at the Center for Interdisciplinary Studies of the 20th Century, University of Coimbra, Portugal.

Carla Patrão holds a PhD in Information Sciences and Technologies in the field of Education for Journalism in the New Media at the Faculty of Sciences and Technology, University of Coimbra, Portugal. She is a researcher at Center for Informatics and Systems of the University of Coimbra and collaborator of CINEP—Center for Innovation and Study of Education in Higher Education. She is a lecturer in the area of Communication Sciences, Organisations and Media, vice-president of the Technical and Scientific Council, director of the degree in Media Studies at the Higher Education School of the Polytechnic Institute of Coimbra and coordinator of the *Letters for Life* Project.

Habeeb Idris Pindiga is Doctoral candidate in Media and Communication at the University of Leicester, UK. His doctoral project investigates the political-economic factors shaping the content and journalistic practices of Nigerian newspapers. Pindiga is a former editor of Nigeria's *Daily Trust* newspaper where he worked first as a reporter before rising through the ranks. He also served as an acting editor for the newspaper's weekend titles, *Weekly Trust* and *Sunday Trust*. He holds a Master's degree in Communications, Media and Public Relations. His previous published research explored the political significance and implications of media framing of presidential illness. His areas of research interest include news production, development communication and media systems.

Bashir Sa'ad Abdullahi is Doctoral Researcher in Media Studies at Communications and Media Research Institute (CAMRI), University of Westminster, UK. Sa'ad Abdullahi's doctoral research focuses on mis- and disinformation ecosystem in Africa, with particular focus on "fake news" and its impact on journalism, governance and coexistence in Nigeria. Bashir Sa'ad Abdullahi was a former editor of the BBC World Service's Abuja bureau in

Nigeria. His previous research focused on new media, development and political communication. Bashir Sa'ad Abdullahi holds a Master's degree in Journalism and another Master's degree in Business Administration.

Radoslaw Sajna-Kunowsky is an assistant professor and head of the Department of Journalism, New Media and Communication at the Kazimierz Wielki University, Bydgoszcz, Poland. He holds an MA in Journalism and a PhD in Political Science from the University of Warsaw, and a post-doc title of "Dr hab." in Political Communication from the University of Wroclaw. Sajna is the author of several books and more than 60 scientific articles in Polish, English and Spanish, published in academic journals and books. He specialises in media systems, political, international and global communication. He is a member of, among others, the IECA (International Environmental Communication Association) and IAMCR (International Association for Media and Communication Research). He was a visiting professor at Granada University, Spain, in 2008 and Kadir Has University, Istanbul, Turkey, in 2012.

Alamira Samah Saleh is an associate professor, media consultant for Cairo University's president and acting dean of Faculty of Mass Communication, Sinai University, Egypt, with more than 17 years of extensive experience in several capacities and media institutes. Saleh holds a PhD in Public Opinion and Collective Insecurity from Cairo University. She was a postdoctoral fellow in both the University of Westminster and Birmingham City University, UK. Among her latest research projects is the one funded by Cairo University on "Social Media Policies in Arab Universities" campuses. Saleh's most recent publications are: Impact of romantic Facebook "crush pages" on the Egyptian youth, *Journal of Humanities and Applied Social Sciences*, 2020. Foreign correspondents between the hammer and the anvil: The case of Egypt during political transitions, *Contemporary Arab Affairs*, 2020. Digitalism, Capitalism, and the contemporary transformation in the academic work: An evaluative study of the risks & opportunities, *Arab, Media & Society*, 2020. Activists' Character Attack in Egypt: ElBaradei as Target, *The Routledge Handbook of Character Assassination and Reputation Management*, 2019. *Dynamics of the Diasporic Syrian Media in Egypt*, Palgrave Macmillan. Saleh's main research interest is the Middle East's media policies and practices with particular reference to its socio-political context and impact on the audience's individual and collective security and freedom.

Noelia Santamaría-Cárdaba holds a PhD scholarship (Predoctoral FPU) in the Department of Sociology and Social Work at the Faculty of Social, Legal and Communication Sciences, University of Valladolid, Spain. She is enrolled at the PhD programme in Transdisciplinary Research in Education, after completing her Grade Primary Education, with a mention in Environment, Nature and Society, and a Master's programme in Social Sciences' Research at the University of Valladolid. She is a member of the Research Group on Education Research and Innovation in Education and Higher Education

Teaching. Her research lines are: "Education for development, Sustainable Development and Education for peace and equality".

Jan Servaes obtained a PhD from the Catholic University of Louvain, Belgium, in 1987. He was UNESCO Chair in Communication for Sustainable Social Change. He has taught International Communication and Communication for Social Change in Australia, Belgium, China, Hong Kong, the United States, The Netherlands and Thailand, in addition to several teaching stints at about 120 universities in 55 countries. Servaes is editor-in-chief of the Elsevier journal *Telematics and Informatics: An Interdisciplinary Journal on the Social Impacts of New Technologies* (http://www.elsevier.com/locate/tele), and an editor of the Lexington Book Series *Communication, Globalization and Cultural Identity* (https://rowman.com/Action/SERIES/LEX/LEXCGC), and the Springer Book Series *Communication, Culture and Change in Asia* (http://www.springer.com/series/13565). Servaes has undertaken research, development and advisory work around the world and is the author of journal articles and books on topics such as international and development communication; ICT and media policies; intercultural communication; participation and social change; and human rights and conflict management. He is known for his coinage of "multiplicity paradigm" in *Communication for Development: One World, Multiple Cultures* (1999). Some of his book titles include: (2016) Servaes, Jan & Oyedemi, Toks (Eds.) *The Praxis of Social Inequality in Media: A Global Perspective.* Lanham, MD; (2016) Servaes, Jan & Oyedemi, Toks (Eds.) *Social Inequalities, Media, and Communication: Theory and Roots.* Lanham, MD; (2014) Jan Servaes (Ed.). *Technological Determinism and Social Change.* Lanham; (2014) Jan Servaes and Patchanee Malikhao. *Communication for Social Change* (in Chinese). Wuhan: Wuhan University Press; (2013) Jan Servaes (Ed.). *Sustainable Development and Green Communication. African and Asian Perspectives,* London/New York: Palgrave Macmillan; (2013) J. Servaes (Ed.). *Sustainability, Participation and Culture in Communication. Theory and Praxis.* Bristol-Chicago; (2008) J. Servaes. *Communication for Development and Social Change.* Los Angeles, London, New Delhi, Singapore; (2007) J. Servaes & Liu S. (Eds.). *Moving Targets. Mapping the Paths Between Communication, Technology and Social Change in Communities.* Penang; (2006) P. Thomas & J. Servaes (Eds.). *Intellectual Property Rights and Communications in Asia.* New Delhi; (2006) J. Servaes & N. Carpentier (Eds.). *Towards A Sustainable European Information Society,* ECCR Book Series. Bristol; (2005) Shi-Xu, Kienpointner M. & J. Servaes (Eds.). *Read the Cultural Other: Forms of Otherness in the Discourses of Hong Kong's Decolonisation.* Berlin; (2003) J. Servaes (Ed.). *The European Information Society: A Reality Check,* ECCR Book Series. Bristol; (2003) J. Servaes (Ed.). *Approaches to Development. Studies on Communication for Development,* Paris; and (2002) J. Servaes. *Communication for Development: One World, Multiple Cultures,* Cresskill NJ.

Dina Soeiro is a lecturer in the area of Psychology and Educational Sciences at the Higher Education School of the Polytechnic Institute of Coimbra, Portugal, and a board member of the European Association for the Education of Adults. She is a researcher at Center for Informatics and Systems of the University of Coimbra and collaborator of CINEP—Center for Innovation and Study of Education in Higher Education. She coordinates intervention projects with elderly people in the degrees in social pedagogy and social gerontology, like *Letters for Life*.

Samantha Stone received a Bachelor's degree in Environmental Studies in 2019 from Humboldt State University (HSU), USA, where she emphasised on the geopolitics of local and global food systems, white hegemony in alternative food movements, and intersections of identity and community organising. She has worked in several education positions through college with HSU's Waste Reduction and Resource Awareness Program and created and facilitated a public workshop series on white privilege and the environment. She is planning to attend graduate school for creative writing.

Toung Eh. Synuanchanh is an ordained Buddhist novice and holds a Postgraduate degree in International Communication from Unitec, New Zealand. His research interests are in Buddhism as an alternative participatory communication practice in sustainable community development in Southeast Asia.

Maria Touri is Lecturer in Communication Studies at the School of Media, Communication and Sociology, University of Leicester, UK. Her research interests lie in the areas of participatory communication practices and alternative media. Her current research focuses on Communication for Development and Social Change (CDSC) in the context of the global food economy and food networks, and on the capacity building of communities in the global South. She is also exploring the role of communication in sustainable development and alternative economic spaces. Her previous work has focused on participatory journalism practices, and the impact of online tools on journalism in Greece. She has written in international journals including the *Journal of International Communication*, *Development in Practice* and *Journalism: Theory, Practice and Criticism*.

Miguel Vicente-Mariño is an associate professor and head of the Department of Sociology and Social Work at the Faculty of Social, Legal and Communication Sciences, University of Valladolid, Spain. He holds a PhD in Audiovisual Communication, a BA in Sociology and in Journalism. He is a member of the Executive Committee of ECREA (European Communication Research and Education Association), deputy director of the Audience section of IAMCR (International Association for Media and Communication Research) and of the Working Group on the History of Communication Research of the Spanish Association of Communication Research. His research topics include the study of mass and social media audiences, environmental communication, public opinion formation processes and communication research methods.

Franzisca Weder obtained her PhD from the Catholic University of Eichstaett-Ingolstadt, Germany. She is a lecturer at the University of Queensland, Australia, and an associate professor at the University of Klagenfurt, Austria (on leave). Her research focuses on organisational communication and PR, public relations research, corporate social responsibility and especially sustainability and environmental communication. She worked as a visiting professor at the University of Alabama, USA; the Catholic University of Eichstaett-Ingolstadt, Germany; the University of Waikato, Hamilton, New Zealand; Royal Melbourne Institute of Technology (RMIT), Melbourne, Australia; and the University of Ilmenau, Germany. Weder is chairwoman of the Austrian Society for Communication Science (ÖGK) and vice-president of the International Environmental Communication Association (IECA).

Jian Xu is Lecturer in Communication in the School of Communication and Creative Arts, Deakin University, Australia. He researches Chinese media politics and culture with a particular focus on digital media. He is the author of *Media Events in Web 2.0 China: Interventions of Online Activism* (2016) and co-editor of *Chinese Social Media: Social, Cultural and Political Implications* (2018). His publications have appeared in *Journal of Contemporary China*, *Asian Studies Review* and *Environmental Communication*.

Kenneth C. C. Yang is a professor in the Department of Communication at the University of Texas, El Paso, USA. Yang's research and teaching interests are emerging information-communication technologies, new media and advertising and consumer behaviour.

Muhammad Jameel Yusha'u is a Lead Strategic Coordinator with the Chief Product and Partnership Officer Directorate at the Islamic Development Bank. He was the Managing Editor of *Africa Policy Journal* and the author of *Regional Parallelism and Corruption Scandals in Nigeria* (Palgrave Macmillan 2018). He was Senior Lecturer in Media and Politics at Northumbria University, Newcastle upon Tyne, UK; a former producer at the BBC World Service, London; Associate Lecturer in Global Journalism at the University of Sheffield; British Correspondent of Deutsche Welle (Hausa Service), as well as Lecturer in Mass Communication at Bayero University, Kano, Nigeria. He holds a PhD in Journalism Studies and an MA in Political Communication from the University of Sheffield, UK, and an MBA from IE Business School, Madrid, Spain. Yusha'u is an alumnus of the Executive Education Programme in Innovation and Entrepreneurship: Policy Considerations, JF Kennedy School of Government, Harvard University, and the Silicon Valley Executive Education Programme in Innovation and Entrepreneurship, Haas School of Business, University of California, Berkeley. His research has been published in leading journals such as *Global Media and Communication*, *African Journalism Studies*, *Journal of African Media Studies* and the *Journal of Arab and Muslim Media Research*. He has written several book chapters on online journalism, corruption and the media, critical discourse analysis and representation of Muslims in the media.

Mahmoud Zaky is an assistant lecturer in the Faculty of Mass Communication at Sinai University, Egypt, where he has been a faculty member since 2019. Zaky completed his undergraduate studies and his Masters at Cairo University. His research interests lie in the area of developmental television, ranging from theory to design to implementation. He has written several articles in Arabic journals about recent research methods such as "Netnography as Qualitative cultural analysis method". In addition, he has collaborated actively with researchers in several other disciplines of Statistics Science, particularly developing solutions to statistical problems faced by several media organisations. Zaky organised a workshop in scientific research methods for novice scholars. Zaky has a previous experience in media research; he previously worked for ten years as a researcher at Arab Radio and Television (ART) channels network. He also passed several online exams in research methodology that made him fully educated and trained to help in teaching research methods and applied statistics. He also worked in the media centre of the Egyptian Ministry of Transport during 2010, where he was responsible for preparing the Ministry's image reports in various media outlets. He is acting as a monitoring unit manager, and also as a quality assurance manager in Sinai University.

He Zhang is a Lecturer in the School of Journalism and Communication, Northwest University, China. She holds a PhD in Media Studies from Curtin University, Australia. Her research focuses on how non-specialist citizen's take-up of digital technology, especially new media technologies, constitutes the practice of cultural citizenship in the digital age.

Lara Zwarun holds a PhD from the University of California, Santa Barbara, USA. She is a University of Missouri System Presidential Engagement Fellow and Associate Professor of Communication at the University of Missouri–St. Louis, USA. Her research focuses on the effects of persuasive media messages, taking into consideration not only their design but the demands of the environment on the audience's motivation and ability to process them.

Abbreviations

ABC	Australian Broadcasting Corporation
BBC	British Broadcasting Corporation
CLC	Community Learning Centre
CLCs	Community Learning Centres
COBET	Complimentary Basic Education
EFA	Education for All
ICBAE	Integrated Community-Based Adult Education
ICT	Information and Communication Technology
IE	Informal Education
IFRC	International Federation of Red Cross and Red Crescent Societies
IGAs	Income Generation Activities
IPPE	Integrated Post-Primary Education
KBC	Kenya Broadcasting Corporation
MDG2	Millennium Development Goal 2
MDGs	Millennium Development Goals
NFE	Non-formal Education
NGOs	Non-governmental Organisations
NTA	Nigeria Television Authority
ODL	Open and Distance Learning
OEC	Office of the Education Council
OECD	Organisation for Economic Co-operation and Development
ONIE	Office of Non-Formal and Informal Education
PISA	Programme for International Student Assessment
REFLECT	Regenerated Freirean Literacy through Empowering Community Techniques
SABC	South African Broadcasting Corporation
SDG4	Sustainable Development Goal 4
SDGs	Sustainable Development Goals
SEP	Sufficiency Economy Philosophy
UIL	UNESCO Institute for Lifelong Learning
UN	United Nations

UN DESD	United Nations Decade of Education for Sustainable Development
UNESCO	United Nations Educational, Scientific and Cultural Organization
UNICEF	United Nations International Children's Emergency Fund
WCED	World Commission on Environment and Development
WEF	World Education Forum

List of Figures

Fig. 1.1	**Cover of *The Economist* of 21 March 2020** following the global lockdown in over 100 countries	11
Fig. 1.2	WHO Director General Dr. Tedros, during COVID-19 media briefing in Geneva, Switzerland	16
Fig. 1.3	*Inside Story* about COVID-19 on Aljazeera English TV Network	19
Fig. 1.4	CNN COVID-19 Elmo Town Hall	21
Fig. 4.1	Dimensions of a new communication framework for sustainable development	95
Fig. 5.1	A holistic spiritual approach to community development through the catalyst of change. (Source: Synuanchanh, 2018)	103
Fig. 5.2	Integration of the IMCFSC model with the BA to development and communication. (Source: Synuanchanh, 2018)	109
Fig. 7.1	Indifference curve of IBF stakeholders	154
Fig. 7.2	Optimal preferences	155
Fig. 7.3	Poverty levels in Indonesia, 1998–2019. (*Source*: BPS 2020 (in Kasri, 2020))	160
Fig. 7.4	Development of Islamic finance in Indonesia, 2015–2019. (*Source*: in Kasri, 2020)	161
Fig. 11.1	Dimension of political action. (*Source:* Melkote and Steeves (2015))	252
Fig. 11.2	P.O.S. model. (Adapted from Melkote and Steeves (2015))	253
Fig. 12.1	The iSDGs discussed in the chapter show the linkages between the various goals as shown here. Overview of the iSDG subsectors. The *outer green* field includes the environment subsectors, the *middle red* field the society subsectors, and the *inner green* field the economy and governance subsectors. Source: Millennium Institute (2016)	267
Fig. 12.2	The diagram illustrates how *Swachh Bharat* (Clean India) meets the iSDG model. Main sectors of the iSDG model. Based on Barney (2002)	282
Fig. 16.1	Emergent multi-stakeholder action research process	352
Fig. 19.1	TV formats of coverage for the Sustainable Development Strategy: Egypt's Vision 2030	429
Fig. 19.2	The dimensions of the Egyptian dream	432

Fig. 19.3	Phases of accomplishing "Egypt's Vision 2030"	437
Fig. 20.1	Scheme of analysis (the authors)	459
Fig. 20.2	Posters from the KNOW YOUR STATUS campaign (Life, 2019b)	461
Fig. 20.3	Posters from the ICH BIN HIV-POSITIV campaign (Aids.at, 2019)	463
Fig. 20.4	Posters from the JUNGES GEMÜSE campaign (BZGA.de, 2016)	466
Fig. 20.5	Posters from the LIEBESORTE campaign (BZGA.de, 2016)	468
Fig. 20.6	Posters from the LOVE LIFE campaign (Love Life, 2019a; Love Life, 2019d)	470
Fig. 22.1	Viewpoints	523
Fig. 23.1	Word cloud. NOTE: on the basis of word frequency. Source: The authors	542
Fig. 23.2	Key phrase extraction. NOTE: minimum=10. Source: The authors	544
Fig. 23.3	"Global Warming" before and after Trump's Presidency. Source: The authors	545
Fig. 23.4	"Carbon Dioxide" before and after Trump's Presidency. Source: The authors	547
Fig. 23.5	"National Security" before and after Trump's Presidency. Source: The authors	547
Fig. 23.6	"Weather Events" before and after Trump's Presidency. Source: The authors	548
Fig. 23.7	"Carbon Emissions" before and after Trump's Presidency. Source: The authors	548
Fig. 23.8	"Caused by Humans" before and after Trump's Presidency. Source: The authors	550
Fig. 23.9	"Adaption and Mitigation" before and after Trump's Presidency. Source: The authors	550
Fig. 24.1	The dominant frames as percentages	572
Fig. 24.2	The use sources by percentage in the two newspapers	575

List of Tables

Table 4.1	Aims	88
Table 4.2	Stakeholders and beneficiaries	90
Table 4.3	Communication strategies	93
Table 5.1	Contextualized indicators from the integration of the IMCFSC model with Buddhist development disciplines	117
Table 7.1	Breakdown of the Global IFSI by sector and region (US$ billion, 2019)	152
Table 7.2	Distribution of Zakat based on types of recipient, 2017–2018	162
Table 7.3	Changes in poverty index of Mustahik in Greater Jakarta	163
Table 7.4	Changes in poverty index of Mustahik in Indonesia	164
Table 7.5	Changes in poverty index of Mustahik under Islamic microfinance programmes in Indonesia	165
Table 8.1	Policies and plans relating to lifelong learning in Tanzania	180
Table 12.1	A comparative chart of Millennium Development Goals and iSDGs	268
Table 12.2	Poverty in Andhra Pradesh and all India	270
Table 12.3	Employment in public and private sectors in Andhra Pradesh (*no. of persons*)	273
Table 12.4	Growth of information technology (Hyderabad)	273
Table 12.5	Growth of IT in tier II locations	275
Table 12.6	Welfare initiatives under social infrastructure. Performance in certain health parameters	275
Table 12.7	Welfare initiatives under social infrastructure. Social welfare institutions	275
Table 12.8	Welfare initiatives under social infrastructure. Girl child protection scheme	276
Table 12.9	Welfare initiatives under social infrastructure. Pensions	276
Table 12.10	Welfare initiatives under social infrastructure. Status of national rural livelihoods mission	277
Table 12.11	Overview of MGNREGS-AP	279
Table 15.1	One-sample *t*-test analysis of fake news exposure among Ghanaians	336
Table 15.2	Independent *t*-test analysis of reasons for fake news vulnerability by gender	338
Table 15.3	ANOVA of reasons for fake news vulnerability by age groups	339

Table 16.1	Ideological precepts of agroecology according to Mr. Javier Carrera	355
Table 16.2	Language frames used by Mr. Roberto Gortaire to define and describe food security versus food sovereignty	356
Table 17.1	Charity foundations and platforms of top ten internet companies in China	377
Table 18.1	Mapping of desired outcomes for pollinator conservation in urban environments to respective SDGs, as well as the proposed communication principles	415
Table 20.1	Summary of the content analysis	473
Table 22.1	Number and percentage of stories by agency type and year	520
Table 22.2	Themes/frames in climate change coverage	521
Table 22.3	Distribution of sources	522
Table 22.4	Frequency of mention of regions	524
Table 23.1	Keyword extraction	543
Table 23.2	Extracted key phrases (Minimum frequency=10)	544
Table 24.1	The SDGs and the number of references to them in the analysed content	568
Table 24.2	Number of appearances of news frames, by newspaper	569
Table 24.3	Main news sources	574
Table 24.4	The journalists interviewed and their newspaper organizations	575
Table 25.1	Media organisations	594
Table 26.1	SDGs scorecard	616

PART I

Introduction: Historical and Theoretical Perspectives

CHAPTER 1

Communication for Sustainable Development in the Age of COVID-19

Muhammad Jameel Yusha'u and Jan Servaes

> "If you ask any public health person before COVID-19, what is the single most important thing in combating an incipient outbreak or pandemic, they will say communication, communication, communication."
> *Dr William Schaffner, Professor of Preventive Medicine in the Department of Health Policy at the University of Vanderbilt during an interview with CNN's Chris Cuomo, July 2020*

Introduction

Since the Spanish Flu of 1918, the world has not seen a pandemic with the same magnitude as COVID-19. When the Spanish Flu was discovered, it began like a normal illness. On 4 March 1914, one Albert Gitchel, a cook at Camp Fuston in Kansas, was experiencing fever, coughing and some headache. His illness ended up being one of the first recorded cases of the Spanish Flu. The Spanish Flu emerged in the middle of World War I, and by the spring of 1918 three-quarters of the French troops fell ill, along with half of British troops. The Spanish Flu spread to North Africa and Mumbai, India, in May 1918; the first cases of the flu were recorded in China in June and by July 1918 the Spanish Flu had reached Australia. Official records showed that at least 50 million people were killed

---

M. J. Yusha'u (✉)
Islamic Development Bank, Jeddah, Saudi Arabia

J. Servaes
KU Leuven, Leuven, Belgium

© The Author(s), under exclusive license to Springer Nature Switzerland AG 2021
M. J. Yusha'u, J. Servaes (eds.), *The Palgrave Handbook of International Communication and Sustainable Development*,
https://doi.org/10.1007/978-3-030-69770-9_1

during the pandemic in addition to massive socio-economic consequences (Honigsbaum, 2020; Martini, Gazzaniga, Bragazzi, & Barberis, 2019).

At the time of the Spanish Flu there were no 24-hour satellite television stations. The Internet was nonexistent. The level of technological advancement was nowhere near the level we are in today. The United Nations as we know it today was not yet born; development communication as a field of study or professional tool to create awareness and lead to behavioural changes, as we know it at present, was not yet conceived; let alone the coalition of experts and diplomats coming together to initiate the Millennium Development Goals (MDGs), or its successor the Sustainable Development Goals (SDGs). So, the rapid spread and casualties recorded by the Spanish Flu was not surprising. Despite the advancement in technology and research that took place between the Spanish Flu and COVID-19, the coronavirus was another shocker to the world, more so to the development community who envisaged a much better world by the year 2030, the dream age to achieve or make substantial progress on the 2030 Agenda for Development. With COVID-19 and the devastating socio-economic impact it has created, the likelihood of attaining the SDGs by 2030 should be subjected to a rigorous review.

According to Singhal (2020) the coronavirus had its origin in bats and was transmitted to human beings through yet-to-be-known intermediary animals in Wuhan, Hubei Province of China, in December 2019. **At the time of writing this chapter in February 2021, over 112 million people were confirmed to have been infected with coronavirus globally. United States had the highest infection with 28.3 million infected people. It was followed by India (11 million), Brazil (10 million), Russia (4.1 million), United Kingdom (4.1 million), France (3.7 million), Spain (3.1 million), Italy (2.8 million), Turkey (2.6 million), Germany (2.4 million), Colombia (2.2 million), Argentina (2.08 million), Mexico (2.060 million), Poland (1.6 million), Iran (1.6 million) and South Africa (1.5 million). These are the top 20 countries with the highest rate of confirmed infections according to Johns Hopkins University Coronavirus Resource Center. The total number of deaths has reached 2.5 million as well.**[1] **The United States had the highest number of casualties as of February 2021 with over 500,000 deaths. Despite the discovery of a vaccine, the number of infections has more than doubled between November 2020 and February 2021 when the global number of infections skyrocketed from 53 million to 112 million.**

Just like the Spanish Flu in 1918, the coronavirus started like a seasonal illness in Wuhan, China. Soon it became a global pandemic that resulted in a massive global lockdown. A health crisis suddenly metamorphosed into economic and social crises that needed massive deployment of a communication approach to help tackle it. Various traditional and digital media were utilized by governments and development institutions in order to curb the spread of COVID-19.

For instance, Sara, Moulik, and Hall (2020) suggested a 10-step communication strategy for the World Bank that can be used to combat the spread of COVID-19 pandemic. The strategy is summarized in the table below:

---

[1] For up-to-date information about the data on coronavirus, see the COVID-19 Dashboard at Johns Hopkins University: https://coronavirus.jhu.edu/map.html.

Ten steps to developing a communication strategy to help combat COVID-19

Step one	**Set up a communication task force**	An agile and action-oriented task force, headed up by a national focal point, is needed to execute the strategy and should include representatives from the Ministry of Health, the private sector, media, behavioural scientists and creative and communication specialists
Step two	Mobilize resources, including from the private sector	Core government funding for COVID communication needs to be mobilized rapidly and can be complemented with help from donors and from the private sector, who have many relevant skills to offer
Step three	Define which behaviours need to change and by whom	Campaigns need to be specific and clear about what behaviour they want people to adopt. Hand hygiene and physical distancing are key to interrupting COVID-19 transmission in the community, as shown below
Step four	Review what is being done internationally and locally	Country programmes need to be aware of global developments, gathered from authoritative sources including WHO, Compass, the World Bank and Hygiene Hub. The task force also needs to map all existing national efforts, as well as quickly counter misinformation
Step five	Review what is known about the risk behaviours and rapidly fill in knowledge gaps	An effective national plan needs to engage the population with messages that are new and surprising in order to grab people's attention. The communication must motivate action by making the behaviour something that people will want to do. Above all, the advocated behaviour has to be possible. Rapid in-depth research into what people are doing and why, especially in vulnerable or marginalized groups, is vital
Step six	Produce a creative brief and theory of change	A creative brief is the guiding document that sets out the problem, purpose, objectives, target behaviours, audience characterization, channels of communication, persuasive argument, tone, personality, measures of impact and the materials required from the creative team
Step seven	Develop a unifying national brand	Governments need to brand their national campaigns to help establish trust and credibility and ensure coherence. The logo should be based on existing government brands but have new, eye-catching elements, while the slogan should encapsulate the primary insight of the campaign
Step eight	**Deploy using the most relevant channels for the target audiences**	Content may take various forms, including TV and radio commercials, memes for social media or content for existing TV and radio shows. The aim is to generate discussion and social media sharing—for messaging to go viral, it must be worth sharing
Step nine	**Rapidly pre-test and continually revise materials**	In emergency conditions, some pre-testing, for example through phone calls with small samples of target audiences, is possible—allowing course corrections before materials are released. Content will need to be revised and refreshed often, since the impact diminishes as surprise fades and circumstances evolve
Step ten	**Monitor, evaluate and share lessons**	Continual monitoring of the effect of communication on behaviour and behavioural indicators is essential, even if the circumstances of a pandemic make this challenging

Source: World Bank—Sara et al. (2020). *Organized and tabulated by authors*

Apart from the World Bank, other development agencies equally came up with a suggested communication framework on how to tackle the COVID-19 pandemic. The International Federation of Red Cross and Red Crescent (IFRC), UNICEF and World Health Organization (WHO) issued a joint Risk Communication and Community Engagement (RCCE) guideline (IFRC, UNICEF, & WHO, 2020). What was unique about this communication guideline is that it encourages flexibility for countries and institutions to adopt it according to their specific need. The RCCE guideline suggested a process on how to prepare and respond to the pandemic as summarized in the table below.

RCCE action plan guidance: COVID-19 preparedness and response

Step one	Assess and collect	Collect existing information and conduct rapid qualitative and/or quantitative assessments to learn about the communities (knowledge, attitudes and perceptions about COVID-19, most at-risk population, communication patterns and channels, language, religion, influencers, health services and situation). With your team, analyse and assess the situation.
Step two	Coordinate	Use existing coordination mechanisms or create new ones to engage with RCCE counterparts in partner organizations at all levels of the response: local, regional and national. These include health authorities, ministries and agencies of other government sectors, international organizations (WHO, UNICEF, IFRC, MSF, etc.), NGOs, academia and so on. Develop and maintain an up-to-date contact list of all partners and their focal points. Regular contact with all partners will help avoid duplication and identify potential gaps in the RCCE response.
Step three	Define	Define and prioritize your key RCCE objectives with your team and partners. Review them regularly to ensure they are responding to your priorities as COVID-19 evolves.
Step four	Identify key audiences and influencers	Identify target audiences and key influencers. These include policy-makers, influential bloggers or other social media leaders, local leaders, women and youth groups, religious and elders' groups, local and international NGOs health experts and practitioners, volunteers and people who have real-life experience with COVID-19 (those who have had COVID-19 or their family members have contracted the virus). Match audiences and influencers with channels and partners that reach them.
Step five	Develop RCCE strategy	Based on the qualitative analysis' results, your defined key objectives and audiences, develop an RCCE strategy that fits into the country's comprehensive COVID-19 response strategy. Adapt to the local context: focus on messages that are tailored to the relevant national and local context, reflecting key audience questions, perceptions, beliefs and practices. Define and prioritize your strategic objectives with your team and partners in alignment with the general objectives of the country's COVID-19 response. Review them regularly with partners and community to ensure they are responding to evolving priorities. Work with the different technical groups of the response to ensure alignment, coordination and internal dialogue between RCCE leadership/field staff and other response teams. Define and describe actions/activities that will contribute to achieve the RCCE objectives. Develop messages and materials to transmit health protection steps and situation updates in line with World Health Organization's message. Messages and materials should be tailored to reflect audience perceptions and knowledge at the level to which the RCCE products are targeted whether national, regional or local (see assessment process in Step one). While defining the list of activities tailored to your country, simultaneously disseminate recommendations from the World Health Organization and your Ministry of Health. These sources provide accurate information that can mitigate concerns and promote prevention actions, even though they are not tailored to local communities. Create relevant information, education and communication (IEC) materials tailored for and pre-tested with representatives of audiences for whom they are intended. Pre-testing messages and materials with target audiences ensure that messages are context-specific and increases ownership from communities and at-risk populations and other stakeholders. As much as possible IEC materials should contain actions that people can take: a. an instruction to follow b. a behaviour to adopt c. information you can share with friends and family

Step six	Implement	Develop and implement the endorsed RCCE plan with relevant partners to engage with identified audiences and community. This should include capacity building and integration of RCCE counterparts from international, national, regional and local groups, ensuring participation and accountability mechanisms are co-defined. Make sure to identify human, material and financial resource needs. Define staff and partners who will do the work (number of people required in the team/organizations) and budget according to the resources. Ensure strong and regular supervision and coordination mechanisms. Close monitoring of field work is essential and mechanisms should be defined before starting implementation. Set up and implement a rumour-tracking system to closely watch misinformation and report to relevant technical partners/sectors. Make sure to respond to rumours and misinformation with evidence-based guidance so that all rumours can be effectively refuted. Adapt materials, messages and methodologies accordingly with the help of the relevant technical group.
Step seven	Monitor	Develop a monitoring plan to evaluate how well the objectives of the RCCE plan are being fulfilled. Identify the activities the RCCE team will perform and the outcomes they are designed to achieve with target audiences (communities, at-risk populations, stakeholders, etc.). Establish a baseline (e.g., note the level of awareness or knowledge of a community at the time before the RCCE plan is implemented). Measure the impact of the RCCE strategy by monitoring changes in the baseline during and after RCCE strategy activities are implemented. If minimal or no positive changes are achieved, find where the problems are: check if the activities are fit for purpose, check the content of the narratives, the methodologies, the quality of work conducted by the teams (it is very important to supervise the way team members conduct the activities). Develop checklists to monitor activities and process indicators for every activity.

Source: World Health Organization. *Organized and tabulated by authors*

The approach of the World Bank, IFRC, UNICEF and WHO centred on the traditional approach to communication for development. This approach is not new, but with the rise of fake news or infodemic relying purely on the old strategy is not enough. The WHO has defined infodemic as "an overabundance of information-some accurate and some not—occurring during an epidemic" (Financial Times, 2020, para. 6).

To be successful in ensuring that communication strategies are effective, they must incorporate a robust strategy to tackle misinformation. To understand why it is vital to put in place a mechanism for tackling misinformation in any communication strategy aimed at tackling a pandemic such as COVID-19, the following examples would be handy. The Director General of WHO Tedros Adhanom Ghebreyesus announced in August 2020 that the world is not just fighting a virus, but it is battling with conspiracy theories that push so much misinformation aimed at undermining the response of the outbreak.

According to the WHO, some of the examples of misinformation include rumours of food scarcity, forcing people to stockpile food stuff. "In the United States of America, a person passed away from ingesting a fish tank cleaning product containing chloroquine after reports mentioned hydroxychloroquine as a possible—yet unproven—remedy for treatment of COVID-19" (WHO, 2020a para. 3). In Iran, hundreds died after drinking methanol alcohol after rumours spread on social media suggesting that it cures COVID-19 (Delirrad & Mohammadi, 2020), while in Germany an anti-vaccine movement emerged which may deter people from being vaccinated (The Atlantic, 2021).

A recent study that examined the vaccination views of 100 million Facebook users globally found that while the pro-vaccination camp (6.9 million people) outnumbered those against vaccination (4.2 million), the anti-vaccine group was less isolated and had more interaction with the individuals (by far the largest group, at 74.1 million) who are undecided about vaccination. (WHO, 2020a para. 4)

Due to the magnitude of the challenge of misinformation, the UN Secretary General had to launch the UN communication response initiative to combat the spread of misinformation (WHO, 2020b). A European Union policy paper on tackling disinformation related to COVID-19 states:

> This 'infodemic' feeds on people's most basic anxieties. Social confinement has obliged millions of people to stay in their homes, increasing the use of social media including as means of access to information, while online platforms, fact-checkers and social media users are reporting millions of false or misleading posts. Given the novelty of the virus, gaps in knowledge have proven to be an ideal breeding ground for false or misleading narratives to spread. (European Commission, 2020, p. 1)

The European Union found several examples of misinformation such as the claim that drinking of bleach or alcohol as a cure for COVID-19. Others were the conspiracy theories that coronavirus was the creation of elites aimed at reducing population growth. One of the wildest rumours was the idea that 5G installations contribute in spreading the virus (European Union 2020). For some people, the virus was created by China deliberately, or it is a plan by Bill Gates to sell vaccines (Naffi, Davidson, & Jawhar, 2020). The exploitation of the pandemic by US President Donald Trump for political purposes during the 2020 US presidential election campaign by calling COVID-19 'China virus' was another challenge in managing and spreading the correct information about the virus. Some of the comments by Donald Trump where aired live on major US television networks.

In the Democratic Republic of Congo, it was a different kind of misinformation: people refused to believe that the virus exists. "According to UNICEF's communication unit in Kinshasa, the most dangerous rumour on social media is that people refuse to believe that the COVID-19 exists in DRC and that it can kill people. This is supported by the findings of a survey by the Kinshasa School of Public Health, which highlighted that 20.2% of people interviewed in the capital did not believe that COVID-19 is real" (Gavi, 2020, para. 6).

It is obvious therefore that communication for development and social change in the age of COVID-19 must deal with the challenge of misinformation in initiating communication responses. It is clear therefore that the communication strategies suggested by the World Bank and IFRC/UNICEF/WHO discussed earlier were not comprehensive enough. First, they did not incorporate the challenges of infodemic and fake news in tackling COVID-19 pandemic. The second shortcoming was that the strategies did not include science communication to sensitize the public about how health experts make decisions and advise the public on their safety.

Lack of basic understanding of science and knowledge on the efficacy of scientific evidence by the public could be attributed to the acceptance of certain aspects of misinformation. The debate about wearing a mask to reduce the potential of spreading COVID-19 in the United States during the 2020 presidential election is one example. Therefore, deploying the tools of development communication without embracing science education in any communication strategy would be inadequate in managing both the pandemic and the infodemic.

Development communication experts should work with policy-makers and the media to get science education out of its elitist box, by making it common knowledge rather than letting it remain in the exclusive domain of university professors and their students and partners in the industry. In the later part of this chapter, a communication framework that addresses these shortcomings would be proposed for tackling pandemics such as COVID-19.

In Sect. 2, this chapter discusses the impact of COVID-19 on the SDGs since the key premise of this book is on the SDGs and the role of communication for development in achieving the 2030 Agenda for Development. Section 3 focuses on the concept of communication for development and dwells on how the COVID-19 pandemic developed a spontaneous reaction from the media and national governments to initiate communication responses aimed at behavioural change. Section 4 discusses the organization of the book and highlights why this book is important and why it is needed at this time; it then concludes with brief information on each section of the book and the specific chapters contributed by various authors from different parts of the globe.

IMPACT OF COVID-19 ON THE SDGs

None of the framers of the SDGs could have envisaged the disruption caused by COVID-19 pandemic on the 2030 Agenda for Development. The era of the MDGs passed largely without a major disruption like the COVID-19 scale. There were wars, natural disasters and other problems, but they were mild compared to the disruption caused by COVID-19. Any discussion on achieving the SDGs must consider the impact of COVID-19 on this journey. Before the outbreak of the pandemic, the UN Secretary General António Guterres had in November 2019 announced that the SDGs were already off-track. He mentioned this in an op-ed published in the *Financial Times* where he made a clarion call to national governments to take the SDGs more seriously. The UN Secretary General was lamenting mainly on the challenge of financing the SDGs as well as the rising living costs and injustices in different parts of the world (UN News, 2020).

A month after the UN Secretary General made this call, Chinese officials announced the discovery of a mystery virus on 12 December 2019 in the city of Wuhan with a population of approximately 11 million people (ABC Australia, 2020). The virus turned out to be the coronavirus. Country after country had to start taking measures to control the spread of the virus. By March 2020 over 100 countries around the world had imposed a lockdown. More strict measures were taken by countries after the WHO declared COVID-19 a pandemic on 11 March 2020. US President Donald Trump blocked all non-essential arrivals from the European Union on 15 March 2020. The European Union followed by blocking visitors from non-Schengen areas. By the end of March 2020 global air traffic had declined by 63 per cent compared to a year earlier (BBC News, 2020).

The lockdowns and curfews imposed by countries across the globe planted the seed that transformed the COVID-19 pandemic from a health crisis to an economic catastrophe. This happened in 2020, the year declared by the United Nations as the decade of action. The timeline expected to accelerate the implementation of the 2030 Agenda for Development and make progress for the remaining ten years (see the conclusion chapter for a discussion on the possibility of achieving the SDGs by 2030).

It suddenly began to dawn on policy-makers that the negative impact on some of the progress made in the implementation of the 2030 Agenda was huge. Already the pandemic had affected SDG3 on healthcare for all. School closure from primary to tertiary levels was a blow on SDG4 on quality education. The economic impact of the pandemic has led to increase in unemployment.

A September 2020 report by the International Labour Organisation (ILO) estimated US $3.5 trillion worth of labour income losses globally. The stimulus gap between low- and middle-income countries was equally wider. "The estimated fiscal stimulus gap is around US$982 billion in low-income and lower-middle-income countries (US$45 billion and US$937 billion, respectively). This gap represents the amount of resources that these countries would need to match the average level of stimulus relative to working-hour losses in high income countries. Significantly, the estimated stimulus gap for low-income countries is less than 1 per cent of the total value of the fiscal stimulus packages announced by high-income countries" (ILO, 2020, p. 2). This economic impact has a direct effect on the attempt to achieve SDG8 on decent work and economic growth. The magnitude of the global lockdown down was captured by the headline of *The Economist* magazine titled: Closed, as indicated in Fig. 1.1.

The IMF has predicted that about 170 countries are facing shrinking GDP while the Asian Development Bank has envisaged that COVID-19 could cost the global economy US $5.8–$8.8 trillion of global GDP, and global employment could fall between 158 million and 242 million jobs (Mukarram, 2020).

In a study on the global impact of COVID-19 on the SDGs, Mukarram (2020, p. 254) states:

1 COMMUNICATION FOR SUSTAINABLE DEVELOPMENT IN THE AGE OF COVID-19

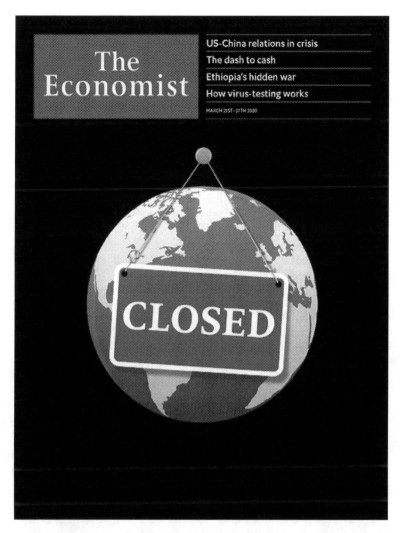

Fig. 1.1 Cover of *The Economist* of **21 March 2020** following the global lockdown in over 100 countries

While all these ongoing efforts on the economic front seem to be very much rational, the world however, must not lose sight of the UN Sustainable Development Goals (SDGs), which are based on 17 goals and 169 targets. The pandemic is very much poised to impact the SDGs in various degrees in different parts of the world, which in turn will have bigger ramifications on the economy, society, and the environment. So, the world must take a holistic and all-encompassing approach with an eye to the overall achievement of SDGs while reformulating the short-term and mid-term policies during and in the post-COVID period.

As we shall discuss in the conclusion chapter of this book, Mukarram (2020) suggests that the level of impact of COVID-19 pandemic on the SDGs could result in a call for revisiting the timeline of the SDGs. But there is one more impact that is as important as the rest. How do the global community and the national and regional governments prepare the minds of the people for the rocky path ahead? Already signs of instability have started manifesting in some countries due to the economic impact of COVID-19. A study by Reinsdorf (2020) on the rise of inflation as a result of COVID-19 pandemic states the challenge ahead could be stiffer. Part of the answer to this gargantuan challenge is by embracing the tenets of communication for development and social change, the subject of the next section.

Communication for Sustainable Development in the Age of COVID-19

Recent efforts to ensure a fair, equitable and just world for the present and future generations stem from the desire to ensure a sustainable world. There have been several initiatives in both the north and global south to achieve economic growth, environmental protection and a just and fair society. Such efforts resulted in the last 20 years to have ambitious goals such as the Millennium Development Goals (MDGs) and the Sustainable Development Goals (SDGs). Ensuring sustainability may not be as easy it sounds because it would require massive adjustment from traditional ways of doing business and changes in behaviour. These adjustments are what communication for development tries to tackle as we shall see in the rest of this book.

But let us start by understanding what sustainable development is. A bit of historical background would be useful in trying to understand the contemporary meaning of sustainable development. Back in 1983, the United Nations General Assembly in its resolution 38/161 of 19 December 1983 welcomed the establishment of the World Commission on Environment and Development. The commission will look at global problems and propose solutions to them up to the year 2000 and beyond (Sustainable Development Goals, 2020).

The former prime minister of Norway, Gro Harlem Brundtland, was saddled with the responsibility of leading the commission. In her foreword to the report of the commission, she stated the following which provides a window on why the issue of sustainability should be taken seriously:

> During the time we met as a Commission, tragedies such as the African famines, the leak at the pesticides factory at Bhopal, India, and the nuclear disaster at Chernobyl, USSR appeared to justify the grave predictions about the human future that were becoming commonplace during the mid-1980s. But at public hearings we held on five continents, we also heard from the individual victims of more chronic, widespread disasters: the debt crisis, stagnating aid to and investment in developing countries, falling commodity prices and falling personal

incomes. We became convinced that major changes were needed, both in attitudes and in the way our societies are organized. (Commission for Environment and Development, 1983, p. 6)

The report of the commission under the section on sustainable development stated that "humanity has the ability to make development sustainable to ensure that it meets the needs of the present without compromising the ability of future generations to meet their own needs." Since then, the latter aspect of this sentence has become the most common definition of sustainable development, meaning, sustainable development is development that "meets the needs of the present without compromising the ability of future generations to meet their own needs" (Commission for Environment and Development, 1983, p. 17). But the report itself was not the first to mention sustainable development.[2]

Other development scholars have elaborated on this definition by looking at sustainable development as "a way of understanding the world and a method of solving global problems" (Sachs, 2015, p. 1). In other words, sustainable development is first "an intellectual pursuit", one that "tried to make sense of the interactions of three complex systems; the world economy, the global society, and the earths physical environment" (Sachs, 2015, p. 3). The focus of sustainable development on economy, society and environment as explained by Sachs (2015) was drawn from the report of the Commission for Environment and Development.

Transforming the three key pillars of sustainable development, that is economy, society and environment, as proposed by the Commission for Environment and Development is not an easy feat. It requires massive reorientation, awareness and stakeholder engagement. "For many scholars, sustainable development implies a participatory, multi-stakeholder approach to policy-making and implementation, mobilizing public and private resources for development and making use of the knowledge, skills, and energy of all social groups concerned with the future of the planet and its people" (Servaes et al., 2012, p. 101). This means more interpersonal communication, persistent media campaigns and persuasive communication. This gap is what communication for development seeks to fill.

This can be seen right from the origin of the discipline and the various theoretical postulations that seek to explain communication for development and social change. Communication for development is thus a social process which aims to consider the need and interest of various groups using the mass media. Servaes and Malikhao (2007) have summarized the different origins, theories and perspectives on communication for development. The early period was between 1958 and 1986 when the Western World saw it as a project to develop Third World countries. At this stage, development communication was greeted with a lot of interest. It was the period of the modernization paradigm. The

---

[2] For more on the historical origin of the term sustainable development, from its use in the ecosystems to earlier reports by the UN, see Sachs (2015, p. 4) or Servaes (2013).

media was seen as an instrument that amplifies the benefit of development. The assumption at this stage was that the mass media can change people from traditional to modern. The most prominent work that espouses this idea was Daniel Lerner's (1958) *The Passing of Traditional Society: Modernizing the Middle East*.

The second stage according to Servaes and Malikhao was from 1987 to 1996 when the modernization theory of Lerner (1958) disappeared and was replaced by the participatory communication model. Modernization theory had a top-down approach to communication. The participatory communication model focuses on the grassroots. It is bottom-top. Change begins from the recipient of the message considering his needs and interests. The third stage in the words of Servaes and Malikhao was when other theories such as knowledge gap, uses and gratification and indirect influence were applied. An important point to note in any discussion on development communication is its interdisciplinary root and approach. It tends to be holistic and wide in the way it approaches communication and behavioural change.

That is why issues such as social justice, community empowerment, development, culture and globalization are part and parcel of communication for development (Melkote & Steeves, 2015). Several approaches and theories of communication for development continue to emerge, particularly those challenging the early approaches of modernization models. The latter theories emerged particularly from Latin American scholars who championed the dependency and underdevelopment theories to challenge the Eurocentric approach of the modernization paradigm. This effort coincided with independence of many developing countries in Africa, Asia and Latin America, resulting in the call for New World Information and Communication Order (Servaes & Malikhao, 2007). The diffusion of innovation theory proposed by Rogers (1962) also gained momentum in communication for development and social change. The prominence of the theory is related to the notion that ideas get momentum or spread through population thereby triggering transformation in society.

The diffusion of innovation theory proposed the five adopter categories to explain how ideas spread. The adopter categories are the innovators; those in this category love testing new ideas by exploring through unchartered territories to bring about social change. The early adopters are the second category; these are the people who are ready to embrace new ideas and are quite receptive to change. Opinion leaders belong to this category. The third category contains an early majority. Those in this category embrace change much later but are quick to do so once there is clear evidence on the benefit of change. The late majority form the fourth category; this is one of the most difficult group, as they hardly embrace new ideas until they are tested, trusted and verified. Much effort using the media and interpersonal communication is needed to convince this group. The laggards are the fifth category. They are very conservative, attached to the past and difficult to appeal to. Their fears must be allayed. More pressure is required from other groups to convince this category (Singer, 2020).

Since then communication for development has been studied and applied in many areas of development: from agriculture, health, education to community empowerment. Such studies looked at various areas of interest such as ICT and globalization (Ogan et al., 2009), empowerment (White, 2004), rural communities (Pade-Khene, Palmer, & Kavhai, 2010) and gender development (Asiedu, 2012). Several scholarly texts such as Servaes (2009), Melkote and Steeves (2015) and the more recent compendium, *Handbook of Communication for Development and Social Change, Volumes I & II* (Servaes, 2020), which is perhaps the largest reference book in this area, have chronicled the most vital information, history, theory, strategy and every application of communication for development and social change.

International development institutions like the World Bank, United Nations Development Programme (UNDP) and several NGOs and civil society have produced books and guides for practical application by development professionals in communication for development. The *Development Communication Source Book* of the World Bank, edited by Mefalopulos (2008) and UNDP's *Communication for Development: A Glimpse at UNDP's Practice* (2009) are few examples.

An interesting point to note during the COVID-19 pandemic was the response of the news media and development institutions. While some media organizations reacted spontaneously through their coverage, others did not. However, development institutions like the WHO responded with immediate urgency because the world was hungry for information about COVID-19. The WHO is one of the most authoritative institutions on matters of public health. Few years back, the WHO would have had to wait for newspapers and television stations to report their press conferences. Due to the advancements in technology, the communication teams in the WHO could organize media briefings without difficulty and do not have to worry about some of the traditional gatekeeping functions of the media which will report the media briefings as decided by the editors. This is a point that communication for development scholars can further explore in future research about media responses to the COVID-19 pandemic.

Examples of such spontaneous reactions include how the World Health Organization (WHO) quickly developed daily briefings on COVID-19 by providing information to the global community on COVID-19 and how the virus spreads. The briefings were conducted under the leadership of the WHO Secretary General Tedros Adhanom Ghebreyesus. The briefings were available in multiple platforms such as the WHO website, LinkedIn, YouTube, Twitter and a host of other channels. Journalists could ask questions from every part of the world, while policy-makers, particularly those in the public health area, benefited immensely from the information provided by the WHO. Although the WHO was criticized heavily by the United States government for being late in declaring COVID-19 a pandemic, the briefings were important in targeting

Fig. 1.2 WHO Director General Dr. Tedros, during COVID-19 media briefing in Geneva, Switzerland

members of the public to practise social distancing measures, wear masks in public and most importantly wash hands regularly to avoid being infected or strengthen the spread of the virus. It is not surprising that the WHO took these measures because the pandemic is a direct attack on the possibility of achieving SDG3 on healthcare for all. As we will see in Chap. 7, it was one of the signs that communication pillars which the UN missed in the SDGs provided the needed impetus for the society during the pandemic (Fig. 1.2).

International News Flow and Communication for Development During COVID-19 Pandemic

One of the phenomena that we have witnessed during the COVID-19 pandemic was a massive flow of international news from the global media in both the global north and the global south. The lockdown and the emergency nature of COVID-19 pandemic forced some of the international media to focus mainly on the COVID-19 pandemic. Coverage of the pandemic made it easier for the news media to focus on one subject, the COVID-19. It provided an opportunity to bring pundits, health experts and correspondents to discuss various issues related to COVID-19. Global news flows and counter flows have been discussed at length by scholars of international communication. These studies include Bagdikian (2004), Boyd-Barrett (2006), Davies (2015), Thussu (2007, 2016, 2018) and Iordache, Van Audenhove, and Loisen (2019), among others.

As we shall see in the examples that will follow shortly, there was convergence on reporting COVID-19 pandemic based on the global media flows which represents the dominant Western media block, as well as the contraflow which represents the media from the global south. They converge on communicating a development challenge. However, there are differences between the dominant Western media and the emerging media from the global south in the editorial direction of the coverage. For instance major commercial news outlets like CNN provided significant coverage on the public health issues on how to mitigate the effects of the pandemic.

A highlight of this was during the global lockdown when CNN journalists like Dr. Sanjay Gupta taught global audiences how to wash hands and make masks at home because of the scarcity of the masks and closure of stores and pharmacies due to the lockdown. Dr. Gupta made the demonstration more personal by informing global audiences how one of his children was able to make the mask herself from clothes. This is communication for development 101. Most people were working from home, yet they could, on their television screens, receive public health instructions which would have been impossible during previous pandemics such as the 1918 Spanish Flu, because the technology for individual journalists to transmit programmes live from home was not available. This is one more reason why it is surprising that the UN missed a goal on communication in the SDGs. Just like COVID-19 is a public emergency, some of the SDGs like eradicating extreme poverty and reducing carbon emission as a result of climate change are equally public emergencies when you weigh their long-term consequences.

Another approach adopted by CNN and other television networks during the COVID-19 pandemic was targeting kids via Elmo Town Hall. It was an engaging programme that appealed to young children. Dr. Sanjay Gupta appears in the programme to answer questions from kids and young members of families. It was a good example of how the power of the mass media can be deployed to tackle key development challenges related to public health safety.

Although the effort of CNN might look neutral on the surface and a casual analysis might suggest that it is done in public interest, there were two major shortcomings in the coverage provided by CNN. First was that the news reporting was heavily skewed on the impact of the pandemic within the United States alone. An international audience that relies on CNN for news might be more informed by the number of infections in New York and Florida than about his or her country or region. The second shortcoming was where the commercial interest becomes clearer. It was heavily critical of Donald Trump's handling of the pandemic. On the right-hand side of the screen was a permanent dashboard with numbers about daily infections and deaths in the United States, while CNN pundits such as Gloria Borger, Sanjay Gupta, Jake Tapper, Van Jones and others discussed how the 2020 elections will be a referendum on Donald Trump's handling of COVID-19. Although Donald Trump was reckless in handling COVID-19, CNN could have been more professional in its reporting, particularly given its global outreach. It should have been more respectful of its audiences outside Europe and North America, as it is a major beneficiary of advertisements from Africa, Asia and Latin America.

A contrast to the perspective of CNN was provided by the English language television channel Aljazeera English. It illustrates the contraflow approach to news as discussed by Thussu (2007). Aljazeera English provides a more global perspective of the coverage with more stories about the pandemic from the global south through its news bulletins and other programmes. The station usually begins programmes by bringing updates from different countries. In one of their daily shows known as *Inside Story*, the audience can have different perspectives on how COVID-19 affects various countries. For example, in the edition of *Inside Story* on 23 August 2020, the programme started by providing an overview of the situation covering countries like India and South Korea.

The pundits invited were equally global with Mathew Fox, a professor of epidemiology at Boston University; Dr. Arisina MA, the president of Hong Kong Public Doctors Association; and Dr. Ahsan Ullah Chaudhry, a frontline medical doctor in the UK's National Health Service, NHS. The composition of the analysts and their location was representative of the global north and south. But due the dominance of the global media and excessive market competition as discussed by Davies (2015), television stations like Aljazeera English are having a hard time penetrating the market in the Western world, particularly in North America.

While a dominant news channel like CNN has a strong American flavour in its coverage, the BBC too had a strong UK and Western 'bias' despite the various global stories featuring on the coronavirus page of the BBC (BBC, 2020). Some of the diversity of the reporting from the global south was illustrated by the China Central Television CCTV. The channel has provided space for covering coronavirus, from a global perspective, with stories such as "Scientists optimistic on making COVID-19 vaccines affordable, equitable despite challenges" (CCTV, 2020a). CCTV also presented stories on what Chinese officials are doing to help tackle COVID-19, with reports such as "Wang Yi addresses UN special session on COVID-19" (CCTV, 2020b). But the coverage of CCTV also highlighted the political tension between the United States and China. Some of the headlines on the CCTV website include, "U.S. hits record-high COVID-19 daily cases, hospitalizations as caseload tops 14 mln" (CCTV, 2020c), or "China willing to work with countries including U.S. to contain COVID-19: spokesperson" (CCTV, 2020d). The constant bullying of China by US President Donald Trump by calling COVID-19 the 'China virus' which aired on US TV networks also received a response through channels like CCTV on equal measure.

The coverage of COVID-19 from the global south was diverse just as the coverage in the global north. While the coverage on the COVID-19 pandemic by the international media might seem like good news for communication for development and social change, the coverage is not necessarily neutral. It was also influenced by local factors and media ownership. Despite this lack of neutrality, key media organizations such as *Deutsche Welle*, which is the public service broadcasting outfit for Germany, *The Economist* as indicated earlier in this chapter, *Le Monde, BBC, The Guardian, El País, The New York Times,*

1 COMMUNICATION FOR SUSTAINABLE DEVELOPMENT IN THE AGE OF COVID-19   19

Fig. 1.3 *Inside Story* about COVID-19 on Aljazeera English TV Network

Washington Post, The Sydney Morning Herald or *The South China Morning Post* have provided space for the coverage of COVID-19. The audience have a choice when it comes to news consumption as long as they read or watch across national borders and are multilingual. There is also diversity and what we might describe as 'intra-global flow' and 'intra-counterflow' in news coverage about the COVID-19 pandemic (Fig. 1.3).

A major lesson from the coverage of COVID-19 in the international media whether from the global south or global north is that in the twenty-first century, major international and local satellite broadcasting stations do not have monopoly. The emergence of video technologies and free Internet channels such as YouTube means that development organizations and individuals can develop similar messages using their expertise to help sensitize the public on safety issues. We have seen that at play during the pandemic. Health professionals in the United Kingdom's National Health Service (NHS) recorded messages on social distancing and the importance of wearing masks which received wide publicity. In countries like Nigeria where multiple languages are spoken, health experts recorded similar video messages targeting the public. Each health professional expresses the same message but in a different language. Even in multilingual Belgium, with its official 3 languages (French, Dutch and German), the Brussels-based NGO Foyer started broadcasting health advice in 11 languages in order to reach as many people as possible (https://www.foyer.be/news/covid-19/). We should not forget that the country is the second-highest in the world for deaths in proportion to its overall population, behind the tiny city state of San Marino (https://www.reuters.com/article/us-health-coronavirus-belgium-idUSKBN29F0BF):"The country, home to the headquarters of the European Union and NATO, has played down comparisons that show it to be one of the world's worst hit by the pandemic, but virologists point to some missteps and systemic problems. A country divided by language, Belgium gives regions substantial autonomy and has nine health ministers."

In Saudi Arabia messages were recorded targeting expatriate workers in languages such as Urdu, Bahasa, Hindi and English (Arab News, 2020). This is how modern technology has made it possible for communication for development to be deployed targeting various local communities. Medical journalists such as Stanford University's Dr. Saima Yasmin who is an academic and a journalist specializing in reporting health epidemics produced blog postings and videos informing the public on how to conquer pandemics like COVID-19 using communication (Stanford Engineering Staff, 2020).

Among policy-makers, the Governor of New York Andrew Cuomo distinguished himself by conducting daily live media briefings informing and educating New Yorkers when the State of New York became the hub of COVID-19. His efforts paid dividend when his aggressive approach to utilizing media and communication helped in curbing the spread of the pandemic. **While the effort of Governor Cuomo was lauded at the peak of the pandemic, serious allegations of underreporting death figures arising from the pandemic appeared in several US media outlets since. The London *Guardian* reported that "deaths of New York nursing home residents were substantially higher than had been recorded by the Cuomo administration. Residents who had fallen sick and died after they were transferred to hospital were mysteriously left off the official count" (The Guardian, 2021, para 27).**

The unravelling of the story on Cuomo's handling of the figures in the pandemic reveals a unique lesson—that communication for development and social change is not and should not be a public relations stunt, but a genuine attempt to use the power of communication to achieve sustainable development. This requires a massive level of transparency and accountability rather than image laundering (Fig. 1.4).

BEYOND COVID-19: A COMMUNICATION FRAMEWORK FOR TACKLING PANDEMICS

What has emerged from the previous sections is that communication for development and social change has continued to evolve in theory and practice. To achieve the 2030 Agenda for Development, the tools of communication for development must be embraced and deployed with the same intensity that they were deployed during COVID-19 pandemic, or at least at near magnitude. In the table below, we propose a communication strategy that could help countries and organizations to manage pandemics of similar magnitude based on the lessons learnt from COVID-19. The communication framework was developed on three key pillars. The first is from the experiences of how governments, institutions and the media took immediate measures to use communication tools for public awareness aimed at tackling COVID-19. The second pillar was the modification of the framework suggested by institutions

1 COMMUNICATION FOR SUSTAINABLE DEVELOPMENT IN THE AGE OF COVID-19

Fig. 1.4 CNN COVID-19 Elmo Town Hall

such as the World Bank, the WHO and so on. We studied the framework, made the necessary modifications and suggest improvements. The third pillar was to provide additional ideas based on the lessons learnt from the first and second pillars. The framework can be adopted and modified as it suits local contexts.

A communication framework for tackling pandemics

Step one	Establish a national communication task force	• Form a task force at the highest level of government comprising senior officials including representatives from the health ministry, major healthcare agencies, finance ministry, ministry of information, senior health experts, researchers, NGOs and media representatives
Step two	Identify target audiences, languages and communication channels	• Identify key target groups, especially those most vulnerable to the pandemics • Develop information guide about the pandemic and define all the channels to be used in reaching the relevant audiences • Launch a robust awareness campaign involving all stakeholders identified in Step one • Translate and conduct campaigns in local languages to ensure effective outreach
Step three	Design misinformation action plan	• Identify all sources of misinformation • Design counter and effective misinformation action plan • Translate messages into local languages • Increase digital literacy and engage community leaders, faith communities and traditional institutions in delegitimizing lies and fake news
Step four	Identify champions, social influencers, faith communities to lead the campaign	• Enlist a group of champions including celebrities, social media influencers, youth groups and community leaders to lead the campaign for behavioural change at the grassroots level

Step five	Develop a unifying rather than fragmented message at national and local levels	• Develop the campaign as national brand rather than a fragmented one • Regional and local authorities to cascade the awareness campaign especially in more diverse and highly populated countries
Step six	Communicating science at the grassroots level	• Make knowledge of science easy and accessible to the general public through the mass media and local and interpersonal channels • Identify groups that resist scientific knowledge and discoveries or are resistant to facts • Design targeted messages for these groups aimed at behavioural change • Build capacity of journalists, NGOs and civil society on science reporting and dissemination
Step seven	Develop coalition of philanthropists, academics and media professionals	• Constitute a major coalition of philanthropists, private sector as well as government resources to fund the campaign for the benefit of the public • Include media professionals and academics in the coalition so that they are privy to all activities related to mobilization of resources and implementation of the campaign. The media and (professional and academic) specialists should be at the table where decisions are made, not just be passive invitees for press conferences or review of documents • Mobilize resources to support national governments due to hardships on the population that could lead to resistance against government efforts • Encourage philanthropists to use own resources through personal initiatives for public good during the pandemic • Utilize the convening power and celebrity status of the philanthropists for public education
Step eight	Evaluate and roll out monitoring and implementation plan	• Design and roll out an effective monitoring and implementation plan • Provide regular update to the public on successes and challenges of the mass awareness campaign during the pandemic • Develop an integrated and proactive health plan focusing on major behavioural changes such as handwashing and social distancing • Pay attention to cultural values that emphasize personal hygiene, volunteering and grassroot campaigns by health officials and civil society organizations as seen from the example of some Asian countries in handling COVID-19 • Evaluate the effectiveness of the campaign and fine-tune it as deemed necessary
Step nine	Establish an advisory team to prepare for the next pandemic	• Establish a foresight advisory team comprising health experts, government agencies and international health experts at the highest level of government to study trends of emerging pandemics and advise relevant authorities
Step ten	Organize annual briefing to inform the public about potential pandemics	• Produce annual documents each year on the work of the advisory team • Conduct media briefing to sensitize the public on the need to be vigilant and always suggest best public health and safety measures

ORGANIZATION OF THE BOOK

There are several books in the area of communication for development, some of which have been cited in this chapter. Other efforts to discuss communication for development within the context of the SDGs include Servaes (2017) and Seneviratne (2018). But the literature on communication for development to achieve SDGs is still not enough to tackle the wide array of issues and debates on the SDGs. This book is a major addition to the pool of research in this area. It focuses purely on the SDGs as you will note from the various chapters, and each chapter discusses at least one of the SDGs or more. The second value addition of this book is that it came out after the COVID-19 outbreak. The content of the book therefore adds to the literature on COVID-19, SDGs and communication for development. The third value addition for this book is that it benefits not just academics and researchers. It is equally valuable to practitioners working for NGOs and civil society organizations. The communication strategies of the development institutions reviewed in this chapter and the newly proposed framework for tackling pandemics are pointers to it. We have also provided several examples from the news media to illustrate our point. Indeed, this book is extremely useful to policy-makers and diplomats in the United Nations because of the constructive criticism and policy recommendations provided in the book in relation to the SDGs.

The book is divided into four parts. Part one provides the introduction, historical and theoretical perspectives. In this part various chapters have discussed the evolution of the Sustainable Development Goals, and the various approaches to understanding communication for development. This chapter has discussed the emergence of the COVID-19 pandemic, communication for development and the impact of the pandemic on SDGs.

In Chap. 2, Jan Servaes provides a historical overview of the transition from the MDGs to SDGs. Servaes provides a critical review of the MDGs and the SDGs, identifies the gaps in both and discusses the successes recorded so far and the challenges ahead.

Chapter 3 is contributed by Muhammad Jameel Yusha'u. The title of the chapter is 'SDG18—The Missing Ventilator: An Introduction to the 2030 Agenda for Development'. This chapter argues that the framers of the 2030 agenda for development have missed one of the most important goals, SDG18 (communication for all). It argues that without SDG18, it is difficult to achieve the targets set in the global goals because each of the SDGs requires an element of communication for development. As the COVID-19 pandemic indicates, the communication infrastructure available the world over served as the 'ventilator' that provided the needed life-support for the global economy during the pandemic. The chapter then provides an overview of each of the SDGs and the challenges of achieving them.

In Chap. 4, Maria Touri, Fani Galatsopoulou, Clio Kenterelidou and Ioanna Kostarella focus on 'Communication for Sustainable Development and Blue Growth: Towards New Theoretical and Empirical Directions'. Drawing on the principles of communication and social change, the chapter offers a mapping of key Blue Growth initiatives in Europe through selected European Union (EU)-funded projects. It reveals the prevalence of a narrow market-orientated approach and one-directional communication strategies that fail to consider the needs and social life of the coastal communities that are most affected.

The subject of Chap. 5 by Toung Eh Synuanchanh and Evangelia Papoutsaki dwells on one of the non-Western perspectives to communication for development and social change. The chapter discusses the 'Buddhist Approach to Participatory Communication and Sustainable Development: A Case Study from Lao PDR'. They look at the role of religion and faith in achieving sustainable development.

In Chap. 6, Anthony Löwstedt and Diana Igropoulou focus on one of the key issues in attaining the SDGs, the issue of climate change. The title of their chapter, 'Between Rights and Diversities: Can the Regulation of Communication Help Prevent Climate Change and Promote Sustainable Development?' says a lot about the current debates on climate change. The chapter specifically looked at how media logic, media effects, mediatization, common journalistic practices, framing, cultural cognition, ideology and prevailing political and cultural economies have acted and interacted to create a global media environment which is unhelpful or hostile to sustainable development, especially with regard to climate change denialism.

One subject that attracted major attention in the formulation of the SDGs was the issue of financing. From the Financing for Development Conference in Addis Ababa in 2015 to various High-Level Political Forums at the United Nations, financing the SDGs was top on the priority of policy-makers. Some of the recommendations of the financing for development conference were to look at non-traditional sources of financing the SDGs. In Chap. 7, Hylmun Izhar and Rahmatina A. Kasri wrote about non-traditional financing by contributing on Islamic finance and SDGs. According to them, the Islamic financial services industry was estimated to be worth US $ 2.5 trillion in 2018 and forecast to reach US $ 3.2 trillion by 2024, which represents a strong potential source of financing the SDGs, fostering development and helping to end poverty.

The focus of Part two of the book is on communicating the global goals or the 2030 Agenda for Development. Various chapters with country case studies have been presented in this section.

The section starts with Chap. 8 by Gwadabe Wada Kurawa who wrote on 'Community Learning Centre as a Promising Medium for Promoting Sustainable Development Goal 4: Lifelong Learning'. The chapter considers participatory communication and adult education and learning philosophies and their importance in the Sustainable Development Goal 4 discourse. Good and promising practices in promoting Sustainable Development Goal 4 at the community level are presented through examples from Tanzania and Thailand.

Noelia Santamaría-Cárdaba and Miguel Vicente-Mariño also wrote on SDG4 in Chap. 9, but with focus on higher education. The aim of their study titled 'Communicating Sustainable Development in Higher Education: Evaluation of Education Experiences and Proposals for Teachers' Orientation' is to identify trends in academic research dealing with sustainable development in higher education over the last five years. The authors suggested strategies on how to achieve SDG4 for global citizens in light of the challenges posed by COVID-19.

Carla Patrão, Dina Soeiro and Sílvia Parreiral also wrote on SDG4 in Chap. 10, titled 'Media, Literacy and Education: Partners for Sustainable Development'. The discussion in this chapter is centred on the partnership of media, literacy and education for sustainable development based on the *Letters for Life*, an adult literacy community project. This example proposes an integrated approach to enhance sustainable development, with impacts on Goal 4.

In Chap. 11, Mohammad Ala-Uddin writes about 'The Paradox in Discourse and Praxis of Gender Equality: A Communicative Framework for Empowerment and Social Justice'. He argues that despite the massive programmatic effort over the past decades, gender-based social disparity is yet at large. While the international communities are set to achieve the goal of gender equality for all women and girls by 2030, no tangible progress has been made thus far. Women and girls across the world are still among the worst victims of poverty, insecurity, violence, conflicts and other forms of unfair social arrangements.

In Chap. 12, C.S.H.N. Murthy wrote on 'Achieving Sustainable Development Goals: An Analytical Overview of Indian Experience (2000–2019)'. The chapter hypothesizes that, albeit the role of communication is central to the developmental processes, the developmental theorists failed so far to suggest a single developmental communication theory that explains the relationship between the communication and sustainable development in highly diverse and pluralistic country like India.

In Chap. 13 the discussion is on SDG5 on gender equality. In this chapter Kanchan K. Malik wrote on 'Fostering Gender-Sensitive Programming and Practices Among Community Radios in India: The Road Ahead'. Kanchan suggested that community radio (CR) in India has played a key role in allowing social groups to negotiate diverse identities and articulate concerns from marginalized perspectives. At present, India has around 245 operational CR stations, over 100 of which are run by NGOs and local communities. Many CR initiatives in India continue to be led by women which will contribute directly to the achievement of key targets of the Sustainable Development Goals (SDGs), particularly SDG5.

Ekaterina Gladkova is the contributor of Chap. 14. She wrote on 'Miscommunication of Harms? A Critique of SDG12: Responsible Consumption and Production Implementation in the Food Sector in Northern Ireland'. The chapter provides a critique of the communication surrounding the implementation of SDG12 by looking at a case study of the Northern Irish leading poultry producer, Moy Park.

Chapter 15 is on SDG16 by Kobby Mensah, Gideon Awini and Gilbert Kofi Mensah. They wrote on an important subject that was earlier discussed in this chapter, that is, fake news. The chapter is titled 'Fake News and SDG16: The Situation in Ghana'. The authors argued that the rise of the fake news phenomenon is seen as a potential barrier to the attainment of SDG16 in Ghana. In their words, unauthentic news that mimics real news with the intent to cause havoc and chaos has the potency to affect the peace and stability of every nation.

Joshua J. Frye and Samantha Stone are the contributors of Chap. 16. The title of their chapter is 'Communication for Sustainable Social Change and the Pursuit of Zero Hunger: The Food Sovereignty Language Frame'. The goal of this chapter is to capture and explain the ideological language framing of food sovereignty by high-level grassroots food movement leaders in Ecuador and by key civil society advocates during official deliberative sessions at the 2014 annual meeting of the Committee on World Food Security (CFS) at the Food and Agriculture Organization in Rome.

Chapter 17 by Jian Xu, Dianlin Huang and He Zhang is on 'Internet Philanthropy as China's "Digital Solution" to the 2030 Agenda for Sustainable Development: Policies, Practices, Politics and Critique'. The chapter examines China's micro-philanthropy wave by looking at its background, practices, platforms and social and political implications.

Chapter 18 is written by Lara Zwarun and Gerardo R. Camilo, titled 'Facts Aren't Enough: Addressing Communication Challenges in the Pollinator Crisis and Beyond'. The chapter states that two-thirds of the world's population will be living in cities by 2050, creating sustainability challenges in terms of biodiversity conservation, ecosystem services and food production in urban environments.

Part three of this book, with the theme International Communication, Journalism and Sustainable Development, provides international perspectives on the SDGs in various countries. The section begins with Chap. 19 by Alamira Samah Saleh and Mahmoud Zaky who provide a country case study to the media coverage of the SDGs. Their chapter is on 'Egyptian TV coverage of the sustainable development strategy (SDS): Egypt's vision 2030'. The chapter explores Egypt's current development trajectory to 2030 across areas of TV content on the representation of sustainable development strategies; it states that the media practices and choices made in Egypt today will shape what the country looks like tomorrow and will determine its ability to meet the development goals outlined in the SDGs and Vision 2030.

Isabell Koinig, Sandra Diehl and Franzisca Weder are the authors of Chap. 20 which focuses on SDG3. Their chapter is on 'Communicating "Health for All" in German-Speaking Countries as Exemplified by HIV/AIDS Advertising Campaigns'. Their chapter highlights how the UN's health goal #3 is communicated as part of national health campaigns for HIV/AIDS prevention. Ensuring quality education at all levels is one of the aims of the SDGs.

In Chap. 21, contributed by Radoslaw Sajna, the author wrote on 'Global Communication and Sustainable Development: From the Earth Summit in Rio 1992 to the Olympic Games in Rio 2016'. The chapter presents a short historical outline of the relationship between media and environment and a study of the global media coverage of the opening ceremony of the Rio Olympic Games.

Chapter 22 focuses on 'A Comparative Analysis of American and Chinese News Media Coverage of Climate Change Issues Over the Period 2007–2015'. The authors of the chapter, Won Y. Jang, Edward Frederick, Eric Jamelske, Wontae Lee and Youngju Kim, present an empirical analysis that compares Chinese and US news agencies' coverage of climate change from 2007 to 2015.

Chapter 23 by Kenneth C. C. Yang and Yowei Kang is also on climate change. The authors ask an interesting question on the theme of the chapter: 'Has Trump's Presidency Changed Climate Change Discourses?: A Text Mining Analysis of Newspaper Contents in the United States'. The authors found noticeable differences before and after Trump's presidency in how US newspapers frame climate change issues, suggesting the possible effect of political changes on the media framing building of climate change issues.

Chapter 24 by Habeeb Idris Pindiga and Bashir Sa'ad Abdullahi studied the coverage of the SDGs in Nigerian newspapers. This chapter examines the reporting of the Sustainable Development Goals (SDGs) in the Nigerian press and the challenges impeding journalists from effectively covering the SDGs. Using content analysis and framing analysis of the news coverage by two national dailies, *Daily Trust* and *Vanguard*, as well as semi-structured interviews with a selection of Nigerian journalists, the chapter seeks to determine the dominant news frames used in representing the SDGs.

Taye C. Obateru's contribution in Chap. 25 is on 'Selected Journalists' Role Perception Towards Achieving *Agenda 2030* in Nigeria'. The theme of the chapter is built on three focus group sessions organized among selected journalists from across Nigeria to investigate their perception of their role towards meeting Agenda 2030.

Part four of the book is the conclusion. In this section, comprising Chap. 26, Muhammad Jameel Yusha'u and Jan Servaes wrap up the book by synthesizing the context of the entire book. It looks at the journey for sustainable development beyond the 2030 Agenda. The chapter provides a critical analysis about the likelihood of achieving the SDGs by 2030. It concludes with several policy recommendations and lessons learnt from this book, including the possibility of reconsidering the timeline for the 2030 Agenda for Development from 2030 to 2050.

References

ABC Australia. (2020). *From Wuhan to Australia: A Timeline of Key Events in the Spread of the Deadly Coronavirus.* Retrieved November 24, 2020, from https://www.abc.net.au/news/2020-01-29/coronavirus-timeline-from-wuhan-china-to-global-crisis/11903298?nw=0

Arab News. (2020). *Saudi Government Messages Experts Over COVID-19 Rules Violations.* Retrieved November 23, 2020, from https://www.arabnews.com/node/1687931/saudi-arabia

Asiedu, C. (2012). Information Communication Technologies for Gender and Development in Africa: The Case for Radio and Technological Blending. *International Communication Gazette, 74*(2), 240–257.

Bagdikian, B. (2004). *The New Media Monopoly* (7th ed.). Boston: Beacon Press.

BBC. (2020). Coronavirus pandemic. Retrieved December 7, 2020, from https://www.bbc.com/news/coronavirus

BBC News. (2020). *Coronavirus: The World in Lockdown in Maps and Charts*. Retrieved November 24, 2020, from https://www.bbc.com/news/world-52103747

Boyd-Barrett, O. (2006). Cyberspace, Globalization and Empire. *Global Media and Communication*, 2(1), 21–41.

CCTV. (2020a). *Scientists Optimistic on Making COVID-19 Vaccines Affordable, Equitable Despite Challenges*. Retrieved December 6, 2020, from https://english.cctv.com/2020/12/06/ARTI0CT0hS1kVcU2iheXoV8P201206.shtml?spm=C69523.PDoRdCIUTBov.S91108.2

CCTV. (2020b). *Wang Yi Addresses UN Special Session on COVID-19*. Retrieved December 7, 2020, from https://english.cctv.com/2020/12/04/ARTIMpzGi4J8PfVQd8elHS5Q201204.shtml?spm=C69523.PDoRdCIUTBov.S91108.44

CCTV. (2020c). *U.S. Hits Record-High COVID-19 Daily Cases, Hospitalizations as Caseload Tops 14 Mln*. Retrieved December 7, 2020, from https://english.cctv.com/2020/12/04/ARTIMD5SRo8DoZZktkg3iBn0201204.shtml?spm=C69523.PDoRdCIUTBov.S91108.65

CCTV. (2020d). *China Willing to Work with Countries Including U.S. to Contain COVID-19: Spokesperson*. Retrieved December 7, 2020, from https://english.cctv.com/2020/12/03/ARTI0TzojeDupAROE61mskih201203.shtml?spm=C69523.PDoRdCIUTBov.S91108.114

Commission for Environment and Development. (1983). *Report of the World Commission on Environment and Development-Our Common World*. Retrieved November 20, 2020, from https://sustainabledevelopment.un.org/content/documents/5987our-common-future.pdf

Davies, I. K. (2015). *International News Contraflow in the United States and Canada. Struggles Over North American Markets and Regulation of Aljazeera and China Central Television*. Unpublished doctoral dissertation, University of Illinois at Urbana-Champaign.

Delirrad, M., & Mohammadi A. B. (2020). New Methanol Poisoning Outbreaks in Iran Following COVID-19 Pandemic. *Alcohol and Alcoholism*. 1–2. https://doi.org/10.1093/alcalc/agaa036

European Commission. (2020). *Tackling COVID-19 Misinformation. Getting Facts Right*. Retrieved November 19, 2020, from https://ec.europa.eu/info/sites/info/files/communication-tackling-covid-19-disinformation-getting-facts-right_en.pdf

European Union. (2020). *Tackling Coronavirus Misinformation: Getting the Facts Right*. Retrieved November 19, 2020, from https://ec.europa.eu/info/sites/info/files/corona_fighting_disinformation.pdf

Financial Times. (2020). *The Real Fake News About COVID-19*. Retrieved November 19, 2020, from https://www.ft.com/content/e5954181-220b-4de5-886c-ef02ee432260

Gavi. (2020). *How Creative Communication Strategies Are Helping Fight COVID-19 Misinformation in DRC*. Retrieved November 19, 2020, from https://www.gavi.org/vaccineswork/how-creative-communication-strategies-helping-fight-covid-19-misinformation-drc

Honigsbaum, M. (2020). *The Pandemic Century. A History of Global Contagion from the Spanish flu to Covid-19*. London: Penguin House.

IFRC, UNICEF, WHO. (2020). *RCCE Action Plan Guidance: COVID-19 Preparedness and Response*. Paris: WHO.

ILO. (2020). *ILO Monitor: COVID-19 and the World of Work. Sixth Edition. Updated Estimates and Analysis.* Retrieved November 24, 2020, from https://www.ilo.org/wcmsp5/groups/public/%2D%2D-dgreports/%2D%2D-dcomm/documents/briefingnote/wcms_755910.pdf

Iordache, C., Van Audenhove, L., & Loisen, J. (2019). Global Media Flows: A Qualitative Review of Research Methods in Audio-Visual Flow Studies. *International Communication Gazette., 81*(6-8), 748–767.

Lerner, D. (1958). *The Passing of Traditional Society: Modernising the Middle East.* Macmillan Co. Pub.

Martini, M., Gazzaniga, V., Bragazzi, N. L., & Barberis, I. (2019). The Spanish Influenza Pandemic: A Lesson From History 100 Years After 1918. *Journal of Preventive Medicine and Hygiene, 60*(1), E64–E67.

Mefalopulos, P. (2008). *Development Communication Source Book. Broadening the Boundaries of Communication.* Washington, DC: World Bank.

Melkote, R. M., & Steeves, H. L. (2015). *Communication for Development. Theory and Practice for Empowerment and Social Justice.* Lon Angeles: Sage.

Mukarram, M. M. (2020). Impact of COVID-19 on the UN Sustainable Development Goals (SDGs). *Strategic Analysis., 44*(3), 253–258.

Naffi, N., Davidson, A., & Jawhar, H. (2020). *5 Ways to Help Stop the 'Infodemic,' the Increasing Misinformation About Coronavirus.* Retrieved November 19, 2020, from https://theconversation.com/5-ways-to-help-stop-the-infodemic-the-increasing-misinformation-about-coronavirus-137561

Ogan, C. L., Bashir, M., Camaj, L., Luo, Y., Gaddie, B., Pennington, R., et al. (2009). Development Communication: The State of Research in an Era of ICTs and Globalization. *The International Communication Gazette, 71*(8), 655–670. https://doi.org/10.1177/1748048509345060

Pade-Khene, C., Palmer, R., & Kavhai, M. (2010). A Baseline Study of a Dwesa Rural Community for the Siyakhula Information and Communication Technology for Development Project: Understanding the Reality on the Ground. *Information Development, 26,* 265.

Reinsdorf, M. (2020). *COVID-19 and CPI: Is Inflation Underestimated?* IMF Working Paper. Retrieved November 24, 2020, from https://www.imf.org/en/Publications/WP/Issues/2020/11/05/COVID-19-and-the-CPI-Is-Inflation-Underestimated-49856

Rogers, E. M. (1962). *Diffusion of innovations.* New York: Free Press of Glencoe. Chicago.

Sachs, J. (2015). *The Age of Sustainable Development.* New York: Columbia University Press.

Sara, J. J., Moulik, S. G., & Hall, M. C. (2020). *10 Steps to Developing a Communication Strategy to Help Combat COVID-19 (Coronavirus).* Retrieved November 15, 2020, from https://blogs.worldbank.org/water/10-steps-developing-communication-strategy-help-combat-covid-19-coronavirus

Seneviratne, K. (2018). *Mindful Communication for Sustainable Development. Perspectives from Asia.* Sage Publications.

Servaes J. (Ed.). (2009). *Communication for Development and Social Change.* Los Angeles, London, New Delhi, Singapore: Sage.

Servaes, J. (2013). Introduction: Imperatives for a Sustainable Future. In J. Servaes (Ed.), *Sustainable Development and Green Communication. African and Asian Perspectives* (pp. 1–39). London and New York: Palgrave and Macmillan.

Servaes, J. (2017). *Sustainable Development Goals in the Asian Context.* Singapore: Springer.

Servaes, J. (2020). *Handbook of Communication for Development and Social Change I & II*. Singapore: Springer.

Servaes, J., & Malikhao P. (2007). Communication for Sustainable Development. In FAO (Eds.), *Communication and Sustainable Development*. Selected papers from the 9th UN Roundtable on Communication for Development. Retrieved November 11, 2020, form http://www.fao.org/3/a-a1476e.pdf

Servaes, J., Polk, E., Shi, S., Reilly, D., & Yakupitijage, T. (2012). Towards a Framework of Sustainability Indicators for 'Communication for Development and Social Change' Projects. *International communication Gazette, 74*(2), 99–123.

Singer, L. (2020). *On the Diffusion of Innovation: How Ideas Spread*. Retrieved November 23, 2020, from https://leif.me/on-the-diffusion-of-innovations-how-new-ideas-spread/

Singhal, T. (2020). A Review of Coronavirus Disease 2019 (COVID-19). *Indian Journal of Pediatrics., 87*(4), 281–286.

Stanford Engineering Staff. (2020). *Seema Yasmin: How to Conquer Pandemic with Communication*. Retrieved November 23, 2020, from https://engineering.stanford.edu/magazine/article/seema-yasmin-how-conquer-pandemic-communication

Sustainable Development Goals. (2020). *Report of the World Commission of Environment and Development-Our Common Future*. Retrieved November 20, 2020, from https://sustainabledevelopment.un.org/milestones/wced

The Atlantic. (2021). *Germany's Anti-vaccination History Is Riddled With Anti-Semitism*. Retrieved from https://www.theatlantic.com/health/archive/2021/05/anti-vaccination-germany-anti-semitism/618777/30/05/2021

The Guardian. (2021). *'Meet the Governor We Have Known All Along': How Cuomo Fell from Grace*. Retrieved February 25, 2020, from https://www.theguardian.com/us-news/2021/feb/20/andrew-cuomo-new-york-pandemic-investigation?fbclid=IwAR1biEnmttJIQy-iWOXg3LKU6i0j3oXm-kZkfCZwlhyGGda47H713hPQqIk

Thussu, D. K. (2007). *Media on the move: Global Flow and Contraflow*. London and New York: Routledge.

Thussu, D. K. (2016). Contra-Flow in Global Media. An Asian Perspective. *Media Asia, 33*(3-4), 123–129.

Thussu, D. K. (2018). International Communication. In *Continuity and Change*. New York: Bloomsbury academic.

UN News. (2020). *Progress Toward Sustainable Development Is Seriously Off-Track*. Retrieved November 23, 2020, from https://news.un.org/en/story/2019/11/1050831

UNDP. (2009). *Communication for Development: A Glimpse at UNDP's Practice*. Retrieved November 22, 2020, from file:///C:/Users/320170/Downloads/Communication%20for%20Development%20A%20Glimpse%20at%20UNDP_s%20Practice%20(2009).pdf

White, R. A. (2004). Is 'Empowerment The Answer?. Current Theory and Research on Development Communication. *The Gazette: The International Journal for Communication Studies., 66*(1), 7–24.

WHO. (2020a). *Immunizing the Public Against Misinformation*. Retrieved November 19, 2020 from https://www.who.int/news-room/feature-stories/detail/immunizing-the-public-against-misinformation

WHO. (2020b). *Managing the Misinformation Infodemic: Promoting Healthy Behaviours and Mitigating the Harm from Misinformation and Disinformation*. Retrieved November 19, 2020, from https://www.who.int/news/item/23-09-2020-managing-the-covid-19-infodemic-promoting-healthy-behaviours-and-mitigating-the-harm-from-misinformation-and-disinformation

CHAPTER 2

The Sustainable Development Goals: A Major Reboot or Just Another Acronym?

Jan Servaes

To make poverty history, you have to understand how history is made
The Economist, 07-07-07: 13

On 25 September 2015, the 70th session of the United Nations General Assembly in New York approved the post-2015 development agenda in the form of 17 Sustainable Development Goals (SDGs), 169 associated targets and 304 indicators (https://sdgs.un.org/goals, SDSN, 2015). These SDGs built on the Millennial Development Goals (MDGs) (https://www.un.org/millenniumgoals/), which were composed of 8 goals and 21 targets expected to be reached by December 2015.

The MDG initiative followed decades of debate over how nations might collaborate on long-term strategies for a global social agenda. Wealthy countries were asked to increase development aid, relieve the debt burden on poor countries and give them fair access to markets and technology. In 2015, 193 nations committed to the SDGs, which set out a transformative agenda that linked human health and prosperity to environmental health and equity.

The new 2030 Agenda for Sustainable Development "is a plan of action for people, planet and prosperity. It also seeks to strengthen universal peace in larger freedom. We recognise that eradicating poverty in all its forms and dimensions, including extreme poverty, is the greatest global challenge and an

J. Servaes (✉)
KU Leuven, Leuven, Belgium

© The Author(s), under exclusive license to Springer Nature Switzerland AG 2021
M. J. Yusha'u, J. Servaes (eds.), *The Palgrave Handbook of International Communication and Sustainable Development*,
https://doi.org/10.1007/978-3-030-69770-9_2

indispensable requirement for sustainable development" (https://sustainabledevelopment.un.org/post2015/transformingourworld).

Some argue that the Sustainable Development Goals (SDGs) are just a sequel to the Millennial Development Goals (MDGs), while others consider them a major reboot. The SDGs are obviously more comprehensive than the MDGs, and resulted from an extensive and participatory process. As a consequence considerably more targets (169 vs. 18) and more words (about 5000 vs. about 300) were needed to spell out the SDGs.

This chapter tries to briefly analyse the history of both acronyms in order to arrive at a critical assessment of their contributions for a global social agenda. In addition to a listing of 'successes' it also outlines the remaining gaps and omissions in the debate.

From MDGs to SDGs

The 'Architects'

Dorine van Norren (2012), Advisory Council on International Affairs at the Dutch Ministry of Foreign Affairs, in an interesting overview of 'the wheel of development' for the Third World Quarterly, outlines four schools of thought regarding the MDGs:

> Optimists (or perhaps one should say 'architects') see the goals as a vehicle for transforming the human condition (including Jeffrey Sachs, leader of the Millennium Project, Vandemoortele and Pronk); strategic realists see the MDGs as essential to achieving and preserving political commitment (Fukuda-Parr and Jolly); sceptics find the MDGs well-intentioned but badly thought out (such as Clemens and Easterly); radical critics see the MDGs as a diversionary manoeuvre to draw attention away from the 'real' issues of growing global inequality and gender disparity (including Antrobus, Eyben, Saith, Pogge and Ziai). UNCTAD describes the fundamental problem of the MDGs as 'the lack of a more inclusive strategy of economic development.' Of course, this division is rudimentary; the position of 'optimists' may be explained by their executive responsibility for the design and/or implementation of MDG policy and not per se by a fundamental disagreement on the analysis of development processes. The position of some, such as Vandemoortele, is evolving over time. (Van Norren, 2012, p. 826)

This Jan Vandemoortele, a Belgian diplomat who worked for over 30 years in different capacities for UNICEF, UNDP, ILO and World Bank, was co-chair of the UN agency group that put the MDGs together. He recounts their history as follows: "The main reason for putting together the MDGs was to prevent the Millennium Declaration from falling into oblivion. A declaration issued by a world summit has a shelf-life of about six months. Beyond that period, its life is reduced to a small world, usually the summit's sponsoring agency. A few months after the Millennium Summit, once the declaration started to fade away, a group of experts from across the United Nations convened to go through the Millennium Declaration. Experts from the Organisation of Economic Co-operation and Development also took part. Eighteen targets were selected and placed verbatim in a stand-alone list. They were grouped under eight goals, and 48 indicators were added for global monitoring. That list of goals, targets and indicators was submitted to the UN General Assembly in late 2001 under the heading Millennium Development Goals. And the rest is history" (Vandemoortele, 2015). The selection took extensive discussions and negotiations, "but it was never the intention to represent a global agenda for development. We simply saw the MDGs as a way to maintain the Millennium Declaration's relevance. Two criteria, though not strictly applied, played a role in the selection: clarity and measurability" (Vandemoortele, 2016).

The MDGs: Too Bureaucratic, Too Ambitious, Too Narrow?

In essence, development is about the development of people and the transformation of society. That was also the objective of the Millennium Declaration of 8 September 2000 (https://www.un.org/en/development/devagenda/millennium.shtml): freedom, equality (of individuals and nations), solidarity, tolerance, respect for nature and shared responsibility were cited as six values fundamental to international relations for the twenty-first century.

Measurable and time-bound global targets, the first of their kind, were adopted to address a number of essential global priorities, such as the reduction of poverty, hunger and disease. They sought to realize the human rights of all and to achieve gender equality and empowerment of all women and girls. They were meant to be integrated and indivisible, and balance the four dimensions of sustainable development: the economic, social, environmental and cultural.

Each MDG had its own set of targets and benchmarks that provide a measurable way to track its implementation (UNDP, 2015). However, various constraints worked against achievement of the MDGs—technical constraints because the MDGs are numerical; operational constraints because they are time bound; and financial constraints because initial cost assumptions did prove false and some eligibility requirements were being imposed. In other words, there were many obstacles to overcome. But the most important obstacle was: *development seen as an 'engineering problem' to be solved from a top-down perspective.* As William Easterly (2006), one of the 'sceptics' in Van Norren's typology, puts it: "Sixty years of countless reform schemes to aid agencies and dozens of different plans, and $2.3 trillion later, the aid industry is still failing to reach the beautiful goal (of making poverty history, JS). The evidence points to an unpopular conclusion: Big Plans will always fail to reach the beautiful goal" (Easterly, 2006, p. 11). In other words, the question should be: What can MDGs do for the poor and 'voiceless'? "Setting a prefixed (and grandiose) goal is irrational because there is no reason to assume that the goal is attainable at a reasonable cost with the available means" (Easterly, ibid.).

We have therefore argued, for instance in Servaes (1999, 2017a, 2020), that it is essential to start from the perspective of local communities and to cooperate with organizations (UN, governmental, NGOs, the public and the private sectors and civil society) that have developed a trust within a community in order to achieve sustainable change in society.

At a more detailed level, questions were also raised about the feasibility and appropriateness of setting the same global targets for governments worldwide: "The MDGs can justly claim to generate a bit of buzz about duties a government might otherwise neglect. ... Sadly, however, they cannot do what they purport to do, which is to provide credible benchmarks against which governments can be judged. ... Some goals cannot be met, others cannot be measured. ... The goals are supposed to be everyone's responsibility, which means they are no one's. Poor countries can blame rich ones for not stumping up enough cash; rich governments can accuse poor ones of failing to deserve more money" (The Economist, 2007, p. 13).

Though co-author of the MDGs Vandemoortele is one of its harshest critics:

> Many saw them as too simplistic and driven by the availability of data, without identifying clear accountability and financing frameworks. Others cautioned against reducing development to a list of targets; potentially leading to a technocratic takeover—by techno-optimists—that would de-politicize the development debate or become a Trojan horse for the Washington Consensus. Still others warned they would reinforce vertical programs and sectoral funding mechanisms. Another common critique was that the MDGs measured progress in terms of national averages, which obscured within-country disparities. Various observers expressed disappointment over the absence of reproductive health in the original MDGs and the inadequate coverage of gender equality and the deficient handling of environmental challenges. (Vandemoortele, 2016)

The World Health Organization (WHO) established an international Task Force to identify health systems research priorities (Bennett et al., 2020; Task Force on Health Systems, 2004). The Task Force employed an interpretive approach to identify a number of broad priority topics. These topics included human resources for health at the district level and below; drugs and diagnostic policies; governance and accountability. With the engagement of policy and decision-makers global priorities for specific domains of health policy and systems research were drafted on health financing, human resources for health, access to medicines and the private health sector. Thanks to this process more specific health goals than the broad domains identified by the Task Force could be identified.

Vandemoortele (2011) sums up: "The basic criticism levelled against the Millennium Development Goals (MDGs) is that they present a reductionist view of development. They are too limited in scope; their definition is too narrowly focused on the social sectors; their sectoral fragmentation leads to vertical silos; their emphasis on quantification is excessive; and they omit fundamental objectives contained in the Millennium Declaration, such as peace and security, human rights, democracy and good governance. The criticism also points out that they fail to underscore universal values such as freedom, tolerance and equality. Too many dimensions are missing (e.g. human rights and economic growth) or the complexity of the dimensions that are included is missed (e.g. gender equality and quality of education)" (Vandemoortele, 2011, p. 8). And he concludes: "Ultimately development is always specific to the space and era in which it unfolds. There are no silver bullets or universal solutions that apply to all countries all the time. Development must be seen as a process of collective self-discovery—in rich and poor countries alike. It cannot be reduced to a set of imported recipes that are limited to the logic of homo economicus. The way in which a country develops is always shaped and influenced by its own specific circumstances. Policy is always embedded in politics, not solely in econometric analysis or technocratic literature. Those who claim that the MDGs should spell out a strategy for reaching the targets merely want to depoliticise the development process by reducing it to a series of standard interventions of a technocratic nature" (Vandemoortele, 2011).

Communication and Culture Missing

In addition, we wondered very early on where communication and culture issues were in all of this (Servaes, 2007a, 2007b, 2008, see also Byrne, Nicholson, & Salem, 2011). Also Silvio Waisbord (2006, p. 3) "cannot help but notice that communication goals are absent. … While everyone seems to think that communication is important, apparently it is not crucial enough to make it into the (MDG) list." This absence of cultural rights, communication freedoms and democracy was confirmed by policymakers within the UN agency system. On 25 June 2007, the Director of UNESCO's Bureau of Strategic Planning urged the Director of the UN Development Group Office (UNDG) in a letter that "while Communication for Development remains critical to achieving the MDGs, it has not been adequately recognized as an essential element in development planning within UN programming exercises in general and CCA/UNDAF in particular. Participants expressed the need to rectify this deficiency and to make it a policy to integrate Communication for Development at field level throughout the planning, implementation and evaluation phases of UN assistance programmes" (quoted in Servaes, 2017a, p. 6).

And so Vandemoortele (2011) argues:

> The MDGs require fundamental transformations in society. Deep-seated changes are required to prioritise the well-being of the most disadvantaged and vulnerable people in society—ethnic minorities, low-caste children and women, slum dwellers, subsistence farmers, and households in the bottom wealth quintiles. They cannot result from the application of the standard recipes that engendered these discriminations in the first place. Einstein's quote comes to mind: 'We can't solve problems by using the same kind of thinking we used when we created them.' Those who call for an overall MDG strategy are implicitly trying to impose their own world-view and ideology onto everyone else.

The 'Successes' of the MDGs

Nevertheless, there is wide agreement that the MDGs have played a significant role in addressing poverty, hunger and disease worldwide. A number of developing countries made considerable progress towards the accomplishment of certain MDGs, but the overall progress was sporadic across goals, countries and regions (Servaes, 2017a).

Some of the most important 'successes' are:

- The world has reduced extreme poverty by half.
- Efforts in the fight against malaria and tuberculosis have shown results.
- Access to improved drinking water source became a reality for 2.3 billion people.
- Disparities in primary school enrolment between boys and girls are being eliminated in all developing regions. Ninety per cent of children in developing regions are attending primary school.
- The political participation of women has continued to increase.
- Development assistance rebounded, the trading system stayed favourable for developing countries and their debt burden remained low.
- Major trends that threaten environmental sustainability continue, but examples of successful global action exist.
- Hunger continues to decline, but immediate additional efforts are needed to reach the MDG target.
- Chronic undernutrition among young children declined, but one in four children is still affected.
- Child mortality has been almost halved, but more progress is needed.
- Much more needs to be done to reduce maternal mortality.
- Antiretroviral therapy is saving lives and must be expanded further.
- Over a quarter of the world's population has gained access to improved sanitation since 1990, yet a billion people still resorted to open defecation.
- (For some more detailed assessments, see McArthur & Rasmussen, 2018, UNECA, 2015, World Vision, 2015)

However, old problems such as poverty, inequality and information gaps have not disappeared. Even the former Secretary-General of the United Nations, Ban Ki Moon (2016, p. 3), admitted: "For all the remarkable gains, I am keenly aware that inequalities persist and that progress has been uneven. The world's poor remain overwhelmingly concentrated in some parts of the world. In 2011, nearly 60 per cent of the world's one billion extremely poor people lived in just five countries. Too many women continue to die during pregnancy or from childbirth-related complications. Progress tends to bypass women and those who are lowest on the economic ladder or are disadvantaged because of their age, disability or ethnicity. Disparities between rural and urban areas remain pronounced. Experiences and evidence from the efforts to achieve the MDGs demonstrate that we know what to do. But further progress will require an unswerving political will, and collective, long-term effort. We need to tackle root causes and do more to integrate the economic, social and environmental dimensions of sustainable development."

The SDGs: Old Wine in New Bottles

While in many respects the MDGs were successful in driving international and national investments, and the world's focus upon the identified goals, they had also been criticized for being insufficiently inclusive in their process of development, providing insufficient justification for why they focused on the issues that they did and for neglecting environmental, communication, indigenous and other issues. The SDGs sought to address these criticisms. They were negotiated in a far more consultative fashion using 13 rounds of discussion within the Open Working Group; they clearly address some of these issues, and they are much broader in terms of the targets identified.

The SDGs follow the Global Partnership for Sustainable Development framework, as outlined in the outcome document of the 3rd International Conference on Financing for Development held in Addis Ababa, Ethiopia, on 16 July 2015 (UNSC, 2015). Additionally, the numerous targets indicated in the SDGs require huge capital investments, not just for the SDGs as a whole but also for its individual components. On a global scale, crude estimates have put the cost of providing a social safety net to eradicate extreme poverty at about US $66 billion a year, while annual investments in improving essential infrastructure could reach US $7 trillion (Ford, 2015).

Jeffrey Sachs, leader of the Millennium Project and listed as one of the 'optimists' or 'architects' in Van Norren's typology mentioned earlier, argued that the complexity and interconnectivity of the SDGs require the mobilization of global knowledge operating across many sectors and regions in order to identify frameworks and systems that would help realize the goals by 2030 (Sachs, 2012). Specifically, effective accountability measures need to be in place, such as annual reviews of specific goals, monitoring systems which gather needed information to support and update conducted projects and follow-up statuses of pre-cursor programmes essential for meeting a specific SDG as initiated by certain stakeholders (SDSN, 2015). According to Hak, Janouskova, and Moldan (2016), the current framework for achieving and monitoring SDGs which rely on triple bottom line parameters and statistics should be improved through robust conceptual and methodological work.

Radical Shift?

For some, the Sustainable Development Goals (SDGs) marked a radical shift in direction from the previous Millennium Development Goals (MDGs). While the MDGs reflected an economic list of relatively narrow targets that addressed low- and middle-income countries alone, the SDGs are more numerous and reflect a more holistic understanding of the nature of sustainable development and its interactions with human health, environmental protection and social justice. Therefore, the SDGs go further than the MDGs, which, aside from having an increased set of agenda to work upon, have more demanding targets (such as the elimination of poverty, instead of reducing its occurrence), as well as closely related and interdependent goals. "In general, it is hoped that by 2030, poverty and hunger are eliminated, quality of life is greatly improved, all forms of capital are intact and functioning under ideal climatic situations, and peace and prosperity is shared by all" (Vandemoortele, 2018).

However, while the UN member-states collectively agreed on the SDGs as equally important global objectives, the same states seemed to prioritize certain SDGs in national implementation. Such cherry-picking defies the "integrated and indivisible" nature of the SDGs and could negatively impact overall progress on sustainable development globally, Forestier and Kim (2020) contend.

Therefore, the Agenda 2030 is not universal in scope because the few targets that are verifiable—those that contain conceptual clarity, numerical outcome and specific deadlines—apply primarily to developing countries. The omission of targets for overweight/obesity and breastfeeding exemplifies, for instance, the reluctance of developed countries to commit themselves to specific, quantitative and time-bound targets. Most SDG targets that are verifiable are actually not dissimilar from the MDGs (Vandemoortele, 2018).

The Agenda 2030 is based on the premise that "eradicating poverty is the greatest global challenge." Logically, the first target is to "eradicate extreme poverty for all people everywhere, currently measured as people living on less than $1.25 a day." Yet, numerous experts and observers argue that extreme poverty no longer constitutes the principal challenge the world is facing today. "That view, they argue, is outdated because of the rise in inequality that has occurred within most countries over the past decades. *The greatest global challenge is extreme inequality*" (Vandemoortele, 2016).

And Jan Vandemoortele elaborates further: "Despite their comprehensiveness and wordy nature, the SDGs lack sufficient specifics to qualify as a major reboot. To be valid, a target must contain three elements: (1) a numerical outcome, (2) a specific deadline and (3) a well-defined domain.

Item 3.1, for example, is a valid target: By 2030, reduce the global maternal mortality ratio to less than 70 per 100,000 live births.

On the other hand, item 17.2 does not contain a deadline: Developed countries to implement fully their ODA commitments, including the commitment by many developed countries to achieve the target of 0.7 per cent of ODA/GNI.

Item 16.5—Substantially reduce corruption and bribery in all their forms—lacks all three elements.

The SDGs actually contain many such items as 16.5. The list is a mixture of ideals and norms, values and principles, generalities and oddities, and some repetitions; a few valid targets are sprinkled in. Indeed, the SDGs may contain 169 bullets, but actually fewer than 30 are concrete targets. Not only does their complexity turn the SDGs into a difficult storyline, but also their fuzziness will create leeway and latitude for non-objective narratives" (Vandemoortele, 2016, see also Vandemoortele, 2017).

The concrete targets are not dissimilar from the MDGs, since they mostly cover issues such as poverty and hunger, child and maternal mortality, safe water, education and gender equality. "In short, the SDGs are not quite a reboot or a paradigm shift. Neither do they represent a universal agenda that addresses inequality and sustainability. Plus ça change, plus c'est la même chose!" (Vandemoortele, 2015).

Beyond Cherry-Picking

Our and Vandemoortele's criticism does not mean that the SDGs have no worth. However, their practical relevance requires that we dig deeper. Implementation needs to start with each country selecting and adapting those aspects of the SDGs that are most relevant to their national context. This is often dismissed as cherry-picking through a non-participatory process. However, in our opinion, besides government, such selection and adaptation need to include civil society, academics, think tanks, trade unions employers federations, ... and the people at large (Servaes, 2007b, 2008, 2017a; Vandemoortele, 2018). The question should also be how global targets make a difference at national and subnational levels? Because, as Bali Swain and Yang-Wallentin argue: "Resources are limited and SDGs are fraught with trade-offs and inconsistencies. Therefore, strategic policy focus on socio-economic development in the developing countries may be a successful short-run policy to achieve sustainable development. Developed countries' results, however, suggest a greater propensity to achieve sustainable development by focus on the environmental and social factors" (Bali Swain & Yang-Wallentin, 2020, p. 105; see also Nilsson et al., 2018).

At the global level, implementation of the SDGs requires addressing three aspects (Vandemoortele, 2015):

First, the way of aggregating the global narrative needs to change radically. This was mostly driven by global statistics and world maps for the MDGs, with off-track countries coloured in red. This time around, the global assessment needs to pay more attention to how global targets make a difference at national and subnational levels.
Second, the choice of indicators must help remedy some of the flaws in the formulation of the SDGs. The inclusion of the Palma ratio, for instance, can fix target 10.1 about inequality. The inclusion of body mass indices can fix target 2.2, which ignores the growing challenge of being overweight or obese.
Third and last, one of the few truly universal targets in the SDGs cannot be left orphaned. It concerns bullet 1.2—by 2030, reduce at least by half the proportion of men, women and children of all ages living in poverty in all its dimensions according to national definitions. The global narrative is already focusing on extreme poverty and hunger, which are not universal targets.

Who will be championing target 1.2? Who will compile the register of national definitions to help clarify the domain?

Gaps and Omissions

Notwithstanding their relevance, the SDGs still contain major omissions and gaps. Let us list a number:

- sustainable development and resiliency;
- the role and place of communication and culture;
- human and indigenous rights;
- the need for an extra SDG 18 on communication for all and digital inclusion; and
- the SDGs and COVID-19.

Sustainable Development

Sustainability and resilience are two of the many concepts currently popular in the academic community, especially with regard to how we understand processes of lasting social change. Indeed, although there is no formal definition of "sustainability," it continues to remain popular in various political, social and economic discourses, particularly those of environmental groups as a call to action to raise awareness around the current depletion of finite natural resources (for recent overviews, see Agyeman, 2013, Farley & Smith, 2014, Foster, 2015, Servaes, 2013, Servaes & Malikhao, 2017, UN, 2013, Zolli & Healy 2012).

Sustainable development is seen as a means of enhancing decision-making so that it provides a more comprehensive assessment of the many multidimensional problems society faces. What is required is an evaluation framework for categorizing programmes, projects, policies and/or decisions as having sustainability potential.

The word is most often associated with being able to meet the needs of the present (socially, economically, environmentally), without compromising the ability of future generations to meet their needs (World Commission on Environment and Development, 1987). The Thai Buddhist monk and philosopher Phra Dhammapidhok (Payutto, 1998) points out that sustainable development in a Western perspective lacks the human development dimension. He states that the Western ideology emphasizes 'competition.' Therefore the concept of 'compromising' is used in the WCED definition. Compromising means lessen the needs of all parties. If the other parties do not want to compromise, you have to compromise your own needs and that will lead to frustration. Development will not be sustained if people are not happy.

He consequently reaches the conclusion that the Western perception of and road to sustainability, based on Western ethics, leads development into a cul-de-sac.

From a Buddhist perspective, sustainability concerns ecology, economy and evolvability. The concept 'evolvability' means the potential of human beings to develop themselves into less selfish persons. The main core of sustainable development is to encourage and convince human beings to live in harmony with their environment, not to control or destroy it. If humans have been socialized correctly, they will express the correct attitude towards nature and the environment and act accordingly. Payutto argues that: "A correct relation system of developed mankind is the acceptance of the fact that human-being is part of the existence of nature and relates to its ecology. Human-being should develop itself to have a higher capacity to help his fellows and other species in the natural domain; to live in a harmonious way and lessen exploitations in order to contribute to a happier world" (Payutto, 1998, p. 189).

This holistic approach of human relates to cultural development in three dimensions:

- Behaviours and lifestyles which do not harm nature;
- Minds in line with (Eastern) ethics, stability of mind, motivation and so forth to see other creatures as companions;
- Wisdom includes knowledge and understanding, attitude, norms and values in order to live in harmony with nature.

Four dimensions are generally recognized as the "pillars" of sustainable development: economic, environmental, social and cultural. "The essence of sustainability therefore, is to take the contextual features of economy, society, and environment—the uncertainty, the multiple competing values, and the distrust among various interest groups—as givens and go on to design a process that guides concerned groups to seek out and ask the right questions as a preventative approach to environmentally and socially regrettable undertakings" (Flint, 2007: IV). Or, in the words of the Thai social philosopher Sulak Sivaraksa: "How much healthier all our societies would be if they were based on value systems that truly advocated sustainability rather than unlimited growth! A society where people help each other out in hard times, a society where power is shared rather than fought over, that reveres and respects nature rather than controlling and using it as a resource, a society unsullied by the poisons of craving (tanha), and a society steeped in spirituality and wisdom" (Sivaraksa, 2009, p. 278).

Over the years, different perspectives—based on both 'Western' and 'Eastern' philosophical starting points—have resulted in a more holistic and integrated vision of sustainable development (Servaes & Malikhao, 2017; Sivaraksa, 2010). At the same time, a unifying theme is that there is no universal development model. Development is an integral, multidimensional and dialectic process that differs from society to society, community to community, context to context. In other words, each society and community must attempt to delineate its own strategy to sustainable development starting with the resources and 'capitals' available (not only physical, financial and environmental but also human, social, institutional etc.), and considering needs and views of the people concerned.

Sustainable development implies a participatory, multi-stakeholder approach to policymaking and implementation, mobilizing public and private resources for development and making use of the knowledge, skills and energy of all social groups concerned with the future of the planet and its people.

Pursuit of this kind of sustainable development requires:

- A political system that secures effective citizen participation in decision-making;
- An economic system that provides for solutions for the tensions arising from disharmonious development;
- A production system that respects the obligation to preserve the ecological base for development;
- A technological system that fosters sustainable patterns of trade and finance;
- An administrative system that is flexible and has the capacity for self-correction;
- A communication system that gets this organized and accepted by all parties concerned at all levels of society.

Communication and Culture

Communication and culture are both keys to sustainable development, at the same time as being development goals in themselves. To date, development has mostly focused on poverty and education but the rapid advancement of Information Communication Technologies (ICTs) is changing that. People can now communicate any time and at any place, catalysing a wider array of opportunities to the development sector. The world today is interconnected and interdependent.

Within this framework, communication and information play a strategic and fundamental role by (a) contributing to the interplay of different development factors, (b) improving the sharing of knowledge and information and (c) encouraging the participation of all concerned. By promoting the free flow of ideas, as is the case in UNESCO's mandate, a truly transformative environment can be enabled through the advancement of communication. Disadvantaged groups can now actively participate in their own community's development.

The challenge for us is to revisit and reposition the field of sustainable development, and include communication and culture, and especially Communication for Sustainable Social Change (CSSC) in it. One important contribution has been made by Lee and Vargas (2020), who, referring to the so-called MacBride report (MacBride, 1980), argue that "it is all the more astonishing that communication and media were not made part and parcel of every SDG or subject to an SDG of their own, since none of the SDGs can be achieved unless people are able to communicate their dreams, concerns and needs—locally, nationally, regionally, globally. The obstacles are many: social, cultural, political, ideological, yet communication can help overcome them all" (Lee & Vargas, 2020, p. 4). They therefore propose another SDG to the list: *SDG 18: Communication for All*, with the goal to "expand and strengthen public civic spaces through equitable and affordable access to communication technologies and platforms, media pluralism, and media diversity" (ibid., p. 5).

Digital Inclusion

In addition, while the digital age is disrupting social systems and driving transformations at a scale and pace unparalleled in history, the SDGs remain quite silent on this topic. Indeed, today digital technologies are shaping what we read and consume, our votes and how we interact with each other and the world around us. Many risks and uncertainties are emerging, including threats to individual rights, social equity and democracy, all amplified by 'the digital divide'—the differential rate of Internet penetration and access to digital technologies around the world.

Therefore, also Amy Luers (2020) pleads for an *18th SDG: Sustainability in the Digital Age*. (https://sustainabilitydigitalage.org/montreal-statement/). This statement calls on society to recognize that tackling the climate crisis, building a sustainable world and working towards a just and equitable digital future are inherently interconnected agendas: The *Montreal Statement on Sustainability in the Digital Age*.

The statement outlines five immediate actions needed to overcome profound risks of the digital age and leverage its transformative capabilities to build a climate-safe, sustainable and equitable world. These include the need to:

- Build a new social contract for the digital age, which addresses individual rights, justice and equity, inclusive access and environmental sustainability;
- Ensure open and transparent access to data and knowledge critical to achieving sustainability and equity;
- Foster public and private collaborations to develop and manage AI and other technologies in support of sustainability and equity;
- Promote research and innovation to steer digital transformations towards sustainability and equity; and
- Support targeted communication, engagement and education to advance the social contract.

Human and Indigenous Rights

It is increasingly recognized that human rights are essential to achieve sustainable development. However, "international human rights treaties are notably absent from the SDGs" (Macchi, 2020). And, furthermore, which 'human rights' are we talking about?

The MDGs served as a proxy for certain economic and social rights but ignored important human right linkages of the so-called third generation: group and collective rights, the right to self-determination, the right to economic and social development, the right to a healthy environment, the right to natural resources, the right to communicate and communication rights, the right to participation in cultural heritage and the rights to intergenerational equity and sustainability (Gupta, 2020; Macklem, 2015) (https://www.coe.int/en/web/compass/the-evolution-of-human-rights). Today, in addition to these solidarity rights, one starts speaking of a fourth generation of human rights: the right to exist digitally, the right to digital reputation and the right to digital identity.

It is fair to say that more human rights principles and standards are now reflected in the ambitious new global development framework, the 2030 Agenda for Sustainable Development (https://sdg.humanrights.dk/).

For instance, Indigenous peoples have a higher profile in the SDG document—they are directly mentioned several times within the text—more than they did in the MDGs. However, "Indigenous Peoples' visions of development were not included in the SDGs and their collective rights were not given sufficient recognition. (...) The SDGs also do not affirm the collective rights of Indigenous Peoples to their lands, territories, and resources" (Kumar Suniwar, 2020, p. 118). Non-discrimination and non-exclusion are cornerstones to the successful application of the 2030 Sustainable Development Agenda. According to current development rhetoric, these must be realized as universal values, which are at the heart of a functioning, stable and peaceful global society (Maclean, 2015).

Therefore, most of the SDGs remain focused on social and economic rights, rather than the cultural and people's rights listed in the third- and fourth-generation human rights. In our opinion, a bottom-up perspective on sustainable development argues in favour of empowerment: the ability of people to influence the wider system and take control of their lives. Therefore, this perspective argues that a communication rights-based approach needs to be explicitly built into development plans and social change projects to ensure that a mutual sharing/learning process is facilitated. Such communicative sharing is deemed the best guarantee for creating successful transformations. Because, all human rights are 'local' (Servaes, 2017b).

SDGs and COVID-19

The magnitude of COVID-19 is forcing us to rethink our strategies and approaches. The pandemic draws attention to the fact that, in order to support those who are hit the hardest and enhance their resilience for the future, our development interventions should be multidimensional (Horton, 2020; The Broker, 2020).

One of the major findings of this year's Sustainable Development Report (SDR; Lafortune, Woelm, Fuller, & Marks, 2020) is that before the COVID-19 outbreak, the world was making progress towards the SDGs. Although no country was on track to achieve the SDGs, the evolution of the SDG Index scores (included in the Sustainable Development Report) between 2010 and 2019 suggests some convergence, with regions and income groups that had lower SDG Index scores in 2010 progressing faster. Due to time lags in data generation and reporting, these results represent the situation before COVID-19. In particular, areas of the Global South, including sub-Saharan Africa, Latin America and the Caribbean, made significant progress during the MDGs period (2000–2015) and also showed progress on the SDGs. However, of all UN regions, East and South Asia demonstrated the most progress on the SDGs (Salsiah et al., 2020a, b).

The report also highlighted significant disparities in progress across the goals and countries. For example, Côte d'Ivoire, Burkina Faso and Cambodia improved the most on the SDGs, while Venezuela, Zimbabwe and the Republic of the Congo regressed the most (Sachs et al. 2020).

However, as argued by Samarajiva (2020), broad categorizations in geographic terms like 'developed' world or the 'industrialized' world or 'advanced' nations make little sense. What does that mean? "How developed are you if you don't have public health? How industrialized are you if you cannot distribute tests and PPE? How advanced are you if your people won't even wear a mask?" Furthermore, appealing to the individual social responsibility of citizens does not seem to work, notwithstanding economic or education levels. Hence, for instance, while in the East the wearing of masks was accepted by the population at large, in the West it was resisted by many with references to ambiguous 'freedom' calls.

Also the discussion about globalization has emerged again with some arguing that 'nation states' have remained important in the corona crisis. While globalization facilitates the rapid spread of viruses around the world, concerted national action by governments, the private sector, civil society and the scientific community has led to different solutions and strategies at national rather than supranational or global levels.

The current crisis, including hostilities among major powers like China versus the USA, raises the *fear of global conflict instead of global cooperation*. Some do also see other trends emerging: "The traditional powers of the west are neither as strong economically, nor as confident of their social and organizational superiority. China, along with developing countries in Asia and Africa that have better weathered COVID storm, will likely increase their global footprint at a much faster rate that they have been doing in the past decades" (Khan & Khan, 2020).

Therefore SDR 2020, in consultation with the Lancet Commission on COVID-19 chaired by SDSN President, Jeffrey Sachs et al. (2020; Sachs, Schmidt-Traub, & Lafortune, 2020), proposes five key global cooperation measures to address the health and economic consequences of the COVID-19 crisis:

- Disseminate best practices rapidly. The world urgently needs to learn from and to emulate the strategies for fighting COVID-19 adopted in the East Asia and the Pacific regions.
- Strengthen financing mechanisms for developing countries. The IMF was created for global crises like this one. Unfortunately, given the global political tensions, it is to be seen whether it can extend credits, either under existing or new programmes. Private creditors may need to refinance or capitalize on debts falling due.
- Address hunger hotspots. We need global support for the lead United Nations agencies, including the Office for the Coordination of Humanitarian Affairs (OCHA), the Food and Agriculture Organisation (FAO) and the World Food Programme (WFP), so that they can best fight impending hunger crises and food insecurity.
- Ensure social protection. As part of any comprehensive response to the pandemic, governments should promote new instruments of social protection. This includes the new *Global Fund for Social Protection* that was proposed to address SDG 1 (No Poverty) even before the pandemic, and is now needed even more so.
- Promote new drugs and vaccines. Financing research and development (R&D) for COVID-19 drugs and vaccines is an urgent global public good. Without global cooperation, R&D will be inadequate and duplicative. And when breakthroughs are achieved, they will in turn require global cooperation to ensure mass uptake.

"The priority of every government must be to continue to contain and suppress the virus. As COVID-19 continues to infect a growing number of people in Africa, Latin America, the Caribbean, and South Asia, strengthening public health systems and providing access to personal protective equipment and large-scale testing is essential in the absence of a treatment or vaccine. Furthermore, international solidarity and partnerships are critical to address and prevent health, economic, and humanitarian crises and to avoid major setbacks on the SDGs in the short and long-term"—Lafortune et al. (2020) conclude their proposal.

Conclusion

We ended an earlier assessment of the SDGs in the Asian context (Servaes, 2017a, p. 164) with the following four questions:

First, how can we bring together the right stakeholders at the right time in the right place?

- Second, how do we make difficult trade-offs?
- Third, how do we build in accountability and transparency for action?
- Fourth, how to organize this in a participatory and democratic way?

These questions remain valid today. In the light of the 2030 Agenda for Sustainable Development, and in order to achieve the goals set within, the global community can no longer participate in a system that highlights division and inequality. All cultures contribute to sustainable development, which is in itself a reflection of the progress made since the implementation of the MDGs. We need to accelerate joint learning and help to overcome the compartmentalization of technical and policy work by promoting integrated approaches to the interconnected economic, social and environmental challenges confronting the world.

Responses to the COVID-19 crisis must be centred on the well-being of people, empowering them and advancing equality. In addition, as Ian Gouch (2017) and others convincingly argued, the pursuit of well-being and social justice is inadequate if it is at the expense of the biosphere and future generations. At the same time, the pursuit of human well-being for some while also respecting planetary limits is unacceptable if it is at the expense of global justice and the poor of the world. Similarly, the pursuit of social justice within planetary limits is inadequate if justice is understood solely in procedural terms, such as greater civic rights and Western democracy, while ignoring more material aspects of well-being.

Therefore, "we need a revolution in policy mind-set and practice. Inclusive and accountable governance systems, adaptive institutions with resilience to future shocks, universal social protection and health insurance and stronger digital infrastructure are part of the transformations needed" (Salsiah, Wignaraja, & Susantono, 2020b) (see also Horton, 2020).

> Rather than abandoning goals that reflect basic human rights and ignoring the need to respect Earth's planetary boundaries, experts should uphold the SDGs and speak truth to power about what is needed to achieve them. (Sachs et al., 2020, p. 344)

In summary, let us return to Jan Vandemoortele (2016) for a final word: "The SDGs offer a better framework than the MDGs, but considerably more work is required to turn their potential into a practical reality." And, ultimately, as Amartya Sen (2000, 2004), who was awarded the Nobel Prize for his contributions to welfare economics in 1998, already warned us some time ago: "The deciding issue has to be one of democracy. An overarching value must be the need for participatory decision-making on the kind of society people want to live in, based on open discussion, with adequate opportunity for the expression of minority positions" (Sen, 2004, p. 20).

References

Agyeman, J. (2013). *Introducing Just Sustainabilities. Policy, Planning and Practice*. London: ZED Books.

Bali Swain, R., & Yang-Wallentin, F. (2020). Achieving Sustainable Development Goals: Predicaments and Strategies. *International Journal of Sustainable Development & World Ecology, 27*(2), 96–106. https://doi.org/10.1080/13504509.2019.1692316

Ban Ki Moon. (2016). http://www.unmultimedia.org/radio/english/2016/07/restore-peoples-trustin-global-economy-by-implementing-sdgs-urges-ban/#.V5xluY78EY0

Bennett, S., Jessani, N., Glandon, D., Qiu, M., Scott, K., Meghani, A., et al. (2020). Understanding the Implications of the Sustainable Development Goals for Health Policy and Systems Research: Results of a Research Priority Setting Exercise. *Global Health, 16*, 5. https://doi.org/10.1186/s12992-019-0534-2

Byrne, E., Nicholson, B., & Salem, F. (2011). Information Communication Technologies and the Millennium Development Goals. *Information Technology for Development, 17*(1), 1–3.

Easterly, W. (2006). *The White Man's Burden. Why the West's Efforts to Aid the Rest Have Done So Much Ill and So Little Good*. New York: Penguin Books.

Farley, H., & Smith, Z. (2014). *Sustainability. If It's Everything, Is It Nothing?* London: Routledge.

Flint, W. (2007). *Sustainability Manifesto. Exploring Sustainability: Getting Inside the Concept*. Retrieved July 21, 2015, from http://www.eeeee.net/sd_manifesto.htm

Ford, L. (2015). Sustainable Development Goals: All You Need to Know. *The Guardian*. Retrieved from http://www.theguardian.com/global-development/2015/jan/19/sustainable-development-goals-united-nations

Forestier, O., & Kim, R. E. (2020). Cherry-Picking the Sustainable Development Goals: Goal Prioritization by National Governments and Implications for Global Governance. *Sustainable Development, 2020*, 1–10. https://doi.org/10.1002/sd.2082

Foster, J. (2015). *After Sustainability. Denial, Hope, Retrieval*. London: Routledge/Earthscan.

Gouch, I. (2017). *Heat, Greed and Human Need. Climate Change, Capitalism and Sustainable Wellbeing*. Cheltenham: Elgar.

Gupta, V. (2020, June 3). *A Simple Plan for Repairing Our Society: We Need New Human Rights, and This Is How We Get Them, Medium*. Retrieved from https://medium.com/@vinay_12336/a-simple-plan-for-repairing-our-society-we-need-new-human-rights-and-this-is-how-we-get-them-cee5d6ededa9

Hak, T., Janouskova, S., & Moldan, B. (2016). Sustainable Development Goals: A Need for Relevant Indicators. *Ecological Indicators, 60*, 565–573.

Horton, R. (2020). *The COVID-19 Catastrophe. What's Gone Wrong and How to Stop It Happening Again* (p. 133). London: Polity Press.

Khan, D., & Khan, L. Y. (2020). Will COVID-19 Change the Global Balance of Power? *IPSnews*. Retrieved from http://www.ipsnews.net/2020/10/will-covid-19-change-global-balance-power/?utm_source=English+-+SDGs&utm_campaign=0a2c7878c2-EMAIL_CAMPAIGN_2020_10_05_08_29_COPY_01&utm_medium=email&utm_term=0_08b3cf317b-0a2c7878c2-4622673

Kumar Suniwar, D. (2020). What Do the SDGs Mean for the World's Indigenous Peoples? In P. Lee & L. Vargas (Eds.), *Expanding Shrinking Communication Spaces* (pp. 115–123).

Lafortune, G., Woelm, F., Fuller, G., & Marks, A. (2020, July 23). *The SDGs, COVID-19 and the Global South: Insights from the Sustainable Development Report 2020 IPSnews. net*. Retrieved from http://www.ipsnews.net/2020/07/sdgs-covid-19-global-south-insights-sustainable-development-report-2020/?utm_source=English%20-%20 SDGs&utm_campaign=e756da33e1-EMAIL_CAMPAIGN_2020_07_20_10_46_ COPY_01&utm_medium=email&utm_term=0_08b3cf317b-e756da33e1-5552745&fbclid=IwAR3BPWLdbYFHM3NTsbfrnNUDs9OIuMcGcxgeCbTWjs-GezZskWGrv9H13MXw

Lee, P., & Vargas, L. (Eds.). (2020). *Expanding Shrinking Communication Spaces*. Penang: Southbound.

Luers, A. (2020). *The Missing SDG: Ensure the Digital Age Supports People, Planet, Prosperity & Peace*. Retrieved from https://www.globalissues.org/news/2020/07/06/26585

MacBride, S. (Ed.). (1980). *Many Voices, One World. Communication and Society. Today and Tomorrow*. Paris: UNESCO.

Macchi, C. (2020, May 18). The SDGs and the Urgency of Human Rights in Times of Crisis. *Blog*. Retrieved from https://www.globalstudies.ugent.be/the-sdgs-and-the-urgency-of-human-rights-in-times-of-crisis/

Macklem, P. (2015). Human Rights in International Law: Three Generations or One? *London Review of International Law, 3*(1), 61–92. https://doi.org/10.1093/lril/lrv001

Maclean, K. (2015). *Cultural Hybridity and the Environment. Strategies to Celebrate Local and Indigenous Knowledge*. Heidelberg: Springer.

McArthur, J., & Rasmussen, K. (2018). Change of Pace: Accelerations and Advances During the Millennium Development Goal Era. *World Development, 105*, 132–143. https://doi.org/10.1016/j.worlddev.2017.12.030

Nilsson, M., Chisholm, E., Griggs, D., Howden-Chapman, P., McCollum, D., Messerli, P., et al. (2018). Mapping Interactions Between the Sustainable Development Goals: Lessons Learned and Ways Forward. *Sustain Sci, 13*, 1489–1503. https://doi.org/10.1007/s11625-018-0604-z

Payutto, P. (1998). *Sustainable Development*. Bangkok: Buddhadham Foundation.

Sachs, J. D. (2012). *From Millennium Development Goals to Sustainable Development Goals*. Cambridge: Cambridge University Press.

Sachs, J., Schmidt-Traub, G., & Lafortune, G. (2020). SDGs: Affordable and More Essential Now. *Nature, 584*(20), 344.

Sachs, J., Schmidt-Traub, G., Kroll, C., Lafortune, G., Fuller, G., & Woelm, F. (2020). The Sustainable Development Goals and COVID-19. Sustainable Development Report 2020. *Lancet, 379*(9832), 2206–2211.

Salsiah, A. A., Wignaraja, K., & Susantono, B. (2020a). Fast-Tracking the SDGs: Driving Asia Pacific Transformations, United Nations (ESCAP), the Asian Development Bank (ADB) and the United Nations Development Programme (UNDP), Bangkok. https://doi.org/10.22617/SPR200149-2

Salsiah, A. A., Wignaraja, K., & Susantono, B. (2020b). A Determined Path to the SDGs in 2030 Despite the COVID 19 Pandemic, *IPS News* http://www.ipsnews.net/2020/07/determined-path-sdgs-2030-despite-covid-19-pandemic/?utm_source=English+-+SDGs&utm_campaign=f0db356886-EMAIL_CAMPAIGN_2020_07_27_06_30_COPY_01&utm_medium=email&utm_term=0_08b3cf317b-f0db356886-5552745

Samarajiva, I. (2020). *The Overwhelming Racism of COVID Coverage. Western Media Cannot Write Western Failure.* Retrieved from https://medium.com/indica/the-overwhelming-racism-of-covid-coverage-78e37e4ce6e8

SDSN. (2015, June 2). *Indicators and a Monitoring Framework for the Sustainable Development Goals.* A Report to the Secretary-General of the United Nations by the Leadership Council of the Sustainable Development Solutions Network, Sustainable Development Solutions Network (SDSN), New York, p. 233. Retrieved from https://sustainabledevelopment.un.org/content/documents/2013150612-FINAL-SDSN-Indicator-Report1.pdf

Sen, A. (2000). *Development as Freedom.* New York: Anchor Books.

Sen, A. (2004). Cultural Liberty and Human Development. In S. Fukuda-Parr (Ed.), *Human Development Report: Cultural Liberty in Today's Diverse World.* New York: United Nations Development Programme.

Servaes, J. (1999). *Communication for Development. One World, Multiple Cultures.* Cresskill: Hampton Press.

Servaes, J. (2007a). Harnessing the UN system into a common approach on Communication for Development. *The International Communication Gazette,* 69(6), 483–507. Retrieved from http://gaz.sagepub.com

Servaes, J. (Ed.). (2007b, October 25–27). *Communication for Development. Making a Difference.* Background Paper for the World Congress on Communication for Development, Rome.

Servaes, J. (2008). Confusion About MDGs and Participatory Diffusion. *Global Journal Communication for Development and Social Change,* 2(3).

Servaes, J. (Ed.). (2013). *Sustainability, Participation and Culture in Communication. Theory and Praxis.* Bristol-Chicago: Intellect-University of Chicago Press.

Servaes, J. (Ed.). (2017a). *The Sustainable Development Goals in an Asian Context* (p. 174). Singapore: Springer. Retrieved from http://www.springer.com/in/book/9789811028144

Servaes, J. (2017b). All Human Rights Are Local. The Resiliency of Social Change. In H. Tumber & S. Waisbord (Eds.), *The Routledge Companion to Media and Human Rights* (pp. 136–146). London: Routledge.

Servaes, J. (Ed.). (2020). *Handbook on Communication for Development and Social Change* (Vol. 1, 2, 9. 1506). Singapore: Springer. Retrieved from https://link.springer.com/referencework/10.1007/978-981-10-7035-8#toc

Servaes, J., & Malikhao, P. (2017). The Role and Place of Communication for Sustainable Social Change (CSSC). *International Social Science Journal,* LXV(217/218), 171–184. Wiley & UNESCO.

Sivaraksa, S. (2009). *Rediscovering Spiritual Value. Alternative to Consumerism from a Siamese Buddhist Perspective.* Bangkok: Sathirakoses-Nagapradipa Foundation.

Sivaraksa, S. (2010). *The Wisdom of Sustainability. Buddhist Economics for the 21st Century.* Chiang Mai: Silkworm Books.

Task Force on Health Systems. (2004). Informed Choices for Attaining the Millennium Development Goals: Towards an International Cooperative Agenda for Health-Systems Research. *The Lancet,* 364(9438), 997–1003. https://doi.org/10.1016/S0140-6736(04)17026-8

The Broker. (2020). *Knowledge Brokering in Times of Crisis: An Online Dossier on COVID-19.* The Hague: The Broker. Retrieved from https://www.thebrokeronline.eu/covid19-dossier/

The Economist. (2007, 7 July). *The Eight Commandments* (pp. 13 & 26–29). The Economist, London.

UN. (2013). *A New Global Partnership: Eradicate Poverty and Transform Economies Through Sustainable Development*. The Report of the High-Level Panel of Eminent Persons on the Post-2015 Development Agenda. New York: United Nations.

UNDP. (2015). *MDG Needs Assessment Tools*. New York: UNDP. Retrieved from https://www.undp.org/content/undp/en/home/librarypage/poverty-reduction/mdg_strategies/mdg_needs_assessmenttools/mdg_needs_assessmenttools.html

UNECA. (2015). *MDG Report 2015—Assessing Progress in Africa toward the Millennium Development Goals. Lessons Learned in Implementing the MDGs*. Addis Ababa: UNECA. Retrieved from https://www.uneca.org/publications/mdg-report-2015-assessing-progress-africa-toward-millennium-development-goals

UNSC. (2015). *Technical Report by the Bureau of the United Nations Statistical Commission on the Process of the Development of an Indicator Framework for the Goals and Targets of the Post-2015 Development Agenda*. Working Draft. Retrieved from https://sustainabledevelopment.un.org/content/documents/6754Technical%20report%20of%20the%20UNSC%20Bureau%20%28final%29.pdf

Van Norren, D. E. (2012). The Wheel of Development: The Millennium Development Goals as a Communication and Development Tool. *Third World Quarterly, 33*(5), 825–836.

Vandemoortele, J. (2015). *Are the SDGs a Major Reboot or a Sequel to the MDGs?* Retrieved from https://www.oecd.org/economy/development-posts-sdg-reboot-or-sequel-mdg.htm

Vandemoortele, J. (2016). *SDGs: The Tyranny of an Acronym?* Retrieved from https://impakter.com/sdgs-tyranny-acronym/

Vandemoortele, J. (2017). From MDGs to SDGs: Critical Reflections on Global Targets and Their Measurement. In *Sustainable Development Goals and Income Inequality*. Cheltenham: Edward Elgar Publishing. https://doi.org/10.4337/9781788110280.00007

Vandemoortele, J. (2018). From Simple-Minded MDGs to Muddle-Headed SDGs. *Development Studies Research, 5*(1), 83–89. https://doi.org/10.1080/21665095.2018.1479647

Vandemoortele, J. (2011). If Not the Millennium Development Goals, Then What? *Third World Quarterly, 32*(1), 9–25.

Waisbord, S. (2006). Where is Communication in the Millennium Development Goals? *Media Development, LIII*(3), 3–6.

World Commission on Environment and Development. (WCED). (1987). *Our Common Future. Published as Annex to General Assembly Document A/42/427, Development and International Co-operation: Environment*. New York: UN.

World Vision. (2015). Were the Millennium Development Goals a Success? Yes! Sort of. Retrieved from https://www.wvi.org/united-nations-and-global-engagement/article/were-mdgs-success

Zolli, A., & Healy, M. (2012). *Resilience: Why Things Bounce Back*. New York, NY: Free Press.

CHAPTER 3

SDG18—The Missing Ventilator: An Introduction to the 2030 Agenda for Development

Muhammad Jameel Yusha'u

INTRODUCTION

If there is one agenda that attracts the attention of policymakers whether at government level or within multilateral institutions like the United Nations, African Union, European Union and among major financial institutions, it is the 2030 Agenda for development known as the global goals or Sustainable Development Goals (SDGs).

The SDGs have formed the key theme for several conferences by the United Nations (UN); they were the key subjects during the annual meetings of multilateral development banks and governments have prioritized the implementation of the SDGs in one way or another in their national development programmes. Yet, as discussed in the introductory chapter of this book, a key pillar that will strengthen the realization of these ambitious goals, that is, the role of communication in its holistic sense was missing. There were only few passing targets in the SDGs that addressed this key function that drives human activity especially in the twenty-first century.

Despite this major omission, even the officials of the United Nations have acknowledged that massive awareness is required to achieve the 2030 Agenda

---

M. J. Yusha'u (✉)
Islamic Development Bank, Jeddah, Saudi Arabia

© The Author(s), under exclusive license to Springer Nature Switzerland AG 2021
M. J. Yusha'u, J. Servaes (eds.), *The Palgrave Handbook of International Communication and Sustainable Development*,
https://doi.org/10.1007/978-3-030-69770-9_3

for development. The former UN Under-Secretary-General for communications and public information Cristina Gallach stated in 2017 that communicating the SDGs is key to achieving global development targets. In her words "The more we communicate about the SDGs and make people aware of the agenda, the more the governments will be accountable and will ensure that it is implemented" (UN News, 2017).

Despite this acknowledgement at the highest level of the UN, an explicit role for communication as a dedicated goal with clear targets in the SDGs was conspicuously absent. Nothing exposes this oversight more than the outbreak of the COVID-19 pandemic. Due to the coronavirus outbreak most countries around the world imposed a lockdown in order to suppress the spread of the virus. Vital economic activities were halted. The airline industry came to an abrupt stop. Universities around the world had to suspend lectures physically and resort to online teaching. Online shopping skyrocketed. Major meetings by different stakeholders and policymakers including preparatory meetings by G20 leaders had to be conducted online. Global conglomerates, corporate organizations, top IT giants all closed their offices. Just 10–20 years ago, this would have been a global catastrophe. Yet the global community survived mainly on the communication infrastructure available. The world survived on the most important SDG that the framers of the 2030 Agenda for development have missed.

The role of communication in tackling COVID-19 became the most important agenda. The role of news media in public education on how to avoid infection from the coronavirus became more critical. The digital component of communication was needed to keep the economy growing, address healthcare challenges and reduce poverty. The SDGs were on a life support, and the missing SDG on communication served as the ventilator for human survival. In essence, the effort of communication scholars on the role of communication for development and social change in achieving development objectives has become more central. As discussed by Servaes and Malikhao (2020), the role of communication in knowledge sharing to achieve consensus on a given action about shared interest is one of the key aims of communication. It is important to note that the criticism by scholars on neglecting the role of communication as a goal did not start with SDGs; similar criticism has been channelled on its predecessor, the Millennium Development Goals (Servaes, 2017).

Suddenly, the issue of inequality which is the premise of SDG10 became even more apparent. Many developing countries do not have the digital infrastructure to move from teaching physically to online tutoring, thereby bringing to the fore the question of digital divide (Yusha'u, 2020). Without communication infrastructure, addressing the digital divide would be a mirage.

Throughout the period of the global lockdown, it became clear that the debate about SDGs is even stronger as expressed in an opinion article jointly published by the President of Ghana, Nana Akufo-Addo, and Ema Solberg, the Prime Minister of Norway. The two leaders stated:

As our world strives to deal with the challenges posed by the pandemic, we ultimately must seek to turn the crisis into an opportunity and ramp up actions necessary to achieve the SDGs. The spirit of solidarity, quick and robust action to defeat the virus that we are witnessing must be brought to bear on the implementation of the Goals. The quantum of stimulus and pecuniary compensation packages that is being made available to deal with the pandemic make it clear that, when it truly matters, the world has the resources to deal with pressing and existential challenges. The SDGs are one such challenge. What is acutely needed is enhanced political will and commitment. Our world has the knowledge, capacity and innovation, and if we are ambitious enough, we can muster the full complement of resources needed to implement successfully the Goals. (Akufo-Addo & Solberg, 2020)

This chapter therefore will discuss the global goals by explaining each of the 17 SDGs (see the list of all the 17 SDGs and their targets at the beginning of this book) and discuss how they will contribute in achieving sustainable development. The chapter will also provide strong critique on the missing SDG, or what would be termed SDG18—*communication for all*, built on the work of Lee and Vargas, *Expanding Shrinking Communication Spaces* (2020). Their work has espoused why an additional goal is necessary if we are to witness a world that is free from poverty, inequality and where issues of climate change and environmental degradation are addressed.

The 17 SDGs: An Overview of the Global Goals

Before delving into discussion about each of the 17 goals, let us start by defining what the SDGs are (see Jan Servaes' chapter on the transition from MDGs to SDGs which is critical in understanding how the SDGs came about).

The SDGs are a set of ambitious goals with identifiable targets "adopted by all United Nations Member States in 2015 as a universal call to action to end poverty, protect the planet and ensure that all people enjoy peace and prosperity by 2030" (UNDP, 2020a, p. 1).

The SDGs, as discussed by Pogge and Sengupta (2016), were designed to carry on from where the MDGs stopped, and try to complete the loopholes left in the implementation of the MDGs and serve as bold statements of aspiration on how to address global challenges. When the SDGs were officially unveiled in 2015, no one envisaged a global crisis like COVID-19; if there is a fear for global challenge, it might be the potential for another economic crisis after the one in 2008, or a regional war that could have debilitating consequences.

Several scholars, researchers and development experts viewed the SDGs from different perspectives. These perspectives include the role of the private sector in achieving development objectives through job creation and innovation (Cheyvens, Banks, & Hughes, 2016), assessing human rights (Pogge & Sengupta, 2016), improving governance (Deacon, 2016), as a framework for countries to come up with economic development plans (Beckline et al., 2018), increasing development freedom (Rosati, 2018), addressing gender issues and migration (Holliday, Hennebry, & Gammage, 2018), postcolonial feminist critique (Struckmann 2018) and enhancing the efficiency of green energy (Alawaneh, 2019).

What this suggests is that the SDGs are viewed as a holistic framework that can serve as an avenue for addressing development challenges. It is ambitious in one sense, but very flexible for countries, institutions and all stakeholders to adapt, localize and then mainstream the SDGs according to the peculiarities of their needs. While the SDGs are big enough to accommodate several interests and development needs, that is where the challenge of implementing them begins. Robust change management, stakeholder engagement and grassroot awareness are needed to achieve the SDGs, hence the inevitability of communications for development which the framers of the SDGs missed. Before discussing how communication for development will serve as a pillar for achieving the SDGs, let us briefly look at each of the 17 SDGs.

SDG1: No Poverty

As pointed out by Doods, Donoghue, and Roesch (2016) in their important book on negotiating the SDGs, "It is important to recognize that the MDGs were the first time that international cooperation would focus around a set of goals to put poverty eradication at the center of a global development agenda. It would acknowledge the multidimensional character of poverty, i.e., that this was beyond just the issue of below US$1.25/day" (p. 1).

"Fundamental to achieving the SDGs will be the recognition that eradicating poverty and inequality, creating inclusive economic growth, preserving the planet and improving population health are not just linked but interdependent" (Chan, 2015 p. III). The key aim of SDG1 is to eradicate extreme poverty in all forms. The confidence of the framers of SDG1 might have emanated from some of the successes recorded in the MDGs where over 1 billion people were lifted out of poverty globally. By 1990, nearly half of the population of developing countries was living on less than $1.25 a day. By 2015, this number dropped by 14 per cent (UN, 2015). By this account, according to the United Nations Development Programme, around 1 billion people have been lifted out of extreme poverty between 1990 and 2015 (UNDP, 2015).

While lifting one billion people out of extreme poverty is worthy of celebration, the figure will be understood better if we look at the regions of the world that recorded this success the most. China is perhaps the biggest success story. Between 1990 and 2011, China lifted 439 million people out of poverty (Huang, 2016), and by 2015 the figure reached 746 million people lifted out of poverty from 1990, accounting for 65.3 per cent of the total number of people lifted out of poverty within that period (UNICEF, 2020). The next biggest success story was India, which had succeeded in reducing poverty from 54.7 per cent to 27.5 per cent between 2005 and 2016 thereby reducing the number of poor people to 271 million by 2018 (India UNDP, 2018).

But how realistic is the dream of eradicating extreme poverty, especially with the challenges posed by COVID-19, which struck exactly a decade before the realization of the 2030 Agenda. According to the 2020 Global Multidimensional Poverty Index, there are 1.3 billion people or 22 per cent of the global population living in extreme poverty across 107 developing countries. In all, 84.3 per cent of the people characterized as multidimensionally poor live in sub-Saharan Africa (558 million) and South Asia (530 million people). The report suggests that many countries were on track to reduce extreme poverty by half by the year 2030 before the COVID-19 pandemic, but 18 countries including some of the poorest are now off track (Human Development Report, 2020).

The World Bank has estimated that as many as 150 million people could be pushed into extreme poverty by 2021 as a result of COVID-19 depending on the severity of economic contraction (World Bank 2020a). SDG1 according to the UN has 7 targets at the core of which is to end extreme poverty for all people by 2030. Yet according to the UN, around 71 million people have been pushed into extreme poverty in 2020 alone. By UN scorecard the world is off track from ending poverty by 2030 (Sustainable Development Goals, 2020). Despite the gloomy picture some of the framers of the SDGs like Jeffrey Sachs believe that it is possible to mobilize enough resources to end extreme poverty. In Jeffrey Sachs' view, apart from governments, there are 2000 billionaires around the world with a net worth of US $10 trillion, and involving these billionaires in the fight against poverty could bring additional successes (Sheldrick, 2018). It is estimated that there is a US $2.5 trillion funding gap to achieve the SDGs in developing countries (UNCTAD, 2014).

SDG2: Zero Hunger

Next in order of priority to achieve the 2030 Agenda for development is SDG2 (zero hunger). The aim of this SDG is ensuring food security, ending hunger, improving nutrition and promoting sustainable agriculture (SDGs, 2020). SDG2 is an essential component of achieving SDG1. The Multidimensional Poverty Index (MPI) has identified three dimensions of poverty measured according to 10 indicators. The three dimensions are health, education and standard of living. The 10 indicators comprise of nutrition, child mortality, years of schooling, school attendance, cooking fuel, sanitation, drinking water, electricity, housing and assets (OPHI, 2020, p. 4). Without zero hunger, it is difficult to achieve such indicators like nutrition, reducing child mortality, providing potable drinking water and sanitation and almost all the indicators. As ambitious as it sounds, without SDG2, it is impossible to talk about eradicating poverty.

According to Blesh et al. (2019, p. 1) "the pathway to achieving zero hunger should center on place-based, adaptive, participatory solutions that simultaneously attend to local institutional capacities, agroecosystem diversification and ecological management, and the quality of local diets." Although the research by Blesh et al. was not about communication for development, they recognized in their research that a participatory solution is required to achieve zero hunger.

SDG2 has at least 8 targets identified by the framers of the SDGs. While some progress was being made before COVID-19 pandemic struck, the challenge remains higher especially with escalating wars and conflicts around the world. The Nobel Prize Committee which awarded the Nobel Peace Prize for 2020 to the UN's World Food Programme was perhaps trying to draw attention to the need to scale-up efforts in achieving zero hunger. According to the Nobel Prize Committee, 135 million people suffered from acute hunger in 2019 alone (The Nobel Prize, 2020). A report on the *State of Food Security and Nutrition in the World* launched by FAO on the sidelines of the High-Level Political Forum (HLPF) in 2019 suggested that there are 820 million people suffering from acute hunger globally (UN News 2019).

SDG3: Good Health and Wellbeing

An interesting study conducted by the International Council of Science concludes that the SDGs interact with each other. The study came to this conclusion following an analysis of SDG3 and found that to achieve good health and wellbeing, there must be progress on equal measure on SDG1, SDG2, SDG8, SDG11 and SDG13. While the focus of SDG3 is on ensuring healthy lives and wellbeing, it cannot be achieved without the required infrastructure or a decent work to pay for healthcare. Also, consideration should be given to the impact of climate change on public health as well as high quality of nutrition (International Council for Science, 2017).

Before COVID-19, some progress was being made on SDG3 according to the UN, but it needs acceleration. Due to the pandemic, achieving this goal by 2030 needs to be reevaluated. Child immunization has been interrupted in 70 countries and cancellation of services could lead to 100 per cent increase in deaths caused by malaria in sub-Saharan Africa (UN SDGs, 2020). In 2018 there were 228 million cases of Malaria globally, and 93 per cent of the cases and 94 per cent of deaths were in the African region (WHO, 2020). The IMF estimated that US $1.3 trillion is needed in 2019–2030 to achieve SDG3 and SDG4 combined. For healthcare alone, an investment of US $370 billion in health is needed annually in low- and middle-income countries (Vorisek & Yu, 2020).

SDG4: Ensure Inclusive and Equitable Quality Education for All and Lifelong Learning

The central aim of SDG4 is to ensure quality education for different segments of society including lifelong learning for all (see Gwadabe Kurawa's chapter in this book on "Community Learning Centre as a Promising Medium for Promoting Sustainable Development Goal 4: Lifelong Learning," for more information). If there is one SDG that attracts significant attention during the COVID-19 pandemic, it is SDG4 on inclusive and equitable quality education. The impact on schools was immediate. A report by UNESCO suggested that at the peak of the lockdown by countries, at least 1.5 billion children were affected by school closures. A third of these children, around 463 million, have no access to remote learning opportunities (UNESCO, 2020).

A breakdown of the figures released by UNESCO on lack of access to remote learning brings the question of digital inequality to the forefront. The region hit hardest was South Asia where 147 million children were affected. Other regions affected according to the UNESCO report were East Asia and the Pacific (80 million), East and Southern Africa (67 million), West and Central Africa (54 million), Middle East and North Africa (37 million), Eastern Europe and Central Asia (25 million) and Latin America and Caribbean (13 million).

Western Europe and North America were the regions least affected by the school closures due to COVID-19. This picture brings out several lessons on the desire of the framers of the SDGs to achieve quality education for all by 2030. First, it is almost impossible to provide access to quality education in the twenty-first century without addressing the gap in digital inequality. Second, there is failure to understand the role of communication as a standalone SDG (see the discussion on SDG18 at the end of this chapter) among the global goals. This is because the digital platforms used to provide access to remote learning are part and parcel of the communication infrastructure needed for the society to function.

Prior to COVID-19, the data on access to quality education was already yearning for financing. According to the Global Education Monitoring Report, to achieve SDG4 by 2030, there is annual financing gap of US $148 billion. With the challenge of COVID-19, the cost could increase by about US $30 billion to $45 billion (Global Education Monitoring Report, 2020). Statistics from the UNESCO Institute of Statistics shows that there are 258 million out-of-school children globally by the end of school year 2018 (UNESCO, 2019).

While each of the SDGs is important, the case of SDG4 is different because it is central to improving human capital. Just an additional year of schooling has the potential to raise earnings by 10 per cent (Patrinos, 2016). In the words of Benjamin Franklin, "an investment in knowledge, always pays the best interest" (Holte, 1978, pp. 99–102).

SDG5: Gender Equality

The aim of SDG5 is to achieve gender equality and empower all women and girls. SDG5 is quite important because it hopes to empower all women economically, create opportunity and contribute to economic growth. "The full incorporation of women's capacities into labor forces would add percentage points to most national growth rates—double digits in many cases. Further, investing in women's empowerment produces the double dividend of benefiting women and children, and is pivotal to the health and social development of families, communities and nations" (SDG Compass, 2020, p. 1).

A key component of SDG5 is reducing violence against women. This has been a subject of discussion and policy briefing during the High-Level Political Forum. The UN Secretary General's Report suggested that there has been some progress in addressing violence against women and legal frameworks have been established aimed at containing it, but there are still challenges such as unpaid work, digital divide and sexual violence. This is one of the SDGs where communications for development and social change would play a crucial role because a lot of the issues affecting women are cultural in nature. Therefore, massive awareness and education are tools in improving the treatment of women and creating opportunities for them to contribute to society.

The COVID-19 pandemic has further exposed the challenges for women. Of course, this does not mean that the pandemic is gender-sensitive, but some of the industries hit hard by the pandemic employ women heavily. A UN report suggests that of the 510 million women employed globally in industries that employ women, such as restaurants and entertainment industries, 40 per cent have been severely affected compared to 36 per cent for men (UN Women, 2020).

Perhaps one of the positives that came out of the COVID-19 pandemic was the type of leadership shown by women in containing the spread of the virus and uniting their countries in dealing with the spread of the pandemic. Although it would be hasty to make conclusions since the pandemic is not yet over at the time of writing this chapter, but the leaders of Germany Angela Merkel, New Zealand's Jacinda Adern and Taiwan's Tsai Ing-Wen have shown remarkable leadership in taking decisive action and limiting the spread of the virus (The Conversation, 2020). This is just one example of how women empowerment could benefit society in line with the goals of SDG5.

SDG6: Clean Water and Sanitation

One of the strengths of the SDGs as discussed earlier is their interconnection. SDG6 which focuses on providing clean water and sanitation is one good example. A critical look at SDG1 on eradicating extreme poverty, SDG2 on zero hunger, SDG3 on good health and wellbeing, SDG4 on quality education and SDG5 on women empowerment suggests one fact, which is improving the quality of life of the individual which in turn reflects in the quality of life of a community and a nation. Clean water and sanitation is a very good measure to assess the quality of life of any given community.

It was right that the framers of the SDGs brought this onboard and highlighted it as an independent goal. According to the United Nations Development Programme, water scarcity affects at least 40 per cent of the global population. By 2015 there were 844 million people globally who lacked even basic drinking water. Also 2.3 billion people lacked basic sanitation, and 892 million people practised open defecation (UNDP, 2020b).

While achieving SDG6 is a noble goal and is connected to other SDGs, achieving it by 2030 is another gargantuan challenge because the targets for SDG6, some of which require energy transformation, might affect climate change issues. Another challenge is funding. A study by Parkinson et al. (2018) suggests that at least $1 trillion is required per annum to achieve SDG6 by 2030. This assessment was done in the pre-COVID-19 world—How can this target be achieved in a post-COVID-19 world when countries are facing constraints in national budgets and struggling to contain the social and economic challenges posed by the pandemic?

SDG7: Affordable and Clean Energy

SDG7 on affordable and clean energy has one of the most ambitious targets among the SDGs. For instance, target 7.1 calls for the need to have universal access to affordable, modern and reliable energy services. Consider such an ambition and compare it with the reality on the ground. According to the UN Environment, there are at least 3 billion people in the world who use charcoal, wood or animal waste for cooking and heating. Since 1990 the emissions of CO_2 at the global level has increased by 46 per cent (UNEP, 2020) thereby highlighting the challenge of creating a balance between affordable energy and decreasing carbon emission.

The challenge is even bigger when you look at the developing countries which are still grappling with issues related to SDG1, SDG2, SDG3, SDG4, SDG5 and SDG6. How can they prioritize the allocation of resources from their national budget? Can developing countries ignore chronic poverty in their countries, or the need to improve health systems or even return out-of-school children back to class, and transfer the resources to the provision of affordable energy, no matter how critical it is? These are some of the questions that require careful but worthy policy prescriptions in order to achieve SDG7.

SDG8: Decent Work and Economic Growth

SDG8 is perhaps the delight or in other words the 'darling' of labour unions, workers and partly development institutions interested in supporting governments to create decent jobs and reduce unemployment. SDG8 calls for promoting inclusive and sustainable economic growth and decent work for all. Perhaps the cliché in the SDGs is the phrase 'for all.' More difficult to achieve is providing decent jobs and creating sustainable economic growth to the 7 billion population of the world. This difficulty has been acknowledged by no other than the International Labour Organisation (ILO). According to ILO, half of the global population lives on less than $2 a day, but more indicting on the attempt to achieve SDG8 is the admission by ILO that having a decent job does not guarantee an escape from poverty (ILO, 2020).

Achieving economic growth and development has been debated thoroughly by economic and development scholars. Such studies include those by the renowned economist and Nobel Prize Winner Joseph Stiglitz whose book *Globalization and its Discontent* (2002) is a major reference in understanding the nuance of development. Others are *Why Nations Fail* (Acemoglu &James 2012), Murat Yulek's *How Nations Succeed* (2018) and the classic work by Justin Yi Fu Lin, former World Bank Chief Economist, and Celestin Monga, Chief Economist for African Development Bank, whose book, *Beating the Odds: Jump-Starting Developing Countries* (2017), thoroughly reviewed how nations develop, and questioned critically how the policy prescriptions given to developing countries by multilateral institutions are counterproductive.

What these works suggested was that development is usually homegrown, propelled by focused policy initiatives and strong political will. How possible is it to have a top-down approach where the UN simply suggests a goal in the name of SDG8 and expects all countries to experience economic growth and provide decent jobs within a period of 15 years from 2015 to 2030? In fact, one of the criticisms against SDG8 is the market-centred approach to economic growth and creation of decent jobs (Frey, 2017).

SDG9: Industry, Innovation and Infrastructure

Unlike the MDGs that were formulated before the massive explosion of technology at the beginning of the millennium, the framers of the SDGs were lucky to come up with the global goals at a time when an unprecedented growth in innovation and technology was taking place. The trend itself is set to continue. As such adding SDG9, which mainly focuses on industry innovation and infrastructure, was the right decision. A number of the SDGs need an enabler, a gigantic vision that could tap human potential to sometimes come up with unimaginable or out-of-the-box solutions. A 2020 report released by the World Economic Forum suggested that 70 per cent of all the SDGs can be achieved by the use of Fourth Industrial Revolution which already exists (WEF, 2020).

For the purpose of this book, it is important to note that SDG9 is one of the SDGs that have some form of role for communications. Target 9.C suggested the need to achieve Universal Access to Information and Communication Technology. It aims to provide universal access to the internet at least in developing countries by the year 2020[1] (The Global Goals, 2020). The other few targets came "under Goal 5 on Gender Equality" to "Enhance the use of enabling technology, in particular information and communications technology, to promote the empowerment of women" and under Goal 16 on "Peace, Justice and Strong Institutions" to "Ensure public access to information and protect fundamental freedoms" (Lee & Vargas, 2020 p. 2).

---

[1] This chapter was written in November 2020. Going by the experience of COVID-19 (see the discussion on SDG4 about the number of school children who missed out on remote access to education), it is clear that this particular target is already off-track.

Here lies the criticism against SDG9. The internet is perhaps the greatest communication tool invented in human history. It was indeed a product of innovation and human ingenuity, and today media, communications and other aspects of human endeavour are made easy or facilitated by the internet. Yet the other components of SDG9, which are industry and infrastructure, could stand alone or be accommodated by SDG8 on decent work and economic growth. It is impossible to achieve industrialization and provide the relevant infrastructure without economic growth.

SDG9 could have been reframed and be the main SDG that focuses on *innovation, technology media and communications* (see the discussion on the missing goal, SDG18 [communication for all]). The COVID-19 experience has further led credence to this argument and highlights the oversight of the framers of the SDGs to ignore the role of media and communications to just one target on the internet under SDG9. Even that was not exhaustive, as it only focuses on the internet rather than on communication as a whole.

SDG10: Reduced Inequality

Joseph Stiglitz's recent work, *The Price of Inequality* (2012), and the more recent *People, Power and Profits* (2020) provide a major critique of capitalism and the widening gap between the rich and the poor in the United States. As suggested by Roberts (2012), Stiglitz tried to bring morality into capitalism due to the control of the US economy by the richest 1 per cent. If Stiglitz was concerned about widening inequality in the United States, the dominant economy in the world, think of the poorest countries who could not even dream of ever reaching the economic might of the United States. The aim of SDG10 is to *reduce inequality within and among countries.*

The idea of leaving no one behind, which has become the slogan of the SDGs or the global goals, is aimed at reducing inequality at individual and national levels. According to the United Nations World Social Report (2020), the world is yet to see an upward trend in reducing inequality. Rather, the share of income for the global 1 per cent of the population has increased in 46 out of 57 countries between 1990 and 2015. The report suggested that two-thirds of the world population live in countries where inequality is growing.

The use of development communication in reducing inequalities is one area where the SDGs can learn from the implementation of the MDGs. During the implementation of the MDGs there was a lot of effort in deploying the power of communications for development to empower communities. OECD's DeVCom and OECD even produced a manual for public affairs and communication specialists in government ministries on how to use information and communication to tackle inequality (OECD, 2014).

To understand the daunting task ahead, it would be relevant to highlight some facts from Oxfam's recent report on global inequality. According to the report, the richest 1 per cent have a wealth which is more than double that of the 6.9 billion people on earth. A section of the 1 per cent is the

2153 billionaires who by the year 2019 have more wealth than 4.6 billion people. By Oxfam's calculation, to amass a fifth of the fortune of the richest billionaires in the world, a person needs to save $10,000 per day since the building of the pyramids of Egypt. This is happening when women and girls are putting 12.5 billion hours of unpaid work every day (Whiting, 2020). So, the $1 trillion question is, how do we reduce inequality and achieve SDG10 by 2030?

SDG11: Sustainable Cities and Communities

The SDGs are quite good in their interconnectedness. By achieving one SDG, other SDGs also benefit. You cannot achieve SDG2 (zero hunger) without addressing SDG1 (no poverty). Similarly, SDG11 whose sole purpose is to *Make Cities and Human Settlements Inclusive, Safe, Resilient and Sustainable* is connected to other SDGs such as SDGs 7–9. The challenge of achieving it by the year 2030 is the biggest task ahead. The challenge can be understood better by looking at the expectation of some of the targets. For instance, target 11.1 wants to ensure access for all to adequate, safe and affordable housing and basic services and upgraded slums (UNODC, 2020).

But what does the reality tell us. Globally cities are becoming more congested, and urban migration is increasing by the day. It is estimated that around 55 per cent of people now live in cities, but that number is expected to grow to 68 per cent by 2050 especially in Africa and Asian countries (Fleming, 2020). A report by the World Economic Forum (2019) suggested that going by the UN data, only 13 per cent of the world cities have affordable housing. The report cited a study by McKinsey which projected that about 1.6 billion people could live in substandard houses by 2025 and the figure could rise to 2.5 billion by 2050. The report added that almost 50 per cent of the population in Africa lives in substandard conditions, while millennials the world over are spending more on housing than any previous generation (WEF, 2019).

A major challenge in achieving SDG11 is the increasing urbanization and managing external factors like conflicts, natural disasters and unexpected crises such as COVID-19 pandemic which has grown from a health challenge to an economic pandemic.

SDG12: Responsible Consumption and Production

The SDGs were not meant to improve human conditions only. They were also meant to improve the environment and help protect the planet. In the MDGs, there was only one goal related to the environment, MDG7. The SDGs were a clear departure with multiple SDGs dealing with environmental issues, and SDG 12 on responsible consumption and production is one of the SDGs aimed at reducing activities that have a negative impact on the environment. Through SDG12, the framers of the global goals would like to see more energy efficiency, sustainable infrastructure, access to basic services and promotion of green and decent jobs (UNOOSA, 2020).

Despite the alarming rate of poverty and hunger in many parts of the world, lack of responsible consumption and waste is a challenge which if tackled diligently could contribute to achieving some of the SDGs. Statistics from the United Nations Development Programme suggested that almost one-third of all food produced, equivalent to 1.3 tonnes worth $1 trillion, ends up as a waste due to poor transportation and harvesting practices. By saving energy bulbs alone according to UNDP the world would save $120 billion annually (UNDP, 2020c).

While achieving all the targets of the SDGs may sometimes sound illusive, SDG12 is one of the targets that the global community could substantially make progress on if communication for development could be embraced by governments, private sector and individuals. Switching light bulbs or reducing waste is substantially about change of behaviour which development communication could help achieve.

SDG13: Climate Action

It would be apt if one describes SDG13 as the action goal. Its key premise is to take urgent action to combat climate change and its impacts (FAO, 2020). SDG13 on climate action is one of the SDGs that received massive publicity due to the interest it attracts especially from young people, NGOs and civil society, but also because of the politics involved by the major global powers such as the United States and China (see the Won Yang et al.'s chapter in this volume on the comparative analysis of American and Chinese coverage of climate change for more information on this subject).

Political dispute aside, what do the facts say about climate change? It is estimated that the concentration of CO_2 in the atmosphere as of May 2020 is the highest it has ever been in human history. About 3.2 billion people are impacted by issues related to environmental degradation, and to successfully combat global warming, about $140 billion is needed annually to make the required adjustment to tackle a warming world (Conservation, 2020).

Unlike many other SDGs, SDG13 has received scholarly and professional attention in the area of communication in general and communications for development in particular. Studies in this area include Ouariachi, Olvera-Lobo, and Gutiérrez-Pérez (2017), Harvey et al. (2012) as well as Filho et al.'s *Handbook of Climate Change Communication* (Filho, Manolas, Azul, Azeiteiro, & McGhie, 2018).

Efforts such as the Yale Programme on Climate Change Communications and having champions like Greta Thunberg and former US Vice President Al Gore calling for behavioural change on climate change issues have significantly drawn attention to the magnitude of the challenges posed by climate change. The elephant in the room though remains whether countries like the United States will return to the climate change agreement following its withdrawal by

US President Donald Trump, and whether United States, China and other countries will agree and fulfil the pledges they made in reducing carbon emission. The change of leadership in the United States following the victory of Joe Biden might signal a new beginning.

SDG14: Life Below Water

An area where SDGs could make massive difference is in expanding the scope of development by looking at the entire terrestrial space. SDG14 aims to do just that by drawing attention to life below water. This is not just to protect nature and improve climate, it is also to protect human beings. Today, there are over three billion people who depend on coastal and marine biodiversity for sustenance (IUCN, 2020).

It is estimated that coastal and marine resources contribute $28 trillion to the global economy each year through ecosystem services. Fishery is another major industry that contributes to the global economy. Despite this, there is a serious threat to the ecosystem because of pollution of land and seas, which is a major threat to land and seas in coastal regions. A major challenge in achieving SDG14 is growing eutrophication. Five large marines' ecosystems are particularly at higher risk. They are the Bay of Bengal, the East China Sea, the Gulf of Mexico, the North Brazil shelf and the South China Sea (Hellenic Statistical Authority, 2020).

SDG15: Life on Land

The architects of the SDGs could have swapped SDG15 with SDG14 by starting with life on land to be followed by life below water. Though this could be a minor thing, nevertheless, it was important that the framers of the SDGs recognized the need to initiate SDG15 which aims to protect, restore and promote sustainable use of terrestrial ecosystems, sustainably manage forests, combat desertification and halt and reverse land degradation and halt biodiversity loss (ISO, 2020).

The magnitude of the challenge in achieving SDG15 could be understood better by looking at the existing facts as indicated below, and sourced from the United Nations Convention to Combat Desertification.

Data and Statistics/Facts and Figures

- Around 1.6 billion people depend on forests for their livelihood.
- Forests are home to more than 80 per cent of all terrestrial species of animals, plants and insects.
- 74 per cent of the poor are directly affected by land degradation globally.
- Of the 8,300 animal breeds known, 8 per cent are extinct and 22 per cent are at risk of extinction.

- Over 80 per cent of the human diet is provided by plants. Only three cereal crops—rice, maize and wheat—provide 60 per cent of energy intake.
- As many as 80 per cent of people living in rural areas in developing countries rely on traditional plant-based medicines for basic healthcare.

Desertification

- 2.6 billion people depend directly on agriculture, but 52 per cent of the land used for agriculture is moderately or severely affected by soil degradation.
- As of 2008, land degradation affected 1.5 billion people globally.
- Arable land loss is estimated at 30 to 35 times the historical rate.
- Due to drought and desertification each year 12 million hectares are lost (23 hectares per minute), where 20 million tons of grain could have been grown.
- 74 per cent of the poor are directly affected by land degradation globally.

Biodiversity

- Of the 8,300 animal breeds known, 8 per cent are extinct and 22 per cent are at risk of extinction.
- Of the over 80,000 tree species, less than 1 per cent have been studied for potential use.
- Fish provide 20 per cent of animal protein to about 3 billion people. Only ten species provide about 30 per cent of marine capture fisheries and ten species provide about 50 per cent of aquaculture production.
- Over 80 per cent of the human diet is provided by plants. Only three cereal crops—rice, maize and wheat—provide 60 per cent of energy intake.
- As many as 80 per cent of people living in rural areas in developing countries rely on traditional plant--based medicines for basic.
- Healthcare
- Micro-organisms and invertebrates are key to ecosystem services, but their contributions are still poorly known and rarely acknowledged.

Forests

- Around 1.6 billion people depend on forests for their livelihood. This includes some 70 million indigenous people.
- Forests are home to more than 80 per cent of all terrestrial species of animals, plants and insects.
- (UNCCD, 2017, p. 1)

SDG16: Peace and Justice and Strong Institutions

SDG16 can be described as the solution or institutional SDG. Others such as Whaites (2016) describe it as the impossible SDG. Human beings have made an unprecedented progress in science, technology, innovation and infrastructure development. Educational systems have been overhauled, and healthcare is being revamped using the power of groundbreaking research and use of technology. Yet, one thing that has eluded the human species is establishing peace, justice and in many parts of the world the strong institutions needed to maintain peace and justice. Without mincing words, none of the SDGs could be sufficiently achieved even in 100 years without peace and justice.

The aim of SDG16 is to promote peaceful and inclusive societies for sustainable development, provide access to justice for all and build effective and accountable institutions at all levels. Yet, according to the United Nation's Department of Social and Economic Affairs, 100 civilians were killed in armed conflicts every day before COVID-19 pandemic. In all 75.9 million people are fleeing war, conflict or persecution, and in the age of COVID-19, 60 per cent of countries suffer from overcrowded prisons (UN, 2020).

So, what would it take to achieve SDG16? According to Whaites (2016) people should not accept defeat due to the unlikelihood of achieving SDG16; rather there should be a move to act politically, that is—"Where politics are the problem not the engine of reform how can and should stakeholders engage?"; innovate radically, meaning "when political space for institutional development does open up then external support has the scope to become a multiplier and accelerator of change"; measure effectively, that is "to accurately capture the changes of behaviour, ethos, process and efficiency that represent real institutional capacity development"; and collaborate differently, suggesting that "SDG16 cannot be delivered by any single community or group. National governments will have the greatest impact, but many actors will be important in making a leap forward to achieve the goal. The question is whether those actors will enhance the impact of each other's efforts or dissipate impact through inchoate approaches" (Whaites, 2016 pp. 1–14).

SDG17: Partnerships to Achieve the Goals

SDG17 is the engine of the global goals. Partnership is essential in achieving the SDGs. No country or institution can drive the 2030 Agenda alone. It requires strong and honest collaboration. The framers of the SDGs foresee a world where international cooperation takes the front row in international development. SDG17 is supposed to be the brother's keeper. Without a spirit of international cooperation, achieving the SDGs would be a mirage.

For instance, according to the United Nations, 79 per cent of imports from developing countries enter developed countries duty free; the debt burden bedevilling developing countries remains stable at 3 per cent; while trade, foreign direct investment and remittances are expected to decline by 40 per cent by 2020 (Sustainable Development Goals, 2020). With COVID-19, the World Bank has projected that remittances to low-income countries would decline by 7 per cent to $508 billion in 2020, and by another 7.5 per cent to $470 billion by 2021 (World Bank 2020). Remittances are major contributors to the economy of many developing countries.

According to the World Bank, as of 2019, the flow of remittances to developing countries was higher than foreign direct investment. The top recipient countries of remittances were India ($79 billion), China ($67 billion), Mexico ($36 billion), Philippines ($34 billion) and Egypt ($29 billion) (World Bank, 2019).

In sub-Saharan Africa for instance, in 2018 remittances from Nigerians in diaspora accounted for 6.1 per cent of the GDP or 83 per cent of the federal budget and was 11 per cent higher than the foreign direct investment of the same period (Nevin, Agbedna, Omosomi, & Asuzu, 2019).

Without a spirit of cooperation, imagine the impact the lack of these remittances could have on the economy of developing countries especially during COVID-19? With the rise of right wing nationalism in Europe, North and Latin America what would be the future of the global goals by 2030?

SDG18: THE MISSING GOAL (COMMUNICATION FOR ALL)

SDG18 is the goal that is conspicuously missing from the global goals despite an acknowledgement by some of the leaders who participated in formulating the 2030 Agenda for development about the inevitability of communication in achieving the SDGs.

Writing in the London *Guardian* during the debates on the post-MDGs agenda, Judith Randel, then Executive Director of *Development Initiative*, stated that "based on our experience and available evidence, we believe the post-2015 settlement must harness the power of technology and information to empower citizens with choice and control over the decisions that impact their lives" (Randel, 2013, p. 1).

During the negotiations on the SDGs, Ireland's permanent representative to the United Nations, David Donoghue, stated that to achieve the SDGs, there is need "in some way to capture the imagination of ordinary people around the world."[2]

Some countries such as The Netherlands have even developed a communication plan for communicating the SDGs at the grassroots level particularly by targeting young people. The SDGs have been integrated in school curricula as part of the strategy for inclusive dialogue and consultation. Indonesia has developed a monitoring dashboard for the SDGs called *Satu Data Initiative* (https://www.satu-indonesia.com/satu/) and the website is available in local

---

[2] See https://www.bic.org/news/Looming-challenge-communicating-Sustainable-Development-Goals%20 retrieved 04/11/2020.

language. Users can visit the dashboard and select any of the SDGs to see the report card on the success recorded so far (Yusha'u, 2019, p. 5).

Communication scholars such as Servaes and Malikhao (2020) and Servaes (2017) have echoed the need to take communication more seriously in achieving the SDGs (see Chap. 2 by Jan Servaes for more information). A critical contribution to this area is the work of Lee and Vargas (2020) who called for adding SDG18, communication for all, to the global goals. According to Lee and Vargas, "no matter the issue—poverty, conflict resolution, self-determination, migration, health, land, housing, the climate crisis—little can be done without effective communication" (Lee & Vargas, 2020, p. 2). They were particularly critical of the failure of the SDGs to appreciate the relevance of free expression as a goal of development and a means to development.

For them, therefore, SDG18 should be one of the SDGs with the following as a goal and targets:

Goal: Expand and strengthen public civic spaces through equitable and affordable access to communication technologies and platforms, media pluralism, and media diversity.

Target 1.1 By 2030, ensure the existence of spaces and resources for men and women, in particular the poor and vulnerable, to engage in transparent, informed, and democratic public dialogue and debate.

Target 1.2 By 2030, ensure the existence of regimes where creative ideas and knowledge are encouraged, can be communicated widely and freely to advance social justice and sustainable development.

Target 1.3 By 2030, ensure protection for the dignity and security of people in relation to communication processes, especially concerning data privacy and freedom from surveillance.

Target **1.4** By 2030, ensure communication spaces for diverse cultures, cultural forms and identities at the individual and social levels.

(Lee & Vargas, 2020, p. 5).

This chapter shares the proposition of Lee and Vargas (2020) and would propose additional targets for SDG18.

1.5 Ensure the use of communication as a tool for economic empowerment and community development by governments, private sector and civil society.

1.6 Use media and communications in promoting accountability, tackling misinformation, strengthening good governance and effective citizen engagement in public affairs.

1.7 Provide communication and technological infrastructure for all to support remote access for citizens in health, education and all public services and economic activities during emergencies.

REFERENCES

Acemoglu, D., & James, A. R. (2012). *Why Nations Fail: The Origins of Power, Prosperity and Poverty*. New York: Crown Publishers.

Akufo-Addo, N., & Solberg, E. (2020). *Amid Coronavirus Pandemic, SDGs are Even More Relevant Today Than Ever Before*. Retrieved June 20, 2020, from http://www.ipsnews.net/2020/04/amid-coronavirus-pandemic-sdgs-even-relevant-today-ever/?utm_source=English+-+SDGs&utm_campaign=2852368cb8-EMAIL_CAMPAIGN_2020_04_21_01_32&utm_medium=email&utm_term=0_08b3cf317b-2852368cb8-4622673

Alawaneh, R. (2019). A New Index for Assessing the Contribution of Energy Efficiency in LEED 2009 Certified Green Buildings to Achieving UN Sustainable Development Goals in Jordan. *International Journal of Green Energy, 16*(6), 490–499.

Beckline, M., Yujun, S., Etongo, D., Saeed, S., Mukete, N., & Richard, T. (2018). Cameroon Must Focus on SDGs in its Economic Development Plans. *Environment: Science and Policy for Sustainable Development, 60*(2), 25–32.

Blesh, J., Hoey, L., Jones, A. D., Friedmann, H., & Perfecto, I. (2019). Development Pathways Toward "Zero Hunger". *World Development, 118*, 1–14.

Chan, M. (2015). Preface. In *Health in 2015: From MDGs to SDGs*. World Health Organisation. Retrieved July 24, 2020, from https://apps.who.int/iris/bitstream/handle/10665/200009/9789241565110_eng.pdf

Cheyvens, R., Banks, G., & Hughes, E. (2016). The Private Sector and the SDGs: The Need to Move Beyond 'Business as Usual. *Sustainable Development., 24*(6), 345–415.

Conservation. (2020). *11 Facts You Need to Know About Climate Change*. Retrieved October 2, 2020, from https://www.conservation.org/stories/11-climate-change-facts-you-need-to-know?utm_campaign=homepage&utm_content=1591716731&utm_medium=social&utm_source=twitter

Deacon, B. (2016). Assessing the SDGs from the Point of View of Global Social Governance. *Journal of International and Comparative Social Policy, 32*(2), 116–130.

Dodds, F; Donoghue, D; Roesch, J L (2016). *Negotiating the Sustainable Development Goals*. London. Routledge

FAO. (2020). *Sustainable Development Goals*. Retrieved November 2, 2020, from http://www.fao.org/sustainable-development-goals/goals/goal-13/en/

Filho, L. W., Manolas, E., Azul, A. M., Azeiteiro, U. M., & McGhie, H. (Eds.). (2018). *Handbook of Climate Change Communication* (Vol. 1). Cham: Springer.

Fleming, S. (2020). *5 Things You Need to Know About Cities in World Cities Day 2020*. Retrieved November 1, 2020, from https://www.weforum.org/agenda/2020/10/world-cities-day-2020-facts-un/

Frey, D. F. (2017). Economic Growth, Full Employment and Decent Work. The Means and Ends in SDG8. *The International Journal of Human Rights, 21*(8), 1164–1184.

Global Education Monitoring Report. (2020). *Act Now: Reduce the Impact of COVID-19 on the Cost of Achieving SDG4*. Retrieved October 15, 2020, from https://unesdoc.unesco.org/ark:/48223/pf0000374163

Harvey, B., Ensor, J., Carlile, L., Garside, B., Patterson, Z., & Naess, L. O. (2012). *Climate Change Communication and Social Learning–Review and Strategy Development for CCAFS*. CCAFS Working Paper No. 22. CGIAR Research Program on Climate Change, Agriculture and Food Security (CCAFS), Copenhagen.

Hellenic Statistical Authority. (2020). *Sustainable Development Goal 14*. Retrieved November 3, 2020, from https://www.statistics.gr/en/sdg14

Holliday, J., Hennebry, J., & Gammage, S. (2018). Achieving the Sustainable Development Goals: Surfacing the Role for Gender Analytic of Migration. *Journal of Ethnic and Migration Studies., 45*(14, Special Issue 1), 2551–2565.

Holte, J. C. (1978). New Writers and New Insights. *MELUS., 5*(4), 99–102.

Huang, C. (2016). *Ending Poverty in China: Lessons for other Countries and the Challenges Ahead*. Retrieved October 8, 2020, from https://blogs.worldbank.org/eastasiapacific/ending-poverty-in-china-lessons-for-other-countries-and-challenges-still-ahead

Human Development Reports. (2020). *The 2020 Global Multidimensional Poverty Index*. Retrieved October 14, 2020, from http://hdr.undp.org/en/2020-MPI

ILO. (2020). *Goal 8: Decent Work and Economic Growth*. Retrieved October 29, 2020, from https://www.ilo.org/global/topics/sdg-2030/goal-8/lang%2D%2Den/index.htm

India UNDP. (2018). *271 Million Less Poor People in India*. Retrieved October 8, 2020, from https://www.in.undp.org/content/india/en/home/sustainable-development/successstories/MultiDimesnionalPovertyIndex.html

International Council for Science. (2017). *A Guide to SDG Interactions: from Science to Implementation*. Paris: International Council for Science. Retrieved October 14, 2020, from http://pure.iiasa.ac.at/id/eprint/14591/

ISO. (2020). *Goal 15: Life on Land*. Retrieved November 3, 2020, from https://www.iso.org/sdg/SDG15.html

IUCN. (2020). *SDG14: Life Blow Water*. Retrieved November 2, 2020, from https://www.iucn.org/theme/global-policy/our-work/sustainable-development-goals/iucn-and-sdgs/sdg-14

Lee, P., & Vargas, L. (2020). *Expanding Shrinking Communication Spaces*. Penang: Southbound, Centre for Communication Rights.

Nevin, Andrew S; Agbedna, O., Omosomi, O., Asuzu, D. (2019): Strength from Abroad: The Power of Nigeria's Diaspora. Retrieved November 3, 2020, from https://www.pwc.com/ng/en/pdf/the-economic-power-of-nigerias-diaspora.pdf

OECD. (2014). *Good Practices in Development Communication*. Retrieved November 1, 2020, from http://www.oecd.org/dev/DevCom%20Publication%20Good%20Practices%20in%20Development%20Communication.pdf

OPHI. (2020). *Charting Pathways out of Multidimensional Poverty: Achieving the SDGs*. Retrieved October 14, 2020, from http://hdr.undp.org/sites/default/files/2020_mpi_report_en.pdf

Ouariachi, T., Olvera-Lobo, M. D., & Gutiérrez-Pérez, J. (2017). Analyzing Climate Change Communication Through Online Games: Development and Application of Validated Criteria. *Science Communication, 39*(1), 10–44.

Parkinson, S., Krey, V., Huppmann, D., Kahil, T., McCollum, D., Fricko, O., et al. (2018). Balancing Clean Water Climate Change Mitigation Trade-Offs. *Environmental Research Letters., 14*(1), 1–11.

Patrinos, H. A. (2016). *Why Education Matters for Economic Development*. Retrieved October 15, 2020, from https://blogs.worldbank.org/education/why-education-matters-economic-development

Pogge, T., & Sengupta, M. (2016). Assessing the Sustainable Development Goals from a Human Rights Perspective. *Journal of International and Comparative Social Policy, 32*(2), 83–97.

Randel, J. (2013). *Why Access to Information Needs to be Central to the Debate About Poverty*. Retrieved November 4, 2020, from https://www.theguardian.com/global-development-professionals-network/2013/jan/18/mdgs-poverty-eradication-information-access

Roberts, Y. (2012). *The Price of Inequality by Joseph Stiglitz-Review*. Retrieved November 1, 2020, from https://www.theguardian.com/books/2012/jul/13/price-inequality-joseph-stiglitz-review

Rosati, C. (2018). Development as Freedom after Flint: A Geographical Approach to Capabilities and Antipoverty Communication. *Journal of Multicultural Discourses, 13*(2), 139–159.

SDG Compass. (2020). *SDG5: Achieve Gender Equality and Empower All Women and Girls*. Retrieved October 25, 2020, from https://sdgcompass.org/sdgs/sdg-5/

SDGs. (2020). *End Hunger, Achieve Food Security and Improve Nutrition and Promote Sustainable Agriculture*. Retrieved October 14, 2020, from https://sdgs.un.org/goals/goal2

Servaes, J. (2017). Introduction: From MDGs to SDGs. In J. Servaes (Ed.), *Sustainable Development Goals in the Asian Context* (pp. 1–22). Singapore: Springer.

Servaes, J., & Malikhao, P. (2020). Communication for Development and Social Change: Three Development Paradigms, Two Communication Models, and Many Applications and Approaches. In J. Servaes (Ed.), *Handbook of Communication for Development and Social Change*. Singapore: Springer.

Sheldrick, M. (2018). *Who Will End Global Poverty?* Retrieved October 14, 2020, from https://oecd-development-matters.org/2018/03/06/who-will-end-global-poverty/

Stiglitz, J. (2002). *Globalisation and Its Discontent*. New York: W.W Norton.

Stiglitz, J. (2012). *The Price of Inequality: How Today's Divided Society Endangers Our Future*. New York: W.W. Norton.

Stiglitz, J. (2020). *People, Power, Profits: Progressive Capitalism for an Age of Discontent*. New York: W.W. Norton.

Struckmann, C. (2018). A Postcolonial Feminist Critique of the 2030 Agenda for Sustainable Development. A South African Application. *Agenda: Empowering Women for Gender Equity, 32*(1), 12–24.

Sustainable Development Goals. (2020). *Goal 17: Revitalize the Global Partnerships for Sustainable Development*. Retrieved November 3, 2020, from https://www.un.org/sustainabledevelopment/globalpartnerships/

The Conversation. (2020). *Are Women Leaders Really Doing Better on Coronavirus? The Data Backs It Up*. Retrieved October 29, 2020, from https://theconversation.com/are-women-leaders-really-doing-better-on-coronavirus-the-data-backs-it-up-144809

The Global Goals. (2020). *9-Industry, Innovation and Infrastructure*. Retrieved October 30, 2020, from https://www.globalgoals.org/9-industry-innovation-and-infrastructure

The Nobel Prize. (2020): *The Nobel Peace Prize for 2020*. Retrieved October 14, 2020, from https://www.nobelprize.org/prizes/peace/2020/press-release/

UN. (2015). *End Poverty. Millennium Development Goals Beyond 2015*. Retrieved October 8, 2020, from https://www.un.org/millenniumgoals/poverty.shtml

UN. (2020). *Goal 16: Peace, Justice and Strong Institutions*. Retrieved November 3, 2020, from https://sdgs.un.org/goals/goal16

UN News. (2017). *Communicating SDGs Key to Achieving Global Development Targets*. Retrieved May 29, 2020, from https://news.un.org/en/story/2017/03/552532-communicating-sdgs-key-achieving-global-development-targets-senior-un-official

UN News. (2019). *Over 820 Million People Suffering From Hunger; New UN Report Reveals Stubborn Realities of 'Immense' Global Challenge*. Retrieved October 14, 2020, from https://news.un.org/en/story/2019/07/1042411

UN SDGs. (2020). *Ensure Healthy Lives and Promote Wellbeing For All at All Ages*. Retrieved October 14, 2020, from https://sdgs.un.org/goals/goal3

UN Women. (2020). *COVID-19 and Its Economic Toll on Women: The Story Behind the Numbers*. Retrieved October 29, 2020, from https://www.unwomen.org/en/news/stories/2020/9/feature-covid-19-economic-impacts-on-women

UNCCD. (2017). *GOAL 15: Life on Land- Facts and Figures, Targets, Why it Matters*. Retrieved November 3, 2020, from https://knowledge.unccd.int/publications/goal-15-life-land-facts-and-figures-targets-why-it-matters

UNCTAD. (2014): *Developing Countries Face $2.5 Trillion Annual Investment Gap in Key Sustainable Development Sectors, UNCTAD Report Estimates*. Retrieved October 14, 2020, from https://unctad.org/press-material/developing-countries-face-25-trillion-annual-investment-gap-key-sustainable

UNDP. (2015). *The Millennium Development Goals Report 2015*. Retrieved October 8, 2020, from https://www.undp.org/content/undp/en/home/sdgoverview/mdg_goals/mdg1.html

UNDP. (2020a). *What Are the Sustainable Development Goals?* Retrieved July 7, 2020, from https://www.undp.org/content/undp/en/home/sustainable-development-goals.html

UNDP. (2020b). *Goal 6: Clean Water and Sanitation*. Retrieved October 28, 2020, from https://www.undp.org/content/undp/en/home/sustainable-development-goals/goal-6-clean-water-and-sanitation.html

UNDP. (2020c). *Goal 12 Targets*. Retrieved November 12, 2020, from https://www.undp.org/content/undp/en/home/sustainable-development-goals/goal-12-responsible-consumption-and-production/targets.html

UNEP. (2020). *Goal 7: Affordable and Clean Energy*. Retrieved October 28, 2020, from https://www.unenvironment.org/explore-topics/sustainable-development-goals/why-do-sustainable-development-goals-matter/goal-7

UNESCO. (2019). *Out of School Children and Youth*. Retrieved October 15, 2020, from http://uis.unesco.org/en/topic/out-school-children-and-youth

UNESCO. (2020). *COVID-19: At Least a Third of the world's School Children Unable to Access Remote Learning During School Closures, New Report Says*. Retrieved October 15, 2020, from https://www.unicef.org/press-releases/covid-19-least-third-worlds-schoolchildren-unable-access-remote-learning-during

Unicef. (2020). *Figure 2.9 Poverty Rate. 1990–2015*. Retrieved October 8, 2020, from https://www.unicef.cn/en/figure-29-poverty-rate-19902015

UNODC. (2020). *SDG 11: Make Cities and Human Settlements Inclusive, Safe, Resilient and Sustainable*. Retrieved November 1, 2020, from https://www.unodc.org/unodc/en/sustainable-development-goals/sdg11_-sustainable-cities-and-communities.html

UNOOSA. (2020). *Sustainable Development Goal 12 12: Responsible Consumption and Production*. Retrieved November 12, 2020, from https://www.unoosa.org/oosa/en/ourwork/space4sdgs/sdg12.html

Vorisek, D., & Yu, S. (2020). *Understanding the Cost of Achieving the Sustainable Development Goals*. Policy Research Working Paper. The World Bank Group. Retrieved October 14, 2020, from http://documents1.worldbank.org/curated/

en/744701582827333101/pdf/Understanding-the-Cost-of-Achieving-the-Sustainable-Development-Goals.pdf

WEF. (2019). *Making Affordable Housing a Reality in Cities.* Retrieved November 1, 2020, from http://www3.weforum.org/docs/WEF_Making_Affordable_Housing_A_Reality_In_Cities_report.pdf

WEF. (2020). *Fourth Industrial Revolution Tech Can Fast Track 70% of the Sustainable Development Goals.* Retrieved October 30, 2020, from https://www.weforum.org/press/2020/01/fourth-industrial-revolution-tech-can-fast-track-70-of-sustainable-development-goals/

Whaites, A. (2016). *Achieving the Impossible. Can We Be SDG16 Believers?* Retrieved November 3, 2020, from http://www.oecd.org/dac/accountable-effective-institutions/Achieving%20the%20Impossible%20can%20we%20be%20SDG16%20believers.pdf

Whiting, K. (2020). *5 Shocking Facts about Inequality, According to Oxfam's Latest Report.* Retrieved November 1, 2020, from https://www.weforum.org/agenda/2020/01/5-shocking-facts-about-inequality-according-to-oxfam-s-latest-report/

WHO. (2020). *Malaria.* Retrieved October 14, 2020, from https://www.who.int/news-room/fact-sheets/detail/malaria

World Bank. (2019). *Record High Remittances Sent Globally in 2018.* Retrieved November 3, 2020, from https://www.worldbank.org/en/news/press-release/2019/04/08/record-high-remittances-sent-globally-in-2018

World Bank. (2020a). *COVID-19 to Add as Many as 150 Million Extreme Poor by 2021.* Retrieved October 14, 2020, from https://www.worldbank.org/en/news/press-release/2020/10/07/covid-19-to-add-as-many-as-150-million-extreme-poor-by-2021

World Bank. (2020b). COVID19: *Remittances to Shrink by 14 % by 2021.* Retrieved November 3, 2020, from https://www.worldbank.org/en/news/press-release/2020/10/29/covid-19-remittance-flows-to-shrink-14-by-2021#:~:text=Remittance%20flows%20to%20low%20and,to%20%24470%20billion%20in%202021

World Social Report. (2020). *Inequality in a Rapidly Changing World.* Retrieved November 1, 2020, from https://www.un.org/development/desa/dspd/wp-content/uploads/sites/22/2020/01/World-Social-Report-2020-FullReport.pdf

Yulek, M. (2018). *How Nations Succeed. Manufacturing, Trade, Industrial Policy and Economic Development.* Singapore: Springer Publishers.

Yusha'u, M. J. (2019). Capturing the Imagination of Ordinary People: Communicating SDGs at the Grassroots Level. *SDGs Digest* (7), p. 5.

Yusha'u, M. J. (2020). COVID-19, Digital Divide and the Rise of Online Education. *SDGs Digest* (11), p. 18. Retrieved May 29, 2020, from https://books.isdb.org/view/383020/18/

CHAPTER 4

Communication for Sustainable Development and Blue Growth: Towards New Theoretical and Empirical Directions

Maria Touri, Fani Galatsopoulou, Clio Kenterelidou, and Ioanna Kostarella

INTRODUCTION

Sustainable development is currently one of the most prominent development paradigms. The United Nations (UN) Sustainable Development Goals (SDGs) reflect the need for strategies that achieve development and economic growth, tackling environmental change and preserving our oceans and forests while enhancing the human aspect. Blue Growth is one of the priorities of the UN's SDGs agenda and of the Europe 2030 strategy to support innovation and sustainable growth in the marine and maritime sectors as a whole (aquaculture, coastal tourism, marine biotechnology, ocean energy, seabed mining), improve maritime safety and security and preserve ecosystems and biodiversity. The concern with healthy oceans and sustainable coastal activity, together with blue awareness and literacy, is being addressed particularly with SDG14 'Life Below Water', but also run through many of the SDGs.

M. Touri (✉)
University of Leicester, Leicester, UK
e-mail: mt141@le.ac.uk

F. Galatsopoulou • C. Kenterelidou • I. Kostarella
Aristotle University of Thessaloniki, Thessaloniki, Greece
e-mail: fgal@jour.auth.gr; ckent@jour.auth.gr; ikostarella@jour.auth.gr

© The Author(s), under exclusive license to Springer Nature Switzerland AG 2021
M. J. Yusha'u, J. Servaes (eds.), *The Palgrave Handbook of International Communication and Sustainable Development*,
https://doi.org/10.1007/978-3-030-69770-9_4

Despite the emergence of new strategies, policy and organisational initiatives to support Blue Growth at a global and national level, there is a noticeable tendency for policymakers, institutions and corporate/business organisations to follow neoliberal strategies that focus on market-based mechanisms and a 'selling nature to save it' reasoning. Such approaches pose major risks to human development as they focus on maximising profits at the detriment of social life and the environment. In essence, there is a need for Blue Growth initiatives to pay more attention to the social dimension of sustainable development, look for the human side of the SDG-related strategies and aim for broader social change and impacts. This tendency is also reflected in the UN initiative launched in 2017, 'Decade of Ocean Science for Sustainable Development 2021-2030', which promotes a common framework for studying and assessing the health of the world's waters, the stakeholders' collaboration and the information sharing and synergetic acts in the blue field.

In this chapter, we argue that the neglected social change aspect in Blue Growth initiatives can be brought to the forefront through a communication perspective to social change, and with the aid of the Communication for Development and Social Change (CDSC) scholarship and practice. The field of CDSC has led to at least two significant realisations concerning social change and sustainable development. First, it has concluded that social change is a multidimensional process that is not limited to income, productivity and gross national product (GNP). Second, there is a consensus that social change requires the grassroots participation of people and communities and should be equated with people's ability to influence the wider system (Servaes & Malikhao, 2016: 174). Such participation requires dialogue and communication, and as we argue in this chapter, communication needs to be integral in Blue Growth and social change projects to ensure that communities and local actors become co-creators in the design of solutions to problems that are too complex to be solved only by institutional interventions.

Drawing on the social dimension of Blue Growth and insights from the field of CDSC, this chapter makes a first attempt at evaluating key Blue Growth initiatives in the European area in terms of the extent to which they promote social change through the employment of strategies and communication practices that take into account the interests of all involved. This is done through a theoretical discussion of Blue Growth in connection to ideas of social innovation, social change and communication. The theoretical discussion is then followed by a mapping of the aims, key stakeholders, beneficiaries and communication practices that are identified in selected Blue Growth projects funded by the European Union (EU). Our discussion demonstrates that the chosen projects promote Blue Growth through a very narrow and market-orientated approach with an emphasis on tourism and resource management with limited consideration of the needs and social life of the coastal communities that are most affected by these strategies. This is also reflected in the communication practices that are driven by a one-directional and top-down rationale, with a low level of participation of the general public and non-institutional actors. We conclude with recommendations for further research opportunities in search of more inclusive solutions.

Sustainable Development and Blue Growth: Concepts and Strategies

Sustainable development has emerged as a prominent development paradigm in the last few decades, with the year 1987 becoming a landmark for the 'sustainability revolution' with the publication of 'The Brundtland report' by the World Commission on Environment and Development (WCED). In this, sustainable development was defined as 'development which meets the needs of the present without compromising the ability of future generations to meet their own needs' (Elliott, 1994: 4), with core issues including development, energy, food security and biodiversity. It can be argued that the Brundtland report was also a landmark for the establishment of what today is called the 'Sustainable Development Goals' (SDGs). The SDGs summarise the agenda agreed by the United Nations' member states to achieve sustainable development between 2015 and 2030, and which continues the Millennium Development Goals (MDGs) that were adopted in 2000.

Sustainable development has also been theorised as a form of growth and social change, 'a social process, which has as its ultimate objective sustainable development at distinct levels of society' (Servaes & Malikhao, 2016: 174; Flint, 2007). Although in the field of social sciences, development has been associated with the development of the economically less advanced countries of the global South, it is now more widely acknowledged that development is no longer reserved for developing countries. Instead, all countries are developing as part of a global process while processes of poverty and marginalisation are also taking place in Europe and the United States of America (Hemer & Tufte, 2005; Ngomba, 2013; Servaes, 2011). It is in this context that this chapter positions Blue Growth as a development process that affects any ocean-dependent regions.

Our focus on Blue Growth is also inspired by the fact that seas and oceans are drivers for the European economy especially in the countries of the Mediterranean Sea, which have been hit the hardest by the economic crisis and the austerity measures of the previous years. The Southern European states (mainly Italy, Spain, Greece and Portugal) were disproportionately impacted by the Eurozone debt crisis and forced to rely on substantial economic relief from the wealthier Northern European states. This divide needs to be addressed through the development of sectors that have a high potential for sustainable jobs and growth, such as the Blue Economy.

The Blue Economy is a notion that has emerged at a time of considerable change in the way ocean spaces are conceived and used (Voyer et al., 2018). The concept of the Blue Economy appeared in the preparatory process of the Rio+20 United Nations Conference on Sustainable Development in 2012.

This conference focused primarily on Green Economy, which was proposed as a solution for 'improved human well-being and social equity while reducing environmental risks and ecological scarcities' (UNEP, 2011). Nature was embraced as a solution that would lead the developed and developing states out of the 2008 financial crisis. The Small Island Developing States (SIDS) and other coastal regions questioned the emphasis on the Green Economy and proposed the 'Blue Economy' for ocean-dependent economies (Mckinley, Aller, Caroline, & Hopkins, 2018). This term was not new, as it was circulated among different actors and was also used at *The Economist* magazine's first World Oceans Summit, four months before Rio+20, where the Blue Growth potential of the oceans drew wider attention (Silver, Gray, Campbell, Fairbanks, & Gruby, 2015). Since then, the oceans and coastal areas are gaining increasing interest as the ocean- and coastal-based economic activities and their associated growth potential are seen as an important driver for bolstering economies around the world (European Commission, 2020; Mckinley et al., 2018). Reports, such as the 'Green Economy in a Blue World' (UNEP, 2012), state the problems of the oceans pollution, overfishing and climate change which threaten the livelihoods of millions of people around the world and analyse how key sectors of the marine and coastal environment can make the transition towards a Green Economy. This report advances and broadens the Green Economy concept as it refers to the 'Blue World' and covers the sectors of shipping, fisheries, tourism, marine-based renewable energies, seabed mining and agriculture. It concludes that 'a shift to sustainability in terms of improved human well-being and social equity can lead to healthier and more economically productive oceans that can simultaneously benefit coastal communities and ocean-linked industries' (UNEP, 2012).

New strategies and policy initiatives are emerging and support the Blue Economy and the Blue Growth concept at a global and national level including the World Bank's Blue Growth Portfolio (Barbesgaard, 2018), and the Blue Growth Initiative (BGI) of the Food and Agricultural Organization (FAO). The FAO BGI was launched in support of food security, poverty alleviation and sustainable management of living aquatic resources (Eikeset et al., 2018). A wide range of countries have also developed and implemented Blue Growth programmes and projects (FAO UN, 2015). The European Union's response was the Blue Growth strategy (European Commission, 2012, 2014), aiming at stimulating economic growth in European seas. The strategy refers to the sectors of aquaculture, biotechnology, energy, coastal and maritime tourism and seabed mining. In terms of actors, the Blue Growth Initiative is based on a partnership approach, bringing together a range of actors, including United Nations (UN) agencies (e.g. UN Environmental Program—UNEP, UN Development Program—UNDP, and Food and Agricultural Organization—FAO), multilateral and national donors (e.g. the Norwegian Agency for Development Cooperation, the World Bank and the Global Environmental Facility), industry coalitions and transnational environmental NGOs (ENGOs) (Barbesgaard, 2018).

The Global Challenge: SDG14 'Life in Water'

The 2030 Agenda for Sustainable Development, adopted by all United Nations member states in 2015, provides a shared blueprint for peace and prosperity for people and the planet, now and into the future. At its heart are the 17 Sustainable Development Goals (SDGs), which are an urgent call for action by all countries in a global partnership. They recognise that ending poverty and other deprivations must go together with strategies that improve health and education, reduce inequality and spur economic growth—all the while tackling climate change and working to preserve our oceans and forests.

SDG14 'Life in Water' is dedicated to the oceans, seas and marine resources, acknowledging the importance of the oceans to life on this planet. It aims at the protection of seas and oceans, as seawater constitutes the world's largest ecosystem. Recognised negative effects of climate change, such as overfishing and pollution, threaten both the intrinsic value of the ecosystem itself and the value and pleasure people get from it. Marine ecosystems are essential for the health and well-being of local coastal communities. They provide food security, protect livelihoods and secure economic development. The fishing sector also provides a social safety net, especially for women, who are occupied in the secondary activities related to marine fisheries and marine aquacultures, such as fish processing and marketing (Mohammed, 2017). SDG14 focuses on conservation and the sustainable use of marine resources and is concerned with human interaction with the oceans. It encompasses all ocean-related activities, including fisheries and aquaculture, land-based sources of pollution, tourism, transportation and new ocean-based industries, such as offshore renewable energy and marine biotechnology. United Nations agencies collaborate with governments, private sector and civil society organisations to harmonise economic development and ocean health (Mohammed, 2017). While improving ocean ecosystem health, it also promotes ocean literacy, which is important in achieving effective conservation practices and sustainable economic development. It recognises the potential economic and social benefits emanating from the development of marine and coastal tourism and broaches the matter of the enhancement of the marine-oriented livelihoods and human well-being (Henderson, 2019).

Contrasting Discourses on Blue Growth and Blue Economy

Despite the multiplicity of programmes and policy proposals that have been and are being developed, scholars such as Barbesgaard (2018) have observed a tendency for policymakers and institutions to follow neoliberal strategies that focus on market-based mechanisms and a 'selling nature to save it' reasoning, posing significant risks to small-scale users. This neoliberal approach is also reflected in the dominant discourses around the Blue Economy. The long-term economic and societal importance of the human interaction with the sea and the potential role of empowered publics in helping to achieve the goals of SDG14 'Life in Water' remain largely untapped and unrecognised (Henderson, 2019). Arbo, Knol, Linke, and Martin (2018) identify distinct discourses such as 'Our sick oceans' discourse, which concerns the climate change and its consequences, the unsustainable fishing practices and the millions of tonnes of plastic litter found in the oceans that endanger the marine ecosystems. In this discourse, the ocean is referred to as humanity's natural and cultural heritage, with emphasis on the need to be protected (Ababouch—FAO-FIPI, 2015). In another dominant discourse, the ocean is framed as a new economic and development frontier, with the riches of the sea being the central point of the Blue Economy (Arbo et al., 2018). The same economic frame is also reflected in the 'Oceans as Good Business' discourse identified by Silver et al. (2015), focusing on problems, preferred solutions and governance actors. Other discourses include the 'Oceans as Natural Capital', 'Oceans as Integral to Pacific SIDS' and 'Oceans as Small-Scale Fisheries Livelihoods'.

Barbesgaard, Franco, and Buxton (2014) draw attention to the way market-based mechanisms in Blue Growth appear to encompass a human-rights-based language focusing on poverty eradication, food security and climate change mitigation. As the authors explain, despite the human rights frames being promoted by many institutions, the underlying principle remains economic deterministic and in opposition to the demands of civil society organisations, since capitalism-driven actors become more and more involved in global policy development for climate change and environmental protection. The conflation of market-based solutions with human rights and environmental protection issues is reflected in the term 'ocean-grabbing', a process involving practices around the use of fishery resources with little concern for the adverse environmental consequences (Barbesgaard, 2018; Barbesgaard et al., 2014; Bennett, Govan, & Satterfield, 2015). This 'enterprising nature' approach epitomises the modernisation logic that continues to characterise development initiatives, especially in the global South, which is predicated on top-down and utilitarian rationality with a clear economistic tendency, aiming to maximise production and profits at the detriment of social life and the environment (Pachon, Bokelmann, & Ramírez, 2016). Moreover, for the most part, Blue Growth strategy is driven by international organisations, governments, investors, scientists and other 'experts', with the voices and requirements of communities being marginalised. In other words, there is an element of social change that is currently undermined in the relevant policies and which merits more attention and investigation.

In the context of Blue Growth, social change has been theorised as social innovation, a concept and process that springs from 'bottom-up initiatives that promote change by so-called enablers, aiming for impacts beyond the individual level, to a broader scope of social and/or ecological contexts' (Soma, van den Burg, Hoefnagel, Stuiver, & van der Heide, 2018: 364). Social innovation is understood as a bottom-up process initiated and advanced by local actors. Murray, Caulier-Grice, and Mulgan (2010) refer to social innovations as innovative 'fixes', as they are seen as responses to societal problems. They underline that in the EU policy context, these social 'fixes' are potential solutions for major macro-level challenges such as achieving carbon-neutral objectives, providing universal healthcare or fighting poverty (Schubert, 2018). The Bureau of European Policy Advisers, in the report 'Empowering People, Driving Change, Social Innovation in the European Union' (European Commission, 2011), refers to social innovation as 'an important option to be enhanced at different levels (local, regional, national, European) and sectors (public, private, civil) as its purpose is to innovate differently (through the active engagement of society itself) and to generate primarily social value' (BEPA, 2010 in Schubert, 2018). Schubert (2018), in his study about social innovation, examines the EU policies and initiatives and underlines the Guide to Social Innovation, published by the European Commission and the Directorate-General for Regional and Urban Policy, which characterises Social Innovation as a process that can be applied to scale up local social innovation to the EU level. This approach sees social innovation as an instrument for social change, as local actors are becoming co-creators for solutions to problems that are too complex to be solved only by top-down interventions. Nevertheless, in the context of Blue Growth, this element of social change is consistently undermined in institutional policies and decisions.

We propose that the neglected social change aspect in Blue Growth initiatives can be brought to the forefront through a communication perspective to social change and with the aid of the Communication for Development and Social Change (CDSC) scholarship and practice. The field of CDSC theorises social change as a multidimensional process that is not limited to income, productivity and gross national product (GNP), and which requires the grassroots participation of people and communities through dialogue and communication. Hence, the field offers valuable tools for theorising and exploring the social dimension of Blue Growth as a type of development and social change that is equated with the ability of people to influence the wider system and take control of their lives, and where communication can play a key role. Although communication is not explicitly mentioned in any of the 17 SDGs, it remains integral in processes that are designed to contribute to sustainable development. It is through communication, transparency and knowledge sharing that global risks can be addressed (Servaes, 2013).

Communication for Development and Social Change: A New Theorisation for Blue Growth

Communication for Development and Social Change (CDSC) is a field of academic and applied research that involves the utilisation of a range of communication tools and media to achieve behaviour change among marginalised groups in order to improve their quality of life. In this context, social change—environmental, political or cultural—happens when communication is used to improve people's lives and promote social justice through dialogue, trust-building and sharing of knowledge (Quarry & Ramírez, 2009; Waisbord, 2015; Wilkins, Tufte, & Obregon, 2014). Overall, the field of CDSC has emerged out of various schools of thought that were developed by scholars and practitioners in different parts of the world. These have also led to the use of different names and discourses, rendering the field a 'chameleon', embedded in international development, changing colours to reflect the development thinking of the day (Quarry & Ramírez, 2009). Among the most dominant discourses are the following: development communication (DevCom), communication for development (ComDev), Latin American alternative communication and communication for social change (CFSC). CDSC has also been practised under the names of Information, Communication and Technology for Development (ICT4D), Learning for Social Change and Social and Behavioral Communication (Thomas & van de Fliert, 2014; Tufte, 2017). In this chapter, the name Communication for Development and Social Change (CDSC) is used as a term that attempts to summarise and encompass the premises of the different approaches broadly.

Over the years, the study of CDSC has witnessed several paradigmatic shifts in theories and models of economic and social development, but as Tufte (2017) notes in his recent book *Communication and Social Change: A citizen's perspective*, two schools of thought have dominated: the diffusion paradigm (Rogers, 1995) and the participatory paradigm (Freire, 2001). Everett Rogers' diffusion theory has informed the use of a broad range of expert-driven communication strategies that focused on facilitating development through the diffusion of knowledge and information to poor communities (Rogers, 1995). In line with theories and discourses that see development through the prism of modernisation and economic growth, the diffusion approach adopts a very linear and top-down process that is based on the creation of effective messages targeting audiences with the aim of persuading them to change their behaviour. The participatory paradigm draws from Paulo Freire, the Brazilian philosopher who conceived of communication as dialogue and participation, with a strong emphasis on the recognition of non-mediated and interpersonal communication, dialogue and persuasion, where communication is a cyclical process of information sharing and leads to individual and collective change (Rodriquez, 2011; Thomas, 2011). These activities enable meaningful knowledge generation and exchange, skill development and establishment of a platform for collective decision-making and action (Thomas & van de Fliert, 2014). In the participatory framework, communication is approached as a meaning-making process that respects and emphasises the cultural contexts and means through which communities understand and act upon their lives (Dutta, 2011). Here, the focus is on the empowerment of communities through their active participation in the identification of problems and solutions and through processes of collective action and reflection (Tufte, 2017). In a nutshell, Communication for Development and Social Change could be described as 'intentional and strategically organised processes of face-to-face and mediated communication aimed at promoting dialogue and action to address inequality, injustice, and insecurity for the common good' (Enghel, 2014: 119).

Communication strategies that have been used in the field of sustainable development interventions also fall under the schools of thought, mentioned earlier. On the one hand, and following the logic of information diffusion, communication campaigns and marketing techniques are used in an attempt to raise awareness and influence attitudes on environmental issues. On the other hand, scholars and practitioners who work in the participatory school of thought tend to focus more on dialogic approaches (see Touri, 2016, 2018) and use more creative and participatory methods such as storytelling and participatory video (Servaes & Lie, 2015). The participatory approach is more effective in terms of achieving project sustainability. Still, it is also less widely applied because it moves away from traditional communication practices that are based on media distributed messages that aim to cause behavioural change (Mefalopulos, 2005). In the case of Blue Growth, and based on the previous discussion, it can be argued that the two main pillars of communication for sustainable development, that is participation and empowerment, are missing since recent efforts to promote sustainable fisheries or blue carbon have not included fisher peoples' movements in the identification of problems, priorities and solutions (Barbesgaard, 2018; Mefalopulos, 2005). In this chapter, we draw on insights from the field of CDSC to provide the first evaluation of key Blue Growth initiatives promoted by selected European Union projects in terms of their social change dimension and the employment of dialogic and participatory communication strategies.

Case Study: Blue Growth in the EU Projects

With 'the blue economy can be a driver for Europe's welfare and prosperity' as the main message of the Blue Growth strategy adopted by the European Commission in 2012 (European Commission, 2012), the related projects held by the member countries of the European Union are a case worth examining. The Blue Growth projects funded by the European Union not only have the potential to contribute to blue policy initiatives, prevention programmes or regulations at national, EU and global level, but they also form the main guide to allow swift reference from strategic policy to practice and implementation and from design to praxis (Karjalainen, Hoeveler, & Draghia-Akli, 2017). These projects demonstrate and encourage policies and innovative projects in coastal areas and the maritime sector, with 22 out of the 27 member states having coastal areas. Thus, they contribute to finding common approaches and planning tools to boost sustainable coastal and maritime tourism in the Mediterranean, Black, North and Baltic Seas and the Atlantic Ocean. They also offer an essential contribution to tackling today's challenges and tensions with regards to the environment (green and blue), poverty, human rights, marginalisation and mobility as they aim to reduce economic and social disparities; to promote sustainable development by creating new business opportunities and managing the resources of oceans, seas and coastal resources in a sustainable manner; and to enhance human well-being as part of the marine ecosystem and as potential economic and societal development factor (European Commission, n.d.-a). In this chapter, we focus on specific projects that were selected through the online tool of the EU-funded projects (European Commission, n.d.-b, n.d.-c, n.d.-d). Our search was guided by the use of specific keywords, 'blue growth' and 'blue economy', and was narrowed to the period between January and February 2019. The final sample included 25 projects. The selected projects had an online profile and presentation through a functioning website in English, German, French, Spanish, Italian or Greek language. The purpose of this mapping was to gain some initial insight into the general strategies and communication practices featured in these projects, rather than offer conclusive answers. Hence, our observations serve as an impetus for future investigation and analysis.

First, and building upon the concept of social change and social innovation, we identify the Blue Growth strategies employed in selected projects in the European area, in terms of their social dimension as it is reflected in their aims, funding sources and opportunities and key stakeholders and target audiences. Through this mapping, we offer some initial insights into whether and to what extent the Blue Growth strategy incorporates promises of technological progress that underestimate the importance of the social dimension of change (Soma et al., 2018); whether it incorporates ideas of social innovation and collaborative action among stakeholders (Soma et al., 2018); whether it aims at long-term sustainable development which is fortified and safeguarded by CEPA interventions (Communication-Education-Participation-Awareness) (Dela, Garnett, Goldstein, & van Kempen, 2007), or at market-based mechanisms and a 'selling nature to save it' reasoning leading to short-term economic benefits and social marketing.

Second, and drawing on ideas from the field of CDSC more specifically, we assess the communication interventions that are integral in the selected projects in terms of their information and communication measures and interventions, the extent to which they take into account the interests of all involved and their capacity to employ a dialogic dimension and facilitate a learning process. Key questions include: How bottom-up or top-down is communication in the EU's Blue Growth programmes? Do the blue communication strategies pitch the public as a participatory co-creator of development and a public communication actor reinforcing social and policy impact into the Blue Growth initiatives?

DISSEMINATING THE IDEA OF BLUE GROWTH IN EUROPE

Aims

The mapping demonstrates that aims are generally driven by the SDGs and the Europe 2030 Agenda for Sustainable Development. They are also driven by the grouping of the Organisation for Economic Co-operation and Development (OECD) and its five (5) Ps[1] that measure the distance to the SDG targets and country contribution to the achievement of the broad 2030 Agenda for Sustainable Development. Common aims include raising awareness, dissemination of the Blue Growth definition, exchanging best practices, networking and clustering, finding common approaches and designing planning tools. Table 4.1 presents selected examples from the sampled projects.

The mapping of the aims has revealed that the Blue Growth concept is approached mainly through the economy prism conceiving the oceans as economically productive and focusing on ocean-linked benefits for the industries and other professional groups, or treating Blue Growth as green growth and relating it to investments or technological products that create jobs and stimulate general growth (e.g. *Hövding* is about a new protective headgear/helmet for cyclists, *InvestInPomerania* is about attracting investment in a region in priority industries—IT, energy, the automotive sector, chemicals and logistics—and helping to increase tax revenues). Overall, the Blue Growth initiatives aim mostly at stimulating economic growth in European seas, leaving behind the conceptualisation of the ocean as humanity's natural and cultural heritage.

Funding, Stakeholders and Target Groups

As the term of Blue Growth has no generally agreed-upon definition (Eikeset et al., 2018), it embodies various meanings and approaches depending on the contexts in which it is used, and on the multiple and diverse stakeholders that are involved. Because sea-basin strategies and initiatives do not have dedicated funds, their implementation requires coordinated use of available *funding* streams, such as the European Maritime and Fisheries Fund (EMFF), Horizon 2020, LIFE, COSME and the European Fund for Strategic Investment (EFSI) (European Commission, 2017). These funding resources associate development mainly with economic or scientific impact.

The engagement of various *stakeholders* is crucial to the design of successful policies and strategies as it creates opportunities to share expertise, data and knowledge. The sea basins in Europe, that is the Baltic Sea, Adriatic and Ionian Sea, Black Sea, Mediterranean Sea, North Sea and the Atlantic Ocean, are all unique sea regions and social settings. These various settings provide a framework for cooperation between the European Union, the member states and their regions and, where appropriate, third countries sharing a sea basin or waters (European Commission, 2017). So, different institutional settings,

---

[1] OECD groups the SDGs into five (5) categories, which are people (goals 1–5: poverty, food, health, education, gender equality), planet (goals 6, 12–15: water, sustainable production, climate, oceans, biodiversity), prosperity (goals 6, 12–15: energy, economy, infrastructure, inequality, cities), peace (goal 16: institutions), partnership (goal 17: implementation). (OECD, retrieved on 26/03/2019, http://www.oecd.org/sdd/measuring-distance-to-the-sdgs-targets.htm)

Table 4.1 Aims

EU project	Aim(s)
4helix+	To strengthen and reinvigorate Blue Economy clusters by offering coaching and funding to improve their competitive strategies through knowledge sharing and innovation.
AMPAMED—marinas protected areas	To promote the role of protected areas for the sustainable development of local economic activities like artisanal, fishing and tourism and to show different approaches in management resources (innovative management, load capacity, criteria) and sustainable development in the Mediterranean basin.
Art Reefs	To promote and facilitate the use of artificial reefs as effective and affordable tools to boost innovative and sustainable coastal and maritime tourism.
BaltCoast	To combine pilot projects and measures across Baltic coast countries with the development of processes and regulations for spatial planning.
BalticRIM	To analyse the relationship between maritime cultural heritage and marine spatial planning, and to build a common database for decision-making processes and management outline.
Blue Growth and relevance of nautical tourism in Sardinia	To raise awareness about Blue Growth concept, introduce nautical tourism (main concepts, definitions and data) and share its relevance in Sardinia.
Blue Net	To facilitate, enhance and develop SMEs collaboration and networking among maritime clusters in the Adriatic, Ionian and Black Seas, for exchanging of good practices of cluster management and development of business sectors; empowering maritime clusters and/or regional centres of competence to become 'blue-innovative'; and enhancing networking among relevant cluster stakeholders.
BLUEMED	To coordinate research and innovation activities so as to support the sustainable management and exploitation of the Mediterranean Sea by the marine and maritime sectors. It also seeks to create synergies between regional, national and EU investments.
BlueTourMed_C3	To enhance the development of a sustainable and responsible coastal and maritime tourism in the Mediterranean area, to enhance jointly solutions for the protection and promotion of natural and cultural resources and to build the thematic community of projects focused on sustainable tourism by helping the synthesis and integration of data, methods and outputs.
Co-Evolve	To promote the co-evolution of human activities and natural systems for the development of sustainable coastal and maritime tourism, and to foster joint development and transferring of approaches, tools, guidelines and best practices.
Columbus	To establish a 'knowledge fellowship' network with knowledge transfer and a blueprint for future activities contributing to sustainable marine and maritime economy.
Deep Blue	To promote collaboration between marine and maritime education, research and training centres in the Western Mediterranean region in order to strengthen relevant skills and increase capacity building for blue career development.

(*continued*)

Table 4.1 (continued)

EU project	Aim(s)
ECOADRIA-FISHERMAN	To make local fishermen the protagonists and enhance sea management by fostering relationships among fishermen in the Adriatic Sea and analysing the feasibility and potential for developing services in the environmental, cultural field and tourism.
IBlue	To contribute to the sustainable relaunch of the yachting sector (shipbuilding, nautical services, tourism), helping the economic upturn by creating a collaborative network.
Maestrale	To lay the foundations for a strategy for the deployment of maritime energy in the Mediterranean area, and to broaden the sharing of knowledge encouraging blue investments.
MedCoast4BG—Med Coasts for Blue Growth	To contribute to finding common approaches and planning tools to boost sustainable coastal and maritime tourism in the Mediterranean.
Medinblue	To promote Blue Economy in the Mediterranean basin, to reinforce the regional dialogue on the Blue Economy/Integrated Maritime Policy and facilitate the elaboration of a Blue Economy regional agenda, to assist with the identification and promotion of initiatives and projects in line with the Mediterranean Blue Economy agenda and to facilitate networking and information sharing among relevant Blue Economy stakeholders.
Mistral	To strengthen transnational partnership, clustering and activity for marine knowledge and blue sustainable innovation.
MUSES_Multi-Use in European Seas	To facilitate sharing marine resources by two or more users, and to highlight multi-use management in overcoming existing barriers and minimise risks (i.e. sectoral demands and vested interests associated with existing political institutions and practices).
Pelagos	To enhance the commercial exploitation of blue energy research and innovation competencies of Mediterranean actors (i.e. marine renewable energy) and increase transnational and trans-sectoral cooperation (maritime industries, private sector, government and social sector).
Proteus	To exploit the growth potential of the emerging maritime surveillance industry as a socio-economic development factor and new job opportunities generator.
Put 'n' Take	To experience sea fishing in a safe and accessible environment and to raise awareness for fisheries.
SpaceTech4Sea	To demonstrate, validate and commercialise an innovative ultralight LNG (liquefied natural gas) fuel tank in the maritime sector, by utilising cutting-edge aerospace technologies and novel shipbuilding techniques in order to boost Blue Economy by removing the obstacles in the implementation of the LNG as marine fuel in EU water basins.
The Sustainable Blue Growth Agenda for the Baltic Sea Region	To identify and discuss in greater depth the processes necessary to realise the Baltic Blue Growth Agenda in the coming years.
Water-Energy-Food-Ecosystem Nexus/Nexus Atlas	To suggest useful examples that reveal the trade-offs and synergies of the water, energy, food and ecosystem sectors in the Mediterranean region.

across market and multiple sectors, and different actors can join in a network in order to lead development and inventiveness for the use and management of marine resources. Because maritime initiatives and policies are collaborative, one of their key features is the implementation of visible deliverables and understandable policies to different *audiences*. Table 4.2 presents the stakeholders, actors involved and target audiences found in the selected EU-funded Blue Growth projects.

The mapping of Blue Growth cases reveals that stakeholders and selected target groups are in line with the core idea and strategy of Blue Growth to foster the future role of seas, coasts and oceans in solving today's challenges and tensions. Specifically, the involved stakeholders, actors and groups are directly involved and have an interest in Blue Growth, and hence they can foster transnational-transregional-transectoral collaborations in specific Blue Growth areas and especially between players in traditional and new or

Table 4.2 Stakeholders and beneficiaries

EU project	Stakeholder(s)	Beneficiary(ies)
ArtReefs		National institutes, national tourism organisations, local governmental authorities
BalticRIM	Tourism, divers, aquaculture, shipping and offshore wind farmers.	Municipalities
Blue Net		Clusters, universities, institutes
BlueTourMed_C3	Regions, universities, local government.	Chambers, councils
Columbus		Pan-European organisations, funding bodies, researchers, communication experts, end-users
Deep Blue		National institutes, universities
IBlue	SMEs, regional development agencies, higher education and research institutions, policymakers at regional level, general public	
MedCoast4BG—Med Coasts for Blue Growth	Regions, institutional and technical partners	Public administrations, national/regional/local private, operators, citizens of coastal areas across the Mediterranean, research institutions/universities, international organizations and networks
Mistral		Leading clusters
MUSES_Multi-Use in European Seas		Submariner network
SpaceTech4Sea		Finance companies, shipping companies
Startup Weekend Piraeus—Blue Growth	Entrepreneurs	

emerging maritime sectors, in order to pool skills, knowledge and resources (e.g. offshore wind farmers, divers). We also found global and multi-stakeholder partnerships that are created in order to enhance the holistic and integrated approach of the public, public-private, civil society partnerships, and the north-south, south-south or triangular, regional and international cooperation on knowledge sharing and capacity building (e.g. public administrations, national/regional/local private operators, citizens of coastal areas across the Mediterranean, research institutions/universities, international organisations and networks).

Yet, the collaboration of the private sector, such as SMEs with the public sector, like universities and research institutions, remains underdeveloped. Although the entrepreneurial and business maritime sector has a strong presence in the European setting, there is a noticeable dichotomy between the public sector and the business world in delivering scientific services and market-oriented products, respectively. This lack of cooperation and coordination between public and private entities is a severe drawback that jeopardises the realisation of collective goals that would enable social change. The projects also exhibit a neoliberal approach since many of the involved stakeholders are governance or institutional actors (Silver et al., 2015). Finally, only two projects refer to grassroots groups by including the end-users or the divers in their frameworks. So, the public and its communities are seen not as the mechanisms for change, but just as the site of the intervention or circulation of information.

In order to engage stakeholders and target audiences more closely with the practices of sustainable development, social change and innovation, the European Commission has undertaken initiatives such as the following (European Commission, 2017):

- The European Maritime Day: an annual meeting point and roadshow for Europe's maritime community to network, discuss and forge joint action in support of the maritime policy and Blue Growth.
- The European Marine Observation and Data network: an initiative that aims to make fragmented and hidden marine data resources available and interoperable.
- The Blue Economy Business and Science Forum: a platform for business, science, finance and policy representatives to exchange knowledge and experiences and discuss opportunities for and barriers to innovation in the blue economy.
- The European Atlas of the Seas: an educational tool highlighting the European common maritime heritage.
- An online maritime forum: a project that was set up to improve communication among stakeholders.

Information and Communication Measures and Interventions

With regards to the core principles of the two competing paradigms in CDSC (diffusion vs. participatory paradigm), communication can focus on delivering messages, information and technologies to target groups (linear communication), or on the process, dialogue and people in which case the target group has a genuine interest in and is invited to be involved in forming actions and policies together with all the actors (horizontal, two-way communication). The mapping of EU projects reveals that the blue communication is static and top-down, one-way and fragmented, not continuous and not consistent, not inviting the public to be engaged but simply throwing out information and data in the digital space. For most of the projects and communication strategies, a diffusion strategy is being implemented, with a relatively low level of participation of non-institutional actors. Social innovation processes are not encouraged, nor are they adopted to enable local actors to be co-creators for solutions to problems. Table 4.3 presents some examples of top-down communication blue strategies in the framework of specific projects.

Community-building activities that stimulate the sharing and co-ownership of data and results are limited to workshops, field exercises or web applications. Media-campaigning is present as it is expected within the framework of dissemination and communication. Most of the projects incorporate social media in their online digital presence and link them to their website page. Yet, they do not activate or exploit the social interaction dimension. Social media accounts are presented and linked to the website without any real interaction taking place in these accounts. Facebook, Twitter and LinkedIn are the main tools (with LinkedIn always being the poorest in interaction), and in fewer cases, we see YouTube, Instagram and Flickr. The website is used as a digital textual announcement board, and the accounts feature very limited information and communication material (creating likes, shares and reposts, commenting and responding). At the same time, no space is provided for community building and interaction (gaining followers, following others, engaging).

Moreover, the structure of the websites is basic, with rudimentary sections like news, events, downloads, documents, media, and no real attempt at fostering communication and public engagement. Only a few adopt infographics and newsletters, and even fewer incorporate interactive measures like innovation vouchers, chat rooms or forums, animations and blogs. Some more creative examples can be found in the projects *BlueTourMed_C3* or *ECOADRIA-FISHERMAN* which include communication practices such as national conference, exhibitions, guided visits, onboard fishing boats, local fish market and educational tours, theatrical performance, artistic sculptures made from rubbish collected at sea (sea rubbish art) or fish tastings with local traditional recipes. The lack of dialogic practices is evident also in the fact that project concepts, ideas and actions-activities do not integrate locations (i.e. coastal and maritime tourism) or sub-sectors (i.e. beach-based and water-based tourism). Further, there is a lack of evidence of cross-sector interaction in the initial design of the

Table 4.3 Communication strategies

EU project	Communication strategy
An online maritime forum	A forum set up to improve communication among stakeholders. It includes summaries of expert group meetings and studies. The material is made available for comments, but there is limited interaction and the networking results are not presented publicly or evaluated.
Art Reefs	Endorsement initiatives, laboratories, conferences.
MedCoast4BG	Development and transferring of tools, guidelines and best practices (all published online in website).
Medinblue	A Mediterranean Blue Economy stakeholder platform with data (all published online in website), conferences, labelling as Medinblue and endorsing regional cooperation projects designated by the respective ministries of foreign affairs.
SpaceTech4Sea	Market consultation and business development through arranged meetings.
The European Atlas of the Seas	An educational tool highlighting the European common maritime heritage. It is deprived of its interactive nature as a digital tool and appears as a static graphical depiction of information without offering the opportunity to the public to enrich these data with information and in real time.
The European Maritime Day	Annual two-day event during which Europe's maritime community meet to network, discuss and forge joint action. It targets maritime professionals, entrepreneurs and ocean leaders. It is a matchmaking event that makes a buzz on social media during those days, but its networking results are not presented publicly or evaluated.
The Sustainable Blue Growth Agenda for the Baltic Sea Region	Development and implementation of a large-scale professional image, marketing and branding campaign for Baltic Sea blue bioeconomy products and services (all published online in website).
Water-Energy-Food-Ecosystem Nexus/ Nexus Atlas	Collection and dissemination of best practices and examples of success stories. The case studies serve as a basis on which to build the narratives of the various development scenarios that will be illustrated in the Atlas (all published online in website).

projects and during its evolvement and actualisation (e.g. cross-sectoral interaction between and among sectors like shipping and ports, oil and gas, pipelines and cables, fishing, marine aquaculture, offshore wind, marine aggregates, conservation, etc.).

CHALLENGING DOMINANT SUSTAINABILITY DISCOURSES THROUGH COMMUNICATION: A FRAMEWORK PROPOSITION

One of the key inferences that can be drawn from this mapping concerns the way in which the examined EU initiatives are permeated by a dominant sustainable development discourse that originates in and is centred primarily on the institutions and economic worldview of the global North. This is a discourse that is predicated on a neoliberal model of development and embodies the power of the North to name, represent and theorise (Escobar, 2001; McEwan,

2008: 165). In the case of the EU programmes examined in this chapter, this discourse is reflected in the emphasis that these programmes place on the economy and the need for visible deliverables and measurable results, in the global or transnational management approach and in the scientific and technological solutions. The recurring reference to the need for supporting tourism and enhancing the commercial exploitation of Blue Growth-related resources highlights the proposed alliance between saving economic growth and saving nature (Pfeifer, 2011). It also demonstrates the utilitarian approach through which Blue Growth is addressed, with emphasis on the services delivered by nature (Woodhouse, 2002). In this case, describing the environment with economic concepts and tools also reflects the tendency by policymakers and environmental experts to assess sustainability based on hard facts, quantifiable data and measurable results (Pfeifer, 2011). This is a tendency that is not unique to Blue Growth initiatives. Instead, it is an ideology that is deeply rooted in well-established neoliberal discourses of development that have underpinned theories and practices of sustainability since the era of colonialism.

The emphasis of EU programmes on global and transnational cooperation and solutions is another manifestation of these discourses. Although global cooperation is paramount for addressing global issues, an overemphasis on a global management approach means that local culture is sidelined in favour of institutionalised and one-size-fits-all solutions (Kothari, Salleh, Escobar, Demaria, & Acosta, 2018). The sidelining of local culture is exacerbated further through the emphasis on the need for investment in cutting-edge technologies. Where modern science and technology becomes a panacea, environmental problems are rendered technical and local needs and knowledge become marginalised (ibid.).

In this context, the prevalence of a static and top-down communication approach is unsurprising. It follows dominant result-oriented, institutionalised approaches that treat communication as an institutionalised and bureaucratic process and fail to consider the importance of local contexts (Enghel, 2014; Wilkins & Enghel, 2013). In line with the dominant sustainable development discourses, communication practices focus on pre-established and tangible quantifiable targets that can be achieved through the transfer of information. As a result, the dynamic, open-ended and often intangible processes and relations that are inherent in development are overshadowed (Tufte, 2017).

Drawing on the principles and lessons from Communication for Development and Social Change, we would propose a new communication framework that is based on a local, small and dialogic approach to communication. In this framework, the 'local' stands for recognition and appreciation of the needs, interests and knowledge of local communities affected by Blue Growth initiatives. The 'small' encompasses the need for small-scale projects working at a regional and local level. Integral in these small programmes is the need for 'dialogic', face-to-face communication and listening to the voices of the communities. We propose that institutions, policymakers and organisations develop

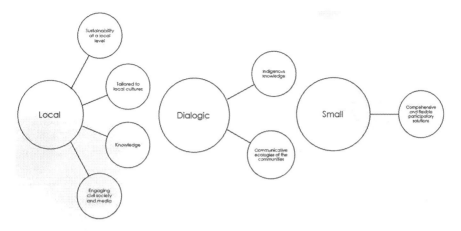

Fig. 4.1 Dimensions of a new communication framework for sustainable development

communication programmes that are based on and incorporate the following principles (Fig. 4.1).

Local

- Well-being and sustainability on a local level
- Culture, habits, needs
- Local knowledge for the identification of communication solutions
- Civil society and collaboration with local NGOs
- Collaboration with local media to report on Blue Growth

Small

- Small-scale communication programmes
- Participatory, inclusive and democratic solutions
- Comprehensible and flexible approaches

Dialogic

- Understanding of the needs, culture and development requirements of communities.
- Identification of the communicative ecologies of the communities, that is the structure of communication and information flows, channels and barriers in peoples' lives and the complete ensemble of resources for communication in a locality (Slater, 2013: 42).
- Listening to and recognition of indigenous knowledge in development

Conclusion

The chapter has offered some preliminary insights into the social dimension of the Blue Growth initiatives implemented by selected EU-funded projects and their capacity to contribute to social change. Drawing on the principles of social innovation and social change, and the significance of dialogic and participatory communication for sustainable development as outlined by the field of CDSC, we have provided a mapping of the aims, key stakeholders, beneficiaries and communication strategies of the selected projects. Our mapping demonstrates that the Blue Growth strategies of the European area that prioritise the UN and European Commission's SDGs and 2030 Agenda and are developed around sustainable Blue Growth and nautical tourism, tend to promote sustainable development through an economistic and market-based approach. Moreover, and based on their communication strategies, the selected projects employ linear and top-down communication approaches with limited evidence of an attempt to engage in dialogue with communities. It can be argued that, by failing to give due consideration to the social dimension of Blue Growth, these EU initiatives undermine a crucial aspect of human development and social change that is tied to ocean life.

It is beyond doubt that more in-depth analysis is needed in order to gain a more nuanced understanding of the contribution that official communication and public engagement activities can make in sustainable development in the area of Blue Growth. Future research should engage with grassroots communities affected by marine life in order to unearth and understand their priorities and needs. Moreover, scholars and practitioners should explore possibilities for incorporating the voice of these communities in future communication strategies and for designing creative bottom-up communication initiatives that engage with a variety of communication channels and methods. The social innovation and social change concepts can be a valuable guide for future communication practices, and for developing a new, improved way of collaborative action. As Soma et al. (2018) point out 'the social innovation concept has an acting component that consists of people with particular attitudes and perceptions about what innovation is, aiming for more societal impacts than making a profit as such, with whom acting involves learning, networking and collaboration' (p.364).

If we are aiming for impacts which can create broader social change beyond the individual level, then we need to concentrate on bottom-up initiatives. If we care about sharing knowledge to understand options for change and their implications, then we need to involve educational and pedagogical practices, which encourage participation in the pursuit of solutions and value-driven strategies and communication praxis. Achieving a more holistic conceptualisation and implementation of Blue Growth, one that is not limited to economic indicators but includes health, gender, social and cultural dimensions, requires more participatory approaches that put people and communities at the centre of policy initiatives and make local actors co-creators in the design of solutions. It is through inclusive and dialogic practices that sustainable, eco-innovative Blue Growth is possible.

Bibliography

Ababouch, L.—Food and Agriculture Organization of the United Nations (FAO UN) & Forest Inventory and Planning Institute (FAO-FIPI). (2015). *Fisheries and Aquaculture in the context of Blue Economy*. Background Paper, in International Conference 'Feeding Africa: an Action Plan for African Agricultural Transformation', (Senegal, Dakar 21-23/10/2015). Retrieved 3, 2019, from https://www.afdb.org/fileadmin/uploads/afdb/Documents/Events/DakAgri2015/Fisheries_and_Aquaculture_in_the_Context_of_Blue_Economy.pdf.

Arbo, P., Knol, M., Linke, S., & Martin, K. S. (2018). The Transformation of the Oceans and the Future of Marine Social Science. *Maritime Studies, 17*, 295–304. https://doi.org/10.3389/fmars.2019.00236

Barbesgaard, M., Franco, J. C., & Buxton, N. (2014). *The Global Ocean Grab: A Primer, TNI Agrarian Justice Programme*, Masifundise and Afrika Kontakt.

Barbesgaard, M. (2018). Blue growth: Saviour or Ocean Grabbing? *The Journal of Peasant Studies, 45*(1), 130–149. https://doi.org/10.1080/03066150.2017.1377186

BEPA. (2010). *Social Innovation. A Decade of Changes*. A BEPA report, Bureau of European Policy Advisers, European Commission. https://ec.europa.eu/migrant-integration/librarydoc/empowering-people-driving-change-social-innovation-in-the-european-union.

Bennett, N. J., Govan, H., & Satterfield, T. (2015). Ocean Grabbing. *Marine Policy, 57*, 61–68. https://doi.org/10.1016/j.marpol.2015.03.026

Dela, J., Garnett, T., Goldstein, W., & van Kempen, P. P. (2007). *Communication, Education and Public Awareness (CEPA): A Toolkit for National Focal Points and NBSAP Coordinators*. Secretariat on the Convention on Biological Diversity. Gland: ICUN Commission on Education and Communication. Retrieved 3, 2019, from https://www.cbd.int/cepa/toolkit/2008/doc/CBD-Toolkit-Complete.pdf.

Dutta, M. (2011). *Communicating Social Change, Structure, Culture and Agency*. New York, London: Routledge.

Enghel, F. (2014). Communication, Development, and Social Change: Future Alternatives. In K. Wilkins, J. Straubhaar, & S. Kumar (Eds.), *Global Communication New Agendas in Communication*. New York, NY: Routledge.

European Commission. (2011). *Empowering People, Driving Change, Social Innovation in the European Union*. European Union: Brussels. Retrieved 3, 2019, from https://ec.europa.eu/migrant-integration/librarydoc/empowering-people-driving-change-social-innovation-in-the-european-union.

European Commission. (2012). *Blue Growth—opportunities for Marine and Maritime Sustainable Growth*, European Union: Brussels, COM(2012). Retrieved 3, 2019, from https://ec.europa.eu/maritimeaffairs/sites/maritimeaffairs/files/docs/body/com_2012_494_en.pdf.

European Commission. (2014). *Innovation in the Blue Economy: Realising the Potential of Our Seas and Oceans for Jobs and Growth*. European Union: Brussels. Retrieved 3, 2019, from https://www.eesc.europa.eu/en/our-work/opinions-information-reports/opinions/innovation-blue-economy-realising-potential-our-seas-and-oceans-jobs-and-growth.

European Commission. (2017). *Report on the Blue Growth Strategy Towards More Sustainable Growth and Jobs in the Blue Economy*, European Union: Brussels. Retrieved 3, 2019, from https://ec.europa.eu/maritimeaffairs/sites/maritimeaffairs/files/swd-2017-128_en.pdf.

European Commission. (2020). *The EU Blue Economy Report 2020*. European Union: Brussels. Retrieved 6, 2019, from https://ec.europa.eu/maritimeaffairs/sites/maritimeaffairs/files/2020_06_blueeconomy-2020-ld_final.pdf.

European Commission. (n.d.-a). *Maritime Affairs—Integrated Maritime Policy Blue Growth*. Retrieved 3, 2019, from https://ec.europa.eu/maritimeaffairs/policy/blue_growth_en.

European Commission. (n.d.-b). *Budget—Examples of EU Funded Projects*. Retrieved 3, 2019, from https://ec.europa.eu/budget/euprojects/search-projects_en.

European Commission. (n.d.-c). *EASME—EMFF Projects*. Retrieved 3, 2019, from https://ec.europa.eu/easme/en/emff-projects.

European Commission. (n.d.-d). *e-Tendering*. Retrieved 3, 2019, from https://etendering.ted.europa.eu/general/page.html?name=home.

Eikeset, A. M., Mazzarella, A. B., Davíðsdóttir, B., Klinger, D. H., Levin, S. A., Rovenskaya, E., et al. (2018). What Is Blue Growth? The Semantics of "Sustainable Development" of Marine Environments. *Marine Policy, 87*(2017), 177–179. https://doi.org/10.1016/j.marpol.2017.10.019

Elliott, J. (1994). *An Introduction to Sustainable Development*. London: Routledge.

Escobar, A. (2001). *Encountering Development: The Making and Unmaking of the Third World*. Princeton New Jersey: Princeton University Press.

Flint, W. (2007). *Sustainability manifesto. Exploring sustainability: getting inside the concept*. Five E's Unlimited: USA. Retrieved 3, 2019, from http://www.eeeee.net/sd_manifesto.htm.

Food and Agriculture Organization of the United Nations (FAO UN). (2015). *FAO Contribution to Part I of the Report of the Secretary-General on Oceans and the Law of the Sea submitted pursuant to General Assembly Draft Resolution A/69/L.29 related to the Topic of Focus of the 16th Meeting of the United Nations Open-Ended Informal Consultative Process on Oceans and the Law of the Sea (ICP 16): 'Oceans and sustainable development: integration of the three dimensions of sustainable development, namely environmental, social and economic'*. FAO UN. Retrieved 3, 2019, from https://www.un.org/depts/los/general_assembly/contributions_2015/FAO.pdf.

Freire, P. (2001). *Pedagogy of the Oppressed*. New York: Continuum.

Hemer, O., & Tufte, T. (Eds.). (2005). *Media and Glocal Change: Rethinking Communication for Development*. Buenos Aires and Gothenburg: CLACSO and NORDICOM.

Henderson, J. (2019). Oceans without History? Marine Cultural Heritage and the Sustainable Development Agenda. *Sustainability, 11*(18) 5080, 1–22. https://doi.org/10.3390/su11185080

Karjalainen, T., Hoeveler, A., & Draghia-Akli, R. (2017). European Union Research in Support of Environment and Health: Building Scientific Evidence Base for Policy. *Environment International, 103*, 51–60. https://doi.org/10.1016/j.envint.2017.03.014

Kothari, A., Salleh, A., Escobar, A., Demaria, F., & Acosta, A. (2018). Introduction: Finding Pluriversal Paths. In A. Kothari, A. Salleh, A. Escobar, F. Demaria, & A. Acosta (Eds.), *Pluriverse: A Post-development Dictionary* (pp. xxi–xl). New Delhi: Tulika Books.

McEwan, C. (2008). *Postcolonialism and Development*. London: Routledge.

Mckinley, E., Aller, O., Caroline, R., & Hopkins, C. R. (2018). Charting the Course for a Blue Economy in Peru: A Research Agenda. *Environment, Development and Sustainability, 21*, 2253–2275. https://doi.org/10.1007/s10668-018-0133-z

Mefalopulos, P. (2005). 'Communication for Sustainable Development: Applications and Challenges'. In, Hemer, O., & Tufte, T. (eds.) *Media and Glocal Change. Rethinking Communication for Development*, CLACSO and NORDICOM, pp. 247-260.

Mohammed, A. (2017). Mobilising the Global Community to Achieve SDG 14. *UN Chronicle*, 54(2). https://doi.org/10.18356/88157e0c-en

Murray, R. Caulier-Grice, J., & Mulgan, G. (2010). *The Open Book of Social Innovation, Social Innovator Series: Ways to Design, Develop and Grow Social Innovation.* NESTA.

Ngomba, T. (2013). Comprehending Social Change in an Era of Austerity: Reflections from a Communication Perspective. *Glocal Times*, 19, https://ojs.mau.se/index.php/glocaltimes/article/view/243/238.

Quarry, W., & Ramírez, R. (2009). *Communication for Another Development: Listening Before Telling.* New York, NY: Zed Books.

Pachon, F. A., Bokelmann, W., & Ramírez, C. M. (2016). *Rural Development Thinking, Moving from the Green Revolution to Food Sovereignty.* Agronomia Colombiana, 34(2), 267–276.

Pfeifer, E. (2011). De-Politicising the Environment: An Inquiry into the Nature of the Sustainable Development Discourse, *Global Politics*. Retrieved 3, 2019, from http://www.globalpolitics.cz/clanky/de-politicizing-the-environment-an-inquiry-into-the-nature-of-the-sustainable-development-discourse.

Rodriquez, C. (2011). *Citizen's Media Against Armed Conflict: Disrupting Violence in Columbia.* Minneapolis: University of Minnesota Press.

Rogers, E. M. (1995). *Diffusion of Innovations.* New York: The Free Press.

Schubert, C. (2018). Social Innovation. In W. Rammert, A. Windeler, H. Knoblauch, & M. Hutter (Eds.), *Innovation Society Today.* Wiesbaden: Springer VS.

Servaes, J. (2011). *Social Change. Oxford Bibliographies Online (OBO).* New York: Oxford University Press.

Servaes, J. (2013). Introduction: The Kaleidoscope of Text and Context in Communication. In J. Servaes (Ed.), *Sustainability, Participation and Culture in Communication: Theory and Praxis* (pp. 1–24). Bristol: Intellect.

Servaes, J., & Lie, R. (2015). New Challenges for Communication for Sustainable Development and Social Change: A Review Essay. *Journal of Multicultural Discourses*, 10(1), 124–148. https://doi.org/10.1080/17447143.2014.982655

Servaes, J., & Malikhao, P. (2016). The Role and Place of Communication for Sustainable Social Change (CSSC). *International Social Science Journal*, 65(217-218), 171–183.

Silver, J. J., Gray, N. J., Campbell, L. M., Fairbanks, L. W., & Gruby, R. L. (2015). Blue Economy and Competing Discourses in International Oceans Governance. *Journal of Environment and Development*, 24(2), 135–160. https://doi.org/10.1177/1070496515580797

Slater, D. (2013). *New Media, Development and Globalization: Making Connections in the Global South.* Cambridge, UK: Polity Press.

Soma, K., van den Burg, S., Hoefnagel, E., Stuiver, M., & van der Heide, M. (2018). Social Innovation—A Future Pathway for Blue Growth? *Marine Policy*, 87, 363–370. https://doi.org/10.1016/j.marpol.2017.10.008

Thomas, P. N., & van de Fliert, E. (2014). *Interrogating the Theory and Practice of Communication for Social Change: The Basis For a Renewal.* New York: Palgrave Macmillan.

Thomas, P. N. (2011). *Negotiating Communication Rights: Case Studies from India*. London, England: Sage.

Touri, M. (2016). Development Communication in Alternative Food Networks: Empowering Indian Farmers Through Market Relations. *Journal of International Communication*, 22(2), 209–228. https://doi.org/10.1080/13216597.2016.1175366

Touri, M. (2018). Development and Communication in Trade Relations: New Synergies in Theory and Practice. *Development in Practice*, 28(3), 388–399. https://doi.org/10.1080/09614524.2018.1432569

Tufte, T. (2017). *Communication and Social Change: A Citizen Perspective*. Cambridge: Polity.

United Nations Environmental Programme (UNEP). (2011). *Towards a Green Economy: Pathways to Sustainable Development and Poverty Eradication*. UNEP/GRID-Arend. Retrieved 3, 2019, from http://all62.jp/ecoacademy/images/15/green_economy_report.pdf.

United Nations Environmental Programme (UNEP). (2012). *Green Economy in a Blue World*. UNEP/GRID-Arend. Retrieved 3, 2019, from https://www.google.com/url?sa=t&rct=j&q=&esrc=s&source=web&cd=&ved=2ahUKEwiSpc-Jmc3qAhXG-aQKHWycDHsQFjABegQIARAB&url=https%3A%2F%2Fwww.undp.org%2Fcontent%2Fdam%2Fundp%2Flibrary%2FEnvironment%2520and%2520Energy%2FWater%2520and%2520Ocean%2520Governance%2FGreen_Economy_Blue_Full.pdf&usg=AOvVaw0QWi1kpfO_ybXtmWt5d6AL.

Waisbord, S. (2015). Three Challenges for Communication and Global Social Change. *Communication Theory*, 25(2), 144–165.

Wilkins, K. G., & Enghel, F. (2013). The Privatisation of Development Through Global Communication Industries: Living Proof? *Media, Culture & Society*, 35(2), 165–181.

Wilkins, K., Tufte, T., & Obregon, R. (Eds.). (2014). *The Handbook of Development Communication and Social Change*. Hoboken, NJ: Wiley-Blackwell.

Woodhouse, P. (2002). Development Policies and Environmental Agendas. In U. Kothari, (ed.), *Development Theory and Practice*. Critical Perspectives, pp. 136–156.

Voyer, M., Quirk, G., Mcilgorm, A., Azmi, K., Quirk, G., Mcilgorm, A., et al. (2018). Shades of Blue: What Do Competing Interpretations of the Blue Economy Mean for Oceans Governance? *Journal of Environmental Policy & Planning*, 20(5), 595–616. https://doi.org/10.1080/1523908X.2018.1473153

CHAPTER 5

A Buddhist Approach to Participatory Communication and Sustainable Development: A Case Study from Lao PDR

Toung Eh. Synuanchanh and Evangelia Papoutsaki

INTRODUCTION

Religion has the potential to become a major socio-economic, political and culture factor for some countries (Tomalin, Haustein, & Kidy, 2019). The significance of Buddhism as a form of religious organization in sustainable development has not been adequately explored, both in practice and in theory. Local and traditional beliefs and culture have been seen as an obstacle to modernity, resulting often in religious communities to be excluded from the development process (Lunn, 2009; Sivaraksa, 2009; Tomalin et al., 2019). Nevertheless, the perception towards religion in development has been changing and its significance in development has been increasingly recognized (Tomalin et al., 2019; Vu, Bailey, & Chen, 2016).

Buddhism, like other religions, has been excluded from the modernization process. The significance of Buddhist values and the role of *Sangha* [Buddhist monastic order] are not sufficiently addressed in the development process, despite the fact that Buddhism is the main religion in many Asian countries and at the centre of community life. Religion plays an influential role in society and

T. E. Synuanchanh (✉)
Unitec Institute of Technology, Auckland, New Zealand

E. Papoutsaki
University of Central Asia, Bishkek, Kyrgyzstan

© The Author(s), under exclusive license to Springer Nature Switzerland AG 2021
M. J. Yusha'u, J. Servaes (eds.), *The Palgrave Handbook of International Communication and Sustainable Development*,
https://doi.org/10.1007/978-3-030-69770-9_5

is a cornerstone of all cultures (King, 2009). Most studies, including those by Boutsavath and Chapelier (1973), Ladwig (2006) and Sengsoulin (2014), concur that Buddhist monasteries (Lao: *Wat*) function as learning and teaching centres where Buddhist monks are instructors. In the current era, *Wats* still remain informal educational institutions alongside other state institutions (Sengsoulin, 2014). Ladwig (2006) and Sengsoulin (2014) confirmed that monks must engage in social work, and helping people reduce their suffering is one of the duties of the *Sangha* (Buddhist community), as it is a primary aim of Buddhism. They have a potential to be a vehicle for change (Boutsavath & Chapelier, 1973).

This chapter is informed by research that sought to explore Buddhism as an alternative approach to participatory communication and sustainable community development. It takes as a case study the Buddhism for Development Project by the Lao Buddhist Fellowship Organization and implemented by Buddhist monks/nuns in local Lao communities. The organization trains the *Sangha*, as well as Buddhist followers, to play a role in social development and change. This chapter discusses the catalyst for change model in the Lao Buddhist context by analysing Buddhist values and the role of Buddhist *Sangha* in community development. It also explores how assimilating the Integrated Model of Communication for Social Change (IMCFSC) by Figueroa, Kincaid, Rani, and Lewis (2002) into the Buddhist development approach (BA) of the Buddhism for Development Project (BDP) (2012) can enhance the Communication for Social Change (CFSC) approaches in community practice and engender social impact which is appropriate to the Buddhist community in Laos.

A Buddhist Holistic Approach to Social Change in the Lao Context

A contextualized holistic Buddhist approach to social change takes into account the social roles of the Buddhist *Dhamma* [teachings], BDP and Buddhist Volunteer Spirit for Community (BVSC) network in *Laos communities*. By exploring the Buddhist catalyst role, this section examines the participatory communication aspects in the Buddhist *Sangha*'s engagement in community development in Laos.

Thomas, Eggins, and Papoutsaki (2016) suggest that community development requires a holistic approach which incorporates the natural environment, respect, reciprocity, beliefs and spirituality. Understanding the Buddhist approach to social change first and foremost requires taking a holistic view of the concept of *paticcasamuppada*. A fundamental to Buddha's teaching, *paticcasamuppada* refers to the law of origination, emphasizing the understanding of the process of existence through interconnectedness or the cause and effect link. In Buddhist view, the four main dimensions of culture and society, nature, technology and economy are interrelated and play dominant roles in the macro-environment, while the micro-environment is more incorporated with cultural dimensions and networks (see Fig. 5.1). In Buddhism, this is recognized as '*paticcasamuppada*' (dependent origination or inter-being). It describes how things are interconnected, so everything arises or falls with causes and effects.

As Hopwood, Mellor, and O'Brien (2005) argue, it is worth devoting close attention to the dependent relationship between society and the environment, in order for sustainable development to flourish, while taking into account that Buddhism is a part of the wider Lao society. Therefore, the value of Buddhist teachings is embedded in the cultural, political, economic and social dimensions of the society.

The Buddhism Project for Development (BDP) represents the Lao Buddhist Fellowship Organisation (LBFO), the highest ranked Buddhist organization in Laos, which engages in social development by training its *Sangha* community and volunteer youth members for community development. The Buddhist

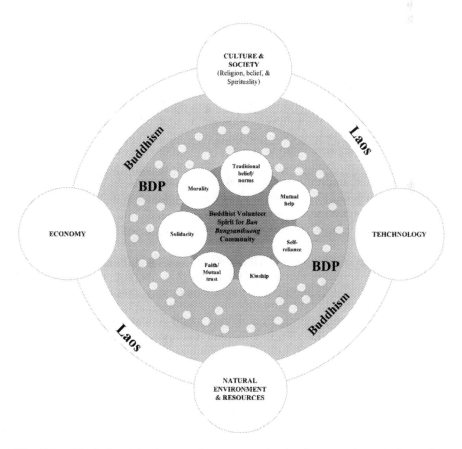

Fig. 5.1 A holistic spiritual approach to community development through the catalyst of change. (Source: Synuanchanh, 2018)

Volunteer Spirit for Community (BVSC) movement is a BDP *Sangha* network implementing grassroots development initiatives in various communities throughout Laos.

BDP acts as a provider of development-oriented monks and volunteers. It provides the BVSC training course, following the Buddhist concept of development from the inside out. As Payutto (2008) argues, one should embark on changing peoples' attitudes towards the environment, economic behaviour, science and technology to initially solve the current issues. In that spirit, BDP aims to empower its *Sangha* community to have the correct attitudes and knowledge before they are exposed to the actual development work. *Sangha* and laypeople find it challenging when combining the traditional teachings with concrete actions (Ladwig, 2006). Thus, they are trained to play the role of a trainer or mentor in their communities, coordinate development and develop a BVSC network. Through its moral teachings the *Sangha* educates people to raise awareness and understanding of the connection between causes, conditions and problems occurring in communities and to spearhead positive changes.

It is commonly perceived that *Sangha* is disciplinarily isolated from the wider society's needs and should not be socially engaged with wider society. Based on the original research, the work of BDP, by educating its *Sangha* community and engaging in development work, has changed this perception. This positive change highlights the importance of Buddhism, especially *Sangha*, as part of the Laos society. According to Vu et al. (2016), an indication of positive change is when participation in religious communities is increased, as these communities were previously seen as opposed to social development and the party's rule. Ladwig (2006) recommends that the power of linking religious organizations, especially Buddhism, with the development process should not be ignored, because doing so emphasizes voices and discourse within a culture.

BDP has also faced criticisms about initial social interventions and the *Sangha*'s involvement. This is because there is a wider, traditional belief that development is a secular, not religious, affair. The duties of *Sangha* are to educate lay followers about *Dhamma* and Buddhist ethics, provide moral support and engage in social activities that eliminate human suffering: the primary goal of Buddhism (Pali: *dukkha*) (Ladwig 2006, 2008). Most spiritual masters, staff members and trainees of the BDP agree that social intervention is crucial for *Sangha* because solving social problems is a principal duty of *Sangha* (Pali: *Dhura*). It is also the ultimate goal of Buddhism, which emphasizes liberation from suffering.

Buddhist Sangha *Volunteer Spirit in Community Development Practice*

Establishing community initiatives is arguably the most productive means of developing social capital (Witten-Hannah, 1999). This sub-section provides evidence of *Sangha* roles in the BVSC project initiatives at the *Ban*

Bungsanthueng, and their importance in popularizing knowledge transfer, moral values, female empowerment and environmental awareness.

Empowering Women

Cernea (1991), as cited in Parks et al. (2005, p. 10), argues that changes can fail to address local needs, to build local assets, to be long-term and to be productive if they lack local ownership. As this research established, the trained monk facilitated power sharing and expression within *Ban Bungsanthueng*'s Women's Handicraft Initiative in order to encourage ownership and control of information and knowledge. According to UN General Assembly (2015), one of the Sustainable Development Goals (SDGs) identifies that women should be able to have equal opportunities to lead and make decision on political, social and economic issues, and have access to information, natural and economic resources and inheritance. The women's group determines how to develop and sustain their local wisdom of '*sad-phue*' (reed mat weaving) as an economic initiative and they are keen to sustain and transfer this knowledge to younger generations. With this activity, the women can control the information and knowledge exchange among group members and other villagers because they *own* the craft knowledge (skills). The monk and the village government act as facilitators and are in agreement with Parks et al.'s (2005) assertion that communication and social change practitioners should transfer ownership to affected communities and facilitate better access to, and control of, information.

Parks et al. (2005) support the notion that both public and private dialogues about social norms increase enrolments of women in education. Schools for adults are missing in most remote villages in Laos. As a result, the *Wat* remains an essential learning centre that provides space for women to demonstrate their information leadership. The villagers, as either individuals or groups, are provided with knowledge, skills and values which are useful for development, participation and action (Servaes & Malikhao, 2007).

The empowerment process facilitated by the *Wat* or *Sangha* contributes to power redistribution amongst groups of women who are considered oppressed within the village (Ife, 2002). Men have traditionally held power in the family and in the community, so women have often been disregarded. This traditional practice obstructs the achievement of above-mentioned SDGs. Following the position of Figueroa et al. (2002), it is arguable here that strengthening the leadership for a particular issue is one of the primary objectives of a social change programme. Women can be catalysts for rural transformation, provided that gender-based constraints be eliminated efficiently (UNCTAD, 2015). With the involvement of and facilitation by monks, village women can lead their own groups or communities, make decision on their activities and sustainably manage their resources and traditional knowledge for their economic improvement, which directly contribute to SDGs 4 and 8.

Catalysing Buddhism and Traditions for Environmental Consciousness
Building on Waisbord's (2005) argument, peasants in many Laos communities have been oppressed and forced to change traditional methods of agricultural practice to unfamiliar processes. These activities have led to massive environmental degradation such as deforestation and soil infertility. Buddhism holds the view that, in order to achieve sustainability, economic development should take place alongside human development and environmental protection (Payutto, 2008). The research from *Ban Bungsanthueng* community shows the trained monks responded to the environmental issues by applying Buddhist ethics and precepts through *Vipassana* meditation practice and *Dhamma* talks. This practice educated and stimulated the villagers into having positive thoughts and actions about sustaining the natural environment. The monks led the villagers to protect the forest with tree ordination and reforestation. The notion of tree ordination is a reinterpretation of Buddhist teachings (Walter 2007). It not only helps to protect the forest but also educates people at a grassroots level, thereby encouraging them to value the conservation of forest resources.

In these activities, the monks engage with traditional beliefs (animism or 'worshiping' *Puta*[1]) and incorporate them into their environmental action. This is supported by Bialek (2014) and Morrow (2011), who also argue that the Buddhist environmental movement is an integration of Buddhist rituals and local beliefs in the spirit and sanctity of the natural world. The *Sangha* environmental practice is built on faith and belief in both spiritual systems and practices. Monks mobilized *Ban Bungsanthueng* villagers to initiate forest ordaining by observing the sacred forest (the location of *Puta's* spirit house) as a protected and conserved area. They ordained the forest by tying monastic robes around tree trunks and planned to place the *Naga*[2] head on the marsh to prevent fishing.

A study by Darlington (1998) indicated gaps in development research, and suggested the impact of Buddhist ecology (especially tree ordination) on socio-economic and political aspects of community development to be examined more closely. Culturally speaking, the forest ordaining gives precedence to the local culture, where all stakeholders have renegotiated their needs in order to reach an agreement on the protection and maintenance of the forest ecosystem. This activity potentially contributes to food security and sustainability for a community with consumption practices based on self-sufficiency. However, most importantly, people became more aware of environmental protection and actively participated in community development, which signifies the political commitment of each village member.

This is strongly supported by Kaza (2000) who argues that the Buddhist principle of *paticcasamuppada* (interdependence) promotes an understanding

---
[1] *Puta* [the guardian spirit of the village] is a Lao term specific to some local communities.
[2] *Naga* is a symbol of sanctity and ordination in Buddhism. It is believed that the *Naga* [an animal] is the protector and king of the river and nether world. The *Naga* (head) can be commonly seen in the Buddhist temple.

of natural systems and the Buddhist ecological movement. This, in turn, indicates that the Buddhist ethics are the backbone of the Buddhist environmental movement. The Five Precepts encourage people to live in harmony with nature, while the Buddhist ideal of interdependence reflects how all living beings are linked.

Integration of IMCFSC Model with the Buddhist Approach to Development and Communication

The Integrated Model of Communication for Social Change (IMCFSC) may be applicable in communities in different regions, but as elsewhere, for the Lao Buddhist communities it would be required to adapt it to the context and traditional practices of local community. IMCFSC can act synergistically with the Buddhist epistemology, through the Buddhist ontology—the Four Noble Truths. Buddhist moral teachings and ethics can effectively regulate the entire process of communication for social change. This section provides an overview of the emerging model and proposes a set of emerging contextualized indicators.

The above model is divided into a four-stage social change process, or what can be referred to as the 'Four Noble Truths for social change process', with two possible outcomes for individual and social change.

The first stage is the **BVSC Training** where members of the *Sangha* and Buddhist community lay followers participate in a BDP training course. The dashed line and arrow show that members attending this course are subject to individual needs, and members of the *Sangha* and various communities can become change agents by adopting the BDP approach.

The **Buddhist catalyst** mainly focuses on internal stimulus, and community members or internal issues may stimulate that dialogue. At the earlier stage, Buddhist change agents work with internal and external *bhavana* (training) to transform people's spirituality and cultivate virtuous values, including compassion and desire to serve others in the name of volunteer spirit and trust building. This stage is particularly important as members learn and cultivate, through interpersonal communication and real-life experience, fundamental knowledge such as interconnection, interdependence and Buddhist ethics. Through this process, the agents gain the trust of the community members who, in turn, can be spiritually transformed by gaining *Samma-sati and Samma-samadhi* (Right Concentration and Right Mindfulness), and *sila* (Right Speech, Right Action and Right Livelihood), so that they are ready to enter into dialogue.

Through learning, understanding and cultivating Buddhist ethical values, the next stage is **participatory dialogic communication**, or **Buddhist ways of analysis (Buddhist ontology)**. In this stage, the Buddhist Four Noble Truths (Pali: *Ariya-sacca*) are incorporated as a method for analysing problems, finding solutions and planning for action, while using Buddhist ethics as a basis for participatory learning and evaluation. The *Sangha* can play a significant role by motivating members to stay together, as conflict or misunderstandings may occur at this point. The *Sangha's* spiritual role remains a key force in holding members together.

At the **collective (harmonious) action** stage, the spiritual need is doubled, requiring mutual trust, solidarity, social harmony and collective consciousness. Here, the Buddhist catalyst (change agent) can demonstrate their leadership to members. Three key community units, *Ban* (village and residents), *Wat* (temple) and *Honghian* (school), are required to work hand-in-hand. At this stage, external actors may be involved in some activities; however, the Buddhists approach values and prioritize self-reliance or independence.

Individual and collective change can take place at every stage of the process. In the BVSC training, changes can take place through the individual *Sangha* members and through the collective *Sangha* community. At the second stage, individual or group members may experience change through spiritual transformation. At the third stage, members are equipped with skills which are based on knowledge of the inter-being[3] of natural systems. Individuals may develop collective consciousness and have ideas about taking action and making a change either individually or collectively. Individuals gain *magga* which leads to changes in morality (Pali: *sila*), concentration (Pali: *samadhi*) and wisdom (Pali: *panna*), in which each aspect of the Noble Eightfold Paths is achieved. Collectively, the community may experience a shared understanding of moral/spiritual norms, social harmony, trust, faith, equitable participation, Right Understanding (Pali: *samma-ditthi*), a sense of collective consciousness, compassionate leadership and self-reliance.

The Emerging Model: The Buddhist Catalyst Roles

The characteristics of the Buddhist catalyst can manifest through the role of a spiritual transformation guide, development facilitator, information influencer and a trusted source. These roles are performed by the *Sangha* members and laity in community development and predominantly act as internal agents of stimulus.

Internal Stimulus/Change Agent

Figueroa et al. (2002) describe the catalyst as either internal or external to the community. In this case, BDP is likely to focus more on the community's internal factors and resources than external ones (see Fig. 5.2). The trainee selection process of the BDP can be considered successful because most BDP trainees and future change agents are likely insiders to communities who know the context of the community's needs and are better equipped to identify barriers, challenges and opportunities. This is consistent with Melkote's (2012) and

---

[3] '*Inter-being*' (Pali: *paticcasamuppada*) refers to the belief of interconnection and interdependence. For instance, economic development (the occurrence) utilizes natural resources (conditions) to promote growth (cause).

5 A BUDDHIST APPROACH TO PARTICIPATORY COMMUNICATION... 109

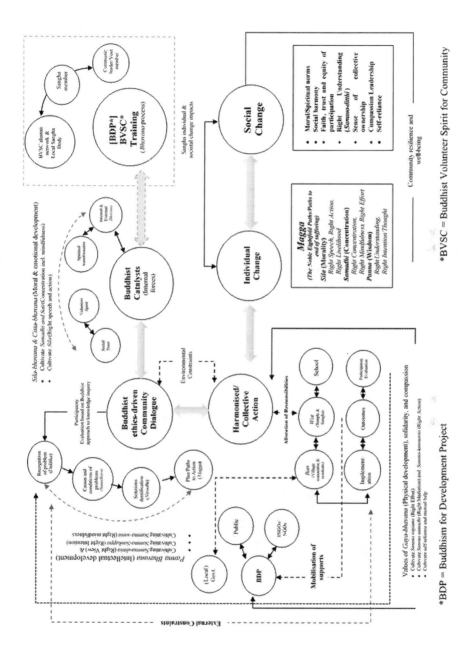

Fig. 5.2 Integration of the IMCFSC model with the BA to development and communication. (Source: Synuanchanh, 2018)

Parks et al.'s (2005) arguments that endogenous efforts and local leaders need to spearhead social transformation using their own practices and act as change agents in order to engender dialogue, promote participation in decision-making processes, emphasize grassroots approaches and facilitate the process. Based on this, it could be argued that the Buddhist catalyst approaches give internal stimulus and resources precedence.

Spiritual Transformer
Apart from traditional tasks, such as meditation and *dhamma* studies, members of the *Sangha* are trained to lead community development initiatives in concurrence with the BDP's goal of consolidating Buddhist knowledge into social work at a grassroots level (Ladwig, 2006, p. 22). In this model, the *Sangha* members are trained to transfer development knowledge (in connection to Buddhist worldviews) to their *Sangha* community by practising internal and external *bhavana* (development or training). Dissanayake (2010) argues that self-transformation is important for understanding the Buddhist way of life, as according to Buddha, social transformation can only take place through spiritual self-transformation. As a result, Buddhism emphasizes that social change must originate in the mind of the individual. This practice both strengthens the mental ability of *Sangha* themselves and helps laypeople to cope with the uncertainties that occur in everyday life.

The original research demonstrates that the *Sangha* guide people to an understanding of natural systems, interdependence and the application of solidarity values for community harmony. The Buddhist value that bears the idea of social harmony is '*Brahma-vihara*' or the Buddhist social emotion (Queen, 2000). This includes "loving-kindness (*metta*), compassion (*karuna*), sympathetic joy (*mudhitha*), and equanimity (*upekkha*)" (Dissanayake, 2010, p. 87; Queen, 2000). This Buddhist value is evidenced in most of the research participants' language, including "the monk is a spiritual leader; the monk changes a bad person to a good one; and the monk promotes solidarity and mutual help in the village". In this context, solidarity and mutual help can be seen as potential social capital which can support the community's sustainability, resilience and peace. Thus, spiritual transformation is significant and deserves to be taken into account in the efforts of building a resilient community.

In addition to the *Sangha*'s role as information transmitter and knowledge translator, they are also considered to be social capital. Ife (2002) and Ladwig (2006) explain that social capital covers a range of social aspects, such as human relationships, religious communities, compassion and generosity, solidarity, trust and reciprocity. In line with this, the *Sangha* are seen as a religious and trusted community that has the promotion of human relationships through the strengthening of solidarity and trust, as a spiritual mandate. By using Buddhist ethics and moral teachings, the *Sangha* trains people to cultivate compassion and generosity, which, in turn, lay the foundation for social harmony and trust. Rawls points out that the village *Wat* connects with the concept of 'distributive justice', because funds donated by the community to the *Wat* support the education of novices from low-income families, which shows *khwamsamakhi* (solidarity) (Rawls, 1971, as cited in Ladwig, 2006). The *Sangha* is thus seen as a body that can effectively intervene in community development by transforming villagers' mental abilities and improving their understanding of *paticcasamuppada* or the inter-being of the natural world. This, in turn, promotes the Buddhist social emotion that can lead to action for change.

Sangha as Information Influencers and People Who Are Trusted
Principally, in the Buddhist Initiative, the information flows better in a cultural context and supports political activity. The village government (headmen) manages political and formal sources of information about development in the community, while the monk deals with the socio-cultural and spiritual framework. The villagers often feel uneasy seeking information from the headmen because this information is primarily limited to circulating within the village committees and is publicly shared sometimes during village meetings or public announcements. Accordingly, the power relationships between the village authority, project members and villagers become constrained by who has access to information, and a dynamic of power is based on exclusiveness rather than on inclusiveness (Internews, 2015).

Catalysts are needed in communities to stimulate dialogue and facilitate concerted action and eventual solutions (Doan-Bao, Papoutsaki, & Dodson, 2018; Figueroa et al., 2002). The original research identified two actors who influence information related to the Buddhist Initiative which is divided into two separate blocks including the government services and the community news. The village headman disseminates information on, and by, government services mostly through *tholakhong* (the announcement speaker) and at village meetings. The trained monk uses *tholakhong* as a tool for educating people with *dhamma* and inviting them to take action. The Internews (2015) study of Myanmar's information ecosystem showed that improving the flow of information is not only a matter of using new tools for information sharing, but also of finding ways to develop the existing practices of information dissemination. In this case, the trained monk uses a traditionally Buddhist method of disseminating information and knowledge by delivering a sermon and *Dhamma* talk. Furthermore, he demonstrates to the villagers how that knowledge can be put into practice, while staying close to them during the entire process. As Tufte and Mefalopulos (2009) point out, Freire's liberating pedagogical approach includes dialogue, voice and reflection. The trained monk deals with spiritual liberation, especially liberating pedagogy and reflection, and provides both spiritual development and experiential learning, so that villagers concurrently learn and gain experience.

Trust is central to the enabler's role because change requires mutual trust (Bacon, 2009). This research indicates that members of the project trust the monk's leadership and knowledge. Significant factors contributing to such trust are the leadership of the monk, his method of knowledge transfer, his position as a respected person and his moral behaviour (especially in regard to the fourth aspect of the Five Precepts—abstaining from false speech). Villagers generally have a conviction that the *Sangha* never speak falsely, so this informs their trust that the project the monk brought to the community will benefit the community in the long run. As Robinson (1999) argues, a high level of trust is key to building social capital, and trust allows various associations or groups to discuss community accounts.

As highly trusted and respected people in Lao society, the *Sangha*'s spiritual leadership allows them to gain attention when they speak *and* ensures that people follow their instructions (Ladwig, 2006; UNICEF EAPRO, 2009). People communicate through everyday interaction, and that is where the role of the *Sangha* can be an important catalyst for change—by building on the social capital that has been generated by their kinship, daily interactions with the community and spiritual leadership role in community development matters. The Buddhist approach itself is focused on human spirituality or mind and takes humans as a start and cornerstone for development. Buddhist ways of teaching are meant to transform human mind towards strong spirituality, morality and human relationship. This supports the idea put forward by Waisbord (2001), that development communication should be more human-focused, rather than media-focused, and aim for strong horizontal communication.

However, the flow of, and access to, information is likely to be interrupted by the endogenous and exogenous environment. Internally, with the neutral position of the *Sangha* afforded by its separation from politics, the challenge is often for the monk to maintain neutrality when making project decisions. To contest the constraint of formal power relationships, the monk could leverage his power with the village headman by using his close relationships with the villagers to renegotiate the power and improve the situation.

Essentially, internal communication flows are vital to successful community development and the role of the catalyst relies heavily on being part of these flows. This corresponds with Waisbord (2001) who refers to Freire's suggestion that development practitioners should make interpersonal communication the priority approach, followed by national media and technologies. The sermon delivery, or *dhamma* talk, is one variety of horizontal and interpersonal communication. In *Ban Bungsanthueng*, interpersonal communication is more effective because of the kinship-based relationships which exist, and because the *Wat* is being used as a space for spiritual refuge and participation.

Buddhist Ethics, Dialogue and Participation

The Buddhist values of moral teachings and ethics can serve positively under the participatory communication for social change approach. This builds on Rajavaramuni's research (cited in Ladwig, 2006, p. 18), which argues that Buddhists practice a very strong belief in social ethics, and on Queen's (2000) suggestion on the four styles of Buddhist ethics (discipline, virtue, altruism and engagement) that can be used as a theoretical framework for discussion.

Social Values of the Five Precepts
Waisbord (2001) argues that true development requires a more holistic approach that is not separated from its socio-cultural and spiritual context. This research indicates that most development agencies consider the Buddhist moral teachings as religious propaganda and choose to ignore its educational potential. Most donors have the opinion that Buddhist moral teaching activities, such as summer novice (student) ordination camps and *Vipassana* meditation practice, have little value for broader societal development.

Comprehending the ethical or moral values for social development requires an understanding of basic Buddhist morality that consists of Five Precepts including abstaining from killing, stealing, sexual misconduct, false speech and intoxicants. The purpose of practicing meditation in *Vipassana* and observing moral teachings is to enable people to put ethics and virtue into practice in their daily lives. The mention of 'virtuous and ethical minds' is based on Lao cultural practices and social norms where Buddhist values have an influential role on the laity. In the Buddhist Initiative, each aspect of the *Sila-ha* encourages villagers to conserve nature, to recognize the relationship between humans and the environment and to conduct community economic activities under natural conditions without exploiting or harming those natural resources. The monk uses this approach to demonstrate the value of individual and collective behavioural change.

Using morality (*Sila*) as a stimulus for change provides a strong sense of ownership of public welfare and a recognition of shared (collective) resources. It also provides people with a platform to discuss activities that are seen as inappropriate or harmful to the community's well-being, through the Buddhist way of knowing (the Fourth Noble Truths). Practising Buddhist ethics is a process of improving the human mind and cultivating social emotions, which, in turn, can promote social harmony. The four Buddhist social emotions known as '*Brahma-vihara*' (divine abodes) are seen as the founding concepts of social harmony (Dissanayake, 2010). Queen (2000) has also put forward a set of Buddhist ethics based on these *Brahma-vihara*, which are further discussed later in the chapter.

Catalysing Buddhist Ethics in Knowledge-Inquiry and Dialogue
Every community, both in developing countries and indigenous communities, has its own ethics which protect its knowledge systems and inquiry (Chilisa, 2012). Just as other religious systems have their own ethics and epistemologies, so too does Buddhism. Buddhism has its own method of comprehending reality, relationships and values, as well as its own philosophy and practices known as 'the Four Noble Truths'. UNICEF EAPRO (2009) believes that the Buddhist notions of suffering and Four Noble Truths can be used to better understand the suffering and challenges of those who live with HIV/AIDS at an individual level, within the family and within the community. This involves using the *Sangha* as agents to practice the notion for change.

Tufte and Mefalopulos (2009) argue that the key element of participatory communication for empowerment is the reflection on the problem, which then leads to action. The BA to knowledge-inquiry through practising the Four Noble Truths is a learning process and provides a framework for villagers to discuss and express ideas in their daily interactions. This research uses the environmental consciousness initiative at *Ban Bungsanthueng* as an example.

The first aspect of the Truths is '*dukkha*' (suffering). In this research, '*dukkha*' is interpreted as an issue that requires understanding, discussion and a solution. Payutto (2002) defines "sufferings as non-tolerant, oppressive, disputed and deficient situations, [with] lack of meanings; and uncertainties causing untrue satisfactoriness or happiness" (p. 90). This first aspect of the Truths emphasizes recognition of the issue, which, from the Buddhist perspective, is called 'awakening'. Therefore, one must first become aware that certain environmental issues exist in their community before acting. This links with the community dialogue in the first stage of the IMCFSC model which perceives community recognition of life-altering problems as essential to the successful process of social change (Figueroa et al., 2002).

The second aspect of the Truths is '*samudaya*' (the origin of sufferings). As UNICEF EAPRO (2009) indicates, *samudaya* "suggests the need to identify the underlying causes of the suffering" in order to "understand and eliminate them" (p. 2). Similarly, *samudaya* draws attention to the underlying causes and conditions of environmental issues and the impact these issues have on people's lives. Consequently, when the underlying causes are identified this leads to finding appropriate ways of stopping the problem. Figueroa et al. (2002) confirm this when they argue that a solution may be identified at the stage of problem identification, essentially because people are unlikely to think about the issue as a problem, if there is no emerging solution in response.

The third aspect of the Truths is '*nirodha*'. It identifies a way to be free from suffering. As UNICEF EAPRO (2009) states, this Noble Truth helps communities to identify resources and mobilize individuals to collaborate and end the suffering. At this stage, both causes *and* stakeholders are identified as being part of the issue, which means this stage provides an opportunity to involve everyone in the discussion for seeking a collective solution and restoring a collective well-being. Cornwall and Jewkes (1995), as cited in Parks et al. (2005), argue that humans should be regarded as agents of change instead of objects, as they are capable of analysing a situation and planning a solution. *Nirodha* is therefore a human-focused approach as it provides a platform for assessing the current situation, brainstorming for resolutions and then planning a course of action. Figueroa et al. (2002) believe that positive outcomes can manifest very soon after a community engages in addressing a critical issue in a communication for social change process. This is because through identification of problems, critical thinking and collaboration, the group members can work towards a solution.

The monk uses the principle of the Truths to explain the linkage between causes and conditions. Somphone (2011) suggests the only way to achieve tranquillity of the mind and happiness is to pursue the essence of education through ethical and spiritual values, because education and development are interconnected and interdependent. Findings indicate that the Buddhist moral teaching approach is deeply embedded in local cultural practices and can promote social change. It is used as a tool for educating people's minds and developing spirituality, which contributes to peace and solidarity and stimulates dialogue and participation. From a Buddhist perspective, human beings should be central to any development, so any development should begin with the human mind.

To illustrate this further, the people of *Ban Bungsanthueng* previously thought that trees growing within their land area were their property, and it was widely accepted that it was their right to cut trees or clear the land to conduct agricultural activities. The monk encouraged villagers to explore the issue and to rethink how their actions would lead to negative impact on the environment and collective village life. The monk also leads the villagers to restore the forest by initiating the reforestation activity. This activity involved taking the sacred forest (the *Puta*'s forest) and growing the trees at the *Vipassana* meditation centre (which is community land) as a community forest. In this case, the monk used the Buddhist Five Precepts as stimulus and '*paticcasamuppada*' (interdependence of inter-being) to educate the villagers about the causes and conditions of such actions.

Collective (Harmonious) Action

The above model is firmly built on Freire's (1970) idea that all stakeholders should be involved in the development process because it is more holistic and corresponds with the BA. In regards to the implementation of sustainable community development, there are three key village institutions: *Ban* (village and residents), *Wat* (or religious bodies) and *Honghian* (educational institutions). Figueroa et al. (2002) point out that collective self-efficacy is the shared belief and confidence that a group of people who join together are capable of taking action and solving problems. In BA the three components of the community enter into discussion and participatory planning, which then leads to concerted action. According to Swiss Agency for Development and Cooperation [SDC] (2016), development communication is used to promote participation for social and political transformation, and it facilitates access to information, stimulates participation, empowers people and influences public policies. Each institution plays its roles, but the village government and monk act as facilitators. Both actors, males in power (Witten-Hannah, 1999), need to have the trust of local groups, need to support local groups with necessary resources for local initiatives and need to facilitate the strengthening of the community's power, so that community members can take control of their own lives.

The village headman is responsible for the coordination and procurement of all necessities required for implementing the activity. Witten-Hannah (1999) suggests that the government also needs to play the role of a facilitator in order to keep local initiatives and growth promoted. Figueroa et al. (2002) point out that social cohesion is the force that encourages members of a group to stay within the group and continue contributing to a collective project. The *Sangha* are seen as a stimulus for community solidarity, and as having social capital, because they act as the glue between villagers, and between the three main institutions within the village. In line with previous studies (Bacon, 2009; Ife, 2002; Witten-Hannah, 1999), trust is needed for social changes, to join people and to bridge gaps in society.

Figueroa et al. (2002) suggest that leaders and members of the community should monitor their assigned work to ensure that the work is on schedule and everyone is doing their work. Through the cooperation of all stakeholders in the community, the BA is likely to be seen as a holistic approach because every member plays a leadership role and fulfils their responsibilities using the spirit of the volunteer. Sustained and efficient leadership must encourage members of the community to voluntarily participate in the programme, must demonstrate a leadership vision for sharing the benefits of the programme and must plan the social change process (Figueroa et al., 2002).

The values of Buddhist ethics and solidarity are put in place at the implementation stage. The essence of participatory communication is how awareness leads to commitment and then to action (Tufte & Mefalopulos, 2009). In the Buddhist context of Lao PDR, the concepts of love, solidarity and harmony play a dominant role in participatory community development. In line with these BA, Freire (1970) suggests that a useful approach for the promotion of community dialogue and participation is one that is founded upon love; dialogue cannot exist without profound love, humility and human faith. Freire articulated that profound love is based on dialogue and a dialogical process because it is a love for the world and people.

The power of Buddhist ethics should not be ignored because they have a significant role in the pre-stage of communication for social change (catalyst approach), particularly through emphasis on the virtue of solidarity and harmony. Bacon (2009) defines community as a collection of all living beings interacting in the same surroundings, sharing an ethos, opportunities and goals. As a result, any actions will have an impact on others in the same environment. The ethical virtue of serving others and feelings of engagement are crucial in BA because they nurture the community members' volunteer spirit, participation and desire to mutually assist in reaching goals (Queen, 2000).

Through the BA to knowledge-inquiry and harmonious implementation process, outcomes can be measured. Speaking in terms of *Dhamma*, members of the community firmly believe that they pursue right meditation, mindfulness, effort action and intention. This demonstrates how external *bhavana* can then link to action. Generally speaking, values of solidarity, mutual help and harmony become aspects of social capital, contributing to peace and social harmony in the community. In summary, the community achieves the goal of self-reliance and resilience because their implementation is based on mutual help and harmony. As everyone in the community has a strong sense of volunteerism the community is likely to be less dependent on external support.

Contextualized Indicators

The original research shows that the BDP's trained *Sangha* play an internal catalyst role in community development in Laos. The merging of the IMCFSC with the BDP's BA to development has generated new indicators which are more holistic and contribute to participatory communication for Buddhist development in Laos. Individual and social change indicators seek the attainment of the last of the Four Noble Truths '*magga*' (path to end suffering or the noble path), which consists of morality (*sila*), concentration (*samadhi*) and wisdom (*panna*). The contextualized social change indicators are discussed in Table 5.1.

The emerging indicators for social impact need to be included in a holistic discussion about community development in Buddhist societies, because they are interrelated and highly contextual. The integrated third column, as seen in the table, takes into consideration the Buddhist values and the IMCFSC; these indicators share equal values.

Moral/Ethical Norms

According to this research, moral norms cover many areas, yet they are all based on the Buddhist ethics, including but not limited to generosity, compassion, love, mindfulness and effort, and most of them are divine abodes (*Brahma-vihara*). Based on the research by Figueroa et al. (2002), social norms are a set of beliefs that shape people's ways of behaving and thinking, whilst also being a judgement of people's action and attitudes. As previously discussed in this chapter, the practice of belief systems in *Ban Bungsanthueng*

Table 5.1 Contextualized indicators from the integration of the IMCFSC model with Buddhist development disciplines

BA indicators	Indicators of IMCFSC social changes	Emerging indicators
• Moral-based society • Social harmony/solidarity • Compassion • Loving-kindness • Mutual help • Self-reliance/Self-help	• Leadership • Degree and equity of participation • Information equity • Collective self-efficacy • Sense of ownership • Social cohesion • Social norms	• Moral/ethical norms • Sense of collective ownership • Social harmony • Faith, trust and equity of participation • Right Understanding (*Samm-ditthi*) • Compassionate leadership • Self-reliance

Source: Synuanchanh (2018)

is a blend of indigenous and Buddhist traditions. Thus, these traditions have become a standard for judging people's behaviour.

Although the village norm sees power and leadership bestowed upon men, the monk provides new approaches to women's empowerment by shedding light on new form of social norms. 'Compassion' can be applied in this context, where men and society should be open to recognizing women's contribution to the improvement of their family and village life. As a result, the spiritual norm of 'generosity' of spirit can lead to a reevaluation of women's involvement in development works or politics.

Sense of Collective Ownership

A sense of ownership can be understood as people's feelings and beliefs about an issue that affects them and their community, and their way of engaging with it (Figueroa et al., 2002). The monk's approach at *Ban Bungsanthueng* has an impact on the village's harmony and sense of ownership. The value of promoting harmony within the village supports the generation of collective ownership. According to Parks et al. (2005), the CFSC process should be controlled by the community and social change activists, especially those who are identified as marginalized groups and can be empowered through a collective sense of ownership. The villagers already have a sense of collective ownership of the *Wat*, and they are therefore likely to voluntarily contribute to any work relating to the *Wat* because they have feelings of ownership and faith (belief). This is in line with Balit (2017) who asserts that the use of existing local communication systems, which generate dialogue and a sense of community ownership and integration, remains a key factor in the success and sustainability of any development programme. This process assures that the community voice is being listened to, and local traditions, languages and cultures are being respected.

Social Harmony

The term 'social harmony' plays a significant role in the Buddhist social order. The Buddhist values within this concept are '*Brahma-vihara*' (divine abodes) or social emotions. Dissanayake (2010) examined the Sarvodaya movement in Sri Lanka and found that the social emotions of loving-kindness, compassion, sympathetic joy and equanimity articulate the concepts of social harmony. Aspects of participatory communication can work well with the concept of 'social cohesion'; according to Figueroa et al. (2002), social cohesiveness refers to the force that stimulates members to stay in the group and carry on contributing to the group's goal, and this includes having a sense of integration, connection and cooperation. For *Ban Bungsanthueng* villagers, social harmony tightly binds them together and motivates them to stay actively engaged in village affairs, especially with regards to *Wat*-related activities or cultural traditions.

If social capital can be compared to the glue that joins people and gaps in society (Ife, 2002; Witten-Hannah, 1999) and enables concerted action to take place (Figueroa et al., 2002), the monk should also be considered part of that social capital. This argument is supported through findings which demonstrated the monk's active contribution to the village's social harmony, and the role of the *Wat* and *Sangha* as a mental/spiritual refuge. This value bridges the relationship gap in the village and brings people together by giving them the same access to collective assets (the *Wat* and *Sangha* in this case). This is witnessed in the number of people participating in religious events.

Faith, Trust and the Equity of Participation

Equity of participation is measured through the participation levels of community members and stakeholders in various activities, including planning, leader selection, decision-making, resource mobilization and management, and outcome evaluation (Figueroa et al., 2002). The degree to which people participate in the Buddhist development activities at *Ban Bungsanthueng* is driven by faith (Lao: *sattha*) in Buddhism and the *Sangha*. The term '*sattha*' itself has many meanings such as trust, confidence and hope. First and foremost, the *Sangha* builds *sattha* and trust among the members of the community. Only when the *Sangha* are trusted will the villagers voluntarily participate in activities conducted by them. According to Ife (2002) and Ladwig (2006), compassion, social obligation, trust, reciprocity and solidarity contribute to social capital. No limit of participation has been set for *sattha*, so it can also be considered as a form of social capital because it can ensure voluntary and equitable participation. *Sattha* may also be viewed as an essential element of a social network as it promotes empowerment and relationships within the community (Robinson, 1999).

Besides the faith in *Tri-ratna* or Triple Gems [Buddha, *Dhamma* and the *Sangha*], the idea that the *Wat* is a collectively owned spiritual refuge lays solid ground for community contributions to the *Wat*. The idea suggests that every member of the village has equal access to participation and utilization of the *Wat*. The *Sangha*, as spiritual transformer or leader, contributes to promoting solidarity and values the participation of every member. Faith and a sense of collective ownership support the flow of information, leadership and harmony.

Right Understanding (Pali: **Samma-Ditthi***)*

Information is the backbone for building a resilient community. One of the BDP's aims for community development is to build well-being and a resilient community. The level of information about an issue, that individuals within a group and between groups in the community are aware of, indicates the equity of information flow (Figueroa et al., 2002). From a Buddhist perspective, people can access information and knowledge and seek solutions through the Four Noble Truths (*Ariya-sacca*)—the Buddhist ways of knowledge, analysis and reflection, the basis of Buddhist ethics or *Sila-dhamma*. The first aspect encourages villagers to be aware of the issue (*dukkha*), the second allows them to explore the causes and conditions of the issue (*samudaya*), the third aspect examines ways to address the issue (*nirodha*) and the last aspect is the step of taking action (*magga*). Balit (2017) argues that knowledge, horizontally communicated, is beyond mere information. In these instances, faith and trust are also applied and contribute to the extent that community members can access the information and trust the information source.

The level of trust and the moral of Right Intention rank high in the villagers' views which implies the monk has demonstrated the Buddhist concepts of '*Samma-Sankappa*' [Right Intention], social faith and trust. As Tufte and Mefalopulos (2009) state, empowerment process is a reflection of the action and the gist of participatory communication is how awareness leads to a commitment to action. Through the practice of the *Ariya-sacca*, the villagers are not only encouraged to be aware of the issue, but to also create conditions for action.

Compassionate Leadership

This research has indicated that spiritual leadership is the accepted Buddhist style of leadership. The *Sanghas* are trained to teach Buddhist morality in order to raise awareness and apply the basic Buddhist precepts in daily life. The practice of morality is to cultivate compassion, an aspect of the Buddhist ethic of virtue (*Brahma-vihara*). The findings from the Buddhist Initiative leaders' perspectives indicate a respected person should carry the leadership in verbal and non-verbal behaviours or should be moral (*sila*). In this case, social trust is applied in leadership as the leader should first gain trust from the community before taking the lead and involving members in community activities. Therefore, leadership is based on the moral of Right Intention, because the members of the community will trust the leader if they see that she/he has good intentions to serve the community.

The *Sangha* is a respected and trusted person in the society (Ladwig, 2008; UNICEF EAPRO, 2009). The BDP trains its own *Sangha* community to develop compassion for others and to volunteer themselves to serve their society in line with the approach '*Jit-asa-sao-Buddha-phue-soumxon*' (Buddhist Volunteer Spirit for Community [BVSC]). The values of volunteer spirit, compassion and leadership work hand-in-hand. As Figueroa et al. (2002) argue, strong leadership encourages community members to volunteer themselves to the programme, demonstrates a leadership vision, shares the benefits of the programme and plans a social change process. In this case, the leader takes the initiative by developing people's compassion and encouraging their desire to serve the other. Dissanayake (2010) refers to the Buddhist notion that all meaningful social changes must first originate within the mind of the individual.

Self-Reliance

Self-reliance is an emerging approach to communication and development. Evidence from this research suggests that the highest goal the BDP wants to achieve is self-reliance. It trains its *Sangha* to serve the community and be its human resource. Some trainees are selected to be trainers at the training centre and in their communities, rather than using external agents.

At *Ban Bungsanthueng*, the monk demonstrates ways of self-reliant living. Self-reliant living has spiritual value and encourages people to stay self-sufficient. Dissanayake (2010) defines self-reliance as a dependence on the natural and human resources of a given country, and a willingness to identify developmental problems, set goals and design strategies based on cultural norms and traditions. The women's handicraft initiative for instance is highly sustainable because the work is based on traditional wisdom that has been transferred down generations and uses resources available in the village. The monk empowers this group by facilitating brainstorming sessions and offering financial advice. The monk has clearly stated that this activity is entirely run using local resources (both knowledge and materials) that are environmentally sustainable.

The development approach of self-reliance includes integrated village or grassroots development, contribution to decision-making processes, effective use of natural resources and maintenance of ecological balance and a willingness to rethink issues in regards to the implication of developments (Dissanayake, 1984). The Buddhist environmental movement is not only about maintaining environmental balance but also about maintaining cultural values and traditions. The conservation of forests through tree and marsh ordaining can contribute to food security and environmental balance in the future.

Conclusion

Based on our research, Buddhist approaches can provide an alternative and more holistic approach to sustainable community development that is more relevant to the Buddhist context of Lao PDR. BDP and BVSC network can play catalyst roles that can stimulate change through being spiritual transformers, information influencers and highly trusted sources or persons in the community. Buddhist ethics are the backbone of BA and can integrate with the IMCFSC model in many regards. Through combining the two approaches (BA and IMCFSC), seven indicators have been developed: (1) moral norms, (2) social harmony, (3) faith, (4) trust and equity of participation, (5) Right Understanding (*Samma-ditthi*), (6) sense of collective ownership and (7) compassionate leadership and self-reliance.

The ethics promote dialogue through a Buddhist epistemology (the Four Noble Truths) and promote participation based on faith, a sense of collective ownership, solidarity and Buddhist virtues. Villagers take the lead in exploring the nature of the issue and inter-being, as well as take action as individuals or as a group. Thus, this research argues that Buddhism, the BDP and the BVSC network (or *Sangha*) can all be catalysts for social change, in the Buddhist context in Lao PDR. *Sangha*'s involvement can be considered as an alternative approach to development in a more holistic human manner for sustainable development where the local people control and lead their own development process.

Appendix 1: List of Buddhist Key Terms and Concepts

Terms	Meanings
Paticcasamuppada	A fundamental to Buddha's teaching, *paticcasamuppada* refers to the law of origination, emphasizing the understanding of the process of existence through interconnectedness or the cause and effect link
Tri-sikkha	The Buddhist Threefold Training or Development
Sila [*Sila-dhamma*]	Buddhist morality or rules
Vinaya	Disciplines practiced by monks, nuns and novices
Brahma-vihara	Buddhist social emotion, the divide abode
Dhamma	It is a Pali term and refers to the term '*dharma*' in Sanskrit language which means the teachings of the Buddha
Sangha	A Buddhist community incorporated by monks, novice, nuns and white ascetics who are ordained in Buddhist life
Vipassana	A kind of Buddhist tradition or practice to cultivate insight and the truth through the nature of reality
Dhura	A Pali term means duty, obligation or responsibility
Magga	The Noble Eightfold Path, a pathway to end sufferings

Source: Synuanchanh (2018)

Appendix 2: Key Elements of Buddhist Philosophy

BUDDHIST CHEATSHEET (minimal edition)

THE NOBLE EIGHTFOLD PATH	THE FOUR NOBLE TRUTHS	THE SEVEN POINTS OF POSTURE
The Buddha taught that to attain liberation one must practice Wholesome: 1. View 5. Livelihood 2. Intention 6. Effort 3. Speech 7. Mindfulness 4. Action 8. Concentration	This was the Buddha's first and fundamental teaching about the nature of our experience and spiritual potential 1. Ordinary life brings about suffering 2. The origin of suffering is attachment 3. The cessation of suffering is attainable 4. Suffering can cease, by following the Eightfold Path	Attend to each in turn when you first take your meditation seat. If you become uncomfortable while sitting, you may go through these points again 1. Legs 5. Hands 2. Shoulders 6. Tongue 3. Back 7. Head 4. Eyes
THE SIX WHOLESOME AND UNWHOLESOME ROOTS OF MIND	THE SIX SENSE DOORS AND THREE FEELING TONES	THE FOUR METTA PHRASES
The mind is always under the influence of one of these states 1. Generosity 4. Greed 2. Love 5. Hatred 3. Wisdom 6. Delusion	Everything we experience comes through these portals 1. Eye (Seeing) 4. Tongue (Tasting) 2. Ear (Hearing) 5. Body (Touching) 3. Nose (Smelling) 6. Mind Experience is felt as one of three tones 1. Pleasant 2. Unpleasant 3. Neutral	Send loving kindness to yourself and others by using these phrases or words that have personal meaning for you 1. May I be free from danger 2. May I be happy 3. May I be healthy 4. May I love with ease
THE EIGHT VICISSITUDES	THE FIVE PRECEPTS	THE FOUR BRAHMA-VIHARAS
According to the Buddha, we will experience these vicissitudes throughout our lives no matter our intentions or actions 1. Pleasure and pain 2. Gain and loss 3. Praise and blame 4. Fame and disrepute	An ethical life is founded on these standards of conduct To refrain from 1. Killing 2. Stealing 3. Sexual Misconduct 4. False, harsh, and idle speech 5. Intoxicants that cloud the mind	These four "best abodes" reflect the mind state of enlightenment 1. Loving Kindness 2. Compassion 3. Joy 4. Equanimity
THE THREE KINDS OF SUFFERING	THE FIVE HINDRANCES	THE SIX STAGES OF METTA
The Buddha taught that we can understand different kinds of suffering through these three categories 1. The suffering of pain 2. The suffering of change 3. The suffering of conditionality	These are the classical hindrances to meditation practice 1. Desire, clinging, craving 2. Aversion, anger, hatred 3. Sleepiness, sloth 4. Restlessness 5. Doubt	Expand your circle of loving kindness by starting with yourself and moving gradually outward 1. Yourself 4. A difficult person 2. A good friend 5. All four 3. A neutral person 6. The entire universe

Source: Hsu et al. (2016)

References

Bacon, J. (2009). *The Art of Community: Building the New Age of Participation.* Sebastopol, CA: O'Reilly Media.

Balit, S. (2017). Communication for Isolated and Marginalized Groups: Blending the Old and the New. In Food and Agriculture Organization [FAO] (Ed.), *Communication and Sustainable Development: Selected Papers from the 9th UN Roundtable on Communication for Development.* Rome, Italy.

Bialek, M. (2014). *Thai Buddhist Ecology Monks: Competing Views of the Forest.* Unpublished Undergraduate Honors Thesis, University of Colorado, Boulder, CO, USA. Retrieved from https://scholar.colorado.edu/cgi/viewcontent.cgi?article=1046&context=honr_theses

Boutsavath, V., & Chapelier, G. (1973). Lao Popular Buddhism and Community Development. *Journal of the Siam Society, 61*(2), 1–38.

Buddhism for Development Project [BDP]. (2012). *Overview of Buddhism for Development Project* (Vol. 2017). Vientiane, Lao PDR.

Chilisa, B. (2012). *Indigenous Research Methodologies.* Thousand Oaks, CA: Sage.

Darlington, S. M. (1998). The Ordination of a Tree: The Buddhist Ecology Movement in Thailand. *Ethnology, 37*(1), 1–15.

Dissanayake, W. (1984). A Buddhist Approach to Development: Sri Lanka Endeavour. In A. Gumucio-Dagron & T. Tufte (Eds.), *Communication for Social Change Anthology: Historical and Contemporary Readings* (pp. 243–245). New Jersey, NJ: Communication for Social Change Consortium.

Dissanayake, W. (2010). Development and Communication in Sri Lanka: A Buddhist Approach. *China Media Research*, 6(3), 85–93.

Doan-Bao, C., Papoutsaki, E., & Dodson, G. (2018). Catalysing Social Change in Ho Chi Minh City, Vietnam: Evaluating the LIN Model of Participatory Community Development. *Community Development Journal*, 7, 1–22. https://doi.org/10.1093/cdj/bsx058

Figueroa, M. E., Kincaid, D. L., Rani, M., & Lewis, G. (2002). *Communication for Social Change: An Integrated Model for Measuring the Process and Its Outcomes*. New York, NY: The Rockefeller Foundation.

Freire, P. (1970). *Pedagogy of the Oppressed* (M. B. Ramose, Trans.). New York, NY: Continuum.

Hopwood, B., Mellor, M., & O'Brien, G. (2005). Sustainable Development: Mapping Different Approaches. *Sustainable Development*, 13(1), 38–52.

Hsu, J., Hsu, J., Pimentel, C., & Vlad. (2016). *A Cheat Sheet to Buddhist Philosophy*. Retrieved from http://thirdmonk.net/lifestyle/buddhist-philosophy-cheat-sheet.html

Ife, J. (2002). *Community Development: Community-Based Alternatives in an Age of Globalisation* (2nd ed.). New South Wales, Australia: Pearson.

Internews. (2015). Why Information Matters: A Foundation for Resilience. *Internews*. Retrieved from https://www.internews.org/sites/default/files/resources/150513-Internews_WhyInformationMatters.pdf

Kaza, S. (2000). To Save All Beings: Buddhist Environmental Activism. In C. S. Queen (Ed.), *Engaged Buddhism in the West* (pp. 159–183). Somerville, MA: Wisdom.

King, S. B. (2009). *Socially Engaged Buddhism*. Honolulu, HI: University of Hawai'i Press.

Ladwig, P. (2006). Applying Dhamma to Contemporary Society: Socially-Engaged Buddhism and Development Work in the Lao PDR. *Juth Pakai*, 7, 16–26. Retrieved from https://www.eth.mpg.de/3466895/Ladwig_Applying_Dhamma_Buddhism_Development_UNDP_.pdf

Ladwig, P. (2008). Between Cultural Preservation and This-Worldly Commitment: Modernization, Social Activism and the Lao Buddhist Sangha. In Y. Goudineau & M. Lorillard (Eds.), *Recherches nouvelles sur le Laos [New research on Laos]* (pp. 465–490). Vientiane: Ecole Française d'Extrême-Orient.

Lunn, J. (2009). The Role of Religion, Spirituality and Faith in Development: A Critical Theory Approach. *Third World Quarterly*, 30(5), 937–951.

Melkote, S. (2012). *Development Communication in Directed Social Change: A Reappraisal of Theory and Practice*. Singapore: Asian Media Information and Communication Centre [AMIC].

Morrow, A. (2011). Tree Ordination as Invented Tradition. *Asian Network Exchange*, 19(1), 53–60.

Parks, W., Gray-Felder, D., Hunt, J., & Byrne, A. (2005). *Who Measures Change? An Introduction to Participatory Monitoring and Evaluation of Communication for Social Change*. New Jersey, NJ: Communication for Social Change Consortium.

Payutto, P. A. (2002). *Dictionary of Buddhism*. Bangkok, Thailand: Sahadharmmic.

Payutto, P. A. (2008). *Karn Patthana Baeb Yuenyong [Sustainable Development]* (D. Bounyavong, Trans.). Vientiane, Laos: Buddhism for Development Project [BDP].
Queen, C. S. (2000). Introduction: A New Buddhism. In C. S. Queen (Ed.), *Engaged Buddhism in the West* (pp. 1–31). Somerville, MA: Wisdom.
Robinson, D. (1999). *Social Capital in Action*. Wellington, New Zealand: Institute of Policy Studies, Victoria University of Wellington.
Sengsoulin, B. (2014). The Lao Sangha of Luang Prabang and Their Social Roles in the Post-1975 Period. In P. J. Bräunlein, M. Dickhardt, K. Klenke, & A. Lauser (Eds.), *Dynamics of Religion in South East Asia Project [DORISEA] Working Paper Series*. Berlin, Germany: University of Gottingen.
Servaes, J., & Malikhao, P. (2007). Communication and Sustainable Development. In J. Servaes & S. Liu (Eds.), *Moving Targets: Mapping the Paths Between Communication, Technology and Social Change in Communities* (pp. 11–42). Penang, Malaysia: Southbound.
Sivaraksa, S. (2009). *The Wisdom of Sustainability: Buddhist Economics in the 21st Century*. London, UK: Souvenir.
Somphone, S. (2011). *Exploring the Heart of Education Through Spirituality and Sustainability: The Way We Live and the Way We Educate Dictate the Future*. Retrieved from http://www.padetc.org/wp-content/uploads/2013/03/Annex-4-TOKYO_TALK-Final-2011.pdf
Swiss Agency for Development and Cooperation [SDC]. (2016). *Communication for Development: A Practical Guide*. Swiss Agency for Development and Cooperation (SDC).
Synuanchanh, T. E. (2018). *Exploring the Role of Buddhist Monks/Nuns' Engagement in Community Development as Catalysts for Social Change and Sustainable Development in Lao People's Democratic Republic: A Case Study of Buddhism for Development Project at Ban Bungsanthueng, Nongbok District, Khammouane Province*. Unpublished Master's Thesis, Unitec Institute of Technology, Auckland, New Zealand.
Thomas, V., Eggins, J., & Papoutsaki, E. (2016). Relational Accountability in Indigenizing Visual Research for Participatory Communication. *SAGE Open, 6*(1), 1–11. https://doi.org/10.1177/2158244015626493
Tomalin, E., Haustein, J., & Kidy, S. (2019). Religion and the Sustainable Development Goals. *The Review of Faith & International Affairs, 17*(2), 102–118. https://doi.org/10.1080/15570274.2019.1608664
Tufte, T., & Mefalopulos, P. (2009). *Participatory Communication: A Practical Guide* (Vol. 170). Washington, DC: World Bank Publications.
UN General Assembly. (2015). *Transforming Our World: The 2030 Agenda for Sustainable Development*, A/RES/70/1. Retrieved April 19, 2020, from https://www.refworld.org/docid/57b6e3e44.html
UNICEF EAPRO. (2009). *Regional Review: Buddhist Leadership Initiative*. Bangkok, Thailand. Retrieved from https://www.unicef.org/eapro/AW_BLI_2Sep09.pdf
United Nations Conference on Trade and Development [UNCTAD]. (2015). *Development Strategies in a Globalised World: Role of Women as a Catalyst for Trade and Development*. Paper Presented at the UNCTAD Board: Sixty-Second Session, Geneva, Switzerland. Retrieved from http://unctad.org/meetings/en/SessionalDocuments/tdb62nonpaper01_en.pdf

Vu, H., Bailey, S., & Chen, J. (2016). Engaging Vietnam and Laos on Religious Freedom. *The Review of Faith & International Affairs*, *14*(2), 86–92. https://doi.org/10.1080/15570274.2016.1184452

Waisbord, S. (2001). *Family Tree of Theories, Methodologies and Strategies in Development Communication*. Retrieved from http://www.comminit.com/global/content/family-tree-theories-methodologies-and-strategies-development-communication-convergences

Waisbord, S. (2005). Five Key Ideas: Coincidences and Challenges in Development Communication. In O. Hemer & T. Tufte (Eds.), *Media & Global Change: Rethinking Communication for Development* (pp. 77–90). Buenos Aires, Argentina: CLACSO.

Walter, P. (2007). Activist Forest Monks, Adult Learning and Buddhist Environment Movement in Thailand. *Journal of Lifelong Education*, *26*(2), 329–345.

Witten-Hannah, S. (1999). Social Capital, Community Initiatives and Local Government. In D. Robinson (Ed.), *Social Capital in Action*. Wellington, New Zealand: Institute of Policy Studies, Victoria University of Wellington.

CHAPTER 6

Between Rights and Diversities: Can the Regulation of Communication Help Prevent Climate Change and Promote Sustainable Development?

Anthony Löwstedt and Diana Igropoulou

INTRODUCTION

The sensationalist dynamics embedded in mainstream journalistic practices serve specific functions in a globalized capitalist economy with strong ("sovereign") nation-state governments. *Events* are reported, sometimes over-reported, whereas *context* and *process* are systematically underreported (Boyd-Barrett, 2008; Payne, 2008). Messages referring to complex and irregular change, such as biodiversity loss and climate change, are therefore structural and perpetual losers in the marketplace of ideas.

The most successful media messages in the market are simple ones, without much context or process. They appeal to the lowest common denominators, to as many people as possible, of all ages, including many with limited knowledge and low levels of literacy. Messages involving sustainable development, on the other hand, are usually complex. To be fully understood, they typically require knowledge and understanding of rich context as well as analytical skills regarding multifactor causalities and multifaceted interaction.

A. Löwstedt (✉) • D. Igropoulou
Department of Media Communications, Webster Vienna Private University, Vienna, Austria
e-mail: Anthony.Loewstedt@webster.ac.at

© The Author(s), under exclusive license to Springer Nature Switzerland AG 2021
M. J. Yusha'u, J. Servaes (eds.), *The Palgrave Handbook of International Communication and Sustainable Development*,
https://doi.org/10.1007/978-3-030-69770-9_6

As the media world struggles to adapt to challenges posed by digitalization, journalistic practices are being transformed, especially in the face of the fragmented and ubiquitous nature of news media. Yet, so far, news media still exhibit a reliance on journalistic practices developed for very different communication landscapes. The literature review in Sections "Media Logic, Effects, Mediatization, and Journalistic Practices" and "Frames, Cultural Cognition, and Ideological Polarization" points to areas that may require rethinking in these regards.

Not only systemic factors, however, are held responsible for climate change denial and unsustainable macro-developments. Individual persons may also be held responsible, so much so that some call for charging corporate CEOs (which could include media executives) and governmental figures with crimes against humanity for knowingly having lied about and covered up these things in public statements (Hertsgaard & Pope, 2019).

Ideology is often embedded in the character of a media outlet, and media logic is itself subject to the ownership of the outlet, stalling efforts for an unbiased reporting of vital subjects such as biodiversity and sustainability. Damaging narratives such as climate change denialism are a manifestation of an increasingly polarized media landscape, demonstrating a sore need for an unbiased third-party agency or body, whether self-regulatory or not, for intervention.

For these reasons, sustainable development is also not easy to define. It is already contentious. We will attempt a rather simple and intuitive definition: Sustainable development does not lead to any net loss of cultural diversity or biodiversity (see Appadurai, 2003, p. 16, for a similar approach).

It is the long run that counts: the sustenance of humankind, of things that make life worth living and of life in general. Often, the two kinds of diversity overlap. In many equatorial regions, where both biodiversity and cultural diversity are threatened the most today, the two are not just allies, but united. The disappearing indigenous Amazon societies, for example, are desperately trying to safeguard the diversity of plants and animals against brutally encroaching monocultures of various kinds (Kolirin, 2020).

However, the two might also contradict rather than complement each other. There is not always a smooth transition from biodiversity to cultural diversity. Under certain conditions, a gain in cultural diversity may result in a net loss of biodiversity, or vice versa. If we should allow more different kinds of sushi to include whale meat, for example, there would most likely be more (sushi) culture but less whale diversity, considering present levels of demand. If all human beings were now to leave South America, for another example, cultural diversity would decrease but biodiversity would increase.

Thus, there are two dangers in the implementation of sustainable development: anthropophilia or anthropocentrism on the one hand, and anthropophobia and the underestimation of the value of cultural diversity on the other. Between Scylla and Charybdis, it would be helpful to identify principles that help balance sustainable development between culture and nature (or life). Should limited clearing of the rainforest, for example, be allowed in order to produce food to keep large populations, such as Brazil's urban poor, from starving? It seems the solutions will depend on political and value priorities. Another dimension of sustainable development, perhaps equally important, is between progress, excellence, and increased diversity on the one hand, and equality and social justice on the other. So, it seems that sustainable development cannot simplistically be reduced to a development that does not lead to any net loss of diversity (period).

Additional dimensions of the difference between bio- and cultural diversity may be well-being and dignity. Castells and Himanen (2014, p. 7) refer to human development as "the self-defined social process by which humans enhance their well-being and assert their dignity." This approach is reflected in the sustainable development goals (SDGs) of the United Nations (2015a). Both progress and social justice are addressed thus, but the dangers of anthropocentrism and of the devaluation of biodiversity also loom large. Apparently, it serves human well-being, but not necessarily the well-being of the biosphere, to mass-produce foods in giant monoculture industries.

Sustainable development may instead be viewed from a non-anthropocentric perspective, perhaps best explained in evolutionary terms. The factors that diminish biodiversity today are anthropogenic as well as natural in origin. They consist of irreversible developments: artificial and natural elimination as well as artificial and natural selection. The more intense the elimination/selection pressures on any population, the less diversity will result. If we treat humankind as just another species, and diversity as essentially biodiversity, we may thus end up with a utilitarian calculation of sustainability, according to which human interests (or even human beings!) would have to be sacrificed in order for the biosphere to keep up its general level of biodiversity (Löwstedt, 1995, pp. 21–23).

One reason that such measures may even be considered is that the biodiversity outlook is increasingly dire: Out of the approximately eight million species of life on this planet, a million species are expected to disappear over the next few decades, largely because of the human impact. Due to the severity of this impact, there is a movement to change the name of our current geological epoch (the Holocene) to the "Anthropocene." Among the numerous causes behind the ongoing mass extinction process, which is also changing basic geological characteristics of the earth's crust, is anthropogenic climate change (Bascompte, Garcia, Ortega, Rezende, & Pironon, 2019).

Climate change may of course be defined in an ethically neutral way—but there is good and bad climate change—and we will use the term here in the (at least potentially) bad or negative sense, meaning climate change that results in or leads to a loss of bio- or cultural diversity. On the other hand, at present, gradual global cooling would be good climate change. This chapter focuses on communication involving negative climate change as one of the main challenges currently facing the sustainability of human and biospheric development. We will look especially at how the news media are communicating information as well as misinformation concerning anthropogenic climate change and how these relate with behaviour. If solutions and principles enabling and ensuring balanced sustainable development be found, that is a balance between enhancing human well-being, dignity, and cultural diversity as well as biodiversity, then these principles still need to be communicated and argued to the people and institutions who enact and decide on any kind of major development. We finally raise the question whether media regulation has been overly concerned with human rights and conclude that biodiversity and cultural diversity also need to be prioritized, along with human rights, in the normative foundations of media law and media ethics.

The literature review that follows concludes that mainstream contemporary news media have so far often minimized reporting on global climate change, but there are signs that things are finally changing (Good, 2017; Krugman, 2020). Despite scientific near-consensus, mainstream commercial news media have systematically reported and debated anthropogenic climate change as if it were a hypothesis next to other hypotheses on climate change which deserve equal or more attention. Moreover, when covering news and hosting debates on the subject, they frequently provided prominent platforms to climate change sceptics and neo-sceptics who downplayed the importance of environmental issues. More or less consciously, they have protected and defended the status quo, in effect drowning out the voices of the 97 or so per cent of the scientific community who emphasize the anthropogenic causes of global climate change since many years already (Klein, 2014; Nuccitelli, 2017). Decades of perpetuated journalistic "balance" in reporting and other standard practices have left audiences perplexed or unsure about the urgency of the subject, thus causing delays in preventive climate change policy and action (Hertsgaard & Pope, 2019; Sheppard, 2012). There are several factors and conditions that have contributed to this miscommunication.

Media Logic, Effects, Mediatization, and Journalistic Practices

The communication theories that emerged with the development of media organizations, alongside the worldwide popularity of writing, radio, sound recording, film, and TV, accompanied and accounted for communication processes prior to digitalization (Hepp, Breiter, & Hasebrink, 2018). For example, media logic and media effects were crystallized as theoretical concepts when television was still analogue. In the face of new possibilities and complications in the digital era, some theorists propose the new concept of mediatization (Couldry & Hepp, 2017; Hepp et al., 2018; Hjarvard, 2008). This is not to say that mediatization theory departs from earlier theories, but rather it is complementary to theories of both media effects and media logic, as well as mediation theory which precedes it. As mediatization theory encompasses both new and digitally transitioned media, it attempts to understand the shift in communication processes and how ICTs socio-construct our realities.

However, some traditional practices of one-to-many communication channels have been influencing public opinion for over seven decades by promoting unhelpful and unprogressive views on both climate change and sustainable development; thus, attention will be given to some of their established communication practices. The study of new media, and interactive platforms such as social media, is more concerned with datafication: how data and digital traces are by-products of our new communication methods, yet raw materials for surveillance, influence, manipulation, and control. In general, new media do not follow traditional rules in communicating climate change, and because of the mobilization of users, such as the public, and the feedback, comments sections, and ability to generate original posts, the one-to-many communication process is disturbed. Does this provide a reason for hope? We are not sure.

Here we examine mediatization as a societal metaprocess and apply its communicative construction of reality on traditional media. Since societal institutions (corporations, markets, governmental agencies, and various other organizations) tailor their content for its consumption by the audience, adaptation plays an important role when sociocultural changes occur, and here one could insert climate change, so that the tailoring process begins anew, shaping the content creation to fit the altered landscape (and seascape).

Readers and consumers may at first have no information on their own and rely entirely on information that is exclusively produced for public opinion to direct its perceptions and societal action (Mormont & Dasnoy, 1995). If we exemplify this lack of information with the increased plastic consumption since the mid-twentieth century, labelled as "a profound revolution ushered by plastic" or "an era of material abundance" amongst other names, we can hardly find a downside, neither in the reporting of plastic nor in the reception of the messages (Parker, 2018). In fact, quite the opposite is true; the cheapness of it—petroleum-made plastic—inspired a wasteful lifestyle, where households favoured plastic products over reusable ones. In 1955, *Life* magazine celebrated the liberation of the American household from drudgery (Parker, 2018). The cover image was a family photograph showing its members throwing plastic cutlery, cups, plates, and so forth into the air. Ordinarily, if these items were made of glass or other fragile materials, they would take up to "40 hours to be cleaned," and under no circumstance could they be thrown out or around, highlighting the superior qualities of plastic, mainly its hassle-free characteristics (Parker, 2018).

The habit of plastic consumption that was nurtured by the perceived absence of any shortcomings is a "communicative construction of reality" that had to be significantly, if not radically, altered, given more recent information about the dangers of micro-plastics, deriving from plastic posing serious threats, especially to marine life and to biodiversity. Here, one can argue that societal institutions have started to actively adapt to meet the new challenge, providing necessary information about the dangers of plastic and highlighting the collective role that the audience (and others) must play to reduce, minimize, and discontinue plastic consumption (SAPEA, 2019, pp. 67–69, 84–89).

Prior to the rise of social media, with their new intermediary role between mass and personal communications, the traditional media stories concerning sustainability and climate change were crafted differently. The one-to-many, top-down reporting of global warming, in US newspapers especially, led to false impressions that scientists are divided about whether climate change was in fact happening (Boykoff & Boykoff, 2004). "For science, objectivity is tentativeness and adherence to evidence in the search for truth. For journalism, objectivity is balance" (Sandman, 1988, p. 37). This was a dominant voice, making objectivity as balance a cornerstone in journalism; not inclusive polylogue, but exclusive dialogue, was the motto. When faced with two opposing accounts of one issue, journalists would fulfil their obligations to objectivity by covering both.

Newsworthiness, another journalistic value, has also distorted, and continues to do so, the reporting on both threats to sustainability and breakthroughs and victories on the road to sustainable development. Distortion occurs because some prospective news stories are more difficult to justify than others.

> While some risks are sudden, immediate and temporary (a volcanic eruption, ash clouds, a quickly contained epidemic, etc.) many issues of risk are creeping issues, or ongoing, slow-burn stories like the spread of AIDS or human-induced environmental changes. These become difficult to fit with the idea of newsworthiness, because for slow-burn issues to warrant continuous news coverage would at least require continuously fresh angles on a story. (Ashe, 2013, p. 14)

To become newsworthy in traditional media, the story must help the journalists meet their obligations, gain editorial and institutional approval, and react in timely ways to related, subsequent events. Their job is to cover events, rather than process or context. Given the fact that sustainability and climate change are slow-burn issues, requiring context and involving complex processes, with few fresh angles to them, they usually appear in the mass media only when certain additional factors are in play: questions of blame, alleged secrets and cover-ups, human interest, links with high-profile issues/persons, conflict, scandal, many people being exposed, strong visual impact, links to sex or crime, and/or death and injury (Pidgeon, 2012).

News stories about sustainability and climate change are reported when journalists can harmonize them with their own concept of newsworthiness. The criteria will differ from journalist to journalist, editor to editor, and media outlet to media outlet, with each negotiating their own understanding of their role. The elements that each will believe necessary in a newsworthy story will also depend on subjective judgements about what the reader, the news institution, the sponsors and funders, and the editors want. It will be based on preconceptions about what grabs audience attention and on learned institutional practices (Ashe, 2013, pp. 13–15).

With regard to health reporting, Picard and Yeo maintain that scientists, journalists, and medical practitioners have dissimilar communication goals: the former to improve public understanding of science, the latter to improve health, and the journalists to achieve "coverage that informs the public about health advances and debates, protects the public against risks, and exposes [injustices]" (Picard & Yeo, 2011, pp. 4–8). Besides, other goals and interests get entangled in media coverage, as media owners, government(s), international organizations, companies, and NGOs will pursue different agendas and influence media coverage (Ashe, 2013, pp. 10–18). Consequently, the interaction between the groups will influence whether and how a story gets covered. For example, environmental NGO activists often stage photogenic protests or time reports to maximize media coverage (Smith, 2005). Their strategy to satisfy news industry needs is often opportunistic and innovative.

The functioning of news media outlets, however, is that most of them are "big business" operators with a tendency to protect the establishment, identify with national and nation-state interests, and ensure that advertisers and corporate owners are happy with the reporting and the choices of stories (Dispensa & Brulle, 2003, pp. 74–82). Such mechanics of the journalism industry are becoming increasingly relevant as advertising capital is relocating, private media ownership is growing and concentrating, and public service ratings are shrinking (Wrabetz, 2017).

Traditionally, journalists also focus on strong viewpoints to create a dramatic tension between various views, hence favouring extreme commentators over the voices of moderation, nuance, and logic (Sandman, 1988, p. 37). This has exacerbated false balancing, for example as journalists tend to give "equal attention to a passionate advocate of a minority position and a comparatively dispassionate representative of the majority position" (Ashe, 2013, p. 15).

Meanwhile, as far as detachment is concerned, it is the job of editors and journalists to simply state the facts and abstain from voicing their opinions, from letting opinions or emotions distort factual representations, and from dictating or advising people what to do or how to behave (Smith, 2005). The principle of detachment is highly valued in journalism and embedded deeply in the profession. In the USA, the principal direction of journalism in the first half of the twentieth century was towards establishing itself as a respectable profession. It was an era when professional schools proliferated, codes of professional ethics were articulated, and the ideology of "objective" reporting matured (Johnstone, Slawski, & Bowman, 1972, p. 524). The commitment to "the identity of a detached observer remains." Especially with conflict situations and disasters, detachment is still considered as essential to ethical journalistic practice (Blastland & Spiegelhalter, 2013, p. 27).

Frames, Cultural Cognition, and Ideological Polarization

Put simply, framing is the angle from which a news story is being told. By covering particular stories and using selected sources, media content providers construct reality from their own or their institution's or their sponsor's point of view (Boykoff, 2008). In general, frames are defined as "the setting of an issue within an appropriate context to achieve a desired interpretation or perspective" and viewed as an inseparable aspect of the act of conveying information (CRED, 2009). Then, framing will be used by readers or listeners to organize ideas, understand why an issue might be problematic, and condense complex information into small clusters. In fact, it is impossible not to offer a frame when discussing a topic and CRED (Center for Research on Environmental Decisions) even offers guidelines for helping to frame information in ways that "maximize comprehension" (2009). The selective process of choosing whether to include or exclude information, depending on whether it is perceived to "fit" inside the frame or not, is a necessary aspect of media framing, and all sides in climate change controversies are subject to it.

Analysing frames allows researchers to consider the factors that influence the journalistic constructions of these frames; the influences can be personal beliefs, organizational outlook, paradigms, ideologies, or sources (Ashe, 2013, p. 12). For example, a framing assessment of news agendas and communicated environmental risks in Sweden found that Swedish media are, for better or for worse, unwilling to "display any kind of scientific uncertainty that would undermine the demand for collective action on the problem" (Olausson, 2009, p. 421).

A major strength of the analytical approach to framing is the acknowledgement that messages are not necessarily transmitted intact from journalist to audience: "there is fluidity to the meanings that individuals may take from a particular presentation of a news story, because each member of the audience will view it from a different perspective" (Ashe, 2013, p. 12). And now, with the new digital media, messages are also transmitted, interpreted, reinterpreted, and misinterpreted much more often, in both directions.

The theory of cultural cognition states that each member of an audience most easily assimilates information that is compatible with their already existing mental model (Ashe, 2013, p. 10; Boykoff, 2008; Ropeik, 2012, p. 4), which is mainly a social construct. "The importance of collective decision-making for human survival means that we will filter our beliefs about the world, even about scientific information, through the perspective of the social groups with which we most closely associate ourselves" (Ropeik, 2012, p. 4).

Complacency and confusion are overt outcomes of the seemingly balanced reporting, while self-approval and general disconnect between cause and effect constitute some of the covert results (Sheppard, 2012, p. 21). It is conspicuous that dissenting views about climate change have been influential in sowing doubt in people's minds and in delaying serious action. As uncertainties allow people to justify inaction, the effect is the adoption of a "wait and see attitude" and "I will do the right thing when I know what the real facts are" (Sheppard, 2012, p. 22).

Climate change communication encounters yet another obstacle—a derivative of balanced reporting—that creates a new category of climate change denial. Proponents of this position argue that climate scientists overblow the risks and tend to be vague in forecasts about effects of climate change in the future. In research, they are frequently mentioned as "neo-sceptics" (Perkins, 2015; Wendel, 2016). While not directly denying anthropogenic global warming, they minimize its projected effects. Then, by diverting their attention from the communicated consequences of climate change to some uncertainties in climate science, neo-sceptics assert their disbelief in mainstream science by accusing it of being unable to pinpoint the precise future of climate change (Perkins, 2015).

The researchers of this new occurrence question the risk communication methods employed by scientists (Stern, Perkins, Sparks, & Knox, 2016). However, all scientists assess risk daily and their methods of communicating it are based on the nature of their subject (Stern et al., 2016). "We're virtually certain" signifies a 99–100 per cent probability in an event occurring, although even such a realistic statement issued by scientists is met with some degree of uncertainty by the public (Gallant, 2013). The neo-sceptic bottom line is that unless the audience is presented with calculated, accurate, and indisputable results, it is well-advised to retain its apathy, disengagement, and detachment (Stern et al., 2016; Wendel, 2016).

On the other hand, there are underlying reasons for perceptual disconnects that are not directly linked with media exposure, for example inherent psychological responses—such as defence mechanisms—that humans exhibit to mentally protect themselves against possible threats when presented with bad news. An outright denial or ignorance of the problem conserves personal energy, reduces stress, and permits routine behaviours to endure uninterrupted (Sheppard, 2012, p. 27). This is a crucial perceptual barrier related to both framing and cultural cognition; we take in information that is available to us selectively, picking the parts that fit our pre-existing beliefs (Sheppard, 2012, p. 30).

Yale researchers have determined that one's "cultural worldview," that is the sum of one's political and paradigmatic leanings and ideological outlook, explains "individuals' beliefs about global warming more powerfully than any other characteristic" (Kahan et al., 2012 p. 735; Klein, 2014). They attribute the correlation between "worldview" and acceptance of climate science to cultural cognition, the process by which we filter new information in ways that will protect our "vision of the good society" (Kahan et al., 2012). If the newly acquired information confirms the "vision," we integrate it more easily (Kahan et al., 2012). However, if it poses a threat to our belief system, "our brain immediately gets to work producing intellectual antibodies designed to repel the unwelcome invasion" (Kahan et al., 2012, p. 734; Klein, 2014).

The interpretation of climate change messages received by the audience certainly does not end with mere exposure to these media messages. The ideological filtering does not stop once media messages reach audiences; it is rather an unfolding process (Horton, 1979). Research on cultural cognition has revealed that individuals will extract the information about climate change that they think matters most to their lives (Carvalho, 2007). This information is most likely to connect them to like-minded people with whom they share ideological standpoints.

The sum of such decoding is sometimes called "ideological polarization." It is reinforced by ideologically specific media usage and selection (Maeseele & Pepermans, 2017). Other theorists call this experience an "activation of confirmation bias," something that makes individuals retreat into their filter bubbles (Pariser, 2011, p. 27). The process of socialization—the individual's personal identity formed by memories and social interactions from childhood onwards—can be shaken (Holtzman & Sharpe, 2015, p. 15). The "social self," a by-product of socialization, builds upon one's sense of belonging to surrounding social groups and community (Holtzman & Sharpe, 2015, p. 15). Now, if the community shifts its values the "social self" will be influenced to revisit the deeply held beliefs and update them (Holtzman & Sharpe, 2015, p. 15). New information may become a threat to one's worldview, and the acceptance of a disconcerting message can drive a wedge between individuals and their peers. Potential disagreement with and disengagement from our social groups are the main reasons "for the strong emotional predisposition to reject [the new messages]" (Kahan et al., 2012, p. 733; see also Klein, 2014, p. 37).

Information Dominance: The Political and Cultural Economy of Climate Change Denialism

Certain nation-state and corporate interests seem to stand to lose the most from a world community achieving sustainable development. Any nation-state, and any individual, may of course find themselves losing out in a transition towards sustainable development, but especially the most powerful and wealthy countries and alliances and groups of countries, as well as many corporations, especially ones dominant in markets involving heavy use of fossil fuels, transport, arms (and many others). They may prepare for not becoming losers, or even for becoming winners in the process, for example by switching from combustion engines to electric engines, or from coal to solar or wind energy. But they will also attempt to cling to proven, traditional assets and means of generating wealth, influence, and power.

In various ways, some of them half-conscious or unconscious, these nation-states, corporations, and individuals may therefore influence the media to allow climate change denialism into the most prominent debates, discussions, and fora on sustainable development, at least as temporary strategies. They will do this for short-term gain, such as profit and enhanced power, midterm reasons such as leaving wealth as inheritance to their descendants, economic growth in general, or prevention of mass unemployment, yet certainly not for long-term humanistic or pro-biospheric reasons. The midterm reasons do serve some public interests, and so corporate and nation-state interests are provided by the news media with legitimate access to the public sphere. But the problem is not that they have access to the public sphere; it is that they dominate it in an almost suffocating way (Herman & Chomsky, 2002, pp. xvii–xix).

In *This Changes Everything*, Klein seeks to provide an adequate explanation for the more than metaphorical question: "What is really preventing us from putting out the fire that is threatening to burn down our collective house?" (Klein, 2014, p. 18). While the pool of potential answers revolves around politics, profit, and ideology, the word "media" is also mentioned repeatedly (Klein, 2014, pp. 18–37). Especially media ownership and control become relevant as Klein states: "We are stuck because the actions that would give us the best chance of averting catastrophe are extremely threatening to an elite minority that has a stranglehold over our economy, our political process, and most of our media outlets" (2014, p. 18).

To immerse herself into the overt and covert motives of Republican think tanks (whose main representatives enjoy frequent coverage by major US media), Klein attended the Heartland Institute's Sixth International Conference on Climate Change (2014, p. 32). The speeches and conversations exchanged during the two-day conference (dubbed "ICCC") included absurdities such as: "Climate change is a plot to steal American freedom," "climate change is a Trojan horse designed to abolish capitalism and replace it with green communitarianism," and the widely circulated statement "one day you will wake up in subsidized government housing, eating subsidized food, while working at your government-assigned job on the bottom floor of your urban transit center village because you have no car [...]" (quoted in Klein, 2014, pp. 32–38).

The importance of this conference is multifaceted. The misleading name ICCC (which can be confused with IPCC, the Intergovernmental Panel on Climate Change), the mimicking of credible scientific conferences with the utilization of mottos such as "Restoring the Scientific Method," and the replacement of scientific expertise on climate change with astronauts and television weathermen who claim to be scientists are all strategies at work to attract media attention through seemingly serious messages (Klein, 2014, p. 33). "The talking points tested here will jam the comment sections beneath every article and YouTube video that contains the phrase 'climate change' and 'global warming'," Joseph Bast, president of the Heartland Institute, admitted to Klein in an interview (quoted in Klein, 2014, p. 34). More importantly, Bast took credit for "thousands of articles and op-eds and speeches [...] that were informed or motivated by somebody attending one of these conferences" (quoted in Klein, 2014, p. 34).

"Information dominance" is a related term used by the US and British militaries since the early twenty-first century (the invasion of Iraq). It is meant as a strategic objective to replace "information superiority," which was seen to be achieved as soon as a 51–49 per cent situation applied. It consists of combinations of censorship and marginalization of enemy communications (to achieve something more like a 99–1 per cent ideal), as well as strategic deception, embedding communicators, and the privatization of weaponized information. And as revolving doors increasingly connect the private sector and the military as well as politics, so do information dominance policies and techniques (Miller, 2003; Nuccitelli, 2017).

Eco-narratives: Contesting Ideologies in Media Representation

Yet the media also provide means to sustainable development. A little-known example is climate fiction, a new type of narrative genre, since around 2002, that addresses a new type of reality. Unlike the science fiction that received critical acclaim since the 1930s and often takes place in a dystopian future—*Brave New World* and *1984* being prime examples—cli-fi happens in a dystopian present. In the scientists' struggle, and often failure, to effectively reach audiences and get their messages across, cli-fi has untapped a way of achieving this, "a way of smuggling some serious topics into the consciousness of readers who may not be following the science" (Curry, 2013). Through narratives and storytelling, novelists tackle climate change in their writing and reach people in ways that the scientific community is unable to do (Curry, 2013). Cambridge University and other prestigious institutions are now teaching climate fiction courses, signalling a larger trend: Despite cli-fi still being considered a niche, it already helps define our culture and current condition. "Looking back at the 21st century, climate change will be one of the major themes in literature" (Stankorb, 2016). From the novelist's point of view, climate change and loss of biodiversity relate to a prevailing sense of gloom and helplessness (Waldman, 2018). The stories that cli-fi authors create, however, also attempt to provide new ways of dealing with the looming changes, adapting to, and perhaps most of all providing hope for, the near future (Waldman, 2018).

In addition, cli-fi may aid in the transition of altering a wasteful lifestyle that characterizes our society and poses as one of the larger threats to the United Nations 2030 Agenda for Sustainable Development. Here, Goal 12, Responsible Consumption and Production, deals with the necessary changes to the consumption and production patterns and habits to prevent more irreversible damage on a global level (U.N., 2015b). The UN considers the change of lifestyle a non-negotiable requirement, since with projections that the total population will be 20 billion by 2050 scientists fear that the natural resources of almost three planets such as ours will be required by then to sustain the only planet that we have (U.N., 2019).

A new UN initiative, the SDG Media Compact, creates an alliance with more than 30 media organizations (consisting of more than 100 media and entertainment outlets) to increase SDG awareness. Across various channels of communication, the participating organizations will benefit by the partnership as the UN promises to increase its efforts to "source and share high-value media content" and "newsworthy opportunities" (U.N., 2019). A representative of Channels Media Group—Nigeria, stated that the group is prepared to hold the government accountable if any of the efforts to tackle the goals of the 2030 Agenda are not being met (U.N., 2019). The traditional virtues of critical, objective, accurate, and investigative reporting still have important roles to play here. But other skills and mechanisms will also be necessary.

Narratology is fast becoming valuable currency in the media world. Transmedia storytelling assures that the message remains unchanged as it travels through various platforms, and as a part of or along with entertainment and marketing it also drives social change (Jenkins, 2006). The rise of social media and the many new formats of how stories are told—for example Instagram stories that expire after 24 hours—force content creators to compete for audiences' engagement by creating new narratives daily. On their social accounts, NGOs as well as big corporations now present sustainability and climate change as a personal target or even priority, often with real-life pictures of catastrophes, and there is always an element of storytelling attached. It can be a hashtag, such as #BeatAirPollution created by the UN environment agency's Instagram account, which in a single post asks the audience to engage by commenting on which one of the three suggested steps it plans on pursuing: (1) plant trees, (2) clean up trash, (3) commute without polluting (U.N.E.P., 2019). Unlike Aristotle's framework that a story has a beginning, a middle, and an end, new formats sometimes provide only a beginning, a start to an ongoing process; with the middle and end to unfold in an uncertain future.

With both traditional and digital media, aesthetics continues to play an important role in captivating audiences. The media can be and sometimes are enablers and supporters of sustainable development. Smith identifies some of the successful elements of a news story on a risk (2005, p. 145):

> There are some common approaches to the way stories are told, [...] respected news craft lies in the choreography of words and images, where pictures make the script both memorable and legitimate. Editorial decision makers manage the kind of stories and the rate of flow around a particular topic.

Studies point to the emergence of new identities in young people (Generation Z and the millennials) attributed largely to social media usage. As news about climate change and loss of biodiversity and cultural diversity challenge our dominant cultural narratives, assumptions, and values, the extension of this challenge translates to changing the sense of self and identity. One new type of identity involves active participation in the collective movements of battling climate change and promoting ethical consumption patterns both online and offline (Norgaard, 2012; Verlie, 2019). It involves appeals to reason based on scientific knowledge, long-term planning and policies, as well as to emotion and passion (Johnstone & Lindh, 2018).

Worldwide, eco-protests have increased tremendously in size and frequency, driven mostly by students who find innovative ways in terms of placards, banners, as well as clothing that often produce a photogenic result (Verlie, 2019). The images of such protests are featured in credible publications, and they travel between various blogs and social media accounts for the wider public to see.

Philosophers such as Foucault and Serres rejected the view of a person having an inner and fixed identity and identified the self as being defined by a continuing discourse in a shifting communication environment (O'Farrell, 2011). It has also been argued that we now live in an "identity vacuum" as digital identities can be adopted and dropped at will (Marcu, 2015). The presence of a plethora of narratives in the media creates tension and difficulty in uniting people with different identities as opposed, for example, to the Enlightenment era when people shared identities largely based on geography (Jameson, 1991), and on the comparative dearth of media messages at that time. Furthermore, the immersive narratives and aesthetically pleasing digital images are used for the selection of identities by members of the audience (O'Farrell, 2011). Perhaps the main obstacle hindering the formation of a transnational, interfaith, trans-cultural, and trans-ideological identity dedicated to sustainable development in an age of simulation and postmodernism is that the narratives so far available to us (with a few exceptions) have not systematically prepared the larger population for the global climate change and diversity crises, nor for the related socio-political and economic problems.

Risk and Uncertainty in Reporting About Sustainability and Climate Change

For most people, knowledge about science comes largely through mass media and not through direct involvement in scientific work or exposure to scientific publications (Ashe, 2013, pp. 6–10; Corbett & Durfee, 2004). Accordingly, as media reports on climate or diversity news are usually based on scientific findings, it becomes crucial for science and for society that the reports are communicated effectively to avoid undesirable effects on audiences, such as misunderstanding, distortion, apathy, or disbelief (Ashe, 2013, pp. 6–10). With climate change, information is related to the scientific terms "risk" and "uncertainty" and is communicated through the media with certain care and rules while also implying recommendations for the future of the discourse on that particular subject (Ashe, 2013, p. 10).

A key question is whether the media's response to risk is proportional and if it fosters a reliable assessment of risk in the public sphere. However, this is a question that favours an objectivist, rather than a cultural relativist understanding of risk. "It presumes risk to be objective and then evaluates media reporting against the paradigm of formal professional risk assessment," Ashe states (2013, p. 9). Then, it happens that the audience becomes more afraid than the evidence suggests, or not as afraid as it ought to be (Ashe, 2013, p. 9; see also Ropeik, 2012, p. 122). News media tend to give more coverage to alarmist perspectives: In 2015 when the WHO classified "processed red meat as a carcinogen" many journalists jumped to the conclusion that all types of red meat can cause cancer (Osterath, 2015). In other instances, however, the media discard sensational elements of scientific press releases, debunking the alarmist stereotype (Ashe, 2013, pp. 9–10). To illustrate, to get more attention by the media, organizations such as People for the Ethical Treatment of Animals (PETA) tend to exaggerate in their press releases. Journalists—to protect the audience from unverified statements—then suppress them by taking the sensational elements out of the story.

Even if journalists could afford the luxury of reporting on all possible environmental and health risk stories, the audience would dismiss them. Ropeik points out that human beings do not assess risk in a rational manner: "most people do not choose to sit down and read dry statistical data about the relative risks of every aspect to our lifestyle" (2012).

Globalism Versus the Rest and Uncritical Pluralism as a Political Problem: Pluralism Versus Diversity

When closely examining Western lifestyles, we can discern a pattern that actively undermines prospects for more sustainable development. Examining the American way of life as a potent ideology is especially important in the context of climate action. It is oftentimes defined as a "non-negotiable right," as an unlimited and ever-expanding ability and privilege of each US citizen to indulge in material consumption (Collomb, 2014). This opinion is embraced by a spectrum of conservatives and liberals from members of the Heartland Foundation to intellectuals and senators, as the mission is to always protect the average consumer from higher prices and regulations (Klein, 2014, p. 24). This becomes evident in the launch of the No Climate Tax Pledge and the labelling of cap and trade policy as a "massive tax hike" (Isaac, 2012, p. 21). The conservative intellectual and author of *Roosters of the Apocalypse*, Rael Jean Isaac, for example, claims that the implementation of the environmental movement's agenda would amount to economic suicide (Isaac, 2012, p. 21).

The American Way of Life is so unconditional that democratic candidates and even presidents also refrain from bargaining with it (Jacquet, Dietrich, & Jost, 2014). In his *Assault on Reason*, Al Gore implies that the American dedication to high consumption and economic growth will not ever be called into question (Gore, 2007, pp. 4–16). On a similar note, Barack Obama postponed and weakened his inaugural promise of protecting the environment due to concerns over its unpopularity in public opinion (Jacquet et al., 2014).

The market economy, consumerism, and capitalism's insatiable hunger for growth have also stressed the need for competition rather than cooperation to achieve growth. If at all, cooperation is systematically rewarded only if it leads to competitive edge, that is to the competitive advantage of a corporation, company, nation-state, or other organization. This triangle of abstract forces either negates or marginalizes sustainabilities and reversibilities in development.

Cooperation beyond market competition and nation-state loyalties is commonly dismissed as Utopian, or dangerous, or both. In a programmatic declaration Donald Trump, President of the USA, addressed (and confronted) the United Nations General Assembly thus:

> We [Americans] reject the ideology of globalism and accept the doctrine of patriotism. ... Sovereign and independent nations are the only vehicle where freedom has ever survived, democracy has ever endured, or peace has ever prospered. (Quoted in Ward, 2018)

This is, however, very far from an exclusively American problem. For example, postmodernism, a dominant intellectual and cultural movement (or condition) emanating especially from western Europe, is aiding an uncritical pluralism, one that marginalizes or negates consensus, unity, and solidarity and reflects a crisis of identity, involving identity vacuums related to the spread and influence of fragmentation, individualism, social atomism, commercialism, capitalism, and market-driven, as well as Western imperialist, globalizations (Löwstedt & Mboti, 2017, pp. 121–123; Sardar, 1998). The responsibility for sustainable development, in contrast, has to be shouldered by all people and all communities (though by some more than others). But the market as well as the international system is built on competition.

With rapidly improving media technologies and increasingly immersive narratives, the media are promoting escape from reality. Yet, they are promoting fantasy as well as escape (Katz & Foulkes, 1962). And fantasy can help provide creative solutions for sustainable development communications as well as for sustainable development itself. Similarly, cooperation without competition seems implausible and perhaps stifling for innovation when we most need it, and, finally, postmodernism is not only bad. It does provide arguments for the protection of minorities, and in some quarters, under some conditions, it also criticizes capitalist ideology as well as imperialist oppression (Löwstedt & Mboti, 2017, pp. 123–124). Nevertheless, it is mainly cooperation, not competition, that now needs to be taken to the next level.

Conclusion: Sustainability and Media Regulation

The correlation between bad climate change and unsustainable human or anthropogenic developments has become virtually irrefutable. Not surprisingly, however, the media work both ways, against and in favour of sustainable development. There are no easy solutions, such as authoritarian censorship or even democratic governmental or intergovernmental control over communications. Especially self-regulation of and by communicators, including media ethics, media literacy, and consistently promoted and safeguarded media diversity and wider cultural diversity, can help the media support sustainable development in sustainable ways. The audience must take some responsibility and not be lazy, and not let the media do the thinking for them. But state or state-like regulation will, unfortunately, also continue to be necessary, especially in the form of anti-trust regulation to ensure media diversity, critical thinking, and multi-perspectivism, and also to stop and prevent hate speech and incitement to violence over the dwindling remaining resources, which are only going to further delay effective sustainability (Löwstedt & Palac, 2019).

State regulation could (and in our view should) include support for public service and community media as well as for self-regulatory bodies, such as press councils. Ultimately, however, it is up to us all to challenge climate change as well as the systems, the authorities, and the elites who endanger or prevent sustainable development. Beyond the international system and the internationalism of the United Nations (which is still centred on the principle of nation-state sovereignty and thus on competition rather than cooperation between nations), the further we develop a functioning global democratic system with "globalization from below" (Falk, 1991), the better the chances will be, in our opinion, to tackle the related problems in a way that is fair to current and future generations of humans as well as to other forms of life.

Media regulation, finally, would be more effective against unsustainable developments if it were not so centred on (individual) rights. Of course, basic human rights such as freedom of expression, freedom of information or the right to privacy need to be at the centre of law and morality, but so do some other values, such as sustainability, biodiversity, and cultural diversity (cf. Babaci-Wilhite, 2013). These are more complex values, as they fundamentally involve both rights and duties. But, like the numerous current invocations of the First Amendment to the US Constitution (1791) and the Universal Declaration of Human Rights (1948), media law and ethics debates and textbooks should start making more use of and more references to the Convention on Biological Diversity (1992), UNESCO's Universal Declaration on Cultural Diversity (2001), and the UN Sustainable Development Goals (2015), among other recent developments of international law and transnational regulation pertaining to both media and sustainability. In our view, media regulation in general needs to reflect a profoundly changed historical reality, both of the media and of the larger contexts. In the long run, human rights, too, will no doubt mainly benefit from being associated more closely with sustainable development and with diversities.

References

Appadurai, A. (2003). *Diversity and Sustainable Development, in United Nations Environment Programme: Cultural Diversity and Biodiversity for Sustainable Development* (pp. 16–20). Nairobi: UNEP. Retrieved April 13, 2020, from https://unesdoc.unesco.org/ark:/48223/pf0000132262_eng

Ashe, T. (2013, October). How the Media Report Scientific Risk and Uncertainty: A Review of the Literature. *The Reuters Institute for the Study of Journalism*. Retrieved May 31, 2019, from www.reutersinstitute.politics.ox.ac.uk

Babaci-Wilhite, Z. (2013). Local Languages of Instruction as a Right in Education for Sustainable Development in Africa. *Sustainability*, 5, 1994–2017. https://doi.org/10.3390/su5051994

Bascompte, J., Garcia, M. B., Ortega, R., Rezende, E. L., & Pironon, S. (2019, May 15). Mutualistic Interactions Reshuffle the Effects of Climate Change on Plants Across the Tree of Life. *Science Advances*, 5(5). https://doi.org/10.1126/sciadv.aav2539

Blastland, M., & Spiegelhalter, D. (2013). *The Norm Chronicles: Stories and Numbers About Danger*. London: Profile Books.

Boyd-Barrett, O. (2008). News Agency Majors: Ownership, Control and Influence Reevaluated. *Journal of Global Mass Communication*, 1(1–2), 57–71.

Boykoff, T. (2008). The Cultural Politics of Climate Change Discourse in UK Tabloids. *Political Geography*, 27, 549–569.

Boykoff, T., & Boykoff, M. (2004). Balance as Bias: Global Warming and the US Prestige Press. *Global Environmental Change, 14*, 125–136.

Carvalho, A. (2007). Ideological Cultures and Media Discourses on Scientific Knowledge: Re-Reading News on Climate Change. *Public Understanding of Science, 16*(2), 223–243.

Castells, M., & Himanen, P. (2014). Introduction. In M. Castells & P. Himanen (Eds.), *Reconceptualizing Development in the Global Information Age* (pp. 1–4). Oxford: Oxford University Press.

Collomb, J.-D. (2014). The Ideology of Climate Change Denial in the United States, *European Journal of American Studies, 9*(1), document 5. https://doi.org/10.4000/ejas.10305

Corbett, J., & Durfee, J. (2004). Testing Public (Un)Certainty of Science: Media Representations of Global Warming. *Science Communication, 26*(2), 129–151.

Couldry, N., & Hepp, A. (2017). *The Mediated Construction of Reality*. Cambridge: Policy Press.

CRED (Center for Research on Environmental Decisions). (2009). *The Psychology of Climate Change Communication: A Guide for Scientists, Journalists, Educators, Political Aides and the Interested Public*. New York: Columbia University. Retrieved May 31, 2019, from http://guide.cred.columbia.edu/pdfs/CREDguide_full-res.pdf

Curry, A. (2013). *Environmental Crisis in Young Adult Fiction*. Houndmills: Palgrave.

Dispensa, J. M., & Brulle, R. J. (2003). Media's Social Construction of Environmental Issues: Focus on Global Warming – A Comparative Study. *International Journal of Sociology and Social Policy, 23*(10), 74–105.

Falk, R. (1991). International Law in a Fragmented World: The Challenge of New Issues and New Actors. In R. Väyrynen (Ed.), *New Directions in Conflict Theory: Conflict Resolution and Conflict Transformation* (pp. 79–107). Newbury Park: Sage.

Gallant, A. (2013). Self-Conscious Emotion: How Two Teachers Explore the Emotional Work of Teaching. *Advances in Research on Teaching, 18*, 163–181. https://doi.org/10.1108/S1479-3687(2013)0000018013

Good, J. (2017, September 18). Putting Hurricanes and Climate Change into the Same Frame. *The Star.*

Gore, A. (2007). *The Assault on Reason*. NY: Penguin Press.

Hepp, A., Breiter, A., & Hasebrink, U. (2018). *Communicating Figurations: Transforming Communications in Times of Deep Mediatization*. Basingstoke: Palgrave Macmillan.

Herman, E. S., & Chomsky, N. (2002). *Manufacturing Consent: The Political Economy of the Mass Media*. London: Pantheon.

Hertsgaard, M., & Pope, K. (2019, April 22). The Media Are Complacent While the World Burns. *Columbia Journalism Review*. Retrieved January 2, 2020, from https://www.cjr.org/special_report/climate-change-media.php

Hjarvard, S. (2008). The Mediatization of Religion: A Theory of the Media as Agents of Religious Change. *Northern Lights: Film & Media Studies Yearbook, 6*(1), 9–26(18). https://doi.org/10.1386/nl.6.1.9_1

Holtzman, L., & Sharpe, L. (2015). *Media Messages* (2nd ed.). New York: Routledge.

Horton, J. (1979). Stuart Hall, et al.: "Policing the Crisis: Mugging, the State, and Law and Order". Book review. *Crime and Social Justice*, (12), 59–63.

Isaac, R. J. (2012). *Roosters of the Apocalypse: How the Junk Science of Global Warming Nearly Bankrupted the Western World*. Chicago: Heartland Institute.

Jacquet, J., Dietrich, M., & Jost, J. (2014, December 18). The Ideological Divide and Climate Change Opinion: 'Top-Down and Bottom-Up Approaches'. *Frontiers in Psychology.* https://doi.org/10.3389/fpsyg.2014.01458

Jameson, F. (1991). *Postmodernism, or, the Cultural Logic of Capitalism.* Durham, NC: Duke University Press.

Jenkins, H. (2006). *Convergence Culture: Where Old and New Media Collide.* New York: New York University Press.

Johnstone, J. W. C., Slawski, E. J., & Bowman, W. W. (1972). The Professional Values of American Newsmen. *Public Opinion Quarterly, 36*(4), 522–540.

Johnstone, L., & Lindh, C. (2018). The Sustainability-Age Dilemma: A Theory of (Un)Planned Behaviour via Influencers. *Journal of Consumer Behaviour, 17*(1), 127–139. https://doi.org/10.1002/cb.1693

Kahan, D. M., Peters, E., Wittlin, M., Slovic, P., Ouellette, L. L., Braman, D., et al. (2012). The Polarizing Impact of Science Literacy and Numeracy on Perceived Climate Change Risks. *Nature Climate Change, 2,* 732–735.

Katz, E., & Foulkes, D. (1962). On the Use of the Mass Media as "Escape": Clarification of a Concept. *The Public Opinion Quarterly, 26*(3), 377–388.

Klein, N. (2014). *This Changes Everything: Capitalism vs. the Climate.* New York: Simon & Schuster.

Kolirin, L. (2020, April 16). 'The Trees Are My Grandparents': The Ecuador Tribe Trying to Save Its Culture. *The Guardian.* Retrieved April 19, 2020, from https://www.theguardian.com/world/2020/apr/16/the-trees-are-my-grandparents-the-ecuador-tribe-trying-to-save-its-culture?fbclid=IwAR1TzAIWkc7DM9SLgm_mcqRJA-BWBL0hTmHX48ulpKeiPy-S7IoV7ZebO3c

Krugman, P. (2020, January 2). Apocalypse Becomes the New Normal. *The New York Times.* Retrieved from https://www.nytimes.com/2020/01/02/opinion/climate-change-australia.html?smid=fb-nytimes&smtyp=cur&fbclid=IwAR2TPTj6XZ2FKYu1D9_k-TctQT9-MBOwnpD4j2p81TJDKBo88GRHkOXiXF8

Löwstedt, A. (1995). *Kultur oder Evolution? Eine Anthropologische Philosophie.* Frankfurt: Lang.

Löwstedt, A., & Mboti, N. (2017). Media Racism: Beyond Modernity and Postmodernity. In A. Löwstedt, M. Schwärzler-Brodesser & B. Wiggins (Eds.). *Power and Media: Ownership, Sponsorship, Censorship, Special Issue, International Journal of Media and Cultural Politics, 13*(1–2), 111–130.

Löwstedt, A., & Palac, J. (2019). Media and Other Biocultural Diversities. In K. Holtzmann, T. Hug, & G. Pallaver (Eds.), *Das Ende der Vielfalt? Zur Diversität der Medien* (pp. 19–34). Innsbruck: Innsbruck University Press.

Maeseele, P., & Pepermans, Y. (2017, April). Ideology in Climate Change Communication. *Oxford Research Encyclopaedias: Climate Science.* https://doi.org/10.1093/acrefore/9780190228620.013.578

Marcu, S. (2015, August). From the Marginal Immigrant to the Mobile Citizen. *Population Space and Place,* 506–517. https://doi.org/10.1002/psp.1845

Miller, D. (2003, December 29). Information Dominance: The Philosophy of Total Propaganda Control? *Scoop Independent News.* Retrieved May 31, 2019, from http://www.scoop.co.nz/stories/HL0312/S00216.htm

Mormont, M., & Dasnoy, C. (1995). Source Strategies and the Mediatization of Climate Change. *Media, Culture & Society, 17*(1), 49–64. https://doi.org/10.1177/016344395017001004

Norgaard, K. M. (2012, July 5). The Everyday Denial of Climate Change. *Bulletin of the Atomic Scientists*. Retrieved May 31, 2019, from https://thebulletin.org/2012/07/the-everyday-denial-of-climate-change/

Nuccitelli, D. (2017, November 29). New Study Uncovers the 'Keystone Domino' Strategy of Climate Denial. *The Guardian*.

O'Farrell, C. (2011). The Identity Game: Michael Foucault's Discourse-Mediated Identity as an Effective Tool of Achieving a Narrative-Based Ethic. *Foucault News*. Retrieved May 31, 2019, from https://michel-foucault.com/2012/02/04/the-identity-game-michel-foucaults-discourse-mediated-identity-as-an-effective-tool-for-achieving-a-narrative-based-ethic-2011/

Olausson, U. (2009, January 21). Global Warming–Global Responsibility? Media Frames of Collective Action and Scientific Certainty. *Public Understanding of Science, 18*(4), 421–436. https://doi.org/10.1177/0963662507081242

Osterath, B. (2015, October 29). No, It Is True That Meat Causes Cancer. *Deutsche Welle*. Retrieved May 31, 2019, from https://www.dw.com/en/no-it-is-true-that-meat-causes-cancer/a-18814721

Pariser, E. (2011). *The Filter Bubble: What the Internet Is Hiding from You*. London: Penguin.

Parker, L. (2018, June). We Made Plastic. We Depend on It. Now We're Drowning in It. *National Geographic*. Retrieved May 31, 2019, from https://www.nationalgeographic.com/magazine/2018/06/plastic-planet-waste-pollution-trash-crisis/

Payne, G. A. (2008). Structural and Social Forces Restricting Media News Content in Democracies: A Critical Perspective. *Journal of Humanities and Social Sciences, 2*(1).

Perkins, J. (2015, June 18). Mitigation Measures: Beware Climate Neo-Scepticism. *Nature, 522*(287).

Picard, P. G., & Yeo, M. (2011, December). Medical and Health News and Information in the UK Media: The Current State of Knowledge. *Reuters Institute for the Study of Journalism*. Retrieved May 31, 2019, from https://reutersinstitute.politics.ox.ac.uk/sites/default/files/2017-11/Media%20and%20UK%20Health.pdf

Pidgeon, N. (2012). Climate Change Risk Perception and Communication: Addressing a Critical Moment? *Risk Analysis, 32*(6), 951–956.

Ropeik, D. (2012). The Perception Gap: Recognizing and Managing the Risks That Arise When We Get Risk Wrong. *Food and Chemical Toxicology, 50*(5), 1222–1225.

Sandman, P. M. (1988). Telling Reporters About Risk. *Civil Engineering–ASCE, 58*(8), 36–38.

SAPEA. (2019, January 21). *A Scientific Perspective on Microplastics in Nature and Society*. Berlin: Science Advice for Policy by European Academies. Retrieved April 25, 2020, from https://www.sapea.info/wp-content/uploads/report-printable.pdf

Sardar, Z. (1998). *Postmodernism and the Other: The New Imperialism of Western Culture*. London: Pluto.

Sheppard, S. (2012). *Visualizing Climate Change: A Guide to Visual Communication of Climate Change*. New York: Routledge.

Smith, J. (2005). Dangerous News: Media Decision Making About Climate Change Risk. *Risk Analysis, 25*(6), 1471–1482.

Stankorb, S. (2016, March 22). Climate Fiction, or 'Cli-Fi,' Is the Hottest New Literary Genre. *Good*. Retrieved May 31, 2019, from https://www.good.is/articles/climate-fiction-cli-fi-genre

Stern, P., Perkins, J., Sparks, R., & Knox, R. A. (2016). The Challenge of Climate-Change Neoskepticism. *Science, 353*, 653–654. https://doi.org/10.1126/science.aaf6675

U.N. (2015a). Sustainable Development Goals. *Sustainable Development Goals.* Retrieved May 31, 2019, from https://sustainabledevelopment.un.org/?menu=1300

U.N. (2015b) Goal 12: Ensure Sustainable Consumption and Production Patterns. *Sustainable Development Goals.* Retrieved May 31, 2019, from https://www.un.org/sustainabledevelopment/sustainable-consumption-production/

U.N. (2019). About the SDGs Media Compact. *Sustainable Development Goals.* Retrieved May 31, 2019, from https://www.un.org/sustainabledevelopment/sdg-media-compact-about/

U.N.E.P. (2019). United Nations Environment Programme. *Instagram.* Retrieved May 31, 2019, from https://www.instagram.com/unenvironment/?hl=el

Verlie, B. (2019, March 14). The Terror of Climate Change Is Transforming Young People's Identity. *The Conversation.* Retrieved May 31, 2019, from https://theconversation.com/the-terror-of-climate-change-is-transforming-young-peoples-identity-113355

Waldman, K. (2018, November 9). How Climate-Change Fiction, or "Cli-Fi," Forces Us to Confront the Incipient Death of the Planet. *The New Yorker.* Retrieved May 31, 2019, from https://www.newyorker.com/books/page-turner/how-climate-change-fiction-or-cli-fi-forces-us-to-confront-the-incipient-death-of-the-planet

Ward, A. (2018, September 25). Read Trump's Speech to the UN General Assembly: "We Reject the Ideology of Globalism and Accept the Doctrine of Patriotism." *Vox.* Retrieved May 31, 2019, from https://www.vox.com/2018/9/25/17901082/trump-un-2018-speech-full-text

Wendel, L. (2016, August 11). Climate Scientists' New Hurdle: Overcoming Climate Change Apathy. *EOS: Earth and Space Science News.* Retrieved May 31, 2019, from https://eos.org/articles/climate-scientists-new-hurdle-overcoming-climate-change-apathy

Wrabetz, A. (2017). Do We Need Public Service Broadcasters? On the Increasing Significance of Public Service Media in the Digital Age. In A. Löwstedt, M. Schwärzler-Brodesser, & B. Wiggins (Eds.). *Power and Media: Ownership, Sponsorship, Censorship, Special Issue, International Journal of Media and Cultural Politics, 13*(1–2), 179–182.

CHAPTER 7

Islamic Finance for SDGs: A Mirage?

Hylmun Izhar and Rahmatina A. Kasri

INTRODUCTION

The world we live in today is without a doubt encountered with omnipresent challenges of poverty, social inequality and environmental adversities that cannot be taken lightly. The 2030 Agenda for Sustainable Development, hence, envisages a revitalized global and unconventional partnership for sustainable development to address such challenges.

The scale and ambition of the 2030 Agenda for Sustainable Development, adopted in 2015, as embodied in the 17 SDGs, call for financial and technical resources, estimated at US $5–$7 trillion, that are far beyond the scope of individual governments and of the multilateral funding agencies. Private sector funding, capabilities and know-how need to be mobilized to sustain the new development agenda, the Global Partnership for Sustainable Development, operationalize the policies and actions outlined in the Addis Ababa Action Agenda and end poverty within a generation.

H. Izhar (✉)
Islamic Development Bank Institute, Islamic Development Bank Group, Jeddah, Saudi Arabia
e-mail: hizhar@isdb.org

R. A. Kasri
Islamic Economics and Business Center (PEBS), Faculty of Economics and Business, Universitas Indonesia, Jakarta, Indonesia
e-mail: rahmatina@ui.ac.id

© The Author(s), under exclusive license to Springer Nature Switzerland AG 2021
M. J. Yusha'u, J. Servaes (eds.), *The Palgrave Handbook of International Communication and Sustainable Development*,
https://doi.org/10.1007/978-3-030-69770-9_7

As reported by State of the Global Islamic Economy Report 2019/2020: Driving the Islamic Economy Revolution 4.0, the Islamic financial services industry was estimated to be worth US $2.5 trillion in 2018 and forecast to reach US $3.2 trillion by 2024[1] which represents a strong potential source of financing the SDGs, fostering development and helping to end poverty. Although Organisation of Islamic Cooperation (OIC) member countries account for 22% of the world population, they house 40% of the world's poor who live on US $1.25 a day or less. Reaching more of those at the bottom of the pyramid by deepening and widening the range of Islamic financing solutions, on offer, especially microfinancing products, would be a major contribution to the 2030 Agenda.

With their rigorous moral and social criteria, their emphasis on inclusiveness and broader understanding of business-society relations, the principles of Islamic finance and SDGs could complement each other. These similarities suggest that bridging the two sectors offers a promising avenue to respond effectively to the growing challenges related to development financing through collaboration, cross-learning and reaching new markets.

The analysis of this chapter is structured as follows: section "Islamic Finance and SDGs" briefly discusses about the alignment of Islamic finance and SDGs, while section "State of Islamic Financial Services Industry (IFSI)" sketches up the states of Islamic financial services industry (IFSI). Incoherent communications emanating from varying degree of preferences among key stakeholders in Islamic finance are addressed in section "Incoherent Communications Emanating from Varying Degree of Preferences Among Key Stakeholders in Islamic Finance". Section "Islamic Finance's Outlook" sheds some light on the outlook of Islamic financial services industry. Section "The Shifting Look of Islamic Finance" analytically investigates the shifting look of Islamic finance over the past few decades. Before the conclusion, section "Can Islamic Finance Help in Achieving SDG 1 and SDG 10? Lessons Learnt from Indonesia" addresses the success story of Indonesia in achieving SDG1 and SDG10 through Islamic social financial instruments.

Islamic Finance and SDGs

Islamic financial institutions have historically been reluctant to look beyond a compliance perspective. A shift to an impact-driven approach with a focus on the objectives of the Sharī'ah would certainly enhance their market outreach and depth. At the same time, this would provide them with an opportunity to participate in the UN-mandated development agenda as responsible global actors. This however requires an enhanced level of awareness about the alignment or otherwise of the objectives (*maqasid*) of the Sharī'ah on one hand, and the development goals of the global community, captured in the SDGs, on the other.

---

[1] State of the Global Islamic Economy Report 2019/2020: Driving the Islamic Economy Revolution 4.0, p. 3.

The Sustainable Development Goals framework reflects the consensus among the global community of policy-makers on major challenges confronting humanity. It sets the direction in which all resources will be channelized over the next decade-and-half with clear targets to be achieved by the year 2030. Adopted by all United Nations member states in 2015, the framework includes 17 SDGs that provide a shared blueprint for peace and prosperity for people and the planet, now and into the future. These are (1) no poverty, (2) zero hunger, (3) good health and well-being, (4) quality education, (5) gender equality, (6) clean water and sanitation, (7) affordable and clean energy, (8) decent work and economic growth, (9) industry, innovation and infrastructure, (10) reducing inequality, (11) sustainable cities and communities, (12) responsible consumption and production, (13) climate action, (14) life below water, (15) life on land, (16) peace, justice and strong institutions and (17) partnerships for the goals.

Since the religion of Islam sets the agenda for development in predominantly Muslim societies, it is not difficult to capture why the principles of Islamic finance are aligned with the SDGs in so many ways. In order to explain the Islamic vision of development, Muslim scholars have come up with a broad framework rooted in what are called the Goals or the *maqasid* of the Sharī'ah; some would also call it Higher Objectives of Sharīʿah (HoS). HoS, as originally presented by the twelfth-century Islamic scholar Al-Ghazzali, are broadly discussed in five categories: protection and enrichment of faith (*din*), self (*nafs*), intellect (*aql*), progeny (*nasl*) and property (*maal*). The deliberation of *maqasid al sharīʿah*, however, is beyond the scope of this article.

STATE OF ISLAMIC FINANCIAL SERVICES INDUSTRY (IFSI)

The central pillars of global financial system have endured a persistent scrutiny in the wake of the continuous changing international economic and political environment. Islamic financial institutions are demonstrating resilience as the world events continue to reshape the landscape of global financial services. The key matter, however, will be the way through which IFSI prepares itself for the opportunities and challenges posed by such a changing global economy. IFSI has demonstrated a remarkable growth, outpacing the growth of its conventional counterparts. The growth in 2019 recorded a y-o-y growth rate of 11.4% compared to the 9.6% growth rate recorded between 2017 and 2018 (The IFSB Stability Report, 2020: 4).[2] Such data are based on disclosed assets by all Islamic finance institutions (full Sharīʿah-compliant as well as those with Sharīʿah "windows") covering commercial banking, funds, *Ṣukūk*, *takāful* and other segments. The IFSB Stability Report 2020 indicates that the breakdown of IFSI by sector can be depicted as follows (Table 7.1).

Data are mostly taken from primary sources (regulatory authorities' statistical databases, annual reports and financial stability reports, official press releases

[2] The IFSB Stability Report 2020, p. 4.

Table 7.1 Breakdown of the Global IFSI by sector and region (US$ billion, 2019)

Region	Banking assets	Ṣukūk outstanding	Islamic funds assets	Takāful contributions	Total	Share %
GCC	854.0	204.5	36.4	11.7	1106.6	45.4%
South-East Asia	240.5	303.3	26.7	3.02	573.5	23.5%
Middle East and South Asia (MESA)	584.3	19.1	16.5	11.36	631.3	25.9%
Africa	33.9	1.8	1.6	0.55	37.9	1.6%
Others	53.1	14.7	21.1	0.44	89.3	3.7%
Total	1765.8	543.4	102.3	27.07	2438.6	100.00%
Share	72.4%	22.3%	4.2%	1.1%	100.0%	

Source: IFSB Stability Report 2020

including the IFSB's prudential and structural Islamic Financial Indicators Database). And for the purpose of regional classification, other than the GCC and Southeast Asian region, a new classification—Middle East and South Asia (MESA)—is used to capture other jurisdictions in Asia. The African region now includes both North Africa and sub-Saharan Africa. Jurisdictions not belonging to any of the four regions are classified as "Others", specifically countries located in Europe, North America, South America and Central Asia regions.

The total worth of the IFSI across its three main segments (banking, capital markets and *takāful*) is estimated at US $2.44 trillion in 2019 marking a y-o-y 11.4% growth in assets in US dollar terms (2018: US $2.19 trillion). All segments contributed to the increased total worth of the global IFSI; however, the key rebound in performance was experienced by the Islamic capital markets and the Islamic banking segments, with steady growth in the prominent Islamic banking jurisdictions as well as emerging countries. The overall growth was achieved despite the heightened uncertainties within the global economic landscape and negative sentiments in the financial market space.

The *ṣukūk* sector ended 2019 with a total *ṣukūk* outstanding worth of US $543.4 billion (2018: US $444.8 billion), thus recording a y-o-y growth of 22.2%. In isolation, the *ṣukūk* sector accounts for 22.3% of global IFSI worth and recorded significant expansion in 2019, bringing its compound annual growth rate (CAGR) over the last 15 years (from 2004 to 2019) to 26%. The expansion recorded in 2019 was due mainly to the strong sovereign and multilateral issuances in key Islamic finance markets aimed at supporting government spending and environmental preservation initiatives, among other reasons. In addition, corporate *ṣukūk* issuances also recorded significant expansion in 2019 in prominent Islamic banking jurisdictions.

The Islamic equity markets also bounced back from the effects of a steep sell-off in December 2018 to a remarkable double-digit growth performance across numerous sectors in 2019, thus recording its strongest performance since the GFC. One likely explanation for such a significant rebound in performance could be the relatively higher exposure of the Islamic indices to the technology sector, which recorded an outstanding performance in 2019. Islamic funds, on the other hand, are still faced with the issues of being largely concentrated and having lack of scale.

Notwithstanding, the sector also recorded noteworthy performance in 2019 in terms of both value of AuM of Islamic funds which grew by 29.8% y-o-y to close at US $102.3 billion at end of 2019 (2018: US $67.1 billion), and the number of Islamic funds, which increased to 1545 (2018: 1489) and grew by 3.8% y-o-y in 2019.

On the basis of the performance of the *ṣukūk*, Islamic equities and Islamic fund sectors in 2019, the Islamic capital market (ICM) segment of the IFSI now accounts for a 26.5% share of global IFSI assets. Over the past three years—from 2016 to 2019—the sector had recorded an increasing share of global IFSI assets at the expense of the Islamic banking segment, which also regained momentum in 2019. The ICM remains a key and viable component of the global IFSI.

In contrast, the growth rate of gross contributions of the global *takāful* industry contracted by 1.1% from 4.3% in 2017 to 3.2% at end of 2018 to close at US $27.07 billion (2017: US $26.23 billion). This resulted in a decrease in the segment's market share in the global IFSI to 1.1% at end of 2018 (2017: 1.3%). Nonetheless, the *takāful* segment recorded a CAGR of 8.5% over the period 2011–2018. Despite its huge potential, the segment still faces a high concentration in key markets and in the general line of business.

The global Islamic banking segment in 2019 experienced an improvement of y-o-y assets growth by 12.7% (2018: 0.9%), with total assets in 3Q19 amounting to US $1.77 trillion (2Q18: US $1.57 trillion). The growth recorded is due to an improvement in the Islamic banking assets in some jurisdictions, especially the GCC region which witnessed significant mergers of Islamic banks to strengthen competitiveness, attract stable deposits and enhance efficiency. The impact of the exchange rate on the nominal assets of the Islamic banking segment in the particular period of reporting has been minimal, compared to the situation reported in 2Q18. Nonetheless, the Islamic banking segment recorded a three-year continuous decline in its share of global IFSI worth, to 72.4% (2Q18: 76.0%), especially as the ICM sector sustained momentum.

Regionally, the GCC retained its position as the largest domicile for Islamic finance assets in 2019; the region experienced a modest increase in its share in global Islamic banking assets to 45.4%. This is followed by the share of the MESA region with 25.9% of global IFSI assets. The Southeast Asian region ranks next with 23.5%, while Africa ranks least with a share of 1.6% of global IFSI assets.

Overall, the global IFSI is well placed to maintain its positive growth trajectory, experiencing asset increases across all three of its main component markets. However, given the continued prevalence of possible downside risks, as well as emerging developments such as the COVID-19 issue, global growth projections for 2020 may have to be revised downwards. The pervasiveness of and speed with which COVID-19 is spreading has affected the global economy through disruptions to both domestic and international trade, travel, supply chains and production linkages.

Incoherent Communications Emanating from Varying Degree of Preferences Among Key Stakeholders in Islamic Finance

Why does there seem to be a different tone, "language" or even ways of communications among the stakeholders in Islamic financial services industry (IFSI)? In order to address this matter, let us first of all revisit how the preferences of stakeholders in IFSI have evolved over time.[3] Using a microeconomic analysis, as shown in Fig. 7.1a, he portrays the indifference curves of *fuqaha* (jurists) that are assumed to be geared towards equity (*al-'adl*) relative to the weight given to considerations of economic efficiency (*al-kafa'a al-iqtisadiyya*). El Gamal contends that such indifference curves by jurists are based on the manifestations of their understanding of the objectives of Islamic law (*maqasid al-sharī'ah*) (El Gamal, 2000: 7). In contrast, it is assumed that the preferences of bankers are more biased towards considerations of efficiency relative to those of Islamic jurists. Hence, the latter preferences are drawn more vertical than the former.

The nature of different preferences between jurists and bankers are clearly depicted in Fig. 7.1a which shows two axes, labelled "efficiency" and "equity", reflecting the trade-offs in any economic system between efficiency (the size of the economic pie to be shared by economic agents) and equity (how justly, and how equally, the pie shares are determined). Another element in Figs. 7.1a and

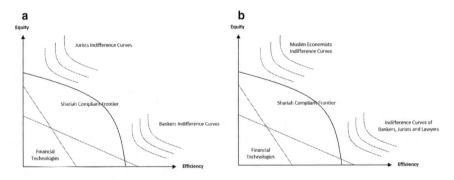

Fig. 7.1 Indifference curve of IBF stakeholders

---

[3] El Gamal, Mahmoud A., "The Economics of 21st Century Islamic Jurisprudence", in *Proceedings of the Fourth Harvard University Forum on Islamic Finance: Islamic Finance: The Task Ahead*, Harvard University, 2000, p. 7.

b is the financial technologies that render certain types of contracts and transactions feasible. Each technology allows for linear trade-offs between efficiency and equity by simply allowing for redistribution schemes. The Sharī'ah boundary, namely Sharī'ah Compliant Frontier, is drawn as a convex set. This is to signify the Islamically permissible set of allocations within the frontier.

While El Gamal's analysis is insightful at the time, such a delineation may no longer reflect the current preferences of IFSI stakeholders. We would argue that the jurists have become more pragmatic in their approach; therefore, their indifference curves, we believe, have shifted towards more efficiency (see Fig. 7.1b). What makes things more interesting now is that the bulk of indifference curves located at the Southeast region of Fig. 7.1b does not only correspond to jurists, but also denotes the preferences of bankers and lawyers. The explanation is very simple and straightforward: the bankers need Sharī'ah scholars (who also are the employees of the banks) to endorse their products; subsequently they will need lawyers to make the products legal so that they can be offered in the market. Moreover, since financial technology evolved, in response to the secular financial needs of economies worldwide, it tends to cater to the banker, jurists and lawyers preferences, thus producing the status quo tangency point Q in the southeast part of the figure, which affords society a high level of economic efficiency, at the expense of low levels of equity (see Fig. 7.2).

The Muslim economists, in contrast, who are now known as being more concerned about the realization of *maqasid al sharī'ah*, aim to describe and analyse the point that is optimal to Islamic economics and finance, that is the tangency point E in the Northwest region (shown in Fig. 7.2).

Nonetheless, recognizing the difficulties surrounding the development of a financial technology that passes through the ideal point E, Muslim economists may compromise by turning to point D, at which the preferences are

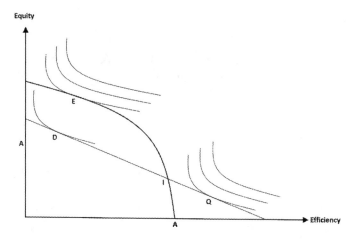

Fig. 7.2 Optimal preferences

maximized subject to the current financial technologies constraints, although this point can easily be viewed by as socially inefficient.

Point I, located at the intersection of the current financial technology and the permissibility frontier, is perhaps closer to the current reality of IFSI as it may be relatively easy to accomplish. This is due to the increasingly prominent role of Sharī'ah scholars in driving the era of Islamic financial engineering.

Thus, it is rather obvious now that coherent initiatives in the development communications have to be solidly put in place to ensure that sharing of knowledge aimed at reaching a consensus for action that takes into account the interests, needs and capacities of all concerned stakeholders can be well aligned (Servaes, 2008: 15).[4]

Islamic Finance's Outlook

Many are of the view that the industrialization of Islamic finance commenced with an establishment of Islamic banks in the mid-1970s. In the earlier stage, the operationalization of Islamic banks was underpinned by the principle of two-tier mudaraba—that is, on the liabilities side of the balance sheet, the depositor would be the financier and the bank the entrepreneur; and on the assets side, the bank would be the financier and the person seeking funding for the entrepreneur. Currently, however, the bulk of assets and liabilities is predominantly under murabaha modes of finance. Following is "a four-stage evolution", that is composed of four distinct phases: (1) the early years (1975–1991); (2) the era of globalization (1991–2001); (3) the post-September 11, 2001 period; and (4) an era after the 2008 global financial crisis;

In spite of an impressive progress of the industry for the last few years, particularly prior to the COVID-19 pandemic, the outlook of Islamic finance industry is characterized by the following (Izhar, et.al, 2018: 89-106).[5]

Considerably Higher Cost of Transactions

Higher cost of transactions is indeed one of the major unresolved issues in IF industry. Some would say that this happens due to the economies of scale that the industry has not yet attained. Others might contend that the problem arises because of lack of legal and regulatory harmonization which contributed to an uneven playing field leading to higher cost of transactions in Islamic financial products. Notwithstanding such arguments, this requires a solid solution, particularly in the area of home financing which is considerably ubiquitous in many Muslim countries and also for the Muslim communities living in non-Muslim countries.

---

[4] The definition of communication development is adopted from Servaes, Jan, "Communication for Development and Social Change", 2008, p. 15.

[5] Izhar, Hylmun et al., "Islamic Finance in a Global Economic Context", in *Global Islamic Finance Report* 2018, p. 89–106.

Limited Options of Risk Management Instruments, Mitigation Techniques and Quantitative Measurement Models

Despite the prominent initiatives by the Islamic Financial Services Board (IFSB) in issuing guidelines relating to risk management, stress testing and capital adequacy standard, a more detailed technical guidance which features the techniques and methodologies of risk assessment taking into account unique risks in IFIs is still required. Furthermore, it was also commonly understood that whilst the definition of risks in IFIs is not substantially different from the ones in their conventional counterparts, a modification in the identification, measurement and mitigation of risks may be required due to some Sharī'ah principles. More importantly, there is a dire need to develop a proper legal environment and suitable regulatory framework for sound practice of risk management in IFIs. In addition, a limited liquidity instrument for Islamic capital markets is another challenge. In response to this, recently, International Islamic Liquidity Management (IILM) has successfully launched "Golden Triangle Ṣukūk" featuring a connection between financial stability, economic development and debt management.

Restricted Legal and Regulatory Framework

A daunting task for the IF industry stakeholders is not only to establish regulatory harmonization between different jurisdictions, but also to conform to the standards and guidance set out by international standard setting bodies such as BCBS, IOSCO and IFRS. Surely, the idea of "one-size-fits-all" is not viable due to the fact that different countries have different institutional and regulatory frameworks.

Lack of Islamic Monetary Policies

At the macro level, the availability of Islamic monetary instruments is indispensable to support the macroeconomic objectives of the Islamic financial system. Another important element of such an instrument is for the purpose of liquidity management. Some countries have initiated the creation of such instruments, such as in Indonesia and Malaysia. However, more efforts need to be undertaken to also allow inter-jurisdictional transactions and liquidity management between the countries implementing interest-free financial system.

Financial Inclusion Gap

Financial inclusion is a concept that gained its importance since the early 2000s, which initially referred to the delivery of financial services to low-income segments of society at affordable cost. However, two distinct features which characterize the concept of financial inclusion from an Islamic perspective are twofold: (a) the notions of risk-sharing and (b) redistribution of wealth

(Mohieldin et al., 2012). Although there is a strong demand for Islamic microfinance services in OIC countries, it is, nevertheless, not met by the supply. A study by Mohieldin et al. (2010) shows that although OIC countries have more microfinance deposits and accounts per thousand adults as compared to non-OIC countries, the values of MFI deposits and loans as percentage of GDP are still much lower in OIC countries (0.61% and 0.79%) compared with developing countries (0.78% and 0.97%) and low-income countries (0.92% and 1.19%). The gap of microfinance in OIC is not only demonstrated by its limited scope, but also by the lack of regulation in OIC countries compared to other developing countries. In MENA region for example, only Egypt, Morocco, Syria, Tunisia and Yemen have specific legislation for microfinance institutions.

Disjointed alignment between industry needs and educational provision

The continuing growth and intensified competition among market players in IF industry has certainly posed quantitative and qualitative human resource problems for the industry. It does not come as a surprise, therefore, that IF industry needs more and better-qualified personnel. However, there is a ubiquitous inverse relationship between a growing number of Islamic finance education programs with the level of absorption of Islamic finance graduates in the job market. One observatory answer could be as follows: although the IF industry has expanded its presence across the globe in a quite great deal, its institutional logic hasn't fundamentally changed; namely it is still essentially a debt creating institution rather than an equitybased stimulating institution, which implies that the skillset and manpower required to manage such debt-creating institutions, consequently, are not fundamentally different than the required skillsets to manage the conventional counterparts. In other words, the need of having Islamic economics informed 'Islamic finance specialists' with a good grasp of Sharī'ah related contractual matters, governance, and fiqh-based financial engineering is not necessarily relevant. As a matter of fact, most of the personnel of the banks and capital markets are just obligated to execute what has been prescribed by the verdict of the respective Sharī'ah boards.

Perceptions About Islamic Finance

Many still think that Islamic finance is basically an industry designed by Muslims and offered to solely Muslims market. Although it appears to be partially the case, nonetheless, the key spirit of Islamic finance is a lot more profound than what has been stated. As a matter a fact, take an example of interest (*riba*) prohibition; it is shared with Judaism and Christianity. It is also interesting to note that charging interest is also prohibited in Buddhism, Hinduism and many other faiths and philosophies.

The Shifting Look of Islamic Finance

Nowadays, where the innovations are characterized by the use of artificial intelligence (AI), fintech and internet of things (IoT), or collectively known as the Fourth Industrial Revolution, Islamic finance, being in its fifth phase of development, is encountered with the situations where such innovations are creating substantial displacements in industry and employment in major economies around the globe.

It is imperative, therefore, that Islamic finance has no other choice but to change. Furthermore, there is also a genuine demand and opportunity to redirect innovations towards services and products that create more economic opportunities, jobs and financial inclusion for those who have been on the sidelines of the Islamic finance revolution. Coincidentally, we are witnessing the propagation of Environmental, Social and Governance (ESG) discourse, which refers to the three central factors in measuring the sustainability and ethical impact of an investment in a company or business, combined with proliferation of the immense potential of Islamic social finance. The terminology "Islamic Social Finance" itself was only prominently introduced in 2014 by Islamic Research and Training Institute through its Islamic Social Finance Report (IRTI ISFR, 2014).[6]

A change in the look and direction in the industry is needed. Malaysia's recent movement of Value-Based Intermediation in Islamic finance can be considered as evidence of such change. Another one is the issuance of Khazanah sustainable and responsible investment (SRI) ṣukūk. Waqf-linked ṣukūk is another breakthrough championed by the Ministry of Finance of Indonesia in partnership with Badan Wakaf Indonesia (BWI) and Bank Indonesia.

It is becoming apparent that the drivers of the change now are no longer driven by an entirely profit-geared motive; rather it emphasizes upon creating social and environmental impact. In other words, it is an admission that that the deviations caused by the operation of Islamic finance in relation to the expected or aspired paradigmatic knowledge, theory and institutional emergence have to be corrected. One way to do that is through the introduction of ESG, impact investing and Islamic social finance.

More importantly, in the wake of the Industrial Revolution 4.0, which is somewhat synonymous with the use of technology and digitalization, we could perhaps hope it would pave the way for Islamic finance to be more appealing for not only its inclusivity but also for the universality of its fundamental principles as an ethical, socially responsible and fair system of finance not just for Muslims but for the whole world.

---

[6] IRTI, *Islamic Social Finance Report*, Islamic Research and Training Institute, (2014).

Can Islamic Finance Help in Achieving SDG1 and SDG10? Lessons Learnt from Indonesia

Indonesia is one of the largest Muslim country worldwide in which around 87% of its 269.6 million population are Muslim. In the past few years, Indonesia has enjoyed a relatively moderate economic growth with the growth rate between 4% and 5% annually. Consistent with this, poverty has also decreased significantly. In the past 10 years, the poverty level has decreased from 13.3% in 2010 to 9.22% in 2019 (Fig. 7.3) (Kasri, 2020).[7]

The past few years have also witnessed promising development of Islamic finance in Indonesia. Data from the Indonesia Financial Services Authority shows that Islamic banking assets grew from 304 trillion rupiah in 2015 to 503.73 trillion rupiah in 2019. This is equivalent to growth rate of 13.6% annually. Similarly, assets of non-banking financial institutions (Islamic insurance, Islamic venture capital, ṣukūk, etc.) also increased by 13.31%. Meanwhile, Islamic capital market enjoys the highest growth of around 26.27% from 318.5 trillion rupiah in 2015 to 801.15 trillion rupiah in 2019. Overall, the market share of Islamic finance in Indonesia accounted to 8.87% in 2019 (Fig. 7.4).[8]

Seminal Role of Islamic Social Finance Instruments

Institutional development in the Islamic financial services industry has taken place at different levels. The industry has achieved its current level of

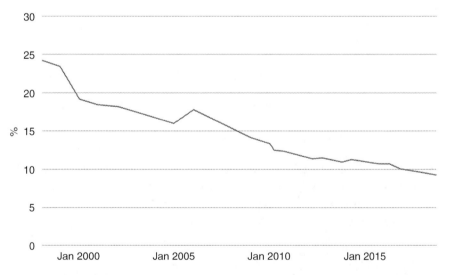

Fig. 7.3 Poverty levels in Indonesia, 1998–2019. (*Source*: BPS 2020 (in Kasri, 2020))

---

[7] In Kasri, Rahmatina Awaliah, *The Impact of COVID-19 on Islamic Finance in Indonesia*, Presentation at FEB UI, 12 May 2020.
[8] Ibid.

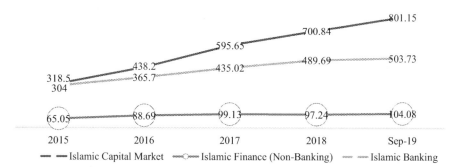

Fig. 7.4 Development of Islamic finance in Indonesia, 2015–2019. (*Source*: in Kasri, 2020)

development through the efforts from mainly profit-geared institutions. One sector that is often overlooked but carries immense potential is Islamic social finance that is proven more resilient and in fact can help in achieving greater financial inclusion. This is due to the fact that the institutions in Islamic social finance require no "regulatory capital" formation as such and therefore operate under fewer constraints than profit-seeking institutions, such as Islamic banks.

Furthermore, the Islamic social finance sector that broadly comprises the traditional Islamic institutions based on philanthropy, for example *zakat*, *sadaqah*, *waqf* and contemporary Islamic not-for-profit microfinance institutions,[9] has huge potential to serve clients that are not "bankable". Since the institutions' formation inherited from Islamic tradition, the way they operate is also subject to a set of Sharī'ah principles that must be adhered to at all times. In addition to this, their financial sustainability should also be maintained in order to ensure that their benefits and impact could run across the next generation.

Development of Islamic social finance in Indonesia, notably zakat and waqf, shows improvement over time. According to *Indonesia Zakat Outlook 2020* published by the National Zakat Board (BAZNAS), the amount of zakat collected has increased from 6.2 trillion rupiah in 2017 to 8.1 trillion rupiah in 2019. Similarly, the amount of zakat fund disbursed has increased from 4.9 trillion rupiah to 6.8 trillion rupiah from 2017 to 2018 (Baznas, 2019).[10] BAZNAS also reported that around 75% of the zakat funds were distributed to the poor and needy, while the rest were distributed to other five groups of zakat recipients or mustahik (see Table 7.2).[11] From the data, it can be inferred that the rate of zakat utilization has increased from around 78% in 2017 to around 84% in 2018. Therefore, it could be suggested that the rates as well as effectiveness of zakat has improved significantly in Indonesia.

---

[9] The definition of Islamic social finance is adopted from IRTI Islamic Social Finance Report 2014 and 2015.
[10] BAZNAS, Outlook Zakat Indonesia 2020, (2019).
[11] Ibid.

Table 7.2 Distribution of Zakat based on types of recipient, 2017–2018

No.	Asnaf	2017	%	2018	%
1	Fakir Miskin	3,356,325,642,451	69.06	2,459,628,416,537	63.3
2	Amil	518,647,467,254	10.67	440,536,648,274	11.34
3	Muallaf	97,156,889,988	2	17,061,510,766	0.44
4	Riqob	21,827,062,720	0.45	1,478,837,467	0.04
5	Gharimin	40,772,744,732	0.84	32,875,372,661	0.85
6	Fi Sabilillah	755,062,496,814	15.54	896,893,187,209	23.08
7	Ibnu Sabil	70,363,020,484	1.45	37,156,093,806	0.96
	Sub Total	**4,860,155,324,445**	**100**	**3,885,630,066,721**	**100**

Source: Puskas BAZNAS 2020

Unlike zakat, waqf is relatively underdeveloped in Indonesia albeit in the last few years some promising development has happened. Based on the data from the Waqf Information System (SIWAK) of the Ministry of Religion Affairs of Indonesia, as of June 2020, waqf land in Indonesia was 51,807 hectares which spread over in 383,490 locations.[12] However, only around 61% of the waqf land has waqf certificate. In terms of usage, around 72.76% of the waqf land is used for mosques/musolla, 14.19% for general and Islamic schools, 4.45% for Islamic cemetery and the rest 8.61% for other social purposes. These imply that the usage of waqf in Indonesia is mostly for traditional purposes. Utilization of waqf for social purposes, such as for building medical clinics/hospital and stores, is rarely found, albeit in the last few years there has been some plans to use waqf land for social purposes which have higher economic value added.

As the Indonesian government is committed to implementing the SDGs, Islamic financial sector is also directed to contribute in achieving the SDGs. In this respect, one of the Islamic financial institutions that has contributed positively in reducing poverty and inequality in Indonesia, and hence contributing to achieving SDG1 and SDG10, is zakat institution. Zakat is an important part of Islamic commercial finance whose primary aim is to help the poor and needy, as directed in the Qur'an. In a broader sense, zakat also aimed to ensure social justice and society's welfare (Kasri, 2016).[13] Another institution that might contribute to achieving SDG1 and SDG10 is Islamic microfinance institution. Both will be elaborated in the following section.

Addressing SDG1 and SDG10 Through Islamic Social Finance Instruments

The zakat management in Indonesia is regulated under Law No 23/2011. Under the law, Indonesia is regarded as adopting a voluntary zakat system, in which zakat payers could pay zakat through various channels, including direct payments to mustahik and indirect payments through zakat organizations. The

---

[12] http://siwak.kemenag.go.id/, Accessed on 26 June 2020.
[13] Kasri, Rahmatina Awaliah, *Effectiveness of Zakat Targeting in Alleviating Poverty in Indonesia*, Al-Iqtisad: Journal of Islamic Economics, 8 (2), (2016) pp. 169–186.

law also outlined that there are two types of zakat institutions in Indonesia, namely the National Amil Zakat Agency (BAZNAS), which is a government zakat institution, and the Amil Zakat Institute (LAZ), which is a nongovernment (private) zakat institution. By 2019, there is one BAZNAS at the national level, 34 BAZNAS at provincial level and 514 BAZNAS at district/city level. Meanwhile, there are 23 national LAZ, 12 provincial LAZ and 33 district/city LAZ (PEBS FEUI Indonesia Sharia Economic Outlook 2020, 2019).[14]

A number of studies documented the positive impact of zakat in reducing poverty and inequality in Indonesia. A study of Kasri (2016) found that the incidence, depth and severity of poverty amongst zakat recipients in Indonesia have decreased due to the contributions of zakat. The empirical study which was conducted on 685 zakat recipients in Greater Jakarta area, which comprises the capital of Indonesia and its surrounding cities, found that the proportions of poor household have decreased from 0.638 (without zakat) to 0.550 (with zakat). This implies an 8.76% decrease in the poverty headcount index amongst the zakat recipient households. It was also estimated that poverty gap, poverty gap index and poverty severity index have been reduced by 18.33%, 4.71% and 3.34%, respectively. These suggested that inequality has also decreased due to the zakat contributions. Moreover, it was found that the average time to exit poverty has decreased from 9.9 years (without zakat) to 9.4 years (with zakat). Albeit the number of years escaping from poverty is still high, the finding suggested a drop in the average exit time of around 0.54 years (6.5 months) due to zakat contribution (Table 7.3).

Quite recently, BAZNAS conducted a nationwide study to investigate the impact of zakat on poverty reduction in Indonesia. The study was conducted in 2019 and included as much as 7052 respondents/mustahik from all 34 provinces of Indonesia. The study found strong evidence that zakat institution has contributed positively in reducing poverty and inequality in the country (Puskas Baznas, 2020b).[15] There are some differences in fresults between provinces in the country. However, the general trends are relatively the same (Table 7.4).

Table 7.3 Changes in poverty index of Mustahik in Greater Jakarta

Poverty Index	Without Zakah	With Zakah	Changes
Headcount index (H)	0.638	0.550	-8.76%
Poverty gap, in rupiah	421,489	344,213	-18.33%
Poverty gap index (P_1)	0.266	0.217	-4.88%
Poverty severity index (P_2)	0.154	0.119	-3.46%
Time to exit poverty (t_g), in years	9.976	9.438	-0.54

Source: Kasri, 2016

[14] PEBS FEB UI, Indonesia Sharia Economic Outlook 2020, (2019).
[15] Puskas BAZNAS, Kaji Dampak Zakat 2019, (2020).

Table 7.4 Changes in poverty index of Mustahik in Indonesia

Poverty index		
H	Before	0.49
	After	0.18
	Δ	−0.31
P1	Before	0.52
	After	0.42
	Δ	−0.10
I	Before	Rp882,783
	After	Rp718,943
	Δ	Rp(163.840)
P2	Before	0.35
	After	0.11
	Δ	−0.24
t	With	12.77
	Without	9.78
	Δ	−2.99

Source: Puskas BAZNAS 2020

In particular, the report estimated that the incidence of poverty amongst the mustahik has decreased significantly from 49% in 2018 to 18% in 2019. This indicates a remarkable drop of around 31% in only one year. Poverty gap, both in nominal and in index values, was also found to decrease by Rp 163,840 or by 10% after receiving zakat assistances. The measure of P2, which indicates severity of poverty, was also reduced by 24%. Additionally, the time taken to exit poverty decreased from 12.77 years to 9.78 years. This remarks a significant drop by 3 years in the time needed by the poor to escape poverty. Overall, these provide strong evidence that zakat institution has contributed positively in reducing poverty and inequality in Indonesia.

Another Islamic financial institution that has contributed positively in realizing SDG1 and SDG10 is Islamic microfinance, which is essentially microfinance institutions which are operating according to Islamic principles. Prior to the issuance of the Law No. 1/2013 concerning microfinance institutions in Indonesia, the Islamic microfinance institution is known by the name Baitul Mal wa Tamwil (BMT) or Sharīʿah Savings and Loan Cooperatives (KSPPS). According to the National Committee for Islamic Economics and Finance (KNEKS) of Indonesia, currently there are around 2000 units of Islamic microfinance institutions in Indonesia (Rahardjo, 2020).[16]

While a nationwide study investigating the impacts of Islamic microfinance on poverty and inequality is hardly found, some reports attempted to provide such evidence. A new report launched by Center of Strategic Research (Puskas) of BAZNAS in early 2020 evaluated and measured the impacts of zakat funds channelled through Islamic microfinance programme (known as BAZNAS microfinance). The number of respondents involved with the impact measurement accounted to 2159 respondents, which constitute zakat recipients from BAZNAS microfinance and other BAZNAS programmes conducted in 2019.

---

[16] Rahardjo, Ventje, *Dampak COVID-19 Terhadap Jasa Keuangan Syariah di Indonesia*, Presentation at FEB UI, 12 May 2020.

Table 7.5 Changes in poverty index of Mustahik under Islamic microfinance programmes in Indonesia

Poverty indicator/index		
H	Before	0.20
	After	0.00
	Δ	-0.20
P1	Before	0.33
	After	0.03
	Δ	-0.30
I	Before	Rp552,837
	After	Rp51,000
	Δ	Rp(501,837)
P2	Before	0.12
	After	0.00
	Δ	-0.12
t	Without Zakat	2.03
	With Zakat	0.00
	Δ	2.03

Source: Puskas BAZNAS 2020

Table 7.5 summarized the changes in poverty conditions of the recipients after receiving zakat through BAZNAS microfinance programmes (Puskas Baznas, 2020a).[17] Prior to getting the zakat funds, the number of poor people amongst the mustahik was 20%. However, after getting the zakat assistance, all 100% of the respondents were able to improve their economic conditions and managed to get out of poverty. Similar result was found with respect to poverty gap, albeit the survey results still reported a gap of Rp 51,000 between the respondents' income and the national poverty line. In line with this, the poverty gap index also decreased significantly from 33% to 3%. Further investigation also reported that the poverty severity index dropped from 12% to 0%, implying that the severity of poverty disappeared after getting zakat assistance. Additionally, time to exit poverty decreased significantly. Indeed, a year after getting zakat assistance from BAZNAS, all recipients of BAZNAS microfinance programmes managed to escape poverty. Taken together, the results of the impact evaluation studies provide evidence regarding the contributions of Islamic microfinance and zakat in reducing poverty and inequality, and hence contributing to achieving SDG1 and SDG10.

Concluding Remarks: Strategy to Bring About the Expected Social Change

The discussion so far indicates that the Islamic financial services industry has evolved over the past four decades, which, after going through a four-stage evolution, has become a real force in some countries' financial system. Nevertheless, the earlier expectation and aspiration upon the industry that it would internalize the social dimension and social justice into its own

---

[17] Puskas BAZNAS, *Dampak Zakat terhadap Tingkat Kesejahteraan Mustahik: Studi Kasus Lembaga-Lembaga Program BAZNAS 2020,* (2020).

operational may not materialize fully. Hence, we witness the altering look of the industry into more inclusive and aligned with the issues of community banking, microfinance, socially responsible investment and the like.

The role of the Islamic financial industry in supporting the SDGs will depend on the extent to which stakeholders can influence its direction. The industry has been driven predominantly by supply-side factors and considerations and demand for it dominated by the household sector, with other sectors, such as institutional investors, corporations and governments, showing varying degrees of interest. There are important factors on the demand side that are likely to change the dynamics of Islamic finance and could link it more profoundly to the SDGs, especially if one of the most distinctive characteristics of Islamic finance—backing financial transactions by real economic activities—is fully operationalized. Some important demand-side factors include the recent rise in demand for Islamic finance products by enterprises across sectors and sizes, as well as the growing demand by sovereign and quasi-sovereign entities for long-term finance based on Islamic principles. It is worth mentioning that a more effective role for Islamic finance in the implementation of the SDGs would require the supply of an innovative mix of products, adequate governance of Islamic finance intermediaries and a supportive legal and regulatory framework. Based on the experience with the MDGs and given the requirements of Islamic finance instruments for better ex-ante and ex-post understanding and scrutiny of transactions, the need for high-quality data cannot be overemphasized.

Islamic finance principles support socially inclusive, environmentally friendly and development-promoting activities. However, in practice, the industry's contribution to these objectives has been below its potential. And even though it has been growing, its share globally remains small, even in Muslim countries. Practical measures are required to enhance the contribution of the Islamic financial sector to achieve the SDGs.

Five tracks through which Islamic finance could support efforts to achieve the SDGs are financial stability, financial inclusion, reducing vulnerability, social and environmental activities and infrastructure finance. Financing for development focuses on four foundational pillars: domestic resource mobilization, better and smarter aid, domestic private finance and external private finance. In this context, Islamic finance has the potential to play a major role in supporting all four of these pillars. Given the magnitude of the SDGs and the important role that can be played by Islamic finance in supporting their implementation and ensuring more robust and inclusive growth, the opportunity to more closely link Islamic finance with sustainable development cannot be overlooked.

The Sustainable Development Goals has given the industry a wakeup call as it provides a platform by which the principles and operationalization of Islamic finance are aligned with the 17 goals set out in SDGs. Thanks to the instruments of Islamic social finance, by which SDG1 and SDG10 are proven to be attainable through the deployment of social finance instruments, such as zakat and Islamic microfinance.

In the context of Indonesia which has been empirically proven, the results suggest that zakat and Islamic microfinance institutions have contributed positively in decreasing the incidence, depth and severity of poverty as indicated by the lower poverty indices after obtaining assistances and getting involved with the institutions. Time to exit poverty also decreased significantly, particularly amongst the recipients of Islamic microfinance programmes. These provide strong evidence regarding the contribution of Islamic finance, particularly Islamic social finance, in achieving SDG1 and SDG10.

* * *

Glossary

maqsad (Maqāṣid al- Sharī'ah*)* Objectives of Islamic law
ribā Usury, interest
ṣadaqāt Charity(ies)
Sharī'ah Islamic law
ṣukūk Equity-based certificates of investment
ṣadaqah jāriyah Perpetual charity
takāful Solidarity, mutual support
waqf (awqāf) Endowment(s), foundation(s), trust(s)
zakāh, zakāt Obligatory contribution to poor due payable by all Muslims having wealth above *nisab* (threshold or exemption limit)

References

BAZNAS. (2019). Outlook Zakat Indonesia 2020.
El Gamal, M. A. (2000). The Economics of 21st Century Islamic Jurisprudence. In *Proceedings of the Fourth Harvard University Forum on Islamic Finance: Islamic Finance: The Task Ahead*. Harvard: University.
IFSB. (2020). *Islamic Financial Services Board Stability Report 2020*. Kuala Lumpur.
IRTI. (2014). *Islamic Social Finance Report*. Jeddah: Islamic Research and Training Institute.
Izhar, H., et al. (2018). Islamic Finance in a Global Economic Context. *Global Islamic Finance Report*.
Kasri, R. A. (2020). *The Impact of COVID-19 on Islamic Finance in Indonesia*. Presentation at FEB UI, 12 May.
Kasri, R. A. (2016). Effectiveness of Zakat Targeting in Alleviating Poverty in Indonesia. *Al-Iqtisad: Journal of Islamic Economics, 8*(2), 169–186.
PEBS FEB UI. (2019). *Indonesia Sharia Economic Outlook 2020*.
Puskas BAZNAS. (2020a). *Dampak Zakat terhadap Tingkat Kesejahteraan Mustahik: Studi Kasus Lembaga-Lembaga Program BAZNAS 2020*.
Puskas BAZNAS. (2020b). *Kaji Dampak Zakat 2019*.

Rahardjo, Ventje. (2020). *Dampak COVID-19 Terhadap Jasa Keuangan Syariah di Indonesia*. Presentation at FEB UI, 12 May.
Retrieved June 26, 2020, from http://siwak.kemenag.go.id/.
Servaes, J. (2008). *Communication for Development and Social Change*. London: Sage Publications.
State of the Global Islamic Economy Report 2019/2020. *Driving the Islamic Economy Revolution 4.0*.

PART II

Communicating the Global Goals

CHAPTER 8

Community Learning Centre as a Promising Medium for Promoting Sustainable Development Goal 4: Lifelong Learning

Gwadabe Kurawa

Introduction

Sustainable development, and the conditions by which it can be maintained, has become a buzzword in both policy and practice, at different levels of government and other institutions and in different sectors including business and education. At the global institutional level, the United Nations has developed the 2030 agenda for sustainable development with its associated 17 goals (UN, 2015). In education, the United Nations Educational, Scientific and Cultural Organization (UNESCO, 2017a) has identified indicative learning objectives for the 17 SDGs and the activities needed to achieve them. SDG4 is dedicated to the provision of inclusive and equitable quality education and lifelong learning opportunities for all.

This chapter is primarily concerned with SDG4—meeting the needs of all children, young persons and adults at local level. The chapter also argues that the concept of lifelong learning for all guides SDG4 and that the community learning centre is an important institutional medium for empowering a learning community for sustainability in African and Asian contexts.

The chapter is structured as follows: It commences with a definition and perspectives of Sustainable Development. Sustainable Development Goal (SDG) 4 is then analysed. This leads to a consideration of the analytical

G. Kurawa (✉)
Independent Researcher, Manchester, UK

© The Author(s), under exclusive license to Springer Nature Switzerland AG 2021
M. J. Yusha'u, J. Servaes (eds.), *The Palgrave Handbook of International Communication and Sustainable Development*,
https://doi.org/10.1007/978-3-030-69770-9_8

framework, participatory communication and adult education and learning approaches discussed in this chapter. This is followed by a description of the community learning centre as a medium for promoting SDG4: lifelong learning. Some promising practices in promoting SDG4 at the community level in Tanzania and Thailand are then presented. The discussion of SDG4 at the community level continues by comparing the two case studies from Tanzania and Thailand. Finally, the chapter concludes that the implementation of SDG4 policies and strategies across Thailand—particularly in areas occupied by vulnerable and marginalised communities—can be regarded as a positive vehicle for sustainable social change relative to the country. The promising practices of widening participation of adults and disaffected youth in alternative education programmes in Tanzania can serve also as an example of a possible course of action to reduce the rate of illiteracy and develop soft and practical skills related to SDG4

Defining Sustainable Development

Sustainable development is a dominant and elusive concept used in contemporary discourse surrounding societal responses to the current depletion of limited natural resources globally. However, although sustainable development is a global issue that is extensively researched in both the Global North and the Global South, Servaes and Malikhao (2016) argue that 'there is no universal development model'. They contend that, although it is possible to enjoy 'a more holistic and integrated vision of sustainable development' across contexts, the reality within each context will be dependent on the strategy, resources and capitals available in addition to the needs and views of the people in that context (Ibid., p. 173). Acknowledging the differences that exist across contexts, and the uniqueness of the overall sustainable development process for each context, an analysis of what sustainable development looks like in Thailand and Tanzania is presented in this chapter. The chapter first establishes the meaning of sustainable development in theory, before exploring media for communicating sustainable development and identifying sustainable development in practice within the case studies.

In its seminal report, titled 'Our Common Future', the World Commission on Environment and Development (WCED) aligns sustainable development with the exploitation of natural resources and associates it predominantly with ways of 'meeting the present needs without compromising the ability of future generations to meet their needs' (WCED, 1987, Sect. 4, Article 27). Concerns have arisen that the strategy discussed in the report reduces sustainable development to unlimited economic growth (Seghezzo, 2009), focuses on environmental issues, downplays (or even discounts) the effect of ecological influences and emphasises competition (Payutto, 1998). He further considers how competition in the report would be characterised. At the very least this may include compromise, which in turn would require reducing the needs of one or both parties. However, compromising their own needs will lead to the frustration of either party and in this sense Payutto (1998) further claims that development will not be sustained if the parties involved are dissatisfied. He therefore concludes that the strategy proposed in the WCED report leads development into a cul-de-sac (see Servaes (2013) for a thorough exposition).

Alternatively, Payutto (1998) characterises sustainability as being equally about ecology, economy and evolvability and as encompassing the following:

> A correct relation system of developed mankind is the acceptance of the fact that human-being is part of the existence of nature and relates to its ecology. Human-being should develop itself to have a higher capacity to help his fellows and other species in the natural domain; to live in a harmonious way and lessen exploitations in order to contribute to a happier world (Payutto, 1998, p. 189).

Here, three key points emerge. First, the definition of sustainability might be driven by behaviours and lifestyles which do not harm nature. Second, the concept of sustainability is partly shaped by the way in which people within the national boundaries have been appropriately socialised. Third, societies or communities should adopt a positive approach towards nature and the environment. Finally, it is suggested that these three aspects can support and influence people to live in harmony with their environment.

Although this reflects a philosophical overview of the Global South of how the concept of sustainability evolved or should evolve, Payutto (1998) provides the least prescriptive definition of sustainability. Such a definition of sustainability has increased the number of pillars of sustainable development, from the initial two (economy and environment) in the WCED report to the four dimensions—economic, environmental, social and cultural—that are now recognised globally. Internationally, development is, as Servaes (2013) indicates, an integral, multidimensional and dialectic process which is peculiar to each society, community or context. This chapter adopts this interpretation of sustainable development as a multidimensional process which can take place at different levels and within different settings. All communication processes of sustainable development, as Servaes (2013) further argues, should be open, inclusive and participatory in order to utilise the knowledge, skills and energy of all stakeholder groups concerned with sustainability. In addition to this, Elias and Merriam (2005) outline educational approaches that promote development and social change while Servaes and Malikhao (2016) describe a participatory communication strategy in which sustainable development can respond to the needs of all social groups in a given context. These educational approaches and communication strategy (used as analytical framework in this chapter) are discussed in subsequent sections of the chapter. Meanwhile, the notion of sustainable development and sustainable development goals are examined next.

SUSTAINABLE DEVELOPMENT GOAL 4: LIFELONG LEARNING

The United Nations Sustainable Development Goals (SDGs) are a set of goals articulated to help the global community to work collectively to make the world a better place in which to live and to implement a more just society (UN, 2015). The ambitious new Agenda for Sustainable Development, titled 'Transforming Our World', increases the number of goals from the initial eight Millennium Development Goals (MDGs), designed in 2000 to be met by 2015, to 17 goals scheduled to be reached by 2030 (ibid.). The 17 SDGs focus on topics related to 'economic growth, social development [and] environmental protection' (ibid., item 9) and are further broken down into 169 targets. SDG4 is devoted to education and lifelong learning.

This indicates that sustainable development has also been attracting political attention in education. For example, the two seminal reports of the United Nations Educational, Scientific and Cultural Organization—'Learning to be: The world of education today and tomorrow' (Faure et al., 1972) and 'Learning: The Treasure Within' (Delors et al., 1996)—represent important planning documents and milestones in the world history of education and lifelong learning. The reports underscore the importance of education in addressing environmental and social problems.

These attempts were re-echoed in the United Nations Decade of Education for Sustainable Development (UN DESD: 2005–2014), which was led by UNESCO, and in the Bonn declaration. The declaration suggests that:

> through education and lifelong learning we can achieve lifestyles based on economic and social justice, food security, ecological integrity, sustainable livelihoods, respect for all life forms and strong values that foster social cohesion, democracy and collective action (UNESCO, 2009, para 5).

These policy packages placed emphasis on active involvement in learning and critical pedagogical approaches aimed at encouraging and empowering learners to change their behaviour and help ensure the concept of sustainability is incorporated within policies globally. UNESCO recently issued 'Learning Objectives' (UNESCO, 2017a) pertinent to the 17 SDGs, including SDG4 which is the focus in this section. These specific learning objectives focus on three domains: cognitive, socio-emotional and behavioural. In other words, the domains comprise the knowledge and skills needed to achieve these objectives, the motivation and attitudes that can support them, and the actions needed to reach them.

It is important to note here that lifelong learning is given greater prominence under the SDGs and Education 2030 than in the MDGs and Education for All (EFA) proposals. The scope, policy focus and the countries targeted under EFA and education-related MDGs are limited compared to SDGs. In terms of scope, EFA and MDG2 placed emphasis on universal and quality basic education to children, youth and adults by 2015. However, the significant percentage of out-of-school children, high illiteracy rates, barriers to education, lack of access to education for marginalised groups and poor infrastructure in some countries (see Kurawa, 2019) suggested that EFA and MDG2 targets have not been achieved. Thus SDG4, which forms part of the 17 SDGs, expanded the focus to all forms of education—basic education, adult education, higher education and technical education—to 'become part of the continuum supported by the global education community in the realisation of sustainability' (Kurawa, 2020).

In regard to geographical coverage, MDG2 generally aimed at ensuring access to and completion of basic education by children in the Global South. This agenda was pursued further by EFA committing to ensure the right to basic 'quality' education for all in both the Global South and the Global North though. The effort was more directed towards countries with high percentage of out-of-school children. This means EFA and MDG2 are not universal agenda. The subsequent SDG4, however, can be viewed as a global programme as it targets all countries across the world. Globally, SDG4 policy focuses, as Kurawa (2020) suggests, on provision of equal opportunity in access to quality forms of education and acquisition of soft and practical skills for the world of work and citizenship. On the other hand, EFA and MDG2 policies are narrowed only to access and quality of basic education. In essence, SDG4, with its associated ten targets, attends to the needs of children, youth and adults and, guided by the concept of lifelong learning, is:

> rooted in the integration of learning and living, covering learning activities for people of all ages (children, young people, adults and the elderly, girls and boys, women and men) in all life-wide contexts (homes, schools, workplace and community among others) and through a variety of modalities (formal, non-formal and informal) which together meet a wide range of learning needs and demands. (UIL, 2015: 2)

This description of lifelong learning, which expresses emancipatory, humanistic and democratic values, is currently perceived as 'a philosophy, a conceptual framework and an organising principle of all forms of education' (UIL, 2012: 5), is aimed at transforming people's lives for the better (UNESCO, 2016). This wide-ranging scope of SDG4 also aims to ensure the provision of equitable education and training opportunities for all individuals throughout their lives. However, it requires economic, communication, cultural and other resources to make learning happen within the home, local libraries, community centres or formal schools (World Education Forum (WEF), 2016). The emancipatory, humanistic and democratic values infused in the concept of lifelong learning are considered in this chapter from participatory communication and adult education and learning approaches.

Participatory Communication, and Adult Education and Learning Approaches

This section presents eclectic philosophical approaches. Instead of exclusively considering one particular approach, the chapter draws from the participatory communication model, and the adult education and learning philosophies. These include radical, humanistic and progressive education, discussed below.

Progressive education places much emphasis on hands-on activities which would lead to social change (Elias & Merriam, 2005), the main concern of progressives being to educate individuals towards democracy and prioritise the learning goals of both the individual and society. The authors also note that, in the process of acquiring knowledge, progressives emphasise the learner experience and view the teacher as a facilitator and co-learner. They further suggest that progressive education encourages community participation and draws the attention of learners to the consequences of their actions and to social reform. This philosophy, as the authors view it, has shifted emphasis towards teaching individuals greater practical life issues such as agriculture, health, vocation and social life. It also moves away from the teacher-centred method to the learner-centred method, which focuses on problem-solving or project-based activities. In this way, education can be (as perceived here) a medium of both individual and societal transformation. The humanist and radical philosophies draw, as shown below, from the progressive movement.

Humanist philosophy focuses on the 'freedom and integrity of the individual in the face of increased bureaucratization in society and its institutions, as well as the whole gamut of human relations' (Elias & Merriam, 2005, p. 113). Humanist philosophy is here summarised as primarily supporting transforming of the human condition and society by individuals attending to their own needs and those of others. In the learning process, teachers serve as facilitators or co-learners. Although this philosophy values self-directed learning, it also encourages group learning and group projects, thus developing a spirit of cooperation and communication (ibid.). Shared learning promotes democratic values, which lead to an increase in acceptance of learning (Oliver, 1987). Learning together with others can also lead to personal meaning making and transformational learning, which allows individuals to create new meanings in their lives (ibid.). Having discussed the humanist tradition, the chapter now moves on to radical adult education philosophy.

Radical philosophy of education is influenced largely by the anarchist and Marxist traditions. The former calls for the restraining of public schooling from educating students to be obedient and compliant in favour of allowing learners to become creative individuals, capable of selecting their own learning goals (Elias & Merriam, 2005). The latter tradition also calls for the emancipation of people from domination, colonialism, cultural imperialism and hegemony (ibid.). This simply advocates for individual freedom and autonomy. Influenced by the three philosophies described above, Freire analyses two educational assumptions—the neutrality of education and the relationship between the teacher and the learners—and concludes that education is not neutral but rather is value-laden (Freire, 1983). He calls for teachers not to exercise power and control over learners as a result of their greater level of knowledge but rather suggests listening to the views of learners in the learning process; engaging learners in education is a welcomed counterbalance to silencing their voices (ibid.). This approach also empowers learners individually and socially which in turn can transform their consciousness and the social structures of the society (Elias & Merriam, 2005). This consciousness-raising should be implemented through dialogue and social activities undertaken during the process of learning (Freire, 1983).

It is important to mention here that this social learning process, which is evident in all the three adult education and learning approaches, closely correlates with the key features of the participatory communication model. The model proposes engaging with a range of perspectives (Servaes & Malikhao, 2016). Specifically, the participatory communication approach provides equal opportunities to diverse stakeholders at all levels—international, national, local and individual—to participate in decision-making process for development (see Servaes, 2013: 19). This can be helpful in achieving an understanding of how to move towards more inclusive ways of working that respond to local needs. Local needs, as Jan Servaes clarifies, should be identified by the local people. He draws on the writing of Paulo Freire and places emphasis on listening to a plurality of voices as one of processes which could bring to the surface features which are important for the successful implementation of development projects. Freire (1983: 76) argued that within a development process there should be a plurality of voices devoid of existing hierarchies of status and privilege:

> This is not the privilege of some few men, but the right of every (wo) man. Consequently, no one can say a true word alone—nor can he say it for another, in a prescriptive act which robs others of their words.

In this sense, listening to the voices is a dialogue or an active process of communication that involves hearing and/or reading, interpreting and constructing meanings, and the understanding of the individuals that results from listening to their voices and is a contextual and interactional aspect explored later in this chapter. This results in a reciprocal relationship in addressing practical life issues such as agriculture, health, vocation and social life of particular cultural and social groups. This chapter also explores how cultural and social groups in Tanzania and Thailand are actively involved in planning and production of media content of their development projects. Of course, it is not feasible to include everyone in its practical implementation however. This chapter is interested to see whether the voices of local people in the two countries are encoded in determining the subjects treated in the messages and in the selection processes. This and other shared features between the participatory communication model and adult education and learning philosophies are analysed in the case studies and discussion sections.

What is emphasised in this section is that the participatory communication and adult education approaches have similar features and are used interchangeably. It is also noted here that sustainable development commences by listening to the perspectives of a local community at a community level or at centres for learning.

COMMUNITY LEARNING CENTRE

A Community Learning Centre (CLC) is a local educational institution typically established and run by grassroots people to provide a range of learning opportunities for individuals and community development (Lee & Kim, 2016). CLCs, which are supported by public and private sectors and non-governmental organisations (NGOs), normally offer literacy and post-literacy programmes, continuing education, income generating and life skills training (Victorino-Soriano, 2016). These learning programmes are often modified to reflect the local needs and contexts of a given community (ibid.).

The purpose of setting up CLCs is to empower diverse local groups and to move forward with community development through lifelong learning for all in the communities (Lee & Kim, 2016). This form of learning particularly helps those social groups with reduced access to learning; for example, pre-school children, out-of-school children, women, youths and the elderly. In other words, CLCs offer new learning pathways through which marginalised social groups may acquire creative and analytical skills to enable them to make improved choices for themselves and their communities (ibid.). The community also chooses and processes the learning resources directly relevant to its needs, reflects on local content and simultaneously learns how to apply the shared knowledge and seek better information (Victorino-Soriano, 2016).

It is important to specify here that CLCs, which are part of non-formal education (NFE), take place outside the formal system. Unlike the formal education system grounded on a conventional curriculum and on standard teaching and assessment methods practised in mainstream schools, NFE is organised in homes, rural libraries, museums or community centres. Informal education (IE) also focuses on everyday human activities related to profession, family or leisure, and takes place within families, religious organisations, community groups and traditional culture. It is similarly provided by news organisations, social media and various forms of entertainment (Fien, 2012; UIL, 2012). This chapter focuses on the provision of IE and NFE in CLCs.

Presently, CLC programmes are mostly operational in 24 Asia-Pacific nations and 10 Arabic-speaking countries (Victorino-Soriano, 2016). Support given to CLCs by countries across the globe has been increasing steadily, however (ibid.). This suggests that CLCs are viewed as a medium for learning, information dissemination and networking to implement the SDGs, especially SDG4. The next section discusses promising practices in the promotion of SDG4: lifelong learning.

Promising Practices in Promoting SDG4 at the Community Level

Case Study 1: Tanzania

Political and Socio-economic Contexts of Tanzania
According to the World Bank Report, Tanzania has sustained relatively high economic growth in the last ten years or so (World Bank, 2019). This has, as the report shows, reduced the poverty rate in the country, but the number of poor households has increased due to the faster rise in the population growth rate. The country is home to an estimated 55 million people, of which 13 million are poor, as held in the report. The report further illustrates that the high population growth rate has undermined the government's attempts to increase access to quality social services such as education, medical care and water. On the other hand, the Mo Ibrahim Index of African Governance demonstrates that the country has, as noted in the report, improved in its overall governance indicators, such as controlling corruption, improving public administration and managing public resources for improved social outcomes, between 2015 and 2018 (ibid.). Conversely, the global index of Governance indicates that the country's scores either dropped or stagnated in those indicators (with the exception of clampdown on corruption) between 2012 and 2017 (ibid.). To put it simply, what are the specific challenges of education in Tanzania?

It follows from the above that, in Tanzania, ensuring universal access to compulsory education for all children remains a challenge. Although primary school enrolment in the country has rapidly been expanded, a significant number of children are dropping out of school or are not attending school at all (UNICEF, 2018). For example, there are nearly 2 million out-of-school primary school-aged children and 1.5 million drop-out in lower secondary school-aged population, and the completion rate of schooling generally is less than 4 per cent (ibid.). In addition to this, provision of equal educational opportunity for all is another challenge to the country (UNICEF, 2017). Girl child, children affected by poverty, children with disabilities and children living in deprived areas are most at risk of discontinuing with their education, exclusion from school or not attending school at all (ibid.).

It is also noted in the document that quality education and its relevance is a big issue to be addressed. For example, the school curriculum was failing children to achieve basic learning outcomes (i.e. numeracy, literacy and entrepreneurial skills) (UNICEF, 2018). These skills determine the future academic performance and earning potentials of children. Research findings on final year primary school students indicated that over 50 per cent cannot read in English properly, or achieve Standard 2 level in mathematics, and they barely had high levels entrepreneurial skills (ibid.).

This chapter argues that this situation calls for transformation of the educational system of the country, to train individuals in the social and functional skills needed to respond to the demands of the labour market and participate in the creation of a peaceful, healthy, secure and green living society. This would, this chapter further contends, improve wellbeing and reduce poverty across the country. Highlighted here is also the role science and technology can play in using educational programmes to develop a skilled labour force for strategic business (Walters, Yang, & Roslander, 2014).

In line with the demands echoed by Recommendation 4 of the UNESCO Institute of Lifelong Learning, on creating a learning society, the government of Tanzania has initiated educational reforms intended to provide effective education, strengthen adult and non-formal education and encourage family and community learning. Table 8.1 below shows the alignment of Tanzanian national policies with lifelong learning.

These national policies reflect the broader scope of SDG4 analysed previously in this chapter. Simply, the policies aim to supplement conventional schooling with a range of flexible non-formal and informal learning and training opportunities for children, young persons and adults throughout their whole lifespan. Equally, transitions between the three forms of education and work and vice versa are, as suggested in SDG4, strengthened in the above policy documents. For example, basic education and literacy standards are expanded and enhanced through various non-formal education initiatives, as evident in the above policies. Simply put, the documents signal that raising the standards of literacy of adults and young persons, their transition back to school and their acquisition of skills and qualities that will increase their earning potential are organised through the following non-formal education programmes: Open and Distance Learning (ODL), Complimentary Basic

Table 8.1 Policies and plans relating to lifelong learning in Tanzania

Policies and plans	Year	Remarks
The Tanzania Development Vision 2025	1999	Focuses on building a prosperous and well-educated society through diverse educational initiatives.
National Youth Development Policy	2007	Promotes learning opportunities for youth through flexible non-formal and continuing educational projects realised in cooperation with various stakeholders.
Education Sector Development Programme 2008–2017	2008	Envisages the establishment of links with civil society organisations and the private sector for the provision of high-quality education and training that correspond to the needs of citizens and labour market.
Adult and Non-Formal Education Development Plan 2012/13–2016/17	2012	Stipulates alternative schooling in order to enable out-of-school youth and adults to complete basic education.
Education and Training Policy	2014	Advocates the improvement of access to educational services for all learners.

Information for the table was taken from the UIL Publications Series on Lifelong Learning Policies and Strategies: No. 5

Education (COBET), Integrated Post Primary Education (IPPE) and Integrated Community-Based Adult Education (ICBAE). ICBAE which is a community learning programme aimed at ensuring community participation in achieving SDG4 or promoting lifelong learning is analysed below.

Tanzanian Integrated Community-Based Adult Education (ICBAE)
Although ICBAE is the focus in this section, a discussion around how the other programmes mentioned above may lead to realisation of SDG4 is presented below, beginning with COBET. This programme provides out-of-school children and youth with alternative education to complete primary education. It also increases the children's and young persons' chances to enrol into secondary and higher institutions (UNICEF, 2018). The programme mainly supports out-of-school children between the ages of 11 and 13 years and those aged 14–18 years (ibid.). Although COBET curriculum can be described as 'loose' or 'easy options', it helps out-of-school and drop-out children and youth acquire social capitals that many professions prefer in this rapidly changing global market economy. Conversely, after reaching some satisfactory levels in the programme, the children are returned to formal primary schools that are required to provide quality and balanced education.

Progression to secondary schools is supported through ODL and Integrated Post Primary Education (IPPE) programme. Both IPPE and ODL programmes provide alternative opportunities to secondary school dropped out and those who are denied access to, and expelled from, secondary school because they could not afford the fees (Do Nascimento & Valdés-Cotera, 2018). The programmes are organised by the Adult Education Institute and the Open University of Tanzania (ibid.). The programmes are accessible to learners irrespective of their socio-economic circumstances and geographical location respectively. In other words, the programmes are often delivered through virtual teaching and learning (Walters et al., 2014). Lessons are pre-recorded and shared with learners through digital mass media (e.g. internet and mobile) and printed media (e.g. textbooks and other teaching materials from rural and mobile libraries and CLCs). CLCs are being developed and expanded and one of the existing community learning is ICBAE.

The ICBAE programme was initiated 23 years ago and has adopted learner-centred and community-based learning approaches in literacy and post-literacy sessions for adults and disaffected youths in the country (Do Nascimento & Valdés-Cotera, 2018). They note that the aim of this existing project is threefold: first, it expands equitable access to, and widens participation in, effective basic education. Second, it supports adults and disaffected young persons to learn literacy skills and achieve a sustainable proficiency level. Third, it enables adults and disengaged youths to acquire soft and practical skills to improve their livelihoods.

This agenda for sustainable development is, as detailed in the above publication, practised across the 25 regions of the country. A typical literacy group comprises 30 learners and a lead facilitator, who may be supplied by public, private or faith organisations (ibid.). The group learning session runs for one year and six months, as also noted in the publication. The group, with its flexible curriculum, focuses on specific local issues affecting the community, plans learning tasks, contributes to the finding of solutions to complex issues and organises income generation activities (IGAs) (Walters et al., 2014). The initial six months of the programme are devoted to shared learning by the group, followed by 12 months putting learning into practice, which then continues following completion of the programme when groups may establish their own IGAs. The founding of new IGAs is encouraged by way of a revolving loan made to the group (Do Nascimento & Valdés-Cotera, 2018).

So far, an estimated four million disaffected youth and adult learners have been provided with increased access to basic education and other learning opportunities through ICBAE (ibid.). From the information presented in this section, it can be argued that ICBAE is in line with the learning society concept. It is shown that lifelong learning, for children, young persons and adults, is being encouraged, through a variety of modalities. Youth and adults were supported to acquire knowledge, attitudes and aptitudes which are required for economic realities. Such qualities would help the re-engaged and re-motivated disaffected youth and adults to actively participate in the process of their individual and community development. IGAs, which are self-initiated community-based learning, seemed to be successful across the regions in Tanzania. This is, of course, not surprising given that the shared learning process, expressed in the ICBAE, promotes a sense of belonging and increases participation in group and community businesses. This prioritisation of community learning and other forms of education to ensure people of all ages return back to school and learning is showing positive result. As Tanzania is not listed in the top ten countries in the world with highest rate of illiteracy and out-of-school children (UNICEF, 2018).

ICBAE has also witnessed a dramatic increase in female participation though. The programme does not lead to qualification. ICBAE is monitored and evaluated through field visits by several personnel from national, district and ward adult education offices (Walters et al., 2014). This is augmented by qualitative feedback gained from learners concerning the quality of ICBAE implementation, obtained during follow-up field visits (Ibid.). These and other successes witnessed through ICBAE programme are considered later in the discussion section along with those identified in CLCs in Thailand.

Case Study 2: Thailand

Political and Socio-economic Contexts of Thailand
Thailand saw relatively high school enrolment and progression between 2000 and 2016 (Lee & Kim, 2016). It is noteworthy however that the country's education system failed to respond appropriately to concerns about inclusion, equity and quality. Over a million 15-year-old students attending schools are

underperforming (Organisation for Economic Cooperation and Development (OECD), 2019). This is evident in its Programme for International Student Assessment (PISA). This shows Thailand slips further in global ranking—from 64th to 66th in reading and 55th to 57th in mathematics. Although it retains its previous 54th position in science on the ranking list, a small percentage of students performed at highest levels of proficiency in science (1 per cent) and mathematics (2 per cent). Equally, a negligible number of students achieved a minimum level of proficiency in English.

In other words, less than 4 per cent of students are demonstrating higher problem-solving and analytical skills compared to 11 per cent on average in the OECD countries (ibid.). This PISA, especially English assessment, suggests that the ratio of functionally illiterate 15-year-old students in Thailand is increasing since 2012. Inclusion and equity in education also require greater attention because most of the underachieving students are from small schools in rural villages (UNESCO, 2017b). In these villages, and perhaps in some urban areas, children from poor backgrounds and those with disabilities are less likely to attend schools (ibid.). This means some children are being denied their right to education and equally the quality of education that other children are receiving is not training them for modern work and life.

Despite Thailand's wealth of culture and history, the country has been troubled by prolonged political instability caused by stark disparities between better-off urban communities, living in and around the capital Bangkok, and worse-off rural communities, living in the agricultural heartland in the northeast of the country (ibid.). In other words, the growing wellbeing and income gaps between urban and rural communities suggest that social and economic developments in the country have not benefitted the disadvantaged. In this context, lifelong learning would be a popular concept in Thailand's education and business sectors.

EDUCATION POLICIES FOR PROMOTING SDG4: LIFELONG LEARNING

The concept of lifelong learning in Thailand is imbedded in its National Education Plan (2017–2036) (Office of the Education Council (OEC), 2017). The plan sets out the government's objective of providing educational opportunities for all citizens for the span of their lives, with much focus on the poorest communities residing in rural and remote districts (Lee & Kim, 2016). The education agenda also adopts equitable non-formal and informal provisions of education and training opportunities through CLCs utilising local resources (Yoruzo, 2017). The operational plan for non-formal education, informal training and CLCs is outlined and supported by the Office of Non-Formal and Informal Education (ONIE) (OEC, 2017). ONIE also raises awareness of the importance of development programmes and creates partnerships with local communities to participate in CLC projects and activities (UNESCO Bangkok, 2013).

Prior to this, the National Education Acts of 1999, 2002 and 2010 implemented initial reforms for equitable educational opportunities (OEC, 2017). These key acts of legislation have promoted the concepts of lifelong learning for all, continuous knowledge development and participation in learning processes by individuals, families, communities and public and private sectors.

Also remarkable in the promotion of lifelong learning was the enactment of the Non-Formal and Informal Education Act of 2008, which supported the development of alternative approaches to education and learning (Yoruzo, 2017). The Act also stipulated the adoption of lifelong learning practices and marked the beginning of the integration of formal, non-formal and informal education (OEC, 2017). This is likely to contribute towards improving individual's lives and social conditions at national and community levels.

Community Learning Centres (CLCs) in Thailand

CLCs, as specified above, are institutional media for non-formal education and informal training, used to promote lifelong learning across Thailand. CLCs are, as also shown above, managed by ONIE through its offices and centres located within each province and district. The non-formal provision focuses on literacy, basic education and continuing education (Yoruzo, 2017). Continuing education equips learners with social skills and the sufficiency economy philosophy (explained below), while basic education provides access to general and vocational training and participation in the literacy project offers access to thousands of 'Smart Book Houses' (UNESCO, 2013). Informal learning, on the other hand, is concerned with the promotion of reading through printed and digital media (OEC, 2017). Both non-formal and informal education at the CLCs are offered to those aged 15–59 years within the working population, particularly those who have previously missed out, or are currently missing out, on opportunities to exercise their right to education (Yoruzo, 2017).

She noted that, so far, CLCs have offered such opportunities to nearly 3.9 million Thais from diverse social backgrounds. Of these figures, 2.5 million learners have participated in informal learning and the remaining 1.4 million in non-formal education. This, of course, reduces the number of out-of-school children in the country. Of the 18 million primary-aged children in Asia-pacific who are out-of-school, Thailand is the third country with the lowest rate of such children (UNESCO, 2019). The country also ranks third with smaller percentage of secondary-aged students missing out from school in the nine countries in Southeast Asia (UNESCO, 2017b)

The number of CLCs has recently risen from 7424 to 8000 spread across a range of provinces and sub-districts, especially areas occupied by ethnic minorities (Victorino-Soriano, 2016). Learning in CLCs focuses on the specific needs and expectations of local communities (Mongsawad, 2010). The communities need access to digital learning, New Theory Farming, democratic values and

Sufficiency Economy Philosophy (SEP). SEP places emphasis on a 'middle path' consisting of three interconnected and interdependent principles of moderation, reasonableness and self-immunity (OEC, 2017). Simply, these principles are a bedrock for developing self-reliance and self-discipline and can be applied at individual, private business or national economic policy levels (Mongsawad, 2010). By applying these principles, Payutto (1998) argues that communities are more likely to live in harmony in a sustainable society and environment.

Sustainable self-development further requires people to acquire Information and Communication Technology (ICT) skills (OEC, 2017). In this way, the Thai government has equipped more than 1600 CLCs with ICTs and a database for education management, in order to develop the capacities of 1.2 million learners (Yoruzo, 2017). Learners—and especially those from agricultural backgrounds—are being supported to utilise New Theory Farming, which promotes organic farming as a minimum (Mongsawad, 2010). This method of farming opposes chemical fertiliser and chemical pesticide use in farming. These chemicals result in soil acidity which lowers crop productivity, kills insects and imperils the environment, which consequently also harms communities. On the other hand, organic farming utilises the natural resources locally available to produce organic fertiliser and insecticide (ibid.). This assists in improving the ecology, preserving the environment and reducing harm to people. To sustain this and other forms of learning, the Thai government resources the CLCs with huge levels of funding and thousands of teachers coached in different pedagogical and knowledge-management approaches, which are subsequently used to collect data for evaluation and improving provision (OEC, 2017). This provision of education at the CLCs in Thailand is compared with ICBAE in Tanzania to allow a deeper understanding to be gained of the different ways in which the two dissimilar countries, from Africa and Asia, are empowering their learning communities for sustainability.

Discussion: Empowering Learning Communities for Sustainability

Many countries have in place an UIL publication series exploring lifelong learning policies and strategies. For example, Yoruzo (2017) examined lifelong learning for social change from the transformative education perspective in 11 Southeast Asian countries and Do Nascimento and Valdés-Cotera (2018) discussed the experiences of five African countries in promoting lifelong learning and their challenges for the future. This UNESCO publications series did not compare the community learning practices for social change in Tanzania and Thailand however and it is important to explore and compare how the two learning practices contribute to social change in dissimilar socio-cultural contexts, as set out in the preceding section.

The practices presented earlier indicate that Tanzanian ICBAE and Thailand's CLCs share certain qualities. For instance, they both value liberal and hands-on activities in learning and learner-centred pedagogy, which are guided by progressive education (Elias & Merriam, 2005). On the other hand, these two learning practices follow different philosophical foundations that closely reflect the different social challenges required to be dealt with in their distinct historical and cultural contexts. Contextually, Tanzanian ICBAE has been affected by the radical education for structural social transformation while Thailand's CLCs underscore how humanistic education for individual development needs to succeed in transforming the society. These points are elaborated upon after comparing the conceptual understanding of lifelong learning and its policies in the two countries.

Although in Thailand the concept of lifelong learning has officially been recognised for some 43 years, it only became popular 21 years ago when the Education Acts of 1999, 2002 and 2010 were enacted (OEC, 2017). The Acts adopted lifelong learning as an organising principle of the whole education system in the country, and encouraged the participation of diverse stakeholders in the lifelong learning processes and in designing learning goals for citizens and society as a whole. An increased focus on lifelong learning was witnessed by the promulgation of the Non-Formal and Informal Education Act of 2008, which calls for the development of unconventional education and learning (Yoruzo, 2017). This Act sanctioned lifelong learning practices and the integration of traditional and alternative education (OEC, 2017), and aimed to enhance the lives of individuals and social situations at country and local levels. These plans were further rooted in the National Education Plan (2017–2036) (OEC, 2017), which places significant emphasis on the ethnic minorities living in rural and isolated areas (Lee & Kim, 2016).

Comparatively, lifelong learning in Tanzania is evolving, as there is no precise definition of lifelong learning found in the country's national policy documents. The notion of learning throughout life has however been indicated in certain national policies and development plans. The Education and Training Policy 2014 and Vision 2025 hint at developing programmes to provide all learners with opportunities for 'continuous learning' (Do Nascimento & Valdés-Cotera, 2018). However, this simply means progression, as a learning outcome, which is only one aspect of a lifelong learning process (ibid.). It is also argued that the prominence given to literacy programmes in NFE, in the 2007 policy and 2008 and 2012 development plans, suggests that lifelong learning is equated with adult learning only (Walters et al., 2014). 'This approach impeded the integration of lifelong learning principles into the education system as a whole, and into wider sectors of society' (Do Nascimento & Valdés-Cotera, 2018: 41).

To sum up, the concept of lifelong learning within Thailand and Tanzania is comparable. It is understood as continuous learning, comprising formal, non-formal and informal learning in Thailand, and as being associated not only with formal education but with a process of learning in Tanzania. The policies and development plans of both countries, as shown previously and hereafter, promote lifelong learning for social change and lifelong learning connecting to local problems. The policies and plans of both countries also underline the experiences of the learners and local people, in addition to democracy within learning and social processes. Both have connected with the Regenerated Freirean Literacy through Empowering Community Techniques (REFLECT). This technique supports flexible curricula and development project activities, allowing learners and local people to focus on issues that affect and interest them as a way in which to effect social change. Examples of practices related to democracy in learning and social processes, as well as learner-centred pedagogy, are briefly summarised below.

For example, the learning themes within ICBAE and the CLCs include the IGAs listed in the previous section. Learning is organised within groups and is based on group projects where each participant's views and opinions are valued. In this way, the participants take turns to share their experiences, and listen to those of others, in relation to the common themes they choose to develop. Civic education linked to IGAs is also discussed during the group seminars facilitated by personnel from government, and international and national NGOs (such as the Seidel Foundation) (Do Nascimento & Valdés-Cotera, 2018). Based on the results of these social interactions and small-scale credit schemes, learners (or local people) can establish their own IGAs.

These IGAs have effectively motivated both the adults and disaffected youth in Tanzania to enrol in the ICBAE programme. The adequate provision of learning resources, chosen and processed by the learners, has improved the quality of the programme and helped facilitators to assess learners through tasks and activities set up in the resources (ibid.). Equally, IGAs enable learners and graduates to access enhanced employment and salary levels, and to acquire greater life skills connected to current changes in the Thai and international communities (Yoruzo, 2017). These benefits are evident as the learners become more aware of the concept of social equity and their surrounding environment. For example, Thai farmers have substituted their chemical fertilisers and chemical pesticides for organic fertilisers and insecticides that help to conserve the environment and do no harm to insects and people (Mongsawad, 2010). In Tanzania, more local people have actively engaged in guarding themselves against negative influences within and outside their community, such as in relation to drugs, sexuality and violence (Walters et al., 2014).

To sum up, dialogue, participation and the sharing of experiences in ICBAE and the CLCs continue today. In both ICBAE and the CLCs, the experiences and socio-cultural backgrounds of the learners are considered. Facilitators are prepared to utilise the learner-centred pedagogy in their facilitation of learning. Learners are given more freedom to design their learning programmes and to reflect on their personal experiences during their social learning process. This also reflects participatory communication and progressive education approaches to social change.

Social change has been developed by Tanzania and Thailand through other participatory communication and adult education philosophies. Tanzania has positive and negative reports on its index of governance indicators (see Case Study 1), which suggests the presence of serious social equity concerns (World Bank, 2019). These issues are discouraging and act to erode the confidence of the people, and especially the disadvantaged, to participate in changing their social conditions. Changing the country into an equal society requires, as Freire (1983) argued, heightened consciousness and collective action. Thus, ICBAE aimed at increasing the awareness of the population (especially the poor), adults and disaffected youth across the country of democracy, governance and human rights. Literacy and post-literacy learning, in this sense, reflect radical participatory communication and adult education philosophies. Radical philosophy places emphasis on 'social empowerment' by bringing together those whose voices have been marginalised in the local communities to collectively address their social problems.

On the other hand, Thailand has comparatively fewer serious social equity problems. The country continues to promote its three principles of SEP—moderation, reasonableness and self-immunity—by providing equitable educational opportunities to all its citizens. Such education opportunities are also provided at CLCs in a democratic, participatory and shared form of learning. This provision of education and the country's philosophy towards sustainable development is clearly affected by humanistic participatory communication and adult education. Humanistic tradition in this chapter emphasises 'individual empowerment' by providing all individuals, regardless of socio-cultural background, with equal opportunities to access an education that supports them in contributing to changing their lives and society.

These societal changes are communicated, as shown in the case studies, through printed and digital media and are being utilised to promote lifelong learning. Textbooks, magazines, newspapers and other local processed learning materials are playing active roles in non-formal and informal education delivered through ICBAE and at CLCs in both countries. In Tanzania, for example, pre-recorded lessons (recently known as lecture capture), email and perhaps text (as learning) messages via chosen media are used in ODL and IPPE programmes. In Thailand, the supply of ICT infrastructure, database and preparation of both teachers and learners in ICT integration at CLCs would contribute in transforming the country towards a learning society.

Conclusion

It follows from the above that implementation of SDG4 policies and strategies across Thailand—particularly in areas occupied by vulnerable and marginalised communities—can be regarded as a positive vehicle for sustainable social change relative to the country. The current and most pressing SDG4 challenge faced by Tanzania concerns the desire to reduce the rate of adult and youth illiteracy. Although a reduction of illiteracy rates would not necessarily evidence the development of soft and practical skills related to SDG4, the promising practices of Tanzania can serve as an example of a possible course of action for illiteracy challenges. The comparison of the two types of learning practices in two countries with dissimilar cultural histories and located in different geographical areas presented in this chapter can also serve as a reminder that 'there is no universal development model' (Servaes & Malikhao, 2016: 180).

Finally, as shown in the two case studies, school enrolments have highly increased in Tanzania and Thailand. In particular, expansions of access to formal, non-formal and informal education are all on their national policies. However, the right to education of children with disabilities is not been given adequate attention in the two countries. Of the 7.9 per cent of such children in Tanzania, less than 1 per cent are enrolled in formal schools (UNICEF, 2018). Similarly, the risk of missing out from school for disabled children is more likely higher than those without disabilities in Thailand (UNESCO, 2017b). Again, formal education, compared to non-formal education, faced other serious challenges in both countries. Formal education values theoretical knowledge expected to be learned perhaps exclusive of its utility. Generally, the curriculum provision, in both countries, is less quality because the breadth of the education and achievement of children are below the expected standards nationally or internationally.

This author, therefore, suggests that access to both forms of education to children with disabilities should be expanded in both countries. The countries should also offer relevant professional development and support to teachers to enable them to respond to the learning needs of all learners. Such learners need curriculum which is more concerned with social, economic and academic goals related to sustainable development.

REFERENCES

Elias, J. L., & Merriam, S. B. (2005). *Philosophical Foundations of Adult Education* (3rd ed.). Malabar, FL: Krieger Publishing Company.

Delors, J., Mutfi, I. A., Amagi, I., Carneiro, R., Chung, F., Geremek, B., et al. (1996). *Learning: The Treasure Within*. Paris: UNESCO.

Do Nascimento, D. V., & Valdés-Cotera, R. (2018). *Promoting Lifelong Learning for All: The Experiences of Ethiopia, Kenya, Namibia, Rwanda and the United Republic of Tanzania*. UIL publications series on lifelong learning policies and strategies: no. 5. UIL, Hamburg: Germany.

Faure, E., Herrera, F., Kaddoura, A. R., Lopes, H., Petrovsky, A. V., Rahnema, M., et al. (1972). *Learning to Be: The World of Education Today and Tomorrow*. Paris: UNESCO.

Fien, J. (2012). *Learning for a Sustainable Future: Maximizing the Synergies Between Quality Education, Learning and Sustainable Human Development*. A paper prepared on behalf of the Inter-Agency Committee for the UN Decade of Education for Sustainable Development.

Freire, P. (1983). *Pedagogy of the Oppressed (revised)*. New York: Continuum.

Kurawa, G. (2019). Examining Teachers' Professional Development for Promoting Inclusive Education in Displacement. In B. M. Rice (Ed.), *Global Perspectives on Inclusive Education*. Hershey, PA: IGI Global.

Kurawa, G. (2020). Study Circles as an Innovative Tool for Promoting Lifelong Learning and Community Empowerment. In E. Sengupta, P. Blessinger, & Y. T. Subhi (Eds.), *Teaching and Learning Strategies for Sustainable Development*. Bingley: Emerald Group Publishing.

Lee, R., & Kim, J. (2016). *Community-Based Lifelong Learning and Adult Education: Situations of Community Learning Centres in 7 Asian Countries*. Paris / Bangkok: UNESCO.

Mongsawad, P. (2010). The Philosophy of the Sufficiency Economy: A Contribution to the Theory of Development. *Asia-Pacific Development Journal, 17*(1), 123–143.

OECD. (2019). *Thailand—Country Note—PISA 2018 Results (Volume 1): What Students Know and Can Do*. Paris: OECD. https://doi.org/10.1787/5f07c754-en

Office of the Education Council (OEC). (2017). *Education in Thailand*. Bangkok: Prigwan Graphic Co., Ltd.

Oliver, L. P. (1987). *Study Circles*. Maryland: Seven Locks Press.

Payutto, P. (1998). *Sustainable Development*. Bangkok: Buddhadham Foundation.

Seghezzo, L. (2009). The Five Dimensions of Sustainability. *Environmental Politics, 18*(4), 539–556.

Servaes, J. (2013). Introduction: Imperatives for a Sustainable Future. In J. Servaes (Ed.), *Sustainable Development and Green Communication: African and Asian Perspectives*. London/New York: Palgrave Macmillan.

Servaes, J., & Malikhao, P. (2016). *The Role and Place Communication for Sustainable Social Change*. Oxford, UK: John Wiley & Sons Ltd.

The World Bank. (2019). *Tanzania at-a-glance: The Overview of the Country*. The world Bank. Retrieved December 2, 2019, from https://www.worldbank.org/en/country/tanzania/overview.

United Nations Educational, Scientific and Cultural Organization (UNESCO). (2009). *Bonn Declaration*. Formulated at the UNESCO World Conference on Education for Sustainable Development held in Bonn, Germany on 31 March to 2 April. Bonn: UNESCO. Retrieved August 8, 2019, from http://unesdoc.unesco.org/images/0018/001887/188799e.pdf.

UIL. (2012). *UNESCO Guidelines for the Recognition, Validation and Accreditation of the Outcomes of Non-formal and Informal Learning*. Hamburg: UIL.

UNESCO. (2013). *Community Learning Centres: Asia-Pacific Regional Conference Report*. Bangkok, UNESCO: Bangkok.

UIL. (2015). *Lifelong Learning. UNESCO Institute for Lifelong Learning Technical Note*. Hamburg: UIL.

UNESCO. (2016). *Education for People and Planet: Creating Sustainable Futures for All. Global Education Monitoring Report 2016*. Paris: UNESCO.

UNESCO. (2017a). *Education for Sustainable Development Goals: Learning Objectives*. Paris: UNESCO.

UNESCO. (2017b). *Situation Analysis of Out-of-School Children in Nine Southeast Asian Countries*. Paris/Bangkok: UNESCO.

UNESCO. (2019). *Out-of-School Children: UNESCO Asia-Pacific In Graphic Detail #9*. Paris/Bangkok: UNESCO.

UNICEF. (2017). *Tanzania: Education Fact Sheet*. New York/Tanzania: UNICEF.

UNICEF. (2018). *Global Initiative on Out-of-school Children: Tanzania Country Report on Out-of-School Children*. New York/Tanzania: UNICEF.

United Nations. (2015). *Transforming Our World: The 2030 Agenda for Sustainable Development*. New York: United Nations.

Victorino-Soriano, C. (2016). *Community-Based Lifelong Learning and Adult Education: Role of Community Learning Centres as Facilitators of Lifelong Learning*. Paris/Bangkok: UNESCO.

Walters, S., Yang, J., & Roslander, P. (2014). *Key issues and Policy Considerations in Promoting Lifelong Learning in Selected African Countries: Ethiopia, Kenya, Namibia, Rwanda and Tanzania*. UIL Publication Series on Lifelong Learning Policies and Strategies. No. 1. Hamburg, UIL.

World Commission on Environment and Development (WCED). (1987). *Our Common Future [The Brundtland Report]*. New York, NY: Oxford University Press.

World Education Forum (WEF). (2016). *Incheon Declaration and Framework for Action for the Implementation of Sustainable Development Goal 4. Towards Inclusive and Equitable Quality Education and Lifelong Learning Opportunities for All. Education 2030*. Paris: UNESCO.

Yoruzo, R. (2017). *Lifelong Learning in Transformation: Promising Practices in Southeast Asia*. UIL Publications Series on Lifelong Learning Policies and Strategies: No. 4. UIL Hamburg: Germany.

CHAPTER 9

Communicating Sustainable Development in Higher Education: Evaluation of Education Experiences and Proposals for Teachers' Orientation

Noelia Santamaría-Cárdaba and Miguel Vicente-Mariño

INTRODUCTION

Sustainable development is an issue of special relevance to international political agendas. The Sustainable Development Goals (SDGs) are a visible sign of the concern raised by this question at the global level (Sachs, 2015). These objectives are part of the Sustainable Development Agenda 2030 and seek to create a committed society that advocates for social and environmental welfare. In doing so, promotion and communication of sustainable development within all levels of education play a key role in supporting sustainability as a common social value, because it must form a global citizenship that defends a more equitable, just and supportive world (Vesterinen et al., 2016). The strategic relevance of SDGs and the Agenda 2030 is widely perceived by global stakeholders, ranging from public to private sectors and covering several levels of decision-making entities, as found by UNESCO, the Global University Network Organization (GUNI, 2019) or the symbolic initiatives emerging from the media and corporate sector, like including SDGs in higher education rankings as Times Higher Education since 2019.

N. Santamaría-Cárdaba (✉) • M. Vicente-Mariño
Universidad de Valladolid, Campus de Segovia, Segovia, Spain
e-mail: noelia.santamaria.cardaba@uva.es; miguel.vicente@uva.es

© The Author(s), under exclusive license to Springer Nature Switzerland AG 2021
M. J. Yusha'u, J. Servaes (eds.), *The Palgrave Handbook of International Communication and Sustainable Development*,
https://doi.org/10.1007/978-3-030-69770-9_9

Servaes (2000) identified three main paradigms of communication and development: first, modernization (1945–1965), based on economic growth and socio-political and technological changes in developed societies; second, dependence (1965–1980), rooted in Latin America, can be understood as "a conditioning situation in which the economy of a group of countries is conditioned by the development and expansion of others" (Dos Santos, 1970, p.231); and third, another development (1980), focused on cultural identity and multidimensionality. Servaes (2012) adds the paradigm of Sustainable Communication for Development and Social Change, which has now become particularly relevant due to its "persistence and its influence on the policy and planning discourse of the main actors in the field of communication for development and social change, both at the theoretical and practical levels" (p.25). This chapter takes this approach as its theoretical anchorage, as communication for development is understood as a tool that promotes strategies for overcoming social problems and citizen participation, and is therefore considered "a guarantee for sustainable, culturally and technologically appropriate human development" (Gumucio-Dagron, 2004, p.4).

This communication for development and social change must encompass issues such as dependence on the natural environment, current environmental problems or the importance of walking towards good living (Barranquero, 2012; Dutta & Zapata, 2019). Making citizens capable of acting in favour of SDGs and understanding the importance of communication for sustainable development is one of the purposes of the educational approach to training critical global citizens (Pashby, Costa, Stein, & Andreotti, 2020; UNESCO, 2015). Consequently, communication for development is categorically linked to the fourth SDG, quality education, as far as the educational field must work on issues related to communication and, of course, to sustainable and human development at all educational levels (Servaes & Lie, 2020). Precisely, the 4.7 target is the one within SDG 4 that most clearly points to the idea promoted by communication for sustainable development, aiming to:

> By 2030, ensure that all learners acquire the knowledge and skills needed to promote sustainable development, including, among others, through education for sustainable development and sustainable lifestyles, human rights, gender equality, promotion of a culture of peace and non-violence, global citizenship and appreciation of cultural diversity and of culture's contribution to sustainable development. (UN, 2015, p.21)

Therefore, all levels of education must promote training in communication for development and focus on educating citizens who not only understand that they live in an interconnected global society, but also act in defence of human rights and in favour of the achievement of the SDGs (Dahama, 2019). Specifically, the higher education environment has an unquestionable relevance for communicating sustainability since universities train future professionals who should be aware of this issue.

Higher education institutions facing the challenge of promoting sustainable development are requested to redesign policies, strategies and curricula increasing the presence of sustainability as a global topic and approach throughout the institutional structure (Aznar & Ull, 2009; Lozano, 2006). Therefore, sustainable development must be transmitted to all actors in the university context (teachers, experts, researchers and students) because it is a sensitive matter for all these audiences (Nhamo & Mjimba, 2020; Servaes & Lie, 2013).

METHOD

This chapter aims to identify trends in the academic research published in leading international journals dealing with sustainable development in higher education over the last five years (2013–2018). Previous works (Wu & Shen, 2016), drawing on similar methods and procedures, identified a gap between research trends and UNESCO priorities, pointing to the need for integration of higher education for sustainable development. Following a similar pathway, we conducted an exploratory analysis based on a systematic literature review, supported by qualitative data analysis software. Systematic literature reviews are vital to identify strengths and weaknesses in a body of published works, as well as emerge contradictions in the available literature (Paré, Trudel, Jaana, & Kitsiou, 2015). With this target in mind, we followed several recommendations included in our previous literature review (Kornhaber, Cross, Betihavas, & Bridgman, 2016; Paré & Kitsiou, 2017).

In this chapter, 56 scientific articles were retrieved from four of the world's leading scientific databases (Google Scholar, Scopus, Proquest and Web of Science) using the following keywords as searching criteria: "education for sustainable development AND higher education" or "sustainable development AND higher education". After conducting a first open coding of the sample during the initial readings, the following four broad categories were identified to classify the articles, being also further applied as a reference during the qualitative analysis:

- Sustainable development in university policies and curricula.
- Communication, Information and Communication Technologies (ICTs) and sustainable development.
- Teachers and students facing sustainable development.
- Initiatives and approaches to work on sustainable development in higher education.

The results obtained in each category return a wide selection of academic research addressing higher education in the area of sustainable development, becoming a valuable repository of good educational practices. Consequently, the systematic study of these educational experiences makes it possible to identify the main trends in ICT usage in the university domain, as well as ways of critically reflecting on the role to be played by social and mass media in raising citizens' awareness of social and environmental risks and challenges.

Therefore, this study aims to contribute in filling the existing gap on identifying educational practices on sustainable development in higher education, since the analysis carried out establishes a series of criteria that must be taken into account when developing educational proposals on this subject.

This chapter is divided into five sections. The first one is dealing with the presence of, and the roles played by, sustainable development in university policies and curricula. The second section tackles the relation between Communication, ICT usage and sustainable development. The third section is focused on students and lecturers, as main actors in the interactive process of education. The fourth one is devoted to projects developed by higher education institutions in the field of sustainable development, aiming to identify good practices to be replicated in the future. This chapter concludes with some recommendations and implications based on the main common findings observed in the systematic literature review.

Sustainable Development in University Policies and Curricula

Education policies in higher education institutions are key to create and consolidate spaces for education and communication for sustainable development. Consequently, higher education institutions are growingly incorporating SDGs into their initiatives, although these proposals are not well coordinated or sufficiently supported (Franco et al., 2018). Facing this problem, Franco et al. (2018) conclude that higher education institutions should integrate sustainable development into their policies, curricula and practices based on the Agenda 2030 promoted by the UN (2015).

Fleacă, Fleacă, and Maiduc (2018) also find difficulties in incorporating sustainable development into all teaching-learning processes; however, higher education institutions must design, promote and adapt specific processes to educate from a sustainability approach in line with the SDGs (UN, 2015). Owens (2017) values the implementation of Agenda 2030 in universities and highlights two key issues to promote sustainable development: publicly funded research and the strategies of higher education institutions.

Following this research line, Holm, Sammalisto, Grindsted, and Vuorisalo (2015a) point to the need to incorporate sustainable development into higher education by providing quality assurance in the teaching learning of this issue. Educational centres must promote concrete actions that encourage the participation of all the people belonging to these institutions. According to this idea, Holm, Sammalisto, and Vuorisalo (2015b) affirm that education for sustainable development must be integrated into all levels of education, and to achieve this, universities must begin their own transformation.

Commitment of higher education institutions to sustainable development was studied by Lozano et al. (2015). Seventy higher education institutions from all over the world participated in this study. Findings reveal the existence of multiple proposals for the implementation of sustainability, which instead of joining forces tended to be fragmented. They point out the need for academic leadership by universities committed to promote policies, strategies and initiatives that guarantee the presence of sustainable development in higher education.

However, Filho, Pallant, Enete, Richter, and Brandli (2018) when studying Sustainable Development planning in higher education institutions find that many universities want to enhance sustainability, but do not have institutional or planning support; therefore, when schools do not have proper planning, they tend to work on sustainability issues on the ground with unqualified staff. Lambrechts, Van Liedekerke, and Petegem (2018) also note that universities need to improve their curricula by clearly integrating competencies for sustainable development. In line with this idea, Vasallo and Arciniegas (2015) point out the importance of embracing sustainable development and social responsibility at university level in order to train professionals with knowledge, skills and citizen values; for this reason, daily training activities should try to develop sustainable habits. Along these lines, Beynaghi et al. (2016) confirm that universities must promote sustainability through social cohesion, research, dissemination and education.

This promotion of social change towards sustainability should be reflected in the universities, as Amador, Martinho, Bacelar-Nicolau, Caeiro, and Oliveira (2015) mention in their study. They designed a series of criteria for curricular evaluation of Education for Sustainable Development in university syllabus, which were tested in a master's degree at the Universidade Aberta in Portugal. This study revealed that the lack of theoretical frameworks that promote sustainable development can lead to a theoretical-practical imbalance; therefore, curricula must be improved by including pedagogical approaches such as service-learning or interdisciplinary collaboration (Lozano & Young, 2012).

Also in Portugal, Fonseca, Ortela, Duarte, Queirós, and Paiva (2018) analyse education for sustainable development in eight higher institutions through a systematic revision of courses and syllabus' contents. They found that sustainability education is divided into different approaches (normative, instrumental), dimensions (social, economic, environmental) and methodologies. Therefore, this difficulty of establishing a single model of education for sustainable development makes it relevant to evaluate its effectiveness in students so that they act as agents of change for sustainability. Farinha, Azeiteiro, and Caeiro (2018) even find that there is a lack of commitment on the side of government institutions to the teaching of education for sustainable development in Portuguese universities.

Katayama, Örnektekin, and Demir (2018) assess the policies of Turkish higher education institutions through a systematic review of existing sustainable development programmes. This analysis identified multiple repetitions of the same activities and lack of interdisciplinary coordination in the exercises, revealing differences between the notion of sustainable development according to European policy initiatives for higher education and the actual practice in Turkish institutions. Crawford-Lee and Wall (2018) also look at educational policies and practices, but focused on UK higher education. Specifically, they find that there is a need for greater integration of education for sustainable development both in higher education institutions and in policies and learning activities; against this background, Crawford-Lee and Wall (2018) point to the importance of mobilizing society and unifying approaches and teaching methods that drive sustainability.

Complementarily, Foo (2013) studies this topic in Malaysia and points to researchers as the key to alert about these problems and helping to drive solutions from various disciplines to environmental challenges. Malaysia has government-promoted policies for sustainability, which it considers important to join forces with non-governmental organizations (NGOs) to mainstream sustainability in environmental education. Policies even promote education for sustainable development through the enactment of environmental protection regulations and sustainable universities.

Other studies such as Holm, Sammalisto and Vourisalo (2015) compare education for sustainable development in universities in the Nordic countries with that in China, concluding that both areas seek to improve training in sustainability. In addition, Holm, Vourisalo and Sammalisto (2015) examined education for sustainable development in the Nordic countries concluding that new strategies are needed to boost sustainability in universities. Dagiliute and Liobikiene (2015) assessed sustainability opportunities at Vytautas Magnus University (Lithuania), determining that training initiatives in sustainability are important for engaging students and that university policies must be coherent and solid in order to continuously promote sustainable development. Verhulst and Lambrechts (2015) focused on a Belgian university and conclude that applying a conceptual model favours the understanding of sustainable development, being therefore necessary to support those who promote sustainability at the university.

Biasutti, Baz, and Alshawa (2016) analyse the incorporation of sustainable development into the curricula of Jordanian higher education institutions. The study shows that in the curricula of Jordanian universities, sustainable consumption, sustainable production, health promotion and values training are the subjects that are most worked on so that students become aware and, by extension, acquire the skills of learning to know and learning to do. Along these lines, Barnard and Merwe (2016) are studying other innovative initiatives aimed at promoting sustainable development at the University of Johannesburg. These authors deduce that various conditions must be met, such as: leadership in the strategic direction on sustainability, continuous monitoring of progress and flexible strategies to promote innovation, since higher education institutions must be capable of adapting to social changes.

The study conducted by Caniglia et al. (2017) questions the type of curricula and teaching-learning environments that should be applied to train university students in sustainability. This study implements a glocal model (global and local) in which new technologies are applied to achieve global cooperation promoted by Arizona State University and Leuphana University of Lüneburg to awaken commitment in students. The results indicate that this type of collaboration creates a teaching-learning environment that favours the understanding of sustainability and promotes an improvement in curricular content.

In this section, we conclude that the policies of higher education institutions must improve four key aspects to properly promote sustainable development: (1) establish coherent policies that promote strategies for sustainable development; (2) provide training for professionals to defend sustainable development; (3) promote research on this subject; and (4) incorporate sustainable development into the curricula. The following section details the findings of the selected articles on the use of ICTs in higher education from a sustainable development perspective.

Communication, ICT and Sustainable Development

Higher education institutions have undergone an adaptation process to integrate the rapid changes emerging from globalization, placing ICT as an unavoidable resource for education. ICTs present an approach linked to sustainable development and ecological problems (Paruchuri, 2009), which is called Green ICT. From a Green ICT perspective, people need to be aware of the environmental harms of ICT and the importance of energy efficiency, and inquire about the solutions that need to be implemented to ensure a sustainable future (James & Hopkinson, 2009). Therefore, the environmental problems linked to climate change affect all countries and it is essential to educate so that action is taken in favour of sustainable development.

Suryawanshi and Narkhede (2015) and Suryawanshi (2019) studied the awareness and use of Green ICT in the training of professionals in the universities of the Pune district in India. In both studies, principals, faculty and students are surveyed regarding their awareness of green ICT. Suryawanshi and Narkhede (2015) found that faculties, staff and students are not motivated to use ICTs from an ecological point of view. They concluded that the lack of motivation coupled with the lack of political momentum is not contributing to reinforce Green ICT centrality and, therefore, strategies should be considered to enhance the sustainable development of ICT. In line with this idea, Suryawanshi (2019) stresses the need to train people to act promoting a sustainable future in which ICTs play a key role, since the results obtained in his study indicate that the students surveyed are less aware when it comes to acting in favour of Green ICT than directors and faculties.

On the other hand, the need to communicate sustainable development in higher education institutions fosters studies like Katiliute, Daunorienė, and Katkutė (2014). Despite the important role of universities in driving change towards more sustainable societies, the spread of sustainable development on the websites of Lithuanian universities is deserving little attention. In other words, the websites of Lithuanian institutions generally neglected the dissemination of sustainability issues and provided little information. Given these results, authors point out to the lack of knowledge to disseminate information on their websites or to the non-recognition of the importance of promoting sustainable development from the university as explanatory causes.

These difficulties of communicating sustainable development in higher education are also studied by Mazo and Macpherson (2018). These authors focused on analysing the communication of sustainable development in three universities located in Canada, Ecuador and Ukraine. They found that universities do not have effective strategic communication plans for all members of educational institutions (teachers, students, staff, etc.). Djordjevic and Cotton (2011) prove in their study that this also occurs in the UK university they analysed. Additionally, Djordjevic and Cotton (2011) point out that there is no successful communication of sustainable development in higher education institutions due to two factors: (1) little shared understanding of sustainability by all members of the educational community, and (2) the differences that may exist in understanding the importance of acting in favour of development due to the values and attitudes of each individual person at an individual level.

One way to spread education beyond the need to mainstream sustainable development is through participation in international conferences. Berchin et al. (2018) analysed 69 academic conferences, which allowed them to prove that these conferences were a relevant strategy for the dissemination, exchange and promotion of initiatives about sustainability. Likewise, Berchin et al. (2018) identify six actions that higher education institutions can implement: (1) creating an institutional agenda, (2) encouraging research on sustainable development, (3) improving the way of teaching by transmitting the need to act according to sustainable development, (4) promoting green campuses, (5) adequately transmitting the importance of sustainability to all members of the educational community, and (6) promoting the dissemination of the actions or knowledge they are obtaining on this issue. In line with this strategy proposal, Lin, Hu, Tseng, Chiu, and Lin (2016) found in Taiwanese institutions that establishing strategic plans to support the communication of sustainable development in higher education is useful for those involved to understand the importance of acting and promoting sustainability.

Moreover, two articles were focused on communicating development issues in order to sensitize all members of the educational community and, by extension, their society. The first research was conducted by Kim, Sadatsafavi, Medal, and Ostergren (2018) who assessed the effectiveness of raising awareness of sustainable development among staff, students and faculty at the University of Washington through various sources of information—news, blogs, social media and local media. Awareness of sustainability in these media had positive results for all participants in this study. Local sources were the least effective, while blogs and social media were the most successful, especially in raising student awareness; however, news was the most effective source for all members of the educational community. The second article (Kang, 2018) tackled communication applied to sustainable urban development. Specifically, it analyses the communication practices of US citizens with storytelling agents. These storytellers are of various types: one-person storytellers (family, friends, etc.), volunteer organizations with which citizens collaborate and act as solution-tellers, and local media as a channel for citizen engagement (Lake & Huckfeldt, 1998; Kim & Ball-Rokeach, 2006, 2011). Specifically, Kang (2018) concludes his study by stating that an active communication of citizens with these agents improves the resolution of the differences between socio-economic development and environmental progress. He also points out the importance of creating proposals from the government that facilitate the communication of policies aimed at promoting sustainable development.

In this section, we confirmed that higher education has an important role to play in developing strategies to raise awareness of sustainable development for the entire educational community; indeed, designing campaigns to raise awareness of the importance of acting for a more sustainable future and energy efficiency through the media tends to be effective. But what does the research on teachers and students highlight about sustainable development? This question points to the focus of the next section.

Teachers and Students Facing Sustainable Development

Teachers and students play a key role within higher education institutions, turning both of them into primary groups for scientific inquiry. Especially since the UN Decade of Education for Sustainable Development (2005–2014), schools began to incorporate this theme in their curricula (Sidiropoulos, 2018).

Sidiropoulos (2018) focuses on investigating the influence of education for sustainable development on the opinions and behaviour of Australian students by incorporating this issue into various disciplines. The results showed that learners saw their attitudes towards more sustainable ones changed. Therefore, current educational approaches must be modified to promote specific didactic strategies that from higher education build global citizens who advocate for sustainable development.

Felgendreher and Löfgren (2018) study the effects of incorporating education for sustainable development into university curricula on students' attitudes and values. This study was carried out at the School of Business, Economics and Law at the University of Gothenburg (Sweden), since this institution promoted "sustainability days" to collectively reflect on their responsibility as consumers and as citizens. The results show that students who participated in these initiatives have a better understanding of the urgency of acting in favour of sustainability than those who did not participate. Felgendreher and Löfgren (2018) conclude that, although activities linked to sustainability do not affect all students homogeneously and their effects may be different, the relationship between everyone's behaviour and established social norms that promote sustainable development must be promoted.

In this line, Shephard et al. (2015) analyse the changes in the world's view of students at the University of Otago (New Zealand) after learning about sustainability issues during their university careers. These authors understand education for sustainable development as a search for affective change and conclude that higher education must clearly articulate its objectives towards sustainable development in order to be able to assess the purposes that are being achieved in the training of students. Crespo, Míguez-Álvarez, Arce, Cuevas, and Míguez (2017) observed the students' capacity to integrate sustainability issues in ten papers produced in the master's degree in Thermal Engineering at the University of Vigo (Spain). This study was carried out by means of the application of a rubric in which issues related to the SDGs were included. The results showed that the students consider economic criteria to a lesser extent, in contrast to the environmental, social and technical issues that were included in most of the works to a greater or lesser extent.

It is worth noting projects covering all members of the educational community, not only students. Peña (2017) explores a formative proposal for sustainable development carried out at the University of Chiapas (Mexico) that promotes the collaboration of all educational members (teachers, students, directors and other educational actors). This proposal is based on the dialogue of three types of knowledge: student, Faculty and community; therefore, it seeks to strengthen this dialogue between university and society, which, according to Leff (2004), takes on special importance to advance towards sustainability. Peña (2017) states in his results that the dialogue between the different sources of knowledge favours that the university students understand the need to change and promote sustainable alternatives to development.

Additionally, research focused on the challenge of educating for sustainable development faced by university faculty is also necessary. This challenge brings with it the concern of higher education institutions to promote education programmes for sustainable development, as noted by Faham, Rezvanfar, Mohammadi, and Rajabi Nohooji (2017). These authors investigate the mechanisms required to develop sustainability competencies in students in order to promote a dynamic model based on the application of strategies that improve the teaching-learning process, the inclusion of sustainability in the curriculum and research on this subject in order to achieve an education that promotes the acquisition of sustainability competencies. Other authors such as Lans, Blok, and Wesselink (2014) focus their study on entrepreneurial higher education and conclude that if sustainability were treated as a specific area, it would stimulate the skills' acquisition by the students.

Dyment and Hill (2015) study the understanding of sustainability in teachers-in-training at an Australian regional university. The study notes that teacher training tends to convey a moderate understanding of sustainability education, although organizational ideas and their curricular inclusion acquire a lower level of understanding. In addition, the work of trainers is essential, and they need to be properly trained so that learners acquire the skills necessary to act in favour of sustainability. For their part, Englund and Price (2018) point out that teachers must act proactively to promote a change in their way of educating for sustainable development in the university; to this end, these authors propose encouraging activities that promote discussion, analysis and critical reflections that lead to a change towards sustainability.

Next, the proposal to work on sustainable development at the university to reinforce collective and individual problems studied by Brunstein and King (2018) focuses on a shift in focus towards transformative learning. This research reveals that applying a commitment-based pedagogy helps teachers and students critically reflect and develop collaborative solutions to sustainable development issues. Teacher training is therefore necessary to educate in sustainability and to value transformation at both the individual and collective levels. Wright and Horst (2013) interviewed Canadian university professors to learn how they understood the issues of sustainable development and sustainable universities. The results show that professors and lecturers generally do reflect on their perception of sustainable development and would like their universities to include sustainability in educational curricula and research.

As a conclusion, Lozano, Lozano, Mulder, Huisingh, and Waas (2013) found that the incorporation of sustainability in higher education institutions is not yet consolidated, and should be highlighted; therefore, professors should be encouraged to collaborate inside and outside universities and initiatives according with sustainable development. In this sense, Longhurst (2014) propose a guide for educators who educate for sustainable development and want their students to understand and take responsibility for their behaviour by trying to foster attitudes in favour of sustainability.

In this section, we emphasized that students improve their attitude if they work in the classroom on issues related to sustainable development. Therefore, it is essential to incorporate this topic into the educational curriculum and include it as one of the objectives of their training. Likewise, teachers need to have adequate training to be able to promote an attitudinal change among students towards sustainable development. But what kinds of initiatives are being developed to educate for sustainable development in higher education?

Working Initiatives and Approaches Towards Sustainable Development in Higher Education

Initiatives related to research and teaching of sustainable development in higher education have increased in recent years, becoming some of them as parts of institutional plans (Lozano, 2006; Lozano et al., 2013). In this sense, the study by Wals (2014) reviews how the issues addressed in the United Nations Decade were integrated by higher education. Wals (2014) proves that higher education institutions are beginning to modify activities, lines of research and community extension focusing in order to take sustainable development into consideration. Specifically, it is perceived that universities are implementing educational reforms, which entail a reconceptualization of learning and the promotion of skills linked to sustainability.

Lozano, Merrill, Sammalisto, Ceulemans, and Lozano (2017) analyse both the competences and the pedagogical approaches to educate promoting sustainable development. Specifically, they highlight the need to integrate sustainable development into university curricula, and to do so, teachers must focus on teaching through pedagogical approaches that improve the acquisition of skills that promote sustainable development. Lozano et al. (2017) defend that approaches to communicating sustainable development should be universal (applicable to various disciplines), aimed at promoting social justice (awakening a sense of belonging to a community) and should educate on environmental issues (environmental education). These authors assert that considering the context of the higher education institution, pedagogical approaches and sustainable development competencies, further training will be achieved through motivating learning techniques such as gambling.

Dealing with approaches to education for sustainable development, Anand, Bisaillon, Webster, and Amor (2015) stress the need to improve the pedagogical approach with various resources and the teacher training approach to learn how to adequately transmit this issue to students. These authors study an educational initiative carried out in two universities and five colleges in Quebec (Canada) with the aim of integrating sustainable development into higher education at the regional level. The project involves several issues: teacher support, programmes and institutional integration, and regional collaboration among academic partners. This initiative helped to develop students' understanding of sustainable development, leading to a change in attitudes towards more sustainable ones.

Another proposal was conducted by the School of Industrial Engineers of the Polytechnic University of Madrid (Spain), as they accepted the challenge to reformulate in a holistic way all the programmed activities to focus them towards sustainability. Yáñez, Uruburu, Moreno, and Lumbreras (2019) verified in this study that the Sustainability Report presented by this institution of higher education has favoured focusing the mission of the centre in accordance with the principles of sustainability, creating new ways of communicating sustainable development and including indicators of the level of sustainability in the global plan. Vaz et al. (2016) focus on analysing curricular, organizational or behavioural issues of members of the educational community (teachers, students and academic staff). Vaz et al. (2016) found that university curricula were too rigid and did not focus on promoting reflection on sustainability; in this sense, these authors state that curricula should have dynamic structures that promote active and applied learning. Therefore, the need to train citizens to reflect and act in favour of sustainable development is necessary to know the activities carried out in higher education, since applying didactic strategies such as learning based on problem solving can facilitate this awareness.

Holm and Martinsen (2016) also study the approaches presented by education for sustainable development in higher education institutions, which have been configured on the basis of the learning discourse. These authors highlight, on the one hand, two approaches: training and qualification. These dimensions are essential for educating for sustainable development as they relate to each other and require qualified solutions to drive sustainability. On the other hand, the approach based on education and lifelong learning refers to the role of universities in educating for problematic situations and their resolution; specifically, sustainable development must be transmitted as a conflictive issue that affects all of us and which must be acted upon to guarantee a sustainable future.

As education is a basic tool to move towards sustainability, then schools are the ideal institutions to convey the importance of being committed to sustainable development. Accordingly, Van and Moore (2015) point out that many educational institutions have promoted plans and initiatives linked to the theme of sustainability; one of the programmes has been called Learning City, which seeks to promote from higher education a reorientation that addresses the problem of current unsustainability. In researching this programme, Van and Moore (2015) prove that through action research interdisciplinary work took place among researchers that culminated in the development of courses, conceptual frameworks and research aimed at studying sustainability in the university.

As Fernandez-Sanchez, Bernaldo, Castillejo, and Manzanero (2015) indicate, education for sustainable development is a worldwide opportunity to teach from universities the effects of human actions to promote a change in attitudes that advocate sustainability. Fernandez-Sanchez et al. (2015) in their study perceive problems such as the need for resources, teacher training and improving the visibility of education for sustainable development within university curricula for which it is essential to have support at the institutional level. In short, it is necessary to promote a comprehensive plan to implement education for sustainable development at the university.

In this section, we verified that there is a need in higher education systems to create more initiatives working on the topic of sustainable development, approached from a perspective linked to social justice and environmental care. In order to make these proposals more effective, there should be more flexible curricula and motivational and participatory teaching methodologies, among other aspects developed in the following section.

Proposals for Universities and Teachers' Orientation

The articles reviewed in the four previous sections explored various aspects linked to the communication and education of sustainable development within universities, allowing us to establish different proposals addressing orientation for both university teaching staff and higher education institutions. These proposals are expected to contribute as valuable drivers to ensure inclusive and equitable quality education and promote lifelong learning opportunities for all, as SDG4 states. The COVID-19 outbreak and the subsequent global crisis will affect these objectives, making them even more vital to draw an equal scenario for the future. The strong impact in both the economies and public health worldwide is expected to deepen some of the existing inequalities in terms of education and communication. Higher education systems are expected to contribute to leverage these unexpected imbalances placing scientific knowledge and education at the forefront of the global recovery plans to be developed during the 2020s.

Universities are an essential pillar for educating for sustainable development and, therefore, they must adapt and apply several modifications that guarantee the formation of sustainable citizens. The study of various prestigious researches on this issue makes it possible to establish a series of orientation proposals to guarantee the inclusion of sustainability, which indicate that higher education institutions should:

- Integrate sustainable development into policies and curricula based on the Agenda 2030 promoted by the UN (2015).
- Design, promote and adapt specific processes to educate from a sustainability approach in accordance with the SDGs.
- Promote sustainable development by financing research with public funds.
- Acquire a commitment that promotes policies, flexible strategies and initiatives that guarantee the teaching of sustainable development and social responsibility in higher education.
- Obtain institutional support to promote sustainability and include it in educational planning.
- Establish environmental protection regulations transforming institutions into sustainable universities.
- Promote local and global collaborations to create a teaching-learning environment that promotes the understanding of sustainability and promotes an improvement in curricular content.
- To motivate citizens through the design of strategies that promote the sustainable development of ICT.
- Adequately disseminate content on sustainability on the websites of higher education institutions.
- Create strategic communication plans to disseminate the relevance of sustainable development among all members of educational institutions through various sources of communication (news, blogs, social networks, etc.).
- Provide resources, teacher training courses and improve the visibility of education for sustainable development within university curricula.

Moreover, this systematic literature review highlights the basic role of teachers in educating for sustainable development in universities. This descriptive analysis makes it possible to establish a series of proposals for improvement aimed at teachers, who should:

- Acquire training that allows them to correctly teach the subject of sustainability so that students acquire the necessary skills and become aware of this issue.
- Teach through educational approaches with specific didactic strategies for students to acquire the necessary skills that awaken their commitment to sustainable development.
- Transmit to the students the relation of the behaviour of each individual with the established social norms that promote sustainable development through a dialogue between the university and society.
- Promote educational programmes for sustainable development based on a dynamic teaching-learning model and the treatment of sustainability in educational curricula.
- Use activities that promote discussion, analysis and critical reflections of students to promote a change in attitudes towards sustainability.
- Apply a pedagogy based on commitment so that students and teachers themselves reflect critically and promote solutions to problems related to sustainability.
- Use didactic strategies to facilitate students' awareness that promote in a balanced way theoretical and practical activity such as: learning based on problem solving, interdisciplinary collaboration or service-learning.
- Collaborate with other teachers to promote interdisciplinary work among researchers.
- Focus their research on issues related to sustainable development in higher education in order to try to improve it.
- Attend research conferences to disseminate the results of their studies on sustainability and learn from the research being carried out by other professionals.

To conclude, the challenges posed by the global COVID-19 outbreak turn all these strategies into something increasingly relevant and urgent, as researchers must work together searching for the common good. Likewise, media actors play a crucial role in reporting national and international news, but it is equally important that citizens think critically to compare the information they can find in different media outlets (Ataguba & Ataguba, 2020). Therefore, if we aim to educate global citizens able to think critically and we are aware of the relevance of the media's commitment to communication for development, then more emphasis should be placed on education by means of the abovementioned strategies. This huge effort and involvement turned into a must to achieve the challenges set by the Agenda 2030 (Ottersen & Engebretsen, 2020). The COVID-19 outbreak has emphasized the urgency of these actions, where an increase in media literacy turns into a valuable key to critically approach our roles as media consumers and, even more relevant, as citizens.

Providing an equal and universal access to education across territories and generations turns into a key for hitting the 2030 target in terms of quality education worldwide.

References

Amador, F., Martinho, A. P., Bacelar-Nicolau, P., Caeiro, S., & Oliveira, C. P. (2015). Education for Sustainable Development in Higher Education: Evaluating Coherence Between Theory and Praxis. *Assessment and Evaluation in Higher Education, 40*(6), 867–882. https://doi.org/10.1080/02602938.2015.1054783

Anand, C. K., Bisaillon, V., Webster, A., & Amor, B. (2015). Integration of Sustainable Development in Higher Education—A Regional Initiative in Quebec (Canada). *Journal of Cleaner Production, 108*, 916–923. https://doi.org/10.1016/j.jclepro.2015.06.134

Ataguba, O. A., & Ataguba, J. E. (2020). Social Determinants of Health: The Role of Effective Communication in the COVID-19 Pandemic in Developing Countries. *Global Health Action, 13*(1), 1788263.

Aznar, P., & Ull, A. (2009). The Formation of Basic Skills for Sustainable Development: The Role of the University. *Journal of Education, 1*, 219–237.

Barnard, Z., & Merwe, D. (2016). International Journal of Sustainability in Higher Education. *International Journal of Sustainability in Higher Education, 17*(2), 228–245. https://doi.org/10.1108/14676371311312905

Barranquero, A. (2012). De la comunicación para el desarrollo a la justicia ecosocial y el buen vivir. *CIC. Cuadernos De Información Y Comunicación, 17*, 63–78.

Berchin, I., Sima, M., Lima, M. A., Biesel, S., Santos, L. P., Ferreira, R. V., et al. (2018). The Importance of International Conferences on Sustainable Development as Higher Education Institutions' Strategies to Promote Sustainability: A Case Study in Brazil. *Journal of Cleaner Production, 171*, 756–772. https://doi.org/10.1016/j.jclepro.2017.10.042

Beynaghi, A., Trencher, G., Moztarzadeh, F., Mozafari, M., Maknoon, R., & Filho, W. (2016). Future Sustainability Scenarios for Universities: Moving Beyond the United Nations Decade of Education for Sustainable Development. *Journal of Cleaner Production, 112*, 3464–3478. https://doi.org/10.1016/j.jclepro.2015.10.117

Biasutti, M., Baz, T., & Alshawa, H. (2016). Assessing the Infusion of Sustainability Principles into University Curricula. *Journal of Teacher Education for Sustainability, 18*(2), 21–40. https://doi.org/10.1515/jtes-2016-0012

Brunstein, J., & King, J. (2018). Organizing Reflection to Address Collective Dilemmas: Engaging Students and Professors with Sustainable Development in Higher Education. *Journal of Cleaner Production, 203*, 153–163. https://doi.org/10.1016/j.jclepro.2018.08.136

Caniglia, G., John, B., Bellina, L., Lang, D., Wiek, A., Cohmer, S., et al. (2017). The Glocal Curriculum: A Model for Transnational Collaboration in Higher Education for Sustainable Development. *Journal of Cleaner Production, 171*, 368–376. https://doi.org/10.1016/j.jclepro.2017.09.207

Crawford-Lee, M., & Wall, T. (2018). Sustainability 2030: A Policy Perspective from the University Vocational Awards Council. *Higher Education, Skills and Work-Based Learning, 8*(3), 233–242. https://doi.org/10.1108/HESWBL-03-2018-0043

Crespo, B., Míguez-Álvarez, C., Arce, M. E., Cuevas, M., & Míguez, J. L. (2017). The Sustainable Development Goals: An Experience on Higher Education. *Sustainability*, *9*(8), 1–15. https://doi.org/10.3390/su9081353

Dagiliute, R., & Liobikiene, G. (2015). University Contributions to Environmental Sustainability: Challenges and Opportunities from the Lithuanian Case. *Journal of Cleaner Production*, *108*, 891–899. https://doi.org/10.1016/j.jclepro.2015.07.015

Dahama, O. P. (2019). *Education and Communication for Development*. New Delhi: Oxford and IBH Publishing.

Djordjevic, A., & Cotton, D. (2011). Communicating the Sustainability Message in Higher Education Institutions. *International Journal of Sustainability in Higher Education*, *12*(4), 381–394. https://doi.org/10.1108/14676371111168296

Dos Santos, T. (1970). The Structure of Dependence. *The American Economic Review*, *60*(2), 231–236.

Dutta, M., & Zapata, B. (2019). *Communicating for Social Change*. London: Palgrave Macmillan.

Dyment, J. E., & Hill, A. (2015). You Mean I Have to Teach Sustainability Too? Initial Teacher Education Students' Perspectives on the Sustainability Cross-curriculum Priority. *Australian Journal of Teacher Education*, *40*(3), 21–35. https://doi.org/10.14221/ajte.2014v40n3.2

Englund, C., & Price, L. (2018). Facilitating Agency: The Change Laboratory as an Intervention for Collaborative Sustainable Development in Higher Education. *International Journal for Academic Development*, *23*(3), 192–205. https://doi.org/10.1080/1360144X.2018.1478837

Faham, E., Rezvanfar, A., Mohammadi, S., & Rajabi Nohooji, M. (2017). Using System Dynamics to Develop Education for Sustainable Development in Higher Education with the Emphasis on the Sustainability Competencies of Students. *Technological Forecasting and Social Change*, *123*, 307–326. https://doi.org/10.1016/j.techfore.2016.03.023

Farinha, C. S., Azeiteiro, U., & Caeiro, S. (2018). Education for Sustainable Development in Portuguese Universities. *International Journal of Sustainability in Higher Education*, *19*(5), 912–941. https://doi.org/10.1108/ijshe-09-2017-0168

Felgendreher, S., & Löfgren, Å. (2018). Higher Education for Sustainability: Can Education Affect Moral Perceptions? *Environmental Education Research*, *24*(4), 479–491. https://doi.org/10.1080/13504622.2017.1307945

Fernandez-Sanchez, G., Bernaldo, M. O., Castillejo, A., & Manzanero, A. M. (2015). Education for Sustainable Development in Higher Education: State-of-the-Art, Barriers, and Challenges. *Higher Learning Research Communications*, *4*(3), 3. https://doi.org/10.18870/hlrc.v4i3.157

Filho, W., Pallant, E., Enete, A., Richter, B., & Brandli, L. L. (2018). Planning and Implementing Sustainability in Higher Education Institutions: An Overview of the Difficulties and Potentials. *International Journal of Sustainable Development and World Ecology*, *25*(8), 712–720. https://doi.org/10.1080/13504509.2018.1461707

Fonseca, L. M., Ortela, A. R., Duarte, B., Queirós, J., & Paiva, L. (2018). Mapping Higher Education for Sustainable Development in Portugal. *Management & Marketing*, *13*(3), 1064–1075. https://doi.org/10.2478/mmcks-2018-0023

Foo, K. Y. (2013). A Vision on the Role of Environmental Higher Education Contributing to the Sustainable Development in Malaysia. *Journal of Cleaner Production*, *61*, 6–12. https://doi.org/10.1016/j.jclepro.2013.05.014

Franco, I., Saito, O., Vaughter, P., Whereat, J., Kanie, N., & Takemoto, K. (2018). Higher Education for Sustainable Development: Actioning the Global Goals in Policy, Curriculum and Practice. *Sustainability Science, 1*, 1–22. https://doi.org/10.1007/s11625-018-0628-4

Fleacă, E., Fleacă, B., & Maiduc, S. (2018). Aligning Strategy with Sustainable Development Goals (SDGs): Process Scoping Diagram for Entrepreneurial Higher Education Institutions (HEIs). *Sustainability (Switzerland), 10*(4), 1–17. https://doi.org/10.3390/su10041032

Gumucio-Dagron, A. (2004). The Fourth Musketeer: Communication for Social Change. *Research and Development, 12*(1), 1–23.

GUNI. (2019). Implementing the 2030 Agenda at Higher Education Institutions: Challenges and Responses. Retrieved from http://www.guninetwork.org/files/guni_publication_-_implementing_the_2030_agenda_at_higher_education_institutions_challenges_and_responses.pdf.

Holm, C., & Martinsen, A. (2016). Mapping the Relationship Between Higher Education and Sustainable Development. *Studia Paedagogica, 20*(4), 71–84. https://doi.org/10.5817/sp2015-4-5

Holm, T., Sammalisto, K., Grindsted, T. S., & Vuorisalo, T. (2015a). Process Framework for Identifying Sustainability Aspects in University Curricula and Integrating Education for Sustainable Development. *Journal of Cleaner Production, 106*, 164–174. https://doi.org/10.1016/j.jclepro.2015.04.059

Holm, T., Sammalisto, K., & Vuorisalo, T. (2015b). Education for Sustainable Development and Quality Assurance in Universities in China and the Nordic Countries: A Comparative Study. *Journal of Cleaner Production, 107*, 529–537. https://doi.org/10.1016/j.jclepro.2014.01.074

James, P., & Hopkinson, L. (2009). *Sustainable ICT in Further and Higher Education*. London: Joint Information Services Committee (JISC).

Kang, S. (2018). Communicating Sustainable Development in the Digital Age: The Relationship Between Citizens' Storytelling and Engagement Intention. *Sustainable Development, 1*, 1–12. https://doi.org/10.1002/sd.1905

Katayama, J., Örnektekin, S., & Demir, S. (2018). Policy into Practice on Sustainable Development Related Teaching in Higher Education in Turkey. *Environmental Education Research, 24*(7), 1017–1030. https://doi.org/10.1080/13504622.2017.1360843

Katiliute, E., Daunoriene, A., & Katkute, J. (2014). Communicating the Sustainability Issues in Higher Education Institutions World Wide Webs. Procedia. *Social and Behavioral Sciences, 156*, 106–110. https://doi.org/10.1016/j.sbspro.2014.11.129

Kim, A., Sadatsafavi, H., Medal, L., & Ostergren, M. J. (2018). 49 Impact of Communication Sources for Achieving Campus Sustainability. *Resources, Conservation and Recycling, 139*, 366–376. https://doi.org/10.1016/j.resconrec.2018.08.024

Kim, Y., & Ball-Rokeach, S. J. (2006). Community Storytelling Network, Neighborhood Context, and Civic Engagement: A Multilevel Approach. *Human Communication Research, 32*(4), 411–439. https://doi.org/10.1111/j.1468-2958.2006.00282

Kornhaber, R., Cross, M., Betihavas, V., & Bridgman, H. (2016). The Benefits and Challenges of Academic Writing Retreats: An Integrative Review. *Higher Education Research & Development, 35*(6), 1210–1227.

Lake, R., & Huckfeldt, R. (1998). Social Capital, Social Networks, and Political Participation. *Political Psychology, 19*(3), 567–584. https://doi.org/10.1111/0162-895X.00118

Lambrechts, W., Van Liedekerke, L., & Petegem, P. (2018). Higher Education for Sustainable Development in Flanders: Balancing Between Normative and Transformative Approaches. *Environmental Education Research, 24*(9), 1284–1300. https://doi.org/10.1080/13504622.2017.1378622

Lans, T., Blok, V., & Wesselink, R. (2014). Learning Apart and Together: Towards an Integrated Competence Framework for Sustainable Entrepreneurship in Higher Education. *Journal of Cleaner Production, 62,* 37–47. https://doi.org/10.1016/j.jclepro.2013.03.036

Leff, E. (2004). Environmental Rationality and Dialogue of Knowledge: Significance and Meaning in the Construction of a Sustainable Future. *Polis. Latin American Journal, 2*(7), 1–35.

Lin, M. H., Hu, J., Tseng, M. L., Chiu, A., & Lin, C. (2016). Sustainable Development in Technological and Vocational Higher Education: Balanced Scorecard Measures with Uncertainty. *Journal of Cleaner Production, 120*(2016), 1–12. https://doi.org/10.1016/j.jclepro.2015.12.054

Longhurst, J. (2014). *Education for Sustainable Development—Guidance for UK Higher Education Providers.* Gloucester: Quality Assurance Agency for Higher Education.

Lozano, R. (2006). Incorporation and Institutionalization of SD into Universities: Breaking Through Barriers to Change. *Journal of Cleaner Production, 14,* 787–796.

Lozano, R., Ceulemans, K., Alonso-Almeida, M., Huisingh, D., Lozano, F. J., Waas, T., Lambrechts, W., Lukman, R., y Hugé, J. (2015). A Review of Commitment and Implementation of Sustainable Development in Higher Education: Results from a Worldwide Survey. *Journal of Cleaner Production, 108,* 1–18. doi:https://doi.org/10.1016/j.jclepro.2014.09.048

Lozano, R., Merrill, M. Y., Sammalisto, K., Ceulemans, K., & Lozano, F. J. (2017). Connecting Competences and Pedagogical Approaches for Sustainable Development in Higher Education: A Literature Review and Framework Proposal. *Sustainability, 9*(10), 1–15. https://doi.org/10.3390/su9101889

Lozano, R., Lozano, F. J., Mulder, K., Huisingh, D., & Waas, T. (2013). Advancing Higher Education for Sustainable Development: International Insights and Critical Reflections. *Journal of Cleaner Production, 48,* 3–9. https://doi.org/10.1016/j.jclepro.2013.03.034

Lozano, R., & Young, W. (2012). Assessing Sustainability in University Curricula: Exploring the Influence of Student Numbers and Course Credits. *Journal of Cleaner Production, 49,* 134–141.

Mazo, L., & Macpherson, I. (2018). A Strategic Communication Model for Sustainable Initiatives in Higher Education Institutions. *Athens Journal of Mass Media and Communications, 3*(4), 321–342. https://doi.org/10.30958/ajmmc/3.4.3

Nhamo, G., & Mjimba, V. (2020). Sustainable Development Goals and Institutions of Higher Education. Springer International Publishing. DOI: https://doi.org/10.1007/978-3-030-26157-3.

Ottersen, O. P., & Engebretsen, E. (2020). COVID-19 Puts the Sustainable Development Goals Center Stage. *Nature Medicine, 1,* 1–1.

Owens, T. L. (2017). Higher Education in the Sustainable Development Goals Framework. *European Journal of Education, 52*(4), 414–420. https://doi.org/10.1111/ejed.12237

Paré, G., & Kitsiou, S. (2017). Methods for Literature Reviews. *Handbook of eHealth Evaluation: An Evidence-based Approach [Internet]*: University of Victoria.

Paré, G., Trudel, M. C., Jaana, M., & Kitsiou, S. (2015). Synthesizing Information Systems Knowledge: A Typology of Literature Reviews. *Information & Management*, 52(2), 183–199.

Paruchuri, V. (2009). Greener ICT: Feasibility of Successful Technologies from Energy Sector. *ISABEL*, *1*, 1–3.

Pashby, K., Costa, M., Stein, S., & Andreotti, V. (2020). A Meta-review of Typologies of Global Citizenship Education. *Comparative Education*, 56(2), 144–164.

Peña, J. (2017). The Training of Professionals in Sustainable Development in an Intercultural Higher Education Program. *Journal of Educational Research*, 25, 265–282.

Sachs, J. (2015). *The Age of Sustainable Development*. New York: Columbia University Press.

Servaes, J. (2000). Comunicación para el desarrollo: tres paradigmas, dos modelos. *Temas y problemas de comunicación*, 8(10), 7–217.

Servaes, J. (2012). Comunicación para el desarrollo sostenible y el cambio social. Una visión general. *CIC. Cuadernos de Información y Comunicación*, 17, 17–40.

Servaes, J., & Lie, R. (2013). Sustainable Social Change and Communication. *Communication Research Trends*, 32(4), 4–30.

Servaes, J., & Lie, R. (2020). Key Concepts, Disciplines, and Fields in Communication for Development and Social Change. J. Servaes (Ed.), *Handbook of Communication for Development and Social Change* (pp. 29-59). Singapore: Springer.

Shephard, K., Harraway, J., Lovelock, B., Mirosa, M., Skeaff, S., Slooten, L., et al. (2015). Seeking Learning Outcomes Appropriate for 'Education for Sustainable Development' and for Higher Education. *Assessment and Evaluation in Higher Education*, 40(6), 855–866. https://doi.org/10.1080/02602938.2015.1009871

Sidiropoulos, E. (2018). The Personal Context of Student Learning for Sustainability: Results of a Multi-university Research Study. *Journal of Cleaner Production*, 181, 537–554. https://doi.org/10.1016/j.jclepro.2018.01.083

Suryawanshi, K. (2019). *Data Management, Analytics and Innovation*. Singapore: Springer.

Suryawanshi, K., & Narkhede, S. (2015). Green ICT for Sustainable Development: A Higher Education Perspective. *Procedia Computer Science*, 70, 701–707. https://doi.org/10.1016/j.procs.2015.10.107

UNESCO. (2015). *Global Citizenship Education: Topics and Learning Objectives*. Paris: UNESCO.

United Nations. (2015). Transforming Our World: The 2030 Agenda for Sustainable development. Retrieved from http://www.un.org/ga/search/view_doc.asp?symbol=A/RES/70/1&Lang=E.

Van, R., & Moore, J. (2015). UN Decade on Education for Sustainable Development (UNDESD): Enabling Sustainability in Higher Education. *Environment, Development and Sustainability*, 17(2), 315–330. https://doi.org/10.1007/s10668-014-9606-x

Vasallo, Y., & Arciniegas, F. (2015). Sustainable Development and Social Responsibility in Higher Education. *San Gregorio Journal*, 2(10), 93–105.

Vaz, C. R., Selig, P. M., Borchardt, M., Bond, A. J., Varvakis, G., Viegas, C. V., et al. (2016). Critical Attributes of Sustainability in Higher Education: A Categorisation from Literature Review. *Journal of Cleaner Production, 126*, 260–276. https://doi.org/10.1016/j.jclepro.2016.02.106

Verhulst, E., & Lambrechts, W. (2015). Fostering the Incorporation of Sustainable Development in Higher Education. Lessons Learned from a Change Management Perspective. *Journal of Cleaner Production, 106*, 189–204. https://doi.org/10.1016/j.jclepro.2014.09.049

Vesterinen, V. M., Tolppanen, S., & Aksela, M. (2016). Toward Citizenship Science Education: What Students Do to Make the World a Better Place? *International Journal of Science Education, 38*(1), 30–50.

Wals, A. (2014). Sustainability in Higher Education in the Context of the un DESD: A Review of Learning and Institutionalization Processes. *Journal of Cleaner Production, 62*, 8–15. https://doi.org/10.1016/j.jclepro.2013.06.007

Wu, Y.-C. J., & Shen, J.-P. (2016). Higher Education for Sustainable Development: A Systematic Review. *International Journal of Sustainability in Higher Education, 17*(5), 633–651. https://doi.org/10.1108/IJSHE-01-2015-0004

Wright, T., & Horst, N. (2013). Exploring the Ambiguity: What Faculty Leaders Really Think of Sustainability in Higher Education. *International Journal of Sustainability in Higher Education, 14*(2), 209–227. https://doi.org/10.1108/14676371311312905

Yáñez, S., Uruburu, Á., Moreno, A., & Lumbreras, J. (2019). The Sustainability Report as an Essential Tool for the Holistic and Strategic Vision of Higher Education Institutions. *Journal of Cleaner Production, 207*, 57–66. https://doi.org/10.1016/j.jclepro.2018.09.171

CHAPTER 10

Media, Literacy and Education: Partners for Sustainable Development

Carla Patrão, Dina Soeiro, and Sílvia Parreiral

Portugal Adult Educational Efforts Towards Sustainable Development

The partnership of media, literacy and education for Sustainable Development is the core of the proposal here presented. In the complex and unpredictable world we live today, we argue that there is a need for an integrated strategy of these partners to reach the Sustainable Development Goals (UN, 2015). Without education we cannot improve literacy, and the media play an active role in promoting literacy.

We witness a social depreciation of the low levels of literacy problem. The negative impacts of this situation are not recognized and socially valued, and the media do not give them the attention they deserve (Rothes, Queirós, & Moreira, 2019). If the media are allies to promote society recognition of this reality, there is more support to fight for strong policies to address the problem.

On the other hand, we need literacy to understand the media, to be able to filter their contents, not just as a consumer, but also as a critical actor towards social change.

C. Patrão (✉) • D. Soeiro • S. Parreiral
University of Coimbra, Coimbra, Portugal

Polytechnic Institute of Coimbra, Coimbra, Portugal
e-mail: cpatrao@esec.pt; disoeiro@esec.pt; scruzp@esec.pt

© The Author(s), under exclusive license to Springer Nature
Switzerland AG 2021
M. J. Yusha'u, J. Servaes (eds.), *The Palgrave Handbook of International Communication and Sustainable Development*,
https://doi.org/10.1007/978-3-030-69770-9_10

The focus of the 4th Global Report is on Adult Learning and Education. Leave no one behind: Participation, Equity and Inclusion (UNESCO, 2019) is on giving everyone a fair chance of having access to lifelong learning opportunities that help them acquire the knowledge and skills needed to exploit opportunities and participate fully in society. However, as consequence of the society's economic organization, which requires an increasingly qualified population, with other types of skills, it further aggravates the difficulty of people with low basic skills of being able to solve, on their own, their everyday problems.

According to DeVita, Milana, and Landri (2019, p. 2), even thought:

1. among the stated key development aims of the United Nations 2030 Agenda for Sustainable Development is the promotion of lifelong learning opportunities for all;
2. and the European Commission has approached the challenge of ensuring that older adults are socially included and able to exercise all their rights by introducing new policies on lifelong learning;
3. and the UNESCO's 2015 Recommendation on Adult Learning and Education insists that governments bear responsibility for promoting inclusive policies that guarantee the right to ongoing education for adults, and the reality of the exclusion and social injustice, faced by so many, makes clear the extent to which these recommendations have been disregarded.

In Portugal, there is a "strong generational penalty in educational terms" (Rothes et al., 2019, p. 52) that demands an urgent response, mobilizing social actors and working together to promote development for all. The Portuguese Government implemented, in 2010, the Basic Skills Training Programme, targeted at aged adults who do not hold literacy, numeracy and ICT skills. The impact was clearly insufficient (Rothes et al., 2019). There are still 895,140 adults (in a total of about 10 million inhabitants) with no education level and almost 500,000 people are illiterate (2011 National Census, INE, 2012). In this regard, Rothes et al. (2019, p. 25) argue that "the illiteracy of 5.2% of the Portuguese population is an expressive phenomenon, reaching, above all, the most deprived groups of resources and power: women, the elderly, agricultural workers, members of families living in especially segregated and impoverished areas and ethnic some minorities". In the 2011 Census, "the illiteracy rate was, in the case of women, much higher than that of men: 6.8% and 3.8%, respectively. The illiterate population was, as expected, essentially elderly—79% were 65 or older" (Rothes et al., 2019, p. 52).

According to the Europe 2020 education indicators in 2019 (Eurostat, 2020a), despite the efforts, Portugal didn't reach Education targets for Europe 2020. The numbers are particularly low for the so-called older adults (55–74 years old): 75.6% have less than primary, primary and lower secondary education (Eurostat, 2020b).

And, if we consider that today's societies are increasingly complex and imposing higher levels of education and education for all as a demand for social justice, compliance with human rights and democratic principles (CNE, 2019), there is no time to waist.

Portugal has been strongly supporting the efforts undertaken by international bodies to implement the Sustainable Development Goals by aligning national policies and instruments to this framework (EAEA, 2018). Education wasn't always one of the top priorities for the Portuguese governments and adult education was even more depreciated and suffered with the policy intermittency over the years. Recently, new developments had created hope in the future of adult education in Portugal (EAEA, 2019).

With a focus on improving basic literacy levels, the National Plan for Adult Literacy is an example of that effort that the Portuguese Government is carrying, in collaboration with the European Commission, the National Agency for Qualification and Professional Training and the European Association for the Education of Adults.

In the Resolution of the Council of Ministers no. 30/2020—Diário da República no. 78/2020, Series I of 2020-04-21, n.d., "It is intended that Portugal is at the forefront of the countries that are best prepared to face the challenges and changes inherent to a global transition, ensuring that it results in greater equality and inclusion of citizens, in strengthening democratic pillars".

This Resolution considers training and digital inclusion of people, with digital education; professional training and requalification; and digital inclusion and literacy. We highlight the Digital Inclusion Program for 1 million adults and the "National Digital Competence Initiative e.2030, Portugal INCoDe.2030, an integrated public policy program that aims to promote digital competences". This initiative intends to guarantee digital literacy and inclusion for the exercise of citizenship (INCoDe.2030, 2018).

Another example is the *Literacy for Democracy* Project, in which several Portuguese civil society organizations collaborate to "educate for citizenship and democratic literacy in order to develop the self-efficacy of communities" (APCEP, 2019).

Focused on the partnership of media, literacy and education for sustainable development, we will present the example of *Letters for Life*, an adult literacy community project.

Adult Literacy Workshops

Maria da Conceição was seven years old when she started guarding sheep and later working in the field. As a girl, she dressed in a grey uniform with a white apron and a cap on her head; she started to be raised to serve. Her salary was just a meal. His brothers, boys, had the opportunity to go to school, but at the time of the dictatorship, it was considered unnecessary for the girls to read and write. Years later her life was dedicated to weed rice. Whole days plucking weeds so that rice would grow faster. The school didn't take place in its toil days. Mary's story is the same as the stories of countless women who instead of attending school went to work to help support families, numerous and poor. Today, at the age of 84, Maria is one of the 185 participants of the community intervention project *Letters for Life*, which promotes literacy, empowerment and social inclusion through adult literacy workshops.

This project is focused on more vulnerable contexts in the central region of Portugal meeting the mission of the Higher School of Education of the Polytechnic Institute of Coimbra, which includes the reciprocity between Higher Education and communities, in a relationship of mutual benefit and proximity.

To achieve this goal, we count on the collaboration and support of 25 partners, such as associations, municipalities, private institutions of social solidarity and companies, and with a team from various areas of knowledge, such as Social Gerontology, Social Pedagogy, Adult Education, Psychology and Media Studies, which have more than 50 facilitators, among teachers, students and volunteers. All facilitators participate both pre-service and in-service training (Soeiro & Parreiral, 2018).

The communities, eager to know how to use new technologies, challenged the team to also create digital literacy workshops, which gave rise to the *Keys for Life*. Here they learn to use the computer, mobile phone, internet or social networks, from a perspective of safe, responsible and aware use of technologies, which goes beyond the utilitarian view. "UNESCO believes that the cultivation of a media-and information-literate population is essential for the sustainable development of any society, requiring the individual person, community, and nation at large to obtain a diverse range of competencies to become information literate and media literate" (UNESCO, 2013, p. 31). In this challenge the elderly cannot be left behind.

Silvino Guedes, with his 91st birthday, enthusiastically integrates one of these workshops to learn how to use the computer. He had a life full of work, was a farmer, repaired roads, built buildings and sold sardines and bread door-to-door. For 30 years he was still a sacristan, witnessing thousands of marriages and baptisms. Although he misses these times, now he is curious and motivated to learn how to write on the "little creature", the name he affectionately gave to the computer. He has already learned to identify the letters and numbers all on the keyboard but confesses that he still has some difficulty in putting the score marks.

The 100 participants who attend digital literacy workshops are between 50 and 95 years old and are motivated by specific needs. Some want to learn how to talk to children or grandchildren who are abroad, others need to know how to access health services, want access to information or even learn how to send a resume to a job. Older age participants, over 70 years of age, value communication with family members who are distant, the younger ones have a more functional perspective and are motivated by the demands of life, which determines their acquisition of digital skills.

In a society where technology prevails, it is vital that everyone acquires critical digital skills in order to improve their lives.

> This opens new horizons for every woman and man to exercise their rights to freedom of opinion, expression and access to information—to be actors in, and beneficiaries of, sustainable development. However, to enjoy these benefits, every citizen needs to be equipped with adequate devices and affordable connectivity. Without this, the gap between the information rich and the information poor will continue to grow—contributing to development gaps that would be unsustainable. (Engida, 2015, p. 9)

Unfortunately, in Portugal, not everyone still has access to technologies, mostly due to the financial situation that does not allow the acquisition of computer equipment.

Although living conditions have improved considerably since Mrs. Conceição was a child, there are still people at risk of poverty, with monthly incomes of less than 460 euros. According to Contemporary Portugal Database (PORDATA, 2020) in 2018, 17.7% of the Portuguese population, aged 65 and over, lives on the threshold of poverty, already including all income of an individual, such as social benefits, pensions, unemployment benefit and social income from insertion.

In the workshops we have participants from disadvantaged social contexts. One of the workshops of *Keys for Life* takes place at the headquarters of a social solidarity institution that works in the fight against poverty, in downtown Coimbra, an aged and abandoned area of the city. According to the Social Diagnosis of the Municipality of Coimbra (2018), the municipality suffered a population decline and the number of elderly people increased, meeting the demographic ageing of the population. The diagnosis points to the elderly who have low economic resources as problematic, many with low-value pensions. These situations of socio-economic vulnerability have several consequences, namely the abdication of health care, the non-acquisition of prescribed medicines and the lack of access to medical care that aggravates the state of health and decreases the quality of life.

According to the report "Health Literacy in Portugal" (Fundação Calouste Gulbenkian, 2016) the level of health literacy of 11% of the population is considered inadequate and that of 38% of the population is considered problematic, with the older population having the lowest level of health literacy. The Health Literacy Action Plan—Portugal 2019–2021 (DGS, 2019) addresses a set of strategic intervention measures for the promotion and sustained increase of health literacy of the Portuguese population.

In addition to the lack of health care, poverty also brings greater vulnerability to situations of violence, social exclusion, isolation and loneliness, situations identified in the diagnosis as problematic for the elderly population living in the municipality of Coimbra.

These most vulnerable groups have inequality in access to information and are unaware of some rights in the area of health, education and social security, among others.

The COVID-19 aggravated the economic situation, and the first-known data on the impact of the pandemic on the labour market, released by the Institute of Employment and Vocational Training (IEFP, 2020), points to 343,761 unemployed people in March of this year, an increase of 8.9% to the previous month. These numbers do not reflect the real scale of the problem because many of the unemployed are not registered with the Employment Institute and are therefore not part of the statistics. As a result of rising unemployment, calls for help and solidarity initiatives arise. In social networks there are several solidarity appeals, especially the initiative "Solidarity Box" which exists throughout the country, by the hand of civil society. Under the motto "take what you need, leave what you want" people leave food in the boxes and those who need it collect the food.

With the confinement, the families stayed at home on remote work and the students moved on to distance learning. This situation has accentuated social inequalities, because many of the students do not have a computer or internet network to attend classes at home, while others must share a computer with family members who are on remote work.

To mitigate social inequalities there have been numerous solutions throughout the country, with municipalities and civil society donating computers to those most in need. But in addition to the computer, it is necessary to have internet which is not a reality in all Portuguese homes.

We have witnessed great dynamism and solidarity of the communities in promoting creative solutions to these challenges.

Letters for Life: A Community-Based Participatory Action Research Approach

Literature has shown that community intervention makes sense when it results from the active participation of community members (Kaplan & Garrett, 2005; Kelly, Snowden, & Munoz, 1977; Kemmis, McTaggart, & Nixon, 2014; Kubisch, Brown, Chaskin, Hirota, & Joseph, 1998; Trickett, 2009).

About the concept "participation", Kemmis et al. (2014, p. 3), by reference to Habermas' (1987) theory of communicative action, and his (Habermas, 1996) views about "public spheres" and "communicative spaces", consider it has a way of "establish the legitimacy and validity of knowledge claims and action aimed at making social practices more rational and reasonable, more productive and sustainable, and more just and inclusive". In this sense, participatory action research is a methodological approach that contributes to the democratization of knowledge (Smith, Bratini, Chambers, Jensen, & Romero, 2010) and is often regarded as a source of empowerment for participants (Kemmis et al., 2014).

Closer to Freire's (1982) perspective who argued that, in the case of action research, we should be "learning to do it by doing it", participating in practice is the best way of understanding and realizing what is important to change in their practices. In turn, Kemmis et al. (2014) refer to "a practice-changing practice" that transforms community members' practices, making them more rational (reasonable, comprehensible, coherent, with individual and collective self-expression), sustainable (participants conduct their practices in an effective, productive and renewable way, immediately or in a long term) and just (the way participants relate to one another in the practice, and to others affected by their practice, don't limit the individual and collective self-determination of those involved and affected). In our understanding these are some principles of a proper community intervention.

Attending these considerations, the methodology of the project *Letters for Life* is person-centred, and according to a participatory action research approach, participants and their human subjectivity are valued and stressed their own consciousness in knowledge creation (Maguire, 1987).

We use an ethnographic lens to share the richness of the participants' life histories, because "the depth of perspective these techniques provide is invaluable in putting the pieces of the puzzle together" (Fetterman, 2010, p. 55) and allows us to understand the obstacles learners face.

Deolinda Ferreira, 80 years old, had never been to school. When she arrived at the workshops, she came very nervous and afraid because she did not know if she was still able to learn. The image she had of the school was from an austere place, with students sitting facing a board, very silent and quiet, listening to a teacher who could give a reprimand if they could not answer any questions. But she found a very different environment than she thought. Participants arrive and are received with affections, with hugs and kisses. Affections are highly valued; hence the project's motto is "Literacy with the Heart!".

According to Patton (1975, cit in Maguire, 1987), this scenario of closeness, empathy, interpersonal exchange and relationships between the team of facilitators and participants gives meaningful insights into their interaction and turns understandable the meaning that both give to their own behaviour. In fact, the *Letters for Life* project is a reciprocal learning context both for participants and for facilitators of the workshops, mostly higher education students in-service learning. These, reviewing the principles and objectives of the project, value it because it is an experiential education approach that promotes contact with people, their needs and motivations. In this regard, we share Bringle and Hatcher's (1996) perspective on in-service learning, in which students participate in an organized activity to serve the needs of the community that allows them to reflect on academic content and promote a sense of civic responsibility (Soeiro & Parreiral, 2018).

After the greetings, they sit around a table with flowers, full of books, dictionaries, almanacs and newspapers, which are chosen according to the preferences of the participants. They like to read the news from regional newspapers, some national reference newspapers and the sports press. Interestingly, the first section of the newspaper they like to read is necrology, to see if someone known or who may be an approximate age of their own has passed away. The computer or tablet is also used to read the information of the day.

Various learning strategies and techniques are used in several non-formal contexts where the workshops occur. The starting point is the knowledge of the participants, what they know instead of what they don't know. If Deolinda Ferreira knows how to make the typical cake of her locality, facilitators ask her to teach how to make it and from there she learns to write the words of the recipe.

One day, Deolinda Ferreira lost the transport that took her to the workshop and as she did not want to miss the session, so she decided to go by bike. She arrived exhausted, but willing to learn and evolve more and more to be included in society that belongs to all. Her motivation is huge. To learn how to read and write is her dream.

Participants can start learning by writing their own name, the name of their children or grandchildren, through the lyrics of some song they like the most or a poem. Both may want to know how to send an email and write a love letter. They realize that they can enter in a process of creation of significative and useful knowledge about their social reality (Fals-Borda & Rahman, 1991).

The sessions are planned according to the interests, needs and potentialities of the participants, through a participatory, active and personalized methodology, based on Paulo Freire's approach, the Pedagogy of Autonomy (Freire, 1996), on Andragogy (Knowles, 1973, 1980), and Self-directed Learning (Knowles, 1975).

By applying a participatory approach, participants and facilitators work together on both planning and evaluation. Being positioned at an equal level by applying the horizontal approach to communication, both improve their learning knowledge and enrich their experience with constructive and consistent support from each other. In addition, active and effective peer-to-peer interaction is encouraged by using Vygotsky's theory of Zone of Proximal Development (Vygotsky, 1978). In this way participants, especially those with differing skill levels, support each other while also improving their own abilities. Based on Freire's literacy approach (Freire, 1967), a series of reading and writing activities are planned and organized in order to promote participants' critical thinking and to contextualize their learning contents. As well as literacy skills, they simultaneously develop social skills, for instance, respect for each other, ICT skills, critical reflection and other skills necessary for personal, social and professional development (Soeiro & Parreiral, 2018).

And as community-based participatory action research, where the concept of uniqueness brings the focus to individuals and groups in their particular social context, the purpose, as literature reminds us, is to enhance local people's understanding and ability to control their own reality (Fals-Borda, 1991; Freire, 1970; Maguire, 1987, 1996).

Participants are helped to improve skills needed for their daily lives, such as knowing how to read a social security form or a supermarket bill, and knowing how to access an online health service, among other activities fundamental to their lives.

To foster reading habits and access to culture, the project promotes visits to municipal public libraries and museums. Some participants had never been in a museum or in a library and did not consider themselves worthy to handle a book with their working hands. For some, books are luxury objects. There are other kinds of visits, with a more convivial nature, such as those going to the beach, that some of them never visited before.

Writing and exchanging letters is one of the activities of the project. Participants write letters to grandchildren and children from elementary schools. Older people teach children how they played, while the younger ones teach the adults to deal with technologies, thus promoting intergenerational learning. Through a collaborative and a participatory exchange, significant learning is a more equally process shared between facilitators and the participants (Maguire, 1996).

In the workshops, participants have the opportunity to express their needs and interests and their perceptions about their learning experiences and, at the same time, their cultures and knowledge are valued. About this, literature refers to the important role of facilitators/researchers for the self-determined social transformation, rather than for the maintenance of inequitable social relations (Fals-Borda, 1991; Kemmis et al., 2014; Maguire, 1987).

Some authors argue that participatory action research "has the explicit intention of collectively investigating reality in order to transform it" (Hall et al., 1982; Fals-Borda, 1977, cit. in Maguire, 1987, p. 3) and "aims to develop critical consciousness to improve the lives of those involved in the research process and to transform fundamental societal structures and relationships" (Maguire, 1987, p. 4). So, we can advance that the *Letters for Life* workshops aim the promotion of civic engagement. As an example, learners have written to the Mayor, Prime Minister and the President of the Republic to voice their concerns over the elderly community and call for support from political leaders.

The project evaluation is inspired on Fetterman's Empowerment Evaluation perspective (Fetterman, 2001, 2005; Fetterman & Wandersman, 2018) and values the diverse contributions of all the direct actors, from the inside, the participants, team and partners, but also from a more external look, from the community of practice that the project promotes, as well as all the critical friends that contact with the project in conferences or technical meetings and share with us valuable feedback on the project.

The project is evaluated on the several dimensions and levels, using mostly a qualitative and formative approach and using triangulation of techniques and instruments, like observation, interviews, photovoice, videovoice and so on.

From a micro-level perspective, the workshops are evaluated at the end of each session and before the completion of each project cycle, in a systematic, continuous and participatory way, using critical discussions, reports, that analyses processes, evolution, products, results and challenges. We promote formative individualized evaluation that includes self-evaluation and content analysis of the materials participants produce.

At a meso level, the partners evaluate each project cycle, discussing a final report in an evaluation meeting and share their insights in the final ceremony, exhibition and party where participants receive their certification, having their family, community, media and even politicians witnessing their accomplishment and celebrating together.

In a macro level, the evaluation from the critical friends of the community of practice and the spheres where stakeholders of the project are interacting are also important. The impact on advocacy for adult education in Portugal is also considered, taking account of the visibility from the national media and the national organizations and government that could influence adult education.

Since 2017, the Project organizes an Annual Meeting Adult Education for Life that brings together academics, practitioners, learners, students, civil society organizations, political actors, partners and potential partners to enrich the critical debate on adult education, promote adult education for all and share good practices in Portugal. This opportunity to discuss our and other project practices and strategies is also very constructive and enhances the quality of adult education response.

The project also benefits from the interest of Master and PhD students, from diverse areas, that invest in researching the processes, results and impact of the project.

CRITICAL READING OF THE WORLD

The challenges of the knowledge and information society are increasing, and the media play a major role in promoting education, training and lifelong learning for all.

> The complexities of modern society demand educated, skilled and critical citizens in many different areas if freedom of expression, democracy and social progress are to be maintained and developed. Some of the knowledge and skills required relate to media and communication culture. Media and Information Literacy (MIL) takes its place alongside other things people need in order to be active citizens: knowledge of how political decisions are taken, the principles of the rule of law, the rights and obligations of citizens, the meaning of universal human rights, national and international security. (Carlsson, 2019, p. 11)

Starting from a perspective based on the critical reading of the world, inspired by Paulo Freire (1989), activities are energized with and for the media such as the promotion of reading and writing, and the use of technologies, as described below.

7 Days with the Media

The national operation *7 Days with the Media* that takes place annually in May, for a week, challenges citizens to think and reflect on the media and role they play in our day-to-day lives. It is an initiative of the Informal Group on Media Literacy open to all people and entities who want to develop their projects with the aim of promoting critical literacy with and for the media.

The participants of *Letters for Life* collaborated on the initiative for the first time in 2017, through various activities of reading, exploring, interpretation and analysis of local, national and sports newspapers and informative magazines, among other publications. The critical discussion of news and articles was promoted, and internet research was conducted resulting from the interests raised by the readings made. For example, regarding a news story they read about vaccination and measles, they conducted research on the reason for using a red cloth to wrap children with measles, which the elderly people participating in the workshop claimed to use.

They also visited the Regional Journal *Diário de Coimbra*, where they followed the entire production process of the newspaper from writing to distribution. As they were unaware of the process, they were impressed by the number of people who are needed for the newspaper to reach newsstands, machinery and printing process, as well as the number of readers and subscribers.

The activity ended with a visit to the centre of audiovisual and multimedia of the Higher School of Education of Coimbra, where participants were interviewed by the students of the Degree in Media Studies. Through these interviews it was possible to understand the perception that participants have about the media and the use they make of them. Most prefer to watch Television, namely news and some entertainment programmes, such as soap operas. Radio is the chosen means to hear the news and specially to feel in company. The reading of newspapers is a daily habit for some, especially the reading of regional newspapers, which bring information about their localities. Sports and cultural news are at the top of preferences over political and economic information.

In the second year of participation in the operation *7 Days with the Media*, the participants of one of the workshops of *Letters for Life* tried to be reporters for a day. It was a unique experience for participants who were not familiar with handling cameras and microphones. This initiative allowed us to promote the understanding of the world, from the perspective of Paulo Freire, through literacy with and for the media. While the participants had the experience of what it is to be a journalist, the students, future professionals, became closer to the sources and the professional knowledge-making, in addition to having developed capacities of civic participation and active citizenship.

Concerns about ethical, security and privacy issues emerging from the new forms of communication led to the realization, in 2019, of the activity to promote critical digital literacy. A reflection and awareness of the risks of the Internet, Fake News and the correct use of social networks was promoted. Participants had the opportunity to clarify some of their doubts, save negative aspects and highlight some positive scans of the internet, such as finding job offers or keeping in touch with family and friends.

After learning some rules for identifying fake news, an exercise was held in which participants had to recognize the veracity of the news presented. This activity confirmed what was already observed in the workshops, participants believe more in the news they read in the traditional newspaper, than in digital. Trust falls in the information that is aired by printed newspapers, especially in regional newspapers that are the ones that they consume the most. They rely more on an online publication that has a paper edition than in an exclusively digital publication. Most participants already know the criteria for identifying fake news, already taking special care to verify the sources of information and content of the news (Patrão, Soeiro, & Parreiral, 2019).

This year, and due to the pandemic COVID-19, the initiative was changed to *7 Days with the Media* without leaving home, face the recommendation of physical distancing and staying at home. As long as there are no safety conditions to develop face-to-face workshops, we will continue to work online beyond the *7 Days* in a regular and systematic base. To support participants in their functional digital needs, the project offers a helpdesk line, but our intervention transcends that.

Given the circumstances the media are fundamental to understand what surrounds us, but we are concerned of the pandemic of disinformation to which we are subject, especially through social networks. To identify the sources of information to which participants use to inform themselves about the current situation, resulting from the pandemic, we conducted a survey on the Facebook page of the Project *Letters for Life* and in the various Facebook and WhatsApp groups of the Workshops *Keys for Life*.

The results show us that participants use different sources to inform themselves about the pandemic situation: 25.9% of the responses point to television news, 22.9% of the answers say they choose the social network Facebook and 17.5% of the answers report that they use the online page of the Portuguese Directorate-General for Health. The online pages of local newspapers are chosen in 17.5% of the answers, while 7% of the answers give preference to the online pages of national newspapers. These numbers represent what we have been checking in the workshops where participants choose more local newspapers, giving value to proximity. Local newspapers have only 2.4% of the answers and there are no answers to the national newspapers. We calculate that these numbers are because people are confined to their homes and do not go out to buy the newspaper, choosing reading online. National radio stations are the choice of 4.8% of the answers while the option for local radios did not obtain answers. Family members and friends were the sources recorded in 6.6% of the answers, and other sources of information, not specified, obtained 5.4% of the answers, while 1.2% of the answers pointed to television programmes other than the news.

Following the collection of this data, the students involved in the project will endorse, through social networks, various challenges related to disinformation, fake news and online security.

Social networks are being flooded with treatments and miracle cures to combat the new COVID-19 coronavirus, which put the public health at risk. Numerous conspiracy theories and myths that need to be demystified are also proliferating in the networks. Scams and online fraud snags have also skyrocketed with the pandemic. The schemes are diverse, ranging from fraudulent text messages and emails with bills to pay for the consumption of water, electricity or telecommunications, non-existent, under penalty of cutting off service or attempting to sell personal protective equipment to fight the virus. With the confinement and the new habits of online consumption it is necessary to alert participants to these situations.

The hate speech that has emerged on the networks is also alarming and must be combated. UN chief, António Guterres, appeals for dealing and combating coronavirus-fuelled hate speech,

> Yet the pandemic continues to unleash a tsunami of hate and xenophobia, scapegoating and scare-mongering. Anti-foreigner sentiment has surged online and in the streets. Anti-Semitic conspiracy theories have spread, and COVID-19-related anti-Muslim attacks have occurred. Migrants and refugees have been vilified as the source of the virus and then denied them access to medical treatment. With older persons among the most vulnerable, contemptible memes have emerged suggesting they are also the most expendable. And journalists, whistleblowers, health professionals, aid workers and human rights defenders are being targeted simply for doing their jobs. We must act now to strengthen the immunity of our societies against the virus of hate. (Guterres, 2020)

Critical digital literacy is increasingly urgent so that we can all fight disinformation and contribute for a conscious and safest online interaction.

Involvement of Media Studies Students

It was through the activity *7 Days with the Media* that the students of the degree in Media Studies began to actively participate in the project *Letters for Life*, continuing through several studies carried out within the scope of curricular units of the course and the performance of curricular internships. In addition to accompanying the workshops, students have conducted interviews, reports, photographic works and documentaries, among others.

The first impact when students arrive in these territories is significant. They find realities that they didn't know and didn't imagine, as there is no internet access or communication system, such as a simple phone. Some of these territories have lost telecommunications infrastructure due to large and serious fires and extreme meteorological phenomena, such as Storm "Leslie", leaving populations even more isolated. They know people who have never seen the sea, who have never even left their village and who for whom school and education is a luxury, much desired and not an acquired right. They might first sing congratulations to someone who had never celebrated his birthday. Some of the participants didn't even know the day they were born. Students feel welcomed, valued and useful, and that makes a difference in people's lives.

By collecting the life stories of the participants, their traditions, memories and customs, students are giving voice to those who were not listened.

One of the communication channels where participants are listened to is on the radio, kind of familiar to them. They are interviewed and participate regularly in the preparation of a radio programme in which they define the contents and share their opinions and stories in collaboration with students.

With the help of students, participants produce written and multimedia content, to feed social networks, always from their interests.

Students in addition to vocational learning enrich their personal and social development. "As a media studies student, I have a responsibility to give voice to the weakest, in this case, to the older ones. They are people who deserve and need our attention and help so that they can be happier and understand the world around them" (Carolina, Media Studies intern).

Through the project, students witness in loco how the right to information is a fundamental right that should be available to everyone. They experience the need for citizens to be informed, to know what is going on around them, so that they can act and make conscious and democratic decisions.

Contributions for the Sustainable Goals

Taking in consideration the "2030 Agenda for Sustainable Development", *Letters for Life* gives a contribution mostly to "Goal 4. Ensure inclusive and equitable quality education and promote lifelong learning opportunities for all" and "Goal 5. Achieve gender equality and empower all women and girls".

Concerning to Education, as the Progress towards the Sustainable Development Goals Report of the Secretary-General (UN, 2019, p. 10) claims, "Refocused efforts are needed to improve learning outcomes for the full life cycle, especially for women, girls and marginalized people in vulnerable settings". Nevertheless, there is no specific commitment to education for older adults.

The focus is still limited on education for productivity, economy and employment:

> investing in education and health and wellbeing for all, including lifelong learning, can improve productivity and maintain economic growth even as the share of working-age population shrinks. (…) As employment is shifting towards jobs that require high-level cognitive and socio-emotional skills in this digital age, more emphasis will need to be placed on lifelong learning to keep up with changes in technology and maintain flexibility in skills. (UN-DESAPD, 2019, p. 27)

That can be contradictory with the demographic ageing reality. In Portugal, one of the most aged countries in the world (UN-DESAPD, 2019), education for the elderly must be an investment.

Leaving no one behind (UN, 2015) is also our pledge. Age shouldn't be a criterion for access and success in Education. We aim to increase the participation of older people in Education. Promoting their access to education is a social justice action. As society we owe them that.

Regarding women empowerment, education can be transformative. Women are the majority of the participants in the *Letters for life* workshops, because they were historically left behind from educational opportunities. They are motivated to learn to write and read because they want to be autonomous and independent. Most of the women participants are over 65 years old, but we have some young Roma women eager to be free, and this educational opportunity represents a ticket to freedom, autonomy and empowerment, not just for them but also for their children who often come to the workshops. These women recognize the value of education and request our support to promote school success for their children. Some of the women participate to enhance their chance to be employee. Most of them are long-term unemployed and the low level of literacy doesn't help them to face the demands of the job market. They realize that they need to invest on their literacy competences. Because of the positive experience in the literacy workshops, some of the younger participants, who were unemployed, were motivated to pursue professional training and got a job.

In the *Keys for Life* workshops devoted to digital literacy, women are interested in using Internet to facilitate their daily lives and mostly to communicate with their relatives abroad. Surprisingly (or not) we have some women participants that come to the workshops without their husband's knowledge. The men are against their digital competence development, accordingly with their wives, because they are afraid that the women learn more and become emancipated, and, perhaps, know more than them.

The content of the workshops is far beyond literacy and digital literacy. Issues like gender equality, domestic violence, education of girls, racism and discrimination emerge in dynamics of the workshops and these are fruitful spaces of critical thinking and awareness. The friendly environment allows the participants to share their life experiences and concerns and to discuss together the challenges they face in life, enlarging their repertoires of behaviour and opening new perspectives. They understand that there is more to live, and their lives can be better.

By developing their critical thinking, they feel able to get more involved in community affairs, especially those that directly concern them. In this way they become participatory, demanding, giving more and more useful to the opportunity to make themselves heard and becoming active actors in the transformation of their community.

The impact on sustainable and local development is verified in the communities' engagement. One of the most satisfying results is the reopening of closed schools. With the decrease in the number of children and the economic vision of the formal educational system, many schools closed, contributing to the isolation and low population density. Within the partnership of local municipalities, we manage to restore the use of the schools for education, opening the schools at different schedules for the workshops. The schools gained a new life, with adults learning in a traditional learning space for children.

Another interesting result is related to decentralized responses, the communication infrastructures and mobility. The communities demanded Internet and transportation for the workshops, creating collaborative solutions between participants and local partners, which allow people to have access to this educational opportunity.

These are some of the results that the *Letters for Life* project has allowed us to achieve with its participants, team and community which we emphasize because they are the ones that, in our opinion, have most contributed to a closer approximation to the goals for sustainable development.

Final Considerations

The sustainable development is a challenging mission, which demands the integrated action of media, literacy and education, as key partners, working together for social change.

Despite the intention of "leaving no one behind", there is no real commitment to education for all. It is urgent to promote participation of older people in education, engaging communities and local governments.

The project gives a contribution in providing equal learning opportunities for the elderly, enhancing intergenerational learning and promoting awareness of the importance of learning at an advanced age and, as a consequence, demonstrating that, at this stage of life, educational offers are not an expense but an investment for social inclusion, active citizenship, well-being and happiness.

Portugal has demonstrated an effort to meet sustainable goals, but we need to analyse this process of achievement in a global and integrated perspective, beyond the current environmental and business dominant focus. We argue that, to understand and foster the progress towards the SDG, it is important to give recognition to the value of education, adult education and non-formal adult education.

There is a risk that the COVID-19 compromises the gains already achieved and makes difficult the progress towards the sustainable development goals. It is necessary to investigate all this impact that the pandemic is bringing to society and mitigate the negative consequences, shield what was conquered and cherish the positive dynamics that emerged from the world in crises.

To strengthen the power that every person and communities have to fight evil and managed fear, now, more than ever, we need Freire's (1992) Pedagogy of Hope.

References

Associação Portuguesa para a Cultura e Educação Permanente (APCEP). (2019). *Literacy for Democracy Project*. Retrieved October 5, 2020, from http://www.apcep.pt/LD_APCEP.php

Bringle, R., & Hatcher, J. (1996). Implementing Service Learning in Higher Education. *The Journal of Higher Education, 67*(2), 221–239.

Carlsson, U. (2019). MIL in the Cause of Social Justice and Democratic Rule. In U. Carlsson (Ed.), *Understanding Media and Information Literacy (MIL) in the Digital Age—A Question of Democracy* (pp. 11–24). Gothenburg: UNESCO.

Conselho Nacional da Educação (CNE). (2019). *Estado da Educação 2018*. Retrieved October 5, 2020, from http://www.cnedu.pt/pt/?fbclid=IwAR2okuFQ7-XlWJuMfR6owSww1ttuZLNPY3K7Qe7NI4sqGcFyNIm_-3InDGM

DeVita, A., Milana, M. & Landri, P. (2019). Responsibility, Participation and Social Justice in Adult Education. *Encyclopaideia—Journal of Phenomenology and Education, 23* (53). Retrieved October 5, 2020, from https://doi.org/10.6092/issn.1825-8670/9362

Direção-Geral da Saúde (DGS). (2019). *Health Literacy Action Plan 2019–2021—Portugal.* Direção de Serviços de Prevenção da Doença e Promoção da Saúde (DSPDPS) Divisão de Literacia, Saúde e Bem-Estar. Retrieved October 5, 2020, from https://www.dgs.pt/documentos-e-publicacoes/plano-de-acao-para-a-literacia-em-saude-2019-2021-pdf.aspx

Engida, G. (2015). Foreword. In J. Sing, A. Grizel, S. J. Yee, & S. H. Culver (Eds.), *MILID Yearbook 2015, Media and Information Literacy for the Sustainable Development Goals* (pp. 9–11). Gothenburg: The International Clearinghouse on Children, Youth and Media Nordicom.

European Association for the Education of Adults (EAEA). (2018). *Adult Education in Europe 2018—A Civil Society View.* Brussels: EAEA. Retrieved October 5, 2020, from https://eaea.org/wp-content/uploads/2018/11/Country_Reports_2018_final.pdf

European Association for the Education of Adults (EAEA) (2019). *Adult Education in Europe 2019—A Civil Society View.* Brussels: EAEA. Retrieved October 5, 2020, from https://eaea.org/wp-content/uploads/2019/12/Country-Reports-2019.pdf

Eurostat. (2020a). *News Release 66/2020—22 April 2020.* Retrieved October 5, 2020, from https://ec.europa.eu/eurostat/documents/2995521/10749941/3-22042020-BP-EN.pdf/04c88d0b-17af-cf7e-7e78-331a67f3fcd5

Eurostat. (2020b). *Population by Educational Attainment Level, Sex and Age (%)—Main Indicators, 55–74 Years.* Retrieved October 5, 2020, from https://appsso.eurostat.ec.europa.eu/nui/submitViewTableAction.do

Fals-Borda, O. (1991). Remaking Knowledge. In O. Fals-Borda & M. A. Rahman (Eds.), *Action and Knowledge: Breaking the Monopoly with Participatory Action Research* (pp. 146–166). New York: Apex.

Fals-Borda, O., & Rahman, M. (1991). *Action and Knowledge: Breaking the Monopoly with Participatory Action Research.* New York: Apex.

Fetterman, D. (2001). *Foundations of Empowerment Evaluation.* Thousand Oaks: Sage.

Fetterman, D. (2005). Empowerment Evaluation Principles in Practice: Assessing Levels of Commitment. In D. Fetterman & A. Wandersman (Eds.), *Empowerment Evaluation: Principles in Practice* (pp. 42–72). New York: Guilford.

Fetterman, D. C. (2010). *Ethnography Step-by-Step.* Thousand Oaks: Sage.

Fetterman, D., & Wandersman, A. (2018). Essentials of Empowerment Evaluation. In D. Fetterman, L. Rodríguez-Campos, & A. Zukoski and Contributors, *Collaborative, Participatory, and Empowerment Evaluation* (pp. 74–89). New York: Guilford.

Freire, P. (1967). *Educação como Prática da Liberdade.* Rio de Janeiro: Paz e Terra.

Freire, P. (1970). *Pedagogy of the Oppressed.* London: Zed Books.

Freire, P. (1982). Creating Alternative Research Methods: Learning to Do It by Doing It. In B. Hall, A. Gillette, & R. Tandon (Eds.), *Creating Knowledge: A Monopoly?* (pp. 29–37). New Delhi: Society for Participatory Research in Asia.

Freire, P. (1989). *A importância do ato de ler: em três artigos que se completam.* São Paulo: Cortez.

Freire, P. (1992). *Pedagogy of Hope: Reliving Pedagogy of the Oppressed.* London: Continuum.

Freire, P. (1996). *Pedagogia da Autonomia. Saberes necessários à prática educative*. São Paulo: Paz e Terra.
Fundação Calouste Gulbenkian. (2016). *Literacia em Saúde em Portugal—Relatório Síntese*. Lisboa: CIES/IUL.
Guterres, A. (2020). *UN chief Global Appeal to Address and Counter COVID-19 Related Hate Speech*. Retrieved October 5, 2020, from https://news.un.org/en/story/2020/05/1063542
Habermas, J. (1987). *Theory of Communicative Action, Volume II: Lifeworld and System: A Critique of Functionalist Reason*. Boston: Beacon.
Habermas, J. (1996). *Between Facts and Norms*. Cambridge: MIT Press.
IEFP. (2020). *Informação Mensal do Mercado de Emprego*. Retrieved October 5, 2020, from https://www.iefp.pt/documents/10181/9766505/Informa%C3%A7%C3%A3o+Mensal+mar%C3%A7o+2020.pdf/910ce737-b43d-41c8-8953-e3aba877ad38
INCoDe.2030. (2018). Brochura Portugal INCoDe.2030 (Versão EN). Retrieved October 5, 2020, from https://www.incode2030.gov.pt/sites/default/files/portugal_incode_en_web_single_0.pdf
INE. (2012). *Censos Portugal 2011*. Lisboa: INE.
Kaplan, S. A., & Garrett, K. E. (2005). The Use of Logic Models by Community-Based Initiatives. *Evaluation and Program Planning, 28*, 167–172.
Kelly, J. C., Snowden, L. R., & Munoz, R. F. (1977). Social and Community Intervention. *Annual Review of Psychology, 38*, 323–361.
Kemmis, S., McTaggart, R., & Nixon, R. (2014). *The Action Research Planner. Doing Critical Participatory Action Research*. London: Springer.
Knowles, M. (1973). *The Adult Learner: A Neglected Species*. Houston: Gulf Publishing Company.
Knowles, M. (1975). *Self-Directed Learning: A Guide for Learners and Teachers*. New York: Associated Press.
Knowles, M. (1980). *The Modern Practice of Adult Education: From Pedagogy to Andragogy*. New York: Association Press.
Kubisch, A. C., Brown, P., Chaskin, R., Hirota, J., & Joseph, M. (1998). *Voices from the Field: Learning from the Early Work of Comprehensive Community Initiatives*. Washington, DC: Aspen Institute.
Maguire, P. (1987). Doing Participatory Research: A Feminist Approach. Participatory. *Research & Practice, 6*, Amherst, MA: University of Massachusetts. Retrieved October 5, 2020, from http://scholarworks.umass.edu/cie_participatoryresearchpractice/1
Maguire, P. (1996). Considering More Feminist Participatory Research: What's Congruency Got to Do with It? *Qualitative Inquiry, 2*, 106–118.
Município de Coimbra. (2018). *Diagnóstico Social do Concelho de Coimbra*. Divisão de Educação e Ação Social da Câmara Municipal de Coimbra. CLAS/C. Retrieved October 5, 2020, from https://www.cm-coimbra.pt/wp-content/uploads/2018/06/Diagno%CC%81stico-Social-2018.pdf
Patrão, C., Soeiro, D., & Parreiral, S. (2019). 'Teclas Prá Vida': a transformar janelas em realidades inclusivas. In S. Pereira (Ed.), *Literacia, Media e Cidadania—Livro de Atas do 5.º congresso* (pp. 302–311). Braga: CECS.
PORDATA. (2020). *Taxa de risco de pobreza após transferências sociais: indivíduos com 65 e mais anos*. Retrieved October 5, 2020, from https://www.pordata.pt/Europa/Taxa+de+risco+de+pobreza+ap%C3%B3s+transfer%C3%AAncias+sociais+indiv%C3%ADduos+com+65+e+mais+anos-2169

Resolução do Conselho de Ministros. (n.d.). n.° 30/2020—*Diário da República n.° 78/2020*, Série I de 2020-04-21.

Rothes, L., Queirós, J., & Moreira, A. (2019). *Plano Nacional de Literacia de Adultos, Relatório de Pesquisa*. Porto. inED—Centro de Investigação & Inovação em Educação, Escola Superior de Educação do Politécnico do Porto.

Smith, L., Bratini, L., Chambers, D.-A., Jensen, R. V., & Romero, L. (2010). Between Idealism and Reality: Meeting the Challenges of Participatory Action Research. *Action Research, 8*(4), 407–425.

Soeiro, D., & Parreiral, S. (2018, 06 de agosto). *Case Study Letters for Life*, Portugal. UNESCO Institute for Lifelong Learning. Retrieved October 5, 2020, from http://uil.unesco.org/case-study/effective-practices-database-litbase-0/letters-life-portugal

Trickett, E. (2009). Multilevel Community-Based Culturally Situated Interventions and Community Impact: An Ecological Perspective. *American Journal of Community Psychology, 43*, 257–266.

UNESCO. (2013). *Global Media and Information Literacy (MIL) Assessment Framework: Country Readiness and Competencies*. Paris: UNESCO. Retrieved October 5, 2020, from https://unesdoc.unesco.org/ark:/48223/pf0000224655

UNESCO. (2019). *4th Global Report on Adult Learning and Education. Leave No One Behind: Participation, Equity and Inclusion*. Institute for Lifelong Learning. Paris: UNESCO. Retrieved October 5, 2020, from https://unesdoc.unesco.org/ark:/48223/pf0000372274

United Nations (UN). (2015). *Transforming Our World: The 2030 Agenda for Sustainable Development, A/RES/70/1*. Retrieved October 5, 2020, from https://sustainabledevelopment.un.org/post2015/transformingourworld/publication

United Nations, Department of Economic and Social Affairs, Population Division (UN-DESAPD). (2019). *World Population Ageing 2019: Highlights* (ST/ESA/SER.A/430). Retrieved October 5, 2020, from https://www.un.org/en/development/desa/population/publications/pdf/ageing/WorldPopulationAgeing2019-Highlights.pdf

United Nations, Economic and Social Council. (2019). *Special Edition: Progress Towards the Sustainable Development Goals Report of the Secretary-General*. Retrieved October 5, 2020, from https://undocs.org/E/2019/68

Vygotsky, L. (1978). *Mind in Society: The Development of Higher Psychological Processes*. Cambridge: Harvard University Press.

CHAPTER 11

The Paradox in Discourse and Praxis of Gender Equality: A Communicative Framework for Sustainable Development

Mohammad Ala-Uddin

> *Anticipations of the future become part of the present, thereby rebounding upon how the future actually develops.*
> —Giddens (1990, pp. 177–178)

INTRODUCTION

In May 2014, two cousin sisters from the *Dalit* ("untouchable") community were allegedly gang-raped and killed by hanging in their scarves with a tree in Badaun of India. Reportedly, the perpetrators picked the minors in the evening from a nearby field where they wanted to relieve themselves as their homes lacked toilet facilities. The local police denied helping the victim's family and filing for the rape and murder (See Dubey, 2018a, 2018b; Burke, 2014). Next year in Baghpat of India, a local *Panchayat* allegedly issued a diktat that two *Dalit* sisters be raped and paraded naked in the blackened face as revenge for

---

An earlier version of this paper was presented at Gender and Communication Section of the 2018 IAMCR Conference in Eugene, Oregon, USA, June 20–24, 2018.

M. Ala-Uddin (✉)
School of Communication Studies, James Madison University,
Harrisonburg, VA, USA
e-mail: alauddmx@jmu.edu

© The Author(s), under exclusive license to Springer Nature
Switzerland AG 2021
M. J. Yusha'u, J. Servaes (eds.), *The Palgrave Handbook of International Communication and Sustainable Development*,
https://doi.org/10.1007/978-3-030-69770-9_11

their brother's elopement with a girl. According to news reports, police abducted and tortured their family members and implicated the boy in a narcotics case. The family was forced to leave the village while the oppressors possessed their house (See Raju, 2015; Bhatia, 2015). According to media reports, Badaun perpetrators were from a higher Hindu caste and ironically included two police constables. The police were also found complicit in the Baghpat incident. Moreover, the *Panchayat* is an unofficial but influential village council system in India, usually managed and led by the senior male members hailing from the local elites.

Both Badaun and Baghpat cases offer several insights. First, in a typical rape incident, perpetrators occasionally kill the victims to avoid being caught. However, the Badaun rapists not only killed the girls but left them hanging with a tree, purportedly to send a strong message to their families that they could do nothing in return. Second, the *Panchayat* rape order revealed the same vulnerability of girls and their families to the power elites. Third, the lack of sanitation facilities at home is more than the mere absence of a material resource. Sanitation is indeed empowerment for some women like in India. Sen (1999) rightly argues that individuals and communities lacking one freedom (e.g., being able to use toilets at home) become vulnerable by other unfreedoms (e.g., being insecure). Finally, both Badaun and Baghpat cases suggest that for women and girls like those in India to live in dignity, equity, and justice, the intricate nature of power to which women become disposable must be addressed in the discourse and practice of social change. As such, this last insight was what brought this chapter into being.

I chose to begin with the above cases not to reduce the issues of gender to a specific sociocultural context, but rather, to make a point that the nature of deprivations inflicted upon women and other marginalized communities is beyond what is generally conceived in the "refined" lexicon of international development. Indeed, these are not isolated incidents in our present globalized society. They represent the chain of persecutions being regularly committed against women and girls, particularly those who live below the power line. In India alone, every 15 minutes a girl is being raped and the crime against women in the nation increased 873% over the past five decades (Dubey, 2018a, 2018b). This is not a problem of just developing countries. Rape is the world's shame and a global pandemic (Equality Now, 2017). According to the US Department of Justice, every 73 seconds, another American is sexually assaulted which includes 10% men while only 5 out of every 1000 perpetrators go to prison (RAINN, n.d.). With about 20 thousand cases, Africa reports the highest female homicides in the world (UNODC, 2018). According to the World Health Organization (WHO, 2017), one in three women experience physical or sexual violence in their lifetime and 38% of murders of women are committed by their intimate partners. This statistic is just the tip of the iceberg. If included the unreported cases, the actual figure may turn several times higher. The rape incidents are usually underreported in developing countries due to various sociocultural, political, and geolocational impediments (Palermo,

Bleck, & Peterman, 2013; Rukmini, 2014). Thus, the mere mention of such statistics may conceal the complex social and political dynamics underlying these incidents.

Apart from the violence against women, the performance of gender equality across the world is deploring and, evidently, the global communities are likely to fail in delivering the promises of gender equality by 2030. According to the 2019 Global Gender Index by Equal Measures 2030, no country has fully achieved that goal so far while the global average of gender equality performance is 65.7 out of 100, which is categorized as "poor," or just a "passing grade" (EM2030, 2019; Connell, Holder, & Kearney, 2020). The Index also specifies that about 1.4 billion (40% of) women and girls of the world live in countries that are performing "very poor" and failed to secure even a "passing grade." That is, gender equality seems to be failing in almost all 17 sustainable development goals (SDGs). For example, the top 20 countries including Denmark, Norway, Germany, Canada, and the UK are doing poorly in the gender climate action (SDG 13) and global partnership for sustainable development (SDG 17). These are also the two least performing SDGs in the spectrum. Similarly, the bottom 40 countries including India, Egypt, and Nigeria are performing "very poor" in almost all the 17 SDGs. In more than 60 countries, regardless of *developed* (e.g., Norway, Switzerland, and Japan) and *developing* (e.g., India, Algeria, and South Africa), a portion of "women agree that husband/partner is justified in beating his wife/partner under certain circumstances" (EM2030, 2019, Indicator 5b). In sum, not a single country has obtained the "excellent" score and thus "no country has reached the last mile on gender equality" (Connell et al., 2020, p. 411). In a most recent report, Equal Measures 2030 predicts that 2.1 billion girls and women live in 67 countries that will not reach any of the five gender equality targets by 2030 at the current pace (EM2030, 2020). Now, the entire 2030 Agenda is interrupted in numerous ways by the ongoing COVID-19 pandemic. For examples, about 47 million women are pushed into poverty due to COVID-19; women being at the heart of care are among the most vulnerable to the infection of COVID-19; and shockingly, there is also a global rise in domestic violence during this pandemic (UN Woman, 2020a, 2020b). Whereas all SDGs are interconnected and interdependent, one way or another, their achievement contributes to the ultimate achievement of gender equality. For instance, the original vision of gender equality (SDG 5) cannot be realized if women and girls are left behind in the SDG 1 (no poverty), SDG 2 (zero hunger), SDG 3 (healthcare for all), and SDG 4 (quality education), to mention a few (McGowan, Stewart, Long, & Grainger, 2019; Ala-Uddin, 2019).

It is evident from the above picture, the world is watering on the branches of a dying tree, instead of its roots, or it is "like throwing darts in the dark" as one advocate once remarked (Connell et al., 2020). The issues of gender equality are much profound than how the global aid agencies conceive it in numerical figures or put effort in the unwarranted places. Taking this as a point of departure, my goal in this chapter is threefold. First, drawing upon a broad-based idea of social justice, I problematize the notions of "equality" and "empowerment" to reveal how they are inadequate in bringing sustainable social change for the marginalized communities. I then follow a critical conversation about the historical formation of gender equality and review its assimilation into the framework of Millennium Development Goals (MDGs) as well as its continuation throughout the Sustainable Development Goals (SDGs). By looking specifically at the conceptual meanings of gender equality and women empowerment within MDGs and SDGs, I was able to point out the paradoxical moments in global development policy and argue that both frameworks inadequately addressed the critical issues relevant to gender inequality and injustice. Finally, this chapter presents a conceptual framework describing the role of communication for development (C4D) that can help tackle the issues of gender inequality and injustice, which may, in turn, inform further the 2030 Agenda for Sustainable Development.

This analysis as well as the resulting conceptual framework is crucial in three broad ways. First, scrutiny of "equality" and "empowerment" from social justice perspective would further our understanding of what constitutes sustainable development and how that could genuinely address the issues of gender, especially within the framework of SDGs. In turn, such an understanding may offer implications for more effective policy formulations towards ensuring justice for all. According to Gardner and Lewis (2000), "The task of deconstructing particular aspects of development discourse can have a direct practical and political outcome" (p. 18). Second, my analysis shed new light on the bearing of nuances and complexities of current social order on women and other marginalized communities being prevented from affording a life that they value. The presence of women in public life, as well as their access to material sources, has increased over the decades; however, "women access to resources does not lead to their greater control over resources; that changes in legal statutes have little influence on practice; and that female political leaders do not necessarily work to promote women's interests" (Malhotra, 2003, p. 3). That is, such a discursive or material endeavour towards improving the fate of the marginalized communities becomes as such "political" by definition, to which is this proposed framework comitted. It comprises a broad-based idea of social justice and addresses the paradoxical moments of social change discourse in gender equality and women empowerment.

EQUALITY, EMPOWERMENT, AND SOCIAL JUSTICE

The notions of equality, empowerment, and justice are infamously fuzzy in social change literature. Although theorized across disciplines, they are interconnected. Their discussion in isolation will not make them less ambiguous. Therefore, the concepts are unpacked and their interconnection is clarified.

Equality Framework

Equality is a "loaded" and "highly contested" concept (Gosepath, 2011). Generally, it has a positive connotation and a rhetorical power. There is no universally agreed-upon definition of equality in literature. The nature of equality is limited to diverse inequalities people experience regularly. Nevertheless, it has at least a *material* (e.g., equality of what?) and a *discursive* dimension. The discussion of equality is integral to the distributive theories of justice. According to Gosepath (2011), equality entails a tripartite relation between (a) *two parties* (e.g., equality among whom?), (b) at least *one quality* (e.g., equality in what respect?), and (c) *a distribution* (e.g., distribution of things among two or more entities). Among the three elements, *distribution* is what makes the process of equality very complicated. How a resource will be allocated generally depends on certain philosophical positions, and the circumstances that characterize the distribution targets. Such allocation, in turn, problematizes the treatment of recipients and allocation of rights and resources while the complexity involved makes the notion of "equality" a point of interdisciplinary discussion.

Social theorists and political philosophers from various disciplinary backgrounds attempt to expand the meaning and construct of equality and its link to justice as well as the principles and rules that mediate it (Eckhoff, 1974; Cook & Hegtvedt, 1983; Gosepath, 2011). To keep it relevant to this chapter, I drew a typology of equality which combines the prominent positions and the pertinent arguments. There are primarily three types of equality. First, *formal equality* provides two individuals equal status in a formal legal or policy framework, at least in one normative respect, while accounting for no difference or circumstances they might have (Gosepath, 2011). Eckhoff (1974) calls this "objective equality." Second, when all are treated in a way that they would receive what they deserve or what is due constitutes *proportional or relative equality* (Eckhoff, 1974; Gosepath, 2011). This type of equality is also called *equity* as a fair exchange (Cook & Hegtvedt, 1983). Third, contrary to the other two, *moral equality* assumes that all people deserve the same dignity and respect even if they are diverse in their attributes and identities (Gosepath, 2011). Moral equality conforms to an egalitarian view of justice (Rawls, 1971).

The above typology renders another way to categorize equality—*formal* equality of opportunities and *substantive* equality of outcomes. The goal of formal equality is to treat men and women equally through legal and policy frameworks. On the other, substantive equality is concerned with the outcomes and consequences of them, because "[e]quality of opportunity need not always be the same thing as equality of *result*, but it cannot lose sight of the fact that opportunity must be *meaningfully* equal" (Stancil, 2016, p. 1638, emphasis original). Stancil adds, "The law might prescribe or proscribe 'equally,' but the law's effects will be felt differentially" (p. 1637). From this, a critical insight can be drawn that an equal opportunity may not produce an equal outcome, for which, equality despite being one of the key properties of justice is not always the same as justice (Lucas, 1980). It is rather the need and context, situations, and circumstances that warrant *varying* support for individuals and communities to enjoy equal opportunities. This "subjective equality" follows a need-based distribution (Eckhoff, 1974; Cook & Hegtvedt, 1983) or difference principles of justice (Rawls, 1971). Such differing characteristics of equality suggest that we cannot embrace either equality or equity uncritically. When used alone, they seem less operative to bring positive change, especially for the marginalized groups. A general approach would be then to integrate *equalities* (formal and moral, e.g., everyone has an equal right to liberty, dignity, and respect) with *equities* (relative and subjective, e.g., give everyone what they deserve as fair distribution or give them what they *need* as their circumstances demand). However, adopting such an integrative framework of equality involves overcoming the "barriers" between different types of equalities, or it would seem less operative at least in a theoretical sense.

Problems of Equality

Now, how can we overcome the perceived "barriers" between different types of equalities to yet employ the equality framework for substantive social progress? But before that, we need to look at the very sources of the barriers. Three interrelated elements constrain the critical use of equality principles: *allocation*, *outcome*, and *exchange*. First, moral and formal equalities ensure, at least in discourse, equal treatment and thereby an equal *allocation* is everyone's natural right to live in dignity and respect, which Brickman, Folger, Goode, and Schul (1981) call "macro justice." Such allocation is problematic in two respects. On the one hand, an equal distribution may not produce equal outcomes because of the different social and political circumstances of the recipients. On the other, equal treatment and equal distribution follow a top-down, one-way allocation process, in which the recipients are least likely to engage in a direct exchange (Cook & Hegtvedt, 1983). These two limitations—sociopolitical circumstances and lack of direct exchange relation—may be partly balanced by an alternative *equitable* distribution, which Brickman et al. (1981) call "microjustice." Finally, although solves the problem of varying social circumstances, it adds one more problem to the list through its allegedly "reverse inequality."

Second, the theories of distributive justice, utilitarian, or egalitarian have limitations in terms of the nature of the *outcomes* they produce (Sen, 1999, 2009). For Sen, mere distribution of primary goods does not guarantee that the recipients will be able to utilize them towards realizing their full potential. He argues that there exist various "disjunctures" between the allocation of a resource and its perceived outcome. For instance, being able to go out and experience bicycling is not the same as owning a bicycle. Sen argues, what if the person has only one leg or what if there is no bike path, or what if again the individual is afraid of traffic? According to Sen, a "just" society, instead of leaving the individual only with resources like a bike, would address the disjunctions and expand human capabilities so that people can enjoy more *functionings*—which is the capability of "being" or "doing" things that individuals in a society value or have reason to value (Sen, 1999).

The third source of barrier in the use of equality framework emerges from the lack of a direct "exchange" relation possible between the allocator and recipients. Eckhoff (1974) makes a clear distinction between "exchange" as reciprocation and "allocation" with an indirect exchange or no exchange at all752. The former is a "mutually beneficial, two-way transfer of valued resources" while the latter is the "one-way distribution of resources across a category or 'circle' of recipients" (Eckhoff, 1974, p. 219). Further, a meaningful exchange can be understood with the possibility of exchange and the quality of exchange. A distribution that is least likely to establish a direct exchange relation with the recipients would be a "top-down" and "one-way" allocation. Sen (2009) criticizes such a distribution for its over-reliance on the institutional guarantee of justice while ignoring human behaviour in the institutions (e.g., the failure of the "trickle-down" model). The next important thing is the quality of the exchange. There might be a two-way transfer of two differently valued resources like positively valued resource followed by a negative one (+, -) or a negatively valued resource followed by a positive one (-, +), or just two negatively valued resources (-, -) (Cook & Hegtvedt, 1983). Any of these transfers lacks the properties of an "exchange" (Eckhoff, 1974). According to the author, for an "exchange" to be genuinely qualitative, the transfer must be of *positively* valued resources from both ends (+, +). That is, it does not rely on a one-way allocation of rights and resources to recipients, for instance, but requires meaningful ownership of the transaction as well as the fulfilment of the terms accompanied.

Capabilities, Communicative, and Relational Dimensions

The sources of barriers—allocation, outcome, and exchange—limiting the integration of *equality* (or macrojustice) and *equity* (or microjustice) pose three fundamental challenges: challenges of capabilities, communication, and relationality. A politically viable, inclusive framework aiming to fight gender-based social injustice must address these challenges. First, it is evident from the discussion in the previous section that equal access to resources may not result in an equal outcome. Sen (1999) finds various "disjunctures" between the access to goods and their actual utility. *Disjunctures* are capabilities deprivations or the lack of capabilities or "opportunity freedom" (Alkire, 2010). In Sen's view, development is thus an expansion of "freedoms" or capabilities and an elimination of the sources of "unfreedoms," or "disjunctures" or capabilities deprivations, to put another way. Such a conception of development enables individuals to opt for certain "lifestyles" from a pool of possibilities, which they genuinely value or have reasons to value. Sen argues that the dominant theories of justice, mostly the utilitarian perspective, did not take the capabilities issue seriously and thereby a practiable framework of social change must address this.

Second, a meaningful "exchange" of two positively valued resources eventually generates a communicative moment. To put another way, the cyclical process of interaction between "macrojustice" and "microjustice" would result in a moment of dialogue between the allocator and recipients. A transaction of this nature seeks active participation and a vigorous exercise of agency and voice of the parties involved in the process. Finally, and most importantly, such dialogic, communicative moments are mediated and inhibited at times by a relational dimension. That is, it necessarily involves a relation of *power*, both material and discursive. A question is inevitable when it comes to equality: *who arbitrates the properties and procedures of equalities?* The question of power is unavoidable in the process of receiving and distributing an "equal" share of a thing. That is, *who lacks and who gives and what exists in between them?* In such a spectrum, those who lack power (a) need to *em*power themselves, at least to secure their share, or (b) need *empowerment* when circumstances are controlled by external forces. As such, the discourse of women's "empowerment" comes from the latter apparatus of power. We can understand what values and politics a particular discourse of *equality* tends to promote if we can locate the nature of the actors involved, the circumstances they are in, and the empowerment they need. Understanding this complex issue problematization of empowerment as a co-discourse with equality, discussed in the following section.

Empowerment

"Empowerment has a curious history, having gained the most expansive semantic range of all, with meanings pouring into development from an enormous diversity of sources, including feminist scholarship ... [it] retains a prominent place in agencies' policies concerning gender" (Cornwall & Brock, 2005, p. 1046). Although overused, the notion "empowerment" seems less critically spelled out. Empowerment originally derives from the concept of *power*. According to Melkote and Steeves (2015), without comprehending the idea of *power*, we may not clearly understand the constructs of "empowerment" and the location of authority and control, neither theoretically nor pragmatically. In Foucault's (1980) conception, power becomes meaningful only in a network of social and political relations. According to Rowlands (1997), such relational concept of power itself has also multiple faces like power *over* (controlling power), the power *to* (generate new possibilities without domination), power *with* (collective power, power created by group process), and power *from within* (spiritual strength that inspires and energizes others). For this analysis, power *over* and power *to* are relevant while other forms of power are also essential in an analysis that is exclusive to power.

Melkote and Steeves (2015) argue that we can realize sustainable social change by addressing the power inequities and facilitating substantive decision-making capabilities to the marginalized individuals, groups, communities, and countries. Empowerment thus means having control and mastery over one's own life stories, social and economic conditions, and democratic participation. Empowerment is more than words. Rowlands (1998) categorizes empowerment into three overlapping levels: *personal empowerment* which raises individual consciousness and confidence to confront oppression and injustice; *relational empowerment* which is an increased ability that helps negotiate and influence relational decisions; and finally, *collective empowerment* which is the collective action of groups or communities at a local or higher level to eliminate oppressive social structures. Although functioned at different levels, the variants of empowerment need entwining to resist any oppressive power structures and ensure a just distribution of opportunities and resources. For instance, personal empowerment seeks competitive individualism, an open marketplace, and meritocracy, which eventually encourages "plutocracy" (Littler, 2013). Indeed, the idea of women's empowerment is predominantly shaped by the discourse of personal empowerment, as informed by libertarian and utilitarian theories of justice.

To summarize the discussion, gender equality fails to negotiate the navigation of macro-and microjustice, and women's empowerment is limited to personal liberty while ignoring the aspects of "power over" and "power to" or relational and collective empowerments, which make the existing framework of gender equality and empowerment implausible. I argue that we need a more comprehensive and politically viable framework is sought to sustainably fight the gender-based social oppression and injustice, which would address all three challenges: capabilities, communication, and power as emerged from the dialectics of resource allocation, outcomes, and exchange. Hence, I make a clear transition here from a discourse of "gender equality" to a discourse of "gender justice," which is conceptualized from a broad-based idea of social justice and empowerment.

Social Justice

Combining Sen's (1999, 2009) idea of development and justice with Giddens' (1990) notion of utopian realism, I adopt a broad-based conception of social justice. Sen's capabilities framework expands the meaning of development. He conceives that development is (a) an expansion of capabilities or "freedoms to" realize the full human potential and (b) the elimination of unfreedoms or "freedoms from" domination. However, Sen's idea of justice or his capabilities approach drew criticism for focusing exclusively on individual capabilities while not accounting for collective capabilities. On the other, Sen also did not provide a list of capabilities that people value or have reasons to value. He left it to the political discretion and decision of society. Thus, Sen equivocally ignored the influence of power on any social and political decisions and perhaps for the same reason, Sen did not provide tools to overcome challenges of power relations.

Giddens' (1990) idea of utopian realism fills the gap in Sen's capabilities framework. Relying on Sen and Giddens, Melkote and Steeves outline two kinds of freedom and politics that constitute a broad-based understanding of social justice: freedom *from* and freedom *to*. According to the authors, a critical development agenda upholding the principles of social justice not only promote freedom *from* underdevelopment or unequal progress, which Giddens labels "emancipatory politics," but also expand another freedom *to* enhance the capacity of individuals so that they can enjoy a full, meaningful life, which Giddens names "life politics." Giddens argues that both *local* and *global* political actions link the politics of emancipation and self-actualization. To relate the arguments to gender, both equality and equity principles aim to provide support to elevate the recipients to a level that they can equally access opportunities and resources and realize their full potential. On the contrary, a social justice framework takes a radical approach and aims to remove the very need or barriers so that the recipients would no longer require additional support.

Taking the above problematics of gender equality, empowerment, and justice into account, next, I present a critical review of the historical formation of gender equality and its eventual assimilation into the most recent 2030 Agenda for Sustainable Development.

Historical Formation of Gender Equality

"Gender equality" and "women empowerment" are among the buzzwords pervading development theory and practice (Rowlands, 1998; Batliwala, 2007). Although the women's struggle for justice is primordial, their discursive entry into the lexicon of international development is recent. Gender issues started to reclaim the development policy space with the mobilization of feminists during the 1980s and 1990s (Cornwall & Rivas, 2015). However, the trajectory of gender equality goes back to the mid-twentieth century. In 1946, the Commission on the Status of Women (CSW), the first official, intergovernmental body under the tutelage of the UN, recognized the issue of gender equality by calling for no gender-based discrimination. It promoted a core principle that "Freedom and equality are essential to human development and whereas a woman is as much human being as man, she is, therefore, entitled to share them with him" (Economic and Social Council, 1947, p. 11). Thus, CSW with a transformative mission for gender equality became a reference point for almost all subsequent international policies and strategies of development.

The discourse of gender equality started to face two types of "paradox" from the outset: *philosophical* and *pragmatic*. Philosophically, the idea of equality is rooted in the instrumental logic of modernity and liberal assumptions (Drolet, 2010), which was highly criticized by later social change scholars. Pragmatically, the UN-led discourse of gender equality did not translate into any specific action plans except the fact that it thinned in the modernization project implemented through post-war development aid programmes, which turned into an expansionist, neocolonial ambition. So, instead of being genuinely motivated to produce positive social change, the modernist agenda equated development with material progress such as securing economic growth in terms of higher GDP and GNP. Moreover, the exponents of modernization also propagated that the economic development would "trickle-down" to society and resolve the problems of underdevelopment, especially in the so-called third world countries, requiring no specific concentration on women as a distinct group (Drolet, 2010; Kabeer, 2003).

From Productive Partner to Development Actor

Admittedly, the CSW worked to raise certain awareness of the conditions of women globally and eliminate the legal barriers to protect women's human rights (United Nations, 2006). However, Boserup (1970), among others, found the modernization approach implausible. The author argued for the inclusion of women's roles in the processes of social change as equal partners with men. This perspective soon became known as *Women In Development* (WID). WID stressed two issues: women's access to resources and their share in economic growth. This approach pursued an aim to establish women as visible actors in the production process, instead of leaving them as passive welfare recipients (Rowlands, 1997). That is, the argument was that the integration of women's instrumental role would make the existing development approach more "efficient" (Kabeer, 1994). Predictably, the WID view did not necessarily question the logic and "viability" of the Western model of development for non-western societies (Drolet, 2010). Hence, the international development framework lacked a "transformative capacity" for sustainable social change (Connelly, Li, MacDondal, & Parpart, 2000).

Beginning in the mid-1970s, in addition to addressing the legal barriers as well as recognizing the women's role in socioeconomic development, active participation of women in development was sought desperately. In contrast to the liberal WID approach, an alternative camp "Women and Development" (WAD) emerged in the early 1980s. This comprised the arguments of socialist, Marxist feminists. Proponents of WAD criticized the view of WID for overlooking the "capitalist" nature of development and its inherent elements that produce inequalities. Thus, the WAD paradigm embraced the epistemic privilege of women and promoted their normative role and responsibility in developmental efforts (Connelly et al., 2000). They also addressed the symbiotic relations of capital and patriarchy, which when band together limit the resources and opportunities for women (Beneria & Sen, 1982).

Some theorists found either WID or WAD unconvincing in that they failed to address the fundamental factors creating and sustaining gender inequalities (Connelly et al., 2000). As a result, they shifted the focus from women alone to the relationships between men and women. This new mode of analysis became known as Gender and Development (GAD). The GAD view accounted for two key aspects: women's material conditions and class position as well as patriarchal structures and ideas that create and uphold their subordination

(Drolet, 2010; Rowlands, 1997). That is, the women's experience of suppression intensifies along with their multitude of identities intersecting race, ethnicity, class, coloniality, culture, and socioeconomic strata (Moser, 1993). Various versions of critical theory like intersectionality, subaltern studies, postcolonial studies addressed these structural issues. They were aimed at reclaiming the critical position of women in development space and influencing the international policy forums.

The Paradoxical Integration into MDGs

Even though the discourses of WAD and GAD were not integrated into the mainstream development agenda, they had already enhanced the feminist understanding of progressive social change and influenced the subsequent policy moments. Among them include the Convention on the Elimination of All Forms of Discrimination against Women or CEDAW (1979), the Declaration on the Elimination of Violence against Women (1993), the Population and Development in Cairo (1994), and the Beijing Declaration and Platform for Action (1995). CEDAW is known for providing a first-ever definition of "discrimination" against women while the Beijing Declaration became a persistent reference point and guidance for the succeeding women empowerment strategies and action plans. In a sense, the intent and commitment of global communities discursively made in the above forums and their outcome documents were robust so much so that they ushered an optimism that the future leaders would radically assimilate the critical perspectives of gender equality. However, the culminating global development policy under the much-awaited millennium development agenda seriously unappreciated the achievements of preceding movements.

Admittedly, one of the eight millennium development goals (MDGs) was dedicated to "Promote Gender Equality and Empower Women" (MDG 3) and there had been some progress under the MDGs framework, especially in areas like education and health (United Nations, 2015a, 2015b). However, the new agenda thrashed the very notions of "equality" and "empowerment." Some even critiqued the MDGs to have borne the legacy of neoliberal capitalism as charted about two decades ago. Mitra and Singh (2007) assert that "high educational attainment alone may not promote gender empowerment unless the social and cultural fabric of a country or state ensures equality of women in all areas of life" (Mitra & Singh, 2007, p. 1227)

To summarize, social change discourse and practice until the end of MDGs nededed to overcome two issues: one at ontological and the other at epistemological levels. Ontologically, the conception of development was reduced to material progress as was the case in the modernization paradigm. On the other, the positivist epistemology shaped the appraisal of progress. As a result, MDGs failed to account for the intricate nature of social problems as well as the play of structural inequality and systematic injustice, while it also disregarded the nuances of local cultures and traditions and indigenous values. The former UN Secretary-General, Ban Ki-moon, correctly admitted while writing his words in the closing report of MDGs that "inequalities" had persisted and the distribution of whatever "progress" had been made by then was "uneven" (United Nations, 2015a, 2015b). For Cornwall and Rivas (2015), the armchair development policy elite followed a top-down approach in developing the MDGs framework, which relegated women to play an "instrumentalist role," instead of letting them work for their development. There was little stress on the underlying structural issues causing gender inequality and disparity (Cornwall & Rivas, 2015). If not acknowledged and directly addressed the originating factors, I argue that future social change would produce similar results.

Gender Equality in the Sustainable Development Agenda

The United Nations General Assembly adopted *The 2030 Agenda for Sustainable Development* in September 2015 to accomplish the unfinished job of MDGs with a renewed commitment (United Nations, 2015a). Comprising 17 goals, 169 targets, and 232 indicators, the new agenda aims to serve *people*, the *planet*, and *prosperity* towards sustainable development. Among the major commitments include anticipation to "eradicate poverty in *all* its forms and dimensions," reduce inequality and injustice, and secure the planet (UN, 2015a, p. 1, emphasis added).

> We envisage a world of universal respect for human rights and human dignity, the rule of law, justice, equality, and non-discrimination; of respect for race, ethnicity and cultural diversity; and of equal opportunity permitting the full realization of human potential and contributing to shared prosperity. A world which invests in its children and in which every child grows up free from violence and exploitation. (Article 8, Sustainable Declarations)

The above excerpt from Article 8 suggests that the 2030 agenda is influential as a declaration of intent to seek a better world while being loaded and ambitious in its scope and agenda. The articulations made both in the preamble and in Article 8 suggest the new generation development agenda seeks to bring a type of progress which is economically giving, environmentally conserving, and socially equalizing. It also aims to create a world where everyone will enjoy equal opportunities to realize their full human potential, irrespective of their intersecting identities such as race, ethnicity, and gender. With such articulations, the sustainable development discourse looks aligned with the principle of "life politics" (or freedom *to*) as comprised in the broad-based idea of social justice argued for in this chapter. However, "[t]he overuse of extreme words throughout the text of Sustainability Declaration renders misgivings about the viability of the SDGs" (Ala-Uddin, 2019, p. 218), explicitly having them implemented over just 15 years. Ala-Uddin rightly states, "the linguistic choices such as 'all forms and dimensions,' 'all countries and all stakeholders,' 'all human beings,' 'applicable to all' and 'everywhere'" make the agenda "oversimplified, ambitious and indivisible" (p. 218).

Vision, Promise, and Goal 5

"The half of the world's population is women, and no social change is sustainable if gender equality, both in principle and strategy, is not integrated throughout the development agenda" (UNDP, 2016). Article 8 of the sustainable declaration envisions:

> A world in which every woman and girl enjoys full gender equality and all legal, social and economic barriers to their empowerment have been removed. A just, equitable, tolerant, open and socially inclusive world in which the needs of the most vulnerable are met. (Article 8, Sustainable Declarations)

With the above, the UN sets a clear vision of establishing a world that is "just," "equitable," "tolerant," "open," and "inclusive." More importantly, it pledges to achieve gender equality in "full" by removing "all" the barriers towards that realization. With such a strong vision, the new agenda dedicates the SDG 5 as it reads: "Achieve gender equality and empower all women and girls." A careful look at their constructs suggests that the SDG 5 seems reframed from its predecessor MDG 3, although not more than a little twist in its wording. For example, MDG 3 aimed to "promote" gender equality and empower women, SDG 5 wants to "*achieve* gender equality and empower *all* women and *girls*" [emphasis added to show the variation from MDG 3]. This modification makes the new agenda bigger in scope and ambitious in action. So, the vision of a "just," "equitable," "tolerant," and "open" global society, as discursively articulated in the Article 8, is not realizable without "gender equality" and "empowerment" of all women and girls.

Targets and Indicators of SDG 5

The UN finalized a total of 9 targets and 13 indicators to realize SDG 5. The targets mainly address the issues of discrimination, violence, harmful practices, unpaid care and domestic works, leadership, sexual and reproductive rights, economic rights, and technology access. The realization of the vision of gender equality and empowerment requires the removal of all the barriers centring around these issues. International communities will measure their achievements in various legal, social, political, and technological interventions as laid out in the 13 indicators. The new agenda integrates the other principle of social justice for women from this discursive sense—"emancipatory politics" (or freedom *from*). It is also equally important to review how the targets are met.

Means of Implementation

The UN has made a clear urge for a robust means of implementation in the preamble and Articles 39–46 of the sustainable declaration. Article 39 states,

> The scale and ambition of the new Agenda require a revitalized Global Partnership to ensure its implementation. We fully commit to this. This Partnership work in

a spirit of global solidarity, in particular, solidarity with the poorest and with people in vulnerable situations. It will facilitate an intensive global engagement in support of the implementation of all the Goals and targets, bringing together Governments, the private sector, civil society, the United Nations system, and other actors and mobilizing all available resources. (Article 39, Sustainable Development Declaration)

The Agenda also dedicates one of the 17 SDGs (Goal 17) for a "revitalized global partnership" as the core of implementation, which is encouraging. As such, the meaning of partnership itself seems based on the integrated, interlinked, and interdependent nature of SDGs.

However, a profound paradox exists between what is discursively articulated in the vision of the new Agenda and how that will be realized, at least in terms of its predominance of economy, non-reactive to power, and omission of political liberty and empowerment (Ala-Uddin, 2019). Whereas the implementation of this broad, ambitious agenda equally warrants a holistic and radical social and political action, the sustainable agenda seems predominantly economic. The goals that pertain to poverty, hunger, industrialization, energy, and growth are conceived in economic terms and thus privilege the economic interest (Ala-Uddin, 2019). Ala-Uddin asserts, "[a]n overly economic dimension of development creates the conditions of inequality and injustice" (p. 222). Second, the Agenda elusively overlooks genuine political liberty and democratic empowerment as the UN aims to execute it primarily through formal, administrative interventions. Finally, the sustainable agenda did not address the structural issues that play a vital role in producing global social inequality and injustice, especially to the marginalized communities.

Based on the discursive commitment and limited means of implementation, I argue that the new agenda accompanies the entire toolbox of seductive buzzwords dominating the today's development discourses. Cornwall and Brock (2005) rightly put,

> The statements of intent that constitute the policies of international development agencies gain the qualities of *myth* precisely because they are born of convictions. They seek to call us to action, name what we can do, and make us into agents of the possible. (p. 1055, emphasis added)

These authors believe that the myths of the development function through emotional appeal, but not through rational choice, thus creating and nourishing the feeling of conviction among people since without such conviction they cannot act. In the abovementioned article, the seeming development myths include "universal respect," "equal opportunity," "full equality," "all" barriers, and so forth (Ala-Uddin, 2019). Although these are utopias as safeguarded by myths, they give us "a feeling of rightness, backed by the creation normative instruments, like MDGs, which serve an almost ceremonial function in bolstering a feeling of togetherness and purposefulness, of a visionary goal toward which to strive" (Cornwall & Brock, 2005, p. 1055).

In short, the new declaration includes myths and utopias while concealing some other agenda behind these myths and utopias. In the guise of equality, it is rather promoting universalism and open space where the privileged are more privileged (Littler, 2013). Among the mythical promises, the vision of "*A just, equitable, tolerant, open and socially inclusive world*" is a big utopia. While reporting "We the People" at the 66th Session of the General Assembly, Ban Ki-moon acknowledged that the potential of women is yet to be realized due to the persisting social, economic, and political inequalities, among other things. The official site of SDGs argues that gender inequalities are deeply rooted in every society and therefore their access to opportunities and resources are limited to those unequal structures. Dolan (2017) states:

> Disproportionately bad and unfair things happen to girls and women around the world, and just as the central moral challenge of the 19th century was slavery, and totalitarianism was the 20th century's, the central moral challenge of this century be *gender inequity*. (Para 8, emphasis added)

That the vision of equality and empowerment for women would remain a mere vision because the notions of equality and empowerment were narrowly conceptualized in economic and legal terms, not in a political sense; neoliberal vision largely shapes the means of implementation; and the indicators and the measuring tools of the progress are also limited to positivist approaches (Ala-Uddin, 2019).

Against this backdrop, the United Nations must first address structural inequality had it authentically aimed to effect positive and sustainable social change. It is undeniable that today's world has become an extremely unequal place and the existing development regime is mostly motivated by a neoliberal economic framework. As such, few countries might have *developed* themselves by implementing the millennium development goals (MDGs); however, many countries have made progress and come out of poverty without putting them into the core of their national development policy. Whereas the neoliberal world system has left damaging effects on the same people, planet, prosperity, and peace, the UN has continued to be the largest flag bearer of this ideology. The agenda is seeking to achieve gender equality and empowerment, but it is alternatively also widening the inequality and gap between the rich and the poor.

Therefore, not just for the case of SDG 5, but for the entire SDG framework, the international bodies must address the paradox and myth of equality and empowerment concerning social justice. I reiterate my argument that the gender equality and empowerment framework is inadequate to bring sustainable change on the face of power, structure, and ideology circuitously promoting inequality and injustice. For a genuine sustainable social change to happen, the dominant, neoliberal discourses of development need to be deconstructed and reconstructed and the lasting gaps of capabilities, communication, and power in development thought need to be directly addressed. To that effort, I provide a conceptual framework to describe what role communication for development (C4D) could play in bringing about "gender justice," which would realistically tackle the issues of inequalities and injustice and fulfil the goals of sustainable development.

Conceptual Framework of Communicative Actions

Giddens (1990) provides one way to approach the future of development by employing the role of critical theory. In his view, we should look beyond the integrated national and global spaces and recognize fundamentally two politics for people: emancipatory politics and life politics of self-actualization in the contexts of the local-global continuum and with the end goals of social justice (Melkote & Steeves, 2015).

Emancipatory Politics and Life Politics

Giddens (1990) operationalizes the outcome of social justice under two broad dimensions of freedoms, freedom *from* and freedom *to*. The former aims to achieve the emancipatory politics towards liberating individuals from the forces of inequalities and servitude while the latter entails the life politics to expand human capabilities towards helping people explore their full potential and live as expressive human beings (Melkote & Steeves, 2015). Giddens provides a schema comprising two intersecting axes, one is emancipatory and life politics and the other is the context for actions and interaction, *global* and *local* (see Fig. 11.1).

Social and Political Action

Giddens advocates for radical social and political actions required for his framework to work. According to the thinker, there are four responses to adjust to any crisis emerged in the global epoch: (1) *pragmatic acceptance* (accept and move on), (2) *sustained optimism* (things be fine), (3) *cynical pessimism* (things are bad), and (4) *radical engagement* (attitude and action). Among them, radical social and political engagement is warranted for genuine empowerment and social justice (Melkote & Steeves, 2015). In Fig. 11.2, the nature of such actions is suggested.

P.O.S. Framework

Figure 11.2 explains the communicative framework what I call the P.O.S. model which comprises three components: Principal Communicative Actions (P), Outcomes of Communicative Actions (O), and sustainable development

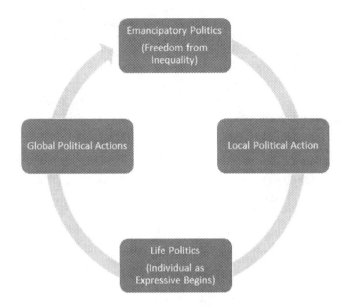

Fig. 11.1 Dimension of political action. (*Source:* Melkote and Steeves (2015))

outcomes for Social Justice (S). The framework promotes a cyclical process and an continuous interaction between the *macro* (e.g., national, regional, global) and *micro* (e.g., place and affinity-based) contexts and between different phases (P, O, and S). They overlap each other. The framework describes the sustainable development goals for social justice outcomes (phase S), which can be achieved and strengthened from the outcomes of the radical social and political engagement (phase O) that are to be realized further through major media and communicative means (phase P).

> The overlapping, reinforcing, and cyclical nature of the actions and outcomes between the various phases of the model and between the macro and micro contexts indicate that the process is neither linear nor teleological. The process is open-ended, multicontextual, dynamic, and ongoing. (Melkote & Steeves, 2015, p. 458)

Principal communicative actions like social and media mobilizations, information politics, and empowerment/resistance communications are taken beyond the administrative and formal institutional arrangements. They result in the empowerment of individuals and communities through active public spheres, public deliberation. Finally, social and political actions shape the macrostructure or macrojustice by recognizing and valuing their rights and ensuring their access to resources and opportunities, contributing to social justice and sustainable development goals. Morever, the cycle continues.

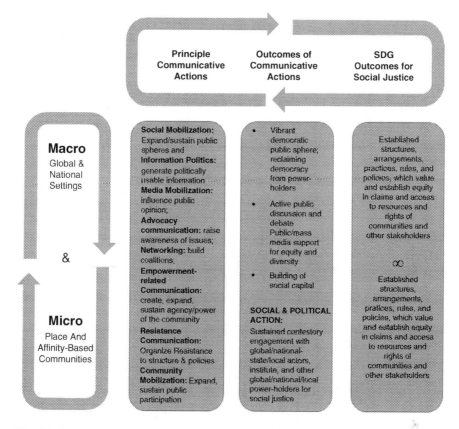

Fig. 11.2 P.O.S. model. (Adapted from Melkote and Steeves (2015))

Conclusion

As I conclude this chapter, there is a deep paradox in the discourse and praxis of gender equality and empowerment, which makes the existing model inadequate, especially in responding to the intricate issues underlying the gender-based social injustice and oppression. I argue that the equality principle in the current discourse and praxis of development is flawed in that an equal distribution of rights and resources does not guarantee the generation of equal outcomes. Alternatively, the principle of an "equitable" distribution does not effectively resolve the issue, as it may produce a reverse inequality.

A general approach to gender equality needs to combine both equality and equity principles. However, the very integration requires overcoming a set of barriers expressed in three fundamental challenges—capabilities, communication, and power. Hence, a more comprehensive framework of empowerment and justice would expand human capabilities while removing the disjunctions that might exist between a people's access to resources and the utilities (Sen, 1999). It would also accommodate strategies to utilize the communicative moments to mediate the relationship between the parties involved in the resource distribution, or between the actors and institutions of macro- and microjustice. Finally, such a framework would interrogate the structures of power and promote radical social and political actions towards open empowerment of individuals and communities. Empowerment, if included individual, relational, and collective goals, is still a politically viable framework in the effort of positive change.

This chapter presented a broad-based idea of social justice and empowerment drawing upon Sen's (1999) idea of development and justice and Giddens' conception of utopian realism, which promotes two overarching principles—"freedom from" and "freedom to," or "emancipatory politics" and "life politics" respectively. Whereas both equality and equity principles provide a support system to the marginalized individuals and communities so that they can equally access opportunities and resources for the realization of their full potential, a broad-based social justice framework takes a radical approach to remove the very "need" or "barriers" so that people would not require additional support anymore.

REFERENCES

Ala-Uddin, M. (2019). 'Sustainable' Discourse: A Critical Analysis of the 2030 Agenda for Sustainable Development. *Asia Pacific Media Educator, 29*(2), 214–224.

Alkire, S. (2010). Instrumental Freedoms and Human Capabilities. In S. L. Esquith & Gifford (Eds.), *Capabilities, Power, and Institutions. Towards a More Critical Development Ethics* (pp. 18–32). Pennsylvania Park: The Pennsylvania State University Press.

Batliwala, S. (2007). Taking the power out of empowerment–an experiential account. *Development in Practice, 17*(4–5), 557–565.

Beneria, L., & Sen, G. (1982). Class and gender inequalities and women's role in economic development: Theoretical and practical implications. *Feminist Studies, 8*(1), 157–176.

Bhatia, I. (2015, August 31). Khap Panchayat's Rape Order of 2 UP Sisters Echoes in UK. *Times of India*. Retrieved November 28, 2020, from https://timesofindia.indiatimes.com/india/Khap-panchayats-rape-order-of-2-UP-sisters-echoes-in-UK/articleshow/48737641.cms

Boserup, E. (1970). *Woman's role in economic development*. London: George Allen & Unwin

Brickman, P., Folger, R., Goode, E., & Schul, Y. (1981). Microjustice and Macrojustice. In M. J. Lerner & S. C. Lerner (Eds.), *The Justice Motive in Social Behavior* (pp. 173–202). New York: Plenum.

Burke, J. (2014, May 30). Indian Minister Criticises Lax Policing in Gang-Rape Case. *The Guardian*. Retrieved November 27, 2020, from https://www.theguardian.com/world/2014/may/30/india-police-gang-rape-katra-uttar-pradesh

Connell, A., Holder, A., & Kearney, H. (2020). Equal Measures 2030: A New Approach for Advocacy and Influencing Beyond Beijing+ 25. *Gender & Development, 28*(2), 405–423.

Cook, K. S., & Hegtvedt, K. A. (1983). Distributive Justice, Equity, and Equality. *Annual Review of Sociology*, 9(1), 217–241.

Cornwall, A., & Brock, K. (2005). What do buzzwords do for development policy? A critical look at 'participation','empowerment'and 'poverty reduction'. *Third world quarterly*, 26(7), 1043–1060.

Cornwall, A., & Rivas, A. M. (2015). From 'Gender Equality and 'Women's Empowerment' to Global Justice: Reclaiming a Transformative Agenda for Gender and Development. *Third World Quarterly*, 36(2), 396–415.

Connelly, M. P., Li, T. M., MacDonald, M., & Parpart, J. L. (2000). Feminism and development: Theoretical perspectives. In P. L. Jane, M. P. Connelly, & V. E. Barriteau (Eds.), *Theoretical perspectives on gender and development* (pp. 51–160). Ottawa: IDRC.

Dolan, S. (2017, February 17). New York Times Columnist Talks Global Gender Equality at USU. *The New York Times*. Retrieved from http://www.nytimes.com

Drolet, J. (2010). Feminist perspectives in development: Implications for women and microcredit. Affilia, 25(3), 212–223.

Dubey, P. (2018a). *No Nation for Women: Reportage on Rape from India, the World's Largest Democracy*. Simon & Schuster.

Dubey, P. (2018b, December 21). Badaun Gang Rape and Murder: This Book Investigates How the CBI Tried to Bury the Case. *Scroll.in*. Retrieved November 27, 2020, from https://scroll.in/article/906291/badaun-gang-rape-and-murder-this-book-investigates-how-the-cbi-tried-to-bury-the-case

Eckhoff, T. (1974). *Justice: Its Determinants in Social Interaction*. Rotterdam University Press.

Economic and Social Council (ECOSOC), Resolution 5(1). (1947, February 25). UN Doc. Retrieved from http://undocs.org/E/281/REV.1

Equal Measures 2030. (2019). *Harnessing the Power of Data for Gender Equality: Introducing the 2019 EM2030 SDG Gender Index*. Equal Measures 2030. Retrieve November 28, 2020, from https://data.em2030.org/wp-content/uploads/2019/07/EM2030_2019_Global_Report_English_WEB.pdf

Equal Measures 2030. (2020). *Bending the Curve Towards Gender Equality by 2030*. Equal Measures 2030. Retrieved November 28, 2020, from https://data.em2030.org/wp-content/uploads/2020/03/EM2030BendingTheCurveReportMarch2020-1.pdf

Equality Now. (2017). The World's Shame, the Global Rape Epidemic, How Laws Around the World are Failing to Protect Women and Girls from Sexual Violence. Retrieved November 28, 2020, from qualityNowRapeLawReport2017_Single_Pages.pdf, 1527096293.

Foucault, M. (1980). *Power/Knowledge: Selected Interviews and Other Writings, 1972–1977*. Pantheon.

Gardner, K., & Lewis, D. (2000). Dominant Paradigms Overturned or 'Business as Usual'? Development Discourse and the White Paper on International Development. *Critique of Anthropology*, 20(1), 15–29.

Giddens, A. (1990). *The Consequences of Modernity*. John Wiley & Sons.

Gosepath, S. (2011). Equality. *Stanford Encyclopedia of Philosophy*. Retrieved from https://plato.stanford.edu/entries/equality/

Kabeer, N. (1994). *Reversed realities: Gender hierarchies in development thought*. Verso.

Kabeer, N. (2003). *Gender Mainstreaming in Poverty Eradication and the Millennium Development Goals: A handbook for policy-makers and other stakeholders.* Commonwealth Secretariat.

Littler, J. (2013). Meritocracy as Plutocracy: The Marketising of Equality Under Neoliberalism. *New Formations, 80*(80), 52–72.

Lucas, J. R. (1980). *On Justice.* Oxford: Clarendon Press.

Malhotra, A. (2003). Conceptualizing and measuring women's empowerment as a variable in international development. In *Measuring Empowerment: Cross-Disciplinary Perspectives*, Washington, DC, 4–5 February.

McGowan, P. J., Stewart, G. B., Long, G., & Grainger, M. J. (2019). An Imperfect Vision of Indivisibility in the Sustainable Development Goals. *Nature Sustainability, 2*(1), 43–45.

Melkote, S. R., & Steeves, H. L. (2015). *Communication for Development: Theory and Practice for Empowerment and Social Justice.* SAGE Publications India.

Mitra, A., & Singh, P. (2007). Human Capital Attainment and Gender Empowerment: The Kerala Paradox. *Social Science Quarterly, 88*(5), 1227–1242.

Moser, C. (1993). *Gender planning and development: Theory, practice and training.* London: Routledge

Palermo, T., Bleck, J., & Peterman, A. (2013). Tip of the Iceberg: Reporting and Gender-based Violence in Developing Countries. *American Journal of Epidemiology, 179*(5), 602–612.

Raju, S. (2015, September 3). Jat Leaders in UP Village Deny Ordering Rape of Dalit Sisters. *The Hindustan Times.* Retrieved November 28, 2020, from https://www.hindustantimes.com/india/jat-leaders-in-up-village-deny-ordering-rape-of-dalit-sisters/story-YT9lHlfxXanfOJ1xQR1K4I.html

Rape, Abuse & Incest National Network (RAINN). (n.d.) Victims-Sexual-Violence | RAINN. Retrieved November 28, 2020, from https://www.rainn.org/statistics/victims-sexual-violence

Rawls, J. (1971). A theory of justice. Cambridge, MA: Harvard University Press.

Rowlands, J. (1997). *Questioning Empowerment: Working with Women in Honduras.* Oxfam.

Rowlands, J. (1998). A Word of the Times, But What Does It Mean? Empowerment in the Discourse and Practice of Development. In *Women and Empowerment* (pp. 11–34). London: Palgrave Macmillan.

Rukmini, S. (2014, October 22). Marital and Other Rapes Grossly Under-Reported. *The Hindu.* Retrieved from http://www.thehindu.com/news/national/marital-and-other-rapes-grossly-underreported/article6524794.ece

Sen, A. (1999). *Development as Freedom.* Oxford University Press.

Sen, A. (2009). *The idea of justice.* Harvard University Press.

Sen, G. (2016). Progress of the World's Women 2015–2016: Transforming Economies, Realizing Rights. *Global Social Policy, 16*(1), 94–96.

Stancil, P. (2016). Substantive Equality and Procedural Justice. *Iowa Law Review, 102,* 1633.

UN Woman. (2020a). *Progress on the Sustainable Development Goals: The Gender Snapshot 2020.* UN Women Headquarters.

UN Woman. (2020b). *COVID-19 and Ending Violence Against Women and Girls.* UN Women Headquarters.

United Nations. (2015a). *Transforming Our World: The 2030 Agenda for Sustainable*. UNGAOR, 70th Sess, UN Doc A/RES/70/1 (25 September 2015). Retrieved April 30, 2017, from undocs.org/A/RES/70/1

United Nations. (2015b). *The Millennium Development Goals Report 2015: Summary*. New York: UN.

United Nations. (2006). The United Nations Commission on the Status of Women - 60 years of work for equality, development and peace. United Nations. https://www.un.org/womenwatch/daw/CSW60YRS/index.htm.

United Nations Development Programme. (2016). *UNDP Support to the Integration of Gender Equality Across the SDGs Including Goal 5*. New York: UNDP. Retrieved from http://www.by.undp.org/content/dam/undp/library/SDGs/5_Gender_Equality_digital.pdf?download

United Nations Office on Drugs and Crime. (2018). *Global Study on Homicide: Gender-related Killing of Women and Girls*. UNODC, United Nations Office on Drugs and Crime.

World Health Organization. (2017). *Violence Against Women*. World Health Organization. Retrieved November 28, 2020, from https://www.who.int/en/news-room/fact-sheets/detail/violence-against-women

CHAPTER 12

Achieving Sustainable Development Goals: An Analytical Overview of Indian Experience (2000–2019)

C. S. H. N. Murthy

INTRODUCTION[1]

Sustainable development demands the peoples' participation. Ever since a resolution to achieve Millennium Development Goals (MDGs), 2000 is drawn, both the developing nations and the developed nations continued to strive hard to achieve them. In the process, both the UNICEF and the World Bank have envisaged a wider role for the media and communication as a connecting agent or tool among various sections of the society of any country. Political processes are communication processes and result—not only through formal elections but also through an ongoing dialogue—between people and their government and through the shaping of public agendas (At the Heart of Change: The Role of Communication in Sustainable Development., 2007, pp. 3–5).

India has been a signatory to the Millennium Development Goals (MDGs) enunciated in 2000 and continued to be a partner in achieving the targets of

---

[1] The State of Andhra Pradesh, with 490 million people as per latest census report 2011, is the eighth largest State in India. It is now called the residual State. The State was last divided into Telangana and Andhra through an enactment of a law in Indian Parliament in March 2013. Earlier it was a combined State and was the fifth largest State in India.

C. S. H. N. Murthy (✉)
Chandigarh University, Punjab, India

© The Author(s), under exclusive license to Springer Nature Switzerland AG 2021
M. J. Yusha'u, J. Servaes (eds.), *The Palgrave Handbook of International Communication and Sustainable Development*,
https://doi.org/10.1007/978-3-030-69770-9_12

integrated Sustainable Development Goals (17 iSDGs). While MDGs have comprised broad 8 goals with 21 targets that all nations must achieve by 2015, the 17 iSDGs have become the extension of MDGs with 169 more specific targets to ensure the development goals of MDGs more inclusive. In other words, MDGs are now more ramified in terms of goals and specific targets to achieve.

This chapter dwells upon various socio-economic and energy-based reforms conceived through different welfare measures (e.g. *Garibi hatao*, nationalization of banks, abolition of privy purses, Clean and Green, *Arogya Sri*, *Anna Canteens*, *Chandranna Bheema*, *Gareeb Kalyan*, *Swachh Bharat*, *Amrit*, etc.) that have begun to creep in to the Indian society in a phased manner both before the ushering in of the MDGs and later within the framework of the MDGs since 2000 (nearly two decades back). Today these welfare measures, highly 'populist' though, are continuing as part of 17 iSDGs aimed to achieve sustainable development (Melokte & Steeves, 2013).

Sustainable development can be defined as a society 'competing for the available resources without exhausting them for future generations' (United Nations Report, 1987). It offers immense opportunities for people to access more information and knowledge, which they use to improve their lives. However, it must be borne in mind that without an operation of a communication paradigm, or a theory, there is no possibility of achieving a 'sustainable development' in any society of any country or any part of the world. Communication paradigm or theory and development issues are mutually and inclusively dependent on each other. In this regard the author wishes to outline some of the concerns that problematize the adoption of a particular communication theory or paradigm for achieving sustainable development in highly culturally diverse Indian contexts.

Accordingly, the chapter discusses first the issues such as problematizing role of communication and sustainable development in terms of its holistic ability to address multilateral issues, real freedoms of a developing society, and how a development is variously interpreted as sustainable in terms of modernization. Further, the chapter reviews in brief some welfare schemes innovatively formulated by both the State of Andhra Pradesh and Central Government of India for achieving a sustainable development both prior to MDGs (i.e. 1970–2000), during MDGs (2000–2015), and iSDGs (2015–2030). The chapter discusses how these schemes from the oldest to the latest reflected the trope of development paradigm in India both before the MDGs, later through the period of MDGs, and iSDGs. The chapter also offers a critical view on the excessive and unscrupulous emphasis on these economic and social reforms, turning them into 'populist measures' and 'vote bank politics', ultimately hindering the development of the State in terms of infrastructural growth, employment, and multilateral development.

Role of Communication for Development in the Changed Context

At the outset, the author opines that there is no need to retell the whole range of discourse surrounding the role of communication and sustainable development. A mention of two most significant works on which the author relied suffices to recapitulate the earlier discourse that stands as a back up to this work: *Communication for Development and Social Change* (Ed. Jan Servaes for UNESCO, 2008) and *Communication for Development in the Third World: Theory and Practice for Empowerment* (Eds. Melokte & Steeves, 2013). For further understanding as to how these theoretical texts helped the author to adopt and relate them to the ongoing social change in India, the author relied on the works of Jan Servaes (1999) (*Communication for Development: One World, Multiple Cultures*) and Jan Servaes (2003) (*Approaches to Development Studies on Communication for Development*).

The most compelling reason for stating this at the outset is that there is no consensus among the development communication scholars as to a unified theory of communication for a sustainable development applicable to all national contexts and cultures (Servaes, 2008a, p.15; Servaes, 2016). Several issues complicated the understanding of an applicability of a single communication model or a theory to a developing context of third world economy in general and India in particular. In fact, the author is of the view that a hybridized model of communication models or theories applies to social contexts in countries like India (Murthy & Das, 2011). At the same time, the results of these models do not exactly follow the western patterns of results. There would be some deviations and limitations. Murthy and Das (2011) combined both Rogers's Diffusion Model (1962/1983) and Bandura's Social Cognitive Theory to explain how social change happens through Indian cinema. Their study also showed how, given the Indian context, the theory of diffusion of innovation in combination with Bandura's theory (2006) deviates from the Rogers's diffusion model.

At the same time, the author would like to remind the communication scholars that it was Contractor, Singhal, and Rogers (1988) who discovered that there are two sub-paradigms of communication model in Indian context. Everett Rogers was one of these team members and the leader of the team as well in this work. Many development scholars perhaps have overlooked this finding of Contractor et al. (1988) before critiquing that innovation diffusion model is simply an effects model and suffers from some limitations. But, in the research of Murthy and Das (2011), it was established that there is no problem with the theory of diffusion of innovation of Rogers's in combination with Bandura's social cognitive theory given due consideration to the two sub-paradigms model of Indian communication system.

The author so far has not come across any paper refuting the discovery of two sub-paradigm model of Contractor et al. (1988) in Indian communication system. In fact, Bandura (2006) stated that there is no single pattern of diffusion, but specifies how different functions of modelling operate, in concert with other sources of influence, in various components of the process of diffusion (p.118). Though many eminent scholars of development communication and social change do not take much cognizance of cinema/film as an agent of change which can influence the behaviour of the masses, Murthy and Das's work, which appeared first in 2011 in *Asian Cinema*, reappeared in the News Letter of *Communication Initiative* on March 8, 2018, published under the editorship of Warren Freek, an eminent development communication scholar (https://www.comminit.com/global/content/social-change-through-diffusion-innovation-indian-popular-cinema-analytical-study-lage-r).

While Melokte and Steeves (2013, p. 46) are of the view that Rogers's innovation diffusion model is linear and hierarchical like Laswell's model of effects, and may not explain the complexity involved in the diffusion of messages, they argued that Kotler's social marketing replaces its weaknesses. At the same time, Servaes (2008a, 2016) offered equal emphasis on innovation diffusions (one of the top-down paradigms mostly related to media effects) as well as the participatory approach (2008a, pp. 16–17). At the same time, he argues in favour of more policy research including institutional analysis of developing agency coordination. Servaes (2008a, b; 2016) opines, therefore, that 'today almost nobody would dare to make the optimistic claims of the early years any longer'. He agrees that 'either implicitly or otherwise, the so-called dominant modernization paradigm still continues to influence the policy and planning-making discourse of major actors in the field of communication for development, both at theoretical and applied levels'.

Against the backdrop, the author intends to take an application approach, than a fundamental research, to the development communication in keeping with the Servaes's (2008a, b; 2016) views expressed above. The author also intends to analyse and relate the ongoing developmental projects and schemes, which are also dearly called in Indian journalistic and political parlance as 'populist schemes' meant to garner votes during elections or convert different sections of society into 'vote banks'. Whatever may be the interpretation of these measures by the general public, the fact is that both the State and Central governments in India implement these schemes in keeping with MDGs (2000–2015) and 17 iSDGs (2015–2030). In the following the author intends to explain the various communication models and networks the governments tend to apply as strategies to give an effective publicity and campaign to their newly announced schemes.

Digital Communication Strategies

Today applying through online or by calling in the information through a toll free number for various State and Central schemes has become a common phenomenon in India (Murthy, 2015). It is the single largest mode of communication for enhancing one's own awareness levels. For each sector of economic and social development that includes medical, health, agriculture, marketing, and insurance, both the State and Central Governments have brought in different toll free numbers (Murthy, 2015). Similarly every service sector, be it private and government, has its own toll free number. *Mee Seva* (in your service—a State government initiative), Internet Kiosks, e-learning through computers at rural NGO centres (Murthy, 2008), Internet penetration, cable television, Direct To Home (DTH), YouTube, *Facebook, Twitter*, and so on have also begun to play a key role in spreading widely the development programmes across rural and semi-urban and urban settings (Murthy, 2015). Information and Communications Technologies (ICTs) and websites have come in quite handy now for giving more access to the rural and urban populace through Internet and mobile facilities. Several self-help groups (SHGs), communities, women, and children associations have now learnt to use mobile, both android and other modes, to elicit information necessary for their upliftment. Mobile has transformed the marketing economy of several rural communities (Murthy, 2009). Compared to a decade ago, today India's digital amenities have multiplied epitomizing the concept of Schramm's 'magic multipliers' today.

Advertising Strategies

Second largest mode of communication for development is the advertising by the State as well as Central governments. The government advertising is the largest source of revenue for print and electronic media. Especially, the advertisements produced by the Films Division of India at the Central level and the State Ministry of Information and Public Relations are usually done by celebrities drawn from the world of film or television or theatre. While some of these are low cost using non-stardom actors/actresses, the others are with actors having a high stardom. At the Central level advertisements such as Prime Minister's pension schemes for unorganized sectors, an eminent actor Amitabh Bachchan portrayed the role of protagonist.

Traditional Strategies

Third most important way of communication of government schemes to rural and urban elite is through posters, pamphlets, and marketing agents, besides announcements through mikes on rickshaws, autos, and in cars. Either the Village *Panchayats*[2] or the Municipal Corporations organize these announcements through its local taxes and funds under self-governance. As for marketing, the agents of Life Insurance Corporation of India (LIC), a government of India undertaking, marketed a number of Government of India schemes through the LIC itself.

Banks also offer ad campaigns through posters and pamphlets in their premises giving effect to various government schemes such as *Jandhan* (a savings

---

[2] *Panchayat* is a smallest democratic parliament at the village level with elected members from the village population. Ward members and a President would constitute this democratic entity. It is an administrative unit of the country to where all the welfare measures and reforms must percolate.

account for a poor woman/man living below poverty line) to whose account Government of India deposits the funds as per their schemes such as *Garib Kalyan. Pradhana Mantri's Kisan Samman Yojana* (Prime Minister's Farmers' Support Plan), *Pradhana Mantri Garib Kalyan Yojana* (Welfare of Poor), Farmers' crop insurance scheme, and so on provide funds from the Central Government to the *Jandhan* account of the poor. For instance in the wake of Corona pandemic in 2020, the Central Government released Rs. 500/- (equivalent to US$ 6–7) for each woman, totalling up to 198.6 million of Indian rupees. Further, Rs. 1000/- (equivalent to US $13–14) was released to each senior citizen to meet the medical expenses during this crisis. Similarly funds up to Rs. 6000/- (equivalent to US $80–81) for raising crops during the onset of monsoon session are released by the Central Government into these schemes.

These schemes have wider publicity not only in the premises of banks but also through FM Radios available on android and non-android mobiles, as well as on radios, community radios, and electronic media and advertising. Besides, the print media which now deeply penetrated in to rural India in vernacular languages (Ninan, 2007) is also offering a lot of information both in the form of news as well as advertisements. In fact the country as a whole witnessed an exponential growth in the traditional media—radio and television. There are about 902 permitted private television channels in India as on March 19, 2019. In addition to these channels, there are cable television channels at regional level in each federal State. Adding up all these, there are totally 1200 television channels in India working 24x7. There are about 369 private radio stations in more than 101 cities in India. The Government-driven All India Radio has more than 450 FM stations covering 52% population of India. There are about 180 community radio stations in India as of now (Murthy, 2010).

India produces the world's highest number of films approximately 1900–2000 a year. Most of these films deal with social issues such as gender, unemployment, psychological complexities of youth, drug addiction, criminal tendencies, OCDs (obsessive compulsive disorders), and so on. In addition there are short films also that attack on the superstitions, occultism, and bigotry.

Manual Strategies

At manual level, the communication flows happen through different hierarchies in India at the central level, and in the federal State of Andhra Pradesh at the regional level. Beginning with the office of the District Collector and Magistrate, the communication flows go downward top to bottom and reach the *Gram Seviks* (Village Assistants), revenue assistants, *Sarpanchs* (Village Secretariat Heads/Presidents), village ward members, *Anganwadis* (village child welfare and communication and service centre), para medical and para sanitation staff, and so on through Regional Development Officers, *Mandal*[3] Development Officers, Block Development Officers, and so on. They in turn

---

[3] *Mandal* is next democratic parliament comprising several village *panchayats*. It is a penultimate unit of country's democratic fabric and acts as a transitory platform to pass on the communication of welfare measures to villages.

conduct meetings with the people through their peer groups leaders, community heads, and women representatives and inform the people about the newly introduced programmes from the government's side, be them from the State of Andhra Pradesh or from the Central Government.

Hybrid Strategies

Thus, due to both the network communications as well as human communication strategies through interpersonal communication flows, development processes spread among the people. With their participation alone the target levels for each specified period are attained. At its heart, the development—if it is to be sustainable—must be a process that allows people to be their own agents of change to act individually and collectively, using their own ingenuity and accessing ideas, practices, and knowledge in the search for ways to fulfil their potential. Melokte and Steeves (2013) viewed that 'communication and information are persuasive tools that can assist in the modernization process' (p. 38). They subscribed to Kotler's social marketing and described the marketing and selling of communication and information as persuasive marketing strategy under social marketing umbrella (p. 39).

Challenges

Servaes and Lie (2014) also outlined the main challenges for the field of communication for development: (a) The differences between good governance and good government and the issues of transparency and accountability; (b) the complexity of the participatory concept; (c) participation taking place at different levels; (d) the reinforcement of independent and pluralistic media; (e) not making full use of potential radio; (f) enabling policy and resources; (g) implementing a legal and supportive framework favouring the right to free expression and the emergence of free and pluralistic information systems; (h) building alliances; and (i) new global partnerships are necessary with the media, development agencies, universities, and governments.

Real Freedoms

Eminent economist and Nobel Laureate Amartya Sen described the free access to communication as 'real freedoms' (Nussbaum & Sen, 1993). Sen viewed the 'real freedom' as 'the capacity for people to participate in a diverse range of decisions that affect them and to enjoy specific "functional" aspects that constitutes a healthy life'. Concentrating more resources on fostering better communication and information processes among people—and between people and governments—will increase the power and ability of individuals to take a meaningful part in debates and decision making that are relevant to their lives (Nussbaum & Sen, 1993).

Thus, the development communication refers to the use of communication to facilitate social development (Quebral, 1972–73). It engages all the relevant stakeholders and government officials, establishes conducive environments, assesses the risks and opportunities, and facilitates exchange of information and communication to generate a positive change which constitutes 'sustainable development'. Quebral expanded the definition of communication development to a scientific realm by saying that 'it is the art of science of human communication applied to the speedy transformation of economy of a country and its masses from poverty to dynamic state of economic potential' (Quebral, 2012). In short, information and communication processes are fundamental to sustainable development and lie at the heart of change (At the Heart of Change: The Role of Communication in Sustainable Development., 2007, p.7, Melokte & Steeves, 2013).

Methodology

The present study is primarily intended to qualitatively examine the genesis, growth, and development of various welfare measures rolled out by the successive governments of India at central level, and of federal State of Andhra Pradesh since 1970 at regional level (i.e. prior to the launch of MDGs in 2000) for poverty reduction, gender development, gender parity, and empowerment in India. It also intends to identify the policy initiatives that acted as accelerating agents or best drivers for implementation of best practices in the wake of liberalization, privatization, and globalization.

As a study covering entire country is beyond the scope of this pilot analysis, it is desired to study these indicators of different targets of MDGs and iSDGs through selected schemes of Central Government as well as the State Government of Andhra Pradesh as case studies. Case study method is one of the common methods in qualitative research (Lindlof & Taylor, 2010). For the purpose of analysis the author uses the method of hermeneutics which allows the research to analyse the government of Andhra Pradesh and *NITI Ayog* reports (SDG India Index-Baseline Report, 2018), online sources, scholarly articles, and so on to document the evidence in support of the hypotheses given in the statement of the problem.

Statement of the Problem

The study problematizes the role of any single theory or paradigm of communication in sustainable development of India. The study assumes that different paradigms of communication are operational in dealing with the issues of sustainable development at different points of time and place in India. The cultural diversities, literacy levels, and traditions play a key role in such matters. The study further argues that hybridized communication paradigms or theories

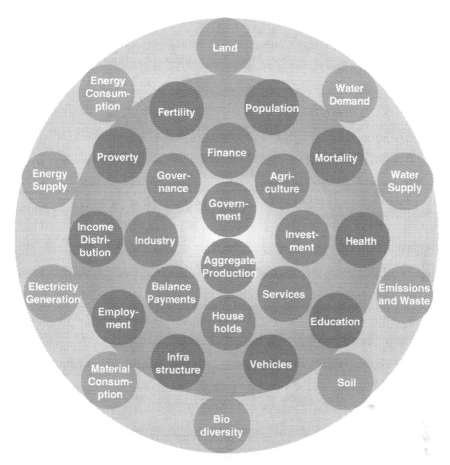

Fig. 12.1 The iSDGs discussed in the chapter show the linkages between the various goals as shown here. Overview of the iSDG subsectors. The *outer green* field includes the environment subsectors, the *middle red* field the society subsectors, and the *inner green* field the economy and governance subsectors. Source: Millennium Institute (2016)

better help explain execution of a developmental programme or scheme but need not follow the same pattern of results as in the West. It further assumes that though India and the State of Andhra Pradesh have been implementing the goals and targets of MDGs (during 2000–2015) and later the 17 iSDGs (during 2015–2019), the manner they were/are implemented in India has become highly controversial giving rise to several questions in terms of economic sustainability of the State's as well as nation's economy and growth, especially in the sectors of infrastructure, expansion of irrigation projects, and generation of employment (Fig. 12.1) (Table 12.1).

Table 12.1 A comparative chart of Millennium Development Goals and iSDGs

Millennium Development Goals 2000–2015	iSDGs 2015–2030
The eight Millennium Development Goals are: • to eradicate extreme poverty and hunger; • to achieve universal primary education; • to promote gender equality and empower women; • to reduce child mortality; • to improve maternal health; • to combat HIV/AIDS, malaria, and other diseases; • to ensure environmental sustainability; and • to develop a global partnership for development.	• Eliminate poverty • Erase hunger • Establish good health and well-being • Provide quality education • Enforce gender equality • Improve clean water and sanitation • Grow affordable and clean energy • Create decent work and economic growth • Increase industry, innovation, and infrastructure • Reduce inequality • Mobilize sustainable cities and communities • Influence responsible consumption and production • Organize climate action • Develop life below water • Advance life on land • Guarantee peace, justice, and strong institutions • Build partnerships for the goals

The Making of a 'Welfare State' Through Communication and Sustainable Development

The concept of 'welfare state' is to 'protect and promote the economic and social well being of its citizens'. The term 'protection' connotes provision of social infrastructure such as health care and prevention of discrimination on the basis of caste, colour and creed, and so on. The term 'promotion' connotes the allotment of state resources through 'redistribution of income gained from taxes for the education, vocation and employment of the depraved, deprived and under privileged/challenged sections of society'. The 'redistribution' of state resources implies offering subsidies, providing ration and free education, and creating avenues for loans at low interests. Thus, the concept of 'welfare state' connotes 'mixed economic' structure of the state as well. In the subsequent parts of this chapter, the author shows how these are being put in place both by the State of Andhra Pradesh and by the Central Government.

The development of a society is also measured in terms of its (society's) ability to offer an 'empowerment'. Melokte and Steeves (2013) defined development in terms of 'empowerment'. Lerner (1958) and Rogers (1962) have developed different paradigms of modernization and defined what they considered as 'development'. Critical perspectives of modernization theories that were developed in the West were expected to blindly give the same results in the East. But, several communication scholars refuted such a blind application of the western development theories to the East (Servaes, 2008, Servaes, 1986; Melokte & Steeves, 2013. p. 34). In fact this has become a 'game changer' or a 'cliff hanger' in the theory of modernization and sustainable development. It has thus become a crucial and critical part of defining the 'development/empowerment' that is more pertinent to the both sides of the hemispheres. The liberation paradigm is the third paradigm of 'development/empowerment' which originated from the Brazilian Educator Paulo Freire, 1970. It is among the most well-known proponents of development as liberation, the basis of which is liberation theology. It prioritizes personal and communal liberation from oppression, as the key to empowerment and self-reliance that is the goal for development (2013, p.34). Eminent scholars from the West such as Servaes (1986), and Haynes, Palermo, and Reidlinger (2016) advocate this model of development communication.

The term 'welfare state' is based on the principles of equality of opportunity, equitable distribution of wealth, and making the public accountable for those who are unable to avail themselves of the minimal provisions for a good life. According to T.H. Marshall (1950), an eminent sociologist, the 'welfare state' is a distinctive combination of democracy, welfare, and capitalism.

Though there are several models of 'welfare state', in addition to what were mentioned in the foregoing, the most commonly and lately referred one is the Nordic model. It relates to the steps taken by the Nordic countries (Iceland, Finland, Sweden, Denmark, and Norway) for the welfare of its citizens (such as old age pensions, transfer of money for meeting domestic expenses, etc.). However, the most widely critiqued, yet used models are based on the pioneering work of Esping-Andersen's (1985, 1990, & 1999) three types of models of welfare state.

As these models are not rigidly followed anywhere, the governments all over the world have shown ample flexibility and re-combinations among these models; however, one that is mostly favoured by the first world countries is the 'liberal' model to which the US economic model also subscribes. India is no exception to this. Though Esping-Andersen's (1990, 1999) model covered communist model, strangely, they seemed to have no knowledge of Gandhian economy model or Nehru's Socialist Model (Misra, 1995) of second largest populous economy in the world. There might be another reason, even if they had known it to ignore, for they were interested more in classifying and studying only highly industrialized first or second world economies. Apparently their interests thus seemed to be stuck there.

The author's contention here is that whatever schemes have been hammered out for the economic upliftment, sustainable development and modernization of Indian society are in compliance with India's commitment to MDGs and 17 iSDGs, signed in 2000 as well as in 2015. However, most of the political leaders and heads of various political parties do not openly admit this. They pretend to show these welfare schemes as their own brainchildren masking the compulsions of MDGs and iSDGs (see NITI Ayog Report, 2018 to ascertain whether these schemes were reflected under the compliance report submitted to the UN body). It is against the backdrop the author intends to deal with the schemes that the federal State Andhra Pradesh as well as the Centre introduced prior to MDGs, during the running of the MDGs (2004–2015) and later during the last five years of iSDGs to drive home the hypotheses laid down in the statement of the problem.

It is five years past since the 17 iSDGs commenced. This transition from MDGs to iSDGs has come into force at a time when National Democratic Alliance (NDA) led by the Prime Minister Narendra Modi formed a stable government with a massive mandate at the Centre (2014–2019), while Nara Chandrababu Naidu has become the first Chief Minister of residual Andhra Pradesh (2014–2019). However, the Chief Minister Chandrababu Naidu has lost the power at the latest polls held in 2019 in the State of Andhra Pradesh. On the other hand, Narendra Modi once again returned to power with a thumping majority at this husting as a Prime Minister for a second term (2019–2024) (Table 12.2).

Table 12.2 Poverty in Andhra Pradesh and all India

Year	Andhra Pradesh			All India		
	Rural	Urban	Combined	Rural	Urban	Combined
1	2	3	4	5	6	7
Percentage of people below poverty line						
1973–1974	48.41	50.61	48.86	56.44	49.01	54.88
1977–1978	38.11	42.55	39.31	53.07	45.24	51.32
1983	26.53	36.30	28.91	45.65	40.79	44.48
1987–1988	20.92	40.11	25.86	39.09	38.20	38.86
1993–1994	15.92	38.33	22.19	37.27	32.36	35.97
2004–2005	11.20	28.00	15.80	23.30	25.70	27.50
1993–1994[a]	48.10	35.20	44.60	50.10	31.80	45.30
2004–2005[a]	32.30	23.40	29.60	42.00	25.50	37.20
2009–2010[a]	22.80	17.70	21.10	33.80	20.90	29.80
Number of people below poverty line						(lakh)
1973–1974	178.21	47.48	225.69	2612.90	600.46	3213.36
1977–1978	149.13	48.41	197.54	2642.47	646.48	3288.95
1983	114.34	50.24	164.58	2519.57	709.40	3228.97
1987–1988	96.38	64.05	160.43	2318.80	751.69	3070.49
1993–1994	79.49	74.47	153.96	2440.31	763.37	3203.68
2004–2005[a]	180.00	55.00	235.10	3258.10	814.10	4072.20
2009–2010[a]	127.90	48.70	176.60	2782.10	764.70	3546.80

Source: Planning Commission, Government of India

Note: [a]As per Tendulkar Committee report

Transition of Indian Economy from Pre-MDGs to Post-MDGs

Pre-MDGs

Pigou (1962) has way back commented that always transfer or redistribution of taxes from the rich to the poor may not give the intended results immediately. He cautioned that sustained transfer for a longer period, till a generation passes out, will only help change the lives of poor demographics. He has modelled his interpretation based on the theory of marginal utility. He argued that 'if the programs launched by the government are not sustainable for the transference of purchase power from rich to poor on a long run, then both the rich and poor will at one time experience same paradoxical situation'. The contentions of Pigou (1962) appear quite pertinent even today to India if one critically examines the scenarios of indiscriminate implementation of the populist measures.

As India, the second largest populous country in the World, has adopted a policy of mixed economy since independence, it has logically followed a 'welfare state' model which is based on the 'liberal' approach (see Melokte & Steeves, 2013 for details of this approach). Jawaharlal Nehru, the first Prime Minister of India, preferred this model, obviously being educated in the UK. Thus, the initial welfare measures of the Government of India reflected in following a public sector economy, where the government has taken the whole responsibility of providing and protecting the citizens through its own administered agencies. During 1947–1970, India followed the then Soviet system of five years plans for development of infrastructure and social support. Government offered pensions to its citizens which lasted till 2004. There was no privatization then. The free market sources were least competitive with the giant government public sectors that were providing goods and services both together. However, the Government provided the ration at subsidized prices.

Some scholars argued that Nehru's ideas on secularism and economic policies evolved over his lifespan, and underscored the relevance of Nehru's vision of secular, democratic, and modern India where inequalities in wealth and status cease to exist. On the contrary, Misra (1995) was of the view that there was no serious comparative study of Gandhi and Nehruvian economic philosophies so far. According to him, the first five-year plan was modelled on the lines of Gandhian economic ideology whereas the second five-year plan completely emerged from the backdrop of Nehru's ideology of economic development. While neither of the plans offered any lasting solutions to the problems of poverty, unemployment, and economic disparities, the planners and policymakers have attempted to develop a third five-year plan by mixing both the ideologies. It was in the third five-year plan that the results have begun to appear.

Bhalla (2005) felt that the Nehruvian policies were quite irrelevant during his own times though his commitment to the development of nation cannot be questioned. It was during Nehru's time that 'license raj' came into existence in the grand name of 'socialist' pattern of economy, where everything is controlled by the State. Nehru's understanding of Indians was also questioned by Bhalla, who felt that Nehru's ideology of economy was that of elite economy on the pattern of US economy. His plans to bridge the gap between the rural poor and urban elite were disoriented with his lopsided industrial and agricultural policy. He was of the view that poor have a right to choose the Prime Minister but have no right to choose what they want for their upliftment.

Contrasting with Nehruvian economics, late Indira Gandhi, the daughter of Nehru, who ascended to power, after a brief tenure of late Lal Bahadur Shastri, in 1970s has been the first Indian leader and the Prime Minister to bring in drivers and policy initiatives for the poverty reduction in India. It was during Indira Gandhi's time that first ever populist schemes, that may be referred to as measures towards building a 'welfare state', have come into existence in India tilting the balance of economy more towards the poor, peasants, and women. Among the important steps she had taken to usher into the 'welfare state' were nationalization of private banks, imposition of moratorium on the loans lent to farmers at high interests by the money lenders/feudalists/middlemen, and finally banning the privy purses to the erstwhile Maharajas. These steps, which had been implemented under the slogan, *'garibi hatao'* (remove poverty) had endeared her epithet *'Indiramma'* (Mother Indira) which is the pet name conferred on her by the poor people of India. She has first come up with a five-point formula for the upliftment of poor but expanded it to 20-point formula later. It was the first ever attempt of an Indian Prime Minister to directly address the issues like poverty, hunger, education, agriculture, unemployment, and health prior to the world coming to the grip of these issues through MDGs and iSDGs. That is reason why Indira Gandhi was called a visionary in the post-independent Indian politics and governance.

It was during her time as Prime Minister, India has launched the first ever Satellite Instructional Television Experiment, called as SITE (1975), that was jointly designed by the technical experts from NASA and ISRO. The experiment covered around 2400 villages of six States. The experiment has taken educational programmes to the door steps of the villages. The experiment proved highly successful and was considered as a pilot project for India's satellite programme. When Indira Gandhi was the Minister of Information and Broadcasting, she has appointed Wilbur Schramm as media advisor to the Government of India. Wilbur Schramm was thus incidentally responsible for founding the India's premium institute—Indian Institute of Mass Communication (IIMC). It is the point of beginning of placing a communication model in the development of the State rural sector (Tables 12.3 and 12.4).

Nehru and Indira's economic reforms have taken a severe beating in the early 1990s, in the wake of collapse of the Soviet Union in 1989. It portended an impending economic blackout for India. Fortunately, the then Prime Minister P.V. Narasimha Rao, who is dearly addressed as the 'Father of Modern Economic Reforms', had gone forward with liberalization, privatization, and globalization in a big way opening flood gates for foreign investments and

Table 12.3 Employment in public and private sectors in Andhra Pradesh *(no. of persons)*

Sl. No.	Years	Public sector	Private sector	Total
1	2	3	4	5
1	March, 1966	656,003	300,738	956,741
2	March, 1970	689,464	294,929	984,393
3	March, 1980	1,106,201	296,700	1,402,901
4	March, 1990	1,368,152	362,500	1,730,652
5	March, 2000	1,503,280	568,362	2,071,642
6	March, 2001	1,489,108	586,154	2,075,262
7	March, 2002	1,462,190	588,541	2,050,731
8	March, 2003	1,475,454	625,335	2,100,789
9	March, 2004	1,443,979	567,666	2,011,645
10	March, 2005	1,395,814	646,966	2,042,780
11	March, 2006	1,374,735	626,719	2,001,454
12	March, 2007	1,393,509	659,633	2,053,142
13	March, 2008	1,365,633	725,298	2,090,931
14	March, 2009	1,357,884	724,916	2,082,800
15	March, 2010	1,350,287	751,357	2,101,644
16	March, 2011	1,277,371	782,457	2,059,828
17	March, 2012	1,276,054	751,854	2,027,908

Table 12.4 Growth of information technology (Hyderabad)

Year	Exports (Rs. crores)	No. of employees (cumulative)
1997–1998	284	8700
1998–1999	574	12,000
1999–2000	1059	25,500
2000–2001	1917	48,700
2001–2002	2907	64,000
2002–2003	3668	71,445
2003–2004	5025	85,945
2004–2005	8270	126,920
2005–2006	12,521	151,789
2006–2007	18,582	187,450
2007–2008	26,122	239,000
2008–2009	32,509	251,786
2009–2010	33,482	264,375
2010–2011	35,022	279,438
2011–2012	40,646	318,624

Source: Software Technology Parks of India, Hyderabad

allowing the entry of multinationals into Indian markets. This is inevitable as economy of any country moves in a cyclical pattern, and whatever we have begun in the 1970s with nationalization has to end with de-nationalization and disinvestment by the 1990s, exactly within two decades. India's transformation and transition from a controlled economy (license raj) to an open market economy during the 1990s stands as an evidence to the contention of the author that the concepts of economic reforms and welfare economics do keep moving in cyclical pattern. What proved to be quite beneficial for the poor Indian peasants in the early 1970s has to give way with the new order global economic changes demanding a different pattern of economic reforms in the place of the older ones.

India has registered for the first time a significant march in communication and sustainable development during 1999–2004 under the vibrant leadership of Atal Bihari Vajpayee who as Prime Minister (1999–2004) has taken forward the economic reforms and liberalization, that P.V. Narasimha Rao founded, to a newer heights.

During MDGs (2000–2015)

The Prime Minister Atal Bihari Vajpayee was leading India when the MDGs have come into existence for the first time in 2000, at the turn of this millennium. During his period the several important developmental policies have come in place including laying down the necessary infrastructure (Golden Quadra Angle Road Construction under National Highways Development Project) for implementation of newly laid policies; significant among them are a revolution in telecommunication policy, airlines policy, radio waves policy, banking and insurance policy, agricultural policy, and industrial policy. For example, *Pradhan Mantri Gram Sadak Yojana* (laying roads to every village in India), *Sarvasiksha Abhiyan* (Universalization of Elementary Education), and so on. Most of these schemes addressed the targets and goals formulated under the Millennium Development Goals (MDGs) to which India became a party in 2000. These new policies have quickly come handy for multinationals as well as indigenous industrial sectors to quickly expand across the country bringing in a new wave of employment potential in India.

Vajpayee's government began to push in second-generation economic reforms to sustain the benefits of the first-generation reforms ushered in during the tenure of P.V. Narasimha Rao. The country registered a staggering growth of GDP exceeding 7% every year from 2003 to 2007. Increasing foreign direct investment, modernizing of public and industrial infrastructure, creating millions of jobs, and promoting high-tech and IT industry have improved the nation's international image. Good crop harvests and strong industrial expansion also helped the economy (Rai, 2004) (Tables 12.5, 12.6, 12.7, 12.8, 12.9, 12.10).

Around this time, the N. Chandrababu Naidu was the Chief Minister of the then combined State of Andhra Pradesh during 1995–2004. He was also the supremo of Telugu Desam Party (TDP) since the revolt of its legislators against the actor-turned Telugu Desam Party (TDP) founder Chief Minister N.T. Rama Rao in 1995. Ever since, Naidu used to work for the development of the State in multipronged manner. During his time, he has implemented several projects and schemes which earned him the epithet—a visionary and hi-tech Chief

Table 12.5 Growth of IT in tier II locations

Centre	Exports (Rs. crores)	No. of employees (cumulative)
Vizag	1200	16,000
Vijayawada	95.6	2558
Kakinada	34.67	1379
Tirupati	4.25	157

Source: Software Technology Parks of India, Hyderabad

Table 12.6 Welfare initiatives under social infrastructure. Performance in certain health parameters

Year	Institutions	Boys	Girls	Total
2008	2358	158,407	89,617	248,024
2009	2358	158,643	86,631	245,274
2010	2358	158,597	88,049	246,646
2011	2358	144,828	86,524	231,352
2012	2358	125,338	71,106	196,444

Source: Social Welfare Department

Table 12.7 Welfare initiatives under social infrastructure. Social welfare institutions

Year	IMR	MMR	Crude birth rate	Crude death rate	Expected life at birth
2001	66	195 (2001–2003)	20.8	8.1	M-64.1
2002	62		20.7	8.1	F-65.4*
2003	59		20.4	8.0	
2004	59	154 (2004–2006)	19.0	7.0	
2005	57		19.1	7.3	
2006	56		18.9	7.3	
2007	54	134 (2007–2009)	18.7	7.4	M-65.4
2008	52		18.4	7.5	F- 69.4 $
2009	49		18.3	7.6	
2010	46		17.9	7.6	
2011	43		17.5	7.5	M-66.9
					F-70.9 @

IMR= No. of Infant deaths during the year per thousand live births.

MMR= Maternal Mortality Ratio is proportion of maternal deaths during the year per 100,000 live births reported.

Crude birth rate =No. of live births during the year per 1000 population. Crude death rate=No. of deaths during the year per 1000 population.

[a]Projections for 2001–2006, $ Projections for 2006–2010 @ Projections for 2011–2015 Source: SRS Bulletins, Registrar General, India

Table 12.8 Welfare initiatives under social infrastructure. Girl child protection scheme

Year	No. of beneficiaries		Total
	Single girl	Two girls	
2005–2006	4914	33,980	38,894
2006–2007	7269	76,801	84,070
2007–2008	6682	86,211	92,893
2008–2009	4684	62,693	67,377
2009–2010	5648	64,654	70,302
2010–2011	6076	85,716	91,792
2011–2012	3648	55,686	59,334
2012–2013 (up to September 2012)	1410	14,112	15,522
Total	40,331	479,853	520,184

Source: Directorate of Women Development & Child Welfare

Table 12.9 Welfare initiatives under social infrastructure. Pensions

Scheme	Existing pensions	
	2011–2012	2012–2013
NOAP (Rs. crores/no. of pensioners)		
Allocation	316.27	368.14
Release	334.45	184.07
Expenditure	380.83	189.12
Pensioners	1,507,891	1,508,163
Indiramma pensions to disabled persons		
Allocation	476.50	546.46
Release	476.50	273.23
Expenditure	477.44	255.27
Pensioners	786,110	784,097
Indiramma pensions to old age persons and widows		
Allocation	1105.60	1239.35
Releases	1105.60	619.68
Expenditure	1202.44	659.94
Pensioners	4,575,946	4,479,671
Toddy tappers		
Allocation	24.48	24.48
Releases	24.48	24.48
Expenditure	8.29	4.22
Pensioners	33,878	33,552
NFBS		
Allocation	10.00	29.00
Releases	32.02	14.50
Expenditure	22.37	17.61
Families assisted	44,739	35,213

Source: SERP–Rural Development Department

Table 12.10 Welfare initiatives under social infrastructure. Status of national rural livelihoods mission

Item/sub item name	Achievement (No.)
No. of individual Swarozgaries assisted	27,717
No. of SC individual Swarozgaries assisted	18,202
No. of ST individual Swarozgaries assisted	5216
No. of disabled individual Swarozgaries assisted	250
Self-help groups Formed under NRLM	20,217
Income-generating activities provided	240,952

Executive Officer of the State. Naidu focused on rural development and poverty eradication through involving people in sustainable development processes accompanied by innovative reforms in the administration. That is the first ever sign of an Indian Chief Minister formulating schemes in keeping with the targets assigned under MDGs.

Two important projects that gathered international attention during his early years of becoming the Chief Minister of the State of Andhra Pradesh were—*Janmabhoomi* (birth place) and Clean and Green projects. Both of them involved public at the grassroots level. Naidu launched the *Janmabhoomi* (birth place) Programme in 1996. The main aim was to involve people in the reconstruction and revitalization of the society. The programme works at a micro level, identifying the problems of people through *Gram Sabha* (Village Parliament) involving public discussions by the regional officers, especially in villages, and to send project proposals to the government to work on. The core areas of concentration were community works, primary school education, drinking water, health, hygiene and hospitals, family welfare, and environmental protection through watershed and joint forest management activities.

In 1997 Naidu launched the 'Clean and Green Campaign' involving school students and teachers for plantation of trees both in the institutions and households in tandem with the government employees. A total of 46 million trees were planted across the entire state. About 3,906,835 people participated in sanitation work, with 1,438,850 persons engaged to remove garbage and 40,921,447 people participated in health awareness rallies (Wikisources). He was instrumental in hammering out programmes such as self-help groups (SHGs) in respect of water user associations, *Vanasamrakshana Samities* (Forest Protection Societies), *Rythu Mithra Groups* (Farmer-friendly groups), Chief Minister Employment Yojana (CMEY) Groups, and School Education Committees, and promoted the 'Development of Women and Children in Rural Areas' (DWCRA) where each group had 10–20 female members and chose a leader who conducted group meetings. The main purpose was to offer microfinance through government and bank linkage that would help rural women to start income-generating activities, know about their rights, and the importance of education. His government supplied one-fifth of a million bicycles to the girls who joined the government high schools as part of women empowerment initiative. He has provided Liquefied Petroleum Gas (LPG) cylinders free to poor rural women for preparing their food at home instead of burning forest wood outside in 1999 under the name *Deepam* (Light).

Forming *Raithu Bazars* (Farmers' Markets), developing a vision document 2020, in which he has clearly indicated his objectives to completely eliminate poverty and hunger from the rural and urban societies, creating water harvesting zones at every house, founding Hyderabad Airports Authority, Cyberabad Development Authority, developing a Multi-Modal Transport System (MMTS), and so on were some of the hallmark welfare and developmental activities that he launched during his time. He has introduced Internet-based *e-seva* (*e-Service* Portal) to eliminate corruption at rural and urban levels. All the document-related certifications are provided at these centres at a nominal price. He has introduced schemes like mapping the State through land digitization. Due to his unwavering determination for development, he has put the State of Andhra Pradesh at the forefront of technology.

Despite all his commitment for the development of the State, both he and the Prime Minister Vajpayee lost power in the elections held in 2004. In the next decade (2004–2014), the Indian National Congress Party, headed by Sonia Gandhi as its Chairman, and Manmohan Singh as the Prime Minister, ruled the country both at the Centre and the State of Andhra Pradesh.

The Congress party has nominated Y.S. Rajasekhara Reddy (popularly known as YSR) as the Chief Minister of the State of Andhra Pradesh for a term of years since 2004–2014. The populist measures the YSR has launched have harvested a rich vote bank among the weaker and poor sections of the society. A cursory glance at the list of some of the most important populist schemes which YSR has offered during his first term in office (2004–2009) as Chief Minister reveals the competitive nature of populist schemes, which are in fact meant to comply with the targets of MDGs. In fact the Congress Party always has looked at the measures taken for complying with the MDGs as 'populist measures' or 'vote bank politics'. In other words, the governments that implemented the MDGs and the World Bank initiatives did not show a neutral attitude with a spirit of national commitment to uplift the poor and deprived societies. On the other hand, they converted them in to political measures (Table 12.11).

Some of the major economic and welfare schemes implemented by the Congress Party during 2004–2014 in keeping with the specific targets of MDGs both at the centre and at the State were: (a) interest-free loans and one-fourth rupee interest for SHGs run by women/weaker sections of society; (b) women's fund credit to women cooperatives has been crucial to empower women meant to free themselves from the evil clutches of microfinancing institutions; (c) Community-Managed Sustainable Agriculture (CMSA) for rural peasant communities has been quite handy with a certain fund earmarked as revolving fund to meet immediate/emergency agricultural needs; (d)

Table 12.11 Overview of MGNREGS-AP

Item	2012–2013 (up to October 2012)	Cumulative
Total no. of job cards issued (lakh)	3.67	128
No. of works completed (lakh)	3.3	23.87
Total expenditure (Rs. crore)	3688	22,834
No. of households provided wage employment (lakh)	54.75	93.7
No. of individuals provided wage employment (lakh)	99.37	189
Person days generated (crore)	27.7	180.35
No. of households completed in 100 days (lakh)	6.5	48.8
Average no. of days employment provided per household	50.61	–
Average wage rate per day per person (Rs.)	105.85	93.37

Source: Rural Development Department

Dairy-Indira Kranthi Patham (IKP) has commenced the initiative of Profitable Dairying by Establishing Milk Procurement Centres in villages and Bulk Milk Cooling Units (BMCUs) at *mandal* level through SHGs and their federations; (e) Knitting Rural Self Help Enterprises (KRUSHE) wing under the Society for Elimination of Rural Poverty (SERP) has been initiated to promote entrepreneurship in farm and non-farm livelihoods among the members of rural SHG households; (f) The Community-Managed Health and Nutrition (CMH&N) intervention offers trained community members in the form of Health Activists (HA) and Community Resource Persons (CRP) to relay messages about maternal, neonatal, infant care practices to SHGs and village organizations; (g) Persons with Disabilities (PWD) are among the poorest and most vulnerable of the poor, the SERP has initiated disability interventions as pilot project in 138 project *mandals* in the State; (h) Social Security Pensions are meant to bring the disbursement of all pensions under one umbrella; (i) *Indira Jeevan Bheema Pathakam* is meant to offer group insurance for the rural landless poor through Life Insurance Corporation of India; (j) *Abhay Hastham* (Assuring Hand) which offers pension to every woman enrolled in SHG at her old age as a social security measure; (k) *Rajiv Arogya Sri* is another scheme which offers health coverage for treatment in corporate hospitals up to a limit of one-fifth of a million (US $2800). The whole expenses for identified diseases would be borne by the State. Even ambulance services 104/108 have been added to this scheme where anyone from anywhere could be carried to a nearest corporate hospital in case of emergency. (l) Fees reimbursement for the children of backward classes and economically backward classes up to post-graduation level in any chosen field/discipline.

When these schemes started rolling out in to public, almost every family in the State appeared to have been benefited by many of them or any one of them in one way or the other. This has acted as a binding substance between the

Congress Party and the people. Especially, YSR has become a god man in human form for masses of the State of Andhra Pradesh. As such it returned the party to power in 2009 elections though this time, the mandate was not as thumping as it was in 2004. Unfortunately, YSR died in a helicopter crash at a village while in the harness in 2009.

The country went to polls in 2014 both at the Central and State level. As a result, the NDA led by the Prime Minister Narendra Modi has come to power at the Centre, while Naidu has become the first Chief Minister of the residual State of Andhra Pradesh. The former capital of the combined State of Andhra Pradesh—Hyderabad—has gone to the newly emerged State of Telangana and the residual State has to identify a new capital for its future building.

Heralding iSDGs (2015–2019)

There is no doubt that India has achieved significant progress, growth, and development in various sectors during the period MDGs were operational between 2000 and 2015. The abovementioned schemes of the State Government of Andhra Pradesh, during the rule of TDP (1999–2004) governance and later under the Congress governance (2004–2014), bear ample testimony to this fact. It is also fact that most of the schemes that the State government of Andhra Pradesh implemented during the last 15 years have received funding from the Central Government led by the BJP and the Congress parties. While the MDGs comprised 8 international development goals with 21 quantifiable targets, the 17 iSDGs have come as an extension of the MDGs with 169 targets.

Recently *NITI Ayog* (formerly known as Planning Commission of India) has brought out a report entitled *SDG India Index—Base line Report 2018*. The report has adequately documented the progress achieved during implementation of MDGs between 2000 and 2015 and the steps envisaged by the Central and State Governments for the implementing 17 iSDGs together with its 169 targets.

With the return of Narendra Modi as the head of the State of Government of India and N. Chandrababu Naidu as the Chief Minister of the State of Andhra Pradesh in 2014 elections, the implementation of the 17 iSDGs have once again assumed groundbreaking significance. In continuation of the welfare schemes the earlier Congress governments implemented between 2004 and 2014, Chandrababu Naidu has once again brought in several new welfare schemes in keeping with the 'vote bank' politics as well as the significance of 'populist measures' that returned him to power after a gap of a decade.

As a first step towards alleviating the farming community from the burden of debt-traps, the Chief Minister Naidu has implemented the loan waiving of farmers to the tune of US $337 billion (24,000 crores). He paid them cash straight into their bank accounts. He has constructed only 187 *Anna Canteens* (brother canteens) as against the promised 282 where people used to have a healthy and hygienic food prepared by *Akshaya Foundation* for just Rs. 5=00

(1/14 of a US$) be it a tiffin or a lunch or a dinner. In other words an individual suffering from hunger and poverty can have his/her two square meals of a day together with breakfast in the morning just for a payment of Rs. 15/- (one-fifth of a US$). He also implemented schemes like *Chandranna Pelli Kanuka* (a gift of Chandrababu on the occasion of a bride's marriage) which offers a cash equivalent to US $700 (Indian rupees 50,000=00) as a onetime gift to the parents of the bride to meet the expenses of the marriages which are performed very traditionally in Andhra Pradesh. Chandranna life insurance worth of US $7100 is created for the unorganized sector such as drivers, *rikshaw* (tri-wheeler) pullers, building construction labour, women, and men in various services where if they encounter an accidental death. The rice of high quality was provided for people living below the poverty line (BPL) as many kilogrammes as they need at ration dealer shops spread across the State at the rate of rupee per kilogramme (1/72 of the cost of a US dollar in Indian currency exchange).

As such he has implemented a galore of schemes for the benefit of the needy and deprived in the State of Andhra Pradesh. Some of his schemes were also having the share of a component of Central Government. He has adopted the scheme of *Mahatma Gandhi Grameen Rojgar Yojana* (Mahatma Gandhi Rural Employment Scheme) on a large scale, and has won the appreciation of the Central Government for procuring the largest sums of investment from the Central Government. During his time, the State image has gone up and it has recorded the highest growth per capita for the State.

Government of India Schemes

Swachh Bharat *(Clean India)*, *AMRIT*, *Smart Cities, and the Like*

In each of the populist scheme implemented by the State Government, for instance, pensions for old people, 50% was given by the Centre and the rest was borne by the State. Similarly if financial interest-free loans are given to women, self-help groups (SHGs), or DWCRA groups, the Centre will bear 60–75% depending on the area and location of the target groups. To commence agricultural operations or its related works during onset of monsoon, the government of India would release its share of Rs. 6000/- (equivalent to US $80). This apart, there are schemes which Centre directly sponsors at its whole expense. Several insurance schemes for the farmers and unorganized sectors fall under this category. Most important one among such schemes is *Swachh Bharat* (Clean India). This is a scheme similar to the 'Clean and Green' scheme of Chandrababu Naidu, implemented during his earlier stint as Chief Minister during 1995–1999, 1999–2004, and 2014–2019.

In addition, the Government of India has launched a number of multifaceted schemes aimed at holistic development. Most important among them are *Swachh Bharat*, *Amrit*, and Smart Cities that seek to revolutionize India's urban and rural settings.

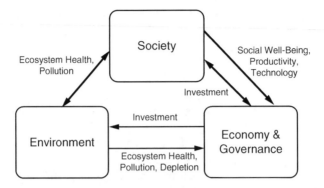

Fig. 12.2 The diagram illustrates how *Swachh Bharat* (Clean India) meets the iSDG model. Main sectors of the iSDG model. Based on Barney (2002)

Swachh Bharat is an eco-friendly, economic, energy-based, environment-friendly, health and hygiene scheme of the Government of India (see Fig. 12.2 to know how it parallels the iSDGs 2030). As soon as Narendra Modi came to power, he has implemented it to keep India clean and hygienic. The scheme is multilateral with far-reaching economic and social outcomes. The government of India invested huge money to keep the country clean at every level from village to urban centres. In the process, the railway stations, the bus stations, the government offices, the municipal and village roads, and so on have come under *Swachh Bharat* programme. Thousands of scavengers and the rural and urban poor have got employment under the scheme and today India looks far better than what it was a decade back.

One of the salient features of the scheme is to maintain good environment at every level keeping the country from village to urban to metro level free from pollution. Due to human wastes lying in the open spaces of lands, along the train tracks and at other places on the road sides, and so on, the air and water are polluted. It is leading to health problems due to contamination. Communicable diseases spread fast. It leads to government spending more money on hospitals to provide medicare for the affected and the needy. A strict implementation and monitoring has resulted in preventing people from being affected by the communicable water and air borne diseases.

Further, the government has implemented a huge plan like collecting garbage from each house. The collected garbage is segregated as wet and dry garbage which are used in processing bio-gas and power. As such the power generated by the burning of dry garbage wastes is about 4–5 MWs per day that meets the per day power requirement of Vijayawada city in Andhra Pradesh. Apart from generating employment for the poor and illiterate rural and urban men and women, it attracted a number of startup initiatives and entrepreneurs to set up small-scale power plants at each district and *mandal* headquarters to generate power that meets the local requirements. The people are mandated to rate the implementation of *Swachh Bharat* by giving their votes at the respective collectorates or municipal corporations. The government constituted *Swachh Survekshan* Committee that would give away ballots to the participating public and elicit their views on the implementation of the scheme. Based on such rating, the Central Government will give away annual awards to the best performing cities, towns, and *mandals* across India.

The Central Government also has rolled out a scheme called *AMRIT (Affordable Medicine and Reliable Implants Treatment)* to support the poor families for the supply of subsidized inputs for treatment. Similarly, the Central Scheme *Ayushman Bharat* (Live Long India) reimburses or bears the entire medical expenditure of the people living below poverty line. The scheme is rolled out as part of National Health Policy. At the State level, the scheme is a parallel to *Arogya Sri*. Further, the Central Government has come up with a scheme called as National Smart City Mission that empowers the small towns and urban centres with all the much-needed infrastructure and digital facilities.

The government of India also implemented schemes to promote girl education—*Beti Bachao and Beti Padhao*—where the educational expenses of the girls are totally borne by the Central Government studying in the State and Central Schools, run by the Central Government funding from primary school level to University level.

It required a critical discussion whether such huge spending of money on populist measures indeed promotes India's objective to attain the iSDGs by 2030. The economic experts argue the matter in a different perspective. However, *NITI Ayog* has brought out a report in 2018 outlining the successful implementation of various schemes and measures under the goals and targets of MDGS as well as 17 iSDGs (see NITI Ayog Report, 2018 available online). That said, there is an urgent need to shift the focus from the competitive politics of populist measures versus sustainability of state's economy in countries like India.

CRITICAL DISCUSSION ON THE COMPETITIVE POLITICS OF iSDGs, SUSTAINABILITY OF STATE'S ECONOMY, AND COMMUNICATION FOR SUSTAINABLE DEVELOPMENT

The foregoing illustrates the fact that political parties competed with each other both at the State and Centre to retain the power or to ascend to the power in hammering out and executing various schemes and populist measures to achieve the goals and targets of the MDGs and 17 iSDGs so far. However, the manner various schemes and welfare measures have come to stay in India raises several pertinent questions, more importantly about the durability of such economic largesse among others. There are issues like what is the budget allocation? What is the source of income? How much of percentage of revenues should be spent on such welfare schemes described as populist schemes? How much of percentage of the GDP (Gross Domestic Product) should be apportioned to construction of infrastructure, industries, and other projects? There should be a scientific criteria within the framework of which the State or the Centre must implement the schemes to meet the targets of iSDGs. What is it? As of now there are no attempts to think in this direction. As a result the State's economy is turning upside down.

As Pigou (1962) discussed that transfer of purchase power from the rich man to poor at the expense of others' costs will have to be evidenced through 'reduction in the drink bill'. If that does not happen, the populist measures of the governments as a result of privatization of economy might jeopardize both the rich and the poor equally. Edwards (2007) argues that 'most academic participants in the ongoing debate over income redistribution are aware that it is not possible, ever, for government to tax one set of persons and redistribute the same amount to a set of subsidy recipients. He further contends that 'one implication of the high cost of government income redistribution comes into focus when costs are understood correctly as alternative opportunities forgone.'

Why the author is compelled to quote this is that the Government of Andhra Pradesh has found that its populist schemes (can also be called as 'charity schemes' from the perspective of the western scholars) are enormously onerous. To meet these enormous over burdening costs, the State resorted to offer cheap alcohol for the people's consumption in every corner of the State (through their own government outlets, licenced marketing outlets, bars in addition to belt shops, etc.). As such the State in its revised estimates is expecting to get whopping revenue of US $281 billion just from the sales of alcohol to the common people, whose income has been augmented by a number of populist schemes by the very State Government. Almost every household in Andhra Pradesh is receiving not less than US $200 either cash or means free from the exchequer of the State and the Central Government. Is this not a paradoxical way of implementation of welfare schemes to attain the targets of the iSDGs?

After all, this is paid from the taxes collected from the people both the rich and the poor. In the name of achieving the targets both during the MDGs and now under the iSDGs, the State revenues are redistributed instead of spending them for income generating sectors such as infrastructure, irrigation projects, and industries that generate both employment and wealth. Now the remedy has become worse than the problem. The people of the State have become addicts to this free income and economic gains under an array of various populist schemes.

Now people of the State of Andhra Pradesh no longer look for development projects and employment generating industrial units that add up to the value of State's wealth. They look for the higher sops from rival political parties competing for power. This criterion has outgrown the earlier concepts of anti-incumbency to a government in office. Now people are voting out of power a duly and well-performed government just because its 'populist schemes' and 'free subsidies' are less beneficial than the schemes of an opposition party that offers higher subsidies and benefits. If a government does not offer these many sops, it will lose power in the next elections. As such there is an unhealthy competition between the rival political parties in promising to bring the heavens down during each term of elections.

Now expansion of agricultural projects, irrigation projects, and hydel power generation units has become secondary due to heavy spending of entire budget on the welfare schemes and populist measures. Even writing off the loans incurred by farmers over period due to crop failures or escalation of cost inputs has not led to a positive result. The government of India's recent economic survey showed that the writing off loans of farmers in fact affected the farming community more than ever. This has affected the banks' ability to lend forward the money besides affecting the borrowing power of the farmers as well. In addition, each of the populist schemes required its own management and thus calls for employment of a number of people for effective implementation. As such the cost inputs incurred on the employment of these people to deliver the schemes have become a threateningly large predator of eating away the actual funds meant for populist schemes (Edwards, 2007: 7).

Both the Government of India and the State of Andhra Pradesh must see through a window free from politics of iSDGs, and assess to whom and how long these measures have to last or end. Though, as hypothesized, the study showed a direct relationship between the communication of welfare schemes and sustainable development with the growing Indian economy, questions do stare into our face on over ambitious planning, crazy promises of welfare schemes in election manifestos, lack of scientific criteria for deciding a percentage of budget or GDP for welfare schemes, and linking the implementation of iSDGs with the politics of 'vote banks' and 'populist measures' that are likely to become decelerators of country's progress and development in the near future.

Conclusions

The chapter overviewed how the communication has played a key role in bringing about the execution of a number of welfare schemes or 'populist measures' to achieve a sustainable development in the State of Andhra Pradesh in general and in India in particular both prior to the launch of MDGs (1970–2000), during the period of MDGs (2000–2015), and later through the period of 17 iSDGs (2015–2030). The study has also highlighted the fact that a hybridized model of communication or theories works better to explain the effective relationship between communication and development in India than a single model of communication. The study also explained how many kinds of communication strategies have been at work in India in executing different welfare schemes from time to time. The State government of Andhra Pradesh has adopted a 'populist' approach in implementing a number of 'populist measures' in the guise of welfare schemes during 2000–2015 under the MDGs and later under the 17 iSDGs. The study argued that in the long course (2000–2019) of implementation of these schemes and measures, the goals and targets of MDGs or iSDGs have been turned into politics of 'vote banks' and 'populist measures'. These goals and targets have become politically competitive in India to ascend to power. In the process, the tax payers' money got distributed among the majority people of the electorate under various schemes that are actually to be afforded to a limited number of people falling below the poverty line. Such unscrupulous implementation of schemes has driven the State to a debt trap destroying the banking sector as well as State's economy.

Finally, the study not only established a direct and positive relationship between communication of welfare schemes and sustainable development at grassroots level, but raised several questions as to the future sustainability of such heavy indiscriminate and unscientific spending on 'populist measures' in order to achieve the targets of the MDGs and 17 iSDGs. It argues for a scientific criterion 'as a percentage of GDP' for such welfare measures, freeing it from the 'vote bank' politics or politics of 'populist schemes'.

References

At the Heart of Change: The Role of Communication in Sustainable Development. (2007), pp. 3–5. London, UK: Panos.

Bandura, A. (2006). On Integrating Social Cognitive and Social Diffusion Theories. In A. Singhal & J. Dearing (Eds.), *In Communication of Innovations: A Journey with EV Rogers* (pp. 111–135). New York: Sage.

Bhalla, S. S. (2005). Nehruvian economics –dean on arrival. *DNA*. Nov. 13.

Contractor, N. S., Singhal, A., & Rogers, E. M. (1988). Meta-theoretical Perspectives on Satellite Television and Development in India. *Journal of Broadcasting and Electronic Media., 33*(2), 129–148.

Edwards, J. R. (2007). The Costs of Public Income Redistribution and Private Charity. *Journal of Libertarian Studies, 21*(2), 3–20.

Esping-Andersen, G. (1985). *Politics Against Markets.* Princeton, NJ: Princeton University Press.

Esping-Andersen, G. (1990). *The Three Worlds of Welfare Capitalism.* Princeton NJ: Princeton University Press.

Esping-Andersen, G. (1999). *Social Foundations of Postindustrial Economies.* Oxford: Oxford University Press.

Freire, P. (1970). *Pedagogy of the Oppressed.* New York: The Seabury Press.

Haynes, E., Palermo, C., & Reidlinger, D. P. (2016). Modified Policy-Delphi Study for Exploring Obesity Prevention Priorities. *BMJ Open, 6*, e011788. https://doi.org/10.1136/bmjopen-2016-011788

Lerner, D. (1958). *The Passing of Traditional Society: Modernizing the Middle East.* New York: Free Press.

Lindlof, T. R., & Taylor, B. C. (2010). *Qualitative Communication Research Methods* (3rd ed.). New York: Sage.

Marshall, T. H. (1950). *Citizenship and Social Class and Other Essays.* Cambridge, UK: CUP.

Melokte, S. R., & Steeves, L. H. (Eds.). (2013). *Communication for the Development in the Third World: Theory and Practice for Empowerment.* California & New Delhi: Sage.

Misra, O. P. (1995). *Economic Thought of Gandhi and Nehru: A Comprehensive Analysis.* New Delhi, India: M.D. Publications Ltd..

Murthy, C. S. H. N. (2008). Designing E-learning Programs for Rural Social Transformation and Poverty Reduction: *Turkish Online Journal of Distance Education.* 9, article no. 11.

Murthy, C. S. H. N. (2009). Use of convergent Mobile Technologies for Sustainable Economic Transformation in the Lives of Small Farmers in Rural India. *Turkish Online Journal of Distance Education, 10*(3), 1.

Murthy, C. S. H. N. (2010). High Film Centricity in Indian TV Channels. Perspectives and Challenges. *Journal of Creative Communication, 5*(3), 153–172.

Murthy, C. S. H. N., & Das, R. (2011). Social Change Through Diffusion of Innovation in Indian Popular Cinema: An Analytical Study of *Lage Raho Munna Bhai* and *Stalin.* Asian Cinema, Fall/Winter, 269–289.

Murthy, C. S. H. N. (2015). Issues of Rural Development In Mainstream Journalism. Exploring New Strategies for Media Intervention. *Journal of Global Communication., 8*(1), 23–35.

Ninan, S. (2007). *Headlines from the Heartland: Reinventing the Hindi Public Sphere.* New Delhi, India: Sage Publications.

NITI Ayog Report. (2018). *SDG-index-baseline Report.* New Delhi, India: Government of India Publications.

Nussbaum, M. C., & Sen, A. K. (1993). *The Quality of Life.* Oxford, UK: Clarendon Press.

Pigou, A. C. (1962). *The Economics of Welfare* (4th ed.). London, UK: Macmillan.

Rai, S. (2004, April 1). India's economy soared by 10% in last quarter of 2003. The New York Times.

Rogers, E. M. (1962/1983). *Diffusion of Innovations* (3rd ed.). New York: The Free Press.

Quebral, N. C. (1972–73). What Do We Mean by Development Communication? *International Development Review, 15*(2), 25–28.

Quebral, N. C. (2012). *Development Communication Primer.* Penang, Malaysia: Southbound.

Servaes, J. (1986). Development Theory and Communication Policy: Power to the People. *European Journal of Communication, 1*(2), 203–209.

Servaes, J. (2008a). *Communication Policies, Good Governance and Development Journalism.* Johannesburg: University of South Africa Press.

Servaes, J. (2008b). *Communication for Development and Social Change.* UNESCO, Paris: Sage.

Servaes, J. (1999). *Communication for Development: One World, Multiple Cultures.* New York: Hampton Press.

Servaes, J. (2003). *Approaches to Development Studies on Communication for Development.* UNESCO, Paris: UNESCO Press.

Servaes, J., & Lie, R. (2014). New Challenges for Communication for Sustainable Development and Social Change: A Review Essay. *Journal of Multicultural Discourses, 10*(1). https://doi.org/10.1080/17447143.2014.982655

Servaes, J. (2016). How 'Sustainable' Is Development Communication Research? *The International Communication Gazette, 78*(7), 701–710.

United Nations. Report. (1987). Report of the World Commission on Environment and Development. General Assembly Resolution 42/187, 11 December 1987. Retrieved April 24, 2020.

CHAPTER 13

Fostering Gender-Sensitive Programming and Practices Among Community Radios in India: The Road Ahead

Kanchan K. Malik

INTRODUCTION: COMMUNITY RADIO IN INDIA AND GENDER

Community radio (CR) in India has played a key role in allowing social groups to negotiate diverse identities and articulate concerns from marginalised perspectives. At present, the country has around 245 operational CR stations, over 100 of which are run by NGOs and local communities. Many CR initiatives in India continue to be led by women, such as Sangham Radio in the state of Telangana and Rudi No Radio in Gujarat. A significant number of NGO- and community-led CR stations work with women and other groups oppressed on grounds of gender. For example, Waqt Ki Awaz, Uttar Pradesh; Gurgaon Ki Awaz, Haryana; Radio Namaskar, Odisha; Alfaz-e-Mewat, Haryana; Radio Active, Karnataka; Tilonia Radio, Rajasthan; Radio Bundelkhand, Madhya Pradesh; Mann Deshi Tarang Vahini, Maharashtra; Radio Mewat, Haryana; Radio Madhuban, Rajasthan; Kalanjiam Samuga Vanoli, Tamil Nadu; and quite a few others have strong gender programming.

From using CR to discuss their domestic and working conditions, to deliberate on how to deal with children, men, the elderly, and women themselves, women across India are tapping CR to create communication spaces for themselves and to be heard. At least one programme in every CR station is dedicated

K. K. Malik (✉)
Department of Communication, University of Hyderabad, Hyderabad, India
e-mail: drkanchan@uohyd.ac.in

© The Author(s), under exclusive license to Springer Nature Switzerland AG 2021
M. J. Yusha'u, J. Servaes (eds.), *The Palgrave Handbook of International Communication and Sustainable Development*,
https://doi.org/10.1007/978-3-030-69770-9_13

to women's everyday concerns within their specific cultural contexts—not something we could say about the mainstream media channels. So, as NGOs set up stations that are run exclusively by women, or those that are making special programming focussed on women, CR exhibits the techno-social potential to empower women—to assert their right to communication spaces; to challenge the socially disempowering gender norms; to participate actively in the development processes; and to aspire for gender equality (Malik, 2020; Malik & Bandelli, 2012; Pavarala & Malik, 2007, 2010; Kadel, 2010; Anwar, 2015; Yalala, 2015).

However, it cannot be ignored that India constitutes a part of the so-called patriarchal belt (Caldwell, 1982; Moghadam, 2005) where women are subordinated to men and their presence in the public realm as well as their representation in the public sphere is low. Even though some progress has been observed in the status of women in the last decade or so (through the efforts of feminist groups, women's movements, progressive government legislations, policy reforms, etc.), clear-cut gender inequities persist, that prevent women from enhancing their capabilities and exercising their agency. There has been progress for women in India over the years, but their status remains problematic, and the contrasting realities cannot be ignored. Sex trafficking, rapes, female foeticide, and dowry deaths are still prevalent. There persists a huge gender gap in access to and control of resources, and the vicious circle of stereotypical roles at home and at work. No doubt, India claims to respect its women, but, is also among the countries that are considered as least gender sensitised (Malik & Bandelli, 2012; Malik, 2020).

Despite the demonstrated importance of CR for empowering women and promoting gender equality in India, even this sector is far from accomplishing equality for men and women in its processes and perspectives. Till date there has been no systematic or conscious attempt to develop tools to build the capacities of CR stations for strengthening gender sensitivity in its policies, practices, and programming, leave alone for understanding gender (and recognising the manifestations of patriarchy). Alternative media, such as community radio, can play a central role in advancement and empowerment of women, but they must themselves first be guided by a gender standpoint to not simply "include women" but to institutionalise measures that reflect gender equity in its practices and programming (Malik, 2020; Malik & Bandelli, 2012; Cornwall, 2003).

As the community radio sector in India beckons an institutional thrust to reinforce gender equality and women's empowerment, the author, as a faculty fellow with the UNESCO Chair on Community Media, University of Hyderabad, is anchoring a participatory project granted by International Programme for the Development of Communication (IPDC), which seeks to address this gap by developing a *Gender Sensitivity Manual for Community Radio*. This manual will seek to help community radio stations reduce gender inequalities, enhance women's participation in every aspect of radio operations, and ensure that stations' editorial content is gender sensitive.

The motivation guiding the project is also that the use of the manual by CR stations will contribute directly to the achievement of certain key targets of the Sustainable Development Goals (SDGs), notably of Goal 5: "Achieve gender equality and empower all women and girls." The target 5.5 of this SDG seeks to "ensure women's full and effective participation and equal opportunities for leadership at all levels" and target 5.B aims to "enhance the use of enabling technology, in particular information and communications technology, to promote the empowerment of women." Finally, women's participation and gender-sensitive programming at CR stations will help "develop effective, accountable and transparent institutions at all levels" and "ensure responsive, inclusive, participatory and representative decision-making at all levels" (SDG 16, Target 16.6 and 16.7).

As a first step towards developing the *Gender Sensitivity Manual for Community Radio*, the author carried out an in-depth desk review of some of the existing guidelines, more significantly, the "Gender-Sensitive Indicators for Media" developed by UNESCO (2012), the "Gender Policy for Community Radio" developed by the World Association of Community Radio Broadcasters (AMARC, 2008), and some others.

This chapter presents a synthesis of some of these guides developed by international organisations with respect to gender issues and engagement of women in media and grassroots interventions that could help frame a roadmap for CR stations to strengthen gender-sensitive policies, practices, and content. By reviewing these guidelines alongside some of the conceptual frameworks on gender, community media, and participatory development, the author builds a preliminary outline of parameters that would eventually help raise pertinent issues for designing the *Gender Sensitivity Manual* through inclusive and participatory consultative and validation workshops planned with the stakeholders.

United Nations and the Focus on Gender Sensitivity

Gender equality and women's empowerment is one of the overarching priorities of the United Nations (UN). Several conventions and declarations have amplified the attention placed on gender equality issues globally.

Chief among these is the Convention on the Elimination of all Forms of Discrimination Against Women (CEDAW), which recognises "that a change in the traditional role of men as well as the role of women in society and in the family is needed to achieve full equality of men and women." It stresses, "To modify the social and cultural patterns of conduct of men and women, with a view to achieving the elimination of prejudices and customary and all other practices which are based on the idea of the inferiority or the superiority of either of the sexes or on stereotyped roles for men and women" (CEDAW, 1979).

Then there is the "Beijing Declaration and Platform for Action," which in 1995 was the outcome of UN's Fourth World Conference on Women in Beijing attended by an unprecedented 17,000 participants and 30,000 activists. Two weeks of debates and discussions followed among remarkably diverse representatives of 189 governments from around the globe with a single point agenda: gender equality and the empowerment of all women, everywhere. The "Beijing Declaration and Platform for Action," one of the most progressive blueprints for advancing women's rights, sought to combat "Stereotyping of women and inequality in women's access to and participation in all communication systems, especially in the media" and "Promote women's full and equal participation in the media, including management, programming, education, training and research" (Section J on "women and the media," Beijing Platform for Action, 1995).

In a historic move, in July 2010 the UN created a new "Entity for Gender Equality and the Empowerment of Women"—to be known as UN Women—to "give women and girls the strong, unified voice they deserve on the world stage" (UN Women, 2010). Then the 2030 Agenda for sustainable development came into effect from January 2016, comprising 17 Sustainable Development Goals (SDGs) that implicate media in advancing the stand-alone goal on gender equality and the empowerment of women and girls. Women (and girls) are both—affected by, and the key to—the aspiration of the proposed SDGs to deliver cross-cutting progress that is inclusive, just, and sustainable.

According to UN Women, gender equality and the empowerment of women and girls lie at the core of each of the 17 SDGs in the 2030 Agenda. They are addressed both in SDG 5 on achieving gender equality and empowering all women and girls, and through the mainstreaming of gender into other goals and targets. This approach signals that gender equality is seen as an objective, as well as a requirement for achieving all development goals, particularly those related to health, education, economic development, and the management of resources (UN Women website). The paragraph 20 of the 2030 Agenda states, "Realizing gender equality and the empowerment of women and girls will make a crucial contribution to progress across all the Goals and targets. The achievement of full human potential and of sustainable development is not possible if one half of humanity continues to be denied its full human rights and opportunities. Women and girls must enjoy equal access to quality education, economic resources and political participation as well as equal opportunities with men and boys for employment, leadership and decision-making at all levels" (UN SDGs website).

Addressing a meeting "Confronting the Crisis in Independent Media: Strategic Approaches for International Donors," the UNESCO director for freedom of expression and media development, Guy Berger, noted, "SDG 16.10 on public access to information and fundamental freedoms cannot be achieved without independent media which can help in achieving all SDGs—whether gender equality, climate change eliminating poverty, reducing inequalities, and sustainable cities." He referenced a discussion paper prepared by UNDP's Oslo Governance Centre and UNESCO's Division for Freedom of Expression and Media Development, which "argues that the SDGs, and especially SDG16, provide a critical entry point through which an independent, professional, diverse and pluralist media, operating in a safe environment, can contribute to the progressive vision articulated in the 2030 Agenda" (UNESCO, 2019).

Community Radio and Women Empowerment: Strengthening Participation and Voice

Community radio has contributed significantly to democratising the media landscape in several regions worldwide, giving voice to the voiceless and opening up spaces for communication to those that are on the fringes of development. Often considered the "third voice" (Servaes, 1999, p. 260), CR provides greater flexibility in dealing with low literacy levels, lack of proficiency with technology, and practical hindrances that entail using other sophisticated media. India, as the first country in the South Asian region to have a dedicated CR policy that allows civil society groups, NGOs, and educational institutions to procure licences, presents itself as an excellent case to study how women and other groups oppressed along grounds of gender engage with community radio as a medium to overcome the inequalities, physical and structural, in everyday life.

Bailey, Cammearts, and Carpentier (2008) in their typology for understanding alternative media differentiate four approaches that characterise the diverse manifestations and practices of community media. These approaches help provide a comprehensive overview of the way CR interventions contribute to social change within the communication for development paradigm. While "serving a community" approach accentuates the community participation as the key defining attribute of CR, the "alternative to mainstream media" positions CR as a site for counter-hegemonic discourses. The third approach focuses on the linkages of CR as a medium that belongs to the "civil society" and is not beholden to the state and market, while the final "alternative media as rhizome" approach broadens the scope by foregrounding the purposive facets of CR that is not so concerned with typecasting, but with the political agenda that they espouse.

The theoretical basis of the transformative potential of community media in the realm of gender is derived from the intersections between development discourses, feminist theorising (Cornwall, 2003; Guijt & Shah, 1998; Parpart, 1999; Pilar Riano, 1994; Kabeer, 1994) and the further linkages of these development and feminist discourses with the emerging community and alternative media scholarship (Gordon, 2012; Howley, 2010; Fuchs, 2010; Forde, Foxwell, & Meadows, 2002; Dagron, 2001; Bailey et al., 2008; Atton, 2002).

The author has carried out this synthesis to build her conceptual basis to comprehend the potential of CR as a tool for collective action and gender-based social change over several years of her engagement in the field of women in community communication. An overview of the gender dimension of community radio, drawn from Malik (2020), Malik and Bandelli (2012), and

Pavarala and Malik (2007, 2010)), follows, and these cited articles may be referred to for deeper readings and case studies.

Gender Equality in Development: Pushing the Boundaries

Gender equality is among the major themes of focus in public debates across India today, and women empowerment figures as a high priority in the list of social goals in the country. Since independence, several programmes have been promoted to improve the condition of women in general, and "poor rural women" in particular. Feminisation of poverty, equal pay, anti-dowry abuse, and domestic violence—all these have been a part of the key struggles of the contemporary women's movements in India. Feminist activists and women's movements in the developing world argue that the conservative ideology of male superiority and the power over productive assets by men act as barriers that hinder women's access to key resources and public spaces, and their participation in decision-making processes and sharing of power. These patriarchal biases also perpetuate regressive social norms and practices that affect women's options and opportunities for a better life.

There is a sustained effort by feminists, women's movements, and poor women's grassroots organisations to mainstream gender in social change discourses—with a view to question the oppressive structures, as well as the existing power relations of patriarchy—by introducing alternative practices and philosophies that challenge the sex-role stereotyping that has led to women's increased marginalisation.

The insights from development frameworks and feminist theorising, especially the Gender and Development (GAD) approach around mid-1980s—that have emerged from the ground-up experiences and research carried out by Third World feminists scholars—cry out for the necessity to create a cultural shift in how social change is epitomised. They stress the need to obtain context and culture-specific understanding of women's concerns based on the lived experiences, and to espouse an empowerment agenda that would question the prevailing social structures that generate and underpin a disadvantageous status for women relative to men—and also affect women's ability to intervene in matters that affect their lives.

Feminist theories of social justice, informed by notions of pluralism, also warn against acceptance of local traditions and practices that violate a woman's agency to take up a way of life that she considers as suitable. Nussbaum (2000) defends a liberal feminist position, even as she indicates sensitivity to cultural dissimilarities and religious freedom, when she argues for an ethical consensus around ideas of human dignity. She identifies certain capabilities as essential to human dignity—those that ascertain the "threshold level of capabilities beneath which truly human functioning is not available." Radical feminist scholars insist that women's subordination—as it is deeply embedded in individual psyches and social practices—is more difficult to change than "class." Third World scholars stress the need to focus on recovering women's silenced voices and knowledge and to involve women meaningfully in policy making roles for any development initiatives that touch their lives significantly.

Women in Community Communications: Forging Subaltern Counterpublics

There is a growing consensus amongst development practitioners, communication scholars, and feminist activists that media and new technologies of communication informed by a gender perspective can play a central role in the empowerment and advancement of women. They are recognising—the involvement of those who have traditionally been socio-culturally marginalised as well as economically and politically disenfranchised—as "partners" in development. The paradigmatic shift in development communication, towards building democratised and decentralised discursive spaces at the grassroots level, appears to offer the prospect of giving all the stakeholders a voice and a choice.

Pilar Riano (1994) argues that women's role as communicative subjects and producers of communication is still being disregarded, and globally, women are the most disadvantaged in terms of access to media, both as receivers and producers of information. This is prevalent owing to various causes such as women tend to be poorer than men; they are more likely to be denied the right to education and impeded from using the media; in patriarchal societies, women are largely confined to domestic chores and care giver roles; there are restrictions of mobility as well as of participation in communicative spaces. Furthermore, like ethnic minorities, poor segments of society, and the disabled, women also must fight to be heard, and whenever they are granted visibility, they are often at the centre of sensationalist and stereotyped news.

Community media, on the other hand, play a key role in facilitating groups to articulate issues from marginalised standpoints. Community media, by definition, are those media that are "about," "by," "of," and "with" the people, and not merely "for" the people. Nancy Fraser (1992, p. 123) designates these parallel discursive arenas as "subaltern counterpublics" and describes them as venues "where members of subordinated social groups invent and circulate counter-discourses, which in turn permit them to formulate oppositional interpretations of their identities, interests, and needs." Gitlin (1998) conceived these as subsets of civil society competing with the dominant public sphere or numerous public "sphericules" to promote democratic citizenship, offsetting the participatory privileges enjoyed by members of dominant social groups.

"Women empowerment" may have become a proverbial mantra in development jargon but remains a complex and contested concept. It has been theorised both as individualised and instrumental empowerment—that is "liberal" empowerment, which focuses on the individual and "liberating" empowerment, which involves collective self-organisation, and is an instrument for challenging patriarchal norms and structures (Sardenberg, 2008, pp. 19–20 as cited in Malik, 2000). Whether conceived as an individual journey or as a collective struggle, both perspectives on empowerment put the accent on women discovering and using their (individual or collective) capability of voice.

Community radio (CR) in India has played a key role in providing women with innovative opportunities to reflect on their own situation and status and to plan for collective campaigns. Studies of CR in India, mentioned above, show that new information enables women to become conscious of their own rights as well as the circumstance of other women, make informed choices, develop creative life-skills, and mobilise group action. CR also provides a platform to build the capacities of women in computer technologies and as journalists and offers the opportunity to establish new interpersonal relations. Women re-define their self-perception, become confident in public speaking, discuss their problems in public meetings, and sometimes even challenge traditional norms.

Challenges for Women to Participate in CR

There is no doubt that CR has proven to be an effective means for women to access information which is relevant to their lives and situations, and in most cases was normally denied or unavailable. Also, CR constitutes an opportunity for women to acquire a voice, which otherwise remains unheard. Community radios are deeply embedded in local communities and are reflective of their linguistic, cultural, and ideological identities. The flow of communication is meant to be, not top-down, but bottom-up and horizontal. This creates prospects for groups with similar interests (such as women) to connect at the grassroots level and to organise themselves. Then, constructing communication gateways for sharing experiences, re-appropriation of public spaces, and strengthening of social bonds become their strategies towards consensus-building and collective action.

However, even when community radio stations are in the process of opening doors wider for women, the process of making them equal partners is hindered; women's role as communicative subjects and producers of content is still being disregarded; and CR in India remains overpoweringly male-dominated. Several factors, such as stereotypical gender roles, disparities of mobility, prejudiced social norms, poverty, rigid cultural beliefs, discriminatory attitudes, sexual harassment, and more, put women in a subordinate position, obstruct their freedom of movement, and consign them to the private sphere (Nussbaum, 2000; Pilar Riano, 1994; Malik & Bandelli, 2012; Malik, 2020).

The traditional patriarchal mindset is internalised by women themselves, because of which they still lack the power to determine the nature and shape of media content or to influence CR policy. These observations during Clemencia Rodríguez's (2001, p. 5) experience with an alternative media training explain this facet, "Women, accustomed to having men 'guide' them and considering this natural, had to reframe their whole outlook on gender relations as they directed male actors for their own alternative soap operas. In some cases, where a woman's subordination to men is the main source of her identity, revising one's convictions about gender relationships implies a complete reformulation of one's entire world view."

For community radio sector in India to accomplish its mandate of enabling gender equality and women empowerment, it must ensure progressive involvement of women and other underrepresented and vulnerable groups in all elements and stages of a CR station and generate communicative prospects for them to be able to participate in different roles and positions. The author argues, based on her earlier research (Malik, 2015, 2020; Malik & Bandelli, 2012; Pavarala & Malik, 2007, 2010), that for this to happen, there needs to be a positive revolution of sorts in the working of community radio stations so as to herald a process of gender mainstreaming and focussing, as a first step, on foregrounding women's and "other" voices, experiences, and expertise as a resource for all programmes, activities, and policy decisions.

For integrating a feminist approach and an empowerment agenda in the working of CR stations in India, it is essential to affirm gender equality, balance, and gender sensitivity in principles, processes, policies, and practices that address all of the following domains:

Listenership and Volunteering

Contemplating on the gender dynamics of direct or uninterrupted access to a radio set is critical for attaining the goal using media for gender equality and women empowerment. Do they have the time or the inclination to listen to radio programmes, given their obligations of household duties and domestic chores? Are they active as audiences, and if motivated, are there supportive and conducive possibilities for them to contribute to programmes as talent or volunteer at the stations? What measures need to be adopted to remedy the listenership and participation imbalance?

Capacity Building and Production

Those who have not had an exposure to media and customarily been treated as second fiddle for eternities cannot be expected to start taking initiatives to produce programmes and willingly discuss their concerns unless they are encouraged to express, and made to feel confident that their perspective matter and their voice has a value. How amenable are the women and underrepresented groups to building their capacities to produce context-specific radio programmes for exercising their right to free speech and expression and are there resources and sensitivities to carry out this prerequisite?

Planning and Management

Few CR stations in India are led by women managers, and one rarely finds stations with minority, rural, semiliterate women, or men, in decision-making roles. Meaningful and undaunted engagement of marginalised groups at all levels in station management and decisions pertaining to day-to-day as well as long-term operations of the station ought to be facilitated. What kind of change in mindset needs to happen for CR stations to exhibit gender equality in representation in forums where crucial matters related to management, production, technology, and policy are decided?

Content and Portrayal

Community radio has a responsibility to address the norms of inequitable gender relations and leverage the use of this platform to support gender-sensitive practices. The wisdom, knowledge, and creativity of women and men as indigenous experts need to be valued and people must be treated as active subjects of engagement rather than passive objects of communication messages. How would community radio be different if it were not to promote gender-informed programming, challenge gender stereotypes, accept women's views, corroborate women's rights, and sponsor a no-tolerance policy for objectification of men/women?

STRENGTHENING GENDER SENSITIVITY IN CR

A review and analysis of the AMARC's "Gender Policy for Community Radio" (2008) and the "Gender-Sensitive Indicators for Media—Framework of Indicators to Gauge Gender Sensitivity in Media Operations and Content" (GSIM) published by UNESCO (2012), among others, blended well with the theoretical reflections and empirical insights of the author on the gender dimension of community radio. What follows is a preliminary outline of some of the key parameters aimed at stimulating community radio stations to identify themselves as crusaders of gender equality and institutions that are gender responsive.

CR as a Space for Gender-Sensitive Practices: Shaping Change

Community radio must signify, represent, and symbolise a space identified with gender-sensitive and inclusive practices. The AMARC (2008, p. 3) gender policy endorses that women's access to the airwaves can be ensured through "a supportive, secure environment in and around the station." It is important to insist on zero tolerance regarding violation of women's dignity or for any forms of discrimination. An anti-sexual harassment policy and complaints mechanism to provide protection for women go hand in hand with a policy of sanctions against anyone found indulging in discrimination. Women and men have a right to work without fear or intimidation, and those visiting a CR station must be able to do so without fear of exclusion or attack. Gender sensitivity in the workplace calls for suitable provision of hygiene facilities for women and men, safe transport, safe working environment, and respectful workstation.

To ensure that there is no breach of established progressive norms, mere drafting of gender-friendly policies for them won't suffice; comprehensive implementing and monitoring mechanisms are essential, including promoting of resources such as internal guides, codes of conduct, and manuals manifesting the pointers for gender sensitivity and acknowledgement of plurality of opinions. Community radios should undertake affirmative action to intensify the participation of women. For this, measures such as flexible working hours, exclusive listening sessions for women, and forums for women to interact and network with other women must be created. CR reporters mobilising women in the community to listen, volunteer, and participate could also be a step forward in this direction and result in cultivation of what Sonia Livingstone (2000) conceptualises as active audience. UNESCO's (2012, p. 24) GSIM pitches for "systems for monitoring and evaluation of gender equality in the workplace." Regular feedback from community, self-assessment by staff, and cyclical reviews of policies would go a long way to fix the gender balance of participants in a CR station.

Gender Balance in Capacity Building and Production

Community radio must give adequate recognition to the capabilities of women to come up with ideas and produce programmes independently. They ought to endeavour to create a social norm within the community they serve around inclusion of women as "partners" and gender equality in all social change initiatives. According to Bicchieri (2006, p. 11), a social norm is a behavioural rule that is followed by individuals in a population "if it is believed that sufficiently many others believe the rule should be followed, and/or may be willing to sanction deviations from it." The AMARC (2008, p. 6) gender policy considers capacity building as a crucial factor for achieving gender parity, "This does not only apply to capacity-building for women involved in the station, but for both men and women so that they can work together to build a safe, nurturing and supportive environment where all feel able to contribute their best to all aspects of the station's success." Women's contribution to production can be supported by simple provisions such as child-care support, flexible recording and broadcast schedules, transport for commuting, and security at the station particularly at night. UNESCO's GSIM (2012, p. 27) recommends putting in place systems for monitoring gender equality in the workplace, for example, by examining if the organisation has transparent pay scale and is "using the same criteria to determine pay structure for men and women."

Women are often neglected as sources of expert opinion and their perspectives are confined to programming on women's issues. These tendencies must be avoided, and conscious efforts made to represent a multiplicity of women's expertise and experiences in the radio programmes. CRs should make special provisions for women to "have access to the airwaves in their full diversity" and "to discuss their issues in an empowering, safe and non-discriminatory environment" and, therefore, reserve airtime for "differently abled women, women from minority ethnic, caste or indigenous backgrounds and women from sexual minorities, such as lesbians and transgenders" (AMARC, 2008, p. 4). Women shy away from handling technology within the radio station. Investing in women friendly studio set up, appropriate technical training, and instructional materials in local languages can pave the way for tackling the gender gap in technology and in due course overcoming the gender *digital divide*. However, the good intentions to be gender responsive in production must be matched with funds for capacity building.

Gender Equality in Decision-Making and Management

Community radios can scale-up the focus on gender equality substantially by redressing the imbalance in management practices and facilitating women's involvement more appropriately and equally at all levels of decision-making. AMARC (2008, p. 5) gender policy warns against mere tokenism in this regard, "Women's participation cannot be measured by the number of women involved in the station. Women must be represented in the production, ownership and decision-making bodies of the station to ensure that women are able to engage meaningfully with policy processes, which could include culturally sensitive supportive environment." While recognising that there exists a glass ceiling in decision-making levels such as senior management, executive, and board, UNESCO's GSIM (2012, p. 24) calls for "equal and transparent recruitment practices (e.g. all interview panels should be gender-balanced, gender officer involved in the recruitment process/programme of the organization at some point)" and indicates that "simply counting totals in any organization did not necessarily reflect the true status of gender equity. Identifying specific career paths within media organizations that are difficult for women to penetrate" (p: 62) would be of greater relevance to understand their real gender gap.

Community radios can contribute to the reversal of women's marginalisation in management by equipping them through capacity building in management and technical skills and the craft of decision-making. For women to be equitably represented at all levels of the community radio station, "quotas for participation need to be set for ownership, management and production, including women's participation in technical management. The ultimate goal is to reach equality between men and women, but quotas of at least 30% women's representation should be set in the interim. To achieve these quotas, it is important to invest in women's skills, to institute leadership and management training aimed at supporting women and achieve gender parity within the station" AMARC (2008, p. 5). It is recommended to induct the practice of an internal "gender audit" of the workforce within the CR station to identify proportions, roles, and responsibilities of women and men at all levels of the organisation. If there is an under-representation of women, men, or marginalised groups in any capacity or level, a review may be undertaken to ensure they have fair and transparent representation. Ross (2018) proposes that "audit should be undertaken on a regular basis in order to identify patterns and trends and to enable progress to be measured year-on-year. The findings from such an audit should be analysed and interpreted and a plan of action developed to monitor and act upon persistent gender imbalances."

Gender-Responsive Content for Social Change

All the above efforts by community radio with regards to gender sensitivity must be backed by a fundamental philosophy of inclusivity and diversity, one that opposes prejudice on the basis of ethnicity; race; language; gender; sexuality; age; physical or mental ability; occupation; and religious, cultural, or political beliefs in the content that the stations produce (Malik, 2015). While addressing gender issues, there must be balanced portrayal of women and men in the content and the CR should "encourage the representation of women in their diversity, instead of emphasising stereotyped roles, such as within the family, for women. Ensure that all people, regardless of gender, ethnicity, class, sexual orientation, etc are treated with respect and dignity in all aspects of the content broadcast on the station, whether as editorial content or advertisements. This includes ensuring that neither men nor women are objectified, physically or otherwise" (AMARC, 2008, pp. 3–4). It is vital that there exists a resources manual for gender-sensitive content such as a stylebook that includes reference to gender representation, and the UNESCO's GSIM (2012, p. 33) considers it necessary that all content production staff, editors, and managers be "made aware of and accept gender/diversity policy, gender and diversity sensitive code of ethics and stylebook/manual." It goes on to further identify the critical concern of programmes with "openly sexist interpretations of the characteristics and roles of women and men in society" and advocates for "multi-dimensional representation/portrayal of men and women (indicating journalistic effort to challenge/counter gender-based stereotypes)" (p. 42).

Community radio stations must invest in encouraging gender-sensitive language and strictly monitor stories with stereotypical depiction of "traditional 'feminine'/'masculine' characteristics and male/female roles, thereby making them appear normal and inevitable." They could also preferably avoid stories that portray "women as victims, e.g., of crime, violence/atrocity, conflict, disaster, poverty, etc." There should be a shift in portrayal from that of a victim to "survivors (i.e., with evidence of active agency despite adverse experiences/circumstances)"—"unless the violence-affected person uses the latter term or has not survived" (UNESCO's GSIM, 2012, p. 42, 45). Avoid using sexist language that reproduces bias, discrimination, or stereotyping based on sex or gender role. Prefer non-judgemental language that does not (a) invade the privacy, (b) denigrate dignity, and/or (c) blame the victim/survivor of the violence on gender/sex lines. While it is advisable to regulate the time and prominence given to stories of gender-based violence, tendency should be to present it with background information as a societal problem rather than as an individual, personal tragedy (UNESCO's GSIM, 2012). Community radio, as gender equality champions, must be the change that they want to see, and there must be dedicated funding available for capacity building in gender-conscious content.

Conclusion

The intention of the author is not to come up with prescriptive or universal parameters, but simply a set of guidelines that could be adapted by the CR stations, in part or as a whole, to effectively espouse gender sensitivity, implement gender-friendly policies, shape codes of conduct that respect social diversity, and build capacities of their members (male and female) to integrate gender awareness into practice. The parameters analysed in the previous section are a work in progress and will be treated as a part of a living document that will later go through a process of participatory and democratic consultation as part of the IPDC project mentioned earlier, to evolve into a manual reflecting plurality of voices and democratic discourse that address local and pertinent and concerns related to gender sensitivity. The purpose of this review/chapter is to create a "dialogue," which will trigger a process of change that can help to lift the "culture of silence" and be the driving force towards "conscientization" often described as "the process of learning to perceive social, political and economic contradictions and taking action against the oppressive elements of reality" (Freire, 2000, p. 35).

The author is also in the process of developing the concept of "voice-capability"—which seeks to unify Couldry's (2010) analysis of "voice that has value" and Amartya Sen's (1999) capability approach. Voice-capability refers to the freedoms that ensure women the agency or choice to speak up, express themselves, and be heard. Women, especially from marginalised groups, who have been deprived of spaces to voice their perspectives for ages, will break their silence only if their opinions are respected, and their voice is considered meaningful (Malik, 2020). By promoting gender-sensitive policies and practices, community radios can become effective conduits of creating voice-capability among women and recast the dominant and gendered public sphere.

References

AMARC. (2008). Gender Policy for Community Radio. Adopted by World General Assembly, AMARC 2010, La Plata, Argentina. Retrieved June 29, 2020, from https://www.isiswomen.org/index.php?option=com_content&view=article&id=1119:gender-policy-for-community-radio&catid=163&Itemid=344

Anwar, M. (2015). Women's Participation in Community Radio in Bangladesh A Thesis presented to The University of Guelph, Ontario, Canada: March. Retrieved June 29, 2020, from https://atrium.lib.uoguelph.ca/xmlui/bitstream/handle/10214/8733/Anwar_Mahmuda_201503_Msc.pdf?sequence=3&isAllowed=y

Atton, C. (2002). *Alternative Media*. London; Thousand Oaks; New Delhi: Sage.

Bailey, O., Cammaerts, B., & Carpentier, N. (2008). *Understanding Alternative Media*. New York: Open University Press.

Bicchieri, C. (2006). *The grammar of society: The nature and dynamics of social norms*. Cambridge University Press.
Caldwell, J. C. (1982). *Theory of fertility decline*. London, UK: Academic Press.
CEDAW. (1979). Convention on the Elimination of All Forms of Discrimination against Women. Retrieved June 29, 2020, from https://www.un.org/womenwatch/daw/cedaw/text/econvention.htm
Cornwall, A. (2003). Whose Voices? Whose Choices? Reflections on Gender and Participatory Development. *World Development*, Elsevier, *31*(8), 1325–1342, August.
Couldry, N. (2010). *Why Voice Matters: Culture and Politics after Neoliberalism*. London: Sage.
Dagron, A. G. (2001). *Making Waves: Stories of Participatory Communication for Social Change*. New York: The Rockefeller Foundation.
Forde, S., Foxwell, K., & Meadows, M. (2002). Creating a Community Public Sphere: Community Radio as a Cultural Resource. *Media International Australia Incorporating Culture and Policy, 103*(1), 56–67. https://doi.org/10.1177/1329878X0210300109
Fraser, N. (1992). Rethinking the Public Sphere: A Contribution to the Critique of Actually Existing Democracy. In C. Calhoun (Ed.), *Habermas and the Public Sphere* (pp. 109–142). Cambridge: MIT Press.
Freire, P. (2000). *Pedagogy of the Oppressed* (30th anniversary ed.). New York: Continuum.
Fuchs, C. (2010). Alternative Media as Critical Media. *European Journal of Social Theory, 13*(2), 173–192.
Gitlin, T. (1998). Public Sphere or Public Sphericules? In T. Liebes & J. Curran (Eds.), *Media, Ritual, Identity* (pp. 168–175). London: Routledge.
Gordon, J. (Ed.). (2012). *Community Radio in the Twenty-First Century*. Switzerland: Peter Lang.
Guijt, I., & Shah, a. M. (1998). Waking Up to Power, Conflict and Process. In I. Guijt & A. M. Shah (Eds.), *The Myth of Community: Gender Issues in Participatory Development* (pp. 1–23). New Delhi: Intermediate Technology Publications.
Howley, K. (2010). Notes on a Theory of Community Radio. In K. Howley (Ed.), *Understanding Community Media* (pp. 63–86). Thousand Oaks, CA: Sage.
Kabeer, N. (1994). *Reversed Realities: Gender Hierarchies in Development Thought*. London: Verso.
Kadel, K. (2010). A Radio by Women for Community: Radio Purbanchal in Nepal. Retrieved June 29, 2020, from http://www.isiswomen.org/index.php?option=com_content&view=article&id=1483
Livingstone, S. (2000). Television and the Active Audience. In D. Fleming (ed.), *Formations: A 21st Century Media Studies Textbook* (pp. 175–193). Manchester, UK: Manchester University Press. ISBN 978-0-71-905845-7
Malik, K. K. (2015). Our Media Our Principles. *Journalism Studies*, 1–15. https://doi.org/10.1080/1461670X.2015.1054195
Malik, K. K. (2020). Women and Community Radio in South Asia: The Participation and Empowerment Conundrum. In K. Malik & V. Pavarala (Eds.), *Community Radio in South Asia: Reclaiming the Airwaves*. London: Routledge India. https://doi.org/10.4324/9781003056232
Malik, K. K., & Bandelli, D. (2012). *Community Radio and Gender—Towards an Inclusive Public Sphere*. Paper at the India Media Symposium: Public Spheres, the Media & Social Change, University of Queensland, Brisbane, Nov 21–23. Retrieved

June 29, 2020, from https://www.researchgate.net/publication/279202551_Community_Radio_and_Gender_-_Towards_an_Inclusive_Public_Sphere

Moghadam, V. M. (2005). *Modernizing Women: Gender and Social Change* (pp. 122–123). New Delhi: Viva Books Private Ltd.

Nussbaum, M. (2000). Women and Work—The Capabilities Approach. *Little Magazine*, Issue I, Retrieved June 29, 2020, from http://www.littlemag.com/2000/martha2.htm

Parpart, J. (1999). Rethinking Participation, Empowerment and Development from a Gender Perspective. In J. Freedman (Ed.), *Transforming Development*. Toronto: University of Toronto Press.

Pavarala, V., & Malik, K. K. (2007). *Other Voices: The Struggle for Community Radio in India*. Sage Publications. [See: Chapter 7: Community Radio for Empowerment: The Gender Dimension].

Pavarala, V., & Malik, K. K. (2010). Community Radio and Women: Forging Subaltern Counterpublics. In C. Rodríguez, D. Kidd, & L. Stein (Eds.), *Making Our Media, Vol. I. Creating New Communication Spaces* (pp. 95–113). New York: Hampton Press.

Riano, P. (Ed.). (1994). *Women in Grassroots Communication*. USA/UK/India: Sage Publications.

Rodríguez, C. (2001). *Fissures in the Mediascape: An International Study of Citizens' Media*. Cresskill: Hampton Press.

Ross, K. (2018). A Hard Ladder to Climb—Women and Power in Media Industries. In *Media Development VOL LXV 1/2018*. World Association for Christian Communication: Canada. ISSN 0143-5558

Sardenberg, C. M. B. (2008). Liberal vs. Liberating Empowerment: A Latin American Feminist Perspective on Conceptualising Women's Empowerment. *IDS Bulletin*, *39*, 18–27.

Sen, A. (1999). *Development as Freedom*. Oxford: Oxford University Press.

Servaes, J. (1999). *Communication for Development: One World, Multiple Cultures*. Cresskill, New Jersey: Hampton Press.

UN SDGs website. Transforming Our World: The 2030 Agenda for Sustainable Development. Retrieved August 13, 2020, from https://sustainabledevelopment.un.org/post2015/transformingourworld

UN Women. (2010). Retrieved June 29, 2020, from https://www.un.org/press/en/2010/dsgsm515.doc.htm

UN Women Website. Women and the Sustainable Development Goals (SDGs). Retrieved August 13, 2020, from https://www.unwomen.org/en/news/in-focus/women-and-the-sdgs

UNESCO. (2012). Gender-Sensitive Indicators for Media—Framework of Indicators to Gauge Gender Sensitivity in Media Operations and Content. ISBN: 978-92-3-001101-7. Retrieved June 29, 2020, from https://unesdoc.unesco.org/ark:/48223/pf0000217831

UNESCO. (2019). Why Independent Media Matter for the Sdgs? Retrieved August 13, 2020, from https://en.unesco.org/news/why-independent-media-matter-sdgs

Yalala, N. (2015). The Role of Community Radio in Empowering Women in India. *Media Asia*, *42*(1–2), 41–46.

CHAPTER 14

Miscommunication of Harms? A Critique of SDG 12: Responsible Consumption and Production Implementation in the Food Sector in Northern Ireland

Ekaterina Gladkova

Introduction

Food is vitally important for human subsistence. The dimensions of its production and consumption provide an insight into the inner workings of the global economy and politics. Food is also an area of concern for the Sustainable Development Goals (SDGs) agenda. FAO (2019) makes a claim that food and agriculture constitute the backbone of the 2030 Agenda for Sustainable Development. Sustainability-related topics in general are relevant in the food sector, where pressure has been building up to address the existing flaws of global food production and re-orient it towards a more sustainable, ecologically sensitive model (Zanasi et al., 2017). Thus, it is important to critically evaluate the current strategies for the SDGs implementation to determine their effectiveness. Food production provides a perfect lens for such evaluation.

SDG 12 aims to ensure sustainable consumption and production patterns and thus also encapsulates the issue of food production. The need to ensure sustainable patterns is more germane for some sectors of food production than for others. For instance, livestock production demands a significant amount of resources: the sector uses large amounts of land, water and nutrients. Reforming

---

E. Gladkova (✉)
Department of Social Sciences, Northumbria University, Newcastle, UK
e-mail: gladkovaka@gmail.com

© The Author(s), under exclusive license to Springer Nature Switzerland AG 2021
M. J. Yusha'u, J. Servaes (eds.), *The Palgrave Handbook of International Communication and Sustainable Development*,
https://doi.org/10.1007/978-3-030-69770-9_14

it can make a substantial contribution to meeting the targets of SDG 12 (FAO, 2018). As a result of this, the intersection of meat production and the SDGs is the focus of this chapter.

Provided that the levels of global consumption of animal products remain unchanged, some estimations predict that it will increase by 70 per cent between 2005 and mid-century (Alexandratos & Bruinsma, 2012). Using this argument, some countries decided to significantly increase domestic livestock production and Northern Ireland is one of them. In 2017, it was reported that Northern Ireland experienced a sharp increase in the number of intensive pig and poultry farms (farms housing at least 40,000 poultry birds or 2000 pigs grown for meat or 750 breeding pigs[1]). The number of farms went up by 68 per cent from 154 in 2011 to 259 in 2017 (The Bureau of Investigative Journalism, 2017). This trend is often linked to the adoption of the Going for Growth (GfG) in 2015, an industry-led strategy that endeavoured to expand the agri-food sector and set out a vision of 'growing a sustainable, profitable and integrated Agri-Food supply chain, focused on delivering the needs of the market' (Agri-Food Strategy Board, 2013, p. 11). Moy Park, the country's largest poultry meat producer, has been particularly successful since the strategy implementation, increasing its production by 20 per cent since 2015 and now supplying 30 per cent of the total UK poultry market (Moy Park, 2018). However, increasing production through intensification is associated with adverse environmental and social impacts (Goodman & Redclift, 1991; Harvey, 2016; Ruhl, 2000) and therefore needs to be weighed against the sustainability objectives laid out by the SDGs.

Communication of sustainability commitments by a business is reported to give an insight into the business strategy (Reilly & Hynan, 2014), thus allowing assessment of the sustainability ethos of a particular company. Yet, sustainability communication can also be tinged with greenwashing (Lyon & Maxwell, 2011; Lyon & Montgomery, 2013), that is, communication that presents a misleadingly positive view of a company's environmental performance, thus concealing harms from production. Therefore, communication around the SDGs implementation needs to be critically assessed to understand whose interests it serves—the interests of the planet or the interests of the companies who may increase their profit margins from embracing the SDGs and communicating a more environmentally friendly image to the public and their stakeholders.

This chapter, therefore, provides a critique of the communication surrounding the implementation of SDG 12 by looking at a case study of the Northern Irish leading poultry producer, Moy Park. Grounded in the green criminological perspective, the chapter argues that communication of the achievement of the SDGs masks the negative effects on the environment and society produced by those doing the communication. Environmentally and socially adverse

---

[1] As determined by the EU Integrated Pollution Prevention and Control (IPPC) guidelines. See http://eippcb.jrc.ec.europa.eu/reference/BREF/irpp_bref_0703.pdf

effects do not feature in the communication due to a disproportionate amount of power wielded by the supporters of the current production system and protection of their vested economic interests. Such 'miscommunication of harms' ultimately results in 'greening' of the capitalist ethos of capital accumulation that is not sustainable in the long term and contradicts the idea of sustainable development in general and the ethos of the SDGs more specifically.

The chapter begins by introducing the theoretical perspective used here—green criminology—and also discusses environmental communication. It follows to introduce SDG 12 and discuss its targets. Furthermore, the chapter presents the implementation of SDG 12 using the case of Moy Park and critically analyses 'selective disclosure' of information released by the company. It concludes by stating that, in the case of this chapter, selective communication around SDG 12 implementation strategies reinforces the green image that allows the company to pursue economic sustainability at the expense of environmental and social sustainability.

GREEN CRIMINOLOGY

The green perspective within criminology emerged in the 1990s and created space for criminologists to discuss and critically evaluate environmental problems and solutions (Lynch & Stretesky, 2014). In a nutshell, it is concerned with studying environmental crimes as well as harmful behaviours positioned beyond the realm of the existing legal frameworks that affect ecosystems, lives of human and non-human animals and the biosphere (Brisman & South, 2018). Considering the current concerns around unsustainable use of the earth's resources addressed by the SDG framework, the spectrum of issues explored by green criminologists is wide. Some of the issues include pollution (air and water), issues surrounding animal welfare and animal rights, harm from global warming, agricultural crimes and harms, harms caused by the illegal disposal of toxic waste (Brisman & South, 2018) and so on.

Green criminology has engaged with the issues of production and consumption directly through the Treadmill of Production (ToP) theory (Schnaiberg, 1980) that examines political economic forces behind relations of production and consumption. ToP underlies the dependence on economic growth and argues that this dependence results in 'ecological disorganisation' where 'human preferences for organizing economic production consistent with the objectives of capitalism are in inherent contradiction with the health of the ecological system' (Lynch et al., 2013, p. 998). ToP also prioritises the analysis of relations that shape production over the relations behind consumption to make sure that the analysis of power relations in the political economy is not obscured (Gould, Pellow, & Schnaiberg, 2003). There are several reasons behind it. First, consumers can only consume that which is first produced. Second, processes of production are in direct relationship with ecosystems (since the resources for what will be produced must be first extracted from natural ecosystems), while the relationship between consumption and ecosystems is indirect (Gould et al., 2003) and therefore has a less significant impact on ecological sustainability. Echoing this argument, Brisman (2009, p. 348) argues that 'whatever environmental benefits are achieved with certain decisions and practices, they may be offset by their limited availability to certain categories of people, and that these exclusive attitudes and behaviours fail to affect other pressing environmental and human health problems'.

Moreover, criminological attention has also been directed towards food production and consumption. Gray and Hinch (2015) regard food as a medium of understanding multifaceted links between humans and ecosystems. Once the concept of food crime was introduced by Croall in 2007, avenues for research included food fraud, food poisoning (Tombs & Whyte, 2010), food mislabelling (Croall, 2012), trade practices and environmental law (Walters, 2006), food pricing, exploitation in food production (Tombs & Whyte, 2007) and cruelty to animals (Agnew, 1998; Yates, 2007). Additionally, critical analyses of harms woven into the fabric of food production have also been analysed by criminologists, including some green criminologists (Gray & Hinch, 2015; Rodríguez Goyes & South, 2016; Sollund, 2015; White, 2012). Regarding food consumption, Agnew (2013) discusses 'ordinary', normalised acts of consumption (such as consuming meat on a regular basis) as contributing to the depletion of the global sustainability fabric. The ordinary nature of such acts ensures their regular repetition. Moreover, as they are deemed acceptable and even desirable, their cumulative effect aggravates environmental problems.

It is evident that green criminology engages with the issues of production and consumption and analyses the impact of current systems of production on sustainability of ecological systems as well as the planet on the whole. Its critical focus makes it a suitable framework through which the implementation of SDG 12 in meat production sector can be examined. Moreover, green criminology also addresses the interplay between sustainable development and communication. Green criminologists have engaged in analysing how experiences of environmental harm are represented and communicated through perspectives of humans and the environment both in reality (Natali & Mcclanahan, 2017) and in fiction (Brisman & South, 2014).

Moreover, green criminologists also take interest in how environmental harms are concealed or miscommunicated and how, while companies allege to be acting in a responsible manner, violation of laws in respect to pollution and use of environmental resources occurs (Nurse, 2014). Considering that environmentally harmful actions are often inseparable from economic development policies and corporate growth (Brisman, South, & White, 2015), it is often in the interests of both the state and corporate actors to diminish the seriousness of harm. Considering their powerful position in society, the state and corporate actors also possess all the necessary resources for doing that, and control over communication is one of such resources. For instance, Bradshaw (2014) demonstrates how the American government implemented a regional blackout of media communications in various capacities to hide the environmental impact of the 2010 Gulf of Mexico oil spill. Some criminologists intersect green criminology and communication by examining the discourses used to legitimise corporate harm. For example, Schally (2017) examines the role of discourse in production and reproduction of environmental harm in the case of a large US agribusiness, Tyson Foods. She shows that the discourse developed by Tyson Foods provides a cultural legitimation of harmful consequences of intensive livestock production and reinforces corporate power wielded by the company. In other cases, the analysis of the strategies for diminishment of the seriousness of harm is based on Sykes and Matza's (1957) neutralisation techniques, which include denial of harm or responsibility over that harm, denial of seriousness of harm and reproaching or blaming the victims of harm. Use of neutralisation techniques results in continuation of harm and perpetuation of the status quo.

It has also been established that Corporate Social Responsibility (CSR) and the move towards the SDGs are often intertwined (Moggi, Bonomi, & Ricciardi, 2018). Some green criminologists review corporate communication on the subject of sustainability through the lens of the CSR. Brisman et al. (2015) conclude that CSR is employed to enhance the image of the harmful projects by drawing attention from serious problems to projects with a development character. CSR can also be the most common tactic in the food industry to make companies appear responsible while precluding any radical change that is needed to cement sustainable development. As a result, Nurse (2014) encourages that CSR principles be implemented in the legal and regulatory justice system to ensure greater accountability.

Green criminology, therefore, serves as a suitable lens to provide critique of the SDG implementation at the intersection of sustainable development and communication. Green criminology uses a critical approach towards understanding of sustainability as well as communication, thus helping to assess whose interests are prioritised in the implementation of SDG 12 agenda. Blaustein et al. (2018, p. 768) argue that criminologists should contribute to the SDGs agenda by playing both a supportive and a critical role in the process of implementation of the goals. This chapter, thus, hopes to address the critical role of criminologists in their engagement with the SDGs.

Environmental Communication

Environmental communication is a thematic subdiscipline that can be distinguished within the field of communication for sustainable development (Lie & Servaes, 2015). Fraser and Villet (1994) suggest that communication for development should change people's lifestyles through awareness and social communication methods to pioneer attitudinal changes. Sustainability implies an equilibrium between economic growth, social equity and the natural environment, and communication is reported to play a decisive role in creating this equilibrium (Lie & Servaes, 2015). Environmental communication, predictably, creates awareness about environmental problems and aims to bring a positive change in one's living conditions. It has been noted that environmental communication scholarship is often linked to mass media production and consumption (Hansen & Cox, 2015), and a close link to journalism has also been identified (Lie & Servaes, 2015). Environmental journalism has a particular importance in the face of climate change and other ecological challenges, and its role in enhancing public understanding of environmental issues is crucial (Smith & McGreavy, 2018). Tong (2015) suggests that investigative environmental journalism constructs an antagonism against state capitalism. Environmental journalism (and investigative journalism in particular) holds the state and corporate actors accountable for environmental destruction and increases transparency around environmental problems. The issues of accountability and transparency are crucial; environmental communication can advance the sustainable development agenda if it is based on sufficient and reliable information and is circulated freely (Zikargae, 2018). The notion of reliability is pertinent for this chapter, as I argue that communication around SDG 12 flowing from the corporate actors may be misleading and not contributing to achieving sustainable development agenda. As it was stated above, CSR can be an important communication tool and can apply to environmental communication. Yet, it needs to be deconstructed, considering that companies may be able to misrepresent themselves as environmental stewards in their own communication (Kingsmith, 2012). Additionally, such communication can perpetuate the elite communication of environmental problems and is, therefore, one-way. The question arises what can replace the elite environmental communication and how one can advance sustainable development agenda through communication. Brulle (2010) suggests that environmental communication needs to aim at developing procedures that involve citizens directly in the policy development process and enhance civic engagement and democratic decision making. Therefore, the role of environmental communication in fostering either elite, one-way communication or a democratic process of change needs to be explored in more depth, and this chapter intends to examine this.

SDG 12

The United Nations (UN) adopted a set of 17 SDGs in 2015 to lay foundations for the Global Agenda 2030. The SDGs galvanise governments, businesses and civil society to take action around a common set of priorities to ensure environmental, social and economic sustainability. The 17 SDGs echo the challenges that humanity faces today (such as ending poverty and hunger) and condenses them into tangible targets and indicators to make sure they can be acted upon.

As it was specified above, SDG 12 aims to consolidate sustainable consumption and production patterns. Discussions on sustainable consumption and production have been appearing on the UN agenda ever since 1972 (Gasper, Shah, & Tankha, 2019). Sustainable consumption and production, as determined by the Oslo Symposium in 1994, refer to 'the use of services and related products, which respond to basic needs and bring a better quality of life while minimising the use of natural resources and toxic materials as well as the emissions of waste and pollutants over the life cycle of the service or product so as not to jeopardize the needs of further generations' (United Nations, 2019).

SDG 12 is operationalised through the following eight targets:

12.1 Implementation of the 10-year framework of programmes on sustainable consumption and production;
12.2 Achievement of the sustainable management and efficient use of natural resources;
12.3 Halving per capita global food waste and reducing food losses in production and supply chains;
12.4 Achievement of environmentally sound management of all wastes in production cycles and reducing their emission into air, water and soil;
12.5 Reducing waste generation;
12.6 Encouragement of adoption of sustainable practices in large and transnational companies;
12.7 Promotion of sustainable public procurement practices;
12.8 Increasing awareness around sustainable development in the general public (United Nations, 2019).

Additionally, the goal features three targets related to the Means of Implementation.

In relation to food, SDG 12 works in conjuncture with other goals. Pohlmann et al. (2019) showcase that sustainable production ensures employment, thus addressing SDG 1 to eliminate poverty. Sustainable food production may also have potential to eradicate hunger and achieve food security (the agenda of SDG 2) and through that promote good health and wellbeing, tackling SDG 3 (Pohlmann et al., 2019). Furthermore, sustainable food production may imply sustainable management of water (SDG 6) and generation of clean energy (SDG 7) (Pohlmann et al., 2019). The latter is particularly relevant for this chapter in the light of the critique of the anaerobic digestion (AD) technology that utilises poultry waste to generate biogas (which will be discussed later). Pohlmann et al. (2019) also discuss interrelations of SDG 12 in the context of food production with SDG 4 (quality education), SDG 5 (gender equality), SDG 10 (reduced inequalities), SDG 15 (life on land), SDG 8 (decent work and economic growth), SDG 9 (industry, innovation and infrastructure) and SDG 17 (partnership for the goals). Moreover, sustainable production and consumption create interlinkages between the inherently complex integrated dimensions of sustainable development challenges, such as climate change (SDG 13) (Akenji & Bengtsson, 2014). This is particularly relevant in the light of this chapter's focus on meat production, as the Food and Agriculture Organization of the United Nations (FAO) has estimated that animal agriculture is responsible for 18 per cent of the total greenhouse gas emissions that contribute to climate change (Steinfeld et al., 2006).

This chapter examines the element of production, rather than consumption, in the implementation of SDG 12, and there are several reasons for it. The goal focuses heavily on the issues of production rather than consumption (with the exception of the target 12.3 that aims to reduce food waste on the consumer level), thus encouraging corporations to see sustainability as a business opportunity rather than a global challenge (Gasper et al., 2019). SDG 12 places a particular focus on production efficiency that can be achieved through technological innovation. Moreover, ambiguous language of the targets and indicators appears to diminish the importance of regulation in achieving sustainability and prioritises voluntary action instead. The latter serves the interests of producers rather than consumers since producers' goal of profitability clashes with the costs of compliance (Nurse, 2014), and this chapter aims to examine the effects of it.

When applied to food production, SDG 12 is concerned with sustainable consumption and production and aims to 'do more and better with less': the aim is to increase gains from all economic activities, while reducing the amount of resources used, and at the same time lowering environmental degradation and pollution (FAO, 2018). More importantly, FAO (2018) states that a key SDG 12 target is improving efficiency in natural resource use in production processes. FAO (2018) recommends that natural resource efficiency in meat production can be enhanced by adopting productivity improvements, for example, improvements in animal health, feeding, reproduction practices, manure management and grazing management. However, resource efficiency is primarily associated with better economic opportunities for profit maximisation and it is evident that the philosophy behind SDG 12 prioritises economic sustainability, while environmental sustainability is seen as a beneficial complementary measure rather than a priority. This trend reflects the direction of the global political economy driven by 'growth fetishism' (Kramer & Michalowski, 2012) where economic development is prioritised over social and environmental sustainability. Therefore, implementation of SDG 12 needs to be analysed more closely, and, as it was stated above, sustainability-related communication enables examination of the relationship between economic and environmental sustainability in more detail. Sustainability-related communication needs to reflect the cross-cutting nature of sustainability issues and communicate changes (Janouskova et al., 2019). Moreover, sustainability-related communication can have a transformative potential: Servaes and Malikhao (2007) state that communication strategies for the implementation of sustainable development can be classified as behaviour change communication, advocacy communication or communication for social change. It is, thus, vital to assess whether current communication around SDGs possesses this transformative potential.

Northern Ireland and Moy Park

As it was stated earlier, Northern Ireland has significantly increased its domestic meat and poultry production, which makes it a suitable case study for analysing how SDG 12 is being implemented by looking at the issues surrounding production. The Going for Growth agri-food strategy aimed to develop a strategic approach to the agri-food sector, drive exports to grow food sales outside Northern Ireland and encourage greater integration of the food supply chain through closer partnership between the industry and the government (Agri-Food Strategy Board, 2013). The strategy was premised on the productionist paradigm and emphasised the importance of efficiency and economies of scale and its ecological and economic sustainability have been called into question (Foord, 2017).

Moy Park, the largest poultry meat producer in Northern Ireland and one of the 15 biggest food companies in the UK, fully embraced the strategy and also developed one of its own—Plan to Grow. For instance, 150 new facilities to house broilers[2] were built in 2014–2015, with another 100 expected to be built (Moy Park, 2015), and farmer producers were actively encouraged to expand their businesses (Haenlein, 2014). Moy Park intended to build 400 poultry houses by the end of 2016 (Clyde Shanks, 2015). Simultaneously, Moy Park repeatedly emphasised that an active approach was and is being taken to reduce their environmental impact stemming from production. The latter resonates with the implementation of the SDGs in general and SDG 12 in particular.

Northern Ireland responded to the call for implementation of the SDGs by submitting several case studies for inclusion in the Northern Ireland reporting to the UK Voluntary National Review Process and summarising the list of projects undertaken by the NGO sector.[3] On the subject of SDG 12, Business in the Community NI is reported to be delivering a 'Circular Economy Business programme which aims to support companies in reducing waste, adopting sustainable use of natural resources, and contributing to local economic growth' (DAERA and NIEL, n.d., p. 5). Business in the Community NI also delivers the annual Northern Ireland Environmental Benchmarking Survey, which assesses how environmentally friendly practices have been embedded in the corporate strategies and encourages improvement in resource efficiency, waste reduction and energy consumption. Businesses participating in the survey are required to provide evidence and analysis of their 'green credentials, environmental management approach and performance' (Farming Life, 2017).

In 2018, Moy Park was awarded a Platinum award, the highest-ranking award in the survey. Moy Park has participated in the survey every year since its inception in 1998 and has been achieving Platinum status for the last six years (Belfast Telegraph, 2018). The company announced that 'as a top UK food

---

[2] The term 'broiler' refers to chicken that is bred and raised for industrial meat production.
[3] UN Sustainable Development Goals—NI Case Studies https://globalgoalsni.org/blog/2019/03/15/un-sustainable-development-goals-ni-case-studies/

company and leading European poultry provider, one of Moy Park's key responsibilities is to demonstrate best practice and leadership. Part of this is helping to drive forward sustainable practices to minimise environmental impact and make a positive contribution to the way people live' (Belfast Telegraph, 2018). Overall, their sustainability agenda includes measures such as 'reducing energy usage and the resultant greenhouse gas emissions; decreasing water consumption and the discharge of effluent; and recycling or diverting waste away from landfill' (Moy Park, 2015, p. 29). In 2017, for instance, when receiving the Northern Ireland Environmental Benchmarking Survey Platinum award Moy Park announced that their electricity intensity was reduced by 8 per cent, water use intensity was reduced by 4 per cent and the achievement of zero waste to landfill was maintained (Farming Life, 2017).

It is evident that Moy Park is articulating its commitment to sustainable development and projecting a green image through the Environmental Benchmarking Survey. Yet, it is also important to emphasise that the company sponsors the survey (Belfast Telegraph, 2018). Therefore, Moy Park consolidates their green reputational capital (Aras & Crowther, 2012) not only through financially backing the survey, but also through getting a top-ranking award in it. Sponsorship of the survey grants Moy Park the power to construct the reality of its environmental performance for the public and other stakeholders and enables the company to continue to exercise material and structural power over ecosystems (Gould et al., 2003). In addition to general sustainability-related commitments, those addressing specifically SDG 12 and Moy Park's production practices need to be analysed.

The company's website lists Moy Park's corporate responsibility commitments, including environmental commitments. They include commitments on climate change, water consumption, and materials and solid waste. SDG 12 is featured in the latter category where Moy Park pledges to 'play our part to reduce food waste by half, in accordance with UN Sustainable Development Goal 12.3' (Moy Park, 2019b). Additionally, although without mentioning it, they also address the target 12.4 through committing 'to manage organic waste responsibly, with the medium/long term objective to drive opportunities to convert it to energy' as well as the target 12.5 through minimising 'waste by optimising use of packaging resources' (Moy Park, 2019b). Moy Park reports to regularly monitor resource efficiency and hold strategic reviews to assess how to enhance these initiatives and develop their business in a sustainable and ethical way (Belfast Telegraph, 2018). While the rhetoric of commitment to the SDGs is being developed, it is important to analyse the substance behind this rhetoric.

In relation to food waste, Moy Park reported to 'have donated more than 100 tonnes of surplus food to those in need, enough for over 250,000 meals' (Moy Park, 2019b) since 2015 as well as having implemented smarter packaging to reduce food waste at home. However, the effectiveness of both of those strategies can be critically evaluated. Devin and Richards (2018) suggest that while donating food can be beneficial to those in need, it does not address the structural problems of the supply chain that drive up waste in the first place. Thus, food donations serve as a smokescreen for concealing the inherently wasteful nature of modern-day food production. Moreover, food waste may also increase a company's financial costs and it is in businesses' strategic interest to cut those costs while also managing their public reputation and projecting an environmentally friendly and socially responsible image (Devin & Richards, 2018). The latter is related to large companies' ability to appear green to prevent any radical change that can threaten their business interests (Lynch & Stretsky, 2003). Similarly, in the case of minimising packaging waste, Moy Park (2019a) reports packaging optimisation measures to reduce the amount of packaging and communicates its commitment to sustainability. However, minimisation of packaging waste is also a business opportunity—DEFRA (2009) reports that packaging optimisation can offer cost-saving opportunities for business and recyclable packaging is also deemed to maximise returns on packaging waste. Economic sustainability, thus, may take priority over environmental and social sustainability.

Moy Park, therefore, may use its desire to embrace the SDGs as an opportunity for increasing profit, thus allowing the production based on an unsustainable economic growth model to continue (Gould et al., 2003). The image of sustainability can also be used for convincing the stakeholders that the company is contributing to delivering good for the environment (May, Cheney, & Roper, 2007). The importance of the latter is emphasised by Moy Park: 'many external stakeholders value outstanding sustainability performance so we believe it's important to continually strive for industry leading practices which go above and beyond mandatory or self-set targets' (Belfast Telegraph, 2018).

However, projection of a green image may also be employed as a strategy for covering the actual activities that are damaging for the environment and thus compromising long-term environmental and social sustainability, as a number of authors researching the greenwashing phenomenon point out (Lyon & Maxwell, 2011; May et al., 2007). Ultimately, greenwashing is about 'telling the truth, but not the whole truth' (Lyon & Maxwell, 2011, p. 9). The case with Moy Park's waste from production illustrates this point.

On the subject of managing organic waste from production, Moy Park aims to increase efficiency by seeking ways 'to use organic waste and implement a commercially viable solution(s)' (Moy Park, 2019b). Around 270,000 tonnes of poultry litter are produced in Northern Ireland every year, and most of it comes from farmers for Moy Park (Macauley, 2019). Moreover, the government predicts that this number can go up to 400,000 tonnes if the industry expands (DAERA, 2014).

It is important to emphasise that waste from agricultural production (animal manure in particular) is already a pressing problem in Northern Ireland. Ammonia emissions from agriculture present a particular challenge. Ammonia is an air pollutant which is known to have a damaging impact on biodiversity as well as human health (DAERA, 2019). When released into the air, ammonia is later deposited onto land and water surfaces in the form of nitrogen. Most of

Northern Ireland, including designated sites and other priority habitats, are receiving levels of nitrogen which are significantly above their 'critical load'— the concentration at which significant ecological damage occurs. Critical levels of ammonia from animal manure are exceeded at 90 per cent of the protected habitats in Northern Ireland (DAERA, 2019). Moreover, ammonia emitted from animal manure mixes with other pollutants in the atmosphere, creating small particles known as particulate matter. Particulate matter is associated with human health impacts—it can be harmful to the lungs when inhaled (DAERA, 2019). Therefore, a strategic implementation of SDG 12 is required to make sure that both environmental and social impacts of expanding production are addressed.

One of the solutions for dealing with waste from the industry proposed by Moy Park is anaerobic digestion (AD) technology. Two large anaerobic digestion plants have been built with financial backing from the Northern Irish government to help address the waste problem: near Ballymena in County Antrim and outside Ballybofey in County Donegal, over the Irish border (Macauley, 2019). AD is a process in which organic matter (pig or cattle slurry, poultry litter, energy crops such as grass silage, and food waste) is broken down by micro-organisms in an oxygen-free environment to make biogas and digestate. Biogas can power on-farm operations or supply the grid while the digestate can be applied straight to land as a replacement for artificial fertiliser.

However, while anaerobic digestion is communicated to be the solution to managing waste from Moy Park's production operations, its environmental impact has been called into question. A report from the Northern Irish Department for Agriculture, Environment and Rural Affairs (DAERA) indicates that anaerobic digestion does not result in the much-needed reduction of ammonia emissions. While the pollution potential of the final product of AD, the digestate, is less than that of the original feedstock, it is still very high (Northern Ireland Fresh Water Taskforce, 2018). As a result, AD plants, while creating renewable energy, are reported to increase ammonia emissions in Northern Ireland, primarily through the storage of digestate, and the spreading of digestate on agricultural land (Bell et al., 2016). Moreover, an investigation conducted by Source Material (2018) found that those living in close proximity to anaerobic digesters complained about the 'vinegary smell' from the plant and pointed out that their eyes and throats became irritated when the plant was in operation.

It is assumed that technological solutions do not stimulate environmental and social change needed for the effective implementation of the SDGs: they simply 'green' capitalism, thus diverting any form of ecological critique (Gould et al., 2003). Power interests safeguard the doctrine of sustainable development, with economically efficient use and management of resources at its core, but manage to dismiss the inherent contradiction between economic production in capitalism and nature, where capitalism must cause ecological disorganisation by polluting nature (Lynch & Stretesky, 2014). Technology might mitigate the harmful impacts of production expansion, but does not challenge or alter the unsustainable nature of the practice.

As it was stated earlier, communication of business performance categorised as greenwashing includes communication of environmentally friendly actions to deflect stakeholders' attention from less ethical business practices (Siano et al., 2017). The case of Moy Park addressing SDG 12 demonstrates a so-called selective disclosure of information, when positive information about dealing with food waste and minimising packaging is openly communicated, while negative information about waste from production is withdrawn (Lyon & Montgomery, 2015). Moreover, technological solutions proposed by Moy Park may not serve their purpose of mitigating environmental externalities adequately. Instead, it may be merely contributing to the image where communication of environmentally friendly actions obscures less ethical business practices, thus being an aspect of marketing (Nurse, 2014, 2016) rather than a genuine commitment. Finally, the strategies for implementing SDG 12 in Moy Park's case prioritise economic sustainability over environmental and social sustainability, which ultimately serves the interests of profit rather than the planet or people.

Conclusion

This chapter provided a critique of SDG 12: Responsible Consumption and Production implementation using a case study of a poultry-producing company Moy Park. It revealed the tension between corporate communication about the SDGs and their prioritisation of economic sustainability at the cost of environmental and social sustainability. This tension also reflects the ethos of the goal itself where economic sustainability serves as the dominant narrative, which is not surprising considering the parameters of the global political economy.

While Moy Park's ambition to increase poultry production within the paradigms of the current economic system may clash with the needs of the environment and society, Moy Park endeavoured to develop an argument that reconciles the polarities between economic growth and environmental externalities. Part of that argument is them addressing SDG 12 and communicating their achievements on that front in relation to reducing food and packaging waste and managing waste from production. However, a closer look at the latter reveals how sustainability rhetoric does not correspond with reality and how environmental externalities associated with the increase in production cannot be eliminated through the use of technology. Therefore, selective communication around the implementation of SDG 12 is not contributing to sustainable development but sustains and reinforces the 'green' image that Moy Park projects to stakeholders and the general public. The latter ultimately enables them to safeguard economic sustainability and continue profit accumulation. The current 'efficient' mode of poultry (and other meat) production lends itself to profit accumulation, but its negative effects can be concealed through a 'scene-stealing argument' (Myerson & Rydin, 1996, p. 194) of sustainable development. Corporate communication, thus, may serve as an enabler for the pursuit of economic sustainability at the cost of environmental and social sustainability. The latter fulfils the ultimate goal of a corporation where 'the social responsibility of business is to increase its profits' (Bisschop, 2010, p. 349).

While there's a danger that economic sustainability may be high-jacking environmental and social sustainability in the SDGs as there are 'direct profit interests in going green' (Bisschop, 2010, p. 356), alternative pathways need to be thought of where economic development is not the dominant paradigm. I suggest that the implementation of the SDGs needs to be critically scrutinised without taking the corporate reporting of it at face value. The broader context in which the implementation of the goals takes place also needs to be further assessed to better understand the goals of all actors involved and the means available to them to achieve those goals. SDGs implementation may benefit from being assessed from a perspective of local communities and organisations familiar with the local community perspective. Furthermore, corporate voluntary action towards the implementation of the SDGs needs to be supplemented with rigorous regulation (Nurse, 2014) to avoid 'deep greenwash'—a strategy advocating for corporate self-regulation at the expense of government policies (Góngora & Lucía, 2013). More regulation around the SDGs will transcend the imprecise and ambiguous language of its targets and indicators, and hopefully contribute to a more balanced idea of sustainability.

The chapter also demonstrates that corporate communication is not an effective medium to achieve sustainable development since it is not aimed at structural social change and, therefore, does not possess the transformative potential. Moreover, such elite environmental communication does not allow for civic engagement and public dialogue. Instead, voices advocating for structural transformation should be given a priority in communication for sustainable development. Considering intersectionality of the goals, advocacy around other SDGs can serve as a powerful tool for transitioning towards more sustainable food systems in general and meat production in particular. Such advocacy can also originate in investigative environmental journalism. In this chapter's case, investigations carried out by The Bureau of Investigative Journalism and Source Material were vital for uncovering the discrepancy between corporate communication in the form of CSR and the reality of the implementation of SDG 12.

References

Agnew, R. (1998). The Causes of Animal Abuse: A Social-Psychological Analysis. *Theoretical Criminology, 2*, 177–209.

Agnew, R. (2013). The Ordinary Acts That Contribute to Ecocide: A Criminological Analysis. In N. South & A. Brisman (Eds.), *Routledge International Handbook of Green Criminology*. London: Routledge.

Agri-Food Strategy Board. (2013). *Going for Growth. A Strategic Action Plan in Support of the Northern Ireland Agri-Food Industry*. Belfast. Retrieved July 31, 2018, from https://www.daera-ni.gov.uk/sites/default/files/publications/dard/going-for-growth.pdf

Akenji, L., & Bengtsson, M. (2014). Making Sustainable Consumption and Production the Core of Sustainable Development Goals. *Sustainability, 6*, 513–529.

Alexandratos, N., & Bruinsma, J. (2012). *World Agriculture Towards 2030/2050: The 2012 Revision*. 12. Rome.

Aras, G., & Crowther, D. (2012). *Governance and Social Responsibility: International Perspectives*. UK: Palgrave Macmillan UK.

Belfast Telegraph. (2018). *Celebrating 20 Years of the Northern Ireland Environmental Benchmarking Survey*. Belfast. Retrieved April 16, 2019, from https://www.bitcni.org.uk/wp-content/uploads/2018/01/181128_NIEBS_20Anniversary_Supplement.pdf

Bell, M. W., et al. (2016). Ammonia Emissions from an Anaerobic Digestion Plant Estimated Using Atmospheric Measurements and Dispersion Modelling. *Waste Management, 56*, 113–124.

Bisschop, L. (2010). Corporate Environmental Responsibility and Criminology. *Crime, Law and Social Change, 53*, 349–364. https://doi.org/10.1007/s10611-009-9227-8

Blaustein, J., et al. (2018). Criminology and the UN Sustainable Development Goals: The Need for Support and Critique. *British Journal of Criminology, 58*, 767–786. https://doi.org/10.1093/bjc/azx061

Bradshaw, E. (2014). State-Corporate Environmental Cover-Up: The Response to the 2010 Gulf of Mexico Oil Spill. *State Crime, 3*(2), 163–181.

Brisman, A. (2009). It Takes Green to Be Green: Environmental Elitism, Ritual Displays, and Conspicuous Non-Consumption. *North Dakota Law Review, 85*, 329–370.

Brisman, A., & South, N. (2014). *Green Cultural Criminology: Constructions of Environmental Harm, Consumerism, and Resistance to Ecocide*. London: Routledge.

Brisman, A., & South, N. (2018). Green Criminology and Environmental Crimes and Harms. *Sociology Compass, 13*, 1–12.

Brisman, A., South, N., & White, R. (2015). *Environmental Crime and Social Conflict. Contemporary and Emerging Issues*. London: Routledge.

Brulle, R. (2010). From Environmental Campaigns to Advancing the Public Dialog: Environmental Communication for Civic Engagement. *Environmental Communication, 4*(1), 82–98.

Clyde Shanks. (2015). *Moy Park Expansion Plans*. Retrieved from http://clydeshanks.com/2015/12/11/moy-park-expansion-plans/

Croall, H. (2012). Food Crime: A Green Criminology Perspective. In N. South & A. Brisman (Eds.), *Routledge International Handbook of Green Criminology*. London: Routledge. https://doi.org/10.4324/9780203093658.ch10

DAERA. (2014). *Review of Alternative Technologies to Fluidised Bed Combustion for Poultry Litter Utilisation/Disposal*. Belfast. Retrieved April 17, 2019, from https://www.daera-ni.gov.uk/sites/default/files/publications/dard/review-of-alternative-technologies-for-poultry-litter-final-jan-2012.pdf

DAERA. (2019). *Ammonia Emissions in Northern Ireland*. Retrieved March 6, 2019, from https://www.daera-ni.gov.uk/articles/ammonia-emissions-northern-ireland

DAERA, & NIEL. (n.d.). *UN Sustainable Development Goals – NI Case Studies*. Belfast. Retrieved from https://globalgoalsni.org/blog/2019/03/15/un-sustainable-development-goals-ni-case-studies/

DEFRA. (2009). *Making the Most of Packaging. A Strategy for a Low-Carbon Economy*. London: Retrieved April 17, 2019, from www.defra.gov.uk

Devin, B., & Richards, C. (2018). Food Waste, Power, and Corporate Social Responsibility in the Australian Food Supply Chain. *Journal of Business Ethics, 150*, 199–210. https://doi.org/10.1007/s10551-016-3181-z

FAO. (2018). *World Livestock: Transforming the Livestock Sector Through the Sustainable Development Goals*. Rome.

FAO. (2019). *Sustainable Development Goals*. Retrieved April 15, 2019, from http://www.fao.org/sustainable-development-goals/en/

Farming Life. (2017). *Moy Park Receives Top Sustainability Status, Farming Life*. Retrieved April 16, 2019, from https://www.farminglife.com/farming-news/moy-park-receives-top-sustainability-status-1-8256753

Foord, W. (2017). *Scenario Planning Methodology and the Politics of Food in Interesting Times – A Northern Ireland Case Study*. Glasgow.

Fraser, C., & Villet, J. (1994). *Communication: A Key to Human Development*. Rome.

Gasper, D., Shah, A., & Tankha, S. (2019). The Framing of Sustainable Consumption and Production in SDG 12. *Global Policy, 10*(1), 83–95.

Góngora, A., & Lucía, C. (2013). Greenwashing: Only the Appearance of Sustainability. *IESE*. Retrieved from https://www.ieseinsight.com/doc.aspx?id=1714&ar=17&idioma=2

Goodman, D., & Redclift, M. (1991). *Refashioning Nature*. London: Routledge.

Gould, K. A., Pellow, D. N., & Schnaiberg, A. (2003). Interrogating the Treadmill of Production: Everything You Wanted to Know About the Treadmill, but Were Afraid to Ask. *Symposium on Environment and the Treadmill of Production*. Madison, pp. 1–84. Retrieved March 11, 2019, from http://www.michaelmbell.net/RC24/papers/gouldpellowschnaiberg.pdf

Gray, A., & Hinch, R. (2015). Agribusiness, Governments and Food Crime: A Critical Perspective. In R. Sollund (Ed.), *Green Harms and Crimes* (pp. 97–116). London: Palgrave Macmillan UK. https://doi.org/10.1057/9781137456267_6

Haenlein, O. (2014). Moy Park Seeks Poultry Farmers to Continue Growth. *Food Manufacture*. Retrieved April 17, 2019, from https://www.foodmanufacture.co.uk/Article/2014/07/31/Moy-Park-seeks-poultry-farmers-to-continue-growth

Hansen, A., & Cox, R. (2015). *The Routledge Handbook of Environment and Communication*. London and New York: Routledge.

Harvey, F. (2016, May 17). Farming Is "Single Biggest Cause" of Worst Air Pollution in Europe. *The Guardian*. https://doi.org/10.1002/2016GL068354

Janouskova, S., et al. (2019). Sustainable Development—A Poorly Communicated Concept by Mass Media. Another Challenge for SDGs? *Sustainability, 11*(11), 1–20.

Kingsmith, A. (2012). Greenwashing: The Corporate Exaggeration of Environmental Consciousness. *The International*.

Kramer, R., & Michalowski, R. (2012). Is Global Warming a State-Corporate Crime? In R. White (Ed.), *Climate Change from a Criminological Perspective*. New York, London: Springer International Publishing.

Lie, R., & Servaes, J. (2015). Disciplines in the Field of Communication for Development and Social Change. *Communication Theory, 25*(2), 244–258.

Lynch, M., & Stretesky, P. (2014). *Exploring Green Criminology: Toward a Green Criminological Revolution.* London: Ashgate Publishing Limited.

Lynch, M., & Stretsky, P. (2003). The Meaning of Green: Contrasting Criminological Perspectives. *Theoretical Criminology, 7*(2), 217–238.

Lynch, M. J., Long, M. A., Barrett, K. L., & Stretesky, P. B. (2013, November). Is it a Crime to Produce Ecological Disorganization? Why Green Criminology and Political Economy Matter in the Analysis of Global Ecological Harms. *The British Journal of Criminology, 53*(6), 997–1016.

Lyon, T., & Maxwell, J. (2011). Greenwash: Corporate Environmental Disclosure Under Threat of Audit. *Journal of Economics & Management Strategy, 20*, 3–41.

Lyon, T., & Montgomery, A. (2013). Tweetjacked: The Impact of Social Media on Corporate Greenwash. *Journal of Business Ethics, 118*, 747–757.

Lyon, T. P., & Montgomery, A. W. (2015). The Means and End of Greenwash. *Organization & Environment, 28*(2), 223–249. https://doi.org/10.1177/1086026615575332

Macauley, C. (2019). Brexit: Poultry Firms Must Plan for Waste Disposal. *BBC News.* Retrieved April 16, 2019, from https://www.bbc.co.uk/news/uk-northern-ireland-47108615

May, S., Cheney, G., & Roper, J. (2007). *The Debate over Corporate Social Responsibility.* Oxford: Oxford University Press.

Moggi, S., Bonomi, S., & Ricciardi, F. (2018). Against Food Waste: CSR for the Social and Environmental Impact Through a Network-Based Organizational Model. *Sustainability, 10*(10).

Moy Park. (2015). *Moy Park 2014/15. Our Business and Our Values.* Belfast. Retrieved April 17, 2019, from https://www.moypark.com/uploads/general/MoyPark_Our_Business_and_Our_Values_2015.pdf

Moy Park. (2018). *Moy Park Achieves Major Production Milestone.* Retrieved April 15, 2019, from https://www.moypark.com/en/news/moy-park-achieves-major-production-milestone

Moy Park. (2019a). *Case Study – Packaging Optimisation.* Retrieved April 17, 2019, from https://www.moypark.com/en/sustainability/case-studies/packaging-optimisation

Moy Park. (2019b). *Food Waste Reduction.* Retrieved April 17, 2019, from https://www.moypark.com/sustainability/case-studies/food-waste-reduction

Myerson, G., & Rydin, Y. (1996). *The Language of Environment. A New Rhetoric.* London: UCL Press.

Natali, L., & Mcclanahan, B. (2017). Perceiving and Communicating Environmental Contamination and Change: Towards a Green Cultural Criminology with Images. *Critical Criminology, 25*, 199–214. https://doi.org/10.1007/s10612-017-9356-9

Northern Ireland Fresh Water Taskforce. (2018). *Environmental Audit Committee: Nitrates Inquiry.* Belfast. Retrieved March 4, 2019, from https://www.cambridge.org/core/journals/proceedings-of-the-royal-society-of-edinburgh-section-b

Nurse, A. (2014). Critical Perspectives on Green Criminology: An Introduction. *Internet Journal of Criminology*, 3–11. Retrieved from www.researchgate.net/publication/280946476_A_Criminological_Exploration_of_the_Industrialisation_of_Pig_Farming

Nurse, A. (2016). Cleaning up Greenwash: A Critical Evaluation of the Activities of Oil Companies in the Niger. In T. Wyatt (Ed.), *Hazardous Waste and Pollution: Detecting and Preventing Green Crimes.* Springer.

Pohlmann, C. R., et al. (2019). The Role of the Focal Company in Sustainable Development Goals: A Brazilian Food Poultry Supply Chain Case Study. *Journal of Cleaner Production, 245*, 1–13.

Reilly, A. H., & Hynan, K. A. (2014). Corporate Communication, Sustainability, and Social Media: It's Not Easy (Really) Being Green. *Business Horizons, 57*(6), 747–758.

Rodríguez Goyes, D., & South, N. (2016). Land-Grabs, Biopiracy and the Inversion of Justice in Colombia. *The British Journal of Criminology, 56*(3), 558–577.

Ruhl, J. B. (2000). Farms, Their Environmental Harms, and Environmental Law. *Ecology Law Quarterly, 27*(2), 263–350. https://doi.org/10.15779/Z38C55S

Schally, J. L. (2017). *Legitimizing Corporate Harm: The Discourse of Contemporary Agribusiness*. USA: Palgrave Macmillan. https://doi.org/10.1007/978-3-319-67879-5

Schnaiberg, A. (1980). *The Environment, from Surplus to Scarcity*. New York: Oxford University Press.

Servaes, J., & Malikhao, P. (2007). *Communication and Sustainable Development*. Rome.

Siano, A., et al. (2017). "More Than Words": Expanding the Taxonomy of Greenwashing After the Volkswagen Scandal. *Journal of Business Research, 71*, 27–37. https://doi.org/10.1016/j.jbusres.2016.11.002

Smith, H., & McGreavy, B. (2018). Editorial: Science and Environmental Journalism: Trends, Boundaries, and Opportunities for a Rapidly Evolving Industry. *Frontiers in Communication, 3*(31), 1–2.

Sollund, R. (2015). *Green Harms and Crimes. Critical Criminological Perspectives*. London: Palgrave Macmillan.

Source Material. (2018). *Muck for Brass*. Retrieved April 17, 2019, from https://www.source-material.org/blog/muck-for-brass

Steinfeld, H., et al. (2006). *Livestock's Long Shadow: Environmental Issues and Options*. Rome.

Sykes, G., & Matza, D. (1957). Techniques of Neutralization: A Theory of Delinquency. *American Sociological Review, 22*(6), 664–670.

The Bureau of Investigative Journalism. (2017). *Intensive Farming in the UK, by Numbers*. Retrieved April 15, 2019, from https://www.thebureauinvestigates.com/stories/2017-07-17/intensive-numbers-of-intensive-farming

Tombs, S., & Whyte, D. (2007). *Safety Crime*. Cullompton: Willan Publishing.

Tombs, S., & Whyte, D. (2010). Crime, Harm and Corporate Power. In J. Muncie, D. Talbot, & R. Walters (Eds.), *Crime: Local and Global* (pp. 137–172). Cullompton: Willan Publishing.

Tong, J. (2015). *Investigative Journalism, Environmental Problems and Modernisation in China*. London: Palgrave Macmillan UK.

United Nations. (2019). *Sustainable Consumption and Production*. Retrieved from https://sustainabledevelopment.un.org/topics/sustainableconsumptionandproduction

Walters, R. (2006). Crime, Bio-Agriculture and the Exploitation of Hunger. *The British Journal of Criminology, 46*(1), 26–45.

White, R. (2012). *Climate Change from a Criminological Perspective*. New York, London: Springer International Publishing.

Yates, R. (2007). Debating "Animal Rights" Online: The Movement-Countermovement Dialectic Revisited. In P. Beirne & N. South (Eds.), *Issues in Green Criminology: Confronting Harms Against Environments, Humanity and Other Animals* (pp. 140–157). Cullompton: Willan Publishing.

Zanasi, C., et al. (2017). An Assessment of the Food Companies Sustainability Policies Through a Greenwashing Indicator. *System Dynamics and Innovation in Food Networks 2017. International Journal on Food System Dynamics.* https://doi.org/10.18461/pfsd.2017.1707

Zikargae, M. (2018). Analysis of Environmental Communication and Its Implication for Sustainable Development in Ethiopia. *Science of the Total Environment, 634,* 1593–1600.

CHAPTER 15

Fake News and SDG16: The Situation in Ghana

Kobby Mensah, Gideon Awini, and Gilbert Kofi Mensah

INTRODUCTION

The sustainable development goal sixteen (SDG16) enjoins the advancement of peaceful and inclusive societies for sustainable development. It further calls for access to justice for all and the building of effective, accountable and inclusive institutions at all levels, ensuring public access to information and the protection of fundamental freedoms in accordance with national legislation and international agreements. This mandate makes communication a strategic instrument to the achievement of goal 16 of the SDGs. It entreats countries to build both institutional and individual communication capacities that will underpin the operationalisation and achievement of the goal. It is agreeable, widely, that advancement in communication has reached most parts of the world and has certainly contributed to the development of not only institutions but the individual, thereby resulting in stronger institutions and more informed individuals than ever before. This development, however, has come with its own challenges that leave people and institutions exposed. Countries in Africa, for example, have formulated and implemented policies such as right to information (RTI) whereas organisations are increasingly implementing data and digital protection measures. Though these are laudable measures in the attempt to protect people and institutions in order to promote world peace and inclusive societies, they are mostly towards institutional capacity building. Citizens are increasingly getting exposed to the negative effects of modern

K. Mensah (✉) • G. Awini • G. K. Mensah
University of Ghana Business School, University of Ghana, Accra, Ghana
e-mail: kobbymensah@ug.edu.gh

© The Author(s), under exclusive license to Springer Nature
Switzerland AG 2021
M. J. Yusha'u, J. Servaes (eds.), *The Palgrave Handbook of International Communication and Sustainable Development*,
https://doi.org/10.1007/978-3-030-69770-9_15

communication, such as manipulation. A classic case study is the activities of Cambridge Analytica and its influence on the 2016 US elections through the manipulation of the American public using fake news (Allcott & Gentzkow, 2017). In Africa, it is reported that Cambridge Analytica pursued a similar agenda in the 2015 Nigerian elections (Kuenzi & Lambright, 2015). It is noted that through fake news, people have been either manipulated or exposed to manipulation on social media, which is arguably the most dominant communication channel globally. This means there is the urgent need to build the communication capacities of people on social media in order that they can detect, report and abstain from the consumption of manipulated information. But what category of people are exposed the most and need the most help? This question is important not only to the agencies responsible for promoting public safety and security, but also to the citizenry in order to ensure personal security and safety. It could help in the targeting of education, with the aim of inoculating the most exposed. Hence, the importance of this topic.

SDG16 AND ITS RELATIONSHIP TO FAKE NEWS

Generally, Sustainable Development Goals (SDGs) are global actions to protect the planet, combat poverty and enhance prosperity, peace and justice for all mankind (United Nations, 2013). This is to state that each and every individual and country on the planet is obliged to play a critical role in fulfilling this global vision. However, among the 17 SDGs, the goal 16, which talks about peace, justice and strong institutions, is arguably the most pertinent among all the goals (Kempe, 2019). This is because without peace, justice and strong institution the other goals such as ending poverty, zero hunger, good health and education cannot be realised. The SDG16 is mostly characterised as the controversial among the 17 goals. It constitutes a 'transformative shifts' from the Millennium Development Goals (MDGs) and highlights the roles that peace, justice and good institutions play in development, and further enhances the collective achievement of the global vision 2030. Peace has broadly been described in the context of SDGs as freedom from violence, both at the hands of state and private actors, including activities that support violence, such as human and arms trafficking. Justice has also been related to the rule of law, non-discrimination and remedies, whereas 'strong institutions' involves lack of corruption, transparency, legal recognition, public participation and an enlightenment on how leaders might be held accountable.

The feasibility of SDG16 in Ghana has been undermined by the upsurge of fake news. A study conducted on fake news revealed that the Ghanaian landscape especially the media are not furnished with systems and specialist to detect and combat the menace of fake news (Penplusbytes, 2018). This makes the situation in Ghana very delicate and alarming since the media is considered the most trusted source of communication channel. The seeming default of trust in information disseminated by media is situated in the source credibility theory, which notes that the source of an information largely embeds credibility in, and therefore acceptance of, that information. Fake news, on the other hand, has been described as deceptive information that mimics news with the intent to misinform and mislead people (Zhang et al., 2019). In recent times, the increased circulation of fake news on both traditional and social media channels have drifted from just manipulating public thinking to a tool of trade for conspiracy and disseminating false information with the intent of spreading hatred against humanity and worst of all, inciting inexcusable violence. This subverts the peace enjoyed by the populace and hinders the objective of SDG16. Further in deterring the peace that SDG16 seeks to achieve, fake news within the context of the study have proven to be a major contributor. For instance, during the current compilation of the voters register in Ghana, a fabricated news from the ruling party (NPP) in the Effutu constituency of the central region reported that a member of parliament has been assaulted and rushed to a nearby health centre. This news was fake but resulted in members of the ruling party in the constituency rushing to the registration centre to retaliate by violently attacking the members of the opposition party (NDC) (Gyamera, 2018). This incidence, precipitated by fake news, undermines the rule of law and access to justice. Socio-economically, the situation described earlier has a detrimental effect on the populace especially the poor, increasing the rate of poverty in the country. This is because not just the accused and abused individuals are affected but also their families, communities and the nation as a whole. What makes the issue of fake news critical in Ghana is the fact that the most trusted sources of information, the media, do not have adequate systems and human capacity to detect false news. More importantly, there is minimal education on the subject from the government and other public service institutions such as the security agencies and the media. A survey conducted by Penplusbytes showed that 82.5% of these institutions do not have programmes for educating the public on fake news. In assessing the capacity of newsrooms to deal with fake news, it came out that most newsrooms (81.7%) did not assign staff to deal with fake news. Arguably, if the issue of fake news is not well managed in Ghana it may cause more havoc than expected especially during election years and this will ruin the peace, justice and the strong institutions the SDG16 seeks to achieve.

UNDERSTANDING THE EFFECT OF FAKE NEWS ON THE SDG16: AN AGENDA FOR DEVELOPMENT COMMUNICATION

Communication is expected to affect the world both in the short and in the long term. Communication is found to have positive and negative bearings on sustainable development, as it facilitates social relations between people and institutions (Servaes, 2020). Communication is not limited to the message or the channels through which message is conveyed, as recent developments, especially in the era of social media, shows that the network and interactivity aspects have become dominant in social relationships. The internet, for example, enhances interactivity, such that it has aided better access to information, education and knowledge in a borderless society, leading to development and social change (Patel, 2020; Servaes, 2020). Development communication therefore means creating mechanisms to broaden public access to information; enabling stakeholder engagement; encouraging inclusive participation (Servaes, 2020). Thus, Jacobson (2016) postulates that communication for development is a social process based on dialogue using a broad range of tools and methods. It is also about seeking change at different levels including listening, building trust, sharing knowledge and skills, building policies, debating and learning for sustained and meaningful change.

According to Servaes (2020) and Thomas (2020) 'development can be described as a significant change of structured social action or of the culture in a given society, community, or context'. The rationality of communication for development and social change is underpinned by different underlying premises (methods and or theories, culture and values). From a culturalist perspective, detailed attention is given to communication in the social change process from the people's perspective (Servaes, 2007). In this direction, for a message to be accepted by people of different cultures, they ought to tolerate, respect and understand each other very well, which goes a long way to stimulate development and social change. The main driver of the SDG16 is to promote peaceful and inclusive societies for sustainable development, provide access to justice for all and build effective, accountable and inclusive institutions at all levels (Khairil, Emrizal, Rizal, Ramli, & Arifin, 2017; Ali, Emrizal, Razman, Ramli, & Arifin, 2017), which communication plays a major role as discussed earlier. That said, fake news is said to be the deliberate spreading of false information for public consumption. It is also considered as misleading information either deliberately or accidentally published as authentic news (Nelson & Taneja, 2018). Fake news results in conflict, insecurity, weak institutions and as well as limiting access to justice.

Review of the Literature on Fake News

Fake news has been studied along four areas: characterisation, creation, circulation and countering (Kalsnes, 2018). In characterisation, what counts as fake is well treated but also disputed in the literature. Creation deals with motivations behind the production of fake news including financial, political or social factors. Circulation concerns itself with the different ways false information is disseminated and amplified. Countering fake news also involves detecting and combating it on different levels including legal, financial and technical approaches. Increasingly, attention is being turned also to the susceptibility to fake news, which this study concerns itself. The Pew Research Centre in 2016 conducted a survey that revealed that about 23% of the US adult population either knowingly or unknowingly shared fake news with relations (Ordway, 2017). Pennycook and Rand (2018) also reported that although there are ideological and political factors underpinning susceptibility to fake news, people who do not apply analytic thinking are overall less able to detect fake from real news. Other studies (Popken, 2019) also contend that age, not politics, is the biggest predictor of who shares fake news on social media. In Africa, concerns about the growing trend of fake news is attributed to four key elements, including the increasing adoption of mobile phones, access to the internet, the youth bulge and the frequency with which political actors attempt to manipulate existing socio-cultural cleavages such as ethnicity and religion (Bajo, 2019). In contrast, studies in Europe and America indicate that young people are more digitally savvy and are far better at identifying and avoiding the peddling of fake news (Ordway, 2017; Popken, 2019). This contradiction demonstrates that whilst concern over fake news is global, contextual differences remain.

The availability of internet has given people the opportunity to utilise online social networking platforms, including Facebook, Instagram and Twitter amongst others, to interact from remote locations. Intuitively, the internet is growing faster than all other communication technologies that came before it. With the internet, millions of people across the globe get to communicate and share information. The global diffusion of the internet and related technologies have boosted knowledge circulation, enhanced communication efficiency, improved political engagement and increased social engagement. Despite these benefits, the internet has some negative effects on users. It is, for example, known to be the single most effective propagator of fake news. Fake news can be defined as the deliberate spreading of false information. It is also considered as misleading information either deliberately or accidentally published as authentic news (Nelson & Taneja, 2018). Tambini (2017) defines fake news as information converted into audio-visual or text file(s) that is/are consciously or unconsciously shared from one source to another for political, economic, social, personal interests or any other purpose. In *The Handbook for Journalism Education and Training*, UNESCO defines misinformation as misleading information created and disseminated without manipulative or malicious intent. Disinformation, however, is false information deliberately created and shared for capricious reasons (Ireton & Posetti, 2018). Although both are problematic, disinformation is however dangerous as it is a deception often planned, well resourced and in recent times scaled to a global proportion aided by advanced technology, as in the case of Cambridge Analytica.

Interestingly, fake news is not new in societies, but the exponential proliferation of its exposure in the age of digital media makes it a constant challenge. Fake news is usually disseminated on the internet and augmented through communication technologies such as social media and search engine optimisation (Allcott & Gentzkow, 2017; Fletcher, Cornia, Graves, & Nielsen, 2018). The characterisation of social media platforms, both in form and content, make them different from previous media technologies, resulting in their capabilities as purveyors of disinformation. For example, content can be relayed among social media users without the editorial judgement inherent in traditional media (Vos, Craft, & Ashley, 2012). Against this backdrop, online news for both consumption and as input raw material in traditional news gathering without considerable fact checking and editorial filtering could have significant consequences. The situation has also resulted in the lack of trust not only in the news media but also in institutions and government communication generally (Ireton & Posetti, 2018), thereby increasing the cost of news media consumption.

Types of Fake News

According to the literature, fake news exists in many forms, including sarcasm, news parody, fabrication and manipulation. Among these, sarcasm or satire is the most common.

Satire is mostly referred to as mock news, applying humour and/or exaggeration to update audience with news. Baym (2005) refers to 'the Daily Show on Comedy Central' in the US as an example of satire news. In Ghana, the satirical 'Weekend City Show' programme on Joy News and the 'The Real News' on UTV are examples. These programmes, which feature talking heads behind news desks with illustrative graphics and videos, are fixated on current issues on television and radio broadcasts, with online streams alongside, as a style to gazette the information. Intuitively these programmes are produced with an equivocal humorous motivation. The rationale is to crave the attention of the younger generation by using sarcastic, wry or 'over-the-top' graphics or comments to arouse their interest. Several studies have noted that satirical programmes are increasingly becoming important to the media ecosystem. Their humorous format is used to critique political, economic or social issues (Tandoc, Lim, & Ling, 2018). Xenos and Becker (2009) note that people who watch satirical programmes are as familiar with current affairs as persons who consume other forms of news media. Satirical programmes are found to have public discourse and political opinion formation as part of their objectives (Brewer, Young, & Morreale, 2013). Their ability to situate daily news pieces within a large context has created a niche for it in the media landscape (Morris, 2009), as evident in 'the Daily Show' for example, which attempts to demonstrate the inconsistencies or contradiction of politicians by comparing their current and past remarks in order to unravel issues. Although research has denoted political news satires as fake news, the definition of their 'fakeness' is in reference to their format (Morris, 2009).

Parody and satire both rely on humour as a medium of attracting audience. Likewise, they use a 'presentation format which mimics mainstream news media'. Parodies on the other hand use non-factual information to inject humour which distinguishes it from satire. Parody plays on the absurdity of issues and as well highlights them by crafting fictitious news stories rather than providing a direct commentary on current issues through humour (Kohut, Morin, & Keeter, 2007). A classic example is that of the parody website in the US called 'The Onion', and the Ghanaian versions of 7news.com and Newsmunews.com. These portals have been mistaken for actual news websites in many instances by unsuspecting readers. According to Xenos and Becker

(2009), the main object of a parody is to play on the equivocal plausibility of the news item, which may not be that obvious to uncritical and unsuspecting readers. That said, Berkowitz and Schwartz (2016) argue that news parodies play a role similar to that of satire, and together they form part of the 'fifth estate' along with non-main-stream media sources such as columnists and bloggers. The fifth estate, they argue, creates an inimitable boundary with mainstream news media to permit critique of both people in power and also of the news media. However, in the case of news parody, the content is fictitious.

Fabrication, as the name suggests, refers to articles that are not factual but are however published in news articles to create legitimacy. When news is fake, there is no implicit comprehension between the reader and the author. Undeniably, the intent is often quite the reverse. The author of the content most often than not has the intention of misinforming. These fictitious items can be gazetted on a legitimate website, blog or on social media platforms (Tandoc et al., 2018). When political organisations publish fabricated stories, they provide it with a façade of objectivity and balanced reporting, making it very difficult to identify as fake news (Palma, 2017). A fabricated news item draws on the pre-existing beliefs and biases of its target audience and weaves them into a narrative in an attempt to lure readers to accept the information as legitimate (Tandoc et al., 2018). The reader faces further exertion in verification since fabricated news is also published by non-news organisations or individuals under a surface of authenticity by adhering to news styles and presentations. The news items can also be shared on social media using its embedded networking and source credibility characteristics, to further gain legitimacy since the sharing parties possess mutual trust. It is imperative to note that every fabricated item relies on pre-existing social tension deliberately exploited by the promoter of the fabricated story on the notion that if the promoter is trusted by the people, they are more likely to accept the story. In this direction, Hunt and Gentzkow (2017) give an example of a fabricated story where Pope Francis was said to have endorsed Donald Trump in the 2016 US general elections. The Trump Campaign was associated with so much surprises that many people failed to examine this news critically before sharing it with others online. Hunt and Gentzkow (2017) note that fabricated news relating to Donald Trump campaign were estimated to have been shared 30 million times on Facebook alone, and those of Hillary Clinton shared 8 million times, with about half of the people believing them.

Photo manipulation is the extensive use of images and videos to conjure a false narrative to catch the attention of the public (Chen, Conroy, & Rubin, 2015). With the advent of digital photos, photo manipulation software and technology, image manipulation has increasingly become common. Modifications can include increasing colour satiety and removing minor elements. Other invasive changes can include eliminating or projecting a person into an image. In mass media, this phenomenon is carried out to catch the attention of the audience. This phenomenon has been studied in the context of citizen journalism (Tandoc et al., 2018), where people fail to verify and authenticate sources of shared information and images.

Zubiaga and Ji (2014) in their study of manipulated photos circulated on Twitter during Hurricane Sandy in 2012 examined many examples of photo manipulation one of which was the Statue of Liberty in New York City being battered by waves, with a superimposed logo that made it appear to originate from a live broadcast. The photo however turned out to be actually a merger of images from a disaster movie and an actual one from Hurricane Sandy. It is however a legitimate practice also that news items could carry what is referred to as file or library pictures using images that are not original to the news item in question but are relevant to the content and which are used in the absence of the original. In this case, the media outlet has the responsibility for disclosure and clarification (Reuters, 2017).

The Proliferation of Fake News

The increasing adoption of social media is perhaps the most obvious reason for the recent proliferation of fake news. New social technologies and photo-sharing apps facilitate rapid information-sharing that can also spread misinformation, or information that is inaccurate or misleading (Nielsen & Graves, 2017). Allcott and Gentzkow (2017) also note that due to substantially reduced editorial quality control in news gathering using online sources, we are seeing a rise in fake news. Vosoughi, Roy, and Ara (2018) look at the algorithm of social media as responsible for the rapid spread of fake news. For example, a rumour cascade begins on twitter, and through the twitter function of retweet other users propagate the rumour, and in most cases without verifying even the authenticity of the source. A rumour's diffusion process can be characterised as having one or more cascades, which can lead to virality, according to Vosoughi et al. (2018). The chain could continue by another individual independently starting a second cascade of the same rumour, embedding their own content to the original thereby becoming a new version independent of the first (Vosoughi et al., 2018).

Fake news is also fuelled by misperceptions and disenchantment with mainstream media. Newman, Fletcher, Kalogeropoulos, Levy, and Nielsen (2017) conducted an in-depth survey and analysis of consumer perceptions of the quality of news in nine countries. The findings suggest that people do not categorically distinguish between 'fake' and 'real' news but rather define it as a continuum, as they continuously see bias, spin, agenda setting in news items every day. There is an overwhelming feeling among people that powerful individuals in society are using the media to push their own interests, rather than representing ordinary citizens. This feeling is most strongly held by young people and by the socio-economically worse off. The functionality of search engines is another factor driving fake news, according to Moraga-González and Vaiva (2013). They observe that because consumers have the tendency to favour top-ranked products and news as a way of reducing search costs, individuals and organisations involved in online manipulation use what is referred to as endogenous ranking in search engine optimisation to push fake news articles to the top of the pile to appear as 'frequently read' in order to achieve legitimisation. By so doing they may push legitimate materials to the bottom and reduce their visibility and readership. This phenomenon is known as superstar and long-tail effects, in search engine optimisation.

Del Vicario, Quattrociocchi, and Zollo (2018) also contend that processes can be used to generate early warning signals on potential themes that could be candidates for fake news. Spreading disinformation on social media is directly related to polarisation and segregation of users, Del Vicario et al. observe. Hence in determining in advance fake news and their potential targets, confirmation bias could be used as proxy as it plays a key role in fostering polarisation. Another theory that can help us detect fake news early is moral emotion. The countenance of moral emotion, according to Brady, Wills, Josr, Tucker, and Van Bavel (2017), leads to the spread of fake news. In a study of social media communication on three polarising moral/political issues, their findings show that moral emotion is critical for the spread of moral and political ideas in online social networks. In this direction, they discovered that the presence of moral-emotional words in messages increased their diffusion by a factor of 20% for each additional word. Moral-emotional language enlarged diffusion more strongly in groups than between groups. This confirms models of social influence and group polarisation as people become increasingly immersed in social media networks. Additionally, fake news is also fuelled by differences in personality. Flynn, Nyhan, and Reifler (2017) explored the psychological motives behind people's retention of false beliefs and the difficulty in persuading them to accept alternative perspectives even in the face of reality. They argue that exposure and consumption of fake news is a directionally motivated reasoning, or planned behaviour that seeks information which reinforces preferences (confirmation bias) and prior attitudes. Although all humans may have confirmation bias playing out when critical decisions are made, people who have ideological stances in political debates easily evoke confirmation bias. For Gentzkow, Shapiro, and Taddy (2016) a significant part of news consumers have their own prior beliefs and ideological preferences, and a significant number of them do not like to be exposed to news that contradicts these beliefs for fear of experiencing cognitive dissonance that may compel them to re-think their convictions and so tend to rather reject the news.

It has also been noted by Jeffrey and Shearer (2016) in the literature that fallen standards in journalism and the low integrity of persons working in media fuel fake news. They opine that a high-quality news producer reports accurately while a normal producer behaves strategically by reporting accurately when it suits their preferred consumers and inaccurately with a 'slant' in other situations. They combine the demand for accuracy, consistency in meeting consumer preferences and sticking to editorial line. Lewandowsky, Ecker, Seifert, Schwarz, and Cook (2012) note that fake news in on the ascendancy. However it is unclear the extent to which the consumption of false news or low-quality news is as a result of lack of media literacy and the ability to judge the credibility of news sources, with some empirical evidence pointing to a link between false news consumption and heavy use of social media (Kamerer, 2013). That could suggest that users who spend more time on social media are more exposed to false news.

Conclusion: Vulnerabilities of Consumers of Fake News

From the literature review, it is obvious that the speed and scale of online diffusion of fake news is on the rise and disturbing cause for concern. The public's vulnerability to false information has grown as a result of the increasing reliance on new media as a source of news, with its minimal gatekeeping and other quality assurance features. The good news, however, is that we have come to know more about the varied factors that facilitate its cultivation and spread, as studies have been widely conducted in many contexts. Some of these factors, according to the literature, include individuals' cognitive abilities (Hambrick & Marquardt, 2018). Cognitive abilities are brain-based skills we need to carry out any task from the simplest to the most complex. They have more to do with the mechanisms of how we learn, remember, problem-solve and pay attention (Michelon, 2006). People with low cognitive abilities have a hard time learning and managing information. They also may have a challenge rejecting misinformation; studies in the literature have shown. These persons may be susceptible to the influences of falsehood even after they are exposed to a proof that the information was false. From the literature, non-digital natives, mainly majority of the adult population are vulnerable to online misinformation. Such people are not particularly new media literate and are prey to the increasing digitisation of news (Lee, 2018). They are susceptible to fake news and fall victim to scams, phishing and other risks faced on digital platforms. Low media literacy is also discussed as another source of vulnerability to fake news. Aufderheide (1993) defines media literacy is an individual's ability to access, analyse and evaluate media. This is evident in people's misrepresentation of what is legitimate news. Flanagin and Metzger (2007) explained that visitors who are unfamiliar with a website's brand may use the sophistication of the website as a mental heuristic to judge its credibility. Fake news outlets create websites that closely mimics legacy news agencies with the aim of securing transfer of legitimacy for validation when an unsuspecting reader is exposed to their platform.

Methodology

This study assessed demographic characteristics and susceptibility to fake news in Ghana. It specifically investigated the demographic characteristics of people vulnerable to fake news and the demographic differences in susceptibility. A quantitative design, using survey instrument of structured questionnaire was adopted and physically distributed to a sample size of 468 respondents in

Accra, Ghana. Convenient sampling was adopted in collecting data for the study. This sampling strategy was used because the accessible population could not be easily estimated, nor could they be accessed in specific locations. A pilot study was conducted with the questionnaires to establish its reliability and also to detect defective items on the questionnaire that might pose challenges for respondents. Twenty respondents from Madina in the La Nkwantanang Municipal Assembly were sampled for this purpose. After the test, some items on the questionnaire were modified and others removed as they elicited repetitive responses. In ethical consideration, consent of respondents was sought prior to their participation in this study. This was by implied consent. According to Berg (2007) implied consent is indicated by the respondent taking the time to complete lengthy questionnaire. In this circumstance, explanations of the study's purpose and potential risks and benefits were explained fully to the respondents before they participated in the study. The respondents were not asked to provide their names and other forms of specific identification on the questionnaires.

Data analysis was performed using descriptive (percentage) analysis, t-test (one-sample and independent) analysis, chi-square test and analysis of variance (ANOVA). The study's sample size of 468 constituted 60.30% male and 39.70% female. Majority of the respondents were between the ages of 19–29 and 30–39. The educational background of the respondents was ascertained to determine their level of knowledge especially with issues concerning the identification of fake news. In this direction the majority of the respondents were diploma and degree holders with their respective percentages being 56.60% and 32.90%. As noted in the literature review, media literacy is one of the key determinants of fake news susceptibility, therefore it was necessary to gather data concerning the frequency at which the participants listened or read the news. The outcome revealed that only a few of the respondents hardly listened to or read the news, with the majority, 87.2% of the respondent stating that they regularly listened to or read the news.

To assess the level of respondents' exposure to fake news, the research employed percentage analysis and one-sample t-test. It was however pertinent that the exposure to fake news be viewed from two perspectives, that is the traditional media and the new media channels, since findings in extant literature have shown increasing use of online sources for news gathering thereby increasing the propensity of fake news in the traditional media channels. In relation to the traditional media, it was found that majority (52.60%) of the respondents indicated they sometimes came across fake news on traditional news media channels, some (29.50%) indicated they very often see fake news and few (16.20%) hardly come across fake news on traditional news media channels. The findings indicate that a significant number of Ghanaians (82.10%) are exposed to news stories on traditional media channels such as TV, radio and newspapers that they perceived as completely made up or fake.

Findings

Findings on exposure to fake news on new media channels such as social media platforms and news websites revealed that more than half (61.80%) of the participants very often come across fake news, 28.20% of the respondents sometimes see fake news and few (2.10%) hardly come across fake news. From the percentage analyses, it can be concluded that majority of Ghanaians come across fake news on both traditional and new media channels. The statistical result of the one-sample t-test analysis is shown below.

Table 15.1 attest to the level of significance of the exposure to fake news among Ghanaians on both the traditional and new media channels. It can be realised from the table that exposure to fake news on traditional news media channel [$t(459) = 10.55, M = 2.37, S.D = 0.75, p < 0.00$] and exposure to fake news on new media channels [t $(430) = 11.76, M = 2.28, S.D = 0.50, p < 0.00$] were statistically significant at 0.1 (0.001%) level of significance.

Findings in relation to Ghanaians' exposure to fake news in both traditional and new media show that exposure to fake news is higher in new media environments. This affirms earlier findings of Bajo (2019), which reported a growing trend of fake news in Africa. As Bajo noted, the surge in fake news stems from the increasing adoption of mobile phones, easy access to the internet, the youthfulness of the continent and the frequency with which political actors are trying to instrumentalise existing categorical differences like ethnicity and religion. This surge in fake news may lead to misinformation and may thus become a threat to evidence-based decision making and traditional journalism.

Furthermore, the studies of Pennycook and Rand (2018) and Lazer et al. (2018) reported that new media in particular contains high doses of fake news. Indeed, some researchers (Allcott & Gentzkow, 2017; Nielsen & Graves, 2017) have cited the proliferation of new media and internet technologies as the most influential factors that have propelled the nascent surge in fake news. Allcott and Gentzkow (2017) are of the view that the increasing adoption of social media is perhaps the most obvious reason for the recent proliferation of fake news. Nielsen and Graves (2017) also argue that new social technologies, notably Twitter, Facebook and photo-sharing apps, facilitate rapid information-sharing and large-scale information cascading that can also spread information that is inaccurate or misleading.

Table 15.1 One-sample t-test analysis of fake news exposure among Ghanaians

Fake news exposure channels	N	Mean (M)	S.D	t	df	p-value
Exposure to fake news in traditional news channels	460	2.37	0.75	10.55	459	0.00
Exposure to fake news in new media channels	431	2.28	0.50	11.76	430	0.00

NB: t-value = 2; ***significant at 0.1% (0.001); maximum = 3, minimum = 1

However, the present research revealed that fake news is present in traditional media too. More than half (52.6%) of the respondents indicated that they are sometimes exposed to fake news in the traditional media like radio and television. Whilst this confirms the assertion that fake news is not only found on new media, it is worrisome to learn that even established news organisations are unable to filter mis/disinformation masquerading as news. This finding is not however entirely surprising because of the fusion of new media sources to the traditional newsroom practices. The study of Nelson and Park (2015) confirms this assertion by stating that 'we are in an age where almost half of all news that consumers receive and share is from online sources, hence false information can reach large audiences by spreading rapidly'. Some journalists and media organisations may be influenced by fake stories in the news ecosystem because they rely on new media ecologies including social media for leads which they use for news meant for traditional news platforms. In addition, some of Ghana's less endowed traditional media outlets do not have sufficient capacity to independently verify the authenticity of their news articles before communicating it to their audience, hence the propensity to broadcast fake news.

It was of essence to probe further in assessing the demography of people who are vulnerable to fake news. This was achieved using cross-tabulation and chi-square analysis. Statistically, it can be said that although exposure to fake news on new media channels such as social media did not differ significantly across demographic groups, exposure to fake news on traditional news media channels differs significantly across different demographic groups, specifically by gender and age. This implies that there is significant association between exposure to fake news and people's gender and age groups.

These findings confirm the study of Krasnova, Veltri, Eling, and Buxmann (2017) as they reported that some are more vulnerable than others based on their demographic characteristics. Krasnova, Veltri, Eling, and Buxmann (2017) argued further that the probability of sharing fake news online is higher in males than females, despite the fact that women use social media more than men. Again, the impact of age on exposure to fake news as reported in this study is in agreement with McGrew, Breakstone, Ortega, Smith, and Wineburg (2018). McGrew et al. (2018) opined that exposure to fake news, particularly those of a political nature increase with age, despite the fact that young people are the majority of internet users. Another reason for the significant influence of age is because people tend to show an increasing interest in news as they get older. For younger users, topics like domestic politics, international politics and economy are seen as less interesting (Costera, 2007), which might explain why older people are more likely to share political fake news online.

In relation to educational background and exposure to fake news, the findings indicate that respondents with degrees very often detect fake news on new media channels compared to other categories of educational level. The rising popularity of social media platforms in terms of news consumption facilitates the dissemination of large volumes of non-supervised content (Jeong, Cho, &

Hwang, 2012). It empowers the misinformation phenomenon and thus provokes the possibility to manipulate the public's perception of reality through the viral spread of fake news. Shu, Sliva, Wang, Tang, and Liu (2017) also agree to this point and added that people with high exposure to social media have a high exposure to fake news, and hence have a high chance of accepting some of the false stories. Further, media audiences may be vulnerable to fake news owing to their ideology and confirmation bias. This is significant because ideology and cognitive bias can cloud people's judgement regardless of educational background. Besides, as Lewandowsky et al. (2012) explain, there is usually a level of emotional intensity attached to fake news and this makes such information spread more easily among people of the same ideological group, providing yet another direct evidence of the strength of confirmation bias.

In probing further to determine the reasons for demographic differences in vulnerability to fake news three reasons were found: ability to detect fake news, difficulty in determining credibility of news and checking with fact-check organisations. It is pertinent to note that fake news exposure does not differ by educational level; hence, reasons for vulnerability of groups of fake news focused on gender and age groups. In other to determine this statistically, independent t-test and ANOVA was employed.

Table 15.2 shows the independent t-test on the reasons for gender vulnerabilities to fake news. From the results, with a maximum value of 3 and minimum of 1, females reported a mean score of 2.34 with a standard deviation of 0.88 compared to the mean value of 1.91 and standard deviation of 0.97 for males on ability to detect fake news. This implies that females are more able to detect fake news compared to their male counterparts. This result is statistically significant at 0.1% level of significance. Thus, males are more vulnerable to fake news than females when it comes to the ability to detect fake news. Similarly, with respect to difficulty in determining credibility and reliability of news, the results revealed that males with a mean score of 2.33 compared to the females of 2.08, find it more difficult to determine the credibility and reliability of doubtful news stories, and hence are more vulnerable to fake news. This difference is statistically significant at 0.1% level of significance. Finally, females (M =

Table 15.2 Independent t-test analysis of reasons for fake news vulnerability by gender

Reasons for fake news vulnerability	Gender	N	Mean	S.D	t	p
Ability to detect fake news	Female	172	2.34	0.88	4.78	0.00
	Male	278	1.91	0.97		
Difficulty in determining credibility of news	Female	168	2.08	0.60	-4.43	0.00
	Male	279	2.33	0.56		
Checking with fact-check organisations	Female	170	2.39	0.55	5.28	0.00
	Male	275	2.091	0.62		

Source: Field survey (2019)

NB: Maximum = 3, minimum = 1, ***significant at 0.1%

2.39; S.D = 0.55) are more likely to check doubtful news with fact-check organisations compared to their male counter parts (M = 2.091, S.D = 0.62).

This implies generally that males are more vulnerable to fake news due to their inability to detect fake news, difficulty in establishing credibility and reliability of doubtful news, as well as less interest in checking doubtful news with fact-check organisations.

Table 15.3 depicts that the ability to detect fake news ($F = 1.20$, $p > 0.05$) is not a major reason why some age groups are vulnerable to fake news. However, the results revealed that the major reasons why some age groups are vulnerable to fake news are: difficulty in determining the credibility and reliability of doubtful news ($F = 2.71$, $p < 0.05$), and low interest in checking doubtful news with fact-check organisations ($F = 2.76$, $p < 0.05$) as these are statistically significant at 5% level of significance. Furthermore, people who are in the age bracket of 60+ years ($M = 2.75$, S.D = 0.50) and followed by those in the age group of 40–49 years ($M = 2.34$, S.D = 0.65) tend to find it most difficult to determine credibility and reliability of doubtful news as well as check with fact-check organisations compared to other age groups.

Finally, the study found that in terms of gender, females claim they are better able to detect fake news compared to their male counterparts. Females are also more likely to check doubtful news with fact-check organisations compared to their male counterparts. In terms of age, the ability to detect fake news is not a major reason why some age groups are vulnerable to fake news. However, the results revealed that some age groups (40–49 years; 60 and above) are vulnerable to fake news because of their difficulty in determining the credibility and reliability of doubtful news and low interest in checking doubtful news with fact-check organisations. Altogether, it was realised that personal difficulty in determining the credibility and reliability of doubtful

Table 15.3 ANOVA of reasons for fake news vulnerability by age groups

Reasons for fake news vulnerability	Age	N	Mean	S.D	F	p
Ability to detect fake news	19–29	242	2.15	0.95	1.20	0.31
	30–39	116	2.04	0.97		
	40–49	64	1.94	0.97		
	50–59	27	1.93	1.00		
	60+	4	1.50	1.00		
Difficulty in determining credibility of news	19–29	242	2.17	0.57	2.71	0.03
	30–39	114	2.32	0.58		
	40–49	63	2.35	0.65		
	50–59	26	2.19	0.57		
	60+	4	2.75	0.50		
Checking with fact-check organisations	19–29	241	2.24	0.61	2.76	0.03
	30–39	115	2.08	0.59		
	40–49	62	2.31	0.62		
	50–59	27	2.15	0.66		
	60+	4	2.75	0.50		

news and low interest in checking doubtful news with fact-check organisations are the main reasons that account for demographic differences in vulnerability to fake news. In lieu of this, the findings of the study support the position of Lee (2018) that vulnerability to fake news may stem from low media literacy, in this case, respondents' ability to evaluate news articles to spot what is fake from what is not. 'Media literacy is an individual's ability to access, analyze, and evaluate media' (Aufderheide, 1993). Non-digital natives are more vulnerable when it comes to online misinformation. They are prone to fake news and fall victim to scams, phishing and other perils on digital platforms.

In contrast with the findings of Bajo (2019) which indicated that that young people in Europe and America are more digitally savvy, have more trust in news and keep up more with current events hence are far better able to avoid fake news. This study reveals, however, that the female respondents appear to be more curious and hence search for confirmation of doubtful news on social media unlike their male counterparts who perhaps overestimate their competency in determining factual from fake news. This is possible given the cultural circumstances and the prevalence of male chauvinism in Ghana.

Conclusion and Recommendations

Findings in this study show that Ghanaians are exposed to fake news in both traditional and new media platforms. However, exposure to fake news is higher in new media environments like social media. This outcome of the study confirms earlier studies that there is a growing trend of fake news in Africa, as observed in other studies, both academic and journalistic, as evident by the Cambridge Analytica scandal in Nigeria, Kenya and other parts of the continent. It is noted that the high exposure of fake news, especially on traditional news platforms, is dangerous to democracy and the wellbeing of the people, hence a barrier to the attainment of the SDG16. The feasibility of SDG16 in Ghana, it is argued in the study, could be undermined by the upsurge of fake news, as evidenced in studies in Ghana. These studies have shown that the increasing circulation of fake news in the media landscape have resulted in the manipulation of public thinking and become a tool for conspiracy with the intent to spread hatred and incite inexcusable violence. Case studies of electoral violence in some parts of the country, Effutu constituency of the central region and some of northern Ghana for example, are noted to be as a result of fake news. The situation ostensibly subverts the peace enjoyed by the people and hinders the achievement of the SDG16.

Fake news has also become an affront to journalism, hence the need for a call to institutions that oversee the journalism standards, such as Ghana Journalist Association (GJA), to initiate campaigns to raise awareness among journalists and the people of the impact of fake news on the institutions and the people. The campaign must also include capacity building of institutions and the people on how to deal with fake news. There must also be the sponsoring of fact-check organisation, and independent or private media organisations must also be encouraged to establish fact-check desks, and strengthen their fact-checking protocols to ensure the reduction of fake news. This fact-checking protocols could be hosted on social media platforms as part of media literacy campaign aimed at the citizens to develop their capacity in dealing with fake news. Future studies using experimental design is encouraged to determine how people deal with fake news in order to adapt the behavioural perspectives to the capacity building.

The findings also note that there are demographic differences in exposure to fake news, especially amongst people in the age bracket of 40–49 (56.90%), who come across fake news more than others, whiles age 19–29 (19.40%) hardly come across fake news in comparison. The findings of the older age bracket being exposed and are likely to share fake news are in line with McGrew et al. (2018) and Aufderheide (1993) studies that show that fake news, especially of political nature, increases with age and among non-digital natives. Hence, despite the fact that young people are the majority of internet users they are mostly unattracted to political content. On education the chi-square test revealed that differences in education is not statistically significant, which affirms earlier studies (Jeong et al., 2012) that regardless of educational level, individuals are exposed to and are likely to be purveyors of fake news due to the rising popularity of social media and its continuous relevance in the lives of media users regardless of educational background. Additionally, other factors such as low media literacy (Lee, 2018), difficulty in determining credibility and reliability of sources of doubtful news and low interest in authenticating doubtful news account for vulnerabilities to fake news. Similar findings were noted by Bajo (2019) that young people in Europe and America were found to be generally digitally savvy and are able to detect fake news and take action against its spread. The departure of this study from Bajo's is that the female samples of the study appear to be more curious and hence search for confirmation of doubtful news on social media than their male counterparts.

REFERENCES

Ali, M. N., Emrizal, R., Razman, M. R., Ramli, Z., & Arifin, K. (2017). Understanding Aggressive Behaviour to Avoid Damages Through the Precautionary Principle Towards the Sustainable Development Goals (SDGs). *Journal of Food, Agriculture & Environment, 15*(1), 52–55.

Allcott, H., & Gentzkow, M. (2017). Social Media and Fake News in the 2016 Election. *Journal of Economic Perspectives, 31*(2), 211–236.

Aufderheide, P. (1993). *Media Literacy: A Report of the National Leadership Conference on Media Literacy.* Aspen, CO: Aspen Institute.

Bajo, C. (2019). Fake News and Censorship in Africa. CCCBLAB. Retrieved May 7, 2019, from http://lab.cccb.org/en/fake-news-and-censorship-in-africa/

Baym, G. (2005). The Daily Show: Discursive Integration and the Reinvention of Political Journalism. *Political Communication, 22*(3), 259–276.

Berg, B. (2007). An Introduction to Content Analysis. In: Berg, B.L., Ed., *Qualitative Research Methods for the Social Sciences,* Allyn and Bacon, Boston, 238–267.

Berkowitz, D., & Schwartz, A. (2016). Miley, CNN and the Onion. *Journalism Practice*, *10*(1), 1–17.

Brady, W. J., Wills, J. A., Josr, J. T., Tucker, J. A., & Van Bavel, J. J. (2017). Emotion Shapes the Diffusion of Moralized Content in Social Networks. *PNAS*, *114*(28), 7313–7318.

Brewer, P. R., Young, D. G., & Morreale, M. (2013). The Impact of Real News about "Fake News": Inter-textual Processes and Political Satire. *International Journal of Public Opinion Research*, *25*(3), 323–343.

Chen, Y. N., Conroy, N. J., & Rubin, V. L. (2015). *Misleading Online Content: Recognizing Clickbait as 'False News'*. Proceedings of the 2015 ACM on Workshop on Multimodal Deception Detection. Seattle, WA: ACM

Costera, I. (2007). The Paradox of Popularity. How Young People Experience the News. *Journalism Studies*, *8*(1), 96–116.

Del Vicario, M., Quattrociocchi, W. A., & Zollo, F. (2018). Polarization and Fake News: Early Warning of Potential Misinformation Targets. *ArXiv New Media*, *1*(1), 1–17.

Flanagin, J., & Metzger, J. (2007). The Role of Site Features, User Attributes, and Information Verification Behaviors on the Perceived Credibility of Web-based Information. *New Media & Society*, *9*(2), 319–342.

Fletcher, R., Cornia, A., Graves, L., & Nielsen, R. K. (2018). Measuring the Reach of "Fake News" and Online Disinformation in Europe. *Factsheets Reuters Institute* https://reutersinstitute.politics.ox.ac.uk/sites/default/files/2018-02/Measuring%20the%20reach%20of%20fake%20news%20and%20online%20distribution%20in%20Europe%20CORRECT%20FLAG.pdf [accessed 26/05/2021]

Flynn, D. J., Nyhan, B., & Reifler, J. (2017). The Nature and Origins of Misperceptions: Understanding False and Unsupported Beliefs about Politics. *Political Psychology*, *38*, 127–150.

Gentzkow, M., Shapiro, J., & Taddy, M. (2016). *Measuring Polarization in High-Dimensional Data: Method and Application to Congressional Speech* (No. Id: 11114).

Gyamera, B. A. R. B. A. R. A. (2018). *Electoral Violence and Democracy in Africa: The Case of Ghana (1992–2012)*. Doctoral dissertation, University of Ghana.

Hambrick, D. Z. & Marquardt, M. (2018). Cognitive Ability and Vulnerability to Fake News. *Scientific American*. Retrieved May 8, 2019, from https://www.scientificamerican.com/article/cognitive-ability-and-vulnerability-to-fake-news/

Hunt, A., & Gentzkow, M. (2017). Social Media and Fake News in the 2016 Election. *Journal of Economic Perspectives*, *31*(2), 211–236.

Ireton, C., & Posetti, J. (2018). *Journalism, Fake News and Disinformation*. Paris: United Nations Educational, Scientific and Cultural Organization.

Jacobson, T. L. (2016). Amartya Sen's Capabilities Approach and Communication for Development and Social Change. *Journal of Communication*, *66*(5), 789–810.

Jeffrey, G., & Shearer, E. (2016). *News Use Across Social Media Platforms 2016*. Washington: Pew Research Center.

Jeong, S., Cho, H., & Hwang, Y. (2012). Media Literacy Interventions: A Meta-Analytic Review. *Journal of Communication*, *62*, 454–472.

Kalsnes, B. (2018). Fake News. *Oxford Research Encyclopedia of Communication*, pp. 1–22.

Kamerer, D. (2013). Media Literacy. *Communication Research Trends*, *32*, 4–25.

Kempe Ronald Hope Sr. (2019). Peace, justice and inclusive institutions: overcoming challenges to the implementation of Sustainable Development Goal 16, Global

Change, Peace & Security, 32:1, 57–77, https://doi.org/10.1080/1478115 8.2019.1667320

Khairil, M., Emrizal, R., Rizal, M., Ramli, Z., & Arifin, K. (2017). Understanding Terrorism Based on Radicalism Idea in Order to Avoid Instability for Achieving Environmental Peace and Justice the Sustainable Development Goals. *Journal of Food, Agriculture & Environment, 15*(1), 48–51.

Kohut, A., Morin, R., & Keeter, S. (2007, April 15). What Americans Know: 1989–2007, Public Knowledge of Current Affairs Little Changed by News and Information Revolutions. *PEW Research Center*.

Krasnova, H., Veltri, N. F., Eling, N., & Buxmann, P. (2017). Why Men and Women Continue to Use Social Networking Sites: The Role of Gender Differences. *The Journal of Strategic Information Systems, 26*(4), 261–284.

Kuenzi, M., & Lambright, G. (2015). Campaign Appeals in Nigeria's 2007 Gubernatorial Elections. *Democratization, 22*(1), 134–156.

Lazer, D. M., Baum, M. A., Benkler, Y., Berinsky, A. J., Greenhill, K. M., Menczer, F., et al. (2018). The Science of Fake News. *Science, 359*(6380), 1094–1096.

Lee, N. M. (2018). Fake News, Phishing, and Fraud: A Call for Research on Digital Media Literacy Education Beyond the Classroom. *Communication Education, 67*(4), 460–466.

Lewandowsky, S., Ecker, U. K. H., Seifert, C. M., Schwarz, N., & Cook, J. (2012). Misinformation and Its Correction: Continued Influence and Successful Debiasing. *Psychological Science in the Public Interest, 13*, 106–131.

McGrew, S., Breakstone, J., Ortega, T., Smith, M., & Wineburg, S. (2018). Can Students Evaluate Online Sources? Learning from Assessments of Civic Online Reasoning. *Theory & Research in Social Education, 46*(2), 165–193.

Michelon, P. (2006). What Are Cognitive Abilities and Skills and How to Boost Them. *Sharp Brains*. Retrieved May 9, 2019, from https://sharpbrains.com/blog/2006/12/18/what-are-cognitive-abilities/

Moraga-González, J. & Vaiva, P. (2013). Search Costs, Demand-Side Economies and the Incentives to Merge under Bertrand Competition. *CEPR Discussion Papers* 9374.

Morris, J. S. (2009). The Daily Show with Jon Stewart and Audience Attitude Change During the 2004 Party Conventions. *Political Behavior, 31*(1), 79–102.

Nelson, J. L., & Taneja, H. (2018). The small, Disloyal Fake News Audience: The Role of Audience Availability in Fake News Consumption. *New Media & Society, 20*(10), 3720–3737.

Nelson, M. R., & Park, J. (2015). Publicity as Covert Marketing? The Role of Persuasion Knowledge and Ethical Perceptions on Beliefs and Credibility in a Video News Release Story. *Journal of Business Ethics, 130*(2), 327–341.

Newman, N., Fletcher, R., Kalogeropoulos, A., Levy, D. A. L., & Nielsen, R. K. (2017). *Reuters Institute Digital News Report 2017*. Oxford: Reuters Institute for the Study of Journalism.

Nielsen, R. K., & Graves, L. (2017). *News You Don't Believe: Audience Perspectives on Fake News*. Oxford: Reuters Institute for the Study of Journalism.

Ordway, D. (2017). *Fake News and the Spread of Misinformation*. Cambridge: Kennedy School on Media, Politics and Public Policy.

Palma, B. (2017). Did Target's Stock 'Crash' Due to Its Transgender Bathroom Policy? Retrieved May 7, 2019, from https://www.researchgate.net/deref/http%3A%2F%2Fwww.snopes.com%2Ftargets-stock-transgender-bathroom-policy%2F

Patel, F. (2020). Glocal Development for Sustainable Social Change. In *Handbook of Communication for Development and Social Change* (pp. 501–517). Springer, Singapore.

Pennycook, G., & Rand, D. G. (2018). Lazy, Not Biased: Susceptibility to Partisan Fake News Is Better Explained by Lack of Reasoning Than by Motivated Reasoning. *Cognition*, 6(11), 1–20.

Penplusbytes (2018). *Media perspectives on fake news in Ghana*, May 2, 2018, https://penplusbytes.org/wp-content/uploads/2018/05/FAKE-NEWS-STUDY.pdf [accessed 26/05/2021]

Popken, B. (2019). Age, Not Politics, Is Biggest Predictor of Who Shares Fake News on Facebook, Study Finds. *NBC News*. Retrieved May 7, 2019, from https://www.nbcnews.com/tech/tech-news/age-not-politics-predicts-who-shares-fake-news-facebook-study-n957246

Reuters. (2017). *A Brief Guide to Standards, Photoshop and Captions. Handbook of Journalism*. Toronto: Reuters News Agency.

Servaes J (Ed.). (2007). *Communication for Development. Making a Difference—A WCCD Background Study*. World Congress on Communication for Development: Lessons, Challenges and the Way Forward.

Servaes, J. (2020). Terms and Definitions in Communication for Development and Social Change. In *Handbook of Communication for Development and Social Change* (pp. 3–13). Springer, Singapore.

Shu, K., Sliva, A., Wang, S., Tang, J., & Liu, H. (2017). Fake News Detection on Social Media: A Data Mining Perspective. *ACM SIGKDD Explorations Newsletter*, 19(1), 22–36.

Tambini, D. (2017). *Fake News: Public Policy Responses. Media Policy Brief 20*. London: Media Policy Project, London School of Economics and Political Science.

Tandoc Jr., E. C., Lim, Z. W., & Ling, R. (2018). Defining "Fake News": A Typology of Scholarly Definitions. *Digital Journalism*, 6(2), 137–153.

Thomas, P. N. (2020). Communication for Social Change, Making Theory Count. *Nordicom Review*, 36(s1), 71–78.

United Nations (2013). *Global Sustainable Development Report – Executive Summary: Building the Common Future We Want*. New York: United Nations Department of Economic and Social Affairs, Division for Sustainable Development. 2013, http://sustainabledevelopment.un.org/globalsdreport/ [accessed 26/05/2021]

Vos, T. P., Craft, S., & Ashley, S. (2012). New Media, Old Criticism: Bloggers' Press Criticism and the Journalistic Field. *Journalism: Theory, Practice & Criticism*, 13(7), 850–868.

Vosoughi, S., Roy, D., & Aral, S. (2018). The spread of true and false news online. *Science*, 359(6380), 1146–1151.

Xenos, M. A., & Becker, A. B. (2009). Moments of Zen: Effects of the Daily Show on Information Seeking and Political Learning. *Political Communication*, 26(3), 317–332.

Zhang, C., Gupta, A., Kauten, C., Deokar, A. V., & Qin, X. (2019). Detecting fake news for reducing misinformation risks using analytics approaches. *European Journal of Operational Research 279*, 1036–1052.

Zubiaga, A., & Ji, H. (2014). Tweet, But Verify: Epistemic Study of Information Verification on Twitter. *Social Network Analysis and Mining*, 4(1), 1–12.

CHAPTER 16

Communication for Sustainable Social Change and the Pursuit of Zero Hunger: The Food Sovereignty Language Frame

Joshua J. Frye and Samantha Stone

INTRODUCTION

In the past several decades, the proliferation of alternative food movement discourse around the world has introduced new language frames such as 'organic food', 'slow food', 'locavorism', 'fair trade' and 'food sovereignty'. How these different language frames get articulated, contested and transformed in preparation for and during the course of policy deliberation, development and implementation yield significant insights into how rhetoric reflects policy and programme tensions and can influence outcomes within the global food system. There are important, but understudied, relationships between framing processes, policy positions and outcomes (Snow & Benford, 1992; Tarrow, 1994).

This chapter examines a particular language frame associated with a powerful global food movement—food sovereignty. The language frame of food sovereignty has recently become dominant discourse in several international food policy arenas.[1] The goal of this research is to compare and contrast the

[1] The creation of dominant discourse is a rhetorical influence process in society. For a more extensive discussion of the process and a contemporary example of this influence process at work with 'food waste' see Frye and Fox (2015).

J. J. Frye (✉) • S. Stone
Humboldt State University, Arcata, CA, USA
e-mail: Joshua.Frye@humboldt.edu

language framing of food sovereignty by grassroots food movement leaders in Ecuador (the first state to legislate food sovereignty) with the rhetorically dynamic framing of food sovereignty during the 2014 annual plenary session of the Committee on World Food Security (CFS) at the Food and Agriculture Organization (FAO) in Rome.

In particular, this chapter argues that the language frame of food security, as reflected by the UN's Sustainable Development Goal 2 of the 2030 Agenda and represented officially by UN committees such as CFS, conflicts in important ways with the language frame of food sovereignty as adopted by UN member states such as Ecuador, Bolivia and Venezuela, and advocated by the Civil Society Mechanism (CSM) within the CFS. The chapter helps to bridge a gap between disparate scholarly literatures such as environmental communication and Communication for Sustainable Social Change. It also utilizes a novel participatory action research approach to enhance understanding of the food sovereignty movement and provides conclusions that can be applied to improve international policymaking for the twenty-first-century global food system.

The chapter begins with a brief review of ideology and language framing, SDGs and food system discourse. Next, the chapter explains the methodology employed by this study. Then a qualitative, rhetorical analysis of field data is provided. Finally, the chapter offers conclusions relevant to global food policymaking and international communication for sustainable development. The significance of this analysis is its ability to illuminate how global policy convergence can encode a specific language frame which subsequently constrains the ability of advocates to legitimize arguments pertaining to disadvantages within the existing policy framework as well as potential advantages to alternative practices.

Language Framing, Food Systems and SDG 2: Zero Hunger

A frame is a composite of ideas and practices that are strategically articulated through language to identify a problem, propose a solution and motivate others to act (Bateson, 1972; Goffman, 1974; Snow, Rochford Jr., Worden, & Benford, 1986). According to Benford and Snow (2000), frame analysis is a dynamic and growing area of research. According to Fairclough (1989), ideology is the most effective when it is the least visible. This happens through language frames because ideological elements are brought to discourse as background assumptions, rather than explicit textual elements. These background assumptions, along with group knowledge, opinions and attitudes (van Djik, 2008), function to lead a text-producer to 'textualize' the world in a particular way as well as interpret that text in certain ways, thereby reproducing an ideology.

Examination of these language frames along with potential disputes reveals stakeholder perceptions, values, tensions and power dynamics as well as future policy possibilities and constraints. These language frames are a key part of the human, communicative and social element involved in forming dominant discourses and the dialectical power struggles between social movements and establishment forces (Morris, 2000). These language frames are important elements to critically examine during the unfolding of a particular discourse's usage, especially if the discourse has probable potency to influence policy and programmes, which food sovereignty clearly does. Locating frame disputes[2] is critical to advancing meaningful dialogue and policy discussions because they function as surrogates to perceptions, values and policy formation. They can occur between different articulations of the same ideology (e.g. two competing articulations of food sovereignty) or between speakers advocating for different things represented by different language frames (e.g. food sovereignty vs. food security).

Since the 1970s, multiple competing ideologies have disputed the language frames within the global food system at an accelerating pace. For example, the United Nations FAO has legitimized the food security language frame through the creation of the CFS in 1974. The CFS was set up as an intergovernmental committee to serve as a deliberative body for review and follow up of food security policies. CFS defines food security as the condition 'when all people, at all times, have physical, social and economic access to sufficient, safe, and nutritious food that meets their dietary needs and food preferences for an active and healthy life' (CFS Brochure, 2013). In turn, the food security language frame grew out of a policy-based approach to alleviating hunger or 'food insecurity'. Many government agencies such as the Committee on World Food Security, the World Food Program and the United States Department of Agriculture have focused their policymaking efforts on food security for decades (Bublitz, Hansen, Peracchio, & Tussler, 2019). The language frame was really popularized in the 1990s by policymakers who endeavoured to develop a standardized way to define hunger and measure hard to access populations (Anderson, 1990; Wunderlich & Norwood, 2006). In the ensuing decades, the United Nations advanced an agenda and framework for global wellbeing. During the first decade of the twenty-first century, this agenda and framework took form as the Millennium Development Goals (MDGs) and were intended to help individual nation states collaborate on long-term strategies for global sustainable development, including poverty, hunger and disease reduction, sustained economic growth, increased gender equality and environmental protections. In 2015 the MDGs were succeeded by Sustainable Development Goals (SDGs) and were intended to increase holistic approaches and reduce compartmentalization of technical and policy work by

---

[2] A frame dispute is the deliberate contestation of a particular linguistic encoding. Frame disputes usually reflect divergent perceptions, values, attitudes and action plans pertaining to a complex social issue. Frame disputes are pervasive in the social construction of meaning and the negotiation of differing conceptualizations between social agents involved in collective action. For further reading on frame disputes see Benford and Snow (2000) and Frye (2009).

acknowledging the interconnected nature of economic, environmental and social challenges facing the world (Servaes, 2016). Among these SDGs is *SDG 2: Zero Hunger*, the complete eradication of hunger on the planet by 2030.

The scope of global food policymaking deliberations has expanded over the past few decades with regard to who constitutes a legitimate voice, who can be involved in what ways, with global food policy discussions. Scope can be an important indicator for what type of symbolic action will or can occur within a given discourse space (Burke, 1945). In 2003 the CFS organized a parallel session for civil society, non-governmental organizations and some government representatives to compliment official policy deliberations by national delegations of UN member states. The motivation was to provide a focus on the issues, approaches and assumptions the food sovereignty ideological frame had created opportunities to explore. Then in 2009 a major reform took place with a vision to have CFS be 'the most inclusive international and intergovernmental platform for all stakeholders to work together' (CFS Brochure, 2013). This means however that radically different ideological value positions have access to deliberate and advocate in this forum including, for instance, representatives from developed and developing countries, Friends of the Earth and Monsanto.

The criterion of inclusivity for the CFS reform in 2009 also suggests the need to counter the tendency to privilege certain voices with the legitimacy to 'speak' during official sessions. The CFS is hosted by FAO, and FAO with other Rome-based agencies makes up the Secretariat. Like any other organization, it will tend to legitimize certain voices and marginalize others (Heath, 2011). According to Brem-Wilson, this dynamic can be seen within the global food policy arena as multi and transnational corporations are actively involved in strategies to augment their 'discursive power' (Brem-Wilson, 2018). Zanella, Goetz, Rist, Schmidt, and Weigelt (2018) call for academic work that includes analysis of differing forms of power that are a part of the social relations in such multi-stakeholder deliberative forums. As a result of the 2009 reform, in part spearheaded by *La Vía Campesína* (Gaarde, 2017), civil society voices have been included as an integral stakeholder to discourse development, policy advice and programme guidelines. And in 2014 an extensive coalition of NGOs, civil society participants, indigenous groups, food sovereignty networks, fisherfolk and agroecology advocates issued a formal statement to the UN claiming their entitlement to not only be invited to the deliberations but to be perceived as definitive stakeholders with the right to determine where agricultural investments go, how they are made and who will benefit:

> Ensuring that investment in agriculture is done responsibly is vital for indigenous peoples, whose identities and cultural survival are inextricably linked to their lands and natural resources. Respecting this link is a fundamental principal in international law and jurisprudence, the recognition of which indigenous peoples have fought for and won and which reaffirms their right to determine the outcome of decision-making that affects them, rather than merely being involved in the process. ('No Compromise', 2014)

Over the past decade, voices from civil society and the private sector have gained increased access and legitimacy to this official deliberative assembly, and stakeholders from other sectors—such as academia—have been invited to observe the deliberations of the CFS. Brem-Wilson (2015) has offered a framework for considering the structural work necessary to transform formal participation into substantive participation for civil society voices within the CFS. This is an important contribution.

Many of these newly included voices have critiqued the food security language frame and as such, it has become a more visibly contested frame similar to the way the language frames of sustainable development and sustainable agriculture did several decades ago (Candel, Breeman, Stiller, & Termeer, 2014; Mooney & Hunt, 2009). Specific member nations of the CFS[3] as well as grassroots food activists and civil society organizations continue to articulate language frames that compete with the dominant frame of food security. The food sovereignty frame has become in recent years the closest competing articulation to food security for policy development in the global food system. Yet, as Higgins (2015) notes, as recently as 2015, the food sovereignty language frame was still in its embryonic stages of articulation and circulation, particularly in the US and UK.

For two decades, activists and scholars across disciplines have been engaging in symbolic interaction to forge the meaning of food sovereignty. *La Vía Campesina*, a coalition representing peasants, smallscale farmers, rural women, farm workers and indigenous peoples, first met in Tlaxcala, Mexico, in 1996 to discuss their common opposition to the neoliberal model of agriculture (Desmarais 2007; Wittman, Desmarais, & Wiebe, 2011). Also in 1996 the food sovereignty language frame was introduced at the World Food Summit in Rome. *La Vía Campesina* (loosely translated as 'the peasant way') has since pioneered an international movement to democratize the food system by building a collective identity, forging alliances with other movements and NGOs, and providing space to develop new legal frameworks around food policy at the national and international level (Desmarais 2007; Wittman et al., 2011). A major achievement for the movement includes reforming Ecuador's constitution in 2008 to include food sovereignty principles (Peña, 2013). Since Ecuador first encoded food sovereignty language into its constitution, many other states have followed. These include Venezuela, Mali, Bolivia, Nepal, Senegal and Egypt (Wittman, Desmarais, & Wiebe, 2010).

Food sovereignty seeks to provide smallscale farmers with a sustainable livelihood, ensure food security for all people, preserve indigenous and traditional epistemologies, achieve gender equality and simultaneously amend the

---

[3] The eligible members of the CFS include all member states of the FAO, the International Fund for Agricultural Development (IFAD) or the World Food Programme (WFP), and non-member states of the FAO that are member states of the United Nations. An exact membership list for CFS as of the 41st annual session can be found in Appendix B of the CFS 41 Final Report at www.fao.org/fileadmin/templates/cfs/Docs1314/CFS41/FinalReport/CFS41_Final_Report_EN.pdf. The list of all of the delegates and observers can be accessed at http://www.fao.org/3/a-ml942t.pdf.

environmental degradation induced by decades of industrial agriculture (Peña, 2013; Wittman et al., 2011) The ambitious and diversified goals pursued by *La Vía Campesina* and the larger food sovereignty movement can be characterized under what Patel refers to as 'big tent' politics, in which disparate groups can recognize their unique struggles within food sovereignty discourse. Patel notes this as a strength, although the wide array of identities seeking representation within the food sovereignty movement has also created unevenness and sometimes contradictions inside its ideological framework (Alonso-Fradejas, Borras, Holmes, Holt-Gimenéz, & Robbins, 2009; Patel, 2009). For example, several authors discuss the 'repeasantization' as the reclaiming of 'peasant' as a politicized identity (Desmarais, 2008).

Due to the social, economic and political complexities of framing and enacting food sovereignty, several scholars iterate that at the heart of food sovereignty is an examination of the social connections inherent in food production and consumption and that the active, ongoing construction of collective identity is critical in unifying the agents of food sovereignty across borders and spurring mobilization (Claeys, 2012). However, care must be taken so as to not homogenize identity as 'peasant' or silence the unique, multi-faceted and dynamic struggles of certain stakeholders within the movement. Politicizing 'peasantry' carries the challenge of resonating with so-called developed world conceptions of contemporary food systems. For instance, where would landless farm workers fit within the agenda of enacting food sovereignty as official agriculture policy? This is a primary tension that arises specifically when considering how food sovereignty might be applied to food systems of the global north, but not exclusively in the global north.

In addition to the work of re-localizing food systems, there is always challenging language framing work that emerges around activist versus governmental articulation of policy issues. Early work in this field analysed the discourse of the first Earth Summit in Rio de Janeiro, Brazil, in 1992 (Meister & Japp, 1998). The authors found that the dominant language frame emerging from this summit was 'sustainable development'. The sustainability language frame, also applied to the domain-specific sector of agriculture, yielded the sustainable agriculture frame, which became dominant discourse in the 1980s and 1990s. In the decades that ensued, frame disputes contesting sustainable agriculture language framing entered public discourse, particularly when organic agriculture became a competing language frame against the sustainable agriculture frame in the 1990s. Organic agriculture posed an ideological challenge to the sustainable agriculture frame (Frye, 2009) and itself became dominant discourse in the late 1990s and 2000s, particularly in the US. This frame dispute eventually transformed the policy arena and subsequent practices when it was encoded in the National Organic Food Production Act (NOFPA) by the USDA. Eventually, the organic frame became so culturally resonant and economically profitable (Loconto & Fouilleux, 2013) that it transcended a domain-specific frame to become a master frame[4] when it surpassed food and began being applied to beverages, health and beauty products, and even lifestyle values. Nevertheless, internationally, the sustainable development and sustainable agriculture language frames are still dominant in much conventional, mainstream discourse, as reflected in the language of SDG 2 of the 2030 Agenda: 'Goal 2: Zero Hunger. "End hunger, achieve *food security* and improved nutrition, and promote *sustainable agriculture*"' (UNDP, 2018, my italics). Yet, as has been noted, sustainable development goals and policies and truly sustainable agriculture practices enacted by family farmers, indigenous communities and peasants may not align seamlessly.

La Vía Campesina draws upon 'old' social movements by utilizing an anti-capitalist rhetoric reminiscent of capitallabour struggles, yet its 'newness' is located in the movement's demand for compensations which surpass what the current neoliberal model can provide (Claeys, 2012; Peña, 2013). Thus, food sovereignty calls for a re-articulation of rights (Claeys, 2012). In so doing, *La Vía Campesina* invokes a flexible rights master frame (Benford, 2013; Claeys, 2012; Patel, 2009; Peña, 2013) and has also been successful at bridging other frames such as 'environmental', and 'sustainability' frames which tend to permeate agrarian movements (Claeys, 2012). Through their discourse of rights, *La Vía Campesina* has provided a centrepiece for the diverse representation of the food sovereignty movement. Their collective identity seeks to bridge the struggles of the indigenous movements, peasants, women and environmentalists (Peña, 2013). Therefore, it is critical to distinguish between their slogan 'right of peoples to food sovereignty' in opposition to the 'right to food' slogan codified by various predecessors in framing conventional food policy (Claeys, 2012), because it reflects *La Vía Campesina's* ideological rejection of the dominant food security language frame.

Food sovereignty language framing recognizes that political reallocation of both resources and rights is a necessary part of achieving a state of true food justice. *La Vía Campesina* defines food sovereignty in part as a 'precondition to genuine food security' (*La Vía Campesina* 1996; Patel, 2009; Rehber, 2012). Thus, food sovereignty arises as a frame dispute to food security discourse namely because of the shortcomings of the food security frame in posing any challenge to existing neoliberal structures. As critiqued by several authors, definitions of food security tend to privilege *access to* food, rather than *control over* food origins, and perceive hunger as an issue which can be solved by advances in trade agreements, technology transfer and distributional reforms.

---

[4] For a full discussion of domain-specific frames and master frames see Benford and Snow (2000) and Benford (1993).

Method/Process

The methodology for this research was emergent, multi-method, multi-stakeholder, participatory action research (see Fig. 16.1). The design for this study was intentionally open-ended, iterative, reflexive and collaborative. As Mohan Jyoti Dutta (2018) explains, 'the concept of evaluating social change communication is plurivocalized, creating anchors for depicting social change from diverse viewpoints, particularly attending to the creation of spaces for knowledge creation from the margins'. According to Dutta (2018, 2019), this novel and unconventional approach to studying communication for social change legitimizes stories, scholars-as-activists and the interrogation of power. Purposive sampling was utilized in the identification and selection of field location and data selection. Purposive sampling (also called quota, deliberate, strategic sampling) is frequently used in exploratory, qualitative research as a technique. This technique carries certain strengths and limitations, as do all data collection techniques. Purposive sampling is a form of convenience sampling where respondents are selected non-randomly based on a particular characteristic (Frey, Botan, & Kreps, 2000; Lindlof & Taylor, 2002). Selection is based on the judgement of the researcher and their knowledge of the phenomenon and population being studied (Babbie, 1999). Purposive sampling is a form of nonprobability sampling, which limits the generalizability of results and makes statistical description and inference impossible. For qualitative research, this does not pose a problem and while admittedly is a limitation of the technique doesn't interfere with the overall quality of a study design. In fact, many qualitative studies have a sample size of $N = 1$. The particular kind of purposive sampling used in this study may be considered *theoretical construct sampling* where the in-depth interview respondents as well as CSM representatives at the CSF 41 were grassroots advocates within the food sovereignty

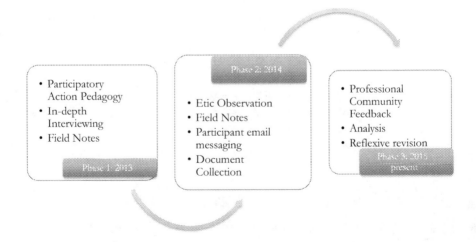

Fig. 16.1 Emergent multi-stakeholder action research process

movement. As such, they met relevant characteristics of the theoretical construct of interest.

Data collection happened in two field sites, including Ecuador and Rome. Ecuador made the precedent-setting move of legislating food sovereignty at the state-level. Interviews with key Ecuadorian community organizers influential in the move for a national food sovereignty policy platform allows for stories to emerge. The FAO in Rome is one of the key deliberative fora for global food policy convergence through the United Nation's Committee on Food Security and as such, a space for scholars to examine knowledge creation that interrogates power. Networking with Ecuadorian activists and the UN allowed this scholarship to combine axiologically with the authors' own commitment to food justice advocacy which makes the methodology for this study a form of participatory action research (Chevalier & Buckles, 2013).

Methodological design began by exploring the connections needed by imagining different pathways to rural Ecuadorians involved in the food sovereignty movement. Fortuitously, the first author discovered a non-profit environmental leadership organization (Sustainable Learning) that offered a field-based experiential education summer programme studying the global food system in Ecuador called 'Seeds of Change'. Sustainable Learning was in the process of hiring Trip Leaders for their summer programmes. The Founder of Sustainable Learning had included in the programme design a two-day workshop with a grassroots farmer-leader—Javier Carrera. Mr. Carrera was directly involved at the national level with the food sovereignty movement in Ecuador.

During the programme in Ecuador an in-depth semi-structured interview was conducted with Mr. Carrera. An additional in-depth semi-structured interview was conducted with Mr. Carrera's colleague, Mr. Roberto Gortaire. Mr. Gortaire was also at the centre of the national food sovereignty movement in Ecuador. Thus, the approach to this targeted and emergent in-depth interviewing was a *grounded form of purposive sampling*.

Phase one (Ecuador fieldwork) was conducted in the summer of 2013 during the Seeds of Change programme. We worked with leading Ecuadorian sustainable agriculture practitioners and food sovereignty advocates. Through participatory action pedagogy, we met and worked with Javier Carrera at his personal home, where students learned about permaculture design and agroecology principles and practices. Mr. Carrera was able to illustrate permaculture and agroecology in practice with our group while in the field and on site at his family home. Mr. Carrera is an agroecologist practitioner and community organizer. He is the founder of the Ecuadorian civil society organization 'Red de Semillias'—Guardians of the Seed (RdS)—which has promoted the rights of agriculturalists through their manifesto and served as an expert group for legislative and judicial actions pertaining to protecting biodiversity, non-transgenic seed and genetic resources vital to the global food system. Mr. Gortaire is engaged on many levels in the Ecuadorian food sovereignty movement. Locally, in the province of Chimborazo, he is involved in a popular social organization that is called UTOPICA. UTOPICA is dedicated to the promotion of agroecology and food sovereignty. The organization does this through the development of a commercial circuit between producers and consumers called 'Canasta Comunitaria', or the community basket. Canasta Comunitaria integrates around 150 families. Nationally, Mr. Gortaire is the National Coordinator of the Agroecological Collective of Ecuador. This collective integrates dozens of peasant farmer agroecological organizations and the food sovereignty movement in many different regions of the country. Mr. Gortaire was also the national representative of the agroecological movement and the member of COPISA (Conferencia Plurinacional e Intercultural de Soberania Alimentaria) for four years. Part of his work was the responsibility to manage a large project, which finalized in the presentation of the 'Law of Agrobiodiversity' and the fomentation of Agroecology to the National Legislative Assembly. The debate to pass national policy regarding food sovereignty, agroecology and Ecuador's food system had been active since 2012. During his time with COPISA Mr. Gortaire was also responsible for the proposal of a law for Responsible Consumption for Food Sovereignty.

Phase two (ethnographic observation of CFS at the FAO) occurred in October 2014. The Committee on Food Security held its annual plenary in Rome in October of 2014. As part of the 2009 CFS reform process, expanded participation to diverse stakeholders, included: (1) members, (2) participants and (3) observers. The first author obtained funding from the SUNY Research Foundation to conduct field-based research during the CFS 41 in Rome and secured permission to attend the annual plenary of the CFS in October 2014 in the role of an invited observer. During CFS 41 official sessions facilitated by the United Nations were attended and etic-based field notes were taken. These sessions included the ten-year retrospective on encoding national-level policy instruments to advance the UN participating countries commitment to providing food as a right to all citizens as well as dialogue and deliberation on advancing policy convergence within the global food system.

Phase three of this project has been ongoing and iterative. After fieldwork in both Ecuador and Rome, there were many data points to organize, synthesize, translate and analyse. This included the interview notes with Ecuadorian food sovereignty advocates, etic-based field notes taken during the CFS 41 in Rome, many textual artefacts from the Ecuadorian food sovereignty movement (e.g. organization websites and government documents), online messages from the CFS and Civil Society Mechanism during the CFS 41 annual plenary, handouts and publications from the CFS and Civil Society Mechanism during the conference. Preliminary analyses of phase one and phase two data were presented to various academic conference audiences in an effort to gather feedback and perspective before undertaking the holistic and integrated analysis that this chapter reflects.

Ecuadorian Food Sovereignty: In-Depth Interview Analysis

The analysis begins by examining the perceptions, values, tensions and policy preferences included in Mr. Carrera and Mr. Gortaire's ideological language framing of food sovereignty. Mr. Carrera sketched a cursory history of the introduction of the language frame of food sovereignty. The food sovereignty frame was first publicly introduced to the international community by *Via Campesína* at the 1996 World Food Summit in Rome (J. Carrera, personal communication, July 15, 2014; Claeys, 2015; Gysel, 2016; Schanbacher, 2010). In 2007 a small village in Mali held the second International Food Sovereignty Forum. This is where the Declaration of Nyéléni[5] was born to advance the work done in 1996 in Tlaxcala, Mexico and to strengthen the global food sovereignty movement. From there, Mr. Carrera went on to suggest that food sovereignty was practically synonymous with agroecology. According to Mr. Carrera, both agroecology and food sovereignty are political frames for agriculture practices and policy whereas permaculture is an apolitical frame. He did include the qualification that these perceptions may be specific to the Latin American context. Mr. Carrera then proceeded to delineate specific agroecology precepts. These included both agricultural and socio-political elements (see Table 16.1).

After delineating the precepts of agroecology Mr. Carrera responded to my question about whether codifying the food sovereignty frame was consequential. There was some inconsistency in Mr. Carrera's perception of the value of codifying food sovereignty in policy discourse. He provided somewhat

Table 16.1 Ideological precepts of agroecology according to Mr. Javier Carrera

Agricultural practices	*Social advocacy mandates*
1. Return all organic matter to the soil.	1. Break up monopolies.
2. Feed the soil, not the plant.	2. Redistribute land.
3. Create biodiversity.	3. Mandate size limits to land ownership.
4. Use crop associations.	4. Establish balance of power between economy, society and environment.
5. Rotate crops.	5. Expand the two-party system.
6. Care for insect populations.	6. Provide public education campaigns on ecological systems.
7. Grow what grows well.	7. Apply continuous social pressure as a managerial technique.
8. Try to use your own seed.	8. Provide incentives.
9. Try to avoid hybrids.	
10. Happy animals will be healthy animals.	
11. Use prevention, not cure.	

---

[5] The Declaration of Nyéléni can be read at www.nyeleni.org/spip.php?article290.

conflicting claims. For example, Mr. Carrera claimed that framing and language are insignificant to advancing the food sovereignty movement, but also that language resonates differently with different people. We interpret the tension in Mr. Carrera's response to this kind of question as an instance of a felt tension for Mr. Carrera between intellectuals and practitioners in the food sovereignty movement. Though he did not want to accentuate this tension during our in-depth interview, its very presence in his response warrants attention. Practitioners and grassroots advocates like Mr. Carrera may believe that academic work addressing symbolic action—such as the language use differences and ideological frame disputes between on-the-ground activists and appointed high-level delegates to the UN—is indulgent rather than useful. Nevertheless, admissions such as the one made by Mr. Carrera regarding tailoring language so that it resonates with people suggest that if this is an aspect of the advocacy practices of effective grassroots activists, it would also obtain as a significant consideration for policy formation and analysis. While some—but not all—language uses will resonate with audiences, so too will language used to frame policy discourse have implications for public perceptions and what counts as legitimate government programmes, agricultural practices and funding decisions and priorities.

Mr. Gortaire's responses to my questions asking for him to define food security and food sovereignty reveal his perception that food security is more of a state-based approach to justice within the global food system while food sovereignty is a collectivist community-based social movement approach to justice within the global food system (see Table 16.2). For example, when Mr. Gortaire was defining food security, he used distancing language, entering the topic with 'I understand it [food security] as', but when asked to define food sovereignty he responded 'it is the right of our communities'. The inclusive language and the more confident tone of this response indicate Mr. Gortaire's emotional attachment and personal, cultural and communal investment in the language of food sovereignty. Furthermore, when responding to the language of food security, he referred to 'legal organizations', 'public health' and 'population'. These terms can be semantically indexed with state-based development models. On the other hand, his language regarding food sovereignty included 'indigenous organizations' and 'campesinos'. This language is also indicative of a greater familiarity, comfort and cultural identification.

Table 16.2 Language frames used by Mr. Roberto Gortaire to define and describe food security versus food sovereignty

	Food security		Food sovereignty
Agency	Legal organizations, public health	vs.	Indigenous organizations
Primary stakeholder	Population	vs.	Campesinos
Impact	Not harmful or offensive	vs.	Culturally appropriate
Primary benefit	Possibility of access to food	vs.	Control of our own agricultural system, access to productive resources

Servaes (2016) has claimed that for sustainable development to be systematic, structural and environmental factors need to be taken into account. In Mr. Gortaire's framing of food sovereignty, both the salience and praxis of Servaes's observation are noticeable. In terms of the structural elements of food security compared with food sovereignty, Mr. Gortaire's responses imply that food security as an ideological language frame would essentially require the development of an organizational field that would engender top-down mechanisms leading from policies to programmes and services providing the possibility for the entire population to have access to food. Food sovereignty, however, in Mr. Gortaire's definition elicits a fundamentally different conceptualization of the global food system. In this paradigm, the state is not even actively present. Rather, communities themselves have rights and ownership. The right to control the food system implies that the state's role is to recognize the sovereignty of its citizens at the community-level. Also, control over productive resources realigns economic relations such that local or regional groups are able to steward basic resources such as water, soil, ecosystems (including plants and animals) and seeds which are the required basis of producing food.

Finally, in terms of the consequences and benefits of these two differing approaches, there is a subtle difference in Mr. Gortaire's responses. The belief that food security includes the conditional provision that the food provided to the population not be harmful or offensive means that there is the absence of deleterious health or cultural effects. Food sovereignty, however, is 'culturally appropriate' and 'preferably agroecological'. In other words, food sovereignty appears to not only protect against deleterious effects but also provide additive elements of both a cultural and ecological nature. These ideological tenets of the Ecuadorian food sovereignty advocates correlate with the most progressive approach to communication for development as presented in the scholarly community. The further adoption and diffusion of food sovereignty movements and policies would disrupt the dominant development paradigm at multiple levels from full authority in anti-hunger programme development at the local level to ecological and economic protections at the institutional and international policy level.

When holding both Mr. Carrera's and Mr. Gortaire's responses together, there are specific ideological elements to both agroecology and food sovereignty that, according to these food sovereignty advocates, distinguish the Ecuadorian food sovereignty movement from other contemporary approaches and discourses of global food policy. One aspect of the in-depth interview data that really stands out is the social, cultural, economic and political mandates emerging from Ecuadorian civil society to pursue a specific constellation of practices and policies. Essentially, according to my interview data, the social advocacy mandates from agroecology and the definitional attributes of food sovereignty are complimentary and commensurate. There are no explicit inconsistencies or contradictions that would create tensions or frame disputes between these ideologies. Agroecology as articulated by Mr. Carrera and food sovereignty as articulated by Mr. Gortaire are not redundant either. These ideological frames complement each other but are not synonymous. When Mr. Carrera and Mr. Gortaire combine these ideologies through the collective agency of the families, communities, networks and organizations that both of these advocates lead they have advanced fundamental changes to the food system. They started at the grassroots level and have worked outwards and upwards from the family and village to the national level and beyond.

An interesting constraint to the framing of this ideological approach to global food policy change would appear to occur at the international level. If and when food sovereignty policy is implemented at the national level within nation states with certain constitutional features, communities are authorized to make autonomous decisions through local democratic organizing and consensus building regarding the control and use of the natural resource base as it pertains to food production. And, according to agroecology social advocacy mandates, all such decisions will necessarily revolve around the fundamental value of protecting the genetic diversity of living biological systems and the food produced. However, when elevated beyond the geopolitical context of a state, international trade laws such as minimizing barriers to importation and the prevalence of genetically modified organisms (GMOs) within the international flows of the global food system clash with the dictates of these ideological tenets. Other scholar-activists working in this area have observed similar structural barriers. For example, Vivero-Pol (2013), working to advance an alternative narrative to our global food system, emphasizes this same type of constraint in the international jurisdiction of our food system:

> A 're-commonification' of food—or, in other words, a transition where we work toward considering food as a commons—is an essential paradigm shift in light of our broken global food system. However, there would of course be practical consequences of this paradigm shift. Food would need to be dealt with outside of trade agreements made for pure private goods, and, as a result, we would need to establish a particular system of governance for the production, distribution, and access to food at a global level.

Interestingly, Mr. Gortaire does not perceive a conflict between food sovereignty and economic globalization. According to Mr. Gortaire, internationalization of food sovereignty

> doesn't mean stopping commercial borders—that is not the concept implied in food sovereignty. The desire of an authentic agriculturalist is to share their product, with the whole village, hopefully with all villages but evidently there is a priority of an order that should be followed: First, family farms, then the closest community, afterward the shortest commercial circuits, and if it is possible, certainly exporting further across regional or national borders, always and when this does not impair your own food capacity.

Gortaire's approach seems to necessitate a restructuring of the global food system. This restructuring would involve decisive changes to international trade policies such as under what local and national conditions food could be imported, higher regulations for trade barriers—especially for environmental protection, a prohibition on genetically engineered organisms in internationally traded food, national-level food sovereignty laws would need to be passed within states participating in this restructured global food system, redefined roles for state agencies and changes in local and regional practices such as land distribution, land use, agricultural technology, crop selection, food distribution and community decision-making. In Mr. Gortaire's words, if the food sovereignty frame is to be successful with broad-scale implementation,

> [w]e only need to break obsolete paradigms of industrial agriculture, fortify the processes of organizing and innovation that mobilize alternative markets, shorten and make more direct and efficient commercial networks. We need urban consumers who are conscientious and active. This is the path for food sovereignty.

Mr. Gortaire's discursive framing in this passage has several notable features. Mr. Gortaire is able to *avoid an ideological frame dispute* with economic globalization with this discursive construction, and although possible, there would need to be multiple interlocking structural, political, economic, social and agricultural changes to both policy and practice for this movement to be consummated. One of the remarkable qualities of Mr. Gortaire's food sovereignty frame is the *motivational appeal to simplicity*, as if breaking the obsolete paradigms of industrial agriculture could swept-up like glass shards from throwing a rock through a window. It is hardly a simple thing to remove the policies and practices enfolded in the industrial agriculture system. But Mr. Gortaire and Mr. Carrera aren't wasting any time bemoaning the barriers of doing this work. Instead, they are getting on with it. They have made incredible advances, especially in Ecuador, but also on both local and global scales.

A small but important rhetorical strategic difference of opinion between these two high-level civil society activists warrants examination. Unlike Mr. Carrera, Mr. Gortaire does seem to believe that for these policy and behaviour changes to occur consistently and without significant tension, the food sovereignty language frame as articulated by these advocates would need to be codified. As Mr. Gortaire noted in his interview response, one of the essential benefits of the success with codifying food sovereignty into Ecuador's national constitution is the ability to invoke food sovereignty in legal disputes. Thus, as a language frame, it has the ability to be used as a judicial tool for food sovereignty advocates if and when legal disputes should happen to occur. In this example, the language frames used to codify ideological movements in the political system have the advantage of using language as a tool—not just to reframe ideas, values and practices, but also to advance political action.

Food Sovereignty Versus Food Security at the CFS 41: Rhetorical Ethnographic Analysis

The 41st annual meeting of the CFS was held at the FAO in Rome from 13 to 18 October 2014. The annual plenary was attended by delegates from 111 Members of the Committee; 10 non-Member States of the Committee and by representatives from 10 United Nations agencies and bodies; 2 international agricultural research organizations; 1 international financial institution; 81 civil society organizations; 73 private sector associations and private philanthropic foundations; 42 observers; and 11 ministers and 2 vice-ministers participated in the session. The structure of CFS 41 featured several plenary sessions, policy roundtables and several side-events. Plenary sessions were attended that were the most relevant to the research focus including a ten-year retrospective on the 'Right to Food' and the Innovation in Family Farming plenary held in conjunction with the Steering Committee for the International Year of Family Farming on World Food Day. Policy Roundtables included Policy Convergence on Food Loss and Food Waste in the Context of Sustainable Agriculture; Agenda for Action for Addressing Food Security in Protracted Crises; Policy Convergence on Sustainable Fisheries and Aquaculture for Food Security and Nutrition; and Policy Convergence on Principles of Responsible Investment in Agriculture and Food Systems. Also attended was the Policy Roundtable on Principles of Responsible Investment in Agriculture and Food Systems as well as two side-events relevant to the research focus. These included a side-event sponsored by the Civil Society Mechanism discussing the FAO's designation of 2014 as the International Year of Family Farming (IYFF) and a side-event on agroecology sponsored by a network of NGOs.

The Right to Food Plenary provided a ten-year retrospective on the adoption of a human rights–based approach to global food policy at the international, national and regional levels. According to many stakeholders at the 2014 CFS the 2004 adoption by CFS delegates of the Voluntary Principles has led to significant progress in hunger reduction through policy mechanisms. During the 2014 CFS, several country representatives invoked the CFS Voluntary Guidelines as helpful in formulating national food policy to eliminate hunger and reduce inequity. Costa Rica said the introduction by the CFS of Voluntary Guidelines ten years ago was progressive because of the rights approach to food policy but it is an unfulfilled mandate. Norway said that the rights-based approach has allowed their country to treat targets not as beneficiaries but as humans with certain entitlements. India said that a rights approach by and for people and movement away from benevolence was progressive. Bangladesh said that the right to food has been included in their national constitution, which is now judicially enforceable. Cape Verde mentioned they are progressing toward including the right to food in their constitution.

The CFS and the FAO reaffirmed and re-committed themselves to the 2004 voluntary principles and rights-based approach to global food policy as well. Special rapporteur (Madame Elver) said a human rights approach to global food system policy is needed. The priority should be ending poverty and injustice, with reference to the UN declaration. The 2004 adoption of voluntary guidelines shifted perspective from technicalities of food system policy to human rights and has led to a 'silent revolution'. Progress since then has been developed by a participatory process with citizens' rights acknowledged. Yet there still exists no well-developed and systematic right to food in moral systems or legal frameworks. The right to food is a new and young right. Madame Elver recommended advocates be vigilant in protecting it and adopt the strongest possible language in national and international guidelines to create a just, equitable and sustainable food system. The CSM representative made the statement that the right to food should lead to the legitimate ability of people to promote policies where governments develop those policies and are held accountable. The fundamental role of rights needs to be reaffirmed and the focus should be on peasants, youth, women, fisherfolk and the landless. These stakeholders within civil society are not on the same terms as the private sector mechanism. International cooperative agreements need to be established. The CSM noted that stakeholders need not congratulate nations for doing what is essentially their obligation. Rather, stakeholders should encourage and call upon nations to continue and expand these efforts. The private sector mechanism (PSM) representative reaffirmed the progress of sustainable development and claimed that key business models exist and should be deployed to reach sustainable development goals. This representative also suggested that the right to food needed to be earned without explaining what that meant. A CSM representative on behalf of *La Vía Campesina* endorsed a public stakeholder approach and suggested that minimalistic entitlements are insufficient. The US and EU through the World Bank need to be exposed. Unfair trade rules (subsidies) need to be condemned. According to this delegate, minimum price mechanisms are a good tool. A reference was made to public stakeholder agenda item in CFS 42 and claimed that the Committee on Food Security should be recognized as the legitimate forum for creating trade rules, not the World Trade Organization.

The tensions between these various stakeholders within the CFS 41st reflect a substantive concern of communication for development scholars. The first concern is whether or not the CFS expansion to include the CSM is ultimately participation-as-a-means or participation as-an-end approach to sustainable development (Melkote, 2003). The former operationalization of communication for development usually results in perpetuating the dominant development paradigm and a top-down approach. This will result in superficial participation from the margins and indigenous communities because it is based on assumptions of the dominant development paradigm that reinforce neoliberal economic drivers and institutional governmental or intergovernmental bureaucracy's agendas to expand cooperation in increasing agricultural production. In this way, the voices of the CSM become co-opted (Melkote & Steeves, 2001).

El Salvador said that there can be no food security without food sovereignty. This was the first time food sovereignty discourse was invoked during the plenary. The CSM immediately supported El Salvador's statement regarding food sovereignty and food security and that food security should not be subordinate to trade policies or international business. Coherence and consistency is needed in terms of how these issues affect food security. El Salvador mentioned its parliament is working on food sovereignty legislation. It is significant to note that the position of both El Salvador and the CSM aligns with the ideological premise articulated by the literature review (*La Vía Campesina* 1996; Patel, 2009; Rehber, 2012).

The official CFS discourse articulates international, national and regional levels of action for policy implementation and coordination. Nowhere in the discourse is the local level identified as operational or relevant. This may pose different kinds of tensions between the food sovereignty language frame and the food security language frame due to the fact that conceptualization and implementation of policy and action for the food sovereignty frame begins with the local and expands outwards geographically, economically and politically.

The Right to Food Plenary ten-year retrospective yielded discourse patterns of the food security frame being challenged by food sovereignty framing. The invocation of the food sovereignty frame happened primarily by Latin American delegates and the Civil Society Mechanism. This observation is consistent with scholarly accounts of Latin American scholars leading the deconstruction of the dominant development paradigm and its attendant communication approaches (Huesca, 2003; Servaes & Malikhao, 2008). Several reports were given of progress in terms of policy adoption and implementation at the national level. A general consensus of positive attributions was made to: (a) the 2004 Voluntary Guidelines; (b) a rights-based approach to food policy; and (c) support for the post 2009 reformed CFS as more participatory and transparent.

The Innovations in Family Farming plenary had strong representation from a network of organizations such as *La Vía Campesina*, the International Federation of Organic Agriculture Movements, Agroecology advocates and the World Rural Forum. Panama discussed a Platform for Food Sovereignty the country was actively building. A strong anti-corporate agriculture tone existed in this session. The dialogue focused on two competing forces in global agriculture: small-scale family farming and large, often multi-national corporate farming. One particularly impassioned speaker offered the following narrative: This year provides answers and strategy to debate the farming of the future. Another discourse—corporate agriculture—has tried to displace family farms, agroecology and food sovereignty. They will continue to try to make as much profit as possible. GMOs are polluting our fields. They will take water from our rivers. They will continue to gain power. But they will not take over the world. Land and water should not be privatized. But we have a UN mandate. Many governments have supported this move. We are waiting for the harvest, but in these forums we have seen the potential for many governments to support us. Governments who want these models of agriculture need to support us. We sell our products to the closest possible market in keeping with the *Via Campesina* (food sovereignty) model. We believe FAO is supporting us. Why should this process be participatory? Otherwise it wouldn't be *public* policy. Dialogue building and transparent, multi-stakeholder participation turns into policies and programmes. We have the right to enrich the discourse and debate the future.

We need more investment, implementation, accountability and monitoring.

The Policy Convergence Roundtable also yielded several discourse patterns: (a) concern for the voluntary nature of CFS principles; (b) contestations of the impossibility of moving forward to progressive policy adoption and implementation due to WTO imposing legal constraints preventing national-level progress in responsible investing in agriculture; and (c) general consensus that academia should be allowed to continue to attend CFS as observers.

At the CSM-sponsored agroecology side-event there were some more invocations of the food sovereignty language frame, the recurrent tension between corporate agriculture and small-scale farming and some discussion of the role of labels and credibility which support the speculation that this diffuse network of stakeholders is deliberate about their use of language in the development of language frames that lead to altered consumer perceptions and innovations in food policymaking. A delegate from Mozambique reflected on this rhetorical dynamic: 'people start to think. They become more aware of the idea of food sovereignty. We've been working to raise awareness of food sovereignty among peasants. We have a peasant-to-peasant model. We've been training people who can communicate in the community' Another stakeholder added that in the 1990s there was an issue with labelling for agroecological and organic. The name issue was about how to receive credibility. This has led to political reflection and resulted in the main lessons of: (1) raising awareness through local and indigenous fairs; (2) building credibility through labelling; (3) trust building between producers and consumers. A representative from the World Alliance of Mobile Pastoralists said there are four world crises of climate, food, jobs and energy. The industrial model contributes to these problems but smallholder farmers contribute to solutions. There is a need to create pride instead of shame for pastoralism.

La Vía Campesina distributed a press release entitled 'October 16th, World Day of Action for Food Sovereignty and Against Transnational Corporations'. It had been published the week before CFS 41, on 9 October 2014. The very first text after the headline is a statement on food sovereignty: 'food sovereignty is the right of the world's peoples to produce and to consume healthy food. Food cannot be reduced to a commodity in the hands of the transnational corporations' (*Via Campesina* Press Release 2014). Further in the press release was an endorsement of agroecological production as the alternative farming practice that is 'consistent with our plans for the future as peasants and family farmers'. It can be seen through this *Via Campesina* press release that agroecology is the preferred agricultural practice by small-scale farmers, the indigenous community, peasants and family farmers in many parts of the world.

This *Via Campesina* document also corroborates the complementarity between the Ecuadorian food sovereignty advocates Javier Carrera and Roberto Gortaire, in terms of the compatibility between food sovereignty as a policy and agroecology as a practice. Interestingly, the press release also stated that the very first official recognition and engagement with agroecology by the FAO was at the *International Symposium on Agroecology for Food and Nutritional Security* held at the FAO in September of 2014. The delegation from *La Vía Campesina* welcomed this opening but 'recommends caution, given the attempts to coopt agroecology that were observed at the event'.

The plenary sessions, responsible investment policy roundtable and agroecology side-event revealed some interesting ideological language framing tensions between food sovereignty and food security as well as subtle indicators of differences in legitimacy between stakeholder voices. CSM repeatedly made appeals to the structure and process of deliberations and policy development, almost petitioning the international community to make good on its agreements of the right to food; CFS as the legitimate decisional forum for global food policy; the need to constrain the corporate agriculture agenda through imposing limitations on the WTO, World Bank, US and EU; increased transparency in policy decisions; and adhering to public stakeholder participation for public policy formation. Numerous stakeholders invoked the food sovereignty ideological frame during all of the aforementioned sessions of CFS 41. While it was a minority of all the stakeholders attending the event, there was evidence of diffusion and amplification of the food sovereignty frame.

A content analysis investigating the presence or absence of the language frames of 'food security' versus 'food sovereignty' in the CFS 41 Final Report reveals the food security language frame is utilized 167 times. Comparatively, the Final Report mentions the food sovereignty language frame only once, and this is in reference to El Salvador's report during the Right to Food plenary session in which El Salvador discussed its constitutional reform to include food sovereignty. Also mentioned only once in the 45 page CFS 41 Final Report is agroecology in Principle 6 of Appendix D which discusses responsible management of natural resources to increase resilience as one of ten principles for responsible investment in agriculture (CFS Final Report 2014). Comparing the frequency with which the CSM representatives invoked the food sovereignty frame during CFS 41 (during plenaries, policy roundtables and side-events) with the official textual representation of the event is noteworthy. Given that the Final Report is the official textual representation of the event, this representation clearly privileges the language frame of food security. The food security language frame's use both during the CFS 41 and in the official textual representation of the meeting is a gauge to how discourse functions ideologically. According to van Djik (2008) the sociocognitive nature of the actors invoking the food security language frame controls the formation, transformation and application of a web of other social cognitions, including social prejudices. Ideology 'assigns coherence among social attitudes which in turn codetermine social practices' (p. 34). In this way, the discourse of food security favours perceptions, interpretations and actions that advance the overall interests of power agents still privileging the dominant development paradigm. Nonetheless, CSM representatives along with several member nation delegates pushed the food sovereignty language frame forward by virtue of invoking this language and sustaining attention on this ideological approach to global food policy.

Conclusions

To date, the most successful language frame used to dispute food security in international political deliberations on global food system policy is the food sovereignty frame. The food sovereignty language frame has ascended to fairly dominant discourse rather rapidly in several national and transnational discourse communities throughout the past few decades. In recent years, several states including Ecuador, Bolivia, Venezuela, Mali, Senegal and Nepal have all inscribed food sovereignty into their national constitutions (McKay, Nehring, & Walsh-Dilley, 2014). During CFS 41, the food security language frame was disputed and the food sovereignty language frame was diffused and amplified in official plenaries through several national delegates and the CSM and affirmed by individual members of NGOs such as *La Vía Campesina*, IFOAM and the World Rural Forum. The food sovereignty language frame made it into the official record of the CFS 41. Even though it appeared only once compared with the 167 instances of food security, it was only in the Final Report because it was invoked during official policy deliberations by legitimized stakeholders in the forum. The food security language frame has been developed and deployed to increase access to foodstuffs for vulnerable and food insecure populations. Yet, a growing number of stakeholders have discovered present shortcomings or have anticipated future sociocultural, ecological and economic problems by relying exclusively on the food security language frame. In particular, the top-down approach to policy and practice within the food security ideology seems firmly rooted in an outmoded (modernization or dependency) development paradigm. Whether this manifests as power agents within the policymaking status quo controlling the parameters for hunger reduction (as in modernization ideology) or perpetuating unhealthy dependency of developing countries and communities on the state and neoliberal economic apparatus (as in dependency ideology), either is problematic. There is a consensus in the early twenty-first century on the need for grassroots participation in bringing about change at both social and individual levels (Servaes, 2016). The food sovereignty language frame can help articulate the ideological dynamics at play between power, governance and local/global ecosystems (Gordon & Hunt, 2019). This chapter has contributed to an enhanced understanding of how it does that communicative work.

Based on my analysis of interview data with Ecuadorian food sovereignty advocates, perceived limitations with the food security language frame revolve around the following: (1) access to food in the food security language frame doesn't equate to local community control and management of the natural resource base; (2) the food security language frame does not equate to addressing the gross inequities between multi-national corporate agribusiness power in the global food system and small-scale family farmers; (3) food security does not integrate agroecology practices or socio-political mandates and therefore does not preserve or protect the environment; and (4) access to food through the food security language frame does not translate into the provision of culturally appropriate food for vastly diverse world populations. These findings support the critique of widely accepted sustainable development practices by the communication for social change (CSC) model (Thomas, 2014). The food sovereignty language frame thus challenges assumptions and expands the thinking of policymakers and practitioners engaged in the multi-vocal dialogue and deliberation addressing ways to reduce malnutrition and hunger and advance the UN's SDG 2 in the 2030 Agenda.

Food sovereignty language framing functions rhetorically as a framing strategy working at the nexus between the structure of the state, neoliberal ideology and global food system policymaking. One of the reasons the sovereignty frame is able to compellingly challenge the dominant discourse of food security is because of its *resonance* (Windfuhr & Jonsen, 2005). The strategic framing adaptation from food security to food sovereignty in global food movement discourse is analogous to the development of the modern state. As Giddens (1989) noted:

> The modern state is inconceivable without a notion of sovereignty. That notion of sovereignty is one that in some sense all of us have mastered. Whenever we use a passport to travel from one country to another, we demonstrate some kind of practical mastery of the notion of sovereignty, of the notion of citizenship, and a range of associated notions. These are not just descriptions of an independently given social world, they have come to constitute what that social world is. They have become absorbed into it and in turn have transformed it. Their impact has been massive in transforming the world.

According to Gaarde's field research (2017), the CFS is a 'political battleground' and civil society inclusion in the CFS led by *La Vía Campesina*'s relentless advocacy of the food sovereignty language frame is not only about influencing the policy outcomes within the global food system. It is also about the subaltern of the world substantively participating in the ongoing negotiation of what democracy means. Seen from this perspective, the sovereignty frame meets the empirical believability criterion theorized as bolstering the potential resonance of a frame.

Part of the success of the global food sovereignty movement is the language strategy itself. Widespread adoption of the food sovereignty language frame by grassroots activists and peasants was an advantageous choice of rhetoric. It has allowed for increasing legitimacy for civil society actors in global deliberative forums such as the CFS and poses a substantive policy alternative to food security discourse. As such, it is an exemplary case of effective communication for social change in the sustainable development arena. The four key principles of CSC practice include dialogue, advocacy, participation and purpose (Thomas & van de Fliert, 2015). As this chapter has shown, this is particularly true for the advocacy component of CSC. *La Vía Campesina* and the food sovereignty movement have empowered local citizens to claim their rights and influence policies at the national and international level. The movement has also advanced meaningful dialogue and has challenged top-down and one-way communication to allow for the development of shared meaning where new understandings regarding the limitations of food security become possible. The CFS has done much to expand participation, but more work is needed to make it a truly inclusive as well as substantive process for previously marginalized stakeholders in agri-food policy deliberations, such as indigenous people, agroecological practitioners and family farmers. This recommendation is corroborated by Padhy (2015) who observed that governments have more work to do to fully realize the potential of participatory forms of communication to advance sustainable development goals. Huesca (2003) reminds us that there are differential levels and intensities of participatory communication within development processes, including: (1) initial access to communication resources; (2) active identification of development issues and goals; and (3) full authority in project governance. This chapter has shown that the food sovereignty language frame is advancing the intermediary level and intensity of participatory communication. If the movement's goals are to be realized at the international level, however, more effort needs to be put into advancing thinking, practice and policymaking to engage the most progressive policy option, which is full authority in project governance. Finally, the food sovereignty language frame has been selected and advanced more and more purposefully because it has been successful in rhetorically challenging conventional modes of policy framing and the underlying problematic dominant development paradigm within the global food system.

REFERENCES

Alonso-Fradejas, A., Borras, S., Holmes, T., Holt-Gimenéz, E., & Robbins, M. (2009, July–August). Agroecology, Small Farms, & Food Sovereignty. *Monthly Review*, 102–113.

Anderson, S. A. (1990). Core Indicators of Nutritional State for Difficult-to-Sample Populations. *Journal of Nutrition, 120*(115), 1555–1600.

Babbie, E. (1999). *The Basics of Social Research*. Belmont, CA: Wadsworth.

Bateson, G. (1972). *Steps to an Ecology of Mind*. New York: Ballantine Books.

Benford, R. D. (1993). Frame Disputes within the Nuclear Disarmament Movement. *Social Forces, 71*, 677–701.

Benford, R. D. (2013). Master Frames. In *Encyclopedia of Social & Political Movements*. Wiley Blackwell. Retrieved February 3, 2017, from http://onlinelibrary.wiley.com/doi/10.1002/9780470674871.wbespm126/full.

Benford, R. D., & Snow, D. A. (2000). Framing Processes and Social Movements: An Overview and Assessment. *Annual Review of Sociology, 26*, 611–639.

Brem-Wilson, J. (2015). Towards food sovereignty: Interrogating peasant voice in the United Nations Committee on World Food Security. *The Journal of Peasant Studies, 42*(1), 73–95.

Brem-Wilson, J. (2018). La Via Campesina and the UN Committee on World Food Security: Affected Publics and institutional dynamics in the nascent transnational public sphere. *Review of International Studies, 43*(2), 302–329.

Bublitz, M. G., Hansen, J., Peracchio, L. A., & Tussler, S. (2019). Hunger and Food Well-Being: Advancing Research and Practice. *Journal of Public Policy & Marketing, 38*(2), 136–153.

Burke, K. (1945). *A Grammar of Motives*. Berkeley: University of California Press.

Candel, J. L., Breeman, G. E., Stiller, S. J., & Termeer, C. J. A. M. (2014). Disentangling the Consensus Frame of Food Security: The Case of the EU Common Agricultural Policy Reform Debate. *Food Policy, 44*, 47–58.

Chevalier, J. M., & Buckles, D. J. (2013). *Participatory Action Research: Theory and Methods for Engaged Inquiry*. New York: Routledge.

Civil Society Mechanism. (2014). No Compromise on the Rights of Indigenous Peoples to FPIC in the CFS!. Email Correspondence to CFS 41 Listserv.

Claeys, P. (2012). The Creation of New Rights by the Food Sovereignty Movement: The Challenge of Institutionalizing Subversion. *Sociology, 46*(5), 844–860.

Claeys, P. (2015). *Human Rights and the Food Sovereignty Movement: Reclaiming Control*. New York: Routledge.

Committee on Food Security. (2009). *Reform of the Committee on World Food Security Final Version*.

Committee on Food Security. (2013). *CFS Brochure*.

Committee on Food Security. (2014). *CFS 41 Final Report. Food and Agriculture Organization, Committee on World Food Security*. http://www.fao.org/cfs/plenary/cfs41/en/

Desmarais, A. A. (2007). *La Via Campesina: Globalization and the power of peasants*. Halifax: Fernwood.

Desmarais, A. A. (2008). The Power of Peasants: Reflections on the Meanings of La Vía Campesina. *Journal of Rural Studies, 24*(2), 138–149.

Dutta, M. J. (2018). Culturally Centering Social Change Communication: Subaltern Critiques of, Resistance to, and Re-imagination of Development. *Journal of Multicultural Discourses, 13*(2), 87–104.

Dutta, M. J., & Zapata, D. B. (Eds.). (2019). *Communicating for Social Change: Meaning, Power, and Resistance*. Singapore: Palgrave Macmillan.

Fairclough, N. (1989). *Language and Power*. Edinburgh Gate, UK: Addison Wesley Longman Limited.

Frey, L. R., Botan, C. H., & Kreps, G. L. (2000). *Investigating Communication: An Introduction to Research Methods*. Needham Heights, MA: Allyn & Bacon.

Frye, J. (2009). *The Origin, Diffusion, and Transformation of 'Organic' Agriculture*. Saarbrüken, Germany: VDM.

Frye, J., & Fox, R. L. (2015). The Rhetorical Construction of Food Waste in US Public Discourse. *Food Studies, 5*, 43–57.

Gaarde, I. (2017). *Peasants Negotiating a Global Policy Space: La Via Campesina in the Committee on World Food Security*. New York and London: Routledge.

Giddens, A. (1989). The Orthodox Consensus and the Emerging Synthesis. In B. Dervin, L. Grossberg, B. O'Keefe, & E. Wartella (Eds.), *Rethinking Communication Vol 1. Issues* (pp. 53–65). Newbury Park, CA: Sage.

Goffman, E. (1974). *Frame Analysis: An Essay on the Organization of the Experience*. New York: Harper Colophon.

Gordon, C., & Hunt, K. (2019). Reform, Justice, and Sovereignty: A Food Systems Agenda for Environmental Communication. *Environmental Communication, 13*(1), 9–22.

Gysel, A. (2016). Food Sovereignty and the Role of the State: The Case of Bolivia. NADEL MAS 2014–2016.

Heath, R. L. (2011). External Organizational Rhetoric: Bridging Management and Sociopolitical Discourse. *Management Communication Quarterly, 25*, 415–435.

Higgins, A. (2015). A War of Words: The Construction of Food Sovereignty in the US & UK. Centre for Rural Economy Discussion Paper Series No. 34. Newcastle University.

Huesca, R. (2003). Participatory Approaches to Communication for Development. In B. Mody (Ed.), *International and Development Communication: A 21st-Century Perspective* (pp. 209–226). Thousand Oaks, CA: Sage.

La Vía Campesina. (1996). *Tlaxcala declaration of the vía campesina*. https://via-campesina.org/en/ii-international-conference-of-the-via-campesina-tlaxcala-mexico-april-18-21/

La Vía Campesina. (2014). October 16th, World Day of Action for Food Sovereignty and Against Transnational Corporations. [Press Release]. Retrieved from https://viacampesina.org/en/event/16th-october-international-day-action-peoples-food-sovereignty-transnational-corporations/.

Lindlof, T. R., & Taylor, B. C. (2002). *Qualitative Communication Research Methods*. Thousand Oaks, CA: Sage.

Loconto, A., & Fouilleux, E. (2013). Politics of Private Regulation: ISEAL and the Shaping of Transnational Sustainability Governance. *Regulation & Governance, 8*(2), 166–185.

McKay, B., Nehring, R., & Walsh-Dilley, M. (2014). The 'State' of Food Sovereignty in Latin America: Political Projects and Alternative Pathways in Venezuela, Ecuador and Bolivia. *The Journal of Peasant Studies, 41*(6), 1175–1200.

Meister, M., & Japp, P. M. (1998). Sustainable Development and the Global Economy: Rhetorical Implications for Improving the Quality of Life. *Communication Research, 25*(4), 399–421.

Melkote, S. R. (2003). Theories of Development Communication. In B. Mody (Ed.), *International and Development Communication: A 21st-Century Perspective* (pp. 129–146). Thousand Oaks, CA: Sage.

Melkote, S. R., & Steeves, H. L. (2001). *Communication for Development in the Third World: Theory and Practice for Empowerment*. Thousand Oaks, CA: Sage.

Mooney, P. H., & Hunt, S. A. (2009). Food Security: The Elaboration of Contested Claims to a Consensus Frame. *Rural Sociology, 74*, 469–497.

Morris, A. (2000). Reflections on Social Movement Theory: Criticisms and Proposals. *Contemporary Sociology, 29*(3), 445–454.

Padhy, M. K. (2015). Poverty Alleviation, Food Security and Environmental Sustainability: The Contribution of Participatory Development Communication. *Journal of Development Communication, 26*(2), 1–14.

Patel, R. (2009). Food Sovereignty. *The Journal of Peasant Studies, 36*(3), 663–706.

Peña, K. (2013). Institutionalizing Food Sovereignty in Ecuador. In *Conference Proceedings, International Conference*, Yale University, September 14–15.

Rehber, E. (2012). Food for Thought: 'four Ss with one F' Security, Safety, Sovereignty, and Shareability of Food. *British Food Journal, 114*(3), 353–371.

Schanbacher, W. B. (2010). *The Politics of Food: The Global Conflict between Food Security and Food Sovereignty*. Santa Barbara: Praeger Security International.

Servaes, J. (2016). Sustainable Development Communication. *Journal of Development Communication, 27*, 1–15.

Servaes, J., & Malikhao, P. (2008). Development Communication Approaches in an International Perspective. In J. Servaes (Ed.), *Communication for Development and Social Change* (pp. 158–179). Los Angeles, CA: Sage.

Snow, D. A., & Benford, R. D. (1992). Master Frames and Cycles of Protest. In A. D. Morris & C. M. Mueller (Eds.), *Frontiers in Social Movement Theory*. New Haven, CT: Yale University Press.

Snow, D. A., Rochford Jr., E. B., Worden, S. K., & Benford, R. D. (1986). Frame Alignment Process, Micromobilization, and Movement Participation. *American Sociological Review, 51*, 464–481.

Tarrow, S. (1994). *Power in Movement: Social Movements and Contentious Politics*. Cambridge and New York: Cambridge University Press.

Thomas, P. N. (2014). Development Communication and Social Change in Historical Context. In K. G. Wilkins, T. Tufte, & R. Obregon (Eds.), *Handbook of Development Communication and Social Change*. Wiley-Blackwell: West Sussex, UK.

Thomas, P. N., & van de Fliert, E. (2015). *Interrogating the Theory and Practice of Communication for Social Change*. UK: Palgrave Macmillan.

United Nations Development Program. (2018). Sustainable Development Goals Knowledge Platform. Retrieved December 19, 2018 from https://sustainabledevelopment.un.org/.

van Djik, T. A. (2008). *Discourse and Power*. New York: Palgrave Macmillan.

Vivero-Pol, J. L. (2013). Food as a Commons: Reframing the Narrative of the Food System. [SSRN Working paper series]. Retrieved from http://papers.ssrn.com/sol3/papers.cfm?abstract_id=2255447.

Windfuhr, M., & Jonsen, J. (2005). *Food Sovereignty: Towards Democracy in Local Food Systems*. ITDG Publishing.

Wittman, H. (2011). Food Sovereignty: A New Rights Framework for Food and Nature? *Environment and Society, 2*, 87–105.

Wittman, H., Desmarais, A., & Wiebe, N. (2010). *Food Sovereignty: Reconnecting Food, Nature and Community*. Oakland, CA: Food First.

Wittman, H., Desmarais, A., & Wiebe, N. (2011). The Origins and Potential of Food Sovereignty. foodfirst.org.

Wunderlich, G. S., & Norwood, J. L. (2006). *Food Insecurity and Hunger in the United States: An Assessment of the Measure*. Washington, DC: The National Academies Press.

Zanella, M. A., Goetz, A., Rist, S., Schmidt, O., & Weigelt, J. (2018). Deliberation in a Multi-stakeholder Participation: A Heuristic Framework Applied to the Committee on World Food Security. *Sustainability, 10*(2), 428.

CHAPTER 17

Internet Philanthropy as China's 'Digital Solution' to the 2030 Agenda for Sustainable Development: Policies, Practices, Politics and Critique

Jian Xu, Dianlin Huang, and He Zhang

INTRODUCTION

Philanthropy has a critical role to play in achieving the 17 Sustainable Development Goals (SDGs) proposed in the 2030 Agenda for Sustainable Development (Ogden, Prasad, & Thompson, 2018). Rather than just a source of money, the philanthropic 'big bets' also support 'big thinking, innovation, risk-taking, and collaboration' that could not only facilitate solution of specific social issues but also propel long-lasting social changes (ibid.). There has

J. Xu (✉)
School of Communication and Creative Arts, Deakin University,
Melbourne, VIC, Australia
e-mail: j.xu@deakin.edu.au

D. Huang
Institute of Communication Studies, Communication University of China,
Beijing, China
e-mail: dianlinhuang@cuc.edu.cn

H. Zhang
School of Journalism and Communication, Northwest University,
Xi'an, Shaanxi Province, China

© The Author(s), under exclusive license to Springer Nature
Switzerland AG 2021
M. J. Yusha'u, J. Servaes (eds.), *The Palgrave Handbook of International Communication and Sustainable Development*,
https://doi.org/10.1007/978-3-030-69770-9_17

already been a global trend to leverage non-state and private philanthropic institutions to influence, deliver and advance the SDGs (Kumi, 2019). For example, SDG Philanthropy Platform (https://www.sdgphilanthropy.org), launched by the Foundation Centre, United Nations Development Programme (UNDP) and Rockefeller Philanthropy Advisors with the support of many other international foundations, has launched work in a few pilot countries, such as Kenya, Columbia, Indonesia and Ghana, to engage philanthropic sector to take actions on the SDGs (Sustainable Development Goals Partnerships Platform, n.d.).

As the world's largest developing nation with the world's largest population, China has attached great importance to the 2030 Agenda and worked collaboratively with other countries to address major common global challenges to ensure sustainable development. In September 2016, China released China's National Plan on Implementation of the 2030 Agenda for Sustainable Development at a high-level symposium on the sidelines of the 71st session of the UN General Assembly, chaired by Chinese Premier Li Keqiang (Paul, 2016). The National Plan elaborates China's concrete actions to implement the 17 SDGs and 169 specific targets as well as the guiding thoughts, overall principles and implementation paths for these actions (Gov.cn, 2016a). In December 2016, the State Council released a notice titled the Development of Innovation Demonstration Zones for Implementation of the 2030 Agenda for Sustainable Development, which greatly pushed the domestic implementation of the 2030 Agenda (Gov.cn, 2016b).

In China, the growing philanthropic sector has been significantly contributing to the achievement of the SDGs by aligning their activities with China's national plan on implementation of SDGs (Xinhua, 2017a). Moreover, China is proactively exporting its philanthropic notions and models to underdeveloped nations, especially those among the 'Belt and Road Initiative' (BRI)[1] countries, to help these nations to advance the SDGs (Xinhua, 2017b).

At the first World Philanthropy Forum held in China in September 2016, the then UN Secretary-General Ban Ki-moon highly praised Chinese philanthropy and the pivotal role it played in achieving SDGs.

> As the world embarks together on implementing the 2030 Agenda for Sustainable Development Goals and Paris Agreement on Climate Change, I attached great important to China's role and Chinese philanthropy. China and its people have a long tradition of giving and Chinese philanthropy has made significant contributions to education, health and the environment. (United Nations, 2016)

In China's dynamic philanthropy sector, internet philanthropy (*hulianwang cishan*) has no doubt become a leading trend. The term 'internet philanthropy'

---

[1] In 2013, the Chinese government adopted BRI, an ambitious global development strategy that aims to significantly expand China's economic, cultural and political influence through infrastructure development and investment in Eurasia and Africa (Aoyama, 2016).

includes traditional philanthropy that uses the internet (e.g. online donation platforms of traditional foundations) as well as the new forms of philanthropy that are enabled by the internet (United Nations Development Programme, 2016). Popular forms of internet-enabled philanthropy include charitable crowdfunding, online peer-to-peer donation of idle items, online charity auctions and donation of walking/running miles. 'E-giving' is the essence of internet philanthropy, which allows low-cost, fast, flexible and transparent donation through digital platforms. Internet philanthropy contrasts with traditional philanthropy in various ways. This includes donor demographics (with internet philanthropists being younger, networked individuals), donation amounts (more varied in size and nature and event- or project-based on the internet), intermediary types (the internet can bypass foundations or involve partners) and relationships between donors and beneficiaries (transparent and interactive on the internet; ibid.). In 2018, 8.46 billion person trips participated in internet philanthropy in China. The total online donation amount for the year was 3.17 billion CNY (about US $450 million) (Xinhua, 2019). As the 2016 report entitled 'Internet Philanthropy in China', released by the United Nations Development Programme (UNDP), positively argues, the rise of China's internet philanthropy 'has necessitated a digital solution in approaching the 17-pronged agenda of the SDGs' (United Nations Development Programme, 2016, p. 1). Therefore, it is crucial to understand internet philanthropy—China's 'digital solution' to achieving the SDGs—if we want to better know about China's potential paths to achieving the 2030 Agenda.

This chapter investigates China's internet philanthropy by looking at its policies, practices, politics and critique. We first examine the internet philanthropy at three different levels. At the macro level, we examine the social, economic and technological background that gave rise to China's internet philanthropy, as well as the policy and regulatory frameworks that influence internet philanthropy. At the meso level, we look at the corporate social responsibilities and initiatives of China's leading internet enterprises that provide the digital infrastructure—online charity platforms, for multiple stakeholders (e.g. foundations, non-government organizations [NGOs] and individuals)—for internet philanthropy. We also identify the targeted and ignored SDGs that China's online charity projects based on the popular internet philanthropy platforms address and fail to address. At the micro level, we study the practice of one of China's most well-known internet philanthropy projects, 'Free Lunch for Children' (FLC; *mianfei wucan*), to look at how it successfully harnesses social media, online donation and crowdfunding platforms to raise funds to support school kids living in poverty-stricken areas. We then discuss the politics of China's internet philanthropy as innovative social governance. Finally, we critique the 'technological solutionism' of leveraging the internet to achieve the SDGs and reflect on the 'going out' of Chinese philanthropy.

Internet Philanthropy: Background, Policy and Regulatory Framework

In the past four decades, China has created an unprecedented economic growth in the world. At the same time, China's economic reform has also led to a series of social problems, such as an excessive gap between rich and poor, environmental degradation, unequal social welfare benefits between urban and rural inhabitants and job loss. These have posed challenges for China's social and political stability and sustainable development (Dollar, 2007) and created a growing need for the Chinese government to develop philanthropy and its associated institutions, such as NGOs and non-profit organizations (NPOs), to tackle social problems caused by government and market failures, through ongoing regulation and management.

The 2008 Sichuan earthquake is widely seen as the trigger for China's philanthropic boom as it witnessed a 'blowout' of unofficial and grassroots philanthropy (ifeng, 2018). In the most destructive disaster since the 1949 founding of the People Republic of China, a total donation of 70 billion CNY (about US $10 billion) was solicited, the largest ever amount of donations in China (Sina, 2008). This could not be achieved without unprecedented scale of participation of unofficial and grassroots philanthropic organizations. The government, for the first time in history, unleashed the philanthropic power of China's emerging civil society and acknowledged the important role of unofficial and grassroots philanthropy as an 'effective supplement' to the traditional philanthropy work led by the Party-state (Gov.cn, 2008). The earthquake thus became a turning point for the government, which changed the restrictive fundraising and policy environment for unofficial and grassroots philanthropic organizations, laying a good foundation for the future development of internet philanthropy.

Technologically speaking, the fast development of China's internet and digital media technologies as well as the dramatic increase of China's internet population since 2008 has created positive conditions for internet philanthropy. Scholars in the field of communication for development and social change (CDSC) have widely examined the role of communication for human development and social change with a particular focus on the innovations of information technologies that could empower citizens and NGOs to articulate and make social, cultural and political changes (Servaes, 2007, 2020; Waisbord, 2014; Wilkins, Tufte, & Obregon, 2014). By conducting case studies in different national contexts, scholars have extensively studied the role of digital media and communication in promoting participatory and creative civic engagement for social changes, such as climate change (Hestres, 2013), environmental protection (Liu, 2011), peace-making (Uzuegbunam & Omenugha, 2018) and human rights campaigns (McPherson, 2017). In the philanthropic sector, the internationally well-known Ice Bucket Challenge in 2014 and China's booming internet philanthropy can both demonstrate the innovation of digital media and communication in transforming the ways of advocating, mobilizing and participating in charities.

Socially speaking, the Guo Meimei and Red Cross scandal further forced the Chinese government to accelerate the steps of reforming philanthropy, creating a favourable political and policy environment for the development of internet philanthropy. In 2011, Guo Meimei, a 20-year-old woman, claimed to be the general manager of a company called Red Cross Commerce, on Sina Weibo, the Chinese version of Twitter, and showed off her luxurious lifestyle online. Furious netizens began to question whether Guo had financed her luxurious lifestyle with money that had been donated to the Red Cross and hunted her down to find out her connection with China's biggest government-backed philanthropic organization (China Daily, 2011). Though Guo and the Red Cross both denied any connection, the online outcry caused the public credibility of and donations to the Red Cross to plummet. The scandal reflected people's long-term discontent over the bureaucracy and lack of transparency of the official philanthropic organizations represented by the Red Cross (China Daily, 2011). To the contrary, several grassroots, internet-based philanthropy projects gained national reputation and momentum that same year due to their efficiency, transparency and reliability, including the most well-known, FLC, which we will examine in detail later (China Development Brief, 2012). Crisis for official philanthropic organizations not only created an opportunity for the rise of the citizen-initiated and internet-enabled grassroots philanthropy but also pushed the government to enhance the transparency and credibility of official philanthropy by harnessing the internet. The year of 2011 therefore opened up the development of China's internet philanthropy.

China's Internet Plus action plan further boosted internet philanthropy to a national scale. Former Premier Li Keqiang first proposed this national initiative in his annual government work report in 2015 (Davidson, 2015). The initiative aims to harness digital technologies to reenergize traditional industries and sectors and boost China's decelerating economy through an all-digital strategy (Pasquier, 2015). As Wu Hequan, former President of the Internet Society of China, pointed out, Internet Plus covers more sectors than its international counterparts—for example, Germany's Industry 4.0 and United States' Industrial Internet of Things—as it is tasked not only with broadening internet's industrial use but also to further explore the internet's potential in stimulating consumption and improving public service (People.cn, 2015). The national initiative was soon applied in the philanthropic sector and 'Internet Plus Philanthropy' was developed to promote the top-down development of internet philanthropy (China-embassy.org, 2015). The government established the China Internet Development Foundation (CIDF) in 2015, a public foundation registered with the Ministry of Civil Affairs and managed by the Cyberspace Administration of China (CAC), as one of the most important actions to implement Internet Plus Philanthropy. At the 2015 World Internet Conference, the CIDF launched an initiative called 'Let the Internet Become a Sea of Love—Proposal to Develop Internet Philanthropy' in collaboration with China's leading internet enterprises and media portals, forming the first national alliance to develop internet philanthropy (Sohu, 2016).

At the same time, the government also strengthened the regulation of internet philanthropy to ensure it runs on the right track. In March 2016, China passed its first Charity Law. The law lowers the bar for public fundraising organizations by allowing all charitable organizations that are lawfully registered for two years and are in good standing to apply for public fundraising status (International Center for Not-for-Profit Law, n.d., p. 3). The law has allowed a growing number of charitable organizations to obtain the public fundraising qualification and solicit donations online. But the law further stipulates that charitable organizations that conduct public fundraising online need to solicit public donation through online charity platforms assigned by the Ministry of Civil Affairs (International Center for Not-for-Profit Law, n.d.). The Ministry of Civil Affairs accredited 13 online charity platforms as online charity platforms in September 2016 (Wu, 2016). In January 2018, nine more online charity platforms received accreditation (Xinhua, 2018). In July 2017, the Ministry of Civil Affairs further issued two standards to strengthen overall supervision of online charity platforms to promote transparency and equity (Ministry of Civil Affairs, 2017; International Center for Not-for-Profit Law, n.d., p. 2). In this way, grassroots internet philanthropy has been gradually incorporated into the government's philanthropic work, with necessary policy support and regulations from the government.

Internet Philanthropy: Platforms, Corporate Social Responsibility and Targeted SDGs

Internet philanthropy is a mission impossible without online charity platforms. China's commercial internet companies own most of these platforms. Our search of China's top ten internet enterprises according to the 2018 China's Top 100 Internet Enterprises (Internet Society of China, 2018) shows that eight of the top ten internet enterprises have established dedicated online charity platforms. Alibaba owns two platforms and the other seven companies own one each. Six of the nine online charity platforms are accredited by the Ministry of Civil Affairs as charity organizations to raise funding. Moreover, eight of the top ten internet enterprises have their own charity foundations (see Table 17.1).

Philanthropy was already one of the main corporate social responsibilities (CSRs) of China's internet giants, including Baidu, Alibaba and Tencent (collectively known as 'BAT'), before the wave of internet philanthropy. Tencent was the first of China's internet enterprises to establish a charity foundation, in 2007 (Tencent Foundation, n.d.). That year Alibaba was the first to release its annual CSR report (China CSR Research Center, 2018). Since the rise of internet philanthropy in 2011, the leading internet enterprises have taken advantage of their platforms, products and users to create online charity platforms, which has not only extended their CSRs but has also greatly promoted the trend of

Table 17.1 Charity foundations and platforms of top ten internet companies in China

Ranking	Company	Charity foundation	Online charity platform
1	Alibaba	Alibaba Foundation	www.gongyi.taobao.com; www.love.alipay.com/donate/index.htm
2	Tencent	Tencent Foundation	www.gongyi.qq.com
3	Baidu	Baidu Foundation	www.gongyi.baidu.com
4	JD	JD Foundation	www.gongyi.jd.com
5	Netease	Netease Lede Foundation	www.gongyi.163.com
6	Sina	Sina Yangfan Foundation	www.gongyi.weibo.com
7	Sohu	Siyuan Focus Foundation	www.gongyi.sohu.com
8	Meituan	N/A	www.gongyi.meituan.com
9	Qihoo 360	360 Charity Foundation	N/A
10	Xiaomi	N/A	N/A

internet philanthropy. Their collective pledge under the call of CIDF to make China's internet a 'Sea of Love' and to develop internet philanthropy at the 2015 World Internet Conference (Sohu, 2016) marks internet philanthropy becoming one of the most important CSRs of China's leading internet enterprises. We will further discuss the rationales of the enthusiasm of the internet enterprises to participate in and promote internet philanthropy later.

Among the internet giants, Tencent is no doubt a pioneer in the promotion of internet philanthropy. In May 2019, Tencent announced that its online charity platform had solicited around 5.3 billion CNY (about US $758 million) from more than 220 million donors by April 2019. Collected donations were used to support more than 50,000 philanthropic projects run by 10,000 charity organizations, with 90% of projects dedicated to poverty alleviation (Sina, 2019). The huge success depends on Tencent's large user base of its popular products, including China's most popular social media, WeChat (the Chinese version of WhatsApp), as well as programmes it runs on its charity platform. For example, the Monthly Donation Plan on its charity platform allows users to regularly donate small amounts of money, for example 10 CNY (about US $1.43) per month, to sponsored philanthropy projects through Tencent's e-payment system. Donators receive a corresponding virtual 'love score' according to the amount of their donations. As their 'love score' increases, donors reach a higher stage in their charity record, from stages 1 to 8 (Baidu Baike n.d.). In addition, in 2015, Tencent initiated China's first charity day on September 9. It conducts a charity campaign from 7 to 9 September every year to solicit donations for philanthropic projects on its charity platform with the participation of celebrities, enterprises, charity organizations and netizens through various festive events online and offline (Zhou, 2018).

Tencent's charity programmes have demonstrated key features of internet philanthropy; they are flexible, mobile, networked, creative and entertaining. Similarly, online charity platforms operated by other internet enterprises as shown in Table 17.1 also run branded charity programmes, including Sina's

Micro Auction and Alibaba's Taobao Charity Shop. These charity platforms and programmes, alongside their social media, e-payment, online news and entertainment products, provide thousands of charitable organizations with the digital means and space to initiate various charity projects to achieve SDGs.

In order to identify what SDGs China's online charity projects aim to address, we analysed the current and past charity projects promoted on the nine online charity platforms listed in Table 17.1. We found that 14 SDGs among the total 17 are targeted. The mostly addressed SDGs in sequence are Goal 1 (No Poverty), Goal 3 (Good Health and Well-being), Goal 4 (Quality Education), Goal 15 (Life on Land), Goal 5 (Gender Equality) and Goal 10 (Reduced Inequality). Three goals are seldom addressed, including Goal 8 (Decent Work and Economic Growth), Goal 13 (Climate Action) and Goal 17 (Partnerships to Achieve the Goal). It can be seen that the internet-facilitated charity projects are predominantly 'inward', dedicating to cope with China's domestic development issues, such as poverty, health, education and environment. It is far from being 'outward' to foster global partnership for sustainable development and combat climate change, one of the most salient global crises, which is incompatible with China's role as one of the major economic players in the world.

Bearing the targeted and ignored SDGs that China's online charity projects address and fail to address in mind, the next section studies one of the most successful online charity projects, FLC, to examine how online charity projects, which are widely called 'micro-philanthropy' (*wei gongyi*) in Chinese, are practised at the micro level.

Doing Micro-philanthropy: Case Study of FLC

Micro-philanthropy projects are called 'micro' because, first, the initiators of the projects are not powerful governmental organizations or rich entrepreneurs usually connected to traditional forms of government-managed and elite-sponsored philanthropy projects, such as Project Hope, which raises funds for rural schooling. Instead, these projects are usually driven by individual activists, grassroots NGOs and ordinary citizens that are relatively powerless and moneyless. Second, these projects encourage each individual's small donation and flexible volunteerism, promoting the notion that 'everyone can do philanthropy at any time'. Third, these projects all harness China's top two social media platforms, Weibo and WeChat (collectively called 'double micro' (*shuang wei*) in Chinese), for publicity, mass mobilization and participation. Therefore, micro-philanthropy is widely seen as a new form of 'altruistic, social-media-enabled, citizen driven, unofficial, sustained and often small-to-large scale civic activism' (Yu, 2018, p. 9) that has profoundly transformed the landscape of China's philanthropic causes. It has been playing an increasingly important role, assisting the Chinese government to achieve SDGs domestically and globally. In order to illustrate how micro-philanthropy project works to promote sustainable development, this section examines FLC as a case study, one of the earliest and most well-known micro-philanthropy initiatives in China.

FLC is a public fundraising organization started in 2011 by Deng Fei, an influential veteran investigative journalist, together with 500 journalists and dozens of domestic mass media. It is officially registered with, and thus subject to, the China Social Welfare Foundation, a national public fundraising foundation under the direct guidance of the Ministry of Civil Affairs.[2] The core issue FLC seeks to address is the poverty-induced malnutrition that affects many schoolchildren in China's underdeveloped rural areas. FLC calls on fellow citizens to donate a small amount of money, initially 3 CNY (about US $0.43), later increased to 4 CNY (about US $0.57) since 2015, per lunch per child, every day to provide free lunch for rural pupils in central and western regions where poverty has not been fully eradicated. According to official statistics, by the end of March 2019, the FLC project had raised 524.49 million CNY (about US $75 million), benefitting 304,570 poverty-stricken children in 1168 schools, across 26 provincial regions (Free Lunch for Children, n.d.).

As a micro-philanthropy initiative, social media and online charity platforms owned by China's leading internet enterprises arguably play the most important role in the successful operation of FLC, from volunteer recruitment, partnership development, information disclosure to fundraising campaigns.

In terms of social media, Weibo plays the leading role. It was launched by Sina Corporation in 2009. By March 2019, the number of Weibo's monthly active users had reached 465 million, among whom 203 million are active on a daily basis (Chinanews, 2019). The microblogging service has unprecedentedly empowered ordinary people's online expression, discussion, community formation and civic participation, though with control and censorship from the government (Xu, 2015, 2016). Deng Fei, the founder of FLC, is a so-called big-V (verified influential user with a large number of followers) on Weibo. His account (https://weibo.com/u/1642326133) has had more than 5 million followers since mid-2019. He is optimistic about Weibo's role in making positive social changes and said in an interview: 'microblogs are our own individual media. They're a loudspeaker, to broadcast yourself. I think microblogs can change our country' (from Lim, 2011). Therefore, since the beginning of his FLC project, a wide and multi-layered Weibo network has been constructed to facilitate the operation of the project. Deng's personal Weibo account and FLC's official Weibo account (https://weibo.com/freelunch) act as the central nodes to raise public awareness of the project and canvass for various forms of symbolic (e.g. likes, comments and reposts) or material support (e.g. fund donations and volunteering). In addition, FLC-sponsored schools are required to set up their own Weibo accounts and post meal details and costs on a daily

---

[2] According to official regulations, establishment of non-governmental organizations in mainland China is subject to a 'dual registration' system. That is, these organizations must be approved by a semi or full official professional 'supervisory unit' (*zhuguan danwei*) before being registered with the Ministry of Civil Affairs (Ministry of Civil Affairs 2013).

basis. Timely information disclosure from the beneficiaries helps enhance the transparency and credibility of the FLC project among the public.

Moreover, celebrity endorsement on Weibo has also greatly contributed to the public awareness of the project. FLC often invites celebrities to record promotional videos and post them on FLC's official Weibo account and celebrities with millions of followers on Weibo directly endorse FLC on their personal accounts. The famous comedian actress Ma Li (https://weibo.com/u/1296492733), who has over 6 million followers, and singer Jackson Yi (https://weibo.com/tfyiyangqianxi, over 73.8 million followers), the youngest member of China's biggest boyband TFBoys, have both promoted FLC on Weibo. The extensive celebrity endorsement of FLC has also inspired millions of fans to exercise fandom philanthropy on behalf of their idols. For example, after one of China's most popular actors, Zhu Yilong (https://weibo.com/zhuyilong, with over 16.3 million followers), expressed his support for FLC, his fans were inspired to follow his path and donated about 1 million CNY (about US $142,170) for FLC's rural projects (Baguaxiaogongju, 2018). Fans, donors and volunteers also actively share their experiences of donating to FLC on their own Weibo accounts, forming a large-scale and loosely connected network for FLC at the grassroots level.

Besides the Weibo network, FLC also harnesses WeChat for its social media strategies. After launching in 2011, the number of monthly active WeChat users has steadily increased, reaching 1.1 billion in the first quarter of 2019 (PRNewswire, 2019). It supports multiple functions, including instant messaging, group messaging and mobile payments to official subscription accounts, and has become the most popular social media app among Chinese people in China and overseas (Chen, Mao, & Qiu, 2018). Official subscription accounts on WeChat have allowed millions of organizations and individuals to update their subscribers with up-to-date information on a regular basis. FLC set up its official WeChat subscription account (ID: freelunchwx) on 8 November 2012. Since then, posts have been sent to its subscribers on an almost daily basis. Posts range from fundraising campaigns, project implementation information to the latest news about the sponsored schools and children. The spot-to-spot communication on WeChat is more effective than the one-to-many communication of Weibo. Subscribers can further share FLC posts on their profile pages or their WeChat groups.

Weibo and WeChat are the two main platforms for FLC to promote the project and solicit donations. Online charity platforms are the actual donation platforms through which people can donate to FLC, including Sina's microphilanthropy, Alibaba's Taobao philanthropy, Tencent Philanthropy and JD Philanthropy (see Table 17.1 for links). Links to these donation sites are embedded in FLC's official Weibo account and WeChat public subscription account and allow social media followers to donate through their mobile phone or other digital devices at anywhere and anytime.

The digitally enabled, networked, flexible and entertaining way of doing micro-philanthropy has quickly made FLC a star philanthropy project with great national impact and has attracted the attention of the central government. In October 2011, just six months after the launch of FLC, former Chinese premier Wen Jiabao declared a Rural Nutrition Improvement Plan, with a pledge of 16 billion CNY (about US $2.27 billion) per year to provide free lunch to 2.6 million students in 699 pilot areas (Deng, 2014). FLC is therefore widely seen to demonstrate that NGOs in China could successfully set the agenda for the government and further influence policymaking if they have a good programme and can implement it strategically, innovatively and effectively.

FLC's huge success in China has pushed Deng Fei and his team to expand FLC's partnership network overseas and export the successful model to Africa to help schoolchildren suffering from hunger. FLC established close ties with the Australian China Education Foundation (ACEF) in 2015, an NPO dedicated to improving education in China's poverty-stricken areas and promoting educational collaboration between China and Australia. By November 2015, after months of fundraising campaigns, the two organizations raised a total of AUD $51,728 (about US $34,160), which was used to finance the first internationally sponsored FLC programme at Dong Gou Primary School in Tianshui County, Gansu Province (Australian China Education Foundation n.d.). The second ACEF-FLC campaign was launched in 2018 and successfully raised AUD $75,300 (about US $49,726) to support the designated Gansu project (Free Lunch for Children, 2018).

In 2017, FLC International commenced its first free meal project in six schools in Nairobi, Kenya, offering free breakfast and lunch to more than 1, 400 Kenyan pupils in slum schools. The project attracted the return of 202 school dropouts and enrolment in the sponsored schools increased dramatically (Sohu, 2018). In order to expand its international scheme, FLC also actively seeks funds from various sources in the United States and Europe. By 2019, FLC's presence and influence in Africa had expanded to 11 countries, including Kenya, Uganda, Ethiopia, Malawi, Tanzania and Jordan (People's Daily, 2017). The 'going-out' of FLC has demonstrated the global aspiration and impact of China's micro-philanthropy, resonating with China's commitment to supporting the achievement of SDGs both at home and abroad. However, Chinese philanthropy 'going out' has also aroused critique which we will further explain later.

Internet Philanthropy as Innovative Social Governance

Why do the government, internet enterprises, charity organizations and ordinary people enthusiastically embrace internet philanthropy? What are the politics behind the trend of internet philanthropy? We argue that internet philanthropy works as 'an effective and legitimate form of societal governance'

(Sorensen & Torfing, 2005, p. 205) in post-reform China, echoing the trend of using third parties to deliver social services in neoliberal societies in the West.

Chinese President Xi Jinping, in his report delivered at the 19th National Congress of the Chinese Communist Party in 2017, stressed the importance of 'establishing a social governance model based on collaboration, participation and common interests'. He argued that it is time to 'shift the focus of social governance to the community level, leverage the role of social organizations, and see that government's governance efforts, on the one hand, and society's self-regulation and residents' self-governance, on the other, reinforce each other' (China Daily, 2017). Internet philanthropy is not only among the first to experiment with the social governance model but also has demonstrated the power and politics of such a model that contributes to China's 'new mentality of government' (Bray & Jeffreys, 2016).

First, in China's socialist market economy, corporations have to pursue economic benefits and undertake social responsibilities at the same time, as required by the Company Law of the People's Republic of China (China Daily, 2006). They are expected to play a pivotal role in constructing a 'harmonious society', a governing philosophy introduced by the Hu-Wen Administration (2003–2013) that aimed to respond to the increasing social injustice and inequality caused by China's rapid economic growth (Zheng & Tok, 2007). China's internet industry has become the growth engine of China's economy, accounting for 6.4% of China's GDP in 2016, the highest proportion in the world (Sohu, 2017). It therefore makes sense to unleash the philanthropic power of the pillar industry that has greatly benefitted from China's economic growth to help the government address social issues. The establishment of the CIDF, which is directly managed by the central governing agency of China's internet, the CAC, demonstrates the centralizing trend of internet philanthropy.

Calling on internet enterprises to embark on internet philanthropy can be seen as a soft approach to governing China's cyberspace. Different from the traditional and hardline internet governance through regulation and censorship (Benny & Xu, 2018; Dong, 2012), this soft approach aims to subtly influence people's use of the internet (doing more social good rather than airing complaints about the status quo of the society) through internet enterprises' collective promotion of philanthropy via their popular digital platforms and products. For the internet enterprises, doing and promoting philanthropy under the call of the government also helps them to exercise good 'corporate citizenship' (Saiia, 2001) and maintain positive roles and responsibilities within society, which is expected by the government. To ingratiate themselves with the state could, in turn, ensure the internet enterprises receive policy and tax revenue support from the state for sustainable economic gain. As Johan Lagerkvist (2011) succinctly put it, the 'state–capitalist power alliance' could not only create a more 'sanitized' cyberspace but also bring 'profitability' to the internet enterprises.

Second, internet philanthropy is also an effective way to mobilize social organizations (e.g. NGOs and NPOs), to participate in social governance. These organizations, which usually seek ways to organize their own institutions for citizen participation and engagement in policymaking, are seen by the government as a potential risk that can deconstruct the social basis for the Party rule if not managed properly (Béja, 2006). Internet philanthropy projects, such as Deng Fei's FLC, are usually initiated by social organizations, but collaborate with public fundraising foundations that are registered with the Ministry of Civil Affairs and are under the direct supervision of governmental institutions. The collaborative model ensures social organizations pursue the government-endorsed agenda and work within the orbit approved by the Party-state. The philanthropic turn of social organizations encourages them to exercise 'embedded activism' that pursues 'gradual transition' and 'incremental political changes' rather than being confronting and radical against the government (Ho, 2007, pp. 187, 189), which is a rule of survival and development for social organizations in China's restrained civil society.

Third, internet philanthropy has also demonstrated its power to engage the mass public in social governance. By mobilizing the kindness and mercy of ordinary people to do philanthropy, the government actually encourages the population to be self-reliant and responsible for sharing the burden of the government to cope with urgent social problems in China's post-socialist transformation. In other words, the government aims to cultivate an 'ideal citizenship' (Yu, 2017) that aligns with the socialist morality (e.g. people-loving, altruistic and dedicated) through philanthropy to energize citizens' self-governing initiatives to make up the deficiencies of state governance.

In doing internet philanthropy, internet enterprises, social organizations and ordinary individuals are all involved in the process of collaborative social governance promoted by the Xi government. The internet has become a central hub that connects multiple stakeholders in philanthropy to 'transmit positive energy to society', a popular political discourse in the Xi era that is widely interpreted to maintain an optimistic attitude and take positive actions to make life, society and the country better (Yang & Tang, 2018). Internet philanthropy thus can be seen as the Chinese government's new 'governmentality' in Foucault's words, the 'art of government' (Foucault, 1991) that uses a wide range of control techniques beyond the state politics, to maintain state power and sovereignty with the assistance of digital technologies.

CRITIQUE OF INTERNET PHILANTHROPY AND CHINESE PHILANTHROPY 'GOING OUT'

As discussed, internet philanthropy is not only an innovation of traditional philanthropy but also an experiment of effective social governance in China's digital era. It has achieved huge success in terms of total solicited donations, social impact and recognition among the public, but can internet philanthropy become a 'digital solution' for the Chinese government to accomplish the SDGs? We argue that it is too optimistic to believe internet philanthropy can solely achieve the SDGs, and those who believe the digital approach can do so are likely to fall into 'technological solutionism'.

Technology critic Evgeny Morozov proposed the term 'technological solutionism' to critique those who enthusiastically embrace digital technology and big data as the solution to a broad range of social problems. He writes that these 'complex social situations [are recast] either as *neatly defined problems with definite, computable solutions or as transparent and self-evident processes that can be easily optimized—if only the right algorithms are in place!*' (Morozov, 2013, p. 5). He argues that technological solutionism embodies 'silicon mentality' and provides 'new problem-solving infrastructure' and 'new types of solutions' to solve social problems that are too complex to be easily fixed only through digital means (Schüll, 2013).

China's 'Internet Plus' initiative has demonstrated the mentality of technological solutionism in policymaking. The great leap forward enthusiastically embraces the internet as a good remedy to fix the problems existing in traditional industries and public service sectors for a long time without fully considering the differences among different sectors and China's digital divide. Internet philanthropy, which has been developed against the backdrop of the 'Internet Plus' initiative and more specifically 'Internet Plus Philanthropy', could only mitigate, rather than completely solve, the problems in Chinese philanthropy, such as the contradiction between the autonomy of NGOs and NPOs and government regulation of philanthropy. Therefore, it is unreasonable to over-depend on internet philanthropy to achieve the SDGs.

On the one hand, problems have already emerged with internet philanthropy and its swift development that have not yet been adequately addressed; fake charity and charity fraud issues have emerged, mainly caused by inadequate supervision of online charity platforms and micro-philanthropy projects (Xinhua, 2017c). On the other hand, achieving the SDGs requires multiple approaches working simultaneously, such as institutional guarantee, social mobilization, resource investment, risk prevention and control, international collaboration, and supervision and evaluation (Gov.cn, 2016a). The achievement of each of the 17 SDGs needs a series of concrete and ongoing actions beyond simple donation. For example, Deng Fei's FLC project has successfully contributed towards achieving the first and second SDGs of eradicating poverty and eliminating hunger. However, to thoroughly realize the two objectives require the Chinese government to, among other things, effectively implement targeted poverty alleviation, improve social welfare and ensure the quantity and quality of cereal products (Gov.cn, 2016a).

We agree that financing is a crucial dimension to achieve the SDGs and the participatory internet philanthropy can significantly contribute to this dimension. But in the meantime, we also warn against falling into a 'technological solutionism' that optimistically thinks achieving the SDGs at home and abroad could be simplified into fund raising through enthusiastic online donation. To gain a critical understanding of China's internet philanthropy, we not only need to unveil the politics of promoting and centralizing internet philanthropy as we did earlier, with the internet philanthropy 'going out' (e.g. FLC's expansion into Africa), we also need to critically understand the politics of China's increasing philanthropic investment overseas.

Since the implementation of the BRI in 2013, China's outward foreign direct investment (OFDI) has significantly increased, especially in the BRI countries (Du & Zhang, 2018). Against the background, China's philanthropic sector is also proactively going out along the New Silk Road. Beyond the traditional 'government-to-government' foreign-aid model, unofficial sectors, such as Chinese enterprises, foundations and NGOs, have become increasingly involved in overseas charitable activities, especially in Africa.

For Chinese enterprises and entrepreneurs, outbound philanthropy can provide effective channels to expand their business empire globally, network with international community and gain credibility and reputation (Yang, 2014). While widely being blamed as a stealer of natural resources or a threat to national security (Knoerich & Vitting, 2018), Chinese enterprises have resorted to increase social investment and charitable engagement overseas to improve public relations and perceptions. For foundations and NGOs, they are encouraged to go abroad to facilitate the outbound philanthropy of Chinese enterprises, help construct China's positive international reputation through unofficial channels, and promote the 'going out' of China's philanthropic culture, notion and model as a part of China's soft power initiative (Deng, 2019; Xinhua, 2017b).

However, Chinese enterprises, foundations and NGOs do not actually work separately, but usually maintain symbiotic relations to promote Chinese philanthropy 'going out'. Lai's research on the China Foundation for Poverty Alleviation's (CFPA) aid in Africa found that donations are mostly sourced from overseas Chinese enterprises in Africa (Lai, 2013). Financially reliant on overseas Chinese enterprises to undertake outbound philanthropy, foundations and NGOs have to promote corporate social responsibility of the enterprises in their philanthropic activities overseas. As former president of the CFPA frankly put it, 'our philanthropic programs (in Africa) also need to support the development of Chinese enterprises in return, not only altruistically benefit African countries' (Zhang, 2014).

In sum, Chinese philanthropy 'going out' is driven by the economic needs of China's internationalizing economic sectors as well as the political needs of the Chinese government to make China a responsible global power. In addition to the economic and political forces, China's cutting-edge digital technology and thriving digital service have also greatly pushed the 'going out' of Chinese philanthropy as shown in the example of FLC in Africa, making China an emerging 'impact powerhouse' in global philanthropy (Khanna, 2019).

Though China's outbound philanthropy is not absolutely altruistic, it would also be unfair to label it as a new form of 'Sino-imperialism' as some Western critiques of China's economic investment and loan in underdeveloped nations often contend (Dok & Thayer, 2019). It is also equally unfair to neglect the positive impacts of Chinese philanthropy on local communities in these supported countries and totally deny the win-win situation. However, in relation to what degree Chinese philanthropy, especially the internet philanthropy, could help these nations to realize their SDGs, it remains an open question that requires further longitudinal empirical research and critical analysis in specific national contexts.

References

Aoyama, R. (2016). 'One Belt, One Road': China's New Global Strategy. *Journal of Contemporary East Asia Studies,* 5(2), 3–22.

Australian China Education Foundation. (n.d.). Free Lunch Campaign. Retrieved from http://www.acefund.org.au/free-lunch-campaign/.

Baguaxiaogongju. (2018). Zhuyilong fensi tigong mianfei wucan gongyi, yi juankuan 90wan, fensi geili luozan [Zhu Yilong's Fans Donated 900, 000 CNY to Support Free Lunch for Children Project, Winning Applause From the Public]. Retrieved from https://kknews.cc/entertainment/2bj4oqg.html.

Baidu Baike. (n.d.). Tengxun yuejuan jihua [Tencent Monthly Donation Plan]. Retrieved from https://baike.baidu.com/item/腾讯月捐计划.

Béja, J. (2006). The Changing Aspects of Civil Society in China. *Social Research,* 73(1), 53–74.

Benny, J., & Xu, J. (2018). The Decline of Sina Weibo: A Technological, Political and Market Analysis. In M. Kent, K. Ellis, & J. Xu (Eds.), *Chinese Social Media: Social, Cultural and Political Implications* (pp. 221–235). London and New York: Routledge.

Bray, D., & Jeffreys, E. (Eds.). (2016). *New Mentalities of Government in China.* London, UK: Routledge.

Chen, Y., Mao, Z., & Qiu, J. L. (2018). *Super-Sticky WeChat and Chinese Society.* Bingley, UK: Emerald Publishing Limited.

China CSR Research Center. (2018). Nengli yueda, zerenyueda, 2017–2018 hulianwang hangye CSR guancha baogao fabu [With Great Power Comes Great Responsibility, 2017–2018 Internet Industry CSR Report Is Released]. Retrieved from http://www.infzm.com/content/137904.

China Daily. (2006). *Company Law of the People's Republic of China (revised).* Retrieved from http://www.chinadaily.com.cn/bizchina/2006-04/17/content_569258.htm.

China Daily. (2011). *Guo Meimei & the Red Cross Society Scandal.* Retrieved from http://www.chinadaily.com.cn/opinion/2011-07/15/content_12912148.htm.

China Daily. (2017). Dang de shijiuda baogao shuangyu quanwen [Bilingual Report of the 19th National Congress of the Communist Party of China]. Retrieved from http://www.chinadaily.com.cn/interface/flipboard/1142846/2017-11-06/cd_34188086.html.

China Development Brief. (2012). 2011nian minjian gongyi pengbo fazhan, Tuidong Chuantong Cishan Tizhi Zhuanxing [Grassroots Philanthropy Thriving in 2011, Pushing Traditional Charity to Transform]. Retrieved from http://www.chinadevelopmentbrief.org.cn/news-4575.html.

China-embassy.org. (2015). Huliwang+ cuisheng zhongguo cishan gongyi xinhuoli [Internet Plus Generates New Energy for China's Charity and Philanthropy]. Retrieved from http://lb.china-embassy.org/chn/whkj/t1298551.htm.

Chinanews. (2019). Weibo yijidu yingshou 26.8yi yue huoyonghu jingzeng 5400wan zhi 4.65yi [Weibo's Revenue in the First Quarter Was 2.68 Billion, and the Number of Monthly Active Users Increased by 54 Million to 465 Million]. Retrieved from http://www.chinanews.com/it/2019/05-24/8846263.shtml.

Davidson, L. E. (2015). *'Internet Plus' and the Salvation of China's Rural Economy*. Retrieved from https://thediplomat.com/2015/07/internet-plus-and-the-salvation-of-chinas-rural-economy/.

Deng, F. (2014). *Mianfei wucan: Rouruan gaibian zhongguo [Free Lunch for Children: Softness Changes China]*. Beijing: Huawen Press.

Deng, G. (2019). Trends in Overseas Philanthropy by Chinese Foundations. *Voluntas, 30*, 678–691.

Dok, A. N. A., & Thayer, B. A. (2019). *China Is Not in Africa for Charity, But to Control Its Resources*. Retrieved from https://nationalinterest.org/blog/buzz/china-not-africa-charity-control-its-resources-97942.

Dollar, D. (2007). *Poverty, Inequality, and Social Disparities during China's Economic Reform*. Policy Research Working Papers. No. WPS 4253. Washington, DC: World Bank. Retrieved from http://documents.worldbank.org/curated/en/182041468241155669/Poverty-inequality-and-social-disparities-during-Chinas-economic-reform.

Dong, F. (2012). Controlling the Internet in China: The Real Story. *Convergence, 18*(4), 403–425.

Du, J., & Zhang, Y. (2018). Does One Belt One Road Initiative Promote Chinese Overseas Direct Investment? *China Economic Review*, Elsevier 47(C), 189–205.

Foucault, M. (1991). Governmentality. In G. Burchell, C. Gordon, & P. Miller (Eds.), *The Foucault Effect: Studies in Governmentality* (pp. 87–104). Hemel Hempstead: Harvester Wheatsheaf.

Free Lunch for Children. (2018). Choukuan da 75300aoyuan! "mianfei wucan aiman aozhou" dierji wanmei shouguan [Donation reached 75, 300 Australian Dollars. The Second Season of Donation Campaign for Free Lunch for Children Was a Huge Success]. Retrieved from http://www.mianfeiwucan.org/infor/detail3/post/1921/.

Free Lunch for Children. (n.d.). About Us. Retrieved from http://www.mianfeiwucan.org/en/aboutus/.

Gov.cn. (2008). Minjian zuzhi jiaru 'jiuzai zongdongyuan', Zaihou Chongjian Gengxian Youshi [Disaster Relief Shows Advantages with Grassroots Organisations Joining the Action]. Retrieved from http://www.gov.cn/jrzg/2008-07/11/content_1041896.htm.

Gov.cn. (2016a). China's National Plan on Implementation of the 2030 Agenda for Sustainable Development. Retrieved from http://www.gov.cn/xinwen/2016-10/13/5118514/files/44cb945589874551a85d49841b568f18.pdf.

Gov.cn. (2016b). Guowuyuan guanyu yinfa zhongguo luoshi 2030nian kechixu fazhan yicheng chuangxin shifanqu jianshe fangan de tongzhi [The Notice to Develop Innovation Demonstration Zones for Implementation of the 2030 Agenda for Sustainable Development, Released by the State Council]. Retrieved from http://www.gov.cn/zhengce/content/2016-12/13/content_5147412.htm.

Hestres, L. E. (2013). Preaching to the Choir: Internet-mediated Advocacy, Issue public Mobilization, and Climate Change. *New Media & Society, 16*(2), 323–339.
Ho, P. (2007). Embedded Activism and Political Change in a Semiauthoritarian Context. *China Information, XXI*(2), 187–209.
ifeng. (2018). Wenchuan dizhen shizhounian xilie: Zhongguo gongyi shinian shuju guancha [The Tenth Anniversary of Wenchuan Earthquake: Statistics of China's Philanthropy over the Past Ten Years]. Retrieved from https://gongyi.ifeng.com/a/20180514/44990609_0.shtml.
International Center for Not-for-Profit Law. (n.d.). FAQ: China's 2016 Charity Law. Retrieved from http://www.icnl.org/research/Philanthropy/FAQ%20-%20Charity%20Law%20final.pdf.
Internet Society of China. (2018). 2018nian zhongguo hulianwang qiye 100qiang bangdan jiexiao [The Ranking of China's Top 100 Internet Enterprises in 2018 is Released]. Retrieved from http://www.isc.org.cn/zxzx/ywsd/listinfo-36191.html.
Khanna, D. (2019). China's Philanthropic Growth Drives World's Next Big Impact Powerhouse. Retrieved from https://www.forbes.com/sites/deepalikhanna/2019/04/14/chinas-philanthropic-growth-drives-worlds-next-big-impact-powerhouse/#52b1adec6ac2.
Knoerich, J., & Vitting, S. (2018). Controversies and Contradictions about Chinese Investments in Europe. Retrieved from https://www.europenowjournal.org/2018/06/04/controversies-and-contradictions-about-chinese-investments-in-europe/.
Kumi, E. (2019). Advancing the Sustainable Development Goals: An Analysis of the Potential Role of Philanthropy in Ghana. *Journal of Asian and African Studies, 54*(7), 1084–1104.
Lagerkvist, J. (2011). New Media Entrepreneurs in China: Allies of the Party-State or Civil Society. *Columbia Journal of International Affairs, 65*, 169–182.
Lai, Y. (2013). Minjian zuzhi congshi duiwai yuanzhu: yi zhongguo fupin jijinhui yuanzhu feizhou weili [NGOs' Engagement in Foreign Aid: A Case Study on China Foundation for Poverty Alleviation's Aid to Africa]. *Guoji luntan [International Forum], 15*(1), 36–42.
Lim, L. (2011). *In China, Dad Uses Social Media to Find Missing Boy.* Retrieved from https://www.npr.org/2011/02/10/133644822/Chinas-Social-Media-Help-To-Rescue-Abducted-Boy.
Liu, J. (2011). Picturing a Green Virtual Public Space for Social Change: A Study of Internet Activism and Web-based Environmental Collective Actions in China. *Chinese Journal of Communication, 4*(2), 137–166.
McPherson, E. (2017). Social Media and Human Rights Advocacy. In H. Tumber & S. Waisbord (Eds.), *The Routledge Companion to Media and Human Rights* (pp. 279–288). London: Routledge.
Ministry of Civil Affairs. (2013). Sehui tuanti dengji guanli tiaoli [The Regulations of Registration of Social Organizations]. Retrieved from http://mjzx.mca.gov.cn/article/zcfg/201304/20130400437175.shtml.
Ministry of Civil Affairs. (2017). Minzhengbu fabu 'Cishan zuzhi hulianwang gongkai mujuan xinxi pingtai jiben jishu guifan' deng 2xiang hangye biaozhun de gonggao [The Ministry of Civil Affairs Issues Two Standards Including 'Basic Technical Specifications for Online Fundraising Platforms for Charitable Organisations']. Retrieved from http://images3.mca.gov.cn/www/file/201707/1501379930753.pdf.

Morozov, E. (2013). *To Save Everything, Click Here: The Folly of Technological Solutionism*. New York: Public Affairs.

Ogden, K., Prasad, S., & Thompson, R. (2018). Philanthropy Bets Big on Sustainable Development Goals. *Stanford Social Innovation Review*. Retrieved from https://ssir.org/articles/entry/philanthropy_bets_big_on_sustainable_development_goals#%201/13.

Pasquier, M. (2015). *Internet Plus: China's Official Strategy for the Uberisation of the Economy*. Retrieved from https://www.innovationiseverywhere.com/internet-plus-chinas-official-strategy-for-the-uberisation-of-the-economy/.

Paul, D. (2016). *China Releases National Implementation Plan on 2030 Agenda*. Retrieved from http://sdg.iisd.org/news/china-releases-national-implementation-plan-on-2030-agenda/.

People.cn. (2015). Wu Hequan yuanshi: Zhongguo hulianwang zhengchu qiansuo weiyou fazhan hao shiqi [Academician Wu Hequan: China's internet is encountering an unprecedented opportunity for development]. Retrieved from http://it.people.com.cn/n1/2015/1218/c1009-27945182.html.

People's Daily. (2017). *Free Lunch for Children's Campaign to Raise Funds Overseas for International Projects*. Retrieved from http://en.people.cn/n3/2017/0621/c90000-9231406.html.

PRNewswire. (2019). *Tencent Announces 2019 First Quarter Results*. Retrieved from https://finance.yahoo.com/news/tencent-announces-2019-first-quarter-114100359.html.

Saiia, H. D. (2001). Philanthropy and Corporate Citizenship: Strategic Philanthropy is Good Corporate Citizenship. *The Journal of Corporate Citizenship*, 2, 57–74.

Schüll, D. N. (2013). *The Folly of Technological Solutionism: An Interview with Evgeny Morozov*. Retrieved from https://www.publicbooks.org/the-folly-of-technological-solutionism-an-interview-with-evgeny-morozov/.

Servaes, J. (2007). *Communication for Development and Social Change*. London: Sage Publications.

Servaes, J. (2020). *Handbook of Communication for Development and Social Change*. Singapore: Springer. https://doi.org/10.1007/978-981-10-7035-8

Sina. (2008). 2008 shi zhongguo gongyi yuannian [2008 is the Year China Enter A Philanthropic Age]. Retrieved from http://news.sina.com.cn/o/2008-11-04/070014675452s.shtml.

Sina. (2019). Tengxun gongyi xuanbu pingtai yiyou 2.2yi renci juankuan 53yiyuan [Tencent Gongyi Announces the Platform have Raised 5.3 Billion CNY in 220 Million Person Times of Donation]. Retrieved from https://finance.sina.com.cn/roll/2019-05-19/doc-ihvhiqax9858610.shtml?source=cj&dv=1.

Sohu. (2016). Rang hulianwang chengwei ai de haiyang—Fazhan wangluo gongyi changyishu [Let the Internet Become a Sea of Love—Proposal to Develop Internet Philanthropy]. Retrieved from http://it.sohu.com/20160111/n434119061.shtml.

Sohu. (2017). Hulianwang chanye zhan GDP bizhong shijie diyi [China's Internet Industry Contributes the Most to the National GDP in the World]. Retrieved from http://www.sohu.com/a/199572900_500856.

Sohu. (2018). He guoji mianfei wucan yiqi wei qinai de haizimen xuge xinnian yuanwang [Make a New Year's Wish for Dear Children with Free Lunch for Children International]. Retrieved from http://www.sohu.com/a/214989470_752332.

Sorensen, E., & Torfing, J. (2005). Network Governance and Post-liberal Democracy. *Administrative Theory & Praxis*, 27(2), 197–237.

Sustainable Development Goals Partnerships Platform. (n.d.). *Achievement at a Glance*. Retrieved from https://sustainabledevelopment.un.org/partnership/?progress&id=330.

Tencent Foundation. (n.d.). *About Us*. Retrieved from https://gongyi.qq.com/jjhgy/about/about.htm.

United Nations. (2016). *Secretary-General, in Message to World Philanthropy Forum, Underlines 2030 Agenda as Exceptional Opportunity to Address Urgent Human Needs across Sectors*. Retrieved from https://www.un.org/press/en/2016/sgsm18033.doc.htm.

United Nations Development Programme. (2016). *Internet Philanthropy in China*. Retrieved from http://www.cn.undp.org/content/china/en/home/library/poverty/internet-philanthropy-in-china-.html.

Uzuegbunam, C. E., & Omenugha, N. O. (2018). Mainstream Media, Social Media and Peace-building in Nigeria: Old Challenges, New Opportunities? *The Nigerian Journal of Communication (TNJC)*, 15(2), 519–534.

Waisbord, S. (2014). The Strategic Politics of Participatory Communication. In K. G. Wilkins, T. Tufte, & R. Obregon (Eds.), *Handbook of Development Communication and Social Change* (pp. 147–167). Chichester: John Wiley & Sons.

Wilkins, K. G., Tufte, T., & Obregon, R. (2014). *Handbook of Development Communication and Social Change*. Chichester: John Wiley & Sons.

Wu, W. (2016). Minzhengbu zhiding 13jia pingtai wei shoupi 'hulianwang mujuan xinxi pingtai' [The Ministry of Civil Affairs Approves 13 Online Charity Platforms to be the First 'Accredited Internet Charity Fundraising Platforms']. Retrieved from http://www.bjnews.com.cn/news/2016/09/01/415450.html.

Xinhua. (2017a). *Chinese Philanthropy Contributes Greatly to Sustainability Goals: UN Official*. Retrieved from http://www.xinhuanet.com//english/2017-10/14/c_136678206.htm.

Xinhua. (2017b). Zhongguo cishan moshi zhengyan yidai yilu zouchuqu [Chinese Philanthropic Model Is Going Out Along the Belt and Road]. Retrieved from http://www.xinhuanet.com//gongyi/2017-08/03/c_129671988.htm.

Xinhua. (2017c). Ruhe rang wangluo cishan zoude genghao [How to Make a Healthy Development of Internet Philanthropy]. Retrieved from http://www.xinhuanet.com/gongyi/2017-03/30/c_129521211.htm.

Xinhua. (2018). Dierpi cishan zuzhi hulianwang mujuan xinxi pingtai gongbu [More Online Charity Platforms Become Accredited Internet Charity Fundraising Platforms]. Retrieved from http://www.xinhuanet.com/gongyi/2018-05/24/c_129879664.htm.

Xinhua. (2019). 2018nian, 84.6yi renci canyu hulianwang cishan [In 2018, 8.46 Billion Person Trips Participated in Internet Philanthropy]. Retrieved from http://www.xinhuanet.com/gongyi/2019-04/08/c_1210102158.htm.

Xu, J. (2015). Online *Weiguan* in Web 2.0 China: Historical Origins, Characteristics, Platforms and Consequences. In G. Yang (Ed.), *China's Contested Internet* (pp. 257–282). Copenhagen: NIAS Press of the University of Copenhagen.

Xu, J. (2016). *Media Events in Web 2.0 China: Interventions of Online Activism*. Brighton: Sussex Academic Press.

Yang, L. (2014). *Chinese Outbound Philanthropy*. Retrieved from https://www.forbes.com/sites/linyang/2014/12/28/chinese-outbound-philanthropy/#ef091bacbcde.

Yang, P., & Tang, L. (2018). 'Positive Energy': Hegemonic Intervention and Online Media Discourse in China's Xi Jinping Era. *China: An International Journal, 16*(1), 1–22.

Yu, H. (2017). Philanthropy on the Move: Mobile Communication and Neoliberal Citizenship in China. *Communication and the Public, 2*(1), 35–49.

Yu, H. (2018). Social Media and the Experience Economy in China's Microphilanthropy. In M. Kent, K. Ellis, & J. Xu (Eds.), *Chinese Social Media: Social, Cultural and Political Implications* (pp. 9–21). London and New York: Routledge.

Zhang, M. (2014). Zhongguo gongyi de feizhou changshi: cong zhengfu dao minjian [Chinese Philanthropy in Africa: From Government to NGOs]. *China Philanthropy Times*. Retrieved from www.gongyishibao.com/html/yaowen/6478.html.

Zheng, Y., & Tok, S. (2007). "Harmonious Society" and "Harmonious World": China's Policy Discourse under Hu Jintao. Briefing Series. Issue 26. China Policy Institute, The University of Nottingham. Retrieved from https://www.nottingham.ac.uk/iaps/documents/cpi/briefings/briefing-26-harmonious-society-and-harmonious-world.pdf.

Zhou, M. (2018). Tencent Charity Day Raises 830 Million Yuan among Internet Users. Retrieved from http://www.chinadaily.com.cn/a/201809/10/WS5b965f86a31033b4f46553e7.html.

CHAPTER 18

Facts Aren't Enough: Addressing Communication Challenges in the Pollinator Crisis and Beyond

Lara Zwarun and Gerardo R. Camilo

INTRODUCTION

In pursuit of the noble purpose of creating the "future we want," all United Nations Member States in 2015 created the 2030 Agenda for Sustainable Development. The plan comprises 17 goals for achieving a better world, by addressing needs that at times seem incompatible: keeping up with an expanding human population while taking care of an overly taxed planet (United Nations, n.d.). The sustainable development goals (SDGs) were developed via multinational collaboration, and recognize the interdependence of economic, social and environmental issues in improving the planet for all its residents. For example, SDG 2 is to end hunger and achieve food security, but the Agenda notes this should be done "while promoting sustainable agriculture," halting biodiversity loss (SDG 15) and making cities sustainable (SDG 11). In other words, actions proposed to address one problem must always be considered in terms of their impact on other concerns.

L. Zwarun (✉)
Department of Communication and Media, University of Missouri–St. Louis, St. Louis, MO, USA
e-mail: zwarunl@umsl.edu

G. R. Camilo
Department of Biology, Saint Louis University, St. Louis, MO, USA
e-mail: gerardo.camilo@slu.edu

© The Author(s), under exclusive license to Springer Nature Switzerland AG 2021
M. J. Yusha'u, J. Servaes (eds.), *The Palgrave Handbook of International Communication and Sustainable Development*,
https://doi.org/10.1007/978-3-030-69770-9_18

The complexity and multi-faceted nature of sustainable growth is well captured by the worldwide pollinator crisis. Due in large part to human development, and ancillary loss of native habitats and increased use of pesticides, pollinator populations are perilously low. The Intergovernmental Science-Policy Platform on Biodiversity and Ecosystem Services (IPBES) estimates that over a third of pollinator species important for human food and fibre production are decreasing in abundance, or worse, considered threatened or endangered (Potts et al., 2016). This threatens the ability of ecosystems to provide essential pollination services (Potts et al., 2016). What's more, this threat to a vital resource is not distributed equally across all people, reflecting unjust disparities within society.

There is a way to address this problem, and it is a solution that addresses not only the pollinator crisis, but a broad range of interconnected problems, by preventing hunger, increasing biodiversity, addressing environmental issues and reducing social disparities by improving the health, diet and economic opportunities of disadvantaged people. Research has shown that pollinators, particularly bees, are doing well in poor urban areas, where residents use vacant space for community gardens and urban farms. Urban agriculture not only facilitates pollinator corridors within cities, it provides fresh food in food deserts, and increases community stability. Moreover, it builds momentum for individual citizens in other neighbourhoods to adjust their lawn care practices to be more pollinator-friendly. Successfully reversing the pollinator decline could therefore exemplify the sort of solution the 2030 Agenda is looking for.

Yet implementation of this, or any, solution is dependent on effective communication. As the 2030 Agenda makes clear, not only does the world face challenges in sustainability, it faces challenges in communicating about them. Human support and action are needed to effect change, and communication is what helps attain support across multiple actors. In this chapter, we will use the pollinator crisis—with a focus on cities, where huge population shifts are expected—to illustrate how communication is a necessary tool for working with and empowering communities while framing the crisis in ways that motivate sustainable development (Kusmanoff et al., 2020). We will first review the threat to biodiversity and food production caused by pollinator decline, then describe some promising news about pollinator diversity and abundance in urban spaces. After that, we will discuss two crucial ways that effective communication can be employed to achieve the objectives set forth by the UN 2030 Agenda for Sustainable Development and to address the pollinator crisis. The first is to use the Communication for Development and Social Change (CDSC) framework to understand and join forces with relevant stakeholders, working with and among individual citizens in a bottom-up approach so as to harness their important contributions. The second is to enlist the expertise of communication scholars and professionals to design tailored, consistent strategic messaging that cuts through limited attention and involvement by appealing to relevant motivations for these audiences. By using these two tactics, those interested in sustainable development will be able to reach the right audience, understand who the "competition" is in battling for individuals' support and design messages that control the narrative rather than allowing it to be reframed. We propose that while the specific application of these techniques will vary across sustainability issues, the underlying communication principles outlined in this chapter are applicable in many global contexts, and are at the heart of fulfilling the sustainable development goals of the UN's 2030 Agenda for Sustainable Development.

Pollinator Declines and Urban Migration

The established consensus in the scientific literature is that we are facing a pollinator crisis of global proportions (FAO, 2018; Koh et al., 2016; National Research Council, 2007; Potts, Imperatriz-Fonseca, Ngo, Biesmeijer, et al., 2016; Potts, Imperatriz-Fonseca, Ngo, Aizen, et al., 2016). Pollinators, particularly native bees such as bumblebees, are required for one-third of the crops that humans consume (Ollerton, Winfree, & Tarrant, 2011). However, the abundance and diversity of bees have been declining for the past two decades (Cameron et al., 2011; Koh et al., 2016; Potts, Imperatriz-Fonseca, Ngo, Biesmeijer, et al., 2016). The causes of these precipitous declines in recent years are attributed to loss of suitable habitat, introduced species and use of pesticides (Cane & Tepedino, 2001; Goulson et al. 2015). The decline threatens the ability to feed the earth's growing population, at the same time that it seems difficult to interrupt given human development (Roubik, 2014).

The current pollinator crisis serves as an excellent example of how methods of protecting and increasing urban biodiversity must simultaneously accommodate the rapid growth of cities worldwide. We are in the midst of a vast human migration towards cities; it is estimated that by 2050, 66% of people will live in an urban area. This will require that the urban infrastructure double by 2050 (Board, 2005; Creutzig et al., 2016; Ferrer, Thomé, & Scavarda, 2018). Nearly 60% of required urban land cover is yet to be built (Angel, Parent, Civco, Blei, & Potere, 2011; Jiang & O'Neill, 2017).

At the same time, many cities also contain "food deserts," areas with few grocery stores and limited options to buy fresh produce and healthy food (Purnell et al., 2014). Food deserts typically occur in parts of cities with slums and poverty, which were neglected after population flight to suburban areas or from loss of jobs and industries (Horst, McClintock, & Hoey, 2017; Raja, Ma, & Yadav, 2008). These neighbourhoods are poorly served by businesses, a symptom of disinvestment in run-down, low-income areas by businesses and grocers (Prener, Braswell, & Monti, 2018). This condition represents a social inequity that contributes to disproportionate health problems in these neighbourhoods (Drewnowski, Aggarwal, Cook, Stewart, & Moudon, 2016; Purnell et al. 2014). Addressing the problem of hunger in urban areas will therefore require addressing problems of inequality and conservation, not just food production or distribution, consistent with the inter-related needs targeted by the SDGs of the 2030 Agenda (Roubik, 2014).

An interesting glimmer of hope in this challenging reality is the recently discovered fact that many cities are refuges for native bees (Baldock et al., 2015; Hall et al., 2017). Despite the current paucity of pollinators, there are places where their populations thrive, including some of the poorest, most neglected neighbourhoods. Post-industrial cities with decrepit infrastructure and vacant lots have bee diversity comparable to native prairies (Hall et al., 2017). In these "shrinking cities," so named because they have lost 1% of their inner urban population annually for at least ten consecutive years, bees have made a vibrant home, succeeding in the tall grasses of un-mowed land and the varied vegetation of the many community gardens that have sprung up on vacant lots. In the United States, this frequently occurs in "rust belt" cities such as Detroit (Glaum, Simao, Vaidya, Fitch, & Iulinao, 2017), Chicago (Lowenstein, Matteson, & Minor, 2015; Tonietto, Fant, Ascher, Ellis, & Larkin, 2011), Cleveland (Gardiner et al., 2013; Turo & Gardiner, 2019) and St. Louis (Camilo, Muñiz, Arduser, & Spevak, 2018), and more specifically, in the most economically disadvantaged neighbourhoods within them. These neighbourhoods have increasingly fallen into disrepair due to public policies, and are often hotbeds of social inequity (e.g. Tighe & Ganning, 2015); however, the same vacant lots and dilapidated buildings that dissuade businesses from building and investing in the community provide the right conditions for many bee species (Anderson & Minor, 2017; Burr, Schaeg, Muñiz, Camilo, & Hall, 2016; Gardiner et al., 2013).

It is not, however, just neglect and decay that help the bees. In cities with large numbers of vacant properties—St. Louis city, for example, has over 120,000 (Prener et al., 2018)—a range of agricultural practices, ranging from individual parcels to community gardens to urban farms, have emerged as a response to the unused space and lack of grocery stores. Community gardens and urban farms have to adapt to a large diversity of spaces and a variety of individual and cultural palettes and needs (Taylor & Lovell, 2014). In a parcel that is less than 100 metres square, it is not uncommon to record over a dozen different crops (Taylor & Lovell, 2014). The large crop diversity in urban agriculture results in large floral diversity and increased habitat heterogeneity, which is highly correlated with increased pollinator diversity (Lowenstein et al., 2015; Lowenstein & Minor, 2016). As a result, bees are thriving in parts of some cities where humans are struggling to thrive. Even cities that are not "shrinking" or that do not have vast expanses of vacant property, such as the booming Sun Belt city of Phoenix, Arizona, tend to possess vibrant bee populations if they possess community gardens or "natural" green spaces (Lowe & Foltz-Sweat, 2017).

Studies of native bees indicate that diverse communities of wild bees persist in cities in many parts of the world, such as Berlin, Germany (Saure et al., 1998); Birmingham, Bristol, Cardiff, Dundee, Edinburg, Glasgow, Hull, Leeds, Leicester, London, Northampton, Reading, Sheffield, Southampton and Swindon in the United Kingdom (Baldock et al., 2015; Goulson et al., 2008; Sirohi et al. 2015); Paris, France (Geslin et al., 2016), Melbourne,

Australia (Threlfall et al., 2015); Guanacaste, Costa Rica (Frankie et al., 2013); and Vancouver (Tommasi, Miro, Higo, & Winston, 2004), Montreal and Quebec City, Canada (Normandin, Vereecken, Buddle, & Fournier, 2017). There are worldwide examples of gardens making use of vacant land, addressing food insecurity and providing resources and habitat for pollinators, while also empowering those who tend and benefit from them, stabilizing the blocks surrounding them and building engagement in the community (Braswell, 2018; Prener et al., 2018). This is why the pollinator crisis and ways to address it in the midst of urban growth are an ideal context within which to examine the interdependent economic, social and environmental issues associated with the 2030 Agenda SDGs, and how communication can be used strategically to advance them.

Pollinators and SDGs

Pollination services are intrinsic to a number of the UN's Sustainable Development Goals. Bees, as well as other pollinators, carry out an essential ecosystem process needed not just by the crops that humans (Ollerton et al., 2011) and their domesticated livestock consume (Delaplane, Mayer, & Mayer, 2000), but that almost all ecosystems on Earth depend upon (Ollerton & Coulthard, 2009). Thus, the conservation of pollinators is directly relevant to Sustainable Development Goal 2—Zero Hunger. A recent review of the literature concluded that pollinators provide a range of services to a variety of urban agriculture forms, from basic home gardens to edible landscapes to rooftop gardens (Nicholls, Ely, Birkin, Basu, & Goulson, 2020). In this way, increased pollinator diversity and abundance are linked to increased local productivity, which translates into decreased hunger (SDG 2.1), decreased malnutrition (SDG 2.2), increased income for farmers (SDG 2.3), sustainable food production (SDG 2.4) and decreased loss of crops' genetic diversity (SDG 2.5).

Nor are pollinators only relevant to SDG 2. In fact, a survey of the scientific literature reports that bees potentially contribute to 15 of the 17 SDGs and at least 30 of their targets, leading the authors to conclude that sustainable pollination systems are essential for meeting SDGs (Patel, Pauli, Biggs, Barbour, & Boruff, 2020). While many of the benefits in this review pertain specifically to the keeping of domesticated honeybees for honey and related products, the conservation of pollinators such as native bees (e.g. bumblebees and squash bees) is linked directly to SDG 15—Life on Land, and more specifically, to the protection of biodiversity (15.5) and integrating ecosystem values into local and national planning (15.9). Both pollination services and beekeeping have resulted in improved livelihoods for small farmers in Kenya (1.5), including Indigenous groups (1.4, 1.5) and women (5.a, 5.5) (Patel et al., 2020). In general, pollination by animals, and specifically bees, is so deeply embedded into all ecosystems that it has been linked to most SDGs (FAO, 2018; Nicholls et al., 2020).

It is worth noting that despite the positive and essential aspects of pollination, Patel et al. (2020) acknowledged the challenge in generating pollinator-friendly practices, and called for increased information exchange and participation among the scientific community, policymakers and the public in general. This directive illustrates the crucial role that communication plays in galvanizing people to address sustainability issues, including the pollinator crisis. One cannot change society without communication (Servaes & Malikhao, 2014). In the case of the pollinator crisis, the general public must be empowered to help solve this issue, both individually (e.g. through responsible lawn and property management), and through reframing of cultural norms and aesthetics as well as support for larger scale policies and initiatives to protect pollinators. Research must be disseminated and translated for policymakers and affected communities. Mass media can be used to promote interactivity between different stakeholders, and play a role through how they frame and prioritize social issues. Analysing how and why communication serves the goal of advancing pollinator protection in urban areas is therefore instructive in examining how communication principles can drive sustainability efforts more generally (Ohlson, 2015).

The Communications for Development and Social Change Paradigm

Communicating is how individuals share thoughts, feelings, intentions and needs; how they persuade each other, inspire one another, inform, educate and debate. This happens at the interpersonal level; through mass communication such as newspapers and radio; and increasingly, in the mediated sphere of digital social networking, from Twitter to blogs to Zoom town halls.

A difficulty that arises from communication about science stems from the tendency to conceive of scientific communication as the process of scientists and "authorities" disseminating ideas to people who need educating. While this is a frequent and necessary aspect of communicating science, it reflects a potentially problematic hierarchy of societal actors—those who know and those who need to be told. Yet communication is often more successful as a dialogue, a multi-directional process with feedback, collaboration and participation by all parties. Particularly when one's goal is social change, communication is best conceived as a social, interactive process, not just messaging directed at people.

In fact, unidirectional communication may be of limited utility in the case of communicating science. It can have the effect of making scientists outsiders to a community, which is problematic when many people distrust both science and outsiders. What's more, the deficit model of science communication—the idea that people need to be educated, and once they are, will behave in a desired way—is not accurate (National Academies, 2017). People are complex, with many motivations for their actions, and simply filling them with certain facts or perspectives will not necessarily result in a desired behaviour. Thus, not only is communicating with an eye towards improving society better conceptualized as a cooperative process, it is more likely to be effective as a cooperative process too.

The interactive, cooperative process described here is known as Communication for Development and Social Change (CDSC), a theoretical framework for how various means of communication can create a favourable environment for social change (Servaes, 2008). This perspective emerged out of decades of well-meaning but not entirely successful endeavours to bring change and improvement to "developing" societies. Servaes and others noted that in these types of situations, it was common for Westerners to arrive in a different culture, prescribe goals and plans and set about strategic messaging to inform and convince the native citizens to embrace and achieve them. Rarely was this entirely successful. The Communication for Development and Social Change model recognizes that people play a crucial role in their own development. While there may be universal human rights, they must be translated into local cultural context, and this is done by allowing people to share their ideas about who they are and how they want to be so that they are heard. Reciprocal collaboration is required so that a dialogue emerges that is not top down, but horizontal. In this model, change is not done to or for a society of people, but with them, by promoting their access to and participation in debates and discussions about the future. Rather than simply disseminating ideas, this method uses ongoing discussion and communication to identify what there is a need for so it can be met, rather than telling people that what they are being told is what they need (Servaes, 2008).

Involving people in their own evolution in an ongoing, culturally relevant way is a framework under which the varied types of communication that characterize current society all fall. Certainly, it encompasses the idea of mass communication in the form of "fair and accurate journalism, including community journalism," and "media programming that builds confidence and counteracts misperceptions," (Servaes, 2008, p. 27), an example of which is edutainment in the form of radio serials or fictional books (Senaratne, 2017). Mass communication scholars have long understood the idea of tailoring messages to audiences, and as digital technology expands the ways in which and reasons why people use different media, this perspective allows for the agility needed to be relevant and compete for scarce attention. It applies as well to mediated interpersonal communication, with its power to rapidly spread ideas through a combination of social media sharing and face-to-face discussion—ideas that may originate from outside the culture or be created by citizens within it. It also captures the importance of direct communication between individuals or groups, through which the knowledge of and involvement with the culture emerges (Lie & Servaes, 2015).

Promoting sustainable development—generally, as well as through protecting pollinators, as discussed here—requires communication of all of these types, as well as a variety of messages, calls to a range of actions, and cultural awareness in different contexts. The principles of the communications for social and developmental change paradigm afford a perspective to unify these and achieve desired goals. Moreover, in the words of Maimunah Mohd Sharif, Executive Director of UN-Habitat, "Cities are the spaces where all SDGs can be integrated to provide holistic solutions to the challenges of poverty, exclusion, climate change and risks" (UN Forum, 2018). The potential for a meaningful way to address the pollinator crisis exists; it involves (indeed, it depends upon) ordinary citizens (in fact, some of the less privileged among them), and it has the potential to address several of the SDGs. Its success is contingent on effective communication in the vein of CDSC.

Strategic Communication of Science

In the case of environmental sustainability, and science more broadly, communication can be a challenge (National Academies, 2017), even after using the principles behind CDSC to establish community goals. The subject matter may include technical or difficult to understand concepts, making it inaccessible for many people. People may not be motivated to expend effort processing this type of information, or they may be sceptical of it for various reasons, or they may not know how to interpret it.

At the same time, messages about science exist in a challenging environment of vast amounts of information. It is difficult to find an attentive audience when so many other messages are competing with yours, particularly if yours is more complex. Scientists tend to speak their own language, of probability and methodology and jargon, and are not trained in how to translate this to people who vary in education, native tongue and cultural norms, or in other communication skills. They work in a realm where jargon, citations and lengthy explanations are desired and the norm. This style of message will never reach regular people, no matter how much it is the intention of the sender to do so.

What's more, communication today occurs not only through traditional media formats like newspapers or television broadcasts but also via social and digital media (Matsa & Mitchell, 2014). The explosion of digital technology, including smart phones, has increased the amount of information available to people astronomically, to the point where it can be overwhelming (Anderson & De Palma, 2012; Pentina & Tarafdar, 2014). As a result, humans have become more likely to preserve cognitive resources by using heuristic cues (Westerman, Spence, & Van Der Heide, 2014). For example, headlines, trending hashtags on Twitter, memes and links to stories, shared via their personal networks, allow people to superficially monitor their environment, without digging deeply into most topics (e.g. Matsa & Mitchell, 2014; Oeldorf-Hirsch, 2018; Pew Research Center, 2019). A consequence of this phenomenon is heightened importance on how a topic is portrayed in the media—not to the careful reader but to the casual observer who may come across it very briefly or distractedly (Gil de Zúñiga, Weeks, & Adrèvol-Abreu, 2017). We live in a world dominated by brands that are infused with personalities and identities by marketing professionals. Science will always be at a disadvantage in such a world unless it can be heard and understood in that same environment: that is to say, to deliver catchy, easy to digest messages that showcase and advance its various ideas and issues needing civic involvement.

When it comes to science, most non-experts get the majority of their knowledge from the mass media (Dahlstrom, 2014). The challenge facing people hoping to advance the cause of sustainable development and biodiversity is not that there is no science in popular culture, but that there is little science deliberately framed and strategically placed by scientists there. Citizens are not sitting around waiting for environmentalists to communicate with them. They can't know what is going on outside their immediate spheres of existence, so the media often fulfils the important function of showing them. In doing so, the media also shape issues; people only have attitudes towards or take action on things after they know they exist. Humanity is currently facing a major challenge in the unprecedented loss of biodiversity, referred to as a "sixth mass extinction" (Ceballos et al., 2015). Given that humans depend on biodiversity for a large range of ecosystem services, from food production to carbon sequestration to disease regulation (Mace, Norris, & Fitter, 2012), it's tremendously important that the general public become aware of and informed about this, not just decision and policymakers. Everyone should have a basic understanding of what is at stake.

For this to happen, scientists and environmentalists must deliver messages that ordinary citizens bump into, that are digestible to a busy, distracted audience and that they control. This requires that they seek out the help of communication experts, who are just as good at messaging as the scientific community is at doing science. Communication scholars and practitioners know how to design messages that are appropriate for lay-people. They understand that less can be more, and sometimes the whole story is not needed, even though this is not how scientists usually communicate. The goal must be on effectively reaching people, not including everything that an enthusiastic scientist might wish to share.

Whether members of the scientific community realize it or not, communication is a social scientific discipline with a rich tradition of scholarship (National Communication Association, 2015; "What is Communication," n.d.). There are many communication scholars who conduct empirical research designing or testing the efficacy of messages and various channels of delivering them, and others who do this sort of work for clients. Many would view collaboration with those promoting sustainability as opportunities to collect data, test hypotheses and develop theories. Funded researchers will find that there are media firms and advertising agencies that wish to work on socially responsible causes, courses and workshops offered in how to develop communication plans, and freelancers with a range of communication education and experience available to hire. It is not unrealistic that collaborations between environmental scientists and communication experts could occur.

As they seek expert help from communicators, people promoting sustainable development are advised to extend their communication efforts beyond journal articles, scholarly conferences with similarly educated people, and "deficit model" didacticism, which assumes that less-knowledgeable people need simply be filled up with information from the scientific community in order to do the right thing. Recognizing the many demands on people in today's world, they are encouraged to design messaging that uses metaphors, narratives and personal anecdotes, and that is shared on social media to attract and maintain interest in their issues, with an emphasis on interesting, timely, practical, surprising, dramatic or emotional frames with geographic or cultural relevance to the audience, as these are more likely to be shared (go viral) (Badenschier & Wormer, 2012; Legagneux et al., 2018).

This strategy is not without risk; it is likely to initially be unappealing to many scientists, who understandably will be worried about inaccuracy, partisanship and sensationalism. That is why it is so important that it be the result of close collaboration between scientists and communication experts. Despite any trepidation, there are serious benefits to capturing the public's attention in this way. Combining the sincerity and accuracy of CDSC and the expertise of the communication discipline has the potential to create powerful, effective communication that competes successfully with other noise in people's media environment. Further, we will illustrate several instances of how this can be successfully employed with respect to the pollinator crisis. While specifics will vary for other issues, we believe the principles they represent generalize to other SDGS, and indeed, to science communication in general.

Communication Principle 1: Identify and Understand Your Diverse Audiences

The idea of tailoring a message for one's audience goes back at least to Aristotle's concept of ethos, so it is nothing new to recommend that messaging around SDGs take into account with whom one is communicating. Whereas Aristotle was committed to the study of persuasion, however, scientists and policymakers concerned with sustainable development are focused on other areas of expertise, and may well have little to no training in effective communication. Passionate about and absorbed in their area of interest, they tend to be more concerned with sharing what they know, without necessarily being inclusive or strategic. Their efforts are further complicated by the need to reach diverse stakeholders with varied motivations, degrees of literacy and levels of trust of science. Yet they hope to reach the goals of engaging the public and getting people to "take urgent and significant action" (SDG 15.1). This requires conducting a complete analysis of the society and culture.

Spending time among and listening to citizens and communities as described in the CDSC paradigm creates the greatest likelihood of advancing the goals of reducing biodiversity loss and protecting pollinators. This increases the likelihood of generating individual attitudes and behaviours that favour these goals.

Individual citizens, who may have no knowledge of or interest in the subject, are an incredibly important audience for messages about protecting pollinators. Whether they realize it or not, humans strongly influence urban biodiversity (McDonnell & Hahs, 2013). Individual residents of cities make decisions that shape the urban environment and profoundly affect its ecology (Aronson et al., 2016). It is unwise to invest resources in shaping policy or behaviour at the community or societal level and not engage individual citizens.

There are several reasons why individuals are such an important part of protecting pollinators. At the most basic level, it is because they make decisions about their own property and how it will be maintained—how often they will mow, whether pesticides will be used and what they will plant. Residential yards constitute a significant portion of US urban landscapes (Minor, Belaire, Davis, Franco, & Lin, 2016). Their varied needs and wants can improve native pollinator diversity and abundance by increasing vegetation resources in the form of forage and habitat in residential yards (Harris, Kendal, Hahs, & Threlfall, 2018). These vegetation attributes strongly influence habitat quality, and can be easily manipulated. High plant species and structural diversity in gardens are the product of individual actions, and likely to play as important a role in urban biodiversity conservation as coordinated actions across large spaces (Goddard, Dougill, & Benton, 2010; Kendal, Williams, & Williams, 2010). Thus, while a city or a neighbourhood as a whole can be seen as an urban refuge, each parcel of land has its own potential to be a refuge of suitable habitat for pollinators.

As previously noted, some of the most important work in addressing the pollinator problem must be done in cities, and resource-poor urban communities are among the most promising locations, due to their abundance and variety of pollinators. These are also communities that have often been ignored in environmental movements, without regard for the many layers of power structures that have created unequal access and opportunities for them, or else that have been viewed as deficient and needing to be saved (Ohlson, 2015). With the pollinator crisis, like many other environmental and social issues, individuals matter and must be involved, invited to be leaders in the work that must be done, not mere beneficiaries of it (Slocum, 2007). Communication is instrumental in accomplishing this (Ohlson, 2015), but to engage people on the topic requires trust on the part of the community, and that may not exist.

A number of explanations have been offered to explain why some people are increasingly distrustful of science and scientists (Goodwin & Dahlstrom, 2014; Wynne, 2006). Some have to do with personal variables, such as socio-economic status and education levels, while others are a function of who is disseminating the information. In terms of personal attributes, valuing scientific authority is more likely to occur among people with higher levels of education, especially when one's perceived knowledge of the issue is low (Brossard & Nisbet, 2007). How much one values scientific authority affects the level of trust one places in science and scientists, which then mediates outcomes such as the degree of attention people pay to guidance from scientific experts and their willingness to act (National Academies, 2017). Distrust in science is also higher when individuals feel their identity or interests are threatened (National Academies, 2017), as may occur in communities that have been marginalized or underserved. In addition, acceptance of scientific information is based on evaluation of who is disseminating it. Actual expertise matters less than perceived expertise, and perceptions of expertise are often rooted in the person or organization's history of being truthful, helpful and fair (National Academies, 2017). Many of the urban communities where bees thrive are populated with citizens who have less formal education than more affluent suburbs, as well as Black and Latinx residents, who have historically been disenfranchised and overlooked in political contexts (Woolf et al., 2015; Wynne, 2006). Moreover, they may have negative histories of being ignored by scientists, or used as temporary locations for data collection, with minimal if any follow-through of sharing or applying results to their community (Corbie-Smith, Thomas, & George, 2002; George, Duran, & Norris, 2014). For all of these reasons, trust in and willingness to work with scientists may be low. Effectively reaching such people requires genuine awareness of who they are, what they believe and the difficulties they face.

Rust Belt cities in the United States where bees are thriving in poor, decimated communities, such as St. Louis, provide an excellent example of how this can work. Telling people they should "save the bees" is not likely to be a particularly effective strategy there, but encouraging participation in the vibrant system of community gardens that already exist in the community, that provide fresh food despite the lack of grocery stores, that lower the cost of feeding a family, and that increase positive neighbourhood involvement despite the large number of vacant properties, is a supportive and relevant approach that meets people where they are and responds to their challenges rather than prescribing values or actions. This arises out of using the Communication for Development and Social Change (CDSC) paradigm's practice of community members expressing what they need, not being told what they should care about.

Moreover, this approach illustrates how CDSC and working with communities of individuals can be used to heed the call of the 2030 Agenda, by expanding the focus of ecologists, urban planners and policymakers to supporting and preserving not only fauna and creatures, but also the growing number of humans. Including and communicating with individual citizens—whether about the pollinator crisis or other environmental issues—helps individuals engage as community members (Legagneux et al., 2018). Engagement is what turns a group of people who live near each other into a community, a network of people who communicate, share interests and generate social capital, "a pillar of a fully functioning democratic society" (Johnson & Lane, 2018). Community engagement can be episodic or relational. The former is centred around a particular issue or topic, and solicits community feedback towards an issue in a more limited feedback loop. Relational engagement is not centred around a particular issue, takes place over a longer period of time and builds trust more than solves specific problems (Johnson & Lane, 2018). In the case of pollination, episodic engagement would refer to communicating with individuals about ways they can nurture pollinators, participate in urban agriculture and grow quality food. Relational engagement would be communication that reminds residents that they are part of a community, solicits their input on the needs of that community and inspires collective support of health, justice and equality (Ohlson, 2015). Both of these can occur if there is a dialogue that includes citizens, scientists and policymakers, all included and listened to about sustainability and developmental issues and other areas of concern and interest (Legagneux et al., 2018). This type of communication greatly increases the likelihood of people supporting pollinators through responsible lawn management practices, particularly in underserved urban areas.

Partnering and communicating with individual communities, as suggested by CDSC, also allows for recognition of the inevitable variation among groups of people. For example, with respect to protecting pollinators, one must be sure to also communicate with community members who will not change their lawn management behaviour, but may be encouraged to have greater tolerance of those who will. In urban areas, this may mean reaching out to individuals who choose or are unable to actively participate in environmentally friendly ventures, and working to increase their awareness of and tolerance for pollinator- and diversity-friendly actions. The goal is to not only motivate some people to engage in responsible practices but also increase awareness of and "buy in" to these behaviours among those who won't or can't participate in them. In more affluent neighbourhoods, there may be pressure to maintain a lawn that is uniform with other neighbours' properties, or compliance with a Homeowners' Association to consider. This is another case where it is not enough to only encourage people to change their lawn maintenance behaviours. One must also encourage non-participants to be more comfortable with diverse non-conventional aesthetics and lawn practices, thereby easing pressure on those who are engaging in them. If people who make changes in their lawn practices feel supported in doing so, this may result in them sharing and bragging about it, further contributing to the spread of these practices. Only by having "feet on the ground" in each community and actively involving citizens in conservation efforts will one recognize and be able to address these and other contingents. As another example, there may be citizens already actively involved in environmentally friendly gardening and lawn care, who are receiving messaging on the subject from other sources, such as organizations to which they belong (e.g. the Audubon Society). Not only will they be identified as another audience for communication, but it will also be possible to design messaging that is consistent with what else they are being told.

Communicating with an audience of "regular people," not just elected officials and policymakers, has the power to be a game changer, since it reflects an evolution from top-down solutions, such as regulations and policies, to more inclusive sustainable development. It is also savvy because, in the case of pollinators and urban spaces, it is unrealistic to assume that sufficient pollinator protection policies will be put in place by governments and municipalities.

There is always a risk that such entities will see vacant lots as unfulfilled areas of human development, in the process pushing for policies that actually compromise the bee habitats (Prener et al., 2018), and therefore, communication with policymakers, politicians and NGOs will also need to be pursued. Communicating with this audience is not a focus of this chapter, as those seeking environmental and sustainability goals tend to already be experienced in this regard; however, we will note that even these opportunities for communication will be improved by being able to more fully and inclusively represent the constituents who will be affected by the policies in the messaging.

Finally, it must be noted that the landscape management practices that are encouraged as pollinator-friendly in the United States—such as mowing less, planting natives and minimizing pesticide use—will differ across countries, and between urban and agricultural areas. We are therefore talking about not only targeting different, unique audiences, but doing so with different, yet compatible messages. While this may sound daunting, it is entirely plausible, and is in fact done for commercial ends by marketers every day. As such marketers know, understanding who you are talking to, determining what behavioural changes to request from them, identifying their motivations for caring about the issue and designing and delivering effective messaging are all made possible only by first conducting a thorough and substantive analysis of the communities in question—an analysis that involves listening as much as talking, responding as much as proposing and cooperating as much as informing.

Communication Principle 2: Combine Audience Insight with Communication Theory and Expertise to Deliver the Right Message(s)

Humans tend not to be interested in hearing much about problems that they think are unsolvable. To learn of something dangerous, harmful or urgent, and then feel that there is nothing they or anyone can do to address it creates dissonance, and a feeling of helplessness that is not likely to inspire positive action. Numerous dual-process theories of communication, such as the Extended Parallel Process Model, note the importance of communicating self-efficacy along with risk when trying to inspire action (Witte, 1992). Thus, communicating with citizens about environmental issues is best done in ways that promote positive emotions and convey that there are tangible ways in which they can make a difference. This can be accomplished by personalizing the pollinator issue, using its relevance to the audience as a source of inspiration.

In recent years, a growing literature in the communication discipline has focused on positive emotions and their potential for cognitive, behavioural and physiological effects (Nabi, 2015). One such positive emotion is hope. There is preliminary support for the idea that hope is a productive emotion that can motivate desired action (Chadwick, 2015) towards important healthy goals (Prestin, 2013). Evidence suggests that the persuasive ability of both fear appeals and evaluations of risk can be increased by increasing self-efficacy through conveyance of hope (Nabi, Gustafson, & Jensen, 2018; Nabi & Myrick, 2018; Yang, Liu, & Popova, 2019). Marketers have long understood the value of using messages with "the motivational fuel of hope" (MacInnis & De Mello, 2005, p. 339). Prestin (2013) suggests social marketers and health promoters should follow suit, harnessing the fact that hope can be a message-generated emotion (Nabi, 2015).

Another attention-getting way to frame issues centres on the positive emotion of pride. The motivational hypothesis of pride says that pride is an incentive to take further action in the area in which recognition has been received (Williams & DeSteno, 2008). This occurs because the acclaim provided by others serves as a social marker of one's value to a social group, motivating people to increase adaptive behaviours. Pride is "a discrete positive state capable of motivating personal development … and may function quite well to impel individuals to develop valuable skills and abilities and in doing so, to take their place as a respected member of their social communities" (Williams & DeSteno, 2008, p. 1014). Pride's motivating power, particularly in light of the importance of perceptions of group identity to group members' self-worth, suggests that providing citizens with something that is recognized in which they can take pride might motivate them towards certain positive behaviours and feelings. Increasing pride could have important consequences for civic behaviour. Practically speaking, to create change in a community, it is also necessary to have the buy-in of all relevant stakeholders, regardless of their level of education or familiarity with formal academic research (Woolf et al., 2015), which means convincing them it matters what they as individuals think and do (Ohlson, 2015).

To illustrate the way this might work with the pollinator crisis, once again consider the success of pollinators in poor urban neighbourhoods. In the case of St. Louis, not only is this something that residents of these neighbourhoods can feel proud of, it is a resource that more affluent parts of cities, with manicured and fertilized acreage, lack (Burr et al., 2016; Burr, Hall, & Schaeg, 2018). It is possible that sharing with community members the success their neighbourhoods and community gardens have already had in supporting pollinators, and the significance of this to their and their community's well-being, will inspire pride in their neighbourhood and in turn, have important consequences for civic behaviour. Pride can be difficult to sustain in neighbourhoods that are typically populated by people with limited socio-economic resources, whose voices have not often been heard, including in discussions of environmental issues (Comfort & Park, 2018; Ohlson, 2015). Imagine ads at bus shelters and on billboards, touting neighbourhoods that have the "best bees in the city," with signs displaying similar colours, fonts and images on public walkways outside community gardens. We propose channels such as transit advertising, signage and social media campaigns with low involvement messages that put certain neighbourhood's thriving bee populations on people's minds in a positive light. Those who want more substantive knowledge can get it, but this won't occur at the expense of the attention of those who do not. A repeating slogan, spokescharacter, jingle or similar peripheral cue saturating a community may go farther than most scientists expect towards increasing awareness of and interest in the environmental issue, and do so in a personally relevant way that increases the likelihood of attitude and behaviour change. Scientists can work closely with strategic communication experts to ensure that while brief or superficial, the messaging is not inaccurate. While such an effort does not educate people on the importance of pollination, or even explain why bees are so successful in these neighbourhoods, it stokes neighbourhood pride in the same way that a sports rivalry might. This could lead to future curiosity about the issue, or it might just generate some low-level awareness of local bee populations.

Because the issue is framed in such a way as to inspire citizens to feel pride about their bountiful bees and gardens, the messaging also may build self-efficacy, by communicating that individuals in these neighbourhoods have accomplished something worth noting and celebrating. This could lead some people to become curious about choosing to take further action, such as becoming involved with a community garden, and might also validate those who already do have association with a garden. Engagement with a garden is associated with a number of benefits, such as improved health from working outside and growing fresh food. It also increases in-person communication with other residents of the neighbourhood, and a particular benefit of the communicative nature of this activity is that it can increase civic engagement. Research shows that talking with people outside of one's immediate family and friends provides valuable non-redundant information not necessarily found in the echo chambers of social media. Like other forms of informational media, these views can promote civic-oriented behaviours by triggering reasoning and political discussion, which subsequently promotes individuals' participation in public affairs and civic action (Eveland, 2004; Gil de Zúñiga & Valenzuela, 2011). All of this starts with hope and self-efficacy, and that starts with "branding the bees." Communication of hope and pride therefore have the potential to address the pollinator crisis, benefit residents who live in food deserts and with food insecurity and provide theoretical insight into how to generate advocacy behaviours in an environmental context. While this particular solution is unique to the pollinator crisis, social advocates working on other sustainability issues are encouraged to seek solutions that foster positive emotions and promote small victories as a means of building involvement (Ohlson, 2015). In addition, they must create and share messages that are strategically designed to register with distracted, busy people, just as all advertisers strive to do.

Communication Principle 3: Be Savvy in Identifying Your "Competition"

Understanding and joining forces with the people whose social and economic development is at stake is a crucial first step towards building the compassion, insight and buy-in that will be needed to accomplish movement towards sustainability. However, this becomes more powerful and effective when a second phase of communication ensues: strategic, professional communication, built through alliances with communication experts. Once again, we will use the pollinator crisis and the importance of individual lawn management decisions to illustrate our point. Partnering with communication experts will result in scientists and environmentalists being encouraged to engage in savvy situation analyses, in which competition or resistance that is not immediately apparent or understood is identified.

Urban neighbourhoods are an important target for messaging that promotes pollinator-friendly behaviours, but so are suburban homeowners, who routinely spend a great deal of time and money on their lawns (Behe et al., 2005; Burr, Hall, & Schaeg, 2018; Groffman et al., 2016). At first consideration, it might seem that an effective strategy would be to inform such homeowners of adjustments they could make that would be better for pollinators and the environment, but that strategy assumes that lack of knowledge is the "enemy" to be battled. In fact, it is often the case that the problem isn't ignorance; it's social pressure from neighbours and aesthetics about what a lawn should look like. It may stem from concern about property values if grass is mowed less frequently. If one doesn't recognize that this social pressure is the stumbling block, and believes instead that people are simply uninformed, communication is likely to be misguided. Professional communicators are trained to unearth these types of insights.

In fact, social norms about how to keep up one's yard are a powerful force. Lawns in the United States occupy over 63,000 square miles (Jenkins, 2005) and are the number one irrigated crop (Milesi et al., 2005). For many homeowners, lawn upkeep can represent 50–70% of the yearly water bill, depending on where they are located. In order to maintain an aesthetically pleasing lawn, many homeowners apply large amounts of fertilizers and pesticides in order to eliminate plants, insects, arachnids and even vertebrates that can disrupt the "perfect" lawn (Nassauer, Wang, & Dayrell, 2009), mow frequently and plant small, neat rows of flowers. This obsession with manicured lawns, free of "weeds" and only containing the desired grasses, has resulted in a large-scale homogenization of urban green spaces with minimal biodiversity (Polsky et al., 2014; Groffman et al., 2016). The negative effects to the environment that highly manicured lawns have are multiple: production of greenhouse gases by gas-powered lawn equipment (Lerman & Contosta, 2019), excessive consumption of water (especially in arid and semi-arid environments), use of nitrogen- and phosphorous-containing fertilizers and use of chemical pesticides (Groffman et al., 2016). Manicured lawns have also been determined to have significant negative effects on bee diversity (Lerman, Contosta, Milam, & Bang, 2018). Despite this, the maintenance of a manicured "green" lawn has been tied to increased property values in the United States for many decades (Irwin, 2002). Homogenization has been coded into neighbourhood association rules and urban municipalities' ordinances (Sisser et al., 2016) in order to ensure increasing property values (Polsky et al., 2014) and to make sure that people moving into the neighbourhood are capable of affording and maintaining those same lawns' features (Grove, Locke, & O'Neil-Dunne, 2014).

Pressure from neighbours and localities to use chemicals and intensive mowing to maintain a highly manicured lawn are echoed in persistent marketing messages from chemical companies that produce fertilizers, pesticides and lawn maintenance services. Through both mass media advertising, such as commercials on radio and television, and marketing efforts targeting individual homes, such as door brochures or offers of "lawn inspections" for homeowners, a message is sent that a "green" lawn will be coveted by neighbours, increase property values and allow for greater enjoyment of your property (Behe et al., 2005). The implication is that lack of compliance with the "green" lawn standards will result in decreased property value and complaints or scorn from the neighbours.

The scientific literature suggests that individual homeowners can contribute to improved overall bee diversity and abundance in cities if they maintain a diversity of native bee-pollinated flowers, increase the inter-mowing interval, leave bare soil and minimize the use of pesticides (Lerman et al., 2018; Lowenstein et al., 2015; Lowenstein & Minor, 2016). Yet, the message that homeowners tend to receive is that those same practices go against established norms, and can disrupt "good" neighbour perceptions (Burr, Hall, & Schaeg, 2018). This message comes through multiple input channels, some formal, like neighbourhood association rules and municipality ordinances, others informal, like conversing with neighbours or browsing at the local home garden store, both reinforced by lawn industry marketing and even real estate agents. Countering this message represents a major communication challenge. It involves not simply convincing individuals that bee-friendly practices are worthwhile and educating them as to what those practices are, but challenging the aesthetic belief that less manicured lawns do not have to mean a lawn that looks neglected or uncared for.

Interestingly, the value associated with the perfect green lawn is driven by cultural norms that vary extensively across countries and cultures (Carrus et al., 2015; Qiu, Lindberg, & Nielsen, 2013). For example, the perception in Japan of a lawn that requires high inputs of chemicals and energy is that it is "fake," with a more "informal" green space being considered "real" (Rupprecht, Byrne, Ueda, & Lo, 2015). This demonstrates that a more environmentally friendly aesthetic is possible, but also shows that it will be difficult to unseat deeply held cultural values. While this may be particularly challenging in suburban subdivisions and well-to-do enclaves, the city has greater potential for malleability in this regard. In several European cities, the aesthetic value of increased biodiversity and structural complexity in green space was correlated with increased cultural diversity (Fischer et al., 2018). Even within neighbourhoods in a city, floral diversity across neighbourhoods changed proportionally to the neighbourhoods' ethnic diversity (Lowenstein & Minor, 2016). What this suggests is that cities, with their diverse citizen bases, may be more receptive to an aesthetic of biodiversity (Goddard et al., 2010). Cities certainly serve as compelling research sites to explore SES patterns and processes to develop responsive sustainability and biodiversity conservation policies and practices (Aronson et al., 2016). This suggests a strategy in which urban neighbourhoods may ultimately be used to evolve tastes and practices in more suburban areas. Again, communication professionals have expertise in these sorts of campaigns, and communication scholars offer theoretical insight into the diffusion of messages and attitudes across populations.

Increased knowledge of plant diversity (Muratet, Pellegrini, Dufour, Arrif, & Chiron, 2015) or participation in gardening activities (Bertoncini, Machon, Pavoine, & Muratet, 2012) also tend to influence the perception of heterogeneity in lawn vegetation in a positive fashion. Efforts to convince people to change their perceptions and their practices therefore require acknowledging that the perception of the "perfect" green lawn seems to be tied to cultural, social and economic forces, all of which are competing for the homeowners' attention. This means that the "enemy" of pollinator-friendly lawns is not just chemicals and homogeneity of vegetation, it is the perception that gardening a different way will result in social judgement and identification as a rule breaker (Burr, Hall, & Schaeg, 2018). Extending beyond pollination issues, all sustainable development efforts should be sure to understand who or what they are positioned against in order to most effectively design their message. Understanding and working to alter the cultural and social forces at play in people's property maintenance decisions is largely a communication problem. It means understanding where they are attitudinally in order to design the most effective persuasion attempt.

One promising way that communication is being used as a solution to social pressure for a "green" lawn are community-based programmes that promote pollinator-friendly management practices of lawns and other green spaces. Many NGOs manage and promote these programmes, like the Audubon Society's "Bring Conservation Home," the Native Wild Plant Society's "Wild Ones," and the Pollinator Partnership's "Milkweeds for Monarchs." All of these programmes provide homeowners with information about native landscaping, what plants are best for their specific environment and climate, as well as how to maintain them with minimal inputs. Properties are inspected and certified for the use of native and pollinator-friendly plants, minimal use of pesticides and other sustainable practices. They also provide homeowners with signage indicating to neighbours and passers-by that they are participating in community conservation programmes which are beneficial for pollinators.

This signage is another example of effectively using communication to address the true threat to the desired behaviour. A sign in the lawn "excuses" grass that is longer than the neighbours', so that people who would like to adhere to a different lawn aesthetic don't have to worry that it will be mistaken for laziness or neglect. In fact, it might even appeal to the sense of pride of many homeowners, by communicating to the neighbours the importance of such landscaping practices and awarding the homeowner status as a leader in this regard. The signage may also serve as a facilitator in order to generate social contagion in the spread of native landscaping in urban residential neighbourhoods, generating curiosity and discussion about pollinator-friendly practices. By addressing social concerns and offering a tangible reward to participating homeowners, positive emotions are invoked, realistic solutions are offered and counter messages are challenged. This is the type of solution that can advance the SDGs effectively.

Communication Principle 4: Control the Narrative or Someone Else Will

The pollinator crisis provides an excellent cautionary tale of a lack of intentional communication leading to an inability to control the narrative in a way that best serves sustainable development. To be clear, this is a two-part problem. The first part is a lack of coverage of biodiversity loss in the press. Legagneux et al. (2018) found that biodiversity was mentioned in the English speaking press 3 to 8 times less frequently than climate change, even when the two issues were generating comparable amounts of scientific research. This leads to audiences having lower perceptions of biodiversity loss as a significant global problem, and less understanding of how and why humans can address it. Even when people are aware of the pollinator crisis specifically, they do not necessarily understand it is an aspect of biodiversity loss—after all, bees can be found in their lawn, whereas "biodiversity" connotes "the rainforest," so the connection is not explicit.

The second part of controlling the narrative for scientists is to stop naively believing that little press on a topic will merely result in its absence from the public's mind. In fact, the problem with not advancing a clear communication strategy for sustainability and biodiversity loss is that the issue will be presented to some people, but in a distorted way due to others controlling the message. As noted earlier, engaging people widely in this day and age requires "selling" the message in a way that will penetrate all the other noise in the environment. We live in an era where topics may be framed in the public's eye by memes and Tweets. This is the arena in which intentional messages from environmentalists must appear. The challenge is that the causes of extinction, according to scientific consensus, are the loss and destruction of natural habitat, overexploitation of natural resources and global climate change, among others (Barnosky et al., 2011). This is a painful and complex reality to convey in attention-grabbing ways. What's more, many, if not most, of the species that drive ecosystem services are not charismatic (Lentz & Nash, 2010). Perhaps that is why the "umbrella" species for biodiversity loss is the panda bear (Barua, 2011; Li & Pimm, 2016). This species has been used in the media as an easily encapsulable and deliverable example of an endangered species and biodiversity loss (Albert, Luque, & Courchamp, 2018). People are captivated by the "cuteness" and the plight of the panda bear. A reason for this is that various NGOs have seized on the charisma of the panda, and have developed a narrative that is easily digestible and appeals to most people (Albert et al., 2018; Wei et al., 2018). Panda bears are featured in the media because there are multiple entities which have vested interests, be it fundraising or projecting a conservation conscious image.

A similar phenomenon has happened in the case of pollinators. While not often conceived of as such, the European honeybee (*Apis mellifera*) is a domesticated species in a manner similar to cows, pigs and chickens (Crane, 1983). Apiculture is the keeping of honeybee hives for the purpose of providing pollinating insects to crops and the harvesting of the honey. In apiculture, and even in casual beekeeping, honeybees are provided with food during the winters, given medicine when diseases are detected and have predators removed from the vicinity of their hives (Crane, 1990). It is estimated that there are at least 5000 commercial beekeepers (300 or more hives) in the United States that own some 2.7 million hives (US Department of Agriculture, 2010). Furthermore, it is estimated that there are an additional 160,000–210,000 amateur (between 10 and 300 hives) and casual (less than 10 hives) beekeepers. Most commercial and many amateur and casual beekeepers organize into local beekeepers associations, which in turn are represented nationally by the American Beekeeping Federation. This trade association represents the beekeepers' interests at the federal and state government levels and lobbies on their behalf. This trade association also promotes their interests in the mass media, food and agricultural industry, as well as to the public in general.

The narrative concerning honeybee conservation in North America parallels that of panda bears. Currently, most of the media stories dealing with the conservation of pollinators are dominated by honeybee "conservation" and related issues, like colony collapse disorder, and not by the reality on the ground of broader pollinator conservation needs (Colla & MacIvor, 2017; Geldmann & González-Varo, 2018). Honeybees are featured as the "poster child" of the pollinator crisis because there are many interests, from small beekeepers to trade organizations to large agricultural industry players, that benefit from such a narrative. This parallels how broader biodiversity loss is dominated by the concept of endangered species, and more specifically, the panda bear. While pandas are featured as important and integral to the functioning of the forest and the local ecosystems (Wei et al., 2018), there is no tangible data that pandas are essential for the functioning of the ecosystem, nor for the provisioning of ecosystem services (Lentz & Nash, 2010). In the same way, honeybees can only pollinate 10–30% of the crops that require bee pollination (Breeze, Bailey, Balcombe, & Potts, 2011; Cunningham, Tyedmers, & Sherren, 2018), so their contribution to human's diets is important, but insufficient. What's more, their presence in an agricultural area will compete with many other bee species who might live there and who could pollinate all of the necessary crops (Hung et al., 2019; Paini, 2004). Put succinctly, saving the honeybees will not solve the pollinator crisis.

Yet honeybees are familiar to humans from childhood, well-known for their yellow and black striped colour scheme. Frequently anthropomorphized into cute characters (e.g. the Honey Nut Cheerios bee), they receive the bulk of the attention about bees and pollination in the media. In part thanks to them, many people are aware that pollinators are in decline or threatened. But because honeybees dominate the public conversation about this crisis, undue attention is focused on "saving honeybees," and many easy and effective techniques that ordinary people could engage in to support and conserve all native bees are not communicated. People doing something to help honeybees are under the impression they are doing the right thing, and are not as open to these measures. As with the panda bear, the narrative that the general public learns is erroneous at best, and misguided at worst. This is a tremendous lost opportunity, since scientific evidence shows that small changes in individuals' property management can improve bee diversity. On the other hand, cultivation of honeybees can actually drive away other types of native bees that pollinate more types of food. By failing to control the narrative about the threat to pollinators, scientists have allowed vital public attention to be diverted to an ineffective solution.

Conclusion

Two-thirds of the world's population will be living in cities by 2050, creating sustainability challenges in terms of biodiversity conservation, ecosystem services and food production in urban environments. It is vital to work with individuals and communities to hear and understand how these problems play out in their lives. This will inform how to communicate the message to people that they can and should help all bees to increase crop pollination, and show them how this might function in their own interest. Leaders and decision-makers in sustainability efforts, such as scientists, advocacy organizations, legislators and urban planners, must be strategic with this communication; after all, we live in a world where countless strategic messages are targeted at us daily, and only a few have any impact. Theories of communication and persuasion should be used to guide efforts, and communication experts and professionals consulted for input and assistance.

We have provided several such principles of effective communication here. Table 18.1 summarizes our ideas and maps them with the respective SDGs, the desired outcomes and the needed communication strategy. While their application here is specific to the pollinator crisis, we believe they represent fundamental techniques that can be adapted to any sustainability issue. Knowing who your audience is, and not forgetting any key contingencies, is wise marketing in any context. With respect to environmental efforts, this often translates to not ignoring the common citizen, even as efforts to develop top-down policies remain essential. This also means speaking in a language that is accessible to a layperson audience, and offering them hope and a sense of possibility that what they do matters. There is promising evidence suggesting the fruits of doing so may extend far beyond motivating individual attitudes and behaviours.

In addition to knowing one's audience and using this knowledge to craft a message, one must also know who one's "competition" is. What is really stopping people from being on your side, and how can you address this? In the

Table 18.1 Mapping of desired outcomes for pollinator conservation in urban environments to respective SDGs, as well as the proposed communication principles

Desired outcome	SDG target	Role of communication	Strategy
Change individual lawn management behaviour (mow less, plant natives, reduce pesticide use)	11.3 13.2 15.5	Use CDSC to identify relevant audiences (Principle 1) and devise right message (Principle 2)	Target individual behaviour change, communicate self-efficacy, establish trust
Increase participation in community gardening	1.4, 1.5 2.1, 2.2, 2.3, 2.4, 2.5 5.a, 5.5 11.7	Use CDSC to devise right message (Principle 2)	Communicate benefits of gardens to community, cultivate hope and pride
Change lawn aesthetics	15.9	Work with communication experts to evaluate competition (Principle 3)	Identify threats, promote signage and affiliation with NGO programmes to counteract HOAs, local ordinances and social pressure
Promote pollinator-friendly policy/collaborate with NGOs	11.7 15.5, 15.9	Use CDSC to understand audience needs (Principle 2) Work with communication experts to control the narrative (Principle 4)	Identify and foster support for policies that benefit pollinators and communities

world of marketing, this might involve recognizing that what laundry soap manufacturers are working against is not really dirty clothes, but an individual's time to devote to chores like laundry. In the realm of the pollinator crisis, it is not necessarily ignorance of what pollinator-friendly lawn practices are, it may be social pressure to conform with the neighbourhood aesthetic of a highly manicured lawn. In another context, it will be something else, but the principle remains: figure out what is realistically needed to persuade people in your favour.

It is a truism in communication that the media do not tell us what to think, they tell us what to think about. In other words, what is being talked about in traditional and social media is what people will think about and be concerned with. In addition, the way that issues are talked about, or framed, is extremely important to what the subsequent discussion about them is. Sustainability advocates ignore this reality at their own peril, as evidenced by the dominance of honeybees in the discussion of the pollinator crisis. Along with knowing one's audience, how to best communicate with them and what the issue is really about in their minds, one must know what message frames are or will be circulating that counter or alter your message. Otherwise, one can achieve awareness and buy-in, and then be faced with a need to re-educate people that what they are doing and feeling good about is not sufficient, and may actually be harmful in terms of a better solution.

Reading through the 17 SDGs in the UN 2030 Agenda is a reminder of how intertwined and substantial the multiple facets of changing the world to be a better place are. This chapter shares some solutions that go a long way to addressing many of these, from inequality to food insecurity to climate change. Additionally, thoughtfully designing strategies to communicate about the pollinator crisis will generate theoretical insights that can inform scientists, policymakers, municipalities and other scientific and governmental entities more broadly about how to improve their communication with various publics.

Despite the gravity of the pollinator crisis and the need for sustainable development overall, much can be accomplished if a majority of urban residents made a few basic adjustments to how they care for the green space around their homes, such as mowing less frequently, planting bee-friendly plants and minimizing pesticide use. Continued support of and participation in community gardens is also a valuable contribution to the solution, and has the added benefit of supporting communities in a number of ways, as the SDGs advocate for. As societies move towards greater appreciation for more sustainable green space, it will be more likely to enact policies and legislation that honour principles of sustainable development as well. The vital role of communication in developing support for this solution cannot be overstated.

References

Albert, C., Luque, G. M., & Courchamp, F. (2018). The Twenty Most Charismatic Species. *PloS One, 13*, e0199149.

Anderson, E. C., & Minor, E. S. (2017). Vacant Lots: An Underexplored Resource for Ecological and Social Benefits in Cities. *Urban Forestry & Urban Greening, 21*, 146–152.

Anderson, S. P., & De Palma, A. (2012). Competition for Attention in the Information (Overload) Age. *The RAND Journal of Economics, 43*, 1–25.

Angel, S., Parent, J., Civco, D. L., Blei, A., & Potere, D. (2011). The Dimensions of Global Urban Expansion: Estimates and Projections for all Countries, 2000–2050. *Progress in Planning, 75*, 53–107.

Aronson, M. F., Nilon, C. H., Lepczyk, C. A., Parker, T. S., Warren, P. S., Cilliers, S. S., et al. (2016). Hierarchical Filters Determine Community Assembly of Urban Species Pools. *Ecology, 97*(11), 2952–2963.

Badenschier, F., & Wormer, H. (2012). Issue Selection in Science Journalism: Towards a Special Theory of News Values for Science News? In S. Rödder, M. Franzen, & P. Weingart (Eds.), *The Sciences' Media Connection: Public Communication and Its Repercussions* (pp. 59–86). London: Springer.

Baldock, K. C., Goddard, M. A., Hicks, D. M., Kunin, W. E., Mitschunas, N., Osgathorpe, L. M., Potts, S. G., Robertson, K.M., Scott, A.V., Stone, G.N.& Vaughan, I.P. (2015). Where is the UK's pollinator biodiversity? The importance of urban areas for flower-visiting insects. *Proceedings of the Royal Society B: Biological Sciences, 282*, 20142849.

Barnosky, A. D., Matzke, N., Tomiya, S., Wogan, G. O., Swartz, B., Quental, T. B., et al. (2011). Has the Earth's Sixth Mass Extinction Already Arrived? *Nature, 471,* 51.

Barua, M. (2011). Mobilizing Metaphors: The Popular Use of Keystone, Flagship and Umbrella Species Concepts. *Biodiversity and Conservation, 20,* 1427.

Behe, B., Hardy, J., Barton, S., Brooker, J., Fernandez, T., Hall, C., et al. (2005). Landscape Plant Material, Size, and Design Sophistication Increase Perceived Home Value. *Journal of Environmental Horticulture, 23,* 127–133.

Bertoncini, A. P., Machon, N., Pavoine, S., & Muratet, A. (2012). Local Gardening Practices Shape Urban Lawn Floristic Communities. *Landscape and Urban Planning, 105,* 53–61.

Board, M. A. (2005). *Millennium Ecosystem Assessment* (p. 13). Washington, DC: New Island.

Braswell, T. H. (2018). Fresh Food, New Faces: Community Gardening as Ecological Gentrification in St. Louis, Missouri. *Agriculture and Human Values, 35,* 809–822.

Breeze, T. D., Bailey, A. P., Balcombe, K. G., & Potts, S. G. (2011). Pollination services in the UK: How Important Are Honeybees? *Agriculture, Ecosystems & Environment, 142,* 137–143.

Brossard, D., & Nisbet, M. C. (2007). Deference to Scientific Authority among a Low Information Public: Understanding US Opinion on Agricultural Biotechnology. *International Journal of Public Opinion Research, 19,* 24–52.

Burr, A., Hall, D. M., & Schaeg, N. (2018). The Perfect Lawn: Exploring Neighborhood Socio-cultural Drivers for Insect Pollinator Habitat. *Urban Ecosystems, 21,* 1123–1137.

Burr, A., Schaeg, N., Muñiz, P., Camilo, G. R., & Hall, D. M. (2016). Wild Bees in the City: Reimagining Urban Spaces for Native Bee Health. *Consilience, 16,* 106–131.

Cameron, S. A., Lozier, J. D., Strange, J. P., Koch, J. B., Cordes, N., Solter, L. F., et al. (2011). Patterns of Widespread Decline in North American Bumble Bees. *Proceedings of the National Academy of Sciences, 108,* 662–667.

Camilo, G. R., Muñiz, P. A., Arduser, M. S., & Spevak, E. M. (2018). A Checklist of the Bees (Hymenoptera: Apoidea) of St. Louis, Missouri, USA. *Journal of the Kansas Entomological Society, 90,* 175–188.

Cane, J. H., & Tepedino, V. J. (2001). Causes and Extent of Declines among Native North American Invertebrate Pollinators: Detection, Evidence, and Consequences. *Conservation Ecology, 5,* 1–7.

Carrus, G., Scopelliti, M., Lafortezza, R., Colangelo, G., Ferrini, F., Salbitano, F., et al. (2015). Go greener, Feel Better? The Positive Effects of Biodiversity on the Well-being of Individuals Visiting Urban and Peri-urban Green Areas. *Landscape and Urban Planning, 134,* 221–228.

Ceballos, G., Ehrlich, P. R., Barnosky, A. D., García, A., Pringle, R. M., & Palmer, T. M. (2015). Accelerated Modern Human-induced Species Losses: Entering the Sixth Mass Extinction. *Science Advances, 1,* e1400253.

Chadwick, A. E. (2015). Toward a Theory of Persuasive Hope: Effects of Cognitive Appraisals, Hope Appeals, and Hope in the Context of Climate Change. *Health Communication, 30,* 598–611.

Colla, S. R., & MacIvor, J. S. (2017). Questioning Public Perception, Conservation Policy, and Recovery Actions for Honeybees in North America. *Conservation Biology, 31,* 1202–1204.

Comfort, S. E., & Park, Y. E. (2018). On the Field of Environmental Communication: A Systematic Review of the Peer-reviewed Literature. *Environmental Communication, 12*, 862–875.

Corbie-Smith, G., Thomas, S. B., & George, D. M. M. S. (2002). Distrust, Race, and research. *Archives of Internal Medicine, 162*, 2458–2463.

Crane, E. (1983). *The Archaeology of Beekeeping*. Duckworth.

Crane, E. (1990). *Bees and Beekeeping: Science, Practice and World Resources*. Heinemann Newnes.

Creutzig, F., Agoston, P., Minx, J. C., Canadell, J. G., Andrew, R. M., Le Quéré, C., et al. (2016). Urban Infrastructure Choices Structure Climate Solutions. *Nature Climate Change, 6*, 1054.

Cunningham, C., Tyedmers, P., & Sherren, K. (2018). Primary Data in Pollination Services Mapping: Potential Service Provision by honey bees (*Apis mellifera*) in Cumberland and Colchester, Nova Scotia. *International Journal of Biodiversity Science, Ecosystem Services & Management, 14*, 60–69.

Dahlstrom, M. F. (2014). Using Narratives and Storytelling to Communicate Science with Nonexpert Audiences. *Proceedings of the National Academy of Sciences, 111*(4), 13614–13620.

Delaplane, K. S., Mayer, D. R., & Mayer, D. F. (2000). *Crop Pollination by Bees*. NY: CABI Publishing.

Drewnowski, A., Aggarwal, A., Cook, A., Stewart, O., & Moudon, A. V. (2016). Geographic Disparities in Healthy Eating Index Scores (HEI–2005 and 2010) by Residential Property Values: Findings from Seattle Obesity Study (SOS). *Preventive Medicine, 83*, 46–55.

Eveland, W. P. (2004). The Effect of Political Discussion in Producing Informed Citizens: The Roles of Information, Motivation, and Elaboration. *Political Communication, 21*, 177–193.

FAO. (2018). *Why bees matter*. Rome: Food and Agriculture Organization of the United Nations.

Ferrer, A. L. C., Thomé, A. M. T., & Scavarda, A. J. (2018). Sustainable Urban Infrastructure: A Review. *Resources, Conservation and Recycling, 128*, 360–372.

Fischer, L. K., Honold, J., Cvejić, R., Delshammar, T., Hilbert, S., Lafortezza, R., et al. (2018). Beyond Green: Broad Support for Biodiversity in Multicultural European Cities. *Global Environmental Change, 49*, 35–45.

Frankie, G.W., Vinson, S.B., Rizzardi, M.A., Griswold, T.L., Coville, R.E., Grayum, M.H., Martinez, L.E.S., Foltz-Sweat, J. & Pawelek, J.C. (2013). Relationships of bees to host ornamental and weedy flowers in urban Northwest Guanacaste Province, Costa Rica. *Journal of the Kansas Entomological Society, 86*, 325–351.

Gardiner, M.M., Burkman, C.E. & Prajzner, S.P. (2013). The value of urban vacant land to support arthropod biodiversity and ecosystem services. *Environmental Entomology, 42*, 1123–1136.

Geldmann, J., & González-Varo, J. P. (2018). Conserving Honey Bees Does Not Help Wildlife. *Science, 359*, 392–393.

George, S., Duran, N., & Norris, K. (2014). A Systematic Review of Barriers and Facilitators to Minority Research Participation among African Americans, Latinos, Asian Americans, and Pacific Islanders. *American Journal of Public Health, 104*, e16–e31.

Geslin, B., Le Féon, V., Folschweiller, M., Flacher, F., Carmignac, D., Motard, E., et al. (2016). The Proportion of Impervious Surfaces at the Landscape Scale Structures wild bee Assemblages in a Densely Populated Region. *Ecology and Evolution*, 6, 6599–6615.

Gil de Zúñiga, H., & Valenzuela, S. (2011). The Mediating Path to a Stronger Citizenship: Online and Offline Networks, Weak Ties, and Civic Engagement. *Communication Research*, 38, 397–421.

Gil de Zúñiga, H., Weeks, B., & Adrèvol-Abreu, A. (2017). Effects of the News-finds-me Perception in Communication: Social Media Use Implications for News Seeking and Learning About Politics. *Journal of Computer-Mediated Communication*, 22, 105–123. https://doi.org/10.1111/jcc4.12185

Glaum, P., Simao, M. C., Vaidya, C., Fitch, G., & Iulinao, B. (2017). Big city Bombus: Using Natural History and Land-use history to find Significant Environmental Drivers in Bumble-bee Declines in Urban Development. *Royal Society Open Science*, 4, 170156.

Goddard, M. A., Dougill, A. J., & Benton, T. G. (2010). Scaling up from Gardens: Biodiversity Conservation in Urban Environments. *Trends in Ecology & Evolution*, 25, 90–98.

Goodwin, J., & Dahlstrom, M. F. (2014). Communication Strategies for Earning Trust in Climate Change debates. *WIREs Climate Change*, 5, 151–160.

Goulson, D., Lye, G.C. & Darvill, B. (2008). Decline and conservation of bumble bees. *Annual Review of Entomology*, 53, 191–208.

Goulson, D., Nicholls, E., Botías, C. & Rotheray, E. L. (2015). Bee declines driven by combined stress from parasites, pesticides, and lack of flowers. *Science*, 347(6229).

Groffman, P. M., Grove, J. M., Polsky, C., Bettez, N. D., Morse, J. L., Cavender-Bares, J., et al. (2016). Satisfaction, Water and Fertilizer Use in the American Residential Macrosystem. *Environmental Research Letters*, 11, 034004.

Grove, J. M., Locke, D. H., & O'Neil-Dunne, J. P. (2014). An Ecology of Prestige in New York City: Examining the Relationships among Population Density, Socio-economic Status, Group Identity, and Residential Canopy Cover. *Environmental Management*, 54, 402–419.

Hall, D.M., Camilo, G. R., Tonietto, R. K., Ollerton, J., Ahrné, K., Arduser, M., Ascher, J. S., Baldock, K. C. R., Fowler, R., Frankie, G., Goulson, D, Gunnarsson, B., Hanley, M. E., Jackson, J. I., Langellotto, G., Lowenstein, D., Minor, E. M., Philpott, S. M., Potts, S. G., Sirohi, M. H., Spevak, E., Stone, G. N. & Threlfall, C. (2017). The city as a refuge for insect pollinators. *Conservation Biology*, 31, 24–29.

Harris, V., Kendal, D., Hahs, A. K., & Threlfall, C. G. (2018). Green Space Context and Vegetation Complexity Shape People's Preferences for Urban Public Parks and Residential Gardens. *Landscape Research*, 43, 150–162.

Horst, M., McClintock, N., & Hoey, L. (2017). The Intersection of Planning, Urban Agriculture, and Food Justice: A Review of the Literature. *Journal of the American Planning Association*, 83, 277–295.

Hung, K. L. J., Kingston, J. M., Lee, A., Holway, D. A., & Kohn, J.R. (2019). Non-native honey bees disproportionally dominate the most abundant floral resources in a biodiversity hotspot. *Proceedings of the Royal Society B*, 286, 20182901.

Irwin, E. G. (2002). The Effects of Open Space on Residential Property Values. *Land Economics*, 78, 465–480.

Jenkins, V. (2005). *The Lawn: A History of an American Obsession*. Washington, DC: Smithsonian Institute.

Jiang, L., & O'Neill, B. C. (2017). Global Urbanization Projections for the Shared Socioeconomic Pathways. *Global Environmental Change*, 42, 193–199.

Johnson, K. A., & Lane, A. B. (2018). Building Relational Capital: The Contribution of Episodic and Relational Community Engagement. *Public Relations Review*, 44, 633–644.

Kendal, D., Williams, N. S. G., & Williams, K. J. H. (2010). Harnessing Diversity in Gardens Through Individual Decision Makers. *Trends in Ecology & Evolution*, 25, 201–202.

Koh, I., Lonsdorf, E. V., Williams, N. M., Brittain, C., Isaacs, R., Gibbs, J., et al. (2016). Modeling the Status, Trends, and Impacts of Wild Bee Abundance in the United States. *Proceedings of the National Academy of Sciences*, 113, 140–145.

Kusmanoff, A. M., Fidler, F., Gordon, A., Garrard, G. E., & Bekessy, S. A. (2020). Five Lessons to Guide More Effective Biodiversity Conservation Message Framing. *Conservation Biology*. https://doi.org/10.1111/cobi.13482

Legagneux, P., Casajus, N., Cazelles, K., Chevallier, C., Chevrinais, M., Guéry, L., et al. (2018). Our House is Burning: Discrepancy in Climate Change vs. Biodiversity Coverage in the Media as Compared to Scientific Literature. *Frontiers in Ecology and Evolution*, 5. https://doi.org/10.3389/fevo.2017.00175

Lentz, J., & Nash, S. (2010). *The Animal Review: The Genius, Mediocrity, and Breathtaking Stupidity that is Nature*. NY: Bloomsbury USA Publishing.

Lerman, S. B., & Contosta, A. R. (2019). Lawn Mowing Frequency and its Effects on Biogenic and Anthropogenic Carbon Dioxide Emissions. *Landscape and Urban Planning*, 182, 114–123.

Lerman, S. B., Contosta, A. R., Milam, J., & Bang, C. (2018). To Mow or to Mow Less: Lawn Mowing Frequency Affects Bee Abundance and Diversity in Suburban yards. *Biological Conservation*, 221, 160–174.

Li, B. V., & Pimm, S. L. (2016). China's Endemic Vertebrates Sheltering under the Protective Umbrella of the Giant Panda. *Conservation Biology*, 30, 329–339.

Lie, R., & Servaes, J. (2015). Disciplines in the Field of Communication for Development and Social Change. *Communication Theory*, 25, 244–258.

Lowe, A. D., & Foltz-Sweat, J. L. (2017). Effect of Floral Diversity and Urbanization on Bee Species Community Composition in Phoenix, Arizona. *Journal of the Arizona-Nevada Academy of Science*, 47, 6–18.

Lowenstein, D. M., Matteson, K. C., & Minor, E. S. (2015). Diversity of Wild Bees Supports Pollination Services in an Urbanized Landscape. *Oecologia*, 179, 811–821.

Lowenstein, D. M., & Minor, E. S. (2016). Diversity in Flowering Plants and their Characteristics: Integrating Humans as a Driver of Urban Floral Resources. *Urban Ecosystems*, 19, 1735–1748.

Mace, G. M., Norris, K., & Fitter, A. H. (2012). Biodiversity and Ecosystem Services: A Multilayered Relationship. *Trends in Ecology & Evolution*, 27, 19–26.

MacInnis, D. J., & De Mello, G. E. (2005). The Concept of Hope and its Relevance to Product Evaluation and Choice. *Journal of Marketing*, 69, 1–14.

Matsa, K. E., & Mitchell, A. (2014). *8 Key Takeaways About Social Media and the News*. Retrieved from http://www.journalism.org/2014/03/26/8-key-takeaways-about-social-media-and-news/

McDonnell, M. J., & Hahs, A. K. (2013). The future of urban biodiversity research: Moving beyond the 'low-hanging fruit'. *Urban Ecosystems*, 16(3), 397–409.

Milesi, C., Running, S. W., Elvidge, C. D., Dietz, J. B., Tuttle, B. T., & Nemani, R. R. (2005). Mapping and Modeling the Biogeochemical Cycling of Turf Grasses in the United States. *Environmental Management*, 36, 426–438. https://doi.org/10.1007/s00267-004-0316-2

Minor, E., Belaire, J. A., Davis, A., Franco, M., & Lin, M. (2016). Socioeconomics and Neighbor Mimicry Drive Yard and Neighborhood Vegetation Patterns. In R. A. Francis, J. D. A. Millington, & M. A. Chadwick (Eds.), *Urban Landscape Ecology: Science, Policy and Practice* (pp. 56–74). Taylor and Francis Inc.. https://doi.org/10.4324/9781315713373

Muratet, A., Pellegrini, P., Dufour, A. B., Arrif, T., & Chiron, F. (2015). Perception and Knowledge of Plant Diversity Among Urban Park Users. *Landscape and Urban Planning, 137*, 95–106.

Nabi, R. L. (2015). Emotional Flow in Persuasive Health Messages. *Health Communication, 30*(2), 114–124.

Nabi, R. L., Gustafson, A., & Jensen, R. (2018). Framing Climate Change: Exploring the Role of Emotion in Generating Advocacy Behavior. *Science Communication, 40*, 442–468.

Nabi, R. L., & Myrick, J. G. (2018). Uplifting Fear Appeals: Considering the Role of Hope in Fear-based Persuasive Messages. *Health Communication*. https://doi.org/10.1080/10410236.2017.1422847

Nassauer, J. I., Wang, Z., & Dayrell, E. (2009). What will the Neighbors Think? Cultural Norms and Ecological Design. *Landscape and Urban Planning, 92*, 282–292.

National Academies of Sciences, Engineering, and Medicine. (2017). *Communicating Science Effectively: A Research Agenda*. Washington, DC: The National Academies Press. https://doi.org/10.17226/23674

National Communication Association. (2015). *Impact Factors, Journal Quality, and Communication Journals*. Washington, DC: NCA.

National Research Council. (2007). *Status of Pollinators in North America*. Washington, DC: National Academies Press.

Nicholls, E., Ely, A., Birkin, L., Basu, P., & Goulson, D. (2020). The Contribution of Small-scale Food Production in urban areas to the sustainable Development Goals: A Review and Case Study. *Sustainability Science*. https://doi.org/10.1007/s11625-020-00792-z

Normandin, É., Vereecken, N. J., Buddle, C. M., & Fournier, V. (2017). Taxonomic and Functional Trait Diversity of Wild Bees in Different Urban Settings. *PeerJ, 5*, e3051.

Oeldorf-Hirsch, A. (2018). The Role of Engagement in Learning from Active and Incidental News Exposure on Social Media. *Mass Communication and Society, 21*, 225–247. https://doi.org/10.1080/15205436.2017.1384022

Ohlson, R. G. (2015). Peripheral no More: Repositioning Narratives for Empowerment and Change in Sustainability Education. *Leadership for Sustainability Education Comprehensive Papers. Paper 9*. Retrieved from http://pdxscholar.library.pdx.edu/lse_comp/9

Ollerton, J., & Coulthard, E. (2009). Evolution of Animal Pollination. *Science, 326*, 808–809.

Ollerton, J., Winfree, R., & Tarrant, S. (2011). How Many Flowering Plants are Pollinated by Animals? *Oikos, 120*, 321–326.

Paini, D. R. (2004). Impact of the Introduced Honey bee (*Apis mellifera*)(Hymenoptera: Apidae) on Native Bees: A Review. *Austral Ecology, 29*, 399–407.

Patel, V., Pauli, N., Biggs, E., Barbour, L., & Boruff, B. (2020). Why Bees are Critical for Achieving Sustainable Development. *Ambio*. https://doi.org/10.1007/s13280-020-01333-9

Pentina, I., & Tarafdar, M. (2014). From "information" to "knowing": Exploring the Role of Social Media in Contemporary News Consumption. *Computers in Human Behavior*, 35, 211–223. https://doi.org/10.1016/j.chb.2014.02.045

Pew Research Center. (2019). Americans are Wary of the Role Social Media Sites Play in Delivering the News.

Polsky, C., Grove, J. M., Knudson, C., Groffman, P. M., Bettez, N., Cavender-Bares, J., et al. (2014). Assessing the Homogenization of Urban Land Management With an Application to US Residential Lawn Care. *Proceedings of the National Academy of Sciences*, 111, 4432–4437.

Potts, S. G., Imperatriz-Fonseca, V., Ngo, H., Biesmeijer, J. C., Breeze, T., Dicks, L., et al. (2016). *Summary for Policymakers of the Assessment Report of the Intergovernmental Science-Policy Platform on Biodiversity and Ecosystem Services (IPBES) on Pollinators, Pollination and Food Production*, No. hal-01946814.

Potts, S. G., Imperatriz-Fonseca, V., Ngo, H. T., Aizen, M. A., Biesmeijer, J. C., Breeze, T. D., et al. (2016). Safeguarding Pollinators and Their Values to Human Well-being. *Nature*, 540, 220–229.

Prener, C. G., Braswell, T. H., & Monti, D. J. (2018). St. Louis's "urban prairie": Vacant Land and the Potential for Revitalization. *Journal of Urban Affairs*, 42, 1–19.

Prestin, A. L. (2013). The Pursuit of Hopefulness: Operationalizing Hope in Entertainment Media Narratives. *Media Psychology*, 16, 318–346.

Purnell, J. Q., Camberos, G. J., & Fields, R. P. (Eds.). (2014). For the Sake of All: A report on the health and well-being of African Americans in St. Louis—and why it matters for everyone. St. Louis, MO: Washington University in St. Louis and Saint Louis University. Available at: http://forthesakeofall.org.

Qiu, L., Lindberg, S., & Nielsen, A. B. (2013). Is Biodiversity Attractive?—On-Site Perception of Recreational and Biodiversity Values in Urban Green Space. *Landscape and Urban Planning*, 119, 136–146.

Raja, S., Ma, C., & Yadav, P. (2008). Beyond Food Deserts: Measuring and Mapping Racial Disparities in Neighborhood Food Environments. *Journal of Planning Education and Research*, 27, 469–482.

Roubik, D. (2014). *Pollinator Safety in Agriculture*. Rome, Italy: Food and Agriculture Organization of the United Nations.

Rupprecht, C. D., Byrne, J. A., Ueda, H., & Lo, A. Y. (2015). It's Real, Not Fake Like a Park': Residents' Perception and Use of Informal Urban Green-space in Brisbane, Australia and Sapporo, Japan. *Landscape and Urban Planning*, 143, 205–218.

Saure, C., Burger, F., & Dathe, H.H. (1998). Die Bienenarten von Branden- burg und Berlin (Hymenoptera: Apidae). *Entomologische Nachrichten und Berichte*, 42, 155–166.

Senaratne, M. (2017). The Transition from MDGs to SDGs: Rethinking Buzzwords. In J. Servaes (Ed.), *Sustainable Development Goals in the Asian Context. Communication, Culture and Change in Asia* (Vol. 2). Singapore: Springer.

Servaes, J. (Ed.). (2008). *Communication for Development and Social Change*. Thousand Oaks, CA: Sage Publications.

Servaes, J., & Malikhao, P. (2014). The Role and Place of Communication for Sustainable Social Change (CSSC). *International Social Science Journal*, 65, 171–183.

Sirohi, M. H., Jackson, J., Edwards, M. & Ollerton, J. (2015). Diversity and abundance of solitary and primitively eusocial bees in an urban centre: a case study from Northampton (England). *Journal of Insect Conservation*, 19, 487–500.

Sisser, J. M., Nelson, K. C., Larson, K. L., Ogden, L. A., Polsky, C., & Chowdhury, R. R. (2016). Lawn enforcement: How municipal policies and neighborhood norms influence homeowner residential landscape management. *Landscape and Urban Planning, 150,* 16–25.

Slocum, R. (2007). Whiteness, Space and Alternative Food Practice. *Geoforum, 38,* 520–533.

Taylor, J. R., & Lovell, S. T. (2014). Urban Home Food Gardens in the Global North: Research Traditions and Future Directions. *Agriculture and Human Values, 31,* 285–305.

Threlfall, C. G., Walker, K., Williams, N. S., Hahs, A. K., Mata, L., Stork, N., et al. (2015). The Conservation Value of Urban Green Space Habitats for Australian Native Bee Communities. *Biological Conservation, 187,* 240–248.

Tighe, J. R., & Ganning, J. P. (2015). The Divergent City: Unequal and Uneven Development in St. Louis. *Urban Geography, 36,* 654–673.

Tommasi, D., Miro, A., Higo, H. A., & Winston, M. L. (2004). Bee diversity and Abundance in an Urban Setting. *The Canadian Entomologist, 136,* 851–869.

Tonietto, R., Fant, J., Ascher, J., Ellis, K., & Larkin, D. (2011). A Comparison of Bee Communities of Chicago Green Roofs, Parks and Prairies. *Landscape and Urban Planning, 103,* 102–108.

Turo, K. J., & Gardiner, M. M. (2019). From Potential to Practical: Conserving Bees in Urban Public Greenspace. *Frontiers in Ecology and the Environment, 16,* 1–9.

UN Forum Spotlights Cities, Where Struggle for Sustainability 'will be Won or Lost.' (2018, July 11). *UN News.* Retrieved from https://news.un.org/en/story/2018/07/1014461

United Nations. (n.d.). Sustainable Development Goals Knowledge Platform. Retrieved from https://sustainabledevelopment.un.org/

United States Department of Agriculture. (2010). *National Agricultural Library.* Retrieved from https://www.nal.usda.gov/afsic/beekeeping

Wei, F., Costanza, R., Dai, Q., Stoeckl, N., Gu, X., Farber, S., et al. (2018). The Value of Ecosystem Services from Giant Panda Reserves. *Current Biology, 28,* 2174–2180.

Westerman, D., Spence, P. R., & Van Der Heide, B. (2014). Social Media as Information Source: Recency of Updates and Credibility of Information. *Journal of Computer-Mediated Communication, 19*(2), 171–183. https://doi.org/10.1111/jcc4.12041

What is Communication? (n.d.). National Communication Association. Retrieved from https://www.natcom.org/about-nca/what-communication

Williams, L. A., & DeSteno, D. (2008). Pride and Perseverance: The Motivational Role of Pride. *Journal of Personality and Social Psychology, 94,* 1007–1017.

Witte, K. (1992). Putting the Fear Back into Fear Appeals: The Extended Parallel Process Model. *Communication Monographs, 59,* 329–349. https://doi.org/10.1080/03637759209376276

Woolf, S. H., Purnell, J. Q., Simon, S. M., Zimmerman, E. B., Camberos, G. J., Haley, A., et al. (2015). Translating Evidence into Population Health Improvement: Strategies and Barriers. *Annual Review of Public Health, 36,* 463–482.

Wynne, B. (2006). Public Engagement as a Means of Restoring Public Trust in Science: Hitting the Notes, but Missing the Music? *Community Genetics, 9,* 211–220.

Yang, B., Liu, J., & Popova, L. (2019). Feeling Hopeful Motivates Change: Emotional Responses to Messages Communicating Comparative Risk of Electronic Cigarettes and Combusted Cigarettes. *Health Education & Behavior, 46,* 471–483. https://doi.org/10.1177/1090198118825236

PART III

International Communication, Journalism and Sustainable Development

CHAPTER 19

Egyptian TV Coverage of the Sustainable Development Strategy (SDS): Egypt Vision 2030

Alamira Samah Saleh and Mahmoud Zaky

INTRODUCTION

In 2015 and during the "Support and Development of the Egyptian Economy" conference in Sharm El-Sheikh, which had witnessed large international participation, President Al-Sisi referred to Egypt's vision 2030, stating: *"The Egyptian economy will not stop at the giant projects. Instead, it will be based on a clear vision and free trend that support the free market economy, which depends on the role of the private sector in the context of a stable economic environment. In this regard, Egypt has developed a long-term sustainable development strategy until 2030, aiming to build a modern and democratic society based on production and openness to the world."*

He added that the government had prepared the strategy according to the planning approach with the participation of the private sector and civil society agencies. Al-Sisi confirmed that "those stakeholders played a central role in preparing the

---

A. S. Saleh (✉)
Faculty of Mass Communication, Cairo University, Cairo, Egypt

M. Zaky
Faculty of Mass Communication, Sinai University, Ismailia, Egypt

© The Author(s), under exclusive license to Springer Nature
Switzerland AG 2021
M. J. Yusha'u, J. Servaes (eds.), *The Palgrave Handbook of International Communication and Sustainable Development*,
https://doi.org/10.1007/978-3-030-69770-9_19

strategy to ensure compliance with the implementation of policies, programmes, and initiatives to be adopted, seeking to achieve the overall Vision goals".[1]

Keeping up with the local and international vision on development, Hala Al-Sa'eed, the Minister of Planning, Monitoring, and Administrative Reform, held a press conference on 13 January 2018 where she announced the "Modernization of the 2030 Sustainable Development Strategy". She declared that the vision goals would be revised depending on the on-ground steps and accomplishments. A self-assessment should be conducted in the second half of this year with the United Nations, in addition to the inclusion of other aspects of the strategy. New areas of interest were centred on, for example, the rates of population-control issues in light of the final population statistics, the new laws of what was called the "financial inclusion" to support the country's strategy to help the poorest segments, and finally the aspect of the scientific research to keep up with aspired progress. Thus, the Sustainable Development Strategy (SDS) "Egypt's Vision 2030" was on the official agendas over time and represented an insisting official orientation.

Based on the previous background, the current analysis was carried out using a purposive sample of the Egyptian televised full programme episodes, particular parts of TV talk shows, official televised information releases, live coverage, news reports, televised public service announcements (PSAs), and documentaries (Fig. 19.1). All of which dealt explicitly with the Sustainable Development Strategy (SDS) goals and the Egyptian governmental achievements. The analysed content was broadcasted on both the Egyptian national and private television channels since the official launch of the strategy in February 2016 till the end of June 2018. The qualitative analysis of the content was done by carefully reviewing the whole selective televised content, then selecting the categories of the analysis. The first stage of this process was done by taking notes and comments on the material, while the second stage was based on classifying the obtained data for qualitative analysis purposes.

THE EGYPTIAN SUSTAINABLE DEVELOPMENT: NEGOTIATING THE MEANING

Concepts such as sustainability and sustainable development, coined by international consultative and policy-making organizations, tend to undergo a complicated process of adaptation and localization within the unique cultural flavour of each national community. There clearly needs to be an intra-national attempt to come to terms with the concepts. Experts and peer groups, as well as leading media within the national community, tend to interpret and enhance the terminologies as part of a cultural adoption process.

The process of meaning negotiation surrounding the concepts of development and sustainability within national and local narratives is currently an increasing trend and relevance in light of their prioritization by national and

---

[1] President Abdel Fattah Al-Sisi during the opening session of "The International Conference to Support the Development of the Egyptian economy", 13 March 2015, https://www.youtube.com/watch?v=D2wgkZbNHfU.

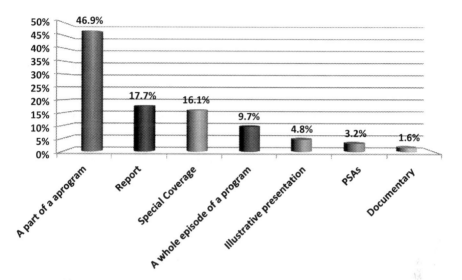

Fig. 19.1 TV formats of coverage for the Sustainable Development Strategy: Egypt's Vision 2030

international agents as well as global initiatives such as the UN Decade of Education for Sustainable Development (2005–2014). Given the various political and cultural agendas that influence media, the question now is what could be the inputs of the agenda for those who wish to promote sustainability (Howson & Cleasby, 1996).

When referring to the Egyptian official formula of sustainable development on the levels of both definition and process, we could go in accordance with the governmental report that had been issued in 2016 by the Ministry of Planning, Monitoring, and Administrative Reform. The report basically defines the strategy as follows:

> The Sustainable Development Strategy: Egypt Vision 2030 represents an essential step in Egypt's extensive development, which seeks to link the present with the future, inspired by the achievements of the ancient Egyptian civilization. It establishes a development procession of an advanced and prosperous nation dominated by economic and social justice. It revives the historic role of Egypt in regional leadership. Moreover, it represents a road map that aims to maximize the use of competitive possibilities and advantages. It also seeks the implementation of the Egyptian people's dreams and aspirations of enjoying a convenient and dignified life. Therefore, it embodies the modern Egyptian constitution, which has as a target for the Egyptian economy to achieve prosperity in Egypt through sustainable development, social justice, and ensuring balanced growth.
>
> The strategy is particularly important in the circumstances prevailing in Egypt, which require revision of development goals in order to keep up with current and future needs and to develop better solutions to deal with them. This should enable Egyptian society to move into the ranks of developed countries and achieve the desired targets for the country. (The Ministry of Planning, Monitoring, and Administrative Reform, 2016)

When trying to answer the questions of the local Egyptian agendas of sustainable development, we could notice that the most significant part of it was mainly concerned with two main broad themes: the first was detailing all that is relevant to the definition, reasons behind, and the strategy concerning promoting it, while the second theme sought to draw the official map that the government would consider for achieving such goals. Consequently, both national and private Egyptian televised narratives were built on the notion that implies the success in achieving sustainable development goals as a non-attainable target unless it is built on a solid, informative base (Abu Ghazi, 2017).

In a televised interview with CBC TV channel[2] Ashraf Al-Arabi, former Minister of Planning, declared that thinking of the "2030 Sustainable Development Document" had begun right after 30 June 2013 Revolution.[3]

In January 2014, he embarked on the actual procedures for the preparation of the strategy and worked on it for the next two whole years. He added that the government was very keen on involving all the social actors to achieve the broadest possible participation with representatives of civil society organizations, the private sector, ministries, academic experts, as well as international partners. Such perspective of participation that would guarantee a sustainable strategy which would not be changed with each cabinet reshuffle and maximizing its outcomes.

This last point concerning "Participatory Planning" was detailed on by Nihal al-Maghrabal, Deputy Minister of Planning, in a TV interview.[4] She added that the ministry is responsible for planning in Egypt for now, but it was not alone in setting the strategy as its role was limited to "organizing and hosting meetings with development partners, namely civil society, the private sector, and international institutions with an effective presence of youth and women" at the beginning of working on the strategy. Then, in a later stage, the ministry acted as a link between all these partners on the one hand and the related ministries on the other hand until it was finally possible to determine the axes of the strategy, its objectives, and indicators.

Therefore, many media messages were directed to interpret the meaning of the sustainable development and the Egyptian vision in this regard as a necessity driven by the priority of preserving the Egyptian state and ensuring its survival, taking into account what the state experienced during the past years and the real threats and conspiracies to bring the state down by emphasizing and exploiting the problems and the challenges it faces from now on.[5]

Moreover, the different media reasoning and justification strategies were built on another aspect of coverage emphasizing that the recent developments

---

[2] The episode was broadcasted on 23 March 2016, Retrieved from https://www.youtube.com/watch?v=nZ7KuYRjXjQ.

[3] He assumed the post of prime minister of Egypt from 9 July 2013 to 24 February 2014.

[4] The episode was broadcasted on 1 June 2016. Retrieved from: https://www.youtube.com/watch?v=gzSL2u4NyFI.

[5] President Abdel Fattah Al-Sisi during his speech in Egypt's Vision 2030 conference, 24 February 2016. Retrieved from: https://www.youtube.com/watch?v=hS8rwgkz4u8

in Egypt at the local, regional, and international levels have made thinking of the future as a popular demand and an official decision to be taken[6] in order to re-attain its unique status: Egypt deserves regionally and globally. A theme which was emphasized repeatedly by many officials who stated that Egypt now is on its way to achieving unprecedented levels of economic development like many countries which overcame the same circumstances and now have become giants (The Asian Tigers were named and meant).[7] On a practical level, the coverage asserted that coordinating the efforts of all the state institutions working in different sectors is now a must so that they could have one goal to achieve either on the plans' level or in the implementation processes with no place for contradictions.

EGYPT'S VISION 2030: A FUTURE PLAN ON SCIENTIFIC BASES?

A national project for the Egyptian state at this historical moment. Hussein Abaza, Adviser to the Minister of Planning

It is the dream espoused and sponsored by the political leadership that recognized the importance of having a dream that people would ever wish to see it come true. So, if the political leaders and their media work hard for it, what is remaining to be achieved is the public support, to ensure its success. Here, the media coverage of SDS was an essential part of drawing the dream in the minds and getting that public help for the one dream embodied in OUR Egypt's Vision 2030.

Four key objectives of the strategy were identified and very well covered by the televised content to be gradually achieved until they are fully completed by 2030. These objectives are illustrated in the following figure (Fig. 19.2).

For the sake of building "the Egyptian dream", the Ministry of Planning, Monitoring, and Administrative Reform sponsored a series of TV advertisements and PSAs that crystalized the concrete steps the ministry made to make the dream clear. The media messages in this context prepared the audience to perceive the ministry as the genuine source of what might be called a "kick-off" and a starting point for the administrative and the institutional flow of work to initiate supporting the Vision 2030, while the civil society, the private sector, and the most related international bodies were considered as "active players". In this regard all the previous list of participants was considered as stakeholders that carry "a noble & a national goal" "over their shoulders which should be translated into achieving sustainability in the various sectors of work". This

---

[6] Deputy Minister of Planning, Monitoring, and Administrative Reform in her televised interview for "Al-Hayat Today" TV programme on Al-Hayat TV channel. The episode was broadcasted on 13 August 2016. Retrieved from: https://www.youtube.com/watch?v=hMEb6OBcTW8.

[7] Sara Kira—an international relations researcher—at the University of San Pablo in Spain in her televised interview in "From Egypt" programme on the Postgraduate Education channel. The episode was broadcasted on 18 March 2016. Retrieved from: https://www.youtube.com/watch?v=BLaS5GoThdw&t=154s.

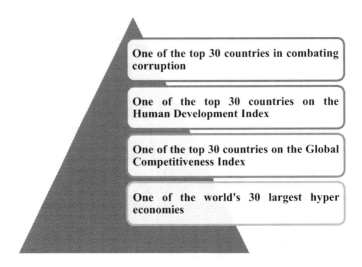

Fig. 19.2 The dimensions of the Egyptian dream

reflects the size of the official keenness to present the strategy as "society and a high state vision rather than a mere ministerial and governmental one".

In a good sense of what might come to mind about whether Egyptians should wait until 2030 to reap the fruits of sustainable development, Prof. Hala Al-Sa'eed, the Minister of Planning, said in one of her speeches during the "Egypt's Vision 2030" session of the Fourth National Conference of Youth in Alexandria[8] that *"[a]chieving the development's goals in the near future requires a good knowledge of the way we are going through & clear multi-stages pathways to achieve them"*.

The same meaning was pointed out by Dr Nihal al-Maghrabal, Deputy Minister of Planning, in a televised interview. She declared that the 2030 specific date does not mean the ultimate goal and the endpoint of achieving the objectives of sustainable development in Egypt, but rather the purpose for which all the medium- and the short-term executive plans are set. "These plans should be reflected in the citizens' lives and the state's economy in a remarkably rapid manner".[9]

Once again, the same meaning was tackled by Dr Ahmed Sa'eed, an expert on the economic and administrative legislation, in his televised interview in a "Start-Up" programme.[10] He said: *"Contrary to what some might think that it is necessary to wait for many years to obtain the results of this plan, the citizens*

---

[8] Egypt's Vision 2030 conference which was broadcasted on 24 July 2017. Retrieved from: https://www.youtube.com/watch?v=hS8rwgkz4u8.
[9] The episode was broadcasted on 13 August 2016.
[10] Episode that was broadcasted on 6 December 2016. Retrieved from: https://www.youtube.com/watch?v=-40fiagp8TA.

should reap the fruits from now as we work continuously in multi fields of development like education, health, and economy".

On concrete bases, President Al-Sisi listed a number of projects and accomplishments which Egypt had witnessed from 2014 to 2016 and which all come under pursuing the goals and the specific plans of Egypt's Vision 2030, which the state strongly supports. Some of these projects are:

- Building 5000 kilometres of roads and working on six more thousand kilometres.
- Constructing 133 bridges in 20 months.
- Solving the problem of frequent power cuts by building several giant power generators.
- Establishing three airports with a capacity of 1.7 million passengers per airport.
- Working on the establishment of three new ports.
- Solving the energy problems in Egypt completely.

Another argument has been thrown on the table of discussions around Egypt's sustainable development goals, which were the worldwide participatory efforts towards the future. A discourse that emphasized the idea of sharing the same experience with other countries that are going through the same process of development: "*We aren't alone; all the developed countries have had a vision for the future, while countries that do not have are floundering in their policies and decisions*".

The same message of internationalization was repeated more and more by many officials and experts who spread their point of view through different media outlets. Remarkable highlights were made by Hala Al-Sa'eed, the Minister of Planning,[11] where she reviewed the experience of South Africa in developing a vision for the future that enabled it to achieve its objectives, in addition to the experience of "Poland" in developing its 2020 vision, as well as the experience of the State of Singapore with its Prime Minister Li Kuan Yew which was believed to be unsuccessful although Singapore has achieved an outstanding economic status.

The official discourse of sharing the development pathway with worldwide players had empathized on the ultimate level when President Al-Sisi confirmed that "*Egypt has actively participated in all stages of drafting the development agenda. We have a clear vision that is strongly urging all the international effort to achieve sustainable development. However, we should assert the uniqueness of each development policy of the different developing countries and their sovereignty. We've to care for their ways in adopting the national economic and social*

---

[11] The speech was given during the "Egypt's Vision 2030" session at the Fourth National Youth Conference, which was held in Alexandria. A televised episode was broadcasted on 24 July 2017.

programs that match its priorities of development, taking into account the specificity of each region and its needs."[12]

In a documentary film which was produced on Egypt's new strategy, Dr Khaled Habib, head of the National Training Academy, has mentioned that although Egypt has been involved in many planning strategies on the national level, however, it was the first time in which Egypt has a comprehensive strategic vision that goes beyond the five-year plans and the idle national projects that prevailed during the 1950s and 1960s.[13]

Additionally, the Egyptian Prime Minister Dr Mostafa Madbouly[14] pointed out during his speech to the House of Representatives[15] that Egypt's vision includes specific programmes and indicators for measuring how successful it is. These measures will be strictly monitored by the current government and all the successive governments.

On a media-wise level, the Egyptian Sustainable Development Strategy (SDS) was represented as an ideal model for future national planning, which is based on scientific fundamentals. Such convictions were declared once again by President Al-Sisi in his speech during the opening of the 9th annual conference of the International Alliance for Financial Inclusion held in Sharm El-Sheikh.[16] He said, "*We embarked on a purely national Egyptian vision, in which we pointed out our situations and problems impartially and honestly. We articulated Egypt's strategy for development until 2030, identified appropriate goals and priorities. We've used very well thought out mechanisms and tools, adhering to specific deadlines, and implementing the necessary policies and decisions, some of which was long-delayed, and some were unavoidable, as we wanted real reform devoid of false promises and slogans.*"

In its way to support all these governmental declarations and steps, the Ministry of Planning has sponsored a series of advertisements and public service announcements in which they embodied in texts and images a very intertwined formula of "an idea and a hope", "the prospectus and the ultimate goal", and the efforts made by the state versus the supposed role of the citizens. Each advertising message was intensive in content and focused on its objectives.

Two versions of the Egypt's Vision 2030 advertisements were presented on all the Egyptian TV channels.[17]

---

[12] Egypt's speech at the United Nations Summit on Sustainable Development. A live broadcast on 25 September 2015. Retrieved from: https://www.youtube.com/watch?v=V_pqfRCkvBg.

[13] The film was broadcasted at the opening session of a conference on 24 February 2016.

[14] Dr Mostafa Madbouly assumed the post of prime minister of Egypt on 7 June 2018, succeeding Eng. Sherif Ismail who launched the strategy during his tenure as prime minister.

[15] It was broadcasted on 3 July 2018. Retrieved from: https://www.youtube.com/watch?v=_UPfQzcSGbk.

[16] A speech, which was broadcasted on 14 September 2017. Retrieved from: https://www.youtube.com/watch?v=jwN09lD5Fzs.

[17] On 22 February 2018, *Al-Dustour* newspaper published that the Minister of Planning, Monitoring, and Administrative Reform Dr Hala Al-Sa'eed announced during the session of the community dialogue hosted by the Ministry on the Sustainable Development Strategy 2018/2019–2021/2022, in the presence of the Minister of Local Development and ten gover-

The first advertisement was a group song performance that lasted for one minute and thirty-five seconds while the second advertisement was presented by the very well-known actor, Hisham Selim. It lasted for one minute and sixteen seconds. The slogan of the two advertisements was "Egypt's Vision 2030. ... Egypt is planning for its future."

As will become evident in the first advertisement,[18] people from all classes and categories of the Egyptian society appeared and took part in drawing the number "2030" in a clear symbolic expression that the society with all its classes is the main component and the target of such a vision. Thus the people should stand behind their leader to portray the future of their country.

فكّرنا نعمل ايه لبلدنا	We thought of what we could do for our country
عشان بنحبها	Because we love her
فكر معانا عشان نفيدها	Think with us to do what is best for her
ونُشرّف اسمها	To honour her name
ايدك فى ايدى ويالله بينا	Put your hand in mine and let's do it
عايزين نثبت لها	We want to prove to her
إن الأمل دلوقتى فينا	That the hope now is in us
عارفين رايحين على فين	We know where we're going to
شايفين 2030	We can see 2030
سابقين لسنين وسنين	Moving ahead for years and years
فى طريق حلمنا ماشيين	On the way of our dream

The song was accompanied by a voice-over which reflected the collective spirit that the advertisement focused on. The commentary presented different images for the Egyptian people, either personal ones showing different working groups in multiple production fields or thematic images for projects that have been or are being implemented.

> *There is no success without planning! Planning means having deliberate plans, well-calculated steps, and priorities. This is precisely Egypt's 2030 Vision.*
> *Egypt is planning her future in all fields; health, education, transport and roads, agriculture, industry, housing, energy, and above all this, Egypt is investing in her youth. All institutions of the state, the private sector will take part in this.*
> *And with proper planning for the first time, we know what we are heading for.*
> *Egypt's 2030 Vision: Egypt is planning her future.*

The combination of both the song and the voice-over commentary reflected the Egyptians with their age, quality, regional, professional, educational, and health differences which are a clear indication that the vision represents the hope of the entire Egyptian society, fulfils the aspirations for a better future, and seeks to create a convenient and co-shared motive for work and

nors, that a campaign for raising awareness of the axes of 2030 strategy is being launched together with short advertisements on TV channels over a week, followed by a series of other advertisements. The news is Retrieved from https://www.dostor.org/2067843.

[18] Retrieved from https://www.youtube.com/watch?V=H-SchWrNpJs.

achievement. On all levels and by all possible means, the advertisement strongly propagated a strategy focusing on guiding the Egyptians towards becoming active and productive members of their nation's future plan that will turn over their whole life to a much better version of their reality.

Rather than a conventional and sensational artistic plot, the rationale message marked the second advertisement. The very well-known actor Hisham Selim took the mission of sending the official point of view on sustainable development to the public with a very special focus on youth.

> *If we follow up the international reports and news, we'll see that the most significant economic institutions bet on Egypt. Do you know why they bet on us?! Do you know that we're going to hit it big?*
>
> *It's all because we started planning and working right. It's also because we have a vision with clear goals and careful steps. And before all, more than 70% of our peoples are mostly young. It's the energy, spirit, and vision of young people that are going to change the status quo.*
>
> *However, the point now is that those young people have to learn and take their chance. … This is Egypt's 2030 Vision. To achieve this, we've built partnerships with the most significant international consulting firms. And for the first time, we're going to have a department for Human Resources Management (HRM), training programs, efficiency-raising programs of civil servants in all stages, and evaluation programs before and after receiving these training programs to ensure that we are on the right track. This all shows that we have a clear vision of the future and that we're planning well for it. Imagine we have a million young Egyptian people who are well trained and well qualified! Well, even if they were only ten, twenty or thirty well trained and qualified ones! Imagine how the future of Egypt will be then!*
>
> *Don't say it's going to take ages because time passes fast, and those who get prepared are the ones who will create it. Egypt's 2030 Vision Egypt: planning the future.*

Here we could notice that the two advertisements sought to market the official state-run media messages on the Egyptian version of sustainable development either using the enthusiastic and the motivational approach or focusing on the logical perspective with another slight specification of the target audience from a general wide umbrella of the Egyptians to a narrow scale one seeking to flirt the majority of the angry youth.

Noteworthy, the launching of this advertising campaign came two years after the official launch of the strategy itself. It could be understood that the Ministry of Planning expected that although the vision's launching had received some media coverage, however, it was not well-absorbed yet to be adopted by the Egyptians and their awareness towards the concept of development and had not been sufficiently linked to the projects underway. Therefore, producing these advertisements together with the use of famous celebrities sought to expand the perspective of these major projects and policies to be borne in the minds of people as part of a broader strategy for the future.

Egypt's Vision 2030: Which Way to Go?!

While dreaming of the future was being shaped, the road to reality was clear in the TV coverage of the Sustainable Development Strategy (SDS) "Egypt's Vision 2030".

The question of "Which way to go?" has always been a concern for the different TV channels covering Sustainable Development Strategy (SDS) "Egypt's Vision 2030". The "goals and objectives" are always followed by an elaboration on "ways and tools" to achieve. The belief in ideas and goals of such magnitude, spatial, and temporal extension, like those contained in the Sustainable Development Strategy (SDS), requires clear and well-articulated pathways. Media voices who were trying to draw the map to the future committed themselves to help the audience identify what will be done with the specification. Truth be told, not everyone was aware enough of how realistic these steps will be or who should specifically monitor and account those claimed achievements. Therefore, the audience here just received different voices with one message that portrayed all relevant issues as fine. You only have to trust what the state is doing for you!

Among the most analysed content, we could categorize how the TV talk shows sought to answer the question of the way to prosperity and development (Fig. 19.3). Evidently, there were three prominent phases of achievements.

Here, Egyptian governmental and private TV channels have given explicit attention to diversifying the forms and genres of coverage, specifically and thematically aired programmes, complete blocks within programmatic episodes, information presentations, live coverage, video reports, TV PSAs, and documentaries.

However, in no equivocal focus and interest, the whole specially designed content of this TV coverage of the strategy seemed to be insufficient compared with the amount of time devoted to other topics/problems in a sense that lacks a solution type of journalism which serves more the crucial issues for a developed society. This lack reflected clearly through the media's inability to translate the holistic, Sustainable Development Strategy into on-ground developmental coverage of projects either those that have been already implemented or the ones under construction as remarkable. Such a kind of coverage

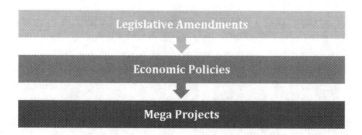

Fig. 19.3 Phases of accomplishing "Egypt's Vision 2030"

of abstract topics, goals, and steps of the sustainable strategy could be a reason behind the lack of recognition of the strategy itself in glaring contrast with the touchable achievements in citizens' everyday life.

While covering the related events and activities of Sustainable Development Strategy (SDS) "Egypt's Vision 2030", the TV coverage focused on hosting former and current officials, experts, and specialists in different interviews with the objective of delivering a convenient level of knowledge and information especially when it comes to complicated numbers, figures, or details that might seem difficult to understand. Moreover, those guests assumed to much better know the history and background of the previous national periods of developmental programmes in Egypt and those of other countries with similar circumstances. These interviews, then, could be a valuable, rich, and informative source of information to different segments of the TV viewers.

Additionally, former and current officials from the Ministry of Planning, Monitoring, and Administrative Reform had a significant presence in such television coverage of SDS. Most of those officials were involved in the various stages of the SDS's preparation, and a variety of time slots during the day were chosen to present the related topics seeking to widely circulate the message of what people should know about SDS. What matters here was the continuation of media interest rather than episodic and seasonal coverage.

Thematically, the analysed TV content of SDS in the current chapter could be classified qualitatively into two categories.

Goals and Objectives: A Dream Building or a Nightmare

This perspective of content has been divided into two main directions, as well; the first one is that the TV messages which provide the viewers with insights and ideas on SDS explain the concept, the reasons for its preparation, its participants, and its significance for the time being and in the future. Finally, this direction gave knowledge about the strategy's dimensions and axes compared with the global planning map.

The second direction of the current category was devoted to build up the dream, inspire the people, and instil hope for the Egyptian state. Noticeably, the role of the Egyptian media in a generic sense and the role of TV content in this specific analysis tended only to propagate, to mobilize the people, and to motivate them to believe in the sustainable development goals rather than running a society debate and dialogue on these goals to let the audience closely monitor the implementation of concrete plans, to guarantee a bottom-up communication and interaction between the ordinary people and the officials. A case that emphasized the very old models of media in which a one-way process of communication took place from the state to the citizens, and which ignored any type of accountability in the road to prosperity and social change.

Although the TV coverage of SDS has been marketed to serve as the "vision of the state and the peoples" rather than a "vision of the authority and the government" only, the reality was different.

"*Don't listen to anybody's words but for me*"[19] President Al-Sisi intimidated the people when he was launching the government's strategic "Egypt Vision 2030" on 24 February 2016.

Look: I know Egypt, as intimately as I can see all of you before me here, and I also know the remedy for her [Egypt], as well as I, can see you before me here. And I say this to everyone listening to me in Egypt: If you please, do not listen to anybody's words but mine! [5 sec. Applause] W I'm utterly serious: don't listen to anybody's words but mine! I'm a man of my words; I don't waver, and I have no other interest in mind than my country. My country alone! [5 sec. Applause] And not only interest other than her—I also have the right understanding of what I'm saying! This program that we are putting in place here was designed to let our young people, for the first time, know what Egypt's true cause is through an 8-month program. We're going to finalize the necessary studies and get a good grip on it … but are we going to rip Egypt to pieces or what? I shall not tolerate this! Watch out! [4 sec. Applause] Watch out! I shall not tolerate this! [Sisi's voice and face take on an increasingly stern expression] No-one should think that my patience and my good nature mean that this country can fall. I swear to God: anyone who tries to trespass on her, I'll erase him from the face of the earth! [17 sec. applause] I'm telling this to all of you, to every Egyptian listening to me … what do you think this is all about!? Do you want to … do you … Who are you anyhow? Who are you? … Ha! … No! … Here's 90 million! [He raises his fist] And I am responsible before Our Lord in that I'll stand before Him on Judgment Day to tell Him: 'I took care of them' [makes a gesture of an enclosure]. If you want to take care of them, with me: welcome! If you don't, well, then please: shut up! (Hofheinz, 2016)

Although the political leadership has given great impetus to this vision, the state officials were careful in more than one television interview to show that the right perception of the future has been dematerialized in favour of enhancing the role of society in planning and implementing the vision and thus gaining its fruits. However, the president positioned himself as the omniscient leader who alone knows and can tell his countrymen how to run Egypt, an expert doctor who alone knows how to remedy what's wrong with her. To listen to anybody else would make the country fall.

And it is at this point that both the above-mentioned TV messages follow the knowledge, attitude, and behaviour (KAB) model of media effects, which seeks to inform the audience in order to create certain attitudes towards a specific idea for the sake of mobilizing people to do a certain behaviour. Although it seems to be an old model of media effects, it still could be used in many contemporary media messages as indicated. Both the governmental and private TV channels supported and backed up the official discourse of the Egyptian state. These channels kept pace with the developmental projects in its various stages of establishment, depending on receiving certain official messages that need to be delivered to the people.

---

[19] President Abdel Fattah Al-Sisi's speech during Egypt's vision for sustainable development's conference ("Egypt's Vision 2030"), 2016, Retrieved from: https://www.youtube.com/watch?v=iiht9hEkiAE&feature=youtu.be&t=677%3E.

The media's role was acknowledged by the former Prime Minister Eng. Sherif Ismail during his meeting with Makram Mohamed Ahmed, the Chairman of the Supreme Council for Media Regulation; Karam Gabr, the President of the National Press Agency; and Hussein Zein, the Head of the National Media Council, in the presence of Hala Al-Sa'eed, the Minister of Planning, Monitoring, and Administrative Reform on 20 August 2017.[20] The prime minister stressed the pivotal role of the media with all its institutions in supporting the state's efforts to achieve the goals of sustainable development in various sectors as well as its role in raising people's awareness.

It is no wonder that such a media tendency makes it difficult to find avenues of mutual exchange of information, interests, and sense of belonging between the government and the public. In such a situation, we could feel familiar with the Macquill's concept of developmental media with its implications which aim to mobilize all efforts for the sake of social cohesion by explaining, interpreting, and commenting on ideas, events, and information which support consensus on different issues and situations, enhancing the social dialogue by showing up the majority culture and the common values. At the same time, the media's content under analysis moved away from Welber Schram's concept of the developmental media functions like the observing function, exploring the horizons, surveillance, and preparing reports on the dangers facing society. Therefore, the Egyptian TV channels here were mere transferring outlets, governmental-oriented, censored ones, and very far away from governance and accountability policies.

Egyptian TV channels did not pay attention to the seriousness of this vast gap between the official discourse presented and the people's views, thoughts, and feedback. Such a lack of counter-argument does not only threaten the professionalism of doing journalism when it turns to be the voice of power but also bear the consequences of the deliberate amplification of people's national hopes and aspirations on the long and medium terms. Such a bright image of a new Egypt with now ways and policies of follow up and accountability could easily be translated into deep disappointments and frustrations as a result of the delayed or the zero returns of the chanted plans and strategies.

More striking is that such a blatant alignment in the TV coverage under analysis with the official discourse had arisen the questions of gaps thawing between the government and the private media, which actually do not exist.

In the end, and because reflecting the authority's view was massive, the media was seen with the government lenses as a highly influential weapon that must be controlled to achieve its goals. Meanwhile, a priceless chance was given to the TV channels which were broadcasting from other countries and were officially classified as "hostile" to question the entire plans and strategies, suspect the integrity and impartially of the Egyptian officials, and point the arrows of condemnation to the government where the local media suffer from the lack of the objective criticism that genuinely cares for the Egyptian viewers' interests.

---

[20] https://www.youm7.com/story/2017/8/21.

Ways and Procedures: Do We Really in the Right Way?!

In describing the means of reaching out the goals and objectives of SDS, the television coverage has attentively regarded the various mega development projects being implemented or have already been achieved by the state. The coverage presented the economic and financial policies and procedures adopted by the state, as well as the legal or regulatory legislative amendments made by the state to fit. All these—apart from what may result from the ongoing reviews and those currently underway for the SDS, including additions or adjustments—fall within the framework of the pathways and procedures utilized to achieve the objectives of sustainable development.

These major projects appeared in various TV coverage as "the guaranteed path" for Egypt towards the future, as it can absorb thousands of Egyptians by providing fair number of work opportunities, both during its founding phase, processing phase, operating phase, and then in managing it. Moreover, these mega projects can facilitate the whole life aspects of the citizens. In addition to all the local benefits, these projects would make Egypt more attractive to foreign and domestic investments, which will open the door for Arab and international partnerships. All of this will contribute to pumping billions of pounds into the country's economy.

However, a huge flow of public criticism has accompanied many of these projects with different criteria in mind. Here, the social media did its role in opposing the mainstream media which was always celebrating the achievements. A parallel role with an alternative voice controlled the scene of covering the SDG of Egypt's Vision 2030 and its ongoing implications. Many examples appeared on social media with different lenses of evaluation as follows:

Social housing project: *Al-Ahram* **newspaper**

Beneficiaries of the project had voiced several criticisms of the government due to the high reservation deposits and violation of the terms of the contract. They claimed the actual apartments, upon delivery, had different specifications to the ones agreed upon in the contract.

Besides, some reservation applicants, who fulfilled the conditions for allocation, were excluded for reasons, which according to their judgement were flawed. In addition, some projects were postponed due to a delay in the delivery of contractors' dues. This, in turn, stopped the implementation of fieldwork. Certain customers added that banks were manipulating them by not handing over the units despite their regular payment of the agreed instalments.

The new administrative capital: *Akhbar Al-Youm* **newspaper**

Perhaps, this project has received the hugest criticisms ever compared to the other projects implemented by the state. It represented a model of non-transparent government policies as it has lacked the community discourse about its implementation cost, its risks to the public budget, and its purpose.

Moreover, the Egyptian government has not presented any feasibility studies on this project, leaving the citizens in a state of fait accompli, yet asking them to support the project, despite their very little—sometimes conflicting—knowledge about it. Real estate development companies ask citizens to buy housing units in the project, with a nationalist-wise propaganda and promises of a better future in this great state project.

Due to the fact that the executing company of the project belongs to the "Armed Forces' Land Projects Organization" and "The National Service Projects Organization" own the New Capital project, the parliament does not have the authority to monitor its actions, and consequently, the parliamentary oversight is also absent.

Reclaiming and cultivating a million and a half acres project: State Information Service

One of the projects, which had the most delays to start and deliver due to disputes between the relevant ministries over jurisdiction and specialization. The disputed parties were mainly the Ministries of Agriculture and Land Reclamation, and the Ministry of Water Resources and Irrigation, where the latter was entrusted with determining the percentages of water used in the cultivation process, regulating the conditions and process of drilling underground wells in some areas, as well as determining the level and reserve of groundwater and the depth of the wells to be drilled.

President Abdel Fattah Al-Sisi had criticized the Al-Reef AlMasry AlGadeed Company and its president, Atir Hanoura, during the opening of a number of projects in El-Marashda in Qena Governorate, on 14 May 2017, because of the company's delay in carrying out its tasks.

The National Roads Network Project: *Al-Ahram* **Newspaper**

This project is one of the least criticized projects for what it has achieved. Despite putting Egypt in a good position on the road of quality index, some defects have been identified in those roads after operation, such as collapses in some areas.

The New Suez Canal Project: *Al-Masry Al-Youm*

This project has received a lot of criticism based on its high cost compared to the returns expected from it, especially in light of indications of the decline in global trade movement and consequently the lack of navigation traffic through the canal.

In addition to that, potential geological effects on marine life in the region have been detected, as well as expected terrorist operations on traffic through the channel.

Airports: *Akhbar Al-Youm*

There were no absent aspects while covering the project of establishing a number of airports, except for highlighting the economic and life feasibility in relation to the Egyptians themselves.

Damietta Furniture City: State Information Service

The project aims to help young manufacturers gather in one place to provide all their needs of raw materials, create new marketing units to sell their products, and raise the rate of exports of the furniture sector.

However, most were unable to move to the city because of the high unit prices, attached lands, and the creation of impossible conditions for obtaining the units. The sale prices of the first stage units are £6000 per square metre for the prefabricated units and £2350 per square metre for the attached lands. The prices have now increased by 10–15%.

Conclusion

Over the past few years, Egypt has witnessed major improvements in society development, including expanding access to education, reducing the burden of diseases, and increasing life expectancy. Today, Egypt is one of the largest economies in the Arab world and home to one of the fastest growing middle classes in the Middle East region. This growth has created its own challenges, typical of developing and growing countries. For instance, an expanding middle class will have higher expectations for public service delivery and a more educated population will expect better jobs. Further, these challenges are compounded in Egypt by a number of factors: economic growth slowed after the unrests began in 2011; high levels of both unemployment and informality persist; the population is still relatively young and growing; and the ability of the government to provide services is constrained by low levels of capacity and transparency. While Egypt is projected to meet a number of its goals by 2030, achieving others will require a more transformative effort even beyond that of the Integrated Push (The Frederick S. Pardee Center for International Futures, 2018).

This chapter has explored Egypt's current development trajectory to 2030 across areas of TV content on the representation of Sustainable Development Strategies. The media practices and choices made in Egypt today will shape what the country looks like tomorrow and will determine its ability to meet the development goals outlined in the SDGs and Vision 2030.

Based on the previous analysis of the most prominent TV coverage of Egypt's Vision 2030, we could conclude that the behaviour of community members is either a stimulating factor and facilitator for sustainable development or a stumbling block against achieving its objectives. This chapter has emphasized the need for making sustainable development communications gear towards behaviour through a harmonious performance that combines the information and ideas' provision and focuses on behavioural models that stimulate individual behaviour.

It is unavoidable to say that while the official efforts are directed at making use of the media and its potentials to achieve the sustainable development goals, those mediums could—unintentionally—turn out to be an obstacle when it is controlled by profitability targets and commercial interests. Therefore, focus is on the consumption-based content based on the dissemination and promotion of consumption-enhancing lifestyles and personal well-being, which can clash with sustainability ideas based on rationalizing consumer behaviour and promoting the values of lasting public benefit and proper use of resources.

Additionally, the previous argument is closely related to the beliefs and visions of the media owners and practitioners in specific, especially television—when it is considered as a heavy-used medium in a literate and developed society—about the idea of sustainability and its on-ground behaviours and people commitments in all sectors of work and life. The clarity of the concept of sustainable development and its executive procedures in the minds of the media professionals was a necessary guarantee for the successful access of development TV messages on the one hand. On the other hand, the media developmental role here could ensure disappearance of contradicted messages with and against the developmental strategies.

Bibliography

Abu Ghazi, E. (2017). The Information System in the Sustainable Development Strategy in Egypt: Perception, Reality, Hope, E'lam Saudi magazine (In Arabic), p. 35. Retrieved from http://www.mandumah.com

Hofheinz, A. (2016). #Sisi_vs_Youth: Who Has a Voice in Egypt? *Journal of Arabic and Islamic Studies, 16*, 327–348.

Howson, J., & Cleasby, A. (1996). Towards a Critical Media. In J. Huckle & S. Sterling (Eds.), *Education for Sustainability* (p. 149). London: Earthscan Publications.

The Frederick S. Pardee Center for International Futures. (2018). *Sustainable Development Goals Report: Egypt 2030*. Denver: The Josef Korbel School of International Studies at the University of Denver. Retrieved from https://www.undp.org/content/dam/egypt/docs/Publications/Docs%20SDGs/Sustainable%20Development%20Goals%20Report.%20Egypt%202030.pdf

The Ministry of Planning, Monitoring, and Administrative reform. (2016). *Sustainable Development Strategy: Egypt's Vision 2030*. Cairo, p. 3. Retrieved from https://www.greengrowthknowledge.org/national-documents/sustainable-development-strategy-egypt-vision-2030

CHAPTER 20

SDG #3: Communicating "Health for All" in German-Speaking Countries as Exemplified by HIV/AIDS Advertising Campaigns

Isabell Koinig, Sandra Diehl, and Franzisca Weder

INTRODUCTION

Following the United Nations Sustainable Development Goals, goal 3 is meant to "ensure healthy lives and promote well-being for all at all ages" (UN, 2017), for health "is a driver, indicator and outcome of sustainable development" (UNDP, 2019). In detail, goal 3 sets out to end the epidemic of infectious and non-communicable diseases as well as reduce malnutrition rates amongst others by 2030 (UN, 2017). While progress has been made over the past decades, which have seen an increase in life expectancy and a success in combatting several diseases (e.g. children's diseases such as measles or adult diseases such as HIV and malaria), new health issues have emerged and need to be addressed. On the UN's agenda, there are a total of nine target strategies (e.g. reducing maternal and premature mortality rates, combatting epidemic diseases like AIDS and malaria and achieving global health coverage) plus an additional four targets that should be achieved by 2030.

Achieving the goal of "health for all" in a mediatized world poses new challenges and opportunities for all stakeholders involved, as mediatization shapes

I. Koinig (✉) • S. Diehl • F. Weder
Department of Media and Communications, Alpen-Adria University of Klagenfurt, Klagenfurt, Austria
e-mail: Isabelle.Koinig@aau.at; Franzisca.Weder@aau.at

© The Author(s), under exclusive license to Springer Nature Switzerland AG 2021
M. J. Yusha'u, J. Servaes (eds.), *The Palgrave Handbook of International Communication and Sustainable Development*,
https://doi.org/10.1007/978-3-030-69770-9_20

the way in which this goal is reflected upon, discussed as well as communicated. In the context of promoting these goals, communication is of uttermost importance. Broadly speaking, health communication refers to "any type of human communication whose content is concerned with health" (Rogers, 1996) and can be directed at both individuals and organizations with the goal of preventing illness and fostering health (Thompson, Parrott, & Nussbaum, 2011). Playing a decisive role in raising awareness, promoting individual acceptance and creating legitimization for the steps needed to work towards achieving "health for all" and regardless of the form it takes (e.g. policies, patient-provider interactions, community projects, public service announcements or advertising), health communication—in form of health campaigns—is concerned with "influencing, engaging and supporting individuals, communities, health professionals, special groups, policy makers and the public to champion, introduce, adopt, or sustain a behavior, practice or policy that will ultimately improve health outcomes" (Schiavo, 2007). Moreover, campaigns are concerned with addressing and improving social problems (Rossmann & Ziegler, 2013).

By means of an extensive content analysis in the German-speaking area (Germany, Austria, Switzerland), the present contribution seeks to highlight how the UN's health goal # 3 is communicated in the three countries as part of national health campaigns for HIV/AIDS prevention, further examining which message aspects are stressed. Successful campaigns are concerned with educating about and creating permanent awareness for HIV/AIDS, also intending to call upon individuals to become involved in their health or assist others in seeking help (e.g. get themselves tested) (Bernhardt, 2004; U.S. Department of Health and Human Services, 2005; Schiavo, 2007). At the same time, stigmatization of diseases and/or the people affected should be reduced.

Amongst others, the contribution sets out to answer the following research questions:

- Which message appeals or design elements are used to attract attention? Is the reasoning rather rational or emotional?
- Which HIV/AIDS frame dominates?
- Are metaphors employed?
- To which extent are elements of selected health theories (Health-Belief-Model, Theory-of-Reasoned-Action and Theory-of-Planned Behaviour) integrated into these messages?
- Do messages differ across different countries?

In conclusion, limitations and directions for future research are addressed.

Communication for Sustainable Development in the Context of Health

Sustainable development, referred to as "one of the most prominent development paradigms" (Servaes & Malikhao, 2016: 317), comprises five areas, namely water/sanitation, human health, energy, agricultural productivity, and biodiversity/ecosystem management (Wallington, 2014). In its 2030 Agenda for Sustainable Development as well as in the accompanying 17 Sustainable Development Goals, the United Nations emphasizes the need to "promote well-being for all ages", which it perceives as a precondition for a "prosperous society" (UN, 2017b). The WHO perceives health as a basic "human right" (WHO, 2013), and as such, prioritizes to grant all individuals access to health, regardless of age, ethnicity, income and geographic location (UN, 2017a). Moreover, sustainability in health entails the social mobilization of a number of stakeholders (Malikhao, 2016). In terms of health promotion, defined as a process to increase individual control over their health (WHO, 1986), similarities to sustainable development can be detected, as both are concerned with equity and sustainability (Fortune et al., 2018). Thereby, it is of uttermost relevance to strengthen individual confidence and involvement in pro-actively shaping the modifiable determinants of health (Edington, Schultz, Pitts, & Camilleri, 2016). The role of communication in achieving sustainability in health is even emphasized by the WHO (2013), who stresses the need to develop communication strategies that empower individuals and "create resilient communities and supportive environments". In this context, communication is seen from a broad perspective, encompassing interpersonal, participatory and mass communication (Servaes & Malikhao, 2016).

In detail, the United Nation's third sustainable development goal comprises nine targets, which address a wide range of health-related topics: (1) reduce maternal mortality rates, (2) reduce deaths of infants and children under the age of five, (3) end different epidemics (e.g. HIV/AIDS, malaria and tuberculosis amongst others), (4) reduce premature mortality by improving mental health and treatments for cardiovascular disease, (5) increase treatment effectiveness for substance abuse, (6) reduce deaths resulting from road traffic accidents, (7) increase access to reproductive health services, (8) provide universal health coverage and (9) reduce the number of deaths caused by hazardous chemicals (SD, 2020). The individual targets are supported by indicators that measure progress. In all areas, significant improvement is meant to be achieved by 2030 (SDUN, 2020).

HIV/AIDS: A Continuing Threat

Identified as one of the most serious threats to public health (HIV.gov, 2019), HIV/AIDS requires commitment by various stakeholders in order to prevent an epidemic outbreak (CDC, 2019). In 2017, almost 37 million people were living with the HIV/AIDS virus around the world; almost 2 million of them were infants or children (WHO, 2019). The number of new infections was estimated at about 1.8 million the same year (HIV.gov, 2019), as approximately one-fourth of people are unaware of their HIV status (UN Aids, 2018). While the number of HIV/AIDS-related deaths has been reduced significantly since 2004 (with 1.4 million people dying that year as compared to 940,000 in 2017; HIV.gov, 2019), it is still of uttermost importance to make people aware of their status to keep the virus from spreading. At the same time, it is essential to familiarize those infected with available treatment options (CDC, 2019). This is why an increasing communicative effort on the risks and effects of HIV/AIDS is required.

Creating Awareness for HIV/AIDS

Following the World Health Organization's 2016 Global Health Strategy Positioning Paper, strategic efforts should be dedicated "towards ending AIDS" (WHO, 2016). The numbers of AIDS infections are concerning, with approximately 17 million people living with the virus; consequently, ending this "epidemic" as part of the UN's sustainable development goals takes priority. The WHO emphasizes the necessity to both "improving the health and well-being of all people living with HIV" and to prevent the spreading of HIV by "enable[ing] people to know their HIV status" (WHO, 2019); at the same time, an end of the stigmatization and discrimination of people living with HIV/AIDS is called for (WHO, 2019). In order to create awareness for HIV/AIDS and achieve the objectives outlined earlier, health communication in general and health campaigns in particular prove to be important concepts.

Health Communication and Health Campaigns

Communication is viable to the health domain, where it is predominantly concerned with communicating and disseminating information on health-related topics to a dispersed mass audience (U.S. Department of Health and Human Services, 2014); moreover, it comprises communication encounters in the health-care setting (i.e. patient-provider interactions; Thompson, 2000; Dutta, 2008). From a rather practical perspective, health communication refers to "the study and use of communication strategies to inform and influence individual and community decisions that enhance health" (Center for Disease Control and Prevention; CDC, 2001; U.S. Department of Health and Human Services, 2005). While health messages can take multiple forms (e.g. health education materials, public or commercial health campaigns; Schiavo, 2007), these materials serve the purpose of "informing, influencing, and motivating individual, institutional, and public audiences about important health issues" (U.S. Department of Health and Human Services, 2000). At the same time, health communication wants to achieve "disease prevention through behavior modification" (Freimuth, Linnan, & Potter, 2000), motivating individuals to drop health-compromising behaviours and pick up health-enhancing behaviours instead (Bernhardt, 2004; U.S. Department of Health and Human Services, 2005; Schiavo, 2007).

While communication is not explicitly addressed as part of sustainable development, it is nonetheless an essential instrument that allows for public participation, information exchange and decision-making (Rioplus, 2008). Communication is particularly essential to raise awareness for health issues, and, hence, presents one of the nine core mechanisms to support sustainable development (OECD, 2001). In detail, it refers to "a dynamic process, integrated in a large-scale initiative that comprises multi-disciplinary and social marketing, non-formal education and public participation, thrives on acting people, aims at the innovative and sustainable change of practices, behaviors and lifestyles, guides communication processes and media interventions within and among social groups, and is a pre-requisite and a tool for change at the same time" (Rioplus, 2008: 7). Strategic communication pursues a long-term vision, prioritizing certain health-related goals and health-enhancing behaviours (Rioplus, 2008). At the same time, mutual understanding should be created (Mulholland, 2019).

Health campaigns "are an essential part of health promotion, [and] can be defined as a systematic effort to change health behaviors [...] within a target population of people who are at risk for a health problem" (Wright, Sparks, & O'Hair, 2008: 233). As such, they pursue a clear objective, address a relatively large, well-defined audience (Rogers & Storey, 1988; Snyder, 2001) and are made up of a series of coordinated activities over a given period of time, as well as across a variety of media channels (Wakefield, Loken, & Hornik, 2010). As such, health communication campaigns are utilized predominantly on a national level to engage individuals in important health issues and increase their influence on health-related outcomes (Kickbusch, 2001).

Up until now, campaign research has focused on major social issues, such as HIV (Niebel & Davidson, 2012), smoking, drug abuse or cancer screening (Jones & Owen, 2006). Additional academic research has investigated the campaigns' success, for example, by increasing immunization rates (Paunio et al., 1991; Porter et al., 2000), elevating knowledge on vaccines (McDivitt, Zimicki, & Hornik, 1997), motivating individuals to do cancer screenings (Ramirez et al., 1999) and enhancing people's disease coping abilities as well as their adherence with either nutrition or fitness regimes (PEW Internet and American Life Project, 2007). Two meta-analyses on health campaigns also support this assumption (Derzon & Lipsey, 2002; Snyder & Hamilton, 2002).

In general, health campaigns "utilize three basic communication processes to move the target audience toward the desired response: awareness, instruction, and persuasion" (Salmon & Atkin, 2003: 455). *Awareness messages* educate people about what to do and identify who should adopt a defined behaviour, offering recipients cues on the time and place of engagement. *Instruction messages* afford recipients with instructional information ("how-to-do-it"; Salmon & Atkin, 2003), whilst *persuasive messages* offer reasons as to why message recipients should take up an advocated action (Salmon & Atkin,

2003). This path is eased once useful information is provided, since "an important objective of health campaigns is getting audiences to seek information, for this indicates that they found campaign content personally relevant enough to take active steps to obtain additional information" (Parrott, 2003: 446).

In the context of health, social marketing campaigns are increasingly utilized. Presenting a core strategic tool of public policymaking, governmental institutions commonly create joint campaigns with civil organizations to increase the visibility of health topics and ultimately change individual behaviour (Gordon, McDermmot, Stead, & Angus, 2006; Grier & Bryant, 2005; Truong, 2014). Moreover, through the utilization of such campaigns, governmental agencies can try to shape individual notions of people living with specific health conditions, contributing to reduce the stigmatization and discrimination these groups are confronted with (Merson, O'Malley, Serwadda, & Apisuk, 2008).

Ad Appeals: Fear Appeals Versus Non-Fear Appeals in Health Communication

Ad appeals describe the way in which advertisers or other commercial parties want to trigger attention in recipients, influencing and shaping their interests and behaviours towards a message or particular product in a favourable manner (Belch & Belch, 1993). Ad appeals are part of the promotional message's overall execution, referring to the cues utilized in messages to attract both recipients' interest and attention, further steering their feelings towards the advertised product or inviting them to reflect about message content (Kinnear, Bernhadt, & Krentler, 1995). Promotional appeals are usually transported through both the ad's headline and the visual, with the body copy backing up as well as building upon these two components (Mueller, 1987). Hereby, two main forms can be distinguished: informative appeals that are explicit and based on hard facts, and emotional appeals that rely on visual stimuli to tell appealing stories and create favourable images in individuals' minds (Leonidou & Leonidou, 2009; Okazaki, Mueller, & Diehl, 2013).

In the context of convincing individuals to change their behaviours, emotional appeals have proven to be effective, since it is particularly a message's persuasive nature that determines its failure or effectiveness (Andsager, Bemker, Choi, & Torwel, 2006). Thereby, positive emotional appeals and negative emotional appeals need to be distinguished. Via joy, happiness, humour and entertainment amongst others (Nabi, 2002), *positive emotional appeals* try to draw in recipients and provoke behavioural change. For instance, humour has been excessively used in health campaigns, where messages employing humor are more frequently recalled than other appeals given their arousing nature (Biener, Ji, Gilpin, & Albers, 2004; Lang, Dhillon, & Dong, 1995). In combination with attractive models or stimulating music, these appeals have proven to be successful (Batra & Ray, 1986).

Negative emotional appeals, on the other hand, include disgust, shame as well as fear (Lupton, 2015; Nabi, 2002). One form that has been extensively used in health communication is fear appeals, defined as "persuasive messages designed to scare people by describing the terrible things that will happen to them if they do not do what the message recommends" (Witte, 1992: 329). Thereby, these consequences can be both physically (e.g. degrading health) or socially harmful (e.g. stigmatization; Hale & Dillard, 1995). These appeals are commonly employed as research has found them to lead recipients to change their attitudes—and ultimately behaviours (Eagly & Chaiken, 1993). As fear appeals usually trigger high levels of arousal and motivate action (LaTour & Zahra, 1989), they also have been commonly used as part of HIV/AIDS communication campaigns (Terblanche-Smit & Terblanche, 2010).

Emotional appeals are renowned to utilize *metaphors* and *frames*, with the health sector not presenting an exception to this rule (Gibbs & Franks, 2002; Sopory, 2005). In general, metaphors describe one concept through another, slightly dissimilar concept (Gibbs, 2008; Kövecses, 2010; Palmer-Wackerly & Krieger, 2015), forming schemas and mental models for how individuals perceive and deal with often complex health issues (Palmer-Wackerly & Krieger, 2015; Sopory, 2005). They are commonly used in patient-provider communication, but also for promotional purposes, as in HIV/AIDS or anti-drug campaigns (Reinarman & Levine, 1995). There, they usually take the form of *visual metaphors* (Lazard, Bamgbade, Sontag, & Brown, 2016), which also encourage recipients to engage in more elaborate thought processes (Gkiouzepas & Hogg, 2011; Phillips & McQuarrie, 2009; Toncar & Munch, 2001). As part of health education messages, metaphors can aid in grabbing individuals' attention and have been found to enhance message recall—and with it, also message effectiveness (Houts, Doak, Doak, & Loscalzo, 2006; Landau, Arndt, & Cameron, 2018; Sopory & Dillard, 2002).

Health communication campaigns are also renowned to present their messages in accordance with existing frames, whereby frames refer to "organizing principles that are socially shared and persistent over time, that work symbolically to meaningfully structure the social world" (Reese, 2001: 11). The present study intends to find out, which character frames (i.e. "affective" frames that are able to evoke emotions and reactions in recipients; Grabe & Bucy, 2009) dominate in health organization's public communication about HIV/AIDS. Generally, four character frames can be distinguished (according to Dan & Coleman, 2014), which have proven to be easily identifiable:

– The victim frame portrays the person affected by a certain disease as suffering and in pain (Lupton, 1999), at times also seeking isolation versus social integration (Cook & Colby, 1992).
– As part of the survivor frame, individuals are characterized as being strong and self-determined (Crossley, 1997), often painting them as heroes or role models (Mezirow, 2000). From these frames, any signs of disease are absent (Campbell, 2008).

- In the carrier frame, individuals are portrayed as having been inflicted with a disease, which now renders them a threat to society (Lupton, 1999). Consequently, their portrayal is full of negative associations (Pratt, Ha, & Pratt, 2002)
- In case of the normal frame, people are presented as ordinary (Grover, 1992), leading an ordinary life surrounded by their loved ones (Scalvini, 2010). They are also commonly shown as being in close (physical) contact with others (Grover, 1992).

Our study will expand the research on these four frames to the German-speaking area. Regardless of the appeal chosen, messages are communicated through both visual and textual elements, which should act in concert in order to engage and "draw in" recipients (Rossiter & Bellman, 2005). Only if individuals rate messages as both appealing and of relevance, corresponding with their demands and eliciting favourable feelings, the ad's inherent intention is fruitful. Illustrations are frequently included to quickly familiarize the target audience with the message's theme and purpose (Leonidou & Leonidou, 2009; Okazaki, Mueller, & Taylor, 2010)—a function that cannot be taken up by written text blocks, which are, nonetheless, regarded as being more formal and credible (Piller, 2001).

In the health context, advertising executives have been advised to only use fear-evoking devices selectively (Piller, 2001), keep their ads' textual components rather short by focusing on the most relevant information, stressing how this information can benefit recipients (Piller, 2001). Textual and visual elements should be geared to each other (Batra, Myers, & Aaker, 1996), while textual elements alone have to be indicative of a common thread as well (headline, slogan and body text; Piller, 2001).

To sum up, it can be claimed that research on the use of fear appeals is contradictory, as suggested by a 2015 meta-analysis: "Overall, we conclude that (a) fear appeals are effective at positively influencing attitude, intentions, and behaviors; (b) there are very few circumstances under which they are not effective; and (c) there are no identified circumstances under which they backfire and lead to undesirable outcomes" (Tannenbaum, 2015: 1178). Therefore, advertisers have started to look into alternatives, often choosing positive emotions over their negative counterparts (Kok, Bartholomew, Parcel, Gottlieb, & Fernandez, 2014). To which extent this trend has been taken up when promoting HIV/AIDS awareness (both textually and visually) in the German-speaking area will be illustrated further.

Integrating Health Theory and/or Targeting an Audience Segment?

Health messages are usually designed keeping theory or audience specifics in mind (Cho, 2012). In order to achieve lasting and positive effects, health communication needs to be carefully crafted. According to Yzer (2012), successful messages can either be based on established health communication theories (following a theory-based message design) or take audience specific into account instead (in line with an audience-based message design).

In terms of *theory-based message design*, the most commonly consulted theories concern the Health-Belief-Model (Rosenstock, 1974), Protection Motivation Theory (Rogers, 1975, 1983), the Theory-of-Planned Behaviour (Ajzen, 1991), the Theory-of-Reasoned Action (Fishbein & Ajzen, 1975), as well as the Extended Parallel Process Model (Witte, 1998). Integrating selected health-theory elements into messages is highly recommended since studies have proven that if health messages are based on theory, they can actually influence recipients to change their behaviours (Yzer, 2012). Several researchers (e.g. Fishbein, 2008) have come to suggest that only a small number of variables need to be considered when predicting, changing or reinforcing a particular behaviour; these variables, however, need to mirror an audience's innate needs. Amongst them, the most prominent ones in the message design context for HIV/AIDS awareness and prevention are perceived susceptibility, perceived severity, perceived benefits, perceived barriers, self-efficacy, behavioural control and cues to action.

- *Perceived susceptibility*—a core element of the Health-Belief-Model, which is known as vulnerability in Protection Motivation Theory (PMT; Rogers, 1983)—refers to the likelihood of an individual being affected by a specific health condition at one point in time (Becker & Rosenstock, 1978). It benefits from personalized (targeted) information as well as detailed descriptions of the risks and risk levels respectively.
- *Perceived severity*—a HBM and PMT component—describes an individual's estimations of both the condition's seriousness and its consequences (Rogers, 1975; Rosenstock, 1974) and is most effective when detailed information on both the risks and consequences are provided.
- Known as response efficacy in PMT (Rogers, 1975), *perceived benefits*—as integrated in the HBM—allude to what an individual is predicted to gain when executing a defined action or taking up a proposed behaviour (Becker, 1974). Therefore, messages highlighting perceived benefits should define the action and describe the positive outcomes that can be achieved when following the recommendations.
- *Perceived barriers*—the opposite end of perceived benefits in the HBM—identify the obstacles an individual might come across, that might prevent them from taking up a suggested action or behaviour (Rosenstock, 1974). In order to reduce barriers, messages should contain incentives to engage in an action or provide assistance on how barriers can be overcome.
- *Self-efficacy*—the most relevant component of the HBM and PMT—highlights the necessity to appeal to individuals' abilities and skills, as their confidence in their ability to undertake a recommended behaviour allows them to play an active role in managing their health (Becker & Rosenstock, 1978; Rogers, 1983). Only if individuals feel that they are in the position to bring about change—on grounds of their own skills and

competences—they will form intentions to adopt a specific behaviour. Training and guiding messages are most effective in this context, and a step-by-step approach is recommended to ensure success (Glanz, Rimer, & Lewis, 2002).
- *Behavioural control*—part of the Theory-of-Reasoned Action (TRA; Ajzen, 1991) and similar to coping appraisal in PMT—refers to people's perceptions of their ability to perform a given behaviour, and their perceptions of whether they are able to master the particularities of their health.
- *Cues to action*—as featured in the HBM—can take multiple forms, all of which are intended to engage individuals and activate their awareness for a specific topic (Becker, 1974). Ideally, through providing information or continuous reminders, individuals feel inclined to take up a specific (health) behaviour.

In our analysis, we will investigate whether these theory-based constructs are taken into consideration in current HIV/AIDS health campaigns. In the case of *audience-based message design*, which aims at reducing health disparities and improving health outcomes amongst a defined target audience by gaining a deep level of understanding together with an inclination to act upon the suggestions provided in the message (Davis & Resnicow, 2012), two concepts are commonly discussed: message targeting and message tailoring. While both are based on audience segmentation (Hawkins et al., 2008), *message targeting* is defined as the use of group-level data to customize health messages for a specific audience (target) group or segment that is relatively homogenous with regard to determinants affecting a specific health outcome (Davis & Resnicow, 2012). *Message tailoring*, on the other hand, follows the same rationale as targeting but consists of a higher degree of customization and audience segmentation, whereby each audience member (or group) receives a unique combination of health messages based on individual- or group-level data (Davis & Resnicow, 2012). Research suggests that tailoring is more effective than targeting (Noar, Benac, & Harris, 2007), as individuals are presumed to behave in certain ways to remain consistent with their in-group norms as well as social roles (Harwood & Giles, 2005). Generally, targeting's effectiveness is subject to each audience members' attentiveness to health messages, their cognitive and emotional processing of these messages and self-referential thinking (Hawkins et al., 2008). If messages are targeted to a particular group or population segment, they have been found to better resonate with these audiences (Casais, Proenca, & Barros, 2019). Thus, we will also include the aspect of message targeting and/or message tailoring in our analysis.

Case Study Analysis of HIV/AIDS Campaigns in the German-Speaking Area

Research has confirmed that the earlier HIV/AIDS is diagnosed and treated, the more effective are therapeutic interventions, leading to a higher life expectancy in the people living with this virus (Rockstroh & Wasmuth, 2017). In order to reduce the number of annual infections, awareness for the necessity to use condoms as well as calls upon message recipients to familiarize themselves with their HIV status take priority to reduce the stigmatization of the people living with HIV/AIDS. In the following, selected campaigns from Germany, Austria and Switzerland are investigated in more detail with regard to how these national campaigns deal with the topic of HIV/AIDS. This is essential, given that raising awareness for health topics requires marketers and government officals to take national characteristics into account (Mulholland, 2019).

For each country, two campaigns which received extensive media coverage were chosen for analysis. Analysis followed a pre-developed scheme of analysis (see Fig. 20.1). Moreover, it was important that the messages originated from official public (health) organizations that have a profound interest in health. In order to get access as well as background on the individual campaigns, organizational websites were consulted.

Austria

The Campaign "Know your status"

For decades, Austria's main affiliation with HIV/AIDS has been established through its annual hosting of the LIFE Ball. It is nitiated by LIFE+ and was first

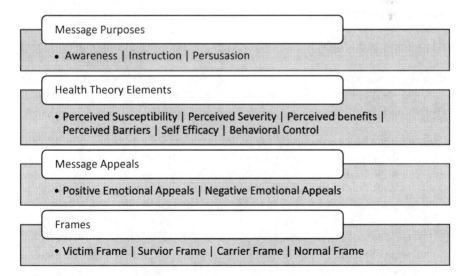

Fig. 20.1 Scheme of analysis (the authors)

hosted in 1992. Claimed to be the largest charity event in Europe, the LIFE Ball expresses support for people affected with HIV and AIDS (Life, 2019a). Moreover, it wants to reduce the exclusion of people living with HIV/AIDS.

Campaign Theme and Execution
The 2018 LIFE Ball Campaign employed the slogan "Know Your Status", which was already utilized the previous year. The campaign's goal is to provide the general public with valuable information so that people are willing to get themselves tested and are aware of whether they carry the virus or not. In order to guarantee public engagement, LIFE+ partnered up with the Austrian AIDS Association to offer immediate access to mobile testing stations (Life, 2019a).

In calling upon individuals to "Know Your Status", the 2018 campaign was in line with the United Nations' Sustainable Development Goals #3 to reduce the infection rates of HIV/AIDS. It was further reflective of the UN's 90-90-90 target, which consists of three stages. It stipulated that 90% of the world population should know their status by 2020 (the campaign goal of 2017 and 2018), and 90% of the people living with AIDS should seek treatment in form of antiretroviral therapy by 2020 (Life, 2019b). The third component refers to the goal that 90% of all people in treatment should live with a fully suppressed viral load.

Besides local and national collaborations, the campaign employed a far-reaching cross-media awareness campaign featuring four internationally renowned celebrities, who were captured by internationally acclaimed photographer Rankin: Philipp Hochmair, Paris Jackson, Eva Herzigová and Aiden Brady. Each celebrity wrote their own campaign message, which was then painted on their bodies. These messages—in line with the "I know my story"-claim in the ad—are reflective of their very own experiences and were accompanied by encouraging hashtags (#behonest, #knowyourstatus_lifeball). The portrayal is reduced to a minimum, but visually appealing due to its body-painting elements (see Fig. 20.2). Besides black and white portrayals, the Life logo in pink is the only pop of colour (Life, 2019b). The campaign text itself is minimalistic and reads as follows: "Everyone has a story. Therefore, everyone has a right to know their HIV-status. Get tested today!". In the videos, each celebrity discloses some personal insights and closes with "I know my status. Do you?".

Campaign Evaluation
The overall purpose, as highlighted on the campaign website as well as across different media channels, is to create *awareness* for the necessity of getting tested. In order to spread *awareness* amongst the public, the message uses the *persuasive* element of conviction (in form of appellation), calling upon individuals to get tested and become "empowered"—as "knowledge (of one's HIV status) equals power". At the same time, the campaign slogan "I know my story. I know my status. Do you know yours?" includes a clear *persuasive* call to action, inviting message recipients to not only tell their stories—as suggested by the testimonials—but also become active themselves and get tested. As

20 SDG #3: COMMUNICATING "HEALTH FOR ALL" IN GERMAN-SPEAKING... 461

Fig. 20.2 Posters from the KNOW YOUR STATUS campaign (Life, 2019b)

such, involvement is created, which is especially enabled through the utilization of the two hashtags #knowyourstatus_lifeball and #behonest.

In terms of message appeal, a *positive emotional* image is utilized. HIV or AIDS is not associated with a social stigma, but the campaign rather wants to weaken the existing negative representation of HIV/AIDS in society (Arendt, Hauck, Mayr, & Negwer, 2019). Even though people who are affected or infected are seen as having power—they are in the position of power because they were tested and now know their HIV/AIDS status. Hence, this knowledge is presented in a positive light, for it empowers individuals, enabling them to seek treatment if necessary. As three ambassadors who do not suffer from HIV/AIDS tell their stories, a normal frame is utilized; in the case of Aiden Brady, a former pornographic actor who is HIV-positive, a carrier frame is employed. Their bodies, upon which each, individualized story is painted, serve as a metaphor for the stories they call their lives, for the roles they see themselves playing. Each message closes with an appellation to get tested, and instead of giving in to the pressures and struggles associated with living with the virus, a positive picture is painted, showing that in spite of being infected, the virus can be controlled, making life definitely worth living.

As it is concerned with creating broad engagement, the campaign itself addresses *the general public*. A moderate form of targeting can be observed, as the campaign material—including posters and campaign videos—are available in multiple languages in order to appeal to a worldwide audience. Moreover, the campaign itself features both international and national (Austrian) celebrities. Content is also adapted to the requirements of the different platforms, which facilitates an easy spreading of the overall message across a variety of media channels.

As to the incorporation of health-message elements, the campaign utilized numerous health-related concepts, such as *perceived susceptibility*—claiming that it is advantageous for everyone to know their HIV status. Besides highlighting the benefits of "knowing" (i.e. being aware of one's HIV/AIDS status; *perceived benefits*), emphasizing the power of the truth and being transparent, the promotion also does not fail to appeal to individuals' *self-efficacy*, calling upon message recipients to become active and get tested. As such, it allocates *behavioural control* with each and every person. Moreover, *cues to action* are two-fold: in addition to being in the know by getting tested, the campaign also encourages monetary donations.

The Campaign "I am HIV-positive. I'm not contagious"

First March has become known as Zero-Discrimination Day, upon which the United Nations invites countries to review their legal regulations for any inconsistency with human rights (UN AIDS, 2019). To celebrate this day, the Austrian Aids Association launched its new cross-media campaign titled "I am HIV-positive. I'm not contagious" in 2019 (Austrian Aids Association, 2019).

Campaign Theme and Execution

As part of its "I am HIV-positive. I'm not contagious" campaign, the Austrian Aids Association composed multiple campaign posters that feature both heterosexual and homosexual couples of different ages together in bed; one poster even depicts a mother with her newborn child. The couples are shown as being close, snuggling or cuddling up—they are having a good time together, enjoying each other's company (see Fig. 20.3). Each appealing visual is accompanied by a short body copy, which reads as follows (messages vary slightly between posters): "An effective therapeutic treatment can inhibit HIV in the body (below detection level). This means that people carrying the HIV-virus cannot pass it on but can continue to enjoy life up until old age" (Austrian Aids Association, 2019). The message closes with the campaign's key message "Fight prejudice with knowledge!" and refers to a hashtag to be employed when spreading the message (#UequalsU–Undetactable = Untransmittable). A similar stance is taken by the campaign video.[1]

Fig. 20.3 Posters from the ICH BIN HIV-POSITIV campaign (Aids.at, 2019)

---

[1] Video text in German: Wir leben … und sind keine Gefahr. Wir können Sex haben … Kinder bekommen und sehen, wie sie aufwachsen. Auch wir können alt werden. All das können wir. Es ist erwiesen, dass HIV-positive Menschen unter Therapie, deren Viruslast unter der Nachweisgrenze ist, HIV nicht übertragen können. Entfache auch du dein Feuer … und bekämpfe Vorurteile mit Wissen (Video available at https://youtu.be/gcis8Q7SJ-k).

Campaign Evaluation

This recently released campaign is—first and foremost—concerned with raising *awareness* for the fact that people affected by HIV/AIDS do not pose a "threat to society" and that their condition does not present any harm if treated with the proper medication. As such, the message also integrates *persuasive* elements—emotional visuals with reduced rational arguments—which intends to end the common stigmatization that is typical for people carrying the virus. Through providing the public with knowledge that the virus can be incubated, the campaign attempts to fight and reduce existing prejudices through education. In presenting people in intimate situations, and by combining a strong visual with only short textual blocks, the campaign utilizes a *positive emotional appeal*, which proclaims that individuals living with HIV/AIDS can still live a normal life and enjoy the intimacy of their loved ones, as the virus they carry is no "threat" if treated properly. As such, it utilizes a positive carrier frame, in which an individual is shown as being close to others, reducing social stigma as to the contagious nature of HIV/AIDS. In case of the elderly couple, even a survivor frame could apply, thus it is a combination of carrier/survivor frame.

The campaign targets a broad and rather *general target audience*, as the message itself is meant to educate the public about the non-contagious nature of HIV/AIDS. Yet, the visuals and textual elements appeal to people in different life situations, suggesting a slightly targeted approach. For instance, visuals depict hetero- and homosexual couples, a mother with her newborn child as well as an elderly couple and are accompanied by corresponding textual elements which indicate that HIV/AIDS cannot be passed on to the child or can enable people to live a long and happy life.

The campaign also references a selective set of health-theory elements, aiming to reduce the threat ascribed to contracting the HIV/AIDS (*perceived severity*) and highlighting the perceived benefits of receiving effective treatment through which the virus can be incubated (*perceived benefits*). As the campaign is of educational nature and wants to get rid of public stigma, *cues to action* predominantly set out to fight existing prejudices by providing the public with relevant and enabling information.

In terms of category, this awareness-raising campaign would qualify as "novel"—as something unusual, something that has not been used before in this context, which is meant to reduce the stigma of people carrying the HIV virus. The use of novel ad appeal elements has been found to trigger positive reactions, leading to greater eye fixation as well as higher attention rates (Pieters, Warlop, & Wedel, 2002; Smith, MacKenzie, Yang, Buchholz, & Darley, 2007); thus, positive effects might occur.

Germany

The Campaign "Auch für junges Gemüse" (engl. "Also for Baby Vegetables")
German Anti-AIDS campaigns have significantly varied in their approaches over time (for an overview, see PKV.de, 2019 or Tümmers, 2013), but one far-reaching media campaign has been employed since 2005, due to a cooperation with the health ministry. Usually short-lived in their theme and execution, visual-driven campaigns want to generate awareness for HIV and AIDS, calling upon recipients to take preventive measures to keep the virus from spreading (PKV.de, 2019). Utilizing the slogan "Mach's mit!" (figuratively and colloquial; referring to the use of a condom), it postulates to use preservatives in order to "Gib Aids keine Chance!" (engl. Don't give AIDS a chance!).

Campaign Theme and Execution
In 2006, the campaign titled "Auch für junges Gemüse" (engl. Also for baby vegetables) was launched and depicted fruit and vegetables wearing condoms. It was developed in cooperation with Darmstadt University and a nationwide creative contest. Each of the six visuals is accompanied by a word-pun matching the vegetable (e.g. in the case of corn, the tagline read "Pop safely") in order to increase the promotional effect (BZGA.de, 2016). The puns referr to either the fruit or vegetable respectively, or the safety gained from using a condom. The choice of visual is meant to create awareness for the increasing number of infections in an appealing and unusual "eye-catcher" manner. The cheeky taglines are chosen to especially appeal to a younger audience (Aerztezeitung, 2006). Vegetables and fruit were deemed suitable as they usually trigger positive associations and are seen as something normal—a meaning that was meant to be transferred to the use of condoms since they were attached to the objects in a natural manner (Kinderkurier, 2006; see Fig. 20.4). Moreover, short body copies appeal to individuals not to give up the fun part of sex, but to be responsible about it, in line with "Don't give AIDS a chance" (Tümmers, 2013).

Campaign Evaluation
This successful cross-media campaign with varying yet content wise mostly identical visual images, first and foremost, sets out to raise *awareness* for the necessity of wearing condoms in order to not contract HIV/AIDS. Through the use of strong visuals (fruit and vegetables wearing condoms) in combination with reduced textual elements (i.e. witty (German) puns or taglines) suggest a reliance on a "novel", metaphoric approach, which was found to have a powerful impact on the German audience by providing them with the instruction to "use condoms" (German: "Mach's mit").

In terms of message appeal, powerful visuals are metaphorically used, while text elements are reduced to a minimum. The visuals do not depict the threat but rather—through visual transfer—take a positive and playful stance towards sexual intercourse. The vivid campaign images are appealing and colourful as

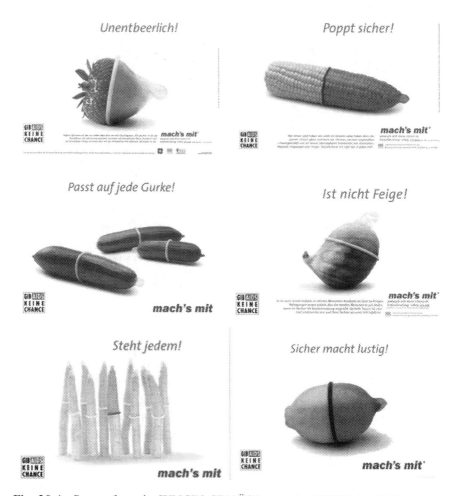

Fig. 20.4 Posters from the JUNGES GEMÜSE campaign (BZGA.de, 2016)

such and are combined with witty statements in order to achieve a maximum effect. As such, a very *positive, emotional appeal* is utilized, which attributes fun, humour and joy to the act of sex—if practised responsibly.

Following the previous examples, also this campaign targets the *general public* instead of selected audience segments. Campaign material is available solely in German. Yet, it can be presumed that the broad range of vegetables and fruit used are most likely meant to resemble the diversity of the (German) target audience.

Albeit the message is kept rather basic and benefits from a reduced amount of text, a number of elements as derived from health theories are incorporated. First and foremost, the *perceived benefits* of using a condom are highlighted by various puns, which either stress that condoms are for everyone (i.e. it fits/suits everyone) respectively the safety they provide (i.e. in stating that they are "essential" or make for "safe sex"). As such, the campaign appeals to individuals' *self-efficacy* and *behavioural control*, reminding both partners to think about condoms for engaging in sex presupposes commitment from both parties. The campaign's tag line—once again—serves as reminder to use condoms when engaging in sexual intercourse (*cue to action*).

The Campaign "Liebesorte" (engl. "Places of Love Making")
Utilizing the same slogan as its predecessor, the 2009 campaign takes a more romantic approach towards sex by showing places of love making—hence the title "Liebesorte" (BZGA.de, 2016). Just like the previous campaign, it was based on a creative contest. The visuals featured range from plain hotel rooms and messy camp sites, over brothel rooms to idyllic and appealing natural sceneries (Sonnenberg-Schwan, 2009)—or, in other words: places, in which people have sex. As such, the campaign tries to convince the target audience to use condoms by rendering it a part of their everyday lives (BZGA.de, 2016).

Campaign Theme and Execution
Instead of featuring real people, only a physical place is depicted, inviting individuals to fill these places with their own memories and experiences (Sonnenberg-Schwan, 2009). Each visual is accompanied by two boxes, that let individuals choose something positive (e.g. enjoying the summer, dreaming in the summer night and getting to know each other) or something negative: "risking AIDS" (see Fig. 20.5). Depending on the image, each short body copy provides some insights into AIDS and the usability of condoms. This is in line with the overall campaign claim: "Sex is great, but AIDS cannot be healed. So, use a condom, do not give AIDS a chance" (Behr, 2009). The "correct" answer is highlighted with a condom instead of a classical tick.

Campaign Evaluation
Set up in a quiz-like format, which invites individuals to make their pick, for the message paints a clear picture of individuals being in power. The campaign aims at creating *awareness* that it is up to individuals whether they contract the disease or not (by wearing condoms). The visuals themselves are clearly *persuasive* in nature, proclaiming that when using a condom, these intimate places will always be associated with fond memories, allowing individuals to enjoy the situation and the feeling it evokes to its fullest.

As suggested by both the visuals and the accompanying text elements, conviction is meant to be achieved through a reliance on powerful visuals (*positive emotional appeal*); text elements, albeit available, are reduced (also in font size), only providing more details upon taking a closer look. The information contained is rather seen as a "back-up" and predominantly concerns statistical data on Germans' uses of condoms, further reassuring message recipients that

Fig. 20.5 Posters from the LIEBESORTE campaign (BZGA.de, 2016)

when condoms are used, HIV and other sexually transmitted diseases can be prevented.

While the message design is not audience-based but rather *general*, the visual campaign strategy appears to be geared towards different target audience segments. The diversity of places featured as part of the campaign seems to be reflective of the diversity of people's life situations and preferences in terms of "romantic places", suggesting a tailoring to some degree. At the same time, these places are presumed to be metaphorically used, resembling memories of individuals' sexual adventures.

In terms of the incorporation of health-message elements, the romantic places featured are not only meant to create memories of (past and present) sexual encounters in similar settings but also trigger identification amongst the target audience, who might have been careless at one point in their time (*perceived susceptibility*). In making "risk AIDS" an answering option, the *perceived severity* of not using a condom is emphasized. The other potential answer—for example, risking feelings, rock'n'roll, loving freely and enjoying summer—then suggests that if condoms are used as protection (through individuals' pro-active and *self-efficient* behaviours), individuals can enjoy their time together to the fullest. As such, choice is allocated to every individual (*behavioural control*). Also, *cues to action* take two forms: on the one hand, they concern a helpline, which can be consulted in case of questions; on the other hand, the ad closes with an appellation to use condoms ("mach's mit!").

Switzerland

The Campaign "Love life, do not regret anything"
In Switzerland, the number of people using condoms still leaves a lot to be desired. For this reason, the most recent campaign (2018/2019) decided to not only encourage people to use a condom, but also combined it with a raffle to obtain higher numbers of engagement. So besides purchasing only a condom, individuals are also given a ticket that can be redeemed online to participate in a sweepstake contest (Love Life.ch, 2019a).

Campaign Theme and Execution
"Love life, do not regret anything"—with this motto, the Swiss AIDS Association starts its manifest on which the present campaign is based (Love Life.ch, 2019b). In detail, the campaign is all about love—love for one's life, one's body. And because of this love, protecting one's health is seen as a priority. On the one hand, the campaign features both homosexual and heterosexual couples who are embracing their time together. On the other hand, it also features a number of short videos, which come with an ambiguous message: people are either at a low point in their life or are not content with what they have; at this moment, they meet someone who has or offers them what they want, which is either love or then linked to the sweepstake initiated by Lifelife.ch (see Fig. 20.6). The third video calls upon individuals to make the safer-sex-check online (Love Life.ch, 2019a). In addition, the campaign includes some banners, which take a slightly different approach. It presumes people not to feel well after having unprotected sexual intercourse, thus encouraging them to go and see a doctor in case they experience flu-like symptoms. The banners themselves are witty and often include puns featuring sex-related terms; clearly, they appeal to individuals' self-efficacy in order to "not regret anything" at a later point (Love Life.ch, 2019c).

Campaign Evaluation
In Switzerland, the campaign sets out to increase condom use and highlights the necessity to do so to not contract the HIV/AIDS virus (*awareness message*). Yet, it seems to pursue two distinct targets afterwards, depending on

Fig. 20.6 Posters from the LOVE LIFE campaign (Love Life, 2019a; Love Life, 2019d)

which campaign message (visually and textually based) is utilized. On the one hand, through a strong visual, the campaign signalizes that if safe sex is practised, people will not be left to regret anything afterwards (*persuasion message*). On the other hand, the message clearly instructs individuals experiencing a set of flu-like symptoms (e.g. sweat, fever and confinement in bed) to immediately consult a doctor in order to seek treatment (*instruction message*).

Likewise, the messages use two distinct *emotional appeals* in order to transport their intended messages. While the visual message utilizes a *positive emotional appeal*, highlighting the fun and pleasure of engaging in sexual intercourse when using protection, a *weak threat* yet *negative emotional appeal* drives the argument of the textual promotion, in which the risks of unprotected sex are thematized. The innate threat is weakened in that consulting a doctor is presented as a solution.

With regard to target audience, the message is directed at the *general public* and does not contain any (textual) elements addressing a particular target segment. When looking at the visual, however, different (target) groups are put at the centre, since both hetero- and homosexual couples are featured. The persons depicted are shown in intimate situations, suggesting the use of a normal frame as there is no indication that they are victims, carriers or survivors. As such, the campaign is targeted to a certain extent, catering to people in different life situations and relationship constellations.

On grounds of its double nature (different messages in the text vs. the picture), the campaign incorporates a number of elements as derived from health theories. For instance, in the negative emotional appeal, *perceived susceptibility* refers to the flu-like symptoms that can occur after engaging in unprotected sex, further underlining the *perceived severity* of these symptoms, for which doctors need to be consulted. In both the negative and positive emotional appeals, the *perceived benefits* of using a condom are emphasized ("do not regret anything"), while the benefits of seeing a doctor are stressed in the negative emotional appeal. These two aspects also are reflective on individuals' *self-efficacy* and *behavioural control*. Finally, calls to play the lottery or go online for further information are integrated into the message as *cues to action*.

The Campaign "Proud to Protect You"

First initiated in 2017 as part of a "Proud to Protect You" campaign and continued in 2018, the Swiss AIDS Association dedicated a considerable amount of attention towards reaching out to the gay community (AIDS.ch, 2018a; Persoenlich, 2018). With this targeted approach and in thematizing the needs of a particular group of recipients, the organization wanted to raise awareness for diseases that specifically affect men having sex with men, calling upon them to not only have themselves tested for sexually transmitted diseases but also to prevent them from being infected with tripper, syphilis or chlamydia (Dr. Gay, 2019).

Campaign Theme and Execution

While the campaign theme is two-fold, with two posters featuring empowering messages (Gain insights! Master the Risk!), the second set of posters put forward more protection-oriented messages (Undetectable[2]! I'm on PrEP[3]!). The first set of messages titled STARMAN, a super hero who can detect sexually transmitted diseases through his specific pair of glasses (Albani, 2018), and SECURION, a gladiator-like figure fighting HIV infections, clearly contain a call to action, appealing to individuals' self-efficacy to get themselves tested for HIV. At the same time, awareness for means to make for safe sex between two men is meant to be created, sensitizing the general public to the risks and

---

[2] HIV-positive but not contagious!
[3] A contraceptive medication (pre-exposure prophylaxis) that—if taken correctly—is as effective as using a condom.

consequences associated with unsafe sex (AIDS.ch, 2018b; Dr. Gay, 2019). The second set of posters emphasizes prevention measures. While the #undetectable claim wants to end the stigmatizing of people infected, who do not bear a risk when taking appropriate treatment (AIDS.ch, 2018c; Dr. Gay, 2018), the latter features not a hero-type figure but an "everybody" informing the public about a new treatment: "I'm on PrEP"—meaning, I come prepared (Albani, 2018).

Campaign Evaluation

Building up its pallet of superheroes successively over the years, this colourful campaign with varying yet mostly identical visual content, first and foremost, sets out to raise *awareness* for different forms of protection. Moreover, through the use of appellations, messages are also meant to both achieve *persuasion* (i.e. know your protection choices, manage the risk) and serve as *instruction* messages (i.e. get tested or retrieve more information online). Allocating power with the individuals (i.e. men) is also implemented visually, suggesting that those being in the know are superheroes.

In terms of message appeal, powerful visuals are metaphorically used, while text elements are reduced to a minimum. The visuals depict strong men, whose names resemble those of superheroes—Starman, Securion, Mr Undetectable and PrEPster. By use of a *positive emotional appeal*, the campaign intends to reduce the stigma associated with people living with HIV/AIDS; instead, the inclusion of superheroes suggests that taking preventive measures and actively addressing the need for prevention amongst sexual partners is key since knowing equals power. As such, each hero stresses unique qualities: Starman (knowing about sexually transmitted diseases; normal frame), Securion (being informed about means of protection; normal frame), Mr Undetectable (reducing the stigma associated with living with HIV/AIDS; carrier frame) and PrEPster (promoting a new therapeutic form to prevent the transmission of HIV; normal and/or carrier frame).

Contrary to the previous examples, which predominantly were targeting the general public, this campaign is *tailored* and solely aiming at homosexual men. Initiated by Dr. Gay, a community for men engaging in sexual intercourse with other men, it explicitly addresses the gay community, promoting issues and solutions that are particular to men.

Across the four different posters, a number of elements as included in health theories are addressed. *Perceived susceptibility* underscores that being infected with HIV/AIDS can happen to men having sex with other men, while the *perceived benefits* stressed by the individual posters are diverse: knowing brings power, so men should get tested; the HIV virus cannot be transmitted with correct treatment; or PrEP is a viable alternative to using condoms. In addition, references to perceived *self-efficacy* (i.e. acquiring knowledge on prevention option is crucial) and individual's *behavioural control* (i.e. get tested; take precautionary measures) can be found. All promotions close with a *cue to action* (i.e. a call to get further information online), whilst two promotions contain additional calls to get tested.

COMPARISON AND EVALUATION

Table 20.1 presents a summary of our findings.

The present study set out to investigate health communication campaigns for HIV/AIDS in the three German-speaking countries of Austria, Germany and Switzerland. With regard to message purpose, awareness and persuasive message elements could be detected in all campaigns. Overall, material is either conceptualized to educate the public as well as create *awareness* (e.g. for the necessity to know their HIV status or regarding the non-communicable nature of HIV/AIDS when medicated properly). Besides using rational arguments, *persuasive* elements are integrated to underline the overall message, whereby strong visuals (e.g. romantic places or intimate situations) invite the public to draw parallels to their own lives. *Instruction* messages are integrated in four out of six campaigns and contain appellations directed to individuals with the goal of getting them to engage in a certain action (e.g. getting tested for HIV) or behaviour (e.g. wearing condoms). As such, the campaigns follow previously established communications patterns for HIV campaigns, which are concerned with reducing HIV transmission through condom use, promoting the non-discrimination of people living with HIV or informing about the availability of testing options (Casais et al., 2019). A "positive sexuality" is put forward (Green & Witte, 2006: 248), which builds on more positive portrayals (Terblanche-Smit & Terblanche, 2010).

Trying to overcome the stigmatization associated with HIV/AIDS, campaigns predominantly utilize *positive emotional appeals*. In five out of six cases, individuals are portrayed as being powerful and in control of their lives, enjoying the company of their loved ones. If people are absent, strong (metaphoric) visuals are employed which are meant to trigger pleasant images in recipients (e.g. romantic places) or tackle the issue of HIV in a humorous fashion. In Switzerland, one campaign addresses the risks of engaging in unprotected sex (e.g. flu-like symptoms) and, thus, serves as an example of a *negative emotional appeal*.

Table 20.1 Summary of the content analysis

Which message appeals or design elements are used to attract attention? Is the reasoning rather rational or emotional?	Predominantly emotional appeals
Which HIV frame dominates?	No clear tendency
Are metaphors employed?	Only in Germany
To which extent are elements of selected health theories (Health-Belief-Model, Theory-of-Reasoned-Action and Theory-of-Planned Behaviour) integrated into these messages?	Between 4 and 5 elements incorporated
Do messages differ across countries?	Yes

In line with the utilization of emotional appeals, which heavily rely on images, both visual frames and metaphors are utilized. Overall, it was observed that if frames are absent, metaphors find use instead. Metaphors are meant to convey complex information through transferring meaning to alternate concepts, leaving a powerful impact on recipients, since they stimulate comprehension. Three campaigns in total (one per country) employ metaphors to reduce the complexity of the health issue and illustrate their arguments in a simplified manner. Frames, on the other hand, occur predominantly in two forms: normal frames (three out of six), in which people are represented in intimate (romantic) scenarios or enjoying and being in power over their lives; and *carrier frames* (three out of six), whereby individuals are shown as neither unhealthy nor suffering, but as being content since they have managed to get a hold of their disease by taking preventive measures. As such, the ads managed to "incubate" the threat that HIV/AIDS poses to the public.

As the topic is of relevance to the general public rather than selected sub-/target-groups, most campaigns (five out of six) are directed towards the *general public* to generate broader awareness and reduce stigmatization on a societal level. If, however, selected issues are addressed and solely concern a sub-group (as it is the case with different means of prevention that are only of interest to men engaging in sex with other men), communication is targeted to fit the needs and requirements of this particular target population. It is only through communication, that interaction and dialogic exchanges can be initiated, and people's perceptions of specific health conditions like HIV/AIDS can be challenged as well as changed sustainably (WHO, 2018). On a national level, policymakers occupy a central role in creating awareness and reducing the stigmatization of affected populations (Rattle, 2010), having the potential to improve the collaboration between stakeholders to mitigate potential global health risks (Servaes & Malikhao, 2016). Besides mass media communication campaigns, other forms of communication (e.g. interpersonal and participatory communication) must not be neglected (Servaes & Malikhao, 2016).

Health campaigns have also been found to benefit from the inclusion of theoretical elements, and HIV/AIDS campaigns in the German-speaking area were found to follow suit. On average, campaigns incorporated four to five theoretical components, the most frequently used elements being *behavioural control* (i.e. appealing to individuals own competencies and assuring them of their abilities to perform a health-enhancing behaviour) and *cues to action* (i.e. providing them with further information or reminders to encourage them to behave or act in a certain manner). Both behavioural control and cues to action are used in all campaigns, while *perceived benefits* (i.e. the advantages of taking up a particular behaviour) and *self-efficacy* (i.e. individuals' confidence in their ability to undertake a recommended behaviour and become more involved in their health) is used in five out of six campaigns. As such, it becomes obvious that after receiving these messages, individuals should feel inclined to play a more (pro-)active and empowered role in their health (Koinig, 2016; Koinig, Diehl, & Mueller, 2017).

Across countries, some differences could be identified. While Austrian and Swiss campaigns depicted people, and utilized both normal and carrier frames (at times even survivor frames), the messages were also designed in a manner to reduce stigma associated with HIV/AIDS by emphasizing its non-contagious nature. The Austrian campaign even relied on celebrity endorsements, which are met with higher rates of awareness (Casais & Proenca, 2012). The German campaigns, on the other hand, were more educational, appealing to individuals to use condoms in order to prevent individuals from getting inflicted with the virus in the first place. Instead of frames, the German campaigns heavily relied on visuals from which individuals were completely absent, leaving it to individuals to fill the blanks and transfer the messages to their very own life situations.

Overall it could be observed that—depending which of the UN's AIDS 90-90-90 targets are prioritized—campaign conceptualization differed widely. While they were all clearly strategic in nature, that is, pursue a long-term orientation and emphasize health-related goals and actions (Rioplus, 2008), German campaigns, for instance, did not take up any of the three identified targets but rather stressed the necessity to practice safer sex. In the case of Austria, the Life Ball's 2018 campaign emphasized the necessity of knowing one's HIV status (stage 1), while the most recent campaign highlighted the fact that HIV is not contagious if treated properly (stage 3). This goal was also addressed by the Life Ball 2019, which followed suit in choosing "Undetectable = Untransmittable" as its slogan (Life, 2019c). As part of Swiss messages, the Love Life campaign calls upon people to not only use condoms, but also get tested in case repercussions surface after having had unprotected sex (stage 1). The diverse Dr. Gay campaigns, however, pursued diverse goals, prompting individuals to get tested (stage 1), seek proper treatment (stage 2) and ensure that the HIV-virus cannot be spread (stage 3).

IMPLICATIONS, LIMITATIONS AND DIRECTIONS FOR FUTURE RESEARCH

The present contribution was able to highlight that while HIV/AIDS campaigns in Austria, Germany and Switzerland show some similarities, such as the use of emotional appeals, there are also some differences on a country basis. Overall, the predominance of emotional appeals confirms the trend that fear appeals no longer prevail, even though they have been shown to trigger stronger behavioural effects than other appeals (Tay, Ozanne, & Santino, 2000). This might be conditioned by the fact that the stigmatization related to HIV/AIDS has decreased in the past years (Arendt et al., 2019). Our results also indicate a reliance on visuals, which are often used in form of metaphors or frames. While the downsides of metaphors as part of health messages have been revealed by previous studies, including recipients' failure to comprehend the message as well as follow instructions (Snowdon, Garcia, & Elbourne, 1997), the plethora of positive effects make metaphors appealing choices in health communication. For example, the positive use of metaphors has led recipients to take up behaviours for the benefits suggested by the message (Rogers, 1983; Witte & Allen, 2000). Thereby, the "fit" of the metaphor with the overall message was found to be an important determinant (Keefer, Landau, Sullivan, & Rothschild, 2014; Landau et al., 2018). Moreover, it is especially visual metaphors that present a promising tool in health communication, since they do not only attract attention but can also stimulate recipients to reflect on the message and beyond (Eppler, 2006; Mohanty & Ratneshwar, 2015), given their "implicit" nature. Despite these positive aspects, it is important to always ensure the comprehensibility of metaphors.

A similar reasoning can be found in support of frames, which are not only easily identifiable by the general public (Dan & Coleman, 2014), but also very common in health communication messages in order to describe and portray people living with a particular health condition, holding the potential to shape public perceptions of and responses towards the disease (Coleman, 2010; Sharf & Vandeford, 2003). In the context of HIV, a shift in framing is characteristic of the past decade, with anti-stigma messages being on the rise (Arendt et al., 2019). While being diagnosed with HIV/AIDS has led to social exclusion in the past, anti-stigma campaigns are commonly used nowadays to generate a more tolerant and open climate for people living with the virus (Brown, Macintryre, & Trujillo, 2003; Mahajan et al., 2008). Consequently, messages have changed in tone, moving away from threat-based message content and carrier or victim frames to more positive portrayals, in which survivor and normal frames prevail. As communication has been part of development communication for over half a century (Malikhao, 2020), it is not surprising that—even though it is not explicitly stated therein—communication is seen as paramount to the United Nations' SDGs. The use of more life-supporting and positive frames might be attributed to efforts on behalf of the United Nations' Sustainable Development Goals, which call for putting an end to the stigmatization associated with HIV/AIDS. This also finds support by the fact that some of the countries have started to address the 90-90-90 targets, with some of them having already moved beyond the first level and now actively advocate the non-contagious nature of HIV. The campaigns are also reflective of this trend, with Austrian and Swiss attempting to reduce the stigmatized view on people living with HIV/AIDS. As part of highly image-driven campaigns, a redefinition of the sick body has occurred (Scalvini, 2010), warranting the application of visual frames. Due to the limited scope of this chapter, a focus was put on message content, however, it would be interesting to analyse which (visual) frames are the most effective ones from the recipients' perspective. Moreover, it is recommended to also go beyond mass media communication effects, as interpersonal communication has been found to be essential to determine the extent to which individuals follow the recommendations presented in health campaign messages (Rogers, 1963). Moreover, it might be fruitful to investigate the role of social media, which might not only reach new and broader audiences, but also increase the visibility of health topics (Koinig & Diehl, 2020).

As outlined earlier, several health-related constructs are considered to be relevant to create effective health communication campaigns. Our content analysis revealed that the most important elements from health communication models, which have been integrated in the HIV/Aids campaigns, are perceived benefits followed by self-efficacy, perceived susceptibility, perceived severity, behavioural control and cues to action. This reflects that advertising practice in the health sector to some extent also integrates theoretical insights (see also Dobrenova, Grabner-Kräuter, Diehl, & Terlutter, 2019), which have to be aligned with national health policies (WHO, 2018). Yet, in order to determine campaign success, campaign results and the stimulated behavioural change need to be monitored in the long run (Wymer, 2011).

There are several limitations to the study at hand. First, only a limited amount of campaigns was scrutinized in detail. Moreover, only message characteristics were studied in detail, blending out individual responses to such messages. Third, the analysis was limited to campaigns in German-speaking countries as well as to a selected set of frames, given the limited scope of the chapter. Hence, further research should be extended to campaigns from other countries, while also looking at national and international campaigns in order to detect potential differences in message design and composition. It might also be interesting to look at messages' activating function in terms of design, composition and frame utilization, while also inquiring individual responses to HIV/AIDS campaigns in order to generate insights into message effectiveness. Responses might also well vary with regard to respondents' demographics, including sex, age and educational level.

References

Aerztezeitung. (2006). Auch für junges Gemüse. Retrieved March 10, 2019, from https://www.aerztezeitung.de/medizin/krankheiten/infektionskrankheiten/aids/article/406047/junges-gemuese.html

Aids.at. (2019). Downloads—Zero Discrimination Day. Retrieved March 7, 2019, from http://www.aids.at/downloads/poster-download-zero-discrimination-day/

AIDS.ch. (2018a). Starman–STI-Testwochen. Retrieved March 13, 2019, from https://www.aids.ch/de/was-wir-tun/kampagnen/starman.php

AIDS.ch. (2018b). SECURION—HIV-Testwochen. Retrieved March 13, 2019, from https://www.aids.ch/de/was-wir-tun/kampagnen/securion.php

AIDS.ch. (2018c). #Undetectable—HIV-positiv, nicht infektiös. Retrieved March 13, 2019, from https://www.aids.ch/de/was-wir-tun/kampagnen/undetectable.php

Ajzen, I. (1991). The Theory of Planned Behavior. *Organizational Behavior and Human Decision Processes, 50*, 179–211.

Albani, V. (2018). Der Erfolg der Superhelden! Retrieved March 13, 2019, from http://www.display-magazin.ch/2018/06/der-erfolg-der-superhelden/

Andsager, J. L., Bemker, V., Choi, H.-L., & Torwel, V. (2006). Perceived Similarity of Exemplar Traits and Behavior: Effects on Message Evaluation. *Communication Research, 33*, 3–18.

Arendt, F., Hauck, P., Mayr, J., & Negwer, F. (2019). Anti-Stigma HIV Related Social Advertising: No Evidence for Side Effects on Condom Use. *Health Communication, 34*(2), 135–138.

Austrian Aids Association. (2019). Am 1. März ist Zero Discrimination Day. Retrieved March 7, 2019, from https://www.aidshilfen.at/node/514

Batra, R., Myers, J. G., & Aaker, D. A. (1996). *Advertising Management* (5th ed.). Upper Saddle River, NJ: Prentice Hall.

Batra, R., & Ray, M. L. (1986). Affective Responses Mediating Acceptance of Advertising. *Journal of Consumer Research, 13*, 234–249.

Becker, M. H. (1974). The Health Belief Model and Preventive Health Behavior. *Health Education Monographs, 2*(4), 354–386.

Becker, M. H., & Rosenstock, I. M. (1978). Compliance with a Medical Regimen for Asthma: A Test of the Health Belief Model. *Public Health Reports, 93*, 68–277.

Behr, A. (2009). Neue Aids-Kampagne: Prävention an allen Liebesorten. Retrieved March 11, 2019, from https://plaforum.pharmazeutische-zeitung.de/index.php?id=777

Belch, G. E., & Belch, M. A. (1993). *Introduction to Advertising and Promotion: An Integrated Marketing Communications Perspective*. Homewood, IL: Irwin.

Bernhardt, J. M. (2004). Communication at the Core of Effective Public Health. *American Journal of Public Health, 94*(2), 2051–2053.

Biener, L., Ji, M., Gilpin, E. A., & Albers, A. B. (2004). The Impact of Emotional Tone, Message, and Broadcast Parameters in Youth Antismoking Advertisements. *Journal of Health Communication, 9*, 259–274.

Brown, L., Macintryre, K., & Trujillo, L. (2003). Interventions to Reduce HIV/AIDS Stigma: What Have We Learned? *AIDS Education and Prevention, 15*, 49–69.

BZGA.de. (2016). HIV/STI-Prävention—im Rückblick. Retrieved March 10, 2019, from https://www.bzga.de/presse/pressemotive/hivsti-praevention-im-rueckblick/

Campbell, D. (2008). The Visual Economy of HIV/AIDS. Retrieved May 28, 2019, from https://www.david-campbell.org/wp-content/documents/Visual_Economy_of_HIV_AIDS.pdf

Casais, B., & Proenca, J. F. (2012). Inhibitions and Implications Associated with Celebrity Participation in Health-Related Social Marketing: An Exploratory Research Focused on HIV Prevention in Portugal. *Health Marketing Quarterly, 29*(3), 206–222.

Casais, B., Proenca, J. F., & Barros, H. (2019). Social Marketing Applied to HIV/AIDS Prevention. The Case of a Five-Year Governmental Response in Portugal. In M. M. Galan-Ladero & H. M. Alves (Eds.), *Case Studies in Social Marketing* (pp. 85–100). Cham: Springer.

CDC. (2001). What is Health Communications? Retrieved February 21, 2019, from http://www.cdc.gov/healthcommunication/healthbasics/whatishc.html

CDC. (2019). Basic Statistics. Retrieved March 1, 2019, from https://www.cdc.gov/hiv/basics/statistics.html

Cho, H. (2012). *Health Communication Message Design: Theory and Practice*. Thousand Oaks, CA: SAGE.

Coleman, R. (2010). Framing the Pictures in Our Heads. Exploring the Framing and Agenda- Setting Effects of Visual Images. In P. D'Angelo & J. A. Kuypers (Eds.), *Doing News Framing Analysis: Empirical and Theoretical Perspectives* (pp. 233–261). New York: Routledge.

Cook, T. E., & Colby, D. E. (1992). The Mass-Mediated Epidemic: The Politics of AIDS on the Nightly Network News. In E. Fee & D. M. Fox (Eds.), *AIDS: The Making of a Chronic Disease* (pp. 84–122). Berkeley: University of California Press.

Crossley, M. L. (1997). Survivors and Victims: Long-Term HIV Positive Individuals and the Ethos of Self-Empowerment. *Social Science and Medicine, 45*(12), 1863–1873.

Dan, V., & Coleman, R. (2014). *Coming down from the Ivory Tower: Visual Frames of HIV/AIDS in the Academic Literature and Broader Society.* Paper presented at the International Communication Association Conference 2014, Seattle, Washington.

Davis, R. E., & Resnicow, K. (2012). The Cultural Variance Framework for Tailoring Health Messages. In H. Cho (Ed.), *Health Communication Message Design: Theory and Practice* (pp. 115–135). SAGE: Thousand Oaks, CA.

Derzon, J. H., & Lipsey, M. W. (2002). A Meta-Analysis of the Effectiveness of Mass-Communication for Changing Substance-use: Knowledge, Attitudes and Behavior. In W. D. Crano & M. Burgoon (Eds.), *Mass Media and Drug Prevention: Classic and Contemporary Theories and Research* (pp. 231–258). Mahwah, London: Lawrence Erlbaum Associates.

Dobrenova, F. V., Grabner-Kräuter, S., Diehl, S., & Terlutter, R. (2019). The Use of Advertising Appeals in Breast Cancer Detection Messages: A Web Content Analysis. *Women and Health.* https://doi.org/10.1080/03630242.2019.1565904

Dr. Gay. (2018). #UNDETECTABLE. Retrieved March 13, 2019, from https://www.drgay.ch/de/deine-gesundheit/undetectable

Dr. Gay. (2019). Securion ist da! Retrieved March 13, 2019, from https://www.drgay.ch/de/securion

Dutta, M. J. (2008). *Communicating Health: A Culture-Centered Approach.* Malden, MA: Policy.

Eagly, A. H., & Chaiken, S. (1993). *The Psychology of Attitudes.* Fort Worth, TX: Harcourt College Publishers.

Edington, D. W., Schultz, A. B., Pitts, J. S., & Camilleri, A. (2016). The Future of Health Promotion in the 21st Century: A Focus on the Working Population. *American Journal of Lifestyle Medicine, 10*(4), 242–252.

Eppler, M. J. (2006). A Comparison Between Concept Maps, Mind Maps, Conceptual Diagrams, and Visual Metaphors as Complementary Tools for Knowledge Construction and Sharing. *Information Visualization, 5,* 202–210.

Fishbein, M. (2008). A Reasoned Action Approach to Health Promotion. *Medical Decision Making, 28*(6), 834–844.

Fishbein, M., & Ajzen, I. (1975). *Belief, Attitude, Intention and Behavior: An Introduction to Theory and Research.* Addison Wesley: Longman.

Fortune, K., Becerra-Posada, F., Buss, P., Galvao, L. A. C., Conteras, A., Murhpy, M., et al. (2018). Health Promotion and the Agenda for Sustainable Development, WHO Region of the Americas. *Bulletin of the World Health Organization, 96,* 621–626.

Freimuth, V., Linnan, H. W., & Potter, P. (2000). Communicating the Threat of Emerging Infections to the Public. *Emerging Infectious Diseases, 6*(4), 337–374.

Gibbs, R. (2008). *The Cambridge Handbook of Metaphor and Thought*. New York, NY: Cambridge University Press.

Gibbs, R. W., & Franks, H. (2002). Embodied Metaphor in Women's Narratives About Their Experiences with Cancer. *Health Communication, 14*, 139–165.

Gkiouzepas, L., & Hogg, M. K. (2011). Articulating a New Framework for Visual Metaphors in Advertising: A Structural, Conceptual, and Pragmatic Investigation. *Journal of Advertising, 40*, 103–120.

Glanz, K., Rimer, B. K., & Lewis, F. M. (2002). *Health Behavior and Health Education. Theory, Research and Practice*. San Francisco: Wiley and Sons.

Gordon, R., McDermmot, L., Stead, M., & Angus, K. (2006). The Effectiveness of Social Marketing Interventions for Health Improvement: What's the Evidence? *Public Health, 120*(12), 1113–11349.

Grabe, M. E., & Bucy, E. P. (2009). *Image Bite Politics: News and the Visual Framing of Elections*. Oxford: Oxford University Press.

Green, C., & Witte, K. (2006). Can Fear Arousal in Public Health Campaigns Contribute to the Decline of HIV Prevalence? *Journal of Health Communication, 11*, 245–259.

Grier, S., & Bryant, C. A. (2005). Social Marketing in Public Health. *Annual Review of Public Health, 26*, 319–339.

Grover, J. Z. (1992). Visible Lesions: Images of PWA in America. In J. Miller (Ed.), *Fluid Exchanges: Artists and Critics in the AIDS crisis* (pp. 23–51). Toronto: Toronto University Press.

Hale, J., & Dillard, J. P. (1995). Fear Appeals in Health Promotion Campaigns: Too Much, Too Little, or Just Right? In E. W. Maibach & R. L. Parrott (Eds.), *Designing Health Messages: Approaches from Communication Theory and Public Health Practice* (pp. 65–81). Thousand Oaks, CA: Sage.

Harwood, J., & Giles, H. (2005). *Intergroup Communication: Multiple Perspectives*. New York: Peter Lang.

Hawkins, J. D., Brown, E. C., Oesterle, S., Arthur, M. W., Abbott, R. D., & Catalano, R. F. (2008). Early Effects of Communities that Care on Targeted Risks and Intention of Delinquent Behavior and Substance Use. *Journal of Adolescent Health, 43*(1), 15–22.

HIV.gov. (2019). Global Statistics. Retrieved March 1, 2019, from https://www.hiv.gov/hiv-basics/overview/data-and-trends/global-statistics

Houts, P. S., Doak, C. C., Doak, L. G., & Loscalzo, M. J. (2006). The Role of Pictures in Improving Health Communication: A Review of Research on Attention, Comprehension, Recall, and Adherence. *Patient Education and Counseling, 61*, 173–190.

Jones, S. C., & Owen, N. (2006). Using fear appeals to promote cancer screening—are we scaring the wrong people? *International Journal of Nonprofit and Voluntary Sector Marketing, 11*(2), 93–103. https://doi.org/10.1002/nvsm.48

Keefer, L. A., Landau, M. J., Sullivan, D., & Rothschild, Z. K. (2014). Embodied Metaphor and Abstract Problem Solving: Testing a Metaphoric Fit Hypothesis in the Health Domain. *Journal of Experimental Social Psychology, 55*, 12–20.

Kickbusch, I. S. (2001). Health Literacy: Addressing the Health and Education Divide. *Health Promotion International, 16*(3), 289–287.

Kinderkuriert. (2006). Mach's mit ... Retrieved March 10, 2019, from https://der-kinderkurier.wordpress.com/2006/07/08/machs-mit/

Kinnear, T. C., Bernhadt, K. L., & Krentler, K. A. (1995). *Principles of Marketing* (4th ed.). New York: Longman.

Koinig, I. (2016). *Pharmaceutical Advertising as a Source of Consumer Self-Empowerment*. Wiesbaden: Springer Fachmedien.

Koinig, I., & Diehl, S. (2020). Designing Sustainable Social Media Health Communication Campaigns for Promoting Rare Diseases. In L. Costa & S. Oliviera (Eds.), *Communicating Rare Diseases and Disorders in the Digital Age* (pp. 113–152). IGI Global.

Koinig, I., Diehl, S., & Mueller, B. (2017). Are Pharmaceutical Ads Affording Consumers a Greater Say in Their Health Care? The Evaluation and Self-Empowerment Effects of Different Ad Appeals in Brazil. *International Journal of Advertising, 36*(6), 945–974.

Kok, G., Bartholomew, L. K., Parcel, G. S., Gottlieb, N. H., & Fernandez, M. E. (2014). Finding Theory—and Evidence-Based Alternatives to Fear Appeals: Intervention Mapping. *International Journal of Psychology, 49*(2), 98–107.

Kövecses, Z. (2010). *Metaphor: A practical introduction*. New York, NY: Oxford University Press.

Landau, M. J., Arndt, J., & Cameron, L. D. (2018). Do Metaphors in Health Messages Work? Exploring Emotional and Cognitive Factors. *Journal of Experimental Social Psychology, 74*, 135–149.

Lang, A., Dhillon, K., & Dong, Q. (1995). Arousal, Emotion, and Memory for Television Messages. *Journal of Broadcasting & Electronic Media, 38*, 1–15.

LaTour, M., & Zahra, S. (1989). Fear Appeals as Advertising Strategy: Should they Be Used? *Journal of Services Marketing, 2*(4), 5–14.

Lazard, A. J., Bamgbade, B. A., Sontag, J. M., & Brown, C. (2016). Using Visual Metaphors in Health Messages: A Strategy to Increase Effectiveness for Mental Illness Communication. *Journal of Health Communication, 21*(12), 1260–1268.

Leonidou, L. C., & Leonidou, C. N. (2009). Rational Versus Emotional Appeals in Newspaper Advertising: Copy, Art, and Layout Differences. *Journal of Promotion Management, 15*, 522–546.

Life. (2019a). Über uns. Retrieved February 27, 2019, from https://lifeplus.org/lifeplus/

Life. (2019b). Know Your Status—the Background. Retrieved February 22, 2019, from https://lifeplus.org/en/know-your-status-2/

Life. (2019c). Know Your Stauts—Die Kampagne 2019. Retrieved May 28, 2019, from https://lifeplus.org/know-your-status/

Love-Life.ch. (2019a). DIE NEUE KAMPAGNE: WER SICH MIT EINEM KONDOM SCHÜTZT, HAT BEREITS GEWONNEN. Retrieved March 12, 2019, from https://www.lovelife.ch/de/kampagne/aktuelle-kampagne/

Love-Life.ch. (2019b). DAS LOVE LIFE MANIFEST. Retrieved March 12, 2019, from https://www.lovelife.ch/de/manifest/

Love-Life.ch. (2019c). KAMPAGNE—INSERATE. Retrieved March 12, 2019, from https://www.lovelife.ch/de/kampagne/archiv/inserate/

Love-Life.ch. (2019d). DIE MODELS ERZÄHLEN: «DARUM WERBEN WIR FÜR LOVE LIFE». Retrieved March 12, 2019, from https://www.lovelife.ch/de/kampagne/archiv/die-models/

Lupton, D. (1999). *Medicine as Culture: Illness, Disease and Culture in Western Societies*. London: Sage.

Lupton, D. (2015). The Pedagogy of Disgust: The Ethical, Moral and Political Implications of Using Disgust in Public Health Campaign. *Critical Public Health*, *25*(1), 4–14.

Mahajan, A., Sayles, J., Pael, V., Remien, R., Ortiz, D., Szekeres, G., et al. (2008). Stigma in the HIV/AIDS Epidemic: A Review of the Literature and Recommendations for the Way Forward. *AIDS*, *22*, 67–79.

Malikhao, P. (2016). *Sex in the Village*. In *Culture, Religion and HIV/AIDS in Thailand*. Silkworm Penang-Chiangmai: Publishers.

Malikhao, P. (2020). Health Communication: Approaches, Strategies, and Ways to Sustainability on Health or Health for All. In J. Servaes (Ed.), *Handbook of Communication for Development and Social Change* (pp. 1015–1037). Singapore: Springer Nature.

McDivitt, J. A., Zimicki, S., & Hornik, R. C. (1997). Explaining the Impact of Communication Campaigns to Change Vaccination Knowledge and Coverage in the Philippines. *Health Communication*, *9*, 95–118.

Merson, M. H., O'Malley, J., Serwadda, D., & Apisuk, C. (2008). The History and Challenge of HIV Prevention. *Lancet*, *372*(9637), 475–488.

Mezirow, J. (2000). *Learning as Transformation: Critical Perspectives on a Theory in Progress*. San Francisco: Jossey-Bass.

Mohanty, P., & Ratneshwar, S. (2015). Did you Get It? Factors Influencing Subjective Comprehension of Visual Metaphors in Advertising. *Journal of Advertising*, *44*, 23–242.

Mueller, B. (1987). Reflections of Culture: An Analysis of Japanese and American Advertising Appeals. *Journal of Advertising Research*, *27*(3), 51–59.

Mulholland, E. (2019). *Communicating Sustainable Development and the SDGs in Europe: Good practice examples from policy, academia, NGOs, and media*. ESDN Quarterly Report 51, January 2019, ESDN Office, Vienna.

Nabi, R. L. (2002). Anger, Fear, Uncertainty, and Attitudes: A Test of the Cognitive-Functional Model. *Communication Monographs*, *69*, 204–216.

Niebel, K., & Davidson, E. (2012). Raising the Bar for HIV Awareness. *Marketing Health Services*, *32*(4), 5–7.

Noar, S. M., Benac, C. N., & Harris, M. S. (2007). Does Tailoring Matter? Meta-Analytic Review of Tailored Print Health Behavior Change Interventions. *Psychological Bulletin*, *133*(4), 673–693.

OECD. (2001). Strategies for Sustainable Development. Practical Guidance for Development Co-operation. Retrieved April 1, 2020, from https://www.oecd.org/dac/environment-development/strategiesforsustainabledevelopment.htm

Okazaki, S., Mueller, B., & Diehl, S. (2013). A Multi-Country Examination of Hard-Sell and Soft-Sell Advertising: Comparing Global Consumer Positioning in Holistic- and Analytic-Thinking Countries. *Journal of Advertising Research*, *53*(3), 258–272.

Okazaki, S., Mueller, B., & Taylor, C. R. (2010). Measuring Soft-Sell Versus Hard-Sell Advertising Appeals. *Journal of Advertising*, *39*(2), 5–20.

Palmer-Wackerly, A. L., & Krieger, J. L. (2015). Dancing Around Infertility: The Use of Metaphors in a Complex Medical Situation. *Health Communication*, *30*, 612–623.

Parrott, R. (2003). Media Issues. In T. L. Thompson, A. M. Dorsey, K. I. Miller, & R. Parrott (Eds.), *Handbook of Health Communication* (pp. 445–448). London: Lawrence Erlbaum Associates.

Paunio, M., Virtanen, M., Poltola, H., Cantell, K., Paunio, P., Valle, M., et al. (1991). Increase of Vaccination Coverage by Mass Media and Individual Approach:

Intensified Measles, Mumps and Rubella Prevention Program in Finland. *American Journal of Epidemiology, 133*(11), 1152–1160.

Persoenlich. (2018). Superhelden machen sich stark für Gays. Retrieved March 13, 2019, from https://www.persoenlich.com/kategorie-werbung/superhelden-machen-sich-stark-fur-gays

PEW Internet and American Life Project. (2007). E-Patients with a Disability or Chronic Disease. Retrieved February 22, 2018, from http://www.pewinternet.org/files/old-media/Files/Reports/2007/EPatients_Chronic_Conditions_2007.pdf.pdf

Phillips, B. J., & McQuarrie, E. F. (2009). Impact of Advertising Metaphor on Consumer Belief: Delineating the Contribution of Comparison Versus Deviation Factors. *Journal of Advertising, 38*, 49–62.

Pieters, R., Warlop, L., & Wedel, M. (2002). Breaking Through the Clutter: Benefits of Advertisement Originality and Familiarity for Brand Attention and Memory. *Management Science, 48*, 765–781. https://doi.org/10.1287/mnsc.48.6.765.192

Piller, I. (2001). Identity Constructions in Multilingual Advertising. *Language in Society, 30*, 153–186.

PKV.de. (2019). Mach's mit–Gib AIDS keine Chance. Retrieved March 10, 2019, from https://www.pkv.de/verband/engagement/praevention/machsmit/

Porter, R. W., Steinglass, R., Kaiser, J., Olkhovsky, P., Rasmuson, M., Dzhatdoeva, F. A., et al. (2000). Role of Health Communication in Russia's Diphtheria Immunization Program. *Journal of Infectious Diseases, 181*, 220–227.

Pratt, C. B., Ha, L., & Pratt, C. A. (2002). Setting the Public Health Agenda on Major Diseases in Sub-Saharan Africa: African Popular Magazines and Medical Journals 1981–1997. *Journal of Communication, 52*, 889–904.

Ramirez, A. G., Villarreal, R., McAlister, A., Gallion, K. J., Suarez, L., & Gomez, P. (1999). Advancing the Role of Participatory Communication in the Diffusion of Cancer Screening Among Hispanics. *Journal of Health Communication, 4*(1), 31–36.

Rattle, R. (2010). *Computing Our Way to Paradise? The Role of Internet and Communication Technologies in Sustainable Consumption and Globalization.* New York: Rowan and Littlefield.

Reese, S. D. (2001). Prologue—Framing Public Life: A Bridging Model for Media Research. In S. D. Reese, O. H. Gandy, & A. E. Grant (Eds.), *Framing Public Life: Perspectives on Media and Our Understanding of the Social World.* Mahwah, NJ: Lawrence Erlbaum.

Reinarman, C., & Levine, H. G. (1995). The Crack Attack: America's Latest Drug Scare, 1986–1992. In J. Best (Ed.), *Images of Issues: Typifying Contemporary Social Problems* (pp. 147–186). New York: de Gruyter.

Rioplus. (2008). Strategic Communication for Sustainable Development A conceptual overview. Retrieved April 1, 2020, from https://www.cbd.int/cepa/toolkit/2008/doc/strategic%20communication%20for%20sustainable%20development.pdf

Rockstroh, J. K., & Wasmuth, J.-C. (2017). HIV-Infektion: Test und Behandlung. *Zentralblatt fur Arbeitsmedizin, Arbeitsschutz und Ergonomie, 67*(1), 49–60.

Rogers, E. M. (1963). *The Diffusion of Innovations.* Los Angeles: Free Press.

Rogers, E. M. (1996). The Field of Health Communication Today: An Up-to-Date Report. *Journal of Health Communication, 1*, 15–23.

Rogers, E. M., & Storey, D. (1988). Communication Campaigns. In C. R. Berger & S. H. Chaffee (Eds.), *Handbook of Communication Science.* SAGE: Newbury Park, CA.

Rogers, R. W. (1975). A Protection Motivation Theory of Fear Appeals and Attitude Change. *Journal of Psychology, 91*, 93–114.

Rogers, R. W. (1983). Cognitive and Physiological Processes in Fear Appeals and Attitude Change: A Revised Theory of Protection Motivation. In J. Cacioppo & R. Petty (Eds.), *Social Psychophysiology: A Sourcebook* (pp. 153–176). New York, NY: Guilford Press.

Rosenstock, I. (1974). Historical Origins of the Health Belief Model. *Health Education Monographs, 2*(4), 328–335.

Rossiter, J. R., & Bellman, S. (2005). *Marketing Communications: Theory and Applications*. French Forest: Pearson Education Australia.

Rossmann, C., & Ziegler, L. (2013). Gesundheitskommunikation: Medienwirkungen im Gesundheitsbereich. In W. Schweiger & A. Fahr (Eds.), *Handbuch Medienwirkungsforschung* (pp. 385–400). Wiesbaden: Springer.

Salmon, C., & Atkin, C. K. (2003). Media Campaigns for Health Promotion. In T. L. Thompson, A. M. Dorsey, K. I. Miller, & R. Parrott (Eds.), *Handbook of Health Communication*. Mahwah, NJ: Lawrence Erlbaum.

Scalvini, M. (2010). Glamorizing Sick Bodies: How Commercial Advertising Has Changed the Representation of HIV/AIDS. *Social Semiotics, 20*(3), 219–231.

Schiavo, R. (2007). *Health Communication: From Theory to Practice*. San Francisco: Wiley and Sons.

SD. (2020). Goal 3: Ensure healthy lives and promote well-being for all at all ages. Retrieved March 26, 2020, from https://www.un.org/sustainabledevelopment/health/

SDUN. (2020). Sustainable Development Goal 3. Retrieved March 26, 2020, from https://sustainabledevelopment.un.org/sdg3

Servaes, J., & Malikhao, P. (2016). Communication is Essential for Global Impact. *Procedia Engineering, 159*, 316–321.

Sharf, B. F., & Vandeford, M. L. (2003). Illness Narratives and the Social Construction of Health. In T. L. Thompson, A. Dorsey, K. I. Miller, & R. Parrot (Eds.), *Handbook of Health Communication* (pp. 9–34). Mahwah, NJ: Lawrence Erlbaum.

Smith, R. E., MacKenzie, S. B., Yang, X., Buchholz, L. M., & Darley, W. K. (2007). Modeling the Determinants and Effects of Creativity in Advertising. *Marketing Science, 26*, 819–833. https://doi.org/10.1287/mksc.1070.0272

Snowdon, C., Garcia, J., & Elbourne, D. (1997). Making Sense of Randomization: Responses of Parents of Critically Ill Babies to Random Allocation of Treatment in a Clinical Trial. *Social Science and Medicine, 45*, 1337–1355.

Snyder, L. B. (2001). Development of Communication Campaigns. In W. B. Gudykunst & B. Mody (Eds.), *Handbook of International and Intercultural Communication* (2nd ed., pp. 457–478). SAGE: Thousand Oaks, CA.

Snyder, L. B., & Hamilton, M. A. (2002). A Meta-Analysis of U.S. Health Campaign Effects on Behavior: Emphasize Enforcement, Exposure, and New Information, and Beware the Secular Trend. In R. C. Hornik (Ed.), *Public Health Communication. Evidence for Behavior Change* (pp. 357–383). London: Lawrence Erlbaum Associates.

Sonnenberg-Schwan, U. (2009). "Liebesorte": Die neue Kampagne der BZgA zur Aidsprävention. Retrieved March 11, 2019, from https://daignet.de/site-content/die-daig/sektionen/aawsall-around-women-special/news/neue-kampagne-der-bzga

Sopory, P. (2005). Metaphor in Formative Evaluation and Message Design: An Application to Relationships and Alcohol Use. *Health Communication, 17*, 149–172.

Sopory, P., & Dillard, J. (2002). The Persuasive Effects of Metaphor: A Meta-Analysis. *Human Communication Research, 28*, 382–419.

Tannenbaum, M. B. (2015). Appealing to Fear: A Meta-Analysis of Fear Appeal Effectiveness and Theories. *Psychological Bulletin, 141*(6), 1178–1204.

Tay, R., Ozanne, L., & Santino, J. (2000). *Advertising and Road Safety.* Proceedings of the ANZMAC 2000, 1248–1251.

Terblanche-Smit, M., & Terblanche, N. (2010). Racial Perceptions in Social Marketing: The Function of Fear in HIV/AIDS communication. *Advances in Advertising Research, 1*, 111–125.

Thompson, T., Parrott, R., & Nussbaum, J. (2011). *The Routledge Handbook of Health Communication* (2nd ed.). New York: Routledge.

Thompson, T. L. (2000). The Nature and Language of Illness Explanations. In B. B. Whaley (Ed.), *Explaining illness: Research, Theory and Strategies* (pp. 3–40). Mahwah, NJ: Erlbaum.

Toncar, M., & Munch, J. (2001). Consumer Responses to Tropes in Print Advertising. *Journal of Advertising, 30*, 55–65.

Truong, V. D. (2014). Social marketing: a systematic review of research 1998–2012. *Social Marketing Quarterly, 20*(1), 15–34.

Tümmers, H. (2013). "GIB AIDS KEINE CHANCE": Eine Präventionsbotschaft in zwei deutschen Staaten. Retrieved March 10, 2019, from https://zeithistorische-forschungen.de/3-2013/id%3D4734

U.S. Department of Health and Human Services. (2000). *Healthy People 2010: Understanding and Improving Health and Objectives for Improving Health.* US Department of Health and Human Services, Washington, DC. Retrieved February 10, 2019, from http://www.cdc.gov/nchs/data/hpdata2010/hp2010_final_review.pdf

U.S. Department of Health and Human Services. (2005). Making Health Communication Programs Work. Retrieved February 10, 2019, from http://www.cancer.gov/publications/health-communication/pink-book.pdf

U.S. Department of Health and Human Services. (2014). What is Health Literacy. Retrieved February 10, 2019, from http://www.health.gov/communication/literacy/

UN. (2017). About the Sustainable Development Goals. Retrieved February 2, 2019, from https://www.un.org/sustainabledevelopment/sustainable-development-goals/

UN. (2017a). Goal 3: Ensure healthy lives and promote well-being for all at all ages. Retrieved from https://www.un.org/sustainabledevelopment/health/

UN. (2017b). Building more inclusive, sustainable and prosperous societies in Europe and Central Asia – A common United Nations vision for the post-2015 development agenda. Retrieved from https://sustainabledevelopment.un.org/index.php?page=view&type=400&nr=1459&menu=1515

UN AIDS. (2018). Global HIV & AIDS statistics — 2018 Fact Sheet. Retrieved March 1, 2019, from http://www.unaids.org/en/resources/fact-sheet

UN AIDS. (2019). Unaids Urges Action to Change Discriminatory Laws In Order to Restore Dignity and Respect and Save Lives. Retrieved March 7, 2019, from http://www.unaids.org/en/2019_ZDD_campaign

UNDP. (2019). Goal 3: Good Health and Well-Being. Retrieved February 2, 2019, from https://www.undp.org/content/undp/en/home/sustainable-development-goals/goal-3-good-health-and-well-being.html

Wakefield, M. A., Loken, B., & Hornik, R. C. (2010). Use of Mass Media Campaigns to Change Health Behaviour. *Lancet, 376*, 1261–1271.

Wallington, S. F. (2014). Health Disparities Research and Practice. The Role of Language and Health Communication. In H. E. Hamilton & W. S. Chou (Eds.), *The Routledge Handbook of Language and Health Communication* (pp. 168–183). London: Routledge.

WHO. (1986). The 1st International Conference on Health Promotion, Ottawa, 1986. Retrieved from https://www.who.int/teams/healthpromotion/enhanced-wellbeing/first-global-conference

WHO. (2013). *A European Policy Framework and Strategy for the 21st Century.* Copenhagen: WHO Regional Office for Europe.

WHO. (2016). Global Health Sector Strategy on HIV 2016–2021: Towards Ending AIDS. Retrieved February 27, 2019, from https://apps.who.int/iris/bitstream/handle/10665/246178/WHO-HIV-2016.05-eng.pdf;jsessionid=F06C41B0389951B87731CCB4F21C2DBB?sequence=1

WHO. (2018). Advancing Public Health for Sustainable Development in the WHO European Region. Retrieved March 26, 2020, from http://www.euro.who.int/de/about-us/governance/regional-committee-for-europe/past-sessions/68th-session/documentation/background-documents/advancing-public-health-for-sustainable-development-in-the-who-european-region

WHO. (2019). HIV/AIDS. Retrieved February 27, 2019, from https://www.who.int/hiv/strategy2016-2021/ghss-hiv/en/

Witte, K. (1992). Putting the Fear Back Into Fear Appeals: The Extended Parallel Process Model. *Communication Monographs, 59*(4), 329–349.

Witte, K., & Allen, M. (2000). A Meta-Analysis of Fear Appeals: Implications for Effective Public Health Campaigns. *Health Education & Behavior, 27*, 608–632.

Witte, K. (1998). Fear as motivator, fear as inhibitor: Using the extended parallel process model to explain fear appeal successes and failures. In P. A. Andersen & L. K. Guerrero (Eds.), Handbook of communication and emotion: Research, theory, applications, and contexts (pp. 423–450). San Diego, CA: Academic Press.

Wright, K. B., Sparks, L., & O'Hair, H. D. (2008). *Health Communication in the 21st Century.* Oxford: Blackwell.

Wymer, W. (2011). Developing More Effective Social Marketing Strategies. *Journal of Social Marketing, 1*(1), 17–31.

Yzer, M. (2012). The Integrative Model of Behavioral Prediction as a Tool for Designing Health Messages. In H. Cho (Ed.), *Health Communication Message Design: Theory and Practice* (pp. 21–40). Los Angeles, CA: Sage.

CHAPTER 21

Global Communication and Sustainable Development: From the Earth Summit in Rio 1992 to the Olympic Games in Rio 2016

Radoslaw Sajna-Kunowsky

INTRODUCTION

Although Rio de Janeiro is associated primarily with the figure of Christ the Redemptorist, the Copacabana beach or Rio Carnival, this large Brazilian city can be called the world capital of sustainable development. This is not because the sustainability principles are implemented in a perfect way there, but because Rio has become a global "center" for promoting the idea of sustainable development. The Earth Summit took place in Rio in 1992, just like the Rio+20 summit 20 years later, and in 2016 the Summer Olympic Games with a "green" opening ceremony focused the attention of people on this metropolis, located in the most biodiverse country in the world. All this in the era of global communication, which allows the promotion of some ideas for the global audience.

The term "global communication" can be associated with various aspects of this phenomenon of modern times, like global media system (McPhail, 2006; Winseck & Pike, 2007; Sajna, 2013), global digital divide (Warschauer, 2004; O'Hara & Stevens, 2006; Rice, 2009), global pluralism (Sajna, 2012, 2016, 2018) and many others. Global communication does not mean, of course, that global media create an "idealistic" global public sphere that serves the development of global society, but allow it, while there are still local public spheres

R. Sajna-Kunowsky (✉)
Kazimierz Wielki University, Bydgoszcz, Poland
e-mail: rs-epp@post.pl; r.sajna@ukw.edu.pl; rsajna@post.pl

© The Author(s), under exclusive license to Springer Nature Switzerland AG 2021
M. J. Yusha'u, J. Servaes (eds.), *The Palgrave Handbook of International Communication and Sustainable Development*,
https://doi.org/10.1007/978-3-030-69770-9_21

interconnected in a global media environment. "Communication globalizes but it also remains local. (...) Global and local belong together. (...) We are global and local citizens and our communication could possibly best be termed *glocal*" (Hamelink, 2015, p. 3). Nevertheless, although global communication is experienced today by people around the world, thanks to the universality of using communication technologies and general understanding, regardless of the place and cultural context, this term has no clear definition (Ociepka, 2016).

Contemporary communication on a global scale is possible thanks to human development, including ideas and technologies, but the same human development is dangerous for the planet. However, the Earth's inhabitants are able to organize themselves to promote sustainable development as "development that meets the needs of the present without compromising the ability of future generations to meet their own needs", as defined in the Report of the World Commission on Environment and Development entitled "Our Common Future", called Brundtland Report (1987). The Chair of this Commission, former Norwegian Prime Minister Gro Harlem Brundtland, was also committed to the first sustainable Winter Olympic Games in Lillehammer 1994. David Goldblatt (2016) in his book *The Games. A Global History of the Olympics* states: "With Prime Minister Gro Harlem Brundtland, the noted environmentalist, in power, there was, at Lillehammer, an unprecedented commitment to thinking through the environmental implications of the games" (p. 370). Since the Olympic Games are the most popular mega sport events, watched by millions of people around the world, there is (thanks to global communication) an enormous potential to promote ideas, including the idea of sustainable development.

Approaches to Media and Development Communication

Many studies on the role of media in development communication or communication for development are known among specialists. There are, of course, many different theories of development (see: Larrain, 1989; Peet & Hartwick, 2015), as well as different definitions and perspectives both on sustainable development and on communication, and the literature on both subjects (treated separately as well as in conjunction) is abundant (see: Servaes, 2013, pp. 1–39). Although in the twentieth century various books dealing with the issue of development communication appeared (by Lerner, Schramm and many others, see: T.L. McPhail, 2009, pp. 6–9), probably the first definition of the term was offered by Nora C. Quebral who, after rethinking the concept, redefined development communication as the "art and science of human communication linked to a society's planned transformation, from a state of poverty to one of dynamic socio-economic growth, that makes for greater equity and the larger unfolding of individual potential" (2002, p. 16). There are at least three methodological and theoretical approaches within communication for development: (1) media for development, (2) media development, (3) participatory and community communication (Manyozo, 2012, pp. 12–20). For this chapter the first approach is relevant, because the role of media to promote the idea of sustainable development and environmental issues on a global scale is analysed, though naturally the environment is only one of many problems of sustainable development (see: UN SDG: https://sustainabledevelopment.un.org).

However, there are various strands in development journalism and two binary perspectives: organic or bottom-up and the external top-down development reporting (Manyozo, 2012, pp. 55–57). In this chapter rather the second perspective is relevant, because the study of the reporting of the "green" opening ceremony of the Rio 2016 Olympic Games is to answer the question: how the media (in this case: prestigious, elite, leading newspapers) in different countries from different continents (and both from the global North and the South) pointed to environmental issues, presented abundantly during the event. Therefore, the global perspective in this chapter is dominant. Although the globalization paradigm in development communication studies is used above all to analyse the role that media and other forms of communication can play in improving the conditions of life for the world's poorest people and confronting the global reality of inequality (see: Sparks, 2007), in this chapter the development is related to the living conditions of the entire global population. Leading newspapers in specific counties influence public opinion which determines social and political life (and changes) in those countries that are connected in multilevel global relations thanks to global communication. In this sense, global communication can be associated with development communication. In this chapter, however, the most important issue is the promotion of the idea of sustainable development on a global scale.

Media and Promotion of Nature, Environmental Issues and Sustainable Development

Some kind of "promotion" of nature and environmental problems in the broad context of human existence could be observed many centuries ago. In ancient Greece and Rome many important works about nature and environment appeared, like Aristotle's books about animals (*Historia Animalium, De Patribus Animalium, De Motu Animalium* etc.), several books of the "father of botany" Theophrastus (*De historia plantarum, De causis plantarum*) or a 37-book encyclopaedia *Historia Naturalis*, written by Pliny the Elder. Mark Neuzil (2008) noticed: "As a journalism forerunner, Pliny demonstrated an awareness of both environmental damage and its causes. (…) Pliny was among the pioneers in writing about exotic species, a popular subject among science and environmental writers of the modern period" (p. 38).

In the Renaissance epoch many ancient works reappeared, but also a lot of new books about nature were written by Leonhart Fuchs, Ulisses Aldrovandi, Pierre Belon, Konrad Gessner and others. Johannes Gutenberg's invention of mechanical printing made possible to produce periodicals that began to appear in Europe in the seventeenth century. During the Enlightenment and the nineteenth century many books and press articles about various aspects of nature were published, and some scientists dealing with natural phenomena became famous, like Carl Linnaeus, Alexander von Humboldt or Charles Darwin, to name only a few of the most important. Many newspapers promoted scientific theories and ideas about nature, agriculture or the environment. Nevertheless, as Libby Lester (2010) states: "There is little agreement on when 'the environment' began. It could have been 1962 when Rachel Carson published *Silent Spring* with its compelling opening fable connecting human activity, science and nature" (p. 17). William Cronon (2008) argues:

> It may be an oversimplification to say that the modern environmental movement began with Rachel Carson's *Silent Spring*, but it is hard to overstate that book's impact. Prior to its publication in 1962, various environmental concerns were becoming more prominent in the years following World War II. (...) But *Silent Spring* was a lightning rod like no other. Gaining visibility first as a series of articles in the *New Yorker* and then as a best-selling book, it catapulted its author (...) into a political firestorm. Carson's indictment of DDT and other insecticides brought heated rebuttals from chemical companies that manufactured these products, from government agencies that promoted their use, and from scientists who believed that their benefits far outweighed their harms. (p. ix)

Shawn William Miller (2007) explains that "with the birth of modern environmentalism in the 1960s, our perceptions of nature changed radically. Nature is no longer simply an object to be conquered by civilization, coerced by conservationists, and consumed by campers. We increasingly see nature as a victim, significantly, a fellow victim, of human overconfidence and excess" (p. 204).

Although different media reported environmental issues before and after the Rachel Carson's book, it was during the Earth Summit in Rio de Janeiro in 1992 when environmental journalism was really born (Parratt, 2006, p. 17) or at least began to develop rapidly. The media not only presented the idea of sustainable development (that became a global issue) to wider audiences, but also began to treat various environmental issues seriously. Of course, many articles on this subject appeared earlier, and in 1991, so before the Earth Summit, a radio programme entitled *Living on Earth* focused on environmental problems, debuted on the American National Public Radio, thanks to the personal interests of the founder of this programme, Steve Curwood. It should be mentioned also that the founder of the first 24-hours TV network, CNN, Ted Turner was interested in these problems too, so some environmental news and documentary shows, such as *Network Earth, Earth Matters* or later *Next@CNN*, was broadcast by TBS or CNN (Neuzil, 2008, pp. 207–216). *Next@CNN* was a weekend TV programme focused on science and technology, including environment, broadcast in 2002–2005 and hosted by Daniel Sieberg, now a senior manager in Google. Naturally, not only in the United States the environmental topics have entered radio and TV programmes. David

Attenborough and his BBC films became famous internationally, and other personalities involved in the promotion of nature and environmental protection appeared in different countries.

In 2006, Davis Guggenheim's documentary film, entitled *An Inconvenient Truth*, about former U.S. Vice President Al Gore's campaign to educate citizens about global warming (followed by the Nobel Peace Prize awarded to Gore in 2007) was released and soon attracted the media's attention to the problem of climate change. As a consequence, the media audiences, not only in the United States, have become more aware of the problem. Indeed, in accordance with a survey of Eurobarometer, conducted in 2007, climate change became the main environmental issue that European citizens were worried about (57 per cent of respondents, while in 2004, before *An Inconvenient Truth*, it was only 45 per cent). Some global surveys have confirmed that concerns about the environment have been growing in the first decade of the twenty-first century on a wider global scale (Hansen, 2010, pp. 163–164). Another Eurobarometer survey from 2017 showed that 92 per cent of the European Union citizens saw climate change as a serious problem and 74 per cent as a "very serious" problem, and, according to the survey: "Nearly nine in ten believe it is important for their national government to set targets to increase renewable energy use by 2030 (89%) and provide support for improving energy efficiency by 2030 (88%)" (see: Eurobarometer 2017 Survey *Citizen support for climate action*: https://ec.europa.eu/clima/citizens/support_en). Another survey, conducted in 2020 in 40 countries (more than 80.000 people surveyed), showed that almost seven in ten think climate change is "a very, or extremely serious, problem", and four out of five countries showing the highest levels of concern were from the global South (see: TheConversation.com, https://theconversation.com/how-much-do-people-around-the-world-care-about-climate-change-we-surveyed-80-000-people-in-40-countries-to-find-out-140801).

Obviously, the media around the world use different frames to interpret the environmental problems, including climate change (see: Painter, 2013). Some kind of global pluralism on the issue of global warming exists, though more emphasis on the problem is laid by the media in the developed countries of Europe and America, than in, for example, poor (however rich in nature), developing countries from other continents (Sajna, 2012, pp. 71–83, 2016, pp. 11–30). As a consequence, citizens' attitudes towards climate change and other environmental problems vary between countries (that could be seen also in the above-mentioned surveys that also show growing concerns in countries of the global South, while in the most developed countries of the North many actions against climate change are visible in the media sphere, so the fears diminish).

The promotion of environmental problems has made environmental journalism (and media) one of the main areas of research in the wider area of environmental communication. Robert Cox (2010) explains: "In many ways, the study of environmental media has become its own subfield. It focuses on the ways in which the news, advertising, commercial programs, and Internet sites portray nature and environmental problems. It is also the study of the *effects* of the media on public attitudes" (p. 17). In fact, the media influence public opinion and attitude to environmental problems. Manuel Castells (2009) in his work *Communication Power* underlines the role of the mass media in transforming environmental issues into a policy issue (p. 316). Thanks to the Internet an alternative public sphere of environmental communication has developed, with environmental blogosphere or many online news services and professional societies for environmental journalists appeared (Cox, 2010, pp. 167–173). New online activists for environmental protection began to influence the new public sphere (see: de Jong, Shaw, & Stammers, 2005; Collins, 2013; Lockwood, 2013; Takahashi, Edwards, Timmons Roberts, & Duan, 2015). As Manuel Castells (2009) concludes: "The Internet has played an increasingly important role in the global movement to prevent global warming" (p. 325). Of course, the Internet has contributed to the global promotion of the idea of sustainable development.

Indeed, between the Earth Summit in Rio (1992) and the Summer Olympic Games in Rio (2016) the media environment has changed dramatically, mainly due to the development of the Internet, but still the major media in specific countries dominate the public sphere. In the global communication environment the messages from different media, traditional and new, mix in conflict spaces and create a new kind of communication reality that can be called "quantum communication" (Sajna, 2013, pp. 88–93). A lot of "quants" of communication create a "communication energy" that can provoke or cause social change. Therefore, it is important to promote ideas through huge "portions" of "communication energy", and every big media event (Summer Olympic Games being probably the biggest) is a "machine" that "produce" a lot of news in different media around the world and a lot of "quants" of communication in the Internet (see many comments, images and other activities in social media and other communication spaces).

The Earth Summit in Rio 1992, Rio+20 and the Media Reactions (Some Examples)

The 1992 Earth Summit was the starting point of global promotion of sustainable development. The most important Summit document Agenda 21, the Rio Declaration on Environment and Development, and the Statement of principles for the Sustainable Management of Forests were adopted by almost 180 Governments at the United Nations Conference on Environment and Development (UNCED) held in Rio de Janeiro, Brazil, 3–14 June 1992. A global vision of the problem was evident in each of the six subsections of the Agenda 21's Preamble (Chap. 1 of the document):

> 1.1. Humanity stands at a defining moment in history. We are confronted with a perpetuation of disparities between and within nations, a worsening of poverty,

hunger, ill health and illiteracy, and the continuing deterioration of the ecosystems on which we depend for our well-being. However, integration of environment and development concerns and greater attention to them will lead to the fulfilment of basic needs, improved living standards for all, better protected and managed ecosystems and a safer, more prosperous future. No nation can achieve this on its own; but together we can—in a global partnership for sustainable development.

1.2. This global partnership must build on the premises of General Assembly resolution 44/228 of 22 December 1989, which was adopted when the nations of the world called for the United Nations Conference on Environment and Development, and on the acceptance of the need to take a balanced and integrated approach to environment and development questions.

1.3. Agenda 21 addresses the pressing problems of today and also aims at preparing the world for the challenges of the next century. It reflects a global consensus and political commitment at the highest level on development and environment cooperation. Its successful implementation is first and foremost the responsibility of Governments. National strategies, plans, policies and processes are crucial in achieving this. International cooperation should support and supplement such national efforts. In this context, the United Nations system has a key role to play. Other international, regional and subregional organizations are also called upon to contribute to this effort. The broadest public participation and the active involvement of the non-governmental organizations and other groups should also be encouraged.

1.4. The developmental and environmental objectives of Agenda 21 will require a substantial flow of new and additional financial resources to developing countries, in order to cover the incremental costs for the actions they have to undertake to deal with global environmental problems and to accelerate sustainable development. Financial resources are also required for strengthening the capacity of international institutions for the implementation of Agenda 21. An indicative order-of-magnitude assessment of costs is included in each of the programme areas. This assessment will need to be examined and refined by the relevant implementing agencies and organizations.

1.5. In the implementation of the relevant programme areas identified in Agenda 21, special attention should be given to the particular circumstances facing the economies in transition. It must also be recognized that these countries are facing unprecedented challenges in transforming their economies, in some cases in the midst of considerable social and political tension.

1.6. The programme areas that constitute Agenda 21 are described in terms of the basis for action, objectives, activities and means of implementation. Agenda 21 is a dynamic programme. It will be carried out by the various actors according to the different situations, capacities and priorities of countries and regions in full respect of all the principles contained in the Rio Declaration on Environment and Development. It could evolve over time in the light of changing needs and circumstances. This process marks the beginning of a new global partnership for sustainable development. (see: https://sustainabledevelopment.un.org/content/documents/Agenda21.pdf)

Of course, this global initiative provoked reactions among politicians and the media. For example, *The Guardian*, the leading liberal-leftist opinion daily from the United Kingdom, on 4 June 1992 published a news article that showed a lot of hope and possible problems:

> The Earth summit of 180 nations opened in Rio yesterday with messages of hope from world leaders, tempered by a warning that new barriers were being erected to insulate the more affluent and privileged from the poor.
>
> Maurice Strong, secretary-general of the summit, warned: *No place on the planet could remain an island of affluence in a sea of misery. We are either going to save the whole world or no one will be saved. One part of the world cannot live in an orgy of unrestrained consumption where the rest destroys its environment just to survive. No one is immune from the effects of the other.*
>
> Mr Strong's speech reflected anxieties that the summit has much to negotiate before it can be counted a success. The United States, in particular, faces heavy pressure to be more positive. But, in their first briefing yesterday, US delegates repeated that they would not sign the convention on bio-diversity. (…)
>
> Britain has yet to announce if it will sign the bio-diversity convention, but is expected to do so today. Although the Government has doubts about the size of the financial commitment, the political gesture to sign is regarded as vital to distance Britain from Washington, although John Major will meet President Bush at Camp David this weekend.
>
> Efforts were being made behind the scenes yesterday to limit the damage done by the US decision. Countries like Malaysia are threatening to refuse to sign the other main convention, on climate change, in retaliation.
>
> There are also fears that other agreements may be under threat. Israel, for example, wants a phrase about *people under occupation* deleted from the Rio Declaration which all heads of government are expected to sign. It was thought that this document had been finalised, but Israel fears this phrase could be used as a weapon by the Palestinians. (…). (https://www.theguardian.com/environment/2012/jun/14/archive-1992-rio-earth-summit-opens)

After the United Nations Conference on Sustainable Development, called Rio+20 (see: Kostadinov & Thaker, 2013, pp. 43–57) and held in Rio de Janeiro on 20–22 June 2012, *The Guardian*, in another news article, entitled "Rio+20 Earth Summit: campaigners decry final document" (with a picture of indigenous protesters), reported:

> Amid doubt, disappointment and division, the world's governments came together in Rio on Friday to declare *a pathway for a sustainable century.*
>
> At the close of the Rio+20 Earth Summit, heads of state and ministers from more than 190 nations signed off on a plan to set global sustainable development goals and other measures to strengthen global environmental management, tighten protection the oceans, improve food security and promote a *green economy.*
>
> After more than a year of negotiations and a 10-day mega-conference involving 45,000 people, the wide-ranging outcome document—The Future We Want—was lambasted by environmentalists and anti-poverty campaigners for

lacking the detail and ambition needed to address the challenges posed by a deteriorating environment, worsening inequality and a global population expected to rise from 7bn to 9bn by 2050. (...). (https://www.theguardian.com/environment/2012/jun/23/rio-20-earth-summit-document)

The New York Times also noticed criticism in an article by Simon Romero and John M. Broder (entitled "Progress on the Sidelines as Rio Conference Ends"), published after the Rio+20 Summit:

Burdened by low expectations, snarled by endless traffic congestion and shunned by President Obama, the United Nations Conference on Sustainable Development ended here as it began, under a shroud of withering criticism.

The antipoverty organization CARE called the meeting *nothing more than a political charade*, and Greenpeace said the gathering was *a failure of epic proportions*. The Pew Environment Group was slightly more charitable. *It would be a mistake to call Rio a failure*, the group said, *but for a once-in-a-decade meeting with so much at stake, it was a far cry from a success.* (...). (Romero & Broder 2012, https://www.nytimes.com/2012/06/24/world/americas/rio20-conference-ends-with-some-progress-on-the-sidelines.html)

Qatar-based pan-Arabic very popular TV news station Al Jazeera broadcast and published on the website a series of news stories and videos after the Rio+20, one of them entitled "Rio+20: A corporate environment?" with a question in the lead: "As business players and activists gather for the environment summit, we ask what corporations are doing for the planet." (https://www.aljazeera.com/programmes/countingthecost/2012/06/2012622135910443825.html)

Another news story, by Preethi Nallu, on the Al Jazeera website was entitled "Alternative voices from Rio+20", and the lead, over a picture of colorful indigenous, explained: "While world leaders negotiate in the Rio+20 meeting halls, thousands of activists have launched 'The People's Summit'." (Nallu 2012, https://www.aljazeera.com/indepth/features/2012/06/2012622175745190650.html)

On 24 June 2015, so three years after Rio+20, *The Guardian* published an article by Greg Harman (independent journalist based in San Antonio, Texas) entitled: "Agenda 21: a conspiracy theory puts sustainability in the crosshairs". In the first paragraphs one could read:

Green space, clean energy, increased urban density ... and global dictatorship. It's hard to see how all of these things could connect, but—according to a popular right wing conspiracy theory—a UN resolution aimed at sustainable development could pave the way.

Theorists argue that Agenda 21, a 23-year-old non-binding UN resolution that suggests ways for governments and NGOs to promote sustainable development, is the linchpin in a plot to subjugate humanity under an eco-totalitarian regime. One of its most outspoken critics, American Policy Center president Tom

DeWeese, has described the resolution as *a new kind of tyranny that, if not stopped, will surely lead us to a new Dark Ages of pain and misery yet unknown to mankind.*

APC is on the political fringes, but anti-Agenda 21 sentiment is moving into the political mainstream. Criticism of the resolution extended to the Republican party's 2012 platform, which stated: *We strongly reject the UN Agenda 21 as erosive of American sovereignty.* (https://www.theguardian.com/sustainable-business/2015/jun/24/agenda-21-conspiracy-theory-sustainability)

These few examples of articles published in *The Guardian*, *The New York Times* and the Al Jazeera website show that the idea of sustainable development is not accepted by everyone, though these British and American dailies are among leading opinion media supporting global action for environmental protection (and counteracting global warming), while Al Jazeera is rather ambivalent. Many media around the world, however, are closer to political groups or parties, which deny global warming and oppose global action.

GLOBAL MEDIA COVERAGE OF THE "GREEN" OPENING CEREMONY OF THE RIO 2016 OLYMPIC GAMES

One of the best examples of promotion of environmental issues and, rather indirectly, the idea of sustainable development, by the media on a global scale was the opening ceremony of the Summer Olympic Games in Rio de Janeiro in 2016. Twenty-four years after the Earth Summit in Rio and 4 years after the Rio+20 Summit this Brazilian city hosted this mega sport event, broadcast to every corner of the planet, and watched by many millions of people around the world. "Green" images (including green Olympic rings or a green peace symbol) and "green" speeches from the opening ceremony of the Games, which took place in the most biodiverse country in the world (with Amazonian forest called "Lungs of the Earth"), were communicated to the global audience through the media from all continents. However, not all media emphasized the "green" message of the ceremony (Sajna, 2018).

Considering the role of the media in global promotion of ideas, this study of the global media coverage of the Rio 2016 Olympics opening ceremony was conducted to answer the question: did the global media coverage of this event serve to promote environmental issues and the idea of sustainable development?

Methods

Various methods are used in studies on environmental communication; however, most studies are focused on Western countries and Western media. In this study, focused on global media coverage of the Rio 2016 Summer Olympic Games opening ceremony, first of all quality content analysis has been used, however with additional quantitative aspects. Various news articles (with pictures) that appeared on official websites of different opinion daily newspapers around the world, directly after the ceremony (on 5–6 August 2016), have been analysed (only the main news article about the ceremony on every newspaper website). A sample of 30 newspapers was selected (by author of this chapter) to represent leading opinion media from different countries and continents or world regions, political biases, languages or cultural and religious backgrounds [see: 'List of the analyzed press articles' after 'References' at the end of this article]. As combating global environmental problems, such as global warming, requires human interaction across the planet, it is important to promote the idea of sustainable development in different countries on different continents. Therefore, this study required a broad (global) selection of media to explore the problem and demonstrate global pluralism in this matter (of course, this selection is subjective and results cannot be generalized).

Since the Olympic Games were held for the first time in South America, a sample from that continent is strongly represented: *O Globo* (Brazil), *La Nación* (Argentina), *El Tiempo* (Colombia), *El Universal* (Venezuela), *El Mercurio* (Chile), *El Comercio* (Peru), *El Universo* (Ecuador) and *ABC Color* (Paraguay). Additionally, two dailies from other Latin American countries were selected: *El Universal* (Mexico) and *Granma* (Cuba), as well as *The New York Times* (USA) and *Le Devoir* (Canada) from North America. From Europe: *The Daily Telegraph* (Great Britain), *Le Figaro* (France), *El Mundo* (Spain), *Diário de Notícias* (Portugal), *Corriere della Sera* (Italy), *Rzeczpospolita* (Poland), *Le Soir* (Belgium), *Le Temps* (Switzerland), *The Irish Independent* (Ireland) and *L'Osservatore Romano* (Vatican). From Asia: *China Daily* (China), *Hindustan Times* (India), *The Jakarta Post* (Indonesia), *The Nation* (Thailand), *The Japan Times* (Japan) and also: the Egyptian daily *Al Ahram*, representing the Middle East, *The Guardian* from the most populous African country that is Nigeria and *The Age* from Australia. Of course, this sample is limited, but representing a wide spectrum of world regions (both from the global North and South), countries and cultures.

The analysis of articles from these online newspapers is based on two steps.

First: headlines of the articles. The question is: did some references to the environmental issues and the idea of sustainable development, presented during the ceremony, appear in the headlines? This is the starting point for analysing the promotional impact of the articles. Using certain words with positive associations makes them positive in the recipient's consciousness. Assuming that the Olympic Games have a generally positive image, using the environmental issues and the idea of sustainable development in conjunction with this global sports event makes them also positive. A quantitative analysis has been appropriate at this stage of the research.

Second: content of the articles (including pictures). The question is: did the articles focus strongly on the environmental issues and the idea of sustainable development, presented during the ceremony? Each article has been read in its entirety to answer this question. Of course, the articles reported the same event, but they could focus on different aspects of the ceremony that lasted several hours. A qualitative analysis has been aimed at determining to what extent the environmental issues and the idea of sustainable development were reflected in the articles. Additional question is: did the pictures show the environmental issues and the idea of sustainable development presented during the ceremony? In this case a visual analysis has been easy and difficult at the same time, because in some cases a gallery of pictures was published, and it has been problematic to determine which photos could be treated as the main pictures of the ceremony. Nevertheless, in most cases, the question regarding this element of the research could be answered.

Results

The environmental references appeared only in six headlines in newspapers from five different continents, though only one reference to the idea of sustainable development (through the word sostenible that means "sustainable" in Spanish) could be found. The Spanish newspaper *El Mundo* (elmundo.es) published a news article with a suggestive headline: "Una ceremonia sostenible entre la selva de atletas" ("A sustainable ceremony among a selva of athletes"). The Paraguayan newspaper *ABC Color* (abc.com.py) posted a headline: "Música, arte y ecologismo en inauguración de Juegos" ("Music, art and environmentalism in the Games inauguration"). On the website of *The Jakarta Post* (thejakartapost.com) from Indonesia one could read the headline: "Rio welcomes world with sultry music, plea for conservation". *The Japan Times* (japantimes.co.jp) posted another headline: "Rio Olympics open with ceremony focused on environment". *The Age* (theage.com.au) from Australia, however, proposed a more metaphorical headline: "First green, now gold: the climate changes in Rio". The Egyptian newspaper *Al Ahram* (english.ahram.org.eg) included a reference to the environment (at least on its English-language website that was analysed) in the headline: "Rio Olympics opening ceremony highlights Brazil, environment". These six headlines made references to the environmental issues explicitly presented during the opening ceremony of the Olympic Games in Rio, while in the rest of the analysed headlines no such mentions could be found.

In several of the analysed articles the environmental elements of the show were underlined; in others at least mentioned in some paragraphs. *The Guardian* (guardian.ng) from Nigeria and *El Universal* (eluniversal.com.mx) from Mexico did not notice any element regarding the environment, abundant in the opening ceremony of the Rio 2016. Naturally, the articles with headlines that made reference to the environmental issues (so the six mentioned earlier) focused most on these aspects of the opening ceremony and the global environmental problems. Nevertheless, other newspapers noticed it too. *Hindustan Times* (hindustantimes.com) from India underlined that Brazil is "home to Amazon, the world's largest rainforest" and "used the ceremony to call on the 3 billion people watching the opening of the world's premiere sporting event to take care of the planet, plant seeds and protect the verdant land that Europeans found here five centuries ago". The Ecuadorian *El Universo* (eluniverso.com) also underlined the natural resources of Brazil, including Amazonas as "the biggest selva of the world", and noticed that the opening ceremony was to ask people, through television, to take care of the planet. The official daily of the Communist Party of Cuba, *Granma* (granma.cu), in the lead paragraph of its article reminded the environmental message of the ceremony: "Pobladores del mundo, salvemos el planeta" ("Inhabitants of the world, let's save the planet"). Also in the lead paragraph of the news article in the Portuguese newspaper *Diário de Notícias* (dn.pt) the importance of the environment was mentioned, though after recalling the arrival of the Portuguese to Brazil, that was presented at the opening ceremony too. Indeed, some nationalistic views were evident in some of the analysed articles. Nevertheless, while the Italian daily newspaper *Corriere della Sera* (corriere.it) offered a picture with the national flag (and no clear references to the environmental issues), in the Vatican newspaper *L'Osservatore Romano* (osservatoreromano.va) the news article entitled "Olimpiade di tutti" ("Olympics for everybody") focused more on the team of refugees that participated in the parade of athletes together with national teams during the opening ceremony. The environmental message was mentioned only in the last paragraph, despite the commitment of Pope Francis to the matter.

Also in other newspapers in the analysed articles only minor references to the environmental issues could be read, like in *The Daily Telegraph* (telegraph.co.uk) from the United Kingdom, *La Nación* (lanacion.com.ar) from Argentina or *The New York Times* (nytimes.com), which however observed "polluted waters" and noticed that "Petrobras, a major emitter of greenhouse gases, is mired in scandal following revelations that Brazil's leaders used the energy behemoth to fund political campaign". In the Swiss *Le Temps* (letemps.ch) a small part of the text was dedicated to the problem of climate change and "the forest of the athletes" created during the opening ceremony. In the Canadian newspaper *Le Devoir* (ledevoir.com) only one sentence, in the middle of the article, informed about allusions to biodiversity and climate change as dangerous for the planet. In *The Nation* (nationmultimedia.com) from Thailand it was mentioned only (in a short paragraph, third after the lead of the text) that "The show is built around the concepts of environmental protection, diversity and joy (...)". In the "official" English-language *China Daily* (chinadaily.com.cn) one could read a news story that was a chronological report of the opening ceremony, so some sentences in the middle of the text were dedicated to the environmental aspects of the show. However, the main photo, published under the headline of the article, presented a spectacular view of the fireworks at the Maracana stadium during the ceremony. A similar picture, but showing Maracana (with huge fireworks) from the outside, even more spectacularly, was published in the Brazilian newspaper, based in Rio de Janeiro, *O Globo* (oglobo.globo.com), also under the headline of a news article, where only some mentions of the environment could be found in the middle of the text reporting the ceremony. Also for the Peruvian *El Comercio* (elcomercio.pe) the fireworks at the Maracana stadium was the most important view of the show. The photo was placed under the headline of the news article that began with the notion that Brazil celebrated its "exuberant natural resources" and mentioned Amazonas and the "save the planet" message in one of the later paragraphs. In the Colombian newspaper *El Tiempo* (eltiempo.com) one could find the same scheme: the fireworks at the Maracana stadium as the main picture and one of the later paragraphs dedicated (not abundantly) to the "green" message from Brazil to the world.

Also in another newspaper some spectacular views from the Maracana stadium were published, though in some cases the fireworks were not only the most important image. Some photos with environmental symbols, present during the ceremony, were placed. In the Venezuelan *El Universal* (eluniversal.com) the first of a series of photos showed a big green pacifist symbol at the Maracana, though the text did not mention the environmental issues. Similarly in the Polish newspaper *Rzeczpospolita* (rp.pl), where a series of photos included big green Olympic rings, made of trees at the Maracana stadium, though without any mention of the environment in the news article. The French newspaper *Le Figaro* (lefigaro.fr) offered "The fifteen images of the ceremony that should not be missing": two images (the 8th and 11th) presented the environmental issues, with appropriate comments, and one of them showed green Olympic rings too. In the Belgian *Le Soir* (lesoir.be) one could see ten images of the ceremony, but none of them showed the environmental aspects of the show. Only one comment under one of the photos mentioned that the environment was among the themes of the ceremony. The Chilean newspaper *El Mercurio* (emol.com) presented a "podium" of the best photos of the ceremony: the Santos Dumont's airplane flying over Rio, fireworks at the Maracana stadium, and finally Indians with green lights, which was an element of the show reviving the history of Brazil, including the nature of Amazonas and the zone of Rio.

In the *Irish Independent* (independent.ie) a photo of the green pacific symbol at the Maracana stadium appeared, but also another green image was placed there: showing green elements of the sweatshirts of the athletes from the "green island" travelling by bus to the opening ceremony. A mention about "ecology" appeared only after a sentence about supermodel Gisele Bundchen, who "made a guest appearance" during the show (and her photos were displayed in different newspapers analysed here): "Celebrating themes of ecology, diversity and joy, the event welcomed 10,500 athletes from more than 200 countries around the world".

Conclusions

In the Preamble to Agenda 21, it is clear that the idea of sustainable development is global, and global action is necessary. Therefore, global promotion is needed to achieve the sustainable development goals. The role of environmental journalism which began to develop rapidly after the Earth Summit in Rio 1992 is very important. The media influence public opinion and attitudes, although politicians and other people should take action ("An Inconvenient Truth" is a very good example of a film that has changed the perception of climate change; will the activism of the teenage "eco-celebrity" Greta Thunberg match the effort of Al Gore or rather ridicule it?).

This chapter only addressed the perspective of top-down communication (from media to society), but in communication for development and social change, other types of communication should also be considered. However, a vision of global communication is necessary to conduct research on the global promotion of sustainable development. It is important to use big global media events for the promotion of ideas but also for research on global pluralism, taking into consideration that people live in about 200 countries on different continents (many scholars forget about it).

Undoubtedly, Summer Olympic Games are among the most global media events in the modern world (not only in the world of sport). The opening ceremony of the Rio 2016 Summer Olympic Games, full of environmental messages, images or allusions, was watched on TV (live or by retransmissions), on computer or mobile devices by millions of viewers around the world and this produced huge communication "energy". The environmental issues were presented to the global audience under the message "let's save the planet!". Media reports in newspapers (in print or online) were read by millions of people on all continents.

After analysing news articles from 30 important newspapers from different countries, it is possible to conclude that the global media coverage of this event could serve to promote environmental issues and, rather indirectly, the idea of sustainable development (of course, not in scientific terms). The environmental aspects were mentioned in most articles, but only in few of them were underlined or treated as a very important message of the ceremony. However, environmental issues were absent from most headlines. Can we say that this is a proof of the failure of communication for development and social change? No, but this is a suggestion that in different contexts some problems seem to be more important for journalists and the media (and their audiences) than the sustainable development goals that reach the future rather than the present.

Global ideas, including sustainable development, are transmitted through media in different ways, depending on various factors, so global pluralism has been noticed in this study. The Olympic Games, being global promotional "machines", not only promote sport and hosting cities/countries but also global ideas, and this is possible thanks to the global communication reality, which should allow us to achieve many of our common goals (however, not accepted by everyone, because of global pluralism, which is also a great value).

References

Agenda 21. UN SDG. Retrieved from https://sustainabledevelopment.un.org/content/documents/Agenda21.pdf

Al Jazeera. Rio+20: A Corporate Environment?, 24 June 2012. Retrieved from https://www.aljazeera.com/programmes/countingthecost/2012/06/2012622135910443825.html

Castells, M. (2009). *Communication Power.* New York: Oxford University Press.
Collins, C. (2013). Clear Cuts on Clearcutting. YouTube, Activist Videos and Narrative Strategies. In: L. Lester, B. Hutchins (Eds.), Environmental Conflict and the Media. New York: Peter Lang.
Cox, R. (2010). *Environmental Communication and the Public Sphere.* Los Angeles: SAGE Publications.
Cronon, W. (2008). Foreword: Silent Spring and the Birth of Modern Environmentalism. In T. R. Dunlap (Ed.), *DDT, Silent Spring, and the Rise of Environmentalism.* Seattle and London: University of Washington Press.
de Jong, W., Shaw, M., & Stammers, N. (2005). Introduction. In W. de Jong, M. Shaw, & N. Stammers (Eds.), *Global Activism, Global Media.* London: Pluto Press.
Eurobarometer 2017 Survey. Citizen Support for Climate Action. Retrieve from https://ec.europa.eu/clima/citizens/support_en
Goldblatt, D. (2016). *The Games. A Global History of the Olympics.* New York, London: W.W. Norton & Company.
Hamelink, C. J. (2015). *Global Communication.* London, Thousand Oaks, New Delhi, Singapore: SAGE Publications.
Hansen, A. (2010). *Environment, Media and Communication.* London and New York: Routledge.
Harman, G. (2015, April 24). Agenda 21: A Conspiracy Theory Puts Sustainability in the Crosshairs. *The Guardian.* Retrieved from https://www.theguardian.com/sustainable-business/2015/jun/24/agenda-21-conspiracy-theory-sustainability.
Kostadinov, K., & Thaker, J. (2013). Sustainable Development and Climate Change: Beyond the Rio + 20 Summit. In J. Servaes (Ed.), *Sustainable Development and Green Communication. African and Asian Perspectives.* London, New York: Palgrave Macmillan.
Larrain, J. (1989). *Theories of Development. Capitalism, Colonialism and Dependency.* Cambridge, Oxford, Malden: Polity Press.
Lester, L. (2010). *Media and Environment. Conflict, Politics and the News.* Cambridge, Malden: Polity Press.
Lockwood, A. (2013). Affecting Environments. Mobilizing Emotion and Twitter in the UK Save Our Forests Campaign. In L. Lester & B. Hutchins (Eds.), *Environmental Conflict and the Media.* New York: Peter Lang.
Manyozo, L. (2012). *Media, Communication and Development. Three Approaches.* Los Angeles, London, New Delhi, Singapore, Washington, DC: SAGE Publications.
McPhail, T. L. (2006). *Global Communication. Theories, Stakeholders, and Trends.* Malden, Oxford, Carlton: Blackwell Publishing.
McPhail, T. L. (2009). Introduction to Development Communication. In T. L. McPhail (Ed.), *Development Communication. Reframing the Role of the Media.* Malden, Oxford, Chichester: Blackwell Publishing Ltd.
Miller, S. W. (2007). *An Environmental History of Latin America.* New York: Cambridge University Press.
Nallu, P. (2012, June 23). Alternative Voices from Rio+20. Al Jazeera Website. Retrieved from https://www.aljazeera.com/indepth/features/2012/06/2012622175745190650.html
Neuzil, M. (2008). *The Environment and the Press. From Adventure Writing to Advocacy.* Evanston: Northwestern University Press.
Ociepka, B. (2016). Komunikowanie globalne—rewizja pojęcia. *Studia Medioznawcze,* 4(67), 11–23.

O'Hara, K., & Stevens, D. (2006). *Inequality.com. Power, Poverty and the Digital Divide.* Oxford: Oneworld Publications.
Painter, J. (2013). *Climate Change in the Media. Reporting Risk and Uncertainty.* London, New York: I.B. Tauris.
Parratt, S. (2006). *Medios de comunicación y medio ambiente.* Madrid: Editorial Fragua.
Peet, R., & Hartwick, E. (2015). *Theories of Development. Contentions, Arguments, Alternatives.* New York: The Guilford Press.
Quebral, N. (2002). *Reflections on Development Communication, 25 Years After.* Los Baños: UPLB College of Development Communication.
Rice, M. F. (2009). The Global Digital Divide. In T. L. McPhail (Ed.), *Development Communication. Reframing the Role of the Media.* Malden, Oxford, Chichester: Blackwell Publishing Ltd.
Romero, S., & Broder, J. M. (2012, June 23). Progress on the Sidelines as Rio Conference Ends. *The New York Times.* Retrieved from https://www.nytimes.com/2012/06/24/world/americas/rio20-conference-ends-with-some-progress-on-the-sidelines.html
Sajna, R. (2012). Planet Earth on the Eve of the Copenhagen Climate Conference 2009: A Study of Prestige Newspapers from Different Continents. *Observatorio Journal,* 6(2), 71–83. Retrieved from http://obs.obercom.pt/index.php/obs/article/view/367
Sajna, R. (2013). *Media w Hispanoameryce w perspektywie komunikowania globalnego.* Bydgoszcz: Wydawnictwo Uniwersytetu Kazimierza Wielkiego.
Sajna, R. (2016). Media i środowisko—stan i perspektywy badań w kontekście pluralizmu globalnego. In I. Biernacka-Ligięza & K. Fil (Eds.), *Człowiek—media—środowisko naturalne—ekologiczny wymiar komunikacji.* Toruń: Wydawnictwo Adam Marszałek.
Sajna, R. (2018). Branding Rio, Brazil and the Environment: A Global Media Coverage of the 2016 Summer Olympics Opening Ceremony. *Observatorio Journal,* 12(2), 47–60. Retrieved from http://obs.obercom.pt/index.php/obs/article/view/1179
Servaes, J. (2013). Introduction: Imperatives for a Sustainable Future. In J. Servaes (Ed.), *Sustainable Development and Green Communication. African and Asian Perspectives.* London, New York: Palgrave Macmillan.
Sparks, C. (2007). *Globalization, Development and the Mass Media.* London: SAGE Publications.
Takahashi, B., Edwards, G., Roberts, J. T., & Duan, R. (2015). Exploring the Use of Online Platforms for Climate Change Policy and Public Engagement by NGOs in Latin America. *Environmental Communication,* 9(2), 228–247.
TheConversation.com. How Much Do People Around the World Care about Climate Change? We Surveyed 80,000 People in 40 Countries to Find Out. Retrieved from https://theconversation.com/how-much-do-people-around-the-world-care-about-climate-change-we-surveyed-80-000-people-in-40-countries-to-find-out-140801
The Guardian. Rio+Earth Summit: Campaigners Decry Final Document. Retrieved from https://www.theguardian.com/environment/2012/jun/23/rio-20-earth-summit-document
The Guardian Archives. Earth Summit: Rio Opens with Plea for Proof of Global Brotherhood. Retrieved from https://www.theguardian.com/environment/2012/jun/14/archive-1992-rio-earth-summit-opens
UN SDG. Retrieved from https://sustainabledevelopment.un.org

Warschauer, M. (2004). *Technology and Social Inclusion. Rethinking the Digital Divide*. Cambridge, London: The MIT Press.
Winseck, D. R., & Pike, R. M. (2007). *Communication and Empire. Media, Markets, and Globalization, 1860–1930*. Durham, London: Duke University Press.

List of the Analysed Press Articles

A Gilded Olympics Begin with the Opening Ceremony in Gritty Rio. Retrieved August 5, 2016, from https://www.nytimes.com/2016/08/06/sports/olympics/summer-games-opening-ceremony-rio.html

Brazil Invokes History, Favelas in a Stunning Rio 2016 Opening Ceremony. Retrieved August 6, 2016, from http://www.hindustantimes.com/olympics/brazil-invokes-history-favelas-in-a-stunning-rio-2016-opening-ceremony/story-P9xUhtkP8UOdgV897KtNhO.html

Ceremonia otwarcia igrzysk. Retrieved August 6, 2016, from http://www.rp.pl/Rio-2016/160809468-Ceremonia-otwarcia-igrzysk.html#ap-1

Del homenaje a Santos Dumont a la historia de Brasil: El podio de las mejores fotos del inicio de los JJ.OO. Retrieved August 6, 2016, from http://www.emol.com/noticias/Deportes/2016/08/06/816042/Del-homenaje-a-Santos-Dumont-al-repaso-a-la-historia-de-Brasil-El-podio-de-las-mejores-fotos-de-la-inauguracion-de-los-JJOO.html

El pebetero olímpico ya está encendido, ¡que empiecen los Juegos!. Retrieved August 5, 2016, from http://www.eltiempo.com/deportes/otros-deportes/el-pebetero-olimpico-ya-esta-encendido-que-empiecen-los-juegos-49349

En marcha la fiesta olímpica de Río 2016. Retrieved August 5, 2016, from http://www.eluniversal.com/noticias/rio-2016/marcha-fiesta-olimpica-rio-2016_430491

Fiesta verdeamarelha en la ceremonia de inauguración de los Juegos Olímpicos. Retrieved August 5, 2016, from http://www.eluniverso.com/deportes/2016/08/05/nota/5726904/ceremonia-inauguracion-juegos-olimpicos-rio-2016-vivo

First Green, Now Gold: The Climate Changes in Rio. Retrieved August 6, 2016, from http://www.theage.com.au/sport/olympics/rio-2016/first-green-now-gold-the-climate-changes-in-rio-20160806-gqmhy8.html

Glittering Ceremony Launches Rio Games. Retrieved August 6, 2016, from https://guardian.ng/sport/olympics-glittering-ceremony-launches-rio-games/

Inauguración Río 2016: revive la espectacular ceremonia. Retrieved August 6, 2016, from http://elcomercio.pe/deporte-total/inauguracion-rio-2016-revive-espectacular-ceremonia-431729

Jogos do Rio abriram em grande. Agora têm a palavra os atletas. Retrieved August 6, 2016, from http://www.dn.pt/desporto/rio-2016/interior/siga-aqui-a-cerimonia-de-abertura-dos-jogos-olimpicos-5324217.html

Le stade de Maracanã vibre au rythme d'une cérémonie colorée. Retrieved August 6, 2016, from http://www.ledevoir.com/sports/actualites-sportives/477198/le-stade-maracana-vibre-au-rythme-d-une-ceremonie-coloree

Les dix imagesqu'il ne fallait pas louper de la cérémonie d'ouverture de JO 2016. Retrieved August 6, 2016, from http://plus.lesoir.be/53587/article/2016-08-06/les-dix-images-quil-ne-fallait-pas-louper-de-la-ceremonie-douverture-des-jo-2016

Les quinze images de la cérémonie qu'il ne fallait pas manquer. Retrieved August 6, 2016, from http://sport24.lefigaro.fr/le-scan-sport/2016/08/06/27001-20160806ARTFIG00008-les-quinze-images-de-la-ceremonie-qu-il-ne-fallait-pas-manquer.php

Música, arte y ecologismo en inauguración de Juegos. Retrieved August 5, 2016, from http://www.abc.com.py/internacionales/musica-arte-y-ecologismo-en-inauguracion-de-rio-2016-1505952.html

Noche carioca para una fiesta mundial. Retrieved August 5, 2016, from http://www.granma.cu/deportes/2016-08-05/noche-carioca-para-una-fiesta-mundial-fotos

Olimpiade di tutti. Retrieved August 6, 2016, from http://www.osservatoreromano.va/it/news/olimpiade-di-tutti

Olimpiadi di Rio 2016, via ai Giochi Samba e colori, la grande festa «Non c'è posto migliore del Brasile». Retrieved August 6, 2016, from http://www.corriere.it/sport/olimpiadi-2016-rio/notizie/olimpiadi-rio-2016-via-giochi-samba-colori-grande-festa-foto-non-c-posto-migliore-brasile-60f8b3a6-5b95-11e6-bfed-33aa6b5e1635.shtml?refresh_ce-cp

Río 2016: "El mejor lugar del mundo es aquí y ahora", ese himno brasileño de Gilberto Gil que se hizo realidad en el Maracaná. Retrieved August 6, 2016, from http://www.lanacion.com.ar/1925460-rio-2016-el-mejor-lugar-del-mundo-es-aqui-y-ahora-ese-himno-brasileno-de-gilberto-gil-que-se-hizo-realidad-en-el-maracana

Rio celebra diversidade e passa mensagem de esperança na abertura dos Jogos na Maracanã. Retrieved August 6, 2016, from https://oglobo.globo.com/esportes/rio-celebra-diversidade-passa-mensagem-de-esperanca-na-abertura-dos-jogos-no-maracana-19866473

Río de Janeiro acoge al mundo. Retrieved August 6, 2016, from http://www.eluniversal.com.mx/articulo/deportes/mas-deportes/2016/08/6/rio-de-janeiro-acoge-al-mundo

Rio Kicks Off Olympic Opening Ceremony. Retrieved August 6, 2016, from http://www.nationmultimedia.com/news/sports/30292293

Rio Leads the World in Glitzy Samba Party at Gala Olympic Parade. Retrieved August 6, 2016, from http://www.independent.ie/sport/rio-2016-olympics/rio-leads-the-world-in-glitzy-samba-party-at-gala-olympic-parade-34943322.html

Rio Olympics Open with Ceremony Focused on Environment. Retrieved August 6, 2016, from http://www.japantimes.co.jp/sports/2016/08/06/olympics/summer-olympics/rio-olympics-open-ceremony-focused-environment/

Rio Olympics 2016 Opening Ceremony Kicks Off with a Vibrant Bang—and Unfortunate Reminders of Troubled Backdrop to the Games. Retrieved August 6, 2016, from http://www.telegraph.co.uk/olympics/2016/08/05/olympics-opening-ceremony-for-rio-2016-live/

Rio Olympics Opening Ceremony Highlights Brazil, Environment. Retrieved August 5, 2016, from http://english.ahram.org.eg/NewsRio/236984.aspx

Rio Opens Olympics with Colors, Curves and Coolness. Retrieved August 6, 2016, from http://www.chinadaily.com.cn/sports/2016rioolympics/2016-08/06/content_26367013.htm

Rio ouvre les Jeux, sans cérémonie. Retrieved August 6, 2016, from https://www.letemps.ch/sport/2016/08/06/rio-ouvre-jeux-ceremonie

Rio Welcomes World with Sultry Music, Plea for Conservation. Retrieved August 6, 2016, from http://www.thejakartapost.com/news/2016/08/06/rio-welcomes-world-with-sultry-music-plea-for-conservation.html

Una ceremonia sostenible entre la selva de atletas. Retrieved August 6, 2016, from http://www.elmundo.es/deportes/2016/08/06/57a5397eca4741a6118b45f3.html

CHAPTER 22

A Comparative Analysis of American and Chinese News Media Coverage of Climate Change Issues over the Period 2007–2015

Won Y. Jang, Edward Frederick, Eric Jamelske, Wontae Lee, and Youngju Kim

In the late 1970s, the global community grew to understand the need to balance a nation's desire for economic growth and social progress with the need to protect the environment and show good stewardship of the world's resources (Servaes, Polk, Shi, Reilly, & Yakupitijage, 2012). Since that time, the international community has championed the concept of Sustainable Development as the key to addressing critical issues such as hunger, poverty, economic growth, and the environment (Yacoumis, 2018). The 1987 Brundtland Commission Report defines Sustainable Development as "development that meets the needs of the present without compromising the ability of future generations to meet their own needs" (WCED, 1987 Chapter 2, para. 1). In 2015, the United

---

W. Y. Jang (✉) • E. Jamelske
University of Wisconsin, Eau Claire, WI, USA
e-mail: jangwy@uwec.edu

E. Frederick
University of Wisconsin-Whitewater, Whitewater, WI, USA

W. Lee
Korea Information Society Development Institute, Jincheon, South Korea

Y. Kim
Korea Press Foundation, Seoul, South Korea

© The Author(s), under exclusive license to Springer Nature Switzerland AG 2021
M. J. Yusha'u, J. Servaes (eds.), *The Palgrave Handbook of International Communication and Sustainable Development*,
https://doi.org/10.1007/978-3-030-69770-9_22

Nations Member States adopted the 2030 Agenda for Sustainable Development. It provides a plan for peace and prosperity for the planet. The plan identifies 17 Sustainable Development Goals (SDGs), one of which is to "take urgent action to combat Climate Change and its impacts" (see: UN Website Sustainable Development Goals, 2020).

As the public discourse over Sustainable Development proceeds, one aspect of the issue, Climate Change, has captured a significant portion of the media's attention (Shehata & Hopmann, 2012). Climate Change has moved from being just a question for the scientific community to debate to a major political issue requiring decisive actions (Giddens, 2009). With its growing position in public discourse, Climate Change has led to intense debates and raised questions with regard to the role of the news media in the development of this issue (Antilla, 2005; Boyce & Lewis, 2009; Boykoff & Boykoff, 2004). The nature of news reporting on Climate Change has wide-ranging implications for public perceptions and opinions about the issue (Entman, 2004; Feldman, Maibach, Roser-Renouf, & Leiserowitz, 2012; Feldman, Myers, Hmielowski, & Leiserowitz, 2014; McCombs, 2004; Scheufele, 1999).

We adopted the Media Propaganda Model and the work of discourse scholars to carry out a cross-national comparison of international news agencies' coverage of Climate Change. Public discourse scholars and mass media researchers contend that the news media play an essential role in the public discussion of contentious public issues such as Sustainable Development and the closely connected issue of Climate Change (Entman, 2004; Gamson & Modigliani, 1989; Iyengar, 1991; McCombs, 2004; Shehata & Hopmann, 2012). News coverage constructs the definition of an issue by shaping and disseminating reports about public events to audience members (Shoemaker, Eichholz, Kim, & Wrigley, 2001).

Because of the global causes and consequences of Climate Change, cooperation between the U.S. and China is essential in implementing successful bilateral and global mitigation policies. Thus, a better understanding of Chinese and American views via their news coverage on domestic and international Climate Change policies is of great interest. We examined the framing of Climate Change by international news agencies based in China and the U.S. and explored whether the agencies' framing of the issue was driven by their respective national socio-political ideologies by looking for differences in their framing of the issue. To that end, we employed Herman and Chomsky's (1988) Media Propaganda Model to argue that the differing hegemonic influences by the two nations' governments and power structures will influence their respective media systems differently and result in differing uses of frames by the two news agencies.

Divergent Positions on Climate Change in the Context of Sustainable Development

The global clash between the hegemonies of the U.S. and China over Sustainable Development is evident in the international efforts to address Climate Change. The relationship has been described as a conflict of two powerful players both of which have great influence over the outcome of the debate (Koehn, 2004). Economic development is strongly linked to energy consumption, and, therefore strongly connected to the issue of Greenhouse Gas (GHG) emissions and Climate Change. Stimulating sustainable economic development, particularly in the poorest countries of the world, requires that Climate Change issues be addressed. Hence, the international agreements to address Climate Change will have direct bearing on Sustainable Development around the globe.

The United Nations Framework Convention on Climate Change (UNFCCC) has instituted a series of international Climate Change negotiations, the Conference of Parties (COP) meetings. The COP is attempting to negotiate international climate policies and assess progress in dealing with Climate Change. The first major outcome of the COP meetings was the Kyoto Protocol. It established legally binding obligations to reduce GHG emissions for developed countries (Annex I parties), but did not call for reductions by developing countries (non-Annex 1 parties). The Kyoto Protocol has largely failed to meet global GHG reduction goals, in part because of the differential treatment of developed and developing nations. The U.S. refused to ratify the treaty because China, as a developing economy, was not asked to reduce GHG emissions under the Kyoto Protocol (Gallagher & Xuan, 2018).

While the U.S. and China both agreed to reduce emissions of GHG for the 2015 UNFCCC in Paris, the clash of the two major superpowers was well illustrated by the outcome of the 2019 COP in Madrid. Most countries were unable to agree on the key initiatives in the establishment of a rule book for the Paris Accord and for designing a global carbon market, in part because of the failure of opposing factions led by the U.S. and China. The attendees agreed only to sign pledges to enhance the Paris emissions reduction targets (Keating, 2019). China and the leading developing economies formed the Basics and called on the U.S. and other wealthier countries to provide more funding to help them cope with the Climate Change crisis (Lau, 2019).

It is not surprising to find different approaches, conflicts, and frictions over the issues of Sustainable Development and Climate Change between the two superpowers. Allison (2017) discussed the hegemonic struggle between the U.S. and China, arguing that the tension between these two countries is inevitable. Allison insisted that China and the U.S. are caught in Thucydides's Trap. China started challenging America's role as a world leader, and the U.S. began to fear losing its pre-eminent position around the world. Allison concluded that the competition between China and the U.S. will result in a cataclysmic war unless the two countries are willing to take difficult steps to avoid it.

One of the arenas in which the two states carry out their competition is in the international news media. Both world powers fight to influence news coverage that encourages advantageous interpretations of issues. We employ Herman and Chomsky's (1988) Media Propaganda Model to explore the influence of the two nations' hegemony on their respective media systems (see

Good, 2008). It seeks to determine whether the media systems tend to adopt their home countries' preferred approach to framing Climate Change.

News as Propaganda

News media coverage is a major influence on the public's perception of the threats posed by Climate Change (Corbett & Durfee, 2004; Lacy, Rife, & Varouhakis, 2007) and the public's primary source for information about sustainability issues in general (Ziemann, 2011). Since the issue of Climate Change emerged three decades ago, mass communication researchers have been studying journalists' presentations of the issue in the U.S. and other countries' media systems. If one applies an Anglo-American Model of journalism (Schudson, 2001) to an analysis of this coverage, one would expect to find an objective and accurate portrayal of the realities of Climate Change and related issues, including Sustainable Development. The model emphasizes the importance of journalists being objective observers who are detached and neutral in their reporting (Schudson, 2001). Under this model, news media are viewed as free from influence from political powers, as watchdogs over the political powers, as objective, and as adhering to professional standards that reinforce the independence of journalism (Mancini, 2005).

However, many scholars argued that the demands of news work, the conventions of journalism, profit motives, and the realities of the news business result in media that do not function as described by the Anglo-American Model (Dimaggio, 2010; Herman & Chomsky, 1988; Iyengar, 1991). Instead, many scholars have argued that the mainstream media in the U.S. participates actively in facilitating the production and reproduction of hegemony, and, as a result, the news reflects and legitimizes dominant discourses, ideologies, and political and business power relations (Althusser, 1971; Block, 2013). Feldman et al. (2012, 2014) examined the relationship between different types of media use and audiences' beliefs about Climate Change issues and policies. They argued that conservative media audiences were less likely than non-conservative media audiences to accept the consensus of the scientific community about Climate Change and to support Climate Change policies (see also Krosnick & MacInnis, 2010).

Herman and Chomsky's (1988) Propaganda Model offers an alternative view of news media that explains why coverage does not match the expectations of the Anglo-American Model for journalism. They identified five factors that filter information as it passes through the media to their audiences and that shape news coverage that aligns with the interests of political and economic elites. The first two filters result from the fact that the vast majority of the U.S. media are rooted in the market system. They pointed out that the American media are mostly for-profit enterprises owned by a few wealthy individuals or corporations. The second filter is that news media organizations derive their incomes from advertising. Herman and Chomsky argued that the advertisers are largely for-profit businesses and that each of these enterprises wants its advertisements "to appear in a supportive selling environment" (p 102). The third filter is the media's reliance on government and business firms as sources. They indicated that the media do so for reasons of efficiency and political expediency. The result, they argued, is too much solidarity between the media, government interests, and the powerful elite business leaders. As a result, interpretations of events that are functional for the government and the powerful tend to dominate news discourse (p. 23). The fourth filter is flak, or the punishment that government and large corporations can bring to bear on the media when the media report negative coverage. The final filter is the influence of the dominant ideology in a socio-political system.

The Propaganda Model has not been without its critics (see Klaehn, 2003, 2009). One of the most important criticisms that has been levelled is aimed at the fact that the model focused on anti-communism as the dominant ideology in the U.S. and, critics argued, was, therefore, limited in scope and application. Critics pointed out that the original conceptualization of this filter focused on the strong anti-communist bent of the ideology of its time. Klaehn (2009) argued that the concept is still quite useful because, in broader terms, it may be used to understand the current dominant ideology's influence on the media's coverage of the merits of capitalism and of the deregulation of private enterprise, as well as its bias against unions. Klaehn's defence demonstrated the value of the Propaganda Model (Klaehn, 2003). At its core it argues that because mass media are businesses as well as socio-political institutions, the media serve the economic, social, and political interests of the elite. Rather than the normative watchdog role for the media, Herman and Chomsky (1988) contend that the media serve the needs and interests of the elite who benefit from policies that are consistent with neo-liberal economic interests.

FRAME AS MECHANISMS OF HEGEMONY

The idea that news coverage frames issues explains, in part, how hegemonic influences and dominant ideologies become incorporated in media reports (Entman, 1993, 2008; Gamson, 1989; Goffman, 1974; Iyengar, 1991). The force of hegemonic ideologies, the values of a profit-driven media, and the professional practices and conventions of journalism all influence the way the news media frame issues (Iyengar, 1991). Gitlin (1980) argued that the strong influence of the powerful elite results from the news media's willingness to allow those in power to define society's "ideological space" (p. 10). Becker (1984) argued that the dominant ideology in a country is deeply embedded within a culture and is a main source of news framing. Many studies have empirically demonstrated that a country's dominant ideology influences how journalists frame issues and events (e.g. Akhavan-Majid & Ramaprasad, 1998, 2000; Jang, 2013; Jang, Hong, & Frederick, 2015; Massey, 2000; Verschueren, 1985).

Discourse scholars argued that much of what audiences learn about public issues stems from how events are framed in the news (Entman, 1993; Han,

2007; Hawdon, Agnich, & Ryan, 2014; Holt & Major, 2010; Li & Liu, 2010; Massey, 2000; Semetko, & Valkenburg, 2000; McGinty, Webster, Jarlenski, & Barry, 2014). News frames are "persistent patterns of cognition, interpretation, and presentation, selection, emphasis, and exclusion, by which symbol-handlers routinely organize discourse, whether verbal or visual" (Gitlin, 1980, p. 7). Tucker (1998) described frames as "familiar and highly ritualized symbolic structures" that "organize the content and serve to close off specific pathways of meaning while promoting others" (p. 143). Other discourse scholars have defined the frame as the central organizing idea to the portrayal of an issue (Gamson & Modigliani, 1989). The news frame is viewed as the smallest single unit of meaning in a news report's portrayal of an issue; it sums up what an issue is about.

Additionally, some discourse scholars have described the news media as arenas of public debate in which those who hold stakes in controversial issues fight to control the language and symbols used to communicate about those issues (Gamson & Modigliani, 1989). The interpretation of an issue is organized around the frames that the news media use (Semetko & Valkenburg, 2000). An issue frame serves several functions. One is to organize information into a coherent whole interpretation (Entman, 1994). Another function that frames perform is "to select some aspects of a perceived reality and make them salient … to promote a particular problem definition, causal interpretation, [and/or] moral evaluation" (Entman, 1993, p. 52).

The interpretations that succeed in dominating the news define the meaning of the issue. Therefore, the news frame shapes how audiences define an issue, attribute causes, and evaluate solutions (Entman, 1993, 2008; Gamson & Lasch, 1983; Gamson & Modigliani, 1989; Iyengar, 1990, 1996; Pan & Kosicki, 1993; Scheufele, 2006). An issue's frame will not absolutely determine an audience member's interpretation or understanding of an issue, but it will set the range of likely interpretations available to the audience member (Greenberg & Knight, 2004), often in ways that support dominant ideologies.

The media's issue frames are constructed during the news reporting process. Mass media scholars argue that when journalists prepare news stories, they engage in a process in which they actively construct reality (Shoemaker et al., 2001). The reporters' choices as to which information to include and which terms and wordings to use help construct the interpretation of the issue that is presented to the audience. The way language, images, and other symbols are used by journalists shapes and defines the meaning of a presented issue (Entman, 1993; Gamson & Modigliani, 1989).

It, however, is not the journalists' work alone that determines the outcome of the news production process. Jowett and O'Donnell (1992) contend that governments use their propaganda capabilities to engage in the debates within these symbolic arenas. Several studies have shown that government propaganda campaigns have influenced the media and have encouraged them to develop reporting that is consistent with the state's dominant ideology and national interests on international issues (Brewer, 2006; Herman & Chomsky, 1988; Jang, 2013; Jang et al., 2015; Lee & Yang, 1996).

In Western nations, framing is a reflective mechanism of ideological influences (Nohrstedt, Kaitatzi-Whitlock, Ottosen, & Riegert, 2000; Snow & Taylor, 2006). News media essentially determine "what issues will be covered and whose voices will be heard" (Giffard & Leuven, 2008, p. 23). Gamson and Modigliani (1989) argued that when an issue first appears in coverage, the news media will apply a variety of frames. However, over time, the frames that resonate most with the dominant ideologies in the culture persevere and end up dominating coverage (Jang, 2013). One reason might be that governments and large corporate entities pursue sophisticated public relations campaigns that help foster their frames for issues (Gamson & Lasch, 1983).

Over the years, in most communist systems, frames that were consistent with the dominant ideology tended to dominate news reporting because, in those systems, the news media has existed to serve the political needs of the ruling political party and state government (Gunaratne & Kim, 2000; Jang, 2013; Jang et al., 2015; Wang, 1991, 1995; Youm, 1991). Jang (2013) found a link between news framing in communist systems' media and the dominant ideology promoted by these states. Jang et al. (2015) found that the Chinese news agency, in reporting on the Six-Party Talks, used frames supportive of national interests. Likewise, Chang and Lin (2014) showed how China used overseas advertising and public relations campaigns in an attempt to manage its image and foster positive international relationships. Simmons (2014) found a similar link in Russia, which is not currently a communist system, but a nation in which many of the vestiges of the past communist system still influence politics. He found that Russian leadership used diplomacy to show a more positive face to the world.

The News Media's Framing of Climate Change

Many mass media scholars have tested the Propaganda Model's assertion that hegemonic influences affect coverage of Sustainable Development and Climate Change.

Yacoumis (2018) carried out a critical analysis of eight Australian newspapers' coverage of Sustainable Development from 2004 to 2013 and concluded that those discourses perpetuated the status quo. Antilla (2005) showed that U.S. news stories tended to frame Climate Change with a focus on controversy, scepticism, and uncertainty (see Zehr, 2009). Carvalho (2005) argued that such framing upholds dominant neo-liberal, free-market capitalist ideologies.

In addition, Foxwell-Norton and Konkes (2019) studied Australian media's framing of efforts to preserve the Great Barrier Reef from the harmful effects of Climate Change. They found that framing switched from a positive "protection" frame to an alternative frame that was consistent with political and industrial interests. Foust and O'Shannon Murphy (2009) used a critical rhetorical analysis to explore U.S. elite media and popular press reporting on Climate

Change. The pair examined the media's use of an "apocalyptic" frame. They found that the media used apocalyptic rhetoric that emphasized a catastrophic end-point that was more or less beyond human agency. Weathers and Kendall (2016) carried out a content analysis of 270 news stories about Climate Change from five U.S. newspapers. Their results showed that the number of articles declined while emphasis on a public health frame for Climate Change increased. They attributed the increase to the standardization and legitimation of the public health frame.

A study of national U.S. newspapers examined a decade of news coverage about Climate Change (Trumbo, 1996). The researchers found that frames emphasizing problems and causes tended to be associated with using scientists as sources, while frames emphasizing judgments and remedies were more associated with political and special interest sources.

Gilley (2012) explained China's response to the Climate Change issue using a theory of Authoritarian Environmentalism. According to this theory, the role of the central government is most important in framing an issue and citizens' perspectives are not important. Adelekan (2009) analysed five years of coverage of Sustainable Development and Climate Change by two of Nigeria's largest newspapers. The researcher found that even though energy issues dominated coverage, Climate Change received little attention. Adelekan points out that the focus on energy issues was supportive of the developing nation's efforts to grow its economy.

Many scholars have undertaken cross-national studies that demonstrate news framing differs across nations' news media systems, supporting the News Propaganda Model's assertion that a region's dominant hegemony will affect framing.

Good (2008) undertook a critical comparative analysis of U.S., Canadian, and international newspapers' framing of the Climate Change issue. Good found that U.S. media tended to avoid this important issue and U.S., Canadian, and international newspapers were all hesitant to use frames that tied the issue to either severe weather changes or oil consumption. Good argued that these frames demonstrated the influence of the powerful elite interests of the energy sectors and the respective governments of the countries in which these media operate.

Brossard, Shanahan, and McComas (2004) used a quantitative content analysis to assess French and U.S. newspapers' framing of the Climate Change issue. They found that the U.S. newspaper emphasized negative consequences of Climate Change more than its French counterpart. They concluded that differences in the two countries' journalism cultures, which arguably reflect their respective nation's dominant ideology, led to the framing differences.

Broadbent et al. (2013) examined the impact the United Nations' efforts to encourage a more shared understanding of Climate Change (including its causes and solutions) in China, India, Japan, South Korea, and Taiwan. They found that the media from the different countries framed the issue differently and concluded the differences were due to divergent domestic factors operating within each country.

Xie (2015) examined news reporting about Climate Change in both U.S. and Chinese newspapers. The results showed that the two countries' newspapers at times used different frames to present the issue, but at other times used similar frames. Xie concluded that each country's socio-political concerns affected how the media framed the issue. Painter and Ashe (2012) examined the inclusion of scepticism about Climate Change in news coverage from the U.S., China, and four other countries. They found that news reporting of scepticism is mostly limited to developed countries, such as the U.S. and the U.K., where it matched the perspective of conservative political leadership.

Although these studies show at least some support for the arguments of the News Propaganda Model, other studies that have undertaken national comparisons of the media's framing of Climate Change failed to find differences, as the model would predict (Howard-Williams, 2009; Shehata & Hopmann, 2012).

Research Questions

Past research has shown that the amount of news coverage is an important measure of media attention (Brossard et al., 2004; Carvalho, 2005; Herman & Chomsky, 1988). According to the Media Propaganda Model, the volume of media coverage will be a reflection of the dominant power structure's preference for whether or not an issue should be covered. If an issue is inconvenient, hegemonic influences would work against frequent coverage. We compared the framing by an international news agency headquartered in China, Xinhua News Agency, with one in the U.S., the Associate Press (AP), to determine whether these news agencies used frames consistent with their respective country's dominant ideologies. Therefore, we pose the following research question:

R1: How does the volume of Climate Change coverage differ between international news media organizations?

The Media Propaganda Model would predict that the two news agencies will frame Climate Change in manners consistent with their respective home political system's dominant ideology. To assess the frames present in the two news agencies' reporting about Climate Change, we adopted a commonly used methodology that determines the framing of an issue by identifying the recurring patterns of common themes present in the news texts (see, e.g., Altheide, 2009; Brossard et al., 2004; Lynn & Williams, 2018; Lawhon & Makina, 2017; Mix, 2009). We pose the following research question as a result:

R2: Will international news media organizations based in different ideological political systems (China and the U.S.) use different frames or themes to cover Climate Change?

Framing is closely linked with the types of sources used in news stories (Trumbo, 1996). Therefore, we also examined the diversity of sources presented as a means of assessing whether coverage offered alternate voices to those of the government and elites (Brossard et al., 2004). In that light, we address the following two research questions:

R3: Are there differences with respect to information source use patterns between international news media organizations?

R4: Does one international news organization's coverage include sources with a wider spectrum of viewpoints on Climate Change than the other organization?

We also determined whether stories were localized as another approach to examining diversity. To judge whether stories were more geographically diverse and provided more localized perspectives, the geographic regions from which reports were filed were identified. The results served as an important indicator as to which perspectives were made part of public discourse (Cohen et al., 2008). We determined whether a variety of regional perspectives were represented (Giffard & Leuven, p. 7). Thus, we ask the following research question:

R5: Is there a difference in the coverage between international news media organizations with respect to how frequently Climate Change stories mention different geographic regions?

In addition, we assessed whether reports provided mobilizing risk information to readers. Mobilizing scholars proposed that news media framing can either legitimize or delegitimize protest movements and their efforts (Ashley & Olson, 1998; Boykoff, 2006; Brasted, 2005; Lynn & Williams, 2018). Media reports, therefore, can play an important role in providing information and facilitating citizen's political participation (e.g. Benford & Snow, 2000; Snow & Benford, 1992). Consequently, the following research question arises:

R6: Is there a difference in coverage between international news media organizations with respect to how frequently Climate Change stories include Personal Mobilizing Information?

Method

To answer these six research questions, we used a quantitative content analysis that identified key themes in coverage (the patterns of those themes reveal the framing of the issue), the amount of coverage, the sources cited in reports, and types of coverage in the news on Climate Change. Content analysis has been a frequently used methodology to explore media reporting on Climate Change (Broadbent et al., 2013; Brossard et al., 2004; Good, 2008; McComas & Shanahan, 1999; Takahashi, 2011; Trumbo, 1996; Ungar, 2000).

Sample

International news agencies are elite media and prominent sources of news about global issues. They set the agenda for other news organizations (Gandy, 1982). They, in particular, have the potential to determine public knowledge and to have strong influences on the global community's perceptions of and attitudes towards environmental issues. We analysed samples of Climate Change media coverage from the Associated Press (AP) in the U.S. and Xinhua News Agency in China. It is also important to point out that the U.S. has long enjoyed democracy and political freedom, while China has a strong authoritarian communist system where most news is controlled and censored by the Communist Party and the government. Recently, the Chinese media have been implementing more flexible and pragmatic strategies to deal with international issues (Jang et al., 2015).

The AP was selected for the study because it is an American independent Western news organization headquartered in New York City. AP often serves as the primary source of foreign news coverage for other news organizations and independent journalists around the world. The Xinhua News Agency was selected because it is China's largest state news agency. It is headquartered in Beijing, and it often serves as the dominant news organization of global news coverage for the domestic and global news services for Chinese and non-Chinese media outlets. The Xinhua News Agency is the mouthpiece of the Chinese Communist Party and serves the political and ideological needs of the Chinese government as the communists' propaganda machine (Hong, 2011).

We sampled stories that were produced by these two news agencies between 2007 and 2015. This period is important because in 2007, the Intergovernmental Panel on Climate Change (IPCC) issued its path-breaking Fourth Annual Report and received the Nobel Peace Prize (Good, 2008), and the first Commitment Period of the Kyoto Protocol was between 2008 and 2012 (Broadbent et al., 2013). Additionally, the 2015 Paris Climate Conference achieved a legally binding and universal agreement on an ambitious global action plan to combat global Climate Change.

Both of the news agencies selected for this analysis are available online through services such as Nexis Uni (formerly known as LexisNexis). The population of interest for this study was all of the news stories primarily dealing with Climate Change issues that were published from 2007 to 2015. The sample was selected from nine time periods that coincided with major international Climate Change summits, including ones organized by the UNFCCC COP. These summits can be regarded as triggering events which generated considerable media stories and attention. Thus, the sample includes all articles containing the words Climate Change, global warming, greenhouse gas, greenhouse effect, or CO_2. These dates were selected to include news reports appearing a few days before and a few days after specific Climate Talks held through the UNFCCC COP. We covered the time period beginning with the

2007 UNFCCC, COP13 held in Bali, Indonesia through the 2015 UNFCCC, COP21 held in Paris. The unit of analysis was the individual articles. A total of 1446 articles were analysed: (1) Xinhua (N = 815, 56.4%) and (2) AP (631, 43.6%).

Coding Instrument

We used the deductive approach (Semetko & Valkenburg, 2000). The coding instrument was developed based on validated approaches used by several scholars (de Beer & Merrill, 2009; Brossard et al., 2004; Cohen et al., 2008; Giffard & Leuven, 2008; McComas & Shanahan, 1999).

We developed a coding scheme to measure the presence of seven frames identified in previous studies of themes of environmental issues: (1) New Evidence or Research Presented; (2) Scientific Background; (3) Consequences; (4) Economics; (5) Domestic Politics; (6) International Relations; and (7) Current Weather (Brossard et al., 2004; McComas & Shanahan, 1999).

The New Evidence or Research Presented frame was considered to be present when the story included some previously unreported scientific data about Climate Change, such as an announcement of a new government study, a new scientific report, or a new environmental group report. The Scientific Background frame was considered present when a story referred to the general scientific and/or technological background of Climate Change, such as a description of a previous study. Another frame was the Consequences frame. This frame was considered present when a statement about the environment, social, or health consequences of Climate Change appeared. This frame did not include statements about the consequences for humans. The Economic frame was indicated when the articles included statements about the costs of the remedy for or solutions to Climate Change. Also, mentions of financial contributions by governments to fight Climate Change were coded under the Economic frame. Two political frames were identified. The Domestic Politics frame was indicated by passages with statements about the debate over environmental policy and mentions of legislation or regulations. If articles contained references to political speeches or campaigns, they were also coded as representing the Domestic Politics frame. The International Relations frame was exhibited by mentions of summits, treaties, or disputes between nations over Climate Change policy. Mentions of U.N.-sponsored research about Climate Change were also coded as representing the International Relations frame. Finally, the Current Weather frame was coded when statements about meteorological patterns, such as abnormal weather, severe storms, drought, heat waves, or floods, were present. Consistent with previous coding schemes (Brossard et al., 2004, p. 367), all stories were examined for the presence of each of the seven respective frames. If a frame was not present, the story receives a "0" or "not present" for that frame. If the frame appeared in any part of the text excluding the lead paragraph, the story received a "1" or "present" for the frame. If the frame was the main focus of the story and appeared in the first paragraph, the story was coded with a "2" or "outstanding focus, or appearing in the lead".

We also coded coverage for an eighth frame, the Personal Behavioural Mobilization frame developed and tested by Cohen et al. (2008). Coders identified whether or not Climate Change stories explicitly described actions readers could take to reduce their own environmental impact or change their behaviour related to Climate Change. Stories were coded for the presence or absence of Personal Behavioural Mobilization information with "0" if such information was absent or a "1" if it was present.

We also coded the sources cited in each news story (Trumbo, 1996). Consistent with Brossard et al. (2004), articles were coded for the presence of the following sources: (1) academic/university professor, researcher, or scientist; (2) resident/citizen "on the street" (i.e., non-expert interview); (3) business/industry group; (4) economists; (5) unnamed experts, celebrity, or officials; (6) unaffiliated or independent research group; (7) governmental sources; and (8) environmental groups. If a source was present at least once in a story, it was coded, with a "1". If a source was not present at least once, it was coded with a "0" for that source. To examine and evaluate sources with a wider spectrum of viewpoints on Climate Change in each news story, a variable "Viewpoints" (minimum = 0, maximum = 7) was created by adding together the number of sources mentioned in an article (Brossard et al., 2004, pp. 367–368).

Coders also evaluated which geographic regions were mentioned in news stories. We adopted a typology of regions used by de Beer and Merrill (2009) in their work. The pair divided the globe into eight major regions: (1) Eastern Europe, Eurasia, the former Yugoslavia and the Balkan States, and Russia; (2) The Middle East and North Africa; (3) Sub-Saharan Africa; (4) Asia and the Pacific region; (5) Latin America and the Caribbean; (6) Western Europe; (7) North America; and (8) Australasia. According to Giffard and Leuven (2008), the geographic regions from which news stories are covered can be an important factor in what perspectives are made part of public discourse (p. 7).

Intercoder Reliability

Four undergraduate student coders with strong academic records read the sample of news stories and indicated which of the themes best represented the central organizing idea of the story (see: Gamson, 1989). Each news story received multiple coding for all frames. That is, if more than one frame appeared in a news story, each one was coded.

Intercoder reliability was assessed by having the coders independently analyse a set of the same news stories (approximately 10% of the sample). Intercoder disagreements were resolved through discussion between independent coders. Intercoder reliability was near or over 90%. Neuendorf (2002) contends that percent agreement is particularly appropriate means for checking coder reliability for nominal-level variables and one of the most popular coefficients used by mass communication researchers. For this study, intercoder reliability across categories also was calculated using Cohen's kappa (Neuendorf, 2002). The statistical result was 0.87. The researchers for this study deemed the analyses as having yielded sufficient intercoder reliability scores.

Results

Research question 1 asked how many Climate Change stories were published. Table 22.1 shows that AP published 631 stories from the sample (43.6% of the total stories collected) and Xinhua published 815 stories from the sample (56.4% of the total stories collected), suggesting that the Chinese media paid more attention to this issue.

Table 22.1 also shows the overall trend in each news agency's coverage. It shows that Climate Change coverage fluctuated over the period of time covered. Xinhua's coverage fluctuated much more than AP's coverage. Climate Change stories appeared more often in AP during 2013–2015. Climate Change stories were most common in 2007 (91.2% in Xinhua vs. 8.8% in AP) and 2010 (66.5% in Xinhua vs. 33.5% in AP) because China and Asian countries produced more news about Climate Change issues (Broadbent et al., 2013). The Chinese government took an active role in international environmental negotiations after the Kyoto Protocol at the Copenhagen Summit in 2009 and the Mexico Summit in 2010 (Broadbent et al., 2013). After the Copenhagen COP15 meeting, a fourth round of talks were held in Tianjin, China, during 2010. The U.S. and China clashed in the Tianjin talks. While it boosted coverage about this issue in China, U.S. and international expectations for the COP16 conference were reduced because of the non-binding Copenhagen Accord in 2009. Both Chinese and U.S. expectations for a future COP conference and climate summit were reduced in 2011 and 2012. The Warsaw Conference in 2013 concluded successfully. The parties adopted key decisions at this conference, including decisions on advancing further the Durban Platform (a new protocol which was finally adopted officially during the 2015

Table 22.1 Number and percentage of stories by agency type and year

Year	All stories N (1446)	AP N (631, 43.6%)		Xinhua N (815, 56.4%)	
2007	136	12	8.8	124	91.2
2008	90	43	47.8	47	52.2
2009	100	50	50	50	50
2010	170	57	33.5	113	66.5
2011	83	55	66.3	38	33.7
2012	94	32	34.0	62	66.0
2013	234	114	48.7	120	51.3
2014	212	127	59.9	85	40.1
2015	327	141	43.1	186	56.9

talks), the Green Climate Fund, and other decisions. Finally, the U.S. and China both committed to emissions reduction for the 2015 UNFCCC Agreement in Paris. Thus, both agencies produced a dramatic increase in news stories about Climate Change issues between 2013 and 2015.

Research question 2 addressed how the two news agencies framed Climate Change. The analysis indicated that International Relations and Domestic Politics frames were the most often reported themes for both agencies. In the end, the issue of Climate Change was primarily framed in terms of International Relations (M = 1.01, SD = .85), followed by Domestic Politics (M = .71, SD = .81), Consequences (M = .52, SD = .62), Scientific Background (M = .52, SD = .58), Economics (M =.50, SD = .63), Current Weather (M = .31, SD = .53), and New Evidence (M =.28, SD = .63).

Independent Samples t-test was used to explore the difference between both agencies' use of the frames. As shown in Table 22.2, AP was significantly different from Xinhua on six of the frames. Some frames were more present in AP coverage, while others were more prominent in Xinhua stories. U.S. coverage was more likely to frame stories about this issue with the Domestic Politics (M = .85, SD = .85), International Relations (M = .79, SD = .86), Consequences (M = .66, SD = .63), Scientific Background (M = .59, SD = .59), Economics (M = .54, SD = .65), and Current Weather (M = .35, SD = .56). Xinhua was more likely to use the International Relations (M = 1.18, SD = .80), Domestic Politics (M = .59, SD = .75), Economics (M = .47, SD = .62), Scientific Background (M = .47, SD = .56), Consequences (M = .41, SD = .59), and Current Weather (M = .27, SD = .51) frames. There was no significant difference for the New Evidence or Research Presented frame because evidence in support of anthropogenic Climate Change is increasingly clear, with the most recent IPCC Fifth Assessment Report (IPCC 2014) attributing at least half of observed surface temperature increases to net human emissions of GHG.

Table 22.2 Themes/frames in climate change coverage

Theme	Agency type				t	
	AP		Xinhua			
	M	SD	M	SD	t	P
New evidence or research presented	.30	.65	.27	.61	1.04	.30
Scientific background	.59	.59	.47	.56	3.98	.000**
Consequences	.66	.63	.41	.59	7.60	.000**
Economics	.54	.65	.47	.62	2.04	.04*
Domestic politics	.85	.85	.59	.75	6.07	.000**
International relations	.79	.86	1.18	.80	-8.77	.000**
Current weather	.35	.56	.27	.51	2.98	.003*

Note: minimum = 0, maximum = 2

*p< .05, **p<.001

Research question 3 addressed which sources were used most by the news agencies. Aggregate figures showed that the two agencies cited primarily government sources (69.4%), followed by environmental groups (26.0%), unnamed experts or officials (23.4%), and academics (18.3%). Neither agencies used Government and Unaffiliated or Independent Research Group sources more than the other. But Chi-square tests indicated significant differences for the other types of sources. As shown in Table 22.3, both agencies relied more heavily on government sources than any other sources (70.2% in AP and 68.8% in Xinhua). However, AP presented more types of sources on the issue of Climate Change than Xinhua. Specifically, AP cited more Environmental Groups ($\chi2 = 39.4$ df = 1, $p = .001$), Academics ($\chi2 = 38.65$ df = 1, $p = .001$), Resident & Citizen ($\chi2 = 20.42$ df = 1, $p = .001$), Business & Industry ($\chi2 = 16.77$ df = 1, $p = .001$), Economists ($\chi2 = 8.84$ df = 1, $p< .05$), and Unnamed Experts or Officials ($\chi2 = 8.34$ df = 1, $p< .05$) sources than Xinhua.

Research question 4 also addressed how many viewpoints were used by each news agency. Figure 22.1 shows that AP used more diverse sources on Climate Change than Xinhua ($F = 136.02$, $p< .001$).

Research question 5 asked how frequently different geographic regions were mentioned in news stories. As shown in Table 22.4, the region most mentioned in news stories was Asia and the Pacific (31.5%). The second most mentioned was North America (26.0%), followed by Western Europe (14.2%). Fourth was the Latin America and the Caribbean (10.4%). The Eastern Europe, Eurasia, and Russia (7.1%) region was fifth. Australia (3.8%) was sixth, Sub-Saharan Africa (2.7%) was seventh, and the Middle East and North Africa (1.4%) was eighth. A large number of stories dealt with Asia and North America because those are the regions in which the two news agencies are headquartered.

Chi-square tests indicated that there were significant differences between the two agencies in the geographic regions mentioned, $X^2(8, N = 1446) = 489.10$, $p< .001$. AP was more likely to mention North America (50.7%), followed by Western Europe (15.7%), Latin America and the Caribbean (9.7%), and the Asia and Pacific (7.9%) regions, while Xinhua was more likely to mention the Asia and Pacific regions (49.8%), followed by

Table 22.3 Distribution of sources

	All stories	AP	Xinhua (%)	X^2 (d.f. = 1)
Academic	18.3	25.5	12.8	38.65**
Resident & citizen	7.4	10.9	4.7	20.42**
Business & industry	13.1	17.3	9.9	16.77**
Economists	2.6	4.0	1.5	8.84*
Unnamed experts or officials	23.4	27.1	20.6	8.34*
Unaffiliated or independent research group	8.6	9.5	8.0	1.06
Government sources	69.4	70.2	68.8	.32
Environmental group	26.0	34.2	19.6	39.40**

*$p< .05$, **$p<.001$

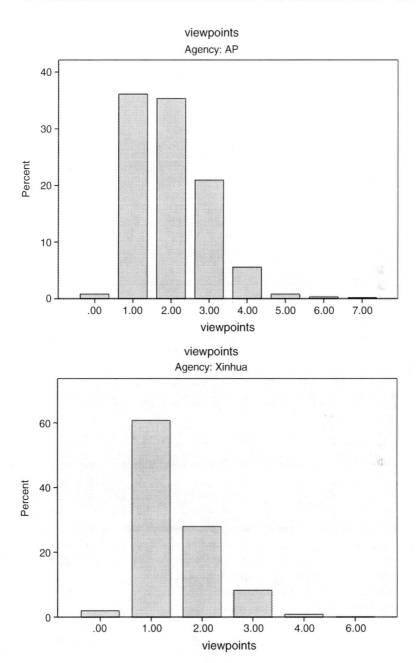

Fig. 22.1 Viewpoints

Table 22.4 Frequency of mention of regions

Year	Agency type					
	All Stories N (%) (1446)		AP N (%) (631, 43.6%)		Xinhua N (%) (815, 56.4%)	
Sub-Saharan Africa	39	2.7	13	2.1	26	3.2
Asia and the Pacific	456	31.5	50	7.9	406	49.8
Middle East & North Africa	20	1.4	12	1.9	8	1.0
Western Europe	205	14.2	99	15.7	106	13.0
Eastern Europe, Eurasia, & Russia	103	7.1	44	7.0	59	7.2
Latin America & the Caribbean	150	10.4	61	9.7	89	10.9
North America	376	26.0	320	50.7	56	6.9
Australasia	55	3.8	8	1.3	47	5.8
None	42	2.9	24	3.8	18	2.2

$X^2(8, N = 1446) = 489.10, p < .001$

Western Europe (13.0%), Latin America and the Caribbean (10.9%), and North America (6.9%) regions.

Research question 6 asked whether there would be differences in the two agencies' use of Personal Mobilizing Information (Cohen et al., 2008). Results showed that Climate Change stories in AP (N = 55, 8.7%) were more likely to include Personal Mobilizing Information than stories in Xinhua (N = 56, 6.9%), but the difference was not statistically significant.

DISCUSSION AND CONCLUSIONS

We focused on how one Chinese and one U.S. news agency framed the issue of Climate Change and whether the frames incorporated in the coverage reflected the dominant ideology and national interests of each agency's home region. Herman and Chomsky's Media Propaganda Model (1988) argues that the media tend to process and present information in ways that foster and promote the dominant ideologies of their respective social systems and that they tend to present pictures of social reality that are functionally advantageous to their respective governments and powerful social elites.

Mass media research has shown that the media set the agenda for the public and prime audiences as to which aspects of an issue deserve attention (McCombs, 2004). The findings of this study showed significant differences between the two news agencies in their coverage about Climate Change. We confirmed some past research which found that the story of Climate Change is told in different ways in different countries (Painter & Ashe, 2012; Zamith, Pinto, & Villar, 2013). Specifically, we showed that the amount of Climate Change news coverage was varied over the period studied. The fluctuations in coverage showed that the news agencies are interested in setting the agenda for discussion. We also found that the U.S. news agency was less likely to cover

Climate Change than its Chinese counterpart. The volume of news coverage is also relatively important to the Climate Change issue within the framework of the Media Propaganda Model (Carvalho, 2005; Good, 2008; Herman & Chomsky, 1988). Our findings suggest that each news agency is more likely to produce news stories that support its respective dominant ideology and help maintain the status quo. It also showed that the news agencies are less likely to tell stories that challenge the privilege and power of the ruling group (Good, 2008; Herman & Chomsky, 1988).

Discourse scholars argued that the way the media frame an issue influences public discourse, which in turn, influences how audiences interpret the issue's meaning (Entman, 2004; Gamson & Modigliani, 1989; Iyengar, 1991; Scheufele, 2006). We analysed the stories for the presence of eight frames and found that each news agency framed the same event in different ways. We contend that of these eight frames, the International Relations and Domestic Politics frames appeared more often. These frames are likely to encourage audience members to learn about and consider Sustainable Development issues, such as Climate Change. In general, each agency frequently covered the international Climate Talks, which arguably increased the salience of the International Relations frame (Brossard et al., 2004). This frame emphasizes the importance of solutions over other aspects of the Climate Change issue. The U.S. and China both want other countries to show more commitment to reducing carbon emission and to bear more of the burden of reducing GHG emissions. For global Climate Change mitigation efforts, each country has a different strategy. The U.S. leadership is polarized over the causes and consequences of Climate Change. Conservatives argue Climate Change is a natural fluctuation in climate trends. Liberals argue sciences indicates that it is the result of human economic development. The Chinese leadership does not face this debate. This perhaps explains the importance given to the frame of Domestic Politics (Carvalho, 2005).

The U.S. media coverage was more likely to use the Consequence frame, but the Chinese news media used the Economics frame more frequently. Because of the political division in the U.S. between conservatives and liberals, news coverage is more likely to report on the debate over Climate Change, criticism of policy, and the potential negative impact on the climate of maintaining economic output. The Chinese media also used the Economic frame which is signalled by content about the costs of solutions for Climate Change. Our results confirmed Wubbeke's finding that the Chinese government argued that "developed countries should be responsible for leading climate change mitigation, while developing countries should mainly continue to pursue their economic development and implement voluntary measures according to their abilities" (2013, p. 8).

Neither news agency used the eighth frame, Personal Behavioural Mobilization, often. The Personal Behaviour Mobilization frame focuses news stories on the actions individuals can take to fight Climate Change. Consequently, there was little mobilizing content ("a crucial cue to action") by news coverage of Climate Change in either agencies' coverage, which supports the status quo and the elite power structure (Cohen et al., 2008, p. 433). Although citizen participation is one of the important pillars for promoting Sustainable Development Goals, both news agencies did not facilitate citizen's participation in the issue. The lack of mobilizing information in coverage would be advantages to the power structures in the two countries.

The third filter of the Media Propaganda Model is the media's reliance on government and business firms as sources. The model argues that this reliance occurs for reasons of efficiency and political expediency. Reliance on officials and business sources is exactly the kind of media behaviour identified by this filter. The result, it is argued, is too much solidarity between the media, government interests, and the powerful elite. As a result, interpretations of events that are functional for the government and the powerful elite tend to dominate the news discourse (p. 23). Our analysis found that both news agencies heavily relied on government sources. Official sources are more likely to present mainstream and status quo perspectives than opinions addressing possible solutions. The results showed that China's media tended to rely heavily on government sources and propaganda when covering Climate Change. Xinhua framed the Climate Change issue in a manner more consistent with government interests and policy. In addition, the AP tended to rely on business and industry sources more than Xinhua, demonstrating that the influence of the third filter was also present in the U.S. coverage.

Both news agencies also relied on environmental groups, as well as academics for information. This is evidence of more balanced reporting regarding this issue. Specifically, AP used more news sources, including both residents & citizens and business & industry. AP articles cited significantly more viewpoints than Xinhua, which is perhaps evidence of the U.S. journalists' efforts to adhere to balance or fairness. Although both agencies cited primarily government sources, AP sought more voices and opinions from more diverse sources.

According to Giffard and Leuven (2008), the geographic focus in the reporting of Climate Change issues reveals whose position and views are being made part of the public discourse (p. 7). We assessed whether a variety of different geographic regions (including the most developed and least developed countries) were represented in coverage. Neither international news agency balanced geographical representation. Each agency tended to focus on its home region as well as developed and developing countries with which their respective home regions had important national interests. We also found that both news agencies frequently mentioned Latin America and the Caribbean because several Climate Change meetings were held in specific countries in these regions. In addition, certain regions were largely ignored by both agencies. Sub-Saharan Africa, the Middle East, and North Africa received little coverage.

In this sense, our findings lend support to previous studies that employed the Media Propaganda Model. Our results indicated that the dominant ideologies and power structures of the nations in which the two media systems operate were able to influence the coverage of Sustainable Development and Climate Change. The findings showed that, as a result of these influences, the news agencies relied on issue frames that were consistent with the ideological principles and social norms of their respective socio-political systems. Thus, we have illuminated the dynamics of framing and the impact of propaganda in a comparative international context and contributed to the further theoretical development of framing in the context of the news media's coverage of Climate Change and Sustainable Development.

This study has the following limitation. Content analysis inevitably requires the analysts' subjective judgments and interpretations, though we took steps to minimize the bias. Future studies are needed to expand this work to a more cross-cultural context and also to explore the efficacy of using more detailed and sophisticated approaches to content analysis. Future research could also move forward to examine how news coverage of controversial issues has influenced the publics' perceptions of and support for policies to address Climate Change.

References

Adelekan, I. (2009). The Nigerian Press and Environmental Information for Sustainable Development. *Local Environment, 14*(4), 297–312.

Akhavan-Majid, R., & Ramaprasad, J. (1998). Framing and Ideology: A Comparative Analysis of U.S. and Chinese Newspaper Coverage of the Fourth United Nations Conference on Women and the NGO Forum. *Mass Communication and Society, 1*(2/3), 131–152.

Akhavan-Majid, R., & Ramaprasad, J. (2000). Framing Beijing: Dominant Ideological Influences on the American Press Coverage of the Fourth UN Conference on Women and the NGO Forum. *International Communication Gazette, 62*(1), 45–59.

Allison, G. (2017). *Destined for War: Can America and China Escape Thucydides's Trap?* Boston: Houghton Mifflin Harcourt.

Altheide, D. (2009). The Columbine Shootings and the Discourse of Fear. *American Behavioral Scientist, 52*(10), 1354–1370.

Althusser, L. (1971). Ideology and Ideological State Apparatuses (Notes Towards an Investigation). In B. Brewster (Ed.), *Lenin and Philosophy and Other Essays*. New York, NY: *Monthly Review Press*.

Antilla, L. (2005). Climate of Skepticism: US Newspaper Coverage of the Science of Climate Change. *Global Environmental Change, 15*(4), 338–352.

Ashley, L., & Olson, B. (1998). Constructing Reality: Print Media's Framing of the Women's Movement. *Journalism and Mass Communication Quarterly, 75*(2), 263–277.

Becker, S. (1984). Marxist Approaches to Media Studies: The British Experience. *Critical Studies in Mass Communication, 1*(1), 66–80.

Benford, R., & Snow, D. (2000). Framing Processes and Social Movements: An Overview and Assessment. *Annual Review of Sociology, 26*, 611–639.

Block, E. (2013). A Culturalist Approach to the Concept of the Mediatization of Politics: The Age of "Media Hegemony". *Communication Theory, 23*(3), 259–278.

Boyce, T., & Lewis, J. (2009). *Climate Change and the Media*. New York: Peter Lang.

Boykoff, J. (2006). Framing Dissent: Mass-Media Coverage of the Global Justice Movement. *New Political Science, 28*(2), 201–228.

Boykoff, M., & Boykoff, J. (2004). Balance as Bias: Global Warming and the US Prestige Press. *Global Environmental Change, 14*(2), 125–136.

Brasted, M. (2005). Framing Protest: The *Chicago Tribune* and *The New York Times* During the 1968 Democratic Convention. *Atlantic Journal of Communication, 13*(1), 1–25.

Brewer, P. R. (2006). National Interest Frames and Public Opinion about World Affairs. *The International Journal of Press/Politics, 11*(4), 89–102.

Broadbent, J., Yun, S.-J., Ku, D., Ikeda, K., Satoh, K., Pellissery, S., et al. (2013). Asian Societies and Climate Change: The Variable Diffusion of Global Norms. *Globality Studies Journal, 32*, 1–24.

Brossard, D., Shanahan, J., & McComas, K. (2004). Are Issue-Cycles Culturally Constructed? A Comparison of French and American Coverage of Global Climate Change. *Mass Communication and Society, 7*(3), 359–377.

Carvalho, A. (2005). Representing the Politics of the Greenhouse Effect: Discursive Strategies in the British Media. *Critical Discourse Studies, 2*, 1–29.

Chang, T., & Lin F. (2014). From Propaganda to Public Diplomacy: Assessing China's International Practice and its Image, 1950–2009. *Public Relations Review, 40*, 450–458.

Cohen, E. L., Caburnay, C. A., Luke, D. A., Rodgers, S., Cameron, G. T., & Kreuter, M. W. (2008). Cancer Coverage in General-Audience and Black Newspapers. *Health Communication, 23*, 427–435.

Corbett, J. B., & Durfee, J. L. (2004). Testing Public (Un)certainty of Science: Media Representations of Global Warming. *Science Communication, 26*, 129–151.

de Beer, A. S., & Merrill, J. C. (2009). *Global Journalism: Topical Issues and Media Systems*. Boston: Pearson, Allyn and Bacon.

Dimaggio, A. (2010). *When Media Goes to War: Hegemonic Discourse, Public Opinion, and the Limits of Dissent*. New York, NY: Monthly Review Press.

Entman, R. M. (1993). Framing: Toward Clarification of a Fractured Paradigm. *Journal of Communication, 43*, 51–58.

Entman, R. M. (1994). Framing: Toward Clarification of a Fractured Paradigm. In M. Levy & M. Gurevitch (Eds.), *Defining Media Studies: Reflections on the Future of the Field*. New York: Oxford University Press.

Entman, R. M. (2004). *Projections of Power. Framing News, Public Opinion, and U.S. Foreign Policy*. Chicago: University of Chicago Press.

Entman, R. M. (2008). Theorizing Mediated Public Diplomacy: The U.S. Case. *The International Journal of Press/Politics, 13*(2), 87–102.

Feldman, L., Maibach, E. W., Roser-Renouf, C., & Leiserowitz, A. (2012). Climate on Cable: The Nature and Impact of Global Warming Coverage on Fox News, CNN, and MSNBC. *The International Journal of Press/Politics, 17*(1), 3–31.

Feldman, L., Myers, T. A., Hmielowski, J. D., & Leiserowitz, A. (2014). The Mutual Reinforcement of Media Selectivity and Effects: Testing the Reinforcing Spirals Framework in the Context of Global Warming. *Journal of Communication, 64*(4), 590–611. https://doi.org/10.1111/jcom.12108

Foust, C., & O'Shannon Murphy, W. (2009). Revealing and Reframing Apocalyptic Tragedy in Global Warming Discourse. *Environmental Communication, 3*(2), 151–167.

Foxwell-Norton, F., & Konkes, C. (2019). The Great Barrier Reef: News Media, Policy and the Politics of Protection. *The International Communication Gazette, 81*(3), 211–234.

Gallagher, K. S., & Xuan, X. (2018). *Titans of the Climate: Explaining Policy Process in the United States and China.* Cambridge: The MIT Press.

Gamson, W. A. (1989). News as Framing: Comments on Graber. *American Behavioral Scientist, 33*(2), 157–161.

Gamson, W. A., & Lasch, K. (1983). The Political Culture of Social Welfare Policy. In S. Spiro & E. Yuchman-Yaar (Eds.), *Evaluating the Welfare State: Social and Political Perspectives* (pp. 397–415). NY: Academic Press.

Gamson, W. A., & Modigliani, A. (1989). Media Discourse and Public Opinion on Nuclear Power: A Constructionist Approach. *American Journal of Sociology, 95*(1), 1–37.

Gandy Jr., O. H. (1982). *Beyond Agenda-Setting: Information Subsidies and Public Policy.* Norwood, NJ: Ablex.

Giddens, A. (2009). *The Politics and Climate Change.* Oxford: Polity.

Giffard, C. A., & Leuven, N. V. (2008). Five Views on Development: How News Agencies Cover the UN Millennium Development Goals. *Journal of Global Mass Communication, 1*(1/2), 22–40.

Gilley, B. (2012). Authoritarian Environmentalism and China's Response to Climate Change. *Environmental Politics, 21*(2), 287–307.

Gitlin, T. (1980). *The Whole World is Watching: Mass Media in the Making and Unmaking of the New Left.* Berkeley, CA: University of California Press.

Goffman, E. (1974). *Frame Analysis: An Essay on the Organization of Experience.* New York: Harper & Row.

Good, J. E. (2008). The Framing of Climate Change in Canadian, American, and International Newspapers: A Media Propaganda Model Analysis. *Canadian Journal of Communication, 33*(2), 233–255.

Greenberg, J., & Knight, G. (2004). Framing Sweatshops: Nike, Global Production, and the American News Media. *Communication & Critical/Cultural Studies, 1*, 151–175.

Gunaratne, S. A., & Kim, S. (2000). North Korea. In S. A. Gunaratne (Eds.), *Handbook of the Media in Asia* (pp. 586–610). Thousand Oaks: Sage Publications.

Han, G. (2007). Mainland China Frames Taiwan: How China's News Websites Covered Taiwan's 2004 Presidential Election. *Asian Journal of Communication, 17*(1), 40–57.

Herman, E., & Chomsky, N. (1988). *Manufacturing Consent: The political Economy of the Mass Media.* New York, NY: Pantheon Books.

Holt, L. F., & Major, L. H. (2010). Frame and Blame: An Analysis of How National and Local Newspapers Framed the Jena 6 Controversy. *Journalism & Mass Communication Quarterly, 87*(3/4), 582–597.

Hong, J. (2011). From the World's Largest Propaganda Machine to A Multi-Functional News Service: The Transformation of Xinhua News Service since 1978. *Journal of Political Communication, 28*(3), 377–393.

Howard-Williams, R. (2009). Ideological Construction of Climate Change in Australian and New Zealand Newspapers. In T. Boyce & J. Lewis (Eds.), *Climate Change and the Media* (pp. 28–40). New York: Peter Lang.

Hawdon, J., Agnich, L. E., & Ryan, J. (2014). Media Framing of a Tragedy: A Content Analysis of Print Media Coverage of the Virginia Tech Tragedy. *Traumatology, 20*(3), 199–208.

Iyengar, S. (1990). Framing Responsibility for Political Issues: The Case of Poverty. *Political Behavior*, 12(1), 19–37.

Iyengar, S. (1991). *Is Anyone Responsible?* Chicago, IL: University of Chicago Press.

Iyengar, S. (1996). Framing Responsibility for Political Issues. *The Annals of the American Academy of Political and Social Science*, 546, 59–70.

Jang, W. (2013). News as Propaganda: A Comparative Analysis of U.S. and Korean Press Coverage of the Six-Party Talks, 2003–2007. *International Communication Gazette*, 75(2), 1–17.

Jang, W., Hong, J., & Frederick, E. (2015). The Framing of the North Korean Six-Party Talks: Communist Propaganda and National INTERESTS. *Media International Australia*, 154, 42–52.

Jowett, G. S., & O'Donnell, V. (1992). *Propaganda and Persuasion*. London: Sage.

Keating, D. (2019, December 15). Failure in Madrid as COP25 Climate Summit ends in disarray. *Forbes*.

Klaehn, J. (2003). Behind the Invisible Curtain of Scholarly Criticism: Revisiting the Propaganda Model. *Journalism Studies*, 4(3), 359–369.

Klaehn, J. (2009). The Propaganda Model: Theoretical and Methodological Considerations. *Canada Westminster Papers in Communication and Culture*, 6(2), 43–58.

Koehn, P. (2004). Sustainable Development Frontiers and Divides: Transnational Actors and US/China Greenhouse Gas Emissions. *The International Journal of Sustainable Development and World Ecology*, 11(4), 380–396.

Krosnick, J. A., & MacInnis, B. (2010). *Frequent Viewers of Fox News Are Less Likely to Accept Scientists' Views of Global Warming*. Technical Paper, Stanford University. Accessed October 1, 2014. http://woods.stanford.edu/sites/default/files/files/Global-Warming-Fox-News.pdf.

Lacy, S., Rife, D., & Varouhakis, M. (2007). Where Do Ohioans Get Their Environmental News? *Newspaper Research Journal*, 28, 70–84.

Lau, S. (2019, December 12). COP25 Summit: China Leads Four-Nation Attack Over 'Imbalances' in UN Climate-Change Negotiations. *South China Morning Post*.

Lawhon, M., & Makina, A. (2017). Assessing Local Discourse on Water in a South African Newspaper. *Local Environment*, 22(2), 240–255.

Lee, C., & Yang, J. (1996). Foreign News and National Interest: Comparing U.S. and Japanes Coverage of a Chinese Student Movement. *International Communication Gazette*, 56(1), 1–18.

Li, X., & Liu, X. (2010). Framing and Coverage of the Same-sex Marriage in U.S. NewsPapers. *The Howard Journal of Communication*, 21, 72–91.

Lynn, T., & Williams, L. (2018). 'Have a Quiet, Orderly, Polite Revolution': Framing Political Protest and Protecting the Status Quo. *Critical Sociology*, 44(4–5), 733–751.

Mancini, P. (2005). Is There a European Model of Journalism? In H. De Burgh (Ed.), *Making Journalists: Diverse Models, Global Issues* (pp. 77–93). London: Routledge.

Massey, B. L. (2000). How Three Southeast-Asian Newspapers Framed 'The Haze' of 1997-98. *Asian Journal of Communication*, 10(1), 72–94.

McComas, K., & Shanahan, J. (1999). Telling Stories About Global Climate Change Measuring the Impact of Narratives on Issue Cycles. *Communication Research*, 26(1), 30–57.

McCombs, M. (2004). *Setting the Agenda: The Mass Media and Public Opinion*. Malden, MA: Polity.

McGinty, E. E., Webster, D. W., Jarlenski, M., & Barry C. L. (2014). News Media Framing of Serious Mental Illness and Gun Violence in the United States, 1997–2012. *American Journal of Public Health, 104*(3), 406–413.

Mix, T. (2009). The Greening of White Separatism: Use of Environmental Themes to Elaborate and Legitimize Extremist Discourse. *Nature and Culture, 4*(2), 138–166.

Neuendorf, K. A. (2002). *The Content Analysis Guidebook*. Thousand Oaks, CA: Sage.

Nohrstedt, S. A., Kaitatzi-Whitlock, S., Ottosen, R., & Riegert, K. (2000). From the Persian Gulf to Kosovo: War Journalism and Propaganda. *European Journal of Communication, 15*(3), 383–404.

Painter, J., & Ashe, T. (2012). Cross-National Comparison of the Presence of Climate Skepticism in the Print Media in Six Countries, 2007–10. *Environmental Research Letters, 7*, 1–8.

Pan, Z., & Kosicki, G. M. (1993). Framing Analysis: An Approach to News Discourse. *Political Communication, 10*(1), 55–75.

Scheufele, B. (2006). Frames, Schemata, and News Reporting. *Communications, 31*, 65–83.

Scheufele, D. (1999). Framing as a Theory of Media Effects. *Journal of Communication, 49*, 103–122.

Schudson, M. (2001). The Objectivity Norm in American Journalism. *Journalism, 2*(2), 149–170.

Semetko, H. A., & Valkenburg, P. M. (2000). Framing European Politics: A Content Analysis of Press and Television News. *Journal of Communication, 50*(2), 93–109.

Servaes, J., Polk, E., Shi, S., Reilly, D., & Yakupitijage, T. (2012). Towards a Framework of Sustainability Indicators for 'Communication for Development and Social Change' Projects. *The International Communication Gazette, 74*(2), 99–123.

Shehata, A., & Hopmann, D. (2012). Framing Climate Change: A Study of US and Swedish Press Coverage of Global Warming. *Journalism Studies, 13*(2), 175–192.

Shoemaker, P., Eichholz, M., Kim, E., & Wrigley, B. (2001). Individual and Routine Forces in Gatekeeping. *Journalism and Mass Communication Quarterly, 78*(2), 233–246.

Simmons, G. (2014). Russian Public Diplomacy in the 21st Century: Structure, Means and Message. *Public Relations Review, 40*, 440–449.

Snow, D., & Benford, R. (1992). Master Frames and Cycles of Protest. In A. Morris & M. Mueller (Eds.), *Frontiers in Social Movement Theory* (pp. 133–155). New Haven, CT: Yale University Press.

Snow, N., & Taylor, P. (2006). The Revival of the Propaganda State: US Propaganda at Home and Abroad Since 9/11. *International Communication Gazette, 68*(5–6), 389–407.

Takahasshi, B. (2011). Framing and Sources: A Study of Mass Media Coverage of Climate Change in Peru During the V ALCUE. *Public Understanding of Science, 20*(4), 543–557.

Trumbo, C. (1996). Constructing Climate Change: Claims and Frames in US News Coverage of an Environmental Issue. *Public Understanding of Science, 5*(3), 269–283.

Tucker, L. R. (1998). The Framing of Calvin Klein: A Frame Analysis of Media Discourse About the August 1995 Calvin Klein Jeans Advertising Campaign. *Critical Studies in Mass Communication, 15*, 141–157.

Ungar, S. (2000). Knowledge, Ignorance and the Popular Culture: Climate Change Versus the Ozone Hole. *Public Understanding of Science, 9*(3), 297–312.

UN Web site Sustainable Development Goals. (January 28, 2020). Retrieved from https://sustainabledevelopment.un.org/sdgs
Verschueren, J. (1985). *International News Reporting: Metapragmatic Metaphors and the U-2*. Amsterdam and Philadelphia: John Benjamins.
Wang, M. (1991). Who is Dominating Whose Ideology? New York Times Reporting on China. *Asian Journal of Communication, 2*(1), 51–69.
Wang, S. (1995). Ideology and Foreign News Coverage: Propaganda Model Re-examined. *Asian Journal of Communication, 5*(1), 110–125.
WCED. (1987). *Our Common Future*. Oxford: United Nations World Commission on Environment and Development. Oxford University Press.
Weathers, M., & Kendall, B. (2016). Developments in the Framing of Climate Change as a Public Health Issue in US Newspapers. *Environmental Communication, 10*(5), 593–611.
Wubbeke, J. (2013). The Science-Politics of Climate Change in China: Development, Equity, and Responsibility. *Nature and Culture, 8*(1), 8–29.
Xie, L. (2015). The Story of Two Big Chimneys: A Frame Analysis of Climate Change in US and Chinese Newspapers. *Journal of Intercultural Communication Research, 44*(2), 151–177.
Yacoumis, P. (2018). Making Progress? Reproducing Hegemony Through Discourses of "Sustainable Development" in the Australian News Media. *Environmental Communication, 12*(6), 840–853.
Youm, K. (1991). Press Laws in North Korea. *Asian Journal of Communication, 2*(1), 70–86.
Zamith, R. Z., Pinto, J., & Villar, M. E. (2013). Constructing Climate Change in the Americas: An Analysis of News Coverage in U.S. and South American Newspapers. *Science Communication, 35*(3), 334–357.
Zehr, S. (2009). An Environmentalist/Economic Hybrid Frame in US Press Coverage of Climate Change, 2000–2008. In T. Boyce & J. Lewis (Eds.), *Climate Change and the Media* (pp. 28–40). New York: Peter Lang.
Ziemann, A. (2011). Communication Theory and Sustainability Discourse. In J. Godemann & G. Michelsen (Eds.), *Sustainability Communication* (pp. 89–96). Houten: Springer.

CHAPTER 23

Running Ahead: Trump's Presidency and Climate Change Discourses. Has Trump's Presidency Changed Climate Change Discourses?: A Text Mining Analysis of Newspaper Contents in the United States

Kenneth C. C. Yang and Yowei Kang

INTRODUCTION

The presidency of Donald Trump began at noon EST on January 20, 2017 as the 45th president of the United States (Johnson, 2017). With a promise to shift Washington power from political elites to ordinary people (*ibid.*), President Trump's "Make America Great Again" (MAGA) rhetoric helped his nomination as a Republican candidate for the 2016 Presidential Election (Qiu, 2016). One of the main agenda to steer Trump's campaign is to bring jobs and factories back to the United States (*ibid.*). As a result, President Trump has reduced the intervention of the federal government in many environmental issues and withdrawn U.S. involvement in global climate change initiatives (Mathiesen, 2017). For example, President Trump has streamlined the operations and

K. C. C. Yang (✉)
University of Texas, El Paso, TX, USA
e-mail: cyang@utep.edu

Y. Kang
National Taiwan Ocean University, Keelung, Taiwan
e-mail: yoweikang@mail.ntou.edu.tw

practices of the Environmental Protection Agency (EPA) (Donald J. Trump for President Inc., n.d.). Furthermore, President Trump also proposed *the Affordable Clean Energy Rule* to replace President Obama's *Clean Power Plan* that is said to increase electricity rates by around 14% (*ibid.*). The methane emissions rule in President Obama's era was also removed to save energy developers about $530 million each year (*ibid.*). EPA also relaxes fuel efficiency standards to save $340 billion in regulatory cost (*ibid.*). Furthermore, the role of scientific research on federal policy-making has been reduced through the cutting down of government funding (Plumer & Davenport, 2019).

The major administrative changes after 2016 Presidential Election have changed American political landscape in terms of foreign policy, immigration, the courts, health care, infrastructure, environment, tax reform, trade, among the few (Zurcher, 2018). One of the causalities is related to human-caused climate change issues that the Trump Administration has dismissed as false (Plumer & Davenport, 2019). Even before his election to the U.S. President, Donald Trump's positions on climate change and other environmental issues have triggered many concerns among environmentalists (Harrington, 2016; Yardley, 2016). Unlike his former competitor, Hilary Clinton, who listed "Protecting Wildlife and Animals" and "Climate Change" as two major topics of her campaign websites, Donald Trump has taken a sceptical view on many claims on climate changes and global warming (Harrington, 2016), yet holds a supportive stance on offshore drilling, fracking, and the construction of Keystone XL pipeline (Zezima & Callahan, 2016). In one of his tweets on November 6, 2016, Trump wrote: "The concept of global warming was created by and for the Chinese in order to make US manufacturing non-competitive" (Trump 2016, as cited in Harrington, 2016). As reported by *The Washington Post* to compare the positions on various campaign issues, Donald Trump was quoted to say "[t]his very expensive global warming bullshit has to stop", while Hilary Clinton said, "I won't let anyone take us backward, deny our economy the benefits of harnessing a clean energy future, or force our children to endure the catastrophe that would result from unchecked climate change" (as cited in Zezima & Callahan, 2016).

Consistent with his position during the 2016 Presidential Election, Trump declared U.S. withdrawal from the Paris Climate Accord in June 2017 (Kaufman, 2017; Liptak & Acosta, 2017; Novak, 2017). The decision is controversial and has led to both positive and negative responses from local land international conservation groups (Kaufman, 2017; Liptak & Acosta, 2017; Mathiesen, 2017; Novak, 2017). For example, Kaufman's (2017) report uses "crushing blow to climate fight" to describe the negative effects of Trump's decision. The Trump Administration has adopted a pro-fossil fuel agenda (BBC News, 2018, November 28). In the end of 2019, President Trump has targeted about 85 environmental rules intended to protect air, land, public health, and water conservation (Newburger, 2019). Some examples include loosening the regulation on methane emissions, removing Obama's cleaning water rules, and reducing offshore drilling regulations (*ibid.*). In March 2020, President Trump continues to dismantle Obama's environmental legacy by lowering the vehicle fuel economy standards by replacing the existing 54 miles (by the year of 2020) with the less stringent 40 miles per gallon fuel efficiency criteria (Brewster, 2020). No wonder, according to a survey report by Statista (2017), 60% of the Americans have agreed that environmentalists will lose their influence during a Trump Presidency. President Trump's positions and actions on climate change, global warming, and other environmental issues have prompted this study to examine whether President Trump's Presidency, as manifestation of political changes due to the "underlying political currents" in the United States (McConnell, 2016, n.p.), has affected how major newspaper media in the United States frame climate change topics before and after his presidency.

Research Objectives and Questions

This book chapter investigates whether climate change discourses may be influenced by political changes marked by the election of President Trump in 2016 because of the political transition from a Democrat to a Republican president that are drastically different in environmental and climate change issues (Alemany, 2017). Trump's election is attributed to what ordinary Americans (not Fortune 500 CEOs and coastal elites) feel about issues on immigration, trade, foreign policies, environment, multiculturalism, and so on (McConnell, 2016). As a result of this great shift in American politics, environmental issues are also at the centre for these debates.

Because of their widespread impacts, about six in ten Americans in 2018 believe that global warming is mostly caused by human activities, according to a longitudinal study by Yale and George Mason University since 2008 (Revkin, 2019). Nevertheless, scholars have pointed out that climate change has long been a bipartisan issue since the 1980s with major stakeholders frame the causes and impacts of climate change differently (refer to Cook, 2019 for review).

While conservation organizations (Greenpeace, n.d.-a, n.d.-b) eagerly advocate the existence of climate change and global warming and attribute their occurrence of human-related activities, academic communities and political elites diverge in their attitudes and perceptions (Cook, 2019). Since mass media will play a significant role in communicating different aspects of climate change debates to shape public opinions, how media organizations frame climate change discourses before and after the Trump's Presidency present an interesting case of learning the frame building by media organizations at the time of historical political transition. Furthermore, the framing of climate change issues was found to influence audience's pro-environmental attitudes and intention (Davis, 1995), which makes the study of media framing building practices relevant and important to conservation campaigns. However, existing research has failed to take advantage of the massive computational data processing capabilities that text mining methods can offer to study this important phenomenon. Therefore, this book chapter attempts to examine how climate change issues have been discussed and represented in major English-language newspaper media in the United States. Employing QDA Miner to conduct a large-scale text mining analysis of over 70 newspaper articles collected from Lexis/Nexis Academic (or Nexis Uni) database, this study aims to answer the following research questions:

Research Question 1: What are the repetitive words and phrases from the English-language newspaper media in the United States when framing climate change issues?

Research Question 2: What will be the most important phrases/frames when framing climate change issues in these English-language newspaper media in the United States before and after Trump's Presidency?

LITERATURE REVIEW

Climate Change Debates in the United States

Climate change has been associated with carbon dioxide emissions created by human activities (Jang & Sol Hart, 2015; Xu, Kang, Zhuang, & Pan, 2010). Historically, carbon dioxide emissions have grown from 5000 million metric tons in 1947 to 36,000 million metric tons in 2017 (Statista, 2019a). As a result, departure from normal temperature (measured in degrees Celsius) has been observed from 0.4 degree in 1990 to 0.7 degree in 2010, to almost one degree in 2017 (*ibid.*). Global warming has often grabbed media attention around the world (Olteanu, Castillo, Diakopoulos, & Aberer, 2015). Movies such as "An Inconvenient Truth", "Carbon Nation" (Lorenz, 2014), and "The Day After Tomorrow" (Lashof, 2004) often ignite much interest among the public. As described in these movies, climate change and global warming often lead to extreme weather catastrophes and have caused significant economic losses and human causalities globally (Statista, 2019a). From 2000 to 2017, an average of US $149.5 billion has been lost due to these weather anomalies (*ibid.*). In addition, many have argued that climate change is also the driver of biodiversity that contributes to the adaptation and mitigation of climate change impacts (UNESCO, n.d.).

In the United States, the debates on climate change are mainly centred on three key areas: (1) scientific consensus on its existence, causes, and outcomes; (2) climate change messaging and framing on the public's attitudes, beliefs, and behaviours; (3) politics and policies. These three areas are interconnected with each other because heightened public concerns, as a result of effective communication of scientific consensus, often lead to possible policy intervention or subsequent political change.

According to a national survey by Yale University, the public consensus on the existence of global warming has reached 67% and 53% of them attribute it to human-related activities (Marlon, Howe, Mildenberger, Leiserowitz, & Wang, 2019). It rises from 48% in an earlier 2016 Pew Research on the public belief on whether climate change is caused by human activities. The public's concerns about climate change have been high, in terms of its potential impacts on animals and plants (69%), future generation (67%), people in developing countries (62%), and people in the United States (57%) (Marlon et al., 2019). While public opinions on climate change are important to garner support for conversation efforts, political changes particularly at the federal level lead to the most imminent impacts on climate change policies.

Unlike President Trump, the previous Obama Administration has placed the deterrence of climate change and global warming as one of his agenda. In his *Climate Action Plan* proposed in 2013, Obama claimed that his plan will "cut carbon pollution, help prepare the United States for the impacts of climate change, and continue to lead international efforts to address global climate change. For the sake of our children and future generations, we must act now" (The White House President Obama, 2013). As a strong believer in the relationship between green gas emissions and global warming, Obama Presidency has focused on the building of a clean energy infrastructure to make the United States more resilient to climate change impacts (The White House President Obama, 2013).

However, in the United States, global warming and climate change have often been an ignored topic in presidential debates (Irfan, 2019). Despite the public belief on the occurrence of global warming has been on the continual rise, an average of 70% between 2008 and 2018 (Statista, 2019b), concerns about rising global temperatures, threatened seashores and properties, irregular rainfall and heat patterns, and deforestation have received scarce attention in televised presidential debates in 2016 (Irfan, 2019). However, increasingly, particularly among Democratic candidates, climate change has increasingly "become a voting issue" according to Senator Sheldon Whitehouse (*ibid.*). Even in China where there is no democratic election, the government has launched the world's largest greenhouse gas emission market that will partially control this problem (Bradsher & Friedman, 2017).

Theoretical Framework: Framing Climate Change

This book chapter focuses on the messaging and framing of climate change issues by mass media organizations. We attempt to explore if political change could have impacts on media organizations' frame building practices. Our theoretical foundation is based on framing theory that has been widely used in analysing media coverage of climate change issues (Aykut, Comby, & Guillemo, 2012; Hase, Engelke, & Kieslich, 2020; Jang & Sol Hart, 2015; Kim, Besley, Sang-Hwa, & Kim, 2014; McKewon, 2012; Nisbet, 2010; Olausson, 2014; Shehata & Hopmann, 2012; Wozniak, Wessler, & Lück, 2017) and other environmental communication topics (D'Angelo & Kuypers, 2010; Davis, 1995; Entman, 1993, 2010). Among these framing studies, both cross-national and longitudinal studies have been used to track the changes in framing climate change or other environmental communication issues (Aykut et al., 2012; Shehata & Hopmann, 2012). For example, Shehata and Hopmann (2012) compare news coverage of climate change topics in Swedish and U.S.

newspapers over a period of ten years, with an intensive focus on Bali and Kyoto Climate Summit as two case studies. Their study concludes a weak influence of national variations in terms of how climate change is covered. It is likely that both countries are eager supporters of environmental agendas. On the other hand, Aykut et al. (2012) investigate the contentions among four different social groups (i.e., journalists, non-governmental organizations, politicians, and scientists) that struggle to set the agendas of climate change issues to affect public perceptions.

Framing is defined as "the ways in which an issue is presented in the media, including the various perspectives and conceptions that people communicate with respect to that issue" (Diakopoulos, Zhang, & Salway, 2013, n.p.). Negatively framed messages are found to have greater impacts on people's judgement (Meyerowitz and Chaiken 1987). News articles on climate change issues traditionally examine the causes, consequences, remedies, and definitions of climate change (Refer to Jang & Sol Hart, 2015 for a detailed review).

Current climate change research has examined the effects of audience's political orientation on the effectiveness of messaging and framing (Marlon et al., 2019; Stecula & Merkley, 2019). For example, a national survey of public opinions observes that the framing of climate change effects does not often lead to concerns about personal harms (only 42%); neither does it lead to people's behavioural change to discuss climate change issue occasionally (36%) (Marlon et al., 2019). It is likely that the politicization of climate change issues is a major factor to undermine many claims about these negative effects (Pew Research Center, 2016). Many because they are undoubtedly interwoven with the public's existing political affiliation and their trust in climate scientists (*ibid.*). While 67% of the U.S. adults believe climate scientists should have a major role in climate-related policies, only 48% among conservative Republicans, but 80% of liberal Democrats, agree with the statement (*ibid.*). Trust in climate scientists as a major of information source that the public learn about the causes of climate changes also varies among conservative Republicans (15%) and liberal Democrats (70%) (*ibid.*). The polarized views on the communication source are likely to affect how climate change issues are debated and communicated to the public.

Existing research on the framing of climate change issues often focuses on the news framing practices of media organizations that "condense complex events into interesting and appealing news reports" (Nisbet, 2010, p.47). This book chapter will focus on how different news organizations (outlets) frame climate change issues either positively or negatively before and after Trump's Presidency. Media have become an importance source of climate change information; 32% of the U.S. adults hear about global warming in the media at least a week, while 66% of them learn about the issue once a month or less often (Marlon et al., 2019). Both traditional and emerging media play an important role in communicating to the public about the severity of climate change issues (Olteanu et al., 2015). About 38% of the U.S. adults surveyed consider mainstream media as trustworthy sources of information on climate change, while about 13% of them trust social media (Statista, 2018). The study of frame building practices of climate change issues in the media is particularly important because a consensus among national and international stakeholders will ultimately affect government policies, regulations, and international collaboration to remedy any global warming effects (Jang & Sol Hart, 2015).

The rapid ascent of emerging media has made these platforms a viable news source to readers to engage with climate change conversations (Ellis, 2019). The recent exponential growth of social media has changed how the public obtains their news about climate change to shape their behaviour, knowledge, and opinion (Anderson, 2017). As a result, scholars have directed their investigation to discuss how conversations and interpersonal interactions facilitated by social media to generate frames about climate change (Jang & Sol Hart, 2015). For example, in a recent tweet against President Trump's stance of clean air, Obama has framed Trump's reduction of fuel efficiency standards as a "climate change denial" and "a delayed response to COVID-19" (Perez, 2020, n.p.).

Conventional framing research of mass media contents mostly emphasizes the identification of salient frames in the media contents (Jang & Sol Hart, 2015). For example, after extensively analysing media contents, five types of risks related to climate changes are identified to discuss the presence, the accuracy, the consequences, the causes, and the remedy of these human-caused risks (as cited in Jang & Sol Hart, 2015, p.12). Shehata and Hopmann (2012) study cross-national news coverage in climate change by examining U.S. and Swedish newspapers by identifying climate change frame and scientific uncertainty frame. Many framing researchers have also attempt to explain variations of frame building in terms of news organizations' political orientation. For example, Jang and Sol Hart (2015) observe the polarization of framing climate changes among Democrat and Republican voters, as well as media outlets along the partisan political stance (Jang & Sol Hart, 2015).

Traditional framing research depends on content analysis method to identify recurrent frames in news contents (Entman, 1993). Content analysis type of framing analysis has often relied on human coders to categorize media contents to generate identifiable and salient frames (Jang & Sol Hart, 2015). In recent years, conventional framing research has also been criticized by its data processing ability to handle a large amount of media data (Lin, Ha, & Liao, 2016; Yang & Kang, 2018). Another criticism is related to the fundamental methodological problem that traditionally framing research often relies on coders' subjective interpretation and judgement of media contents (Trilling & Jonkman, 2018) in the data categorization process. Increasingly, computational text processing methods, or commonly known as text mining methods, have gained wide applications in framing research to facilitate the identification of frames (Lin et al., 2016; Odijk, Burscher, Vliegenthart, & de Rijke, 2013; Yang & Kang, 2018). Because of the inherent methodological problems of traditional content analysis and coding, Hase et al. (2020) employ a combination of unsupervised machine learning and manual coding to identify themes and topics in news contents in both the United States and the United Kingdom for a period of 28 years.

Research Method

Using Text Mining Methods in Framing Research

To provide answers to our research questions to examine if Trump's Presidency has influenced the frame building practices among U.S. news organizations. We used a computational framing technique (Hase et al., 2020) to extract repetitive words, phrases, and topics from the newspaper articles and examine their pre- and post-Trump differences. Recent advances in computational data processing have enabled environmental communication researchers to analyse a large amount of data systematically, without biases, without coders' errors, and more objectively (Diakopoulos et al., 2013; Yang & Kang, 2018) to identify common topics in the media corpus (Hase et al., 2020). This research technique also allows researcher to "explore and structure corpora as a form of *distant reading*" (*ibid.*).

Furthermore, computational research methods allow many framing researchers of climate change topics to extract recurrent words and phrases and contextualize them in media texts to answer our research questions (Trilling & Jonkman, 2018)—a function similar to many traditional framing research used in climate change studies (Aykut et al., 2012; Kim et al., 2014; McKewon, 2012). Among various computational methods, the text mining techniques are most relevant to environmental communication researchers who attempt to extract meaningful, repetitive, and useful insights and patterns from unstructured textual data (He, Zha, & Li, 2013). Particularly, the topic modelling procedure help identify and reveal topical patterns in the media corpus (Rathore & Roy, 2014)—a function similar to the human coding of salient categories, themes, and topics in traditional framing research using content analysis methods (Hase et al., 2020). Researchers who have adopted text mining methods have applauded their effectiveness in terms of the automatic generation of frames and the methodological improvement from traditional framing research (Yang & Kang, 2018).

Sampling Method, Sample Characteristics, and Pre-processing Media Corpus

This study used QDA Miner and its add-on program, WORDStat, to analyse media data collected from the mainstream English-language media. As the first step to pre-process data, we compiled the media corpus, based on one key phrase search, "climate change", from the Lexis/Nexis database. The first search has generated 654 articles that include all major international news sources. Six duplicate cases were filtered and removed from the media corpus as part of the pre-processing procedure. In the end, a total of 648 articles were included in our media corpus. Since the study focuses on the U.S. media outlets only, we employed the case filter function to select only media outlets published in the United States. Seventy cases (N=70) were identified to be included in the text mining analysis.

Unlike previous framing research that often sampled from major media outlets (i.e., *The Washington Post* and *USA Today*) (Olausson, 2014), this study has collected from a wide variety of newspapers, both national and local, in the United States. Given the limited number of articles available, we did not filter the collected newspapers on the basis of their political ideologies. For example, two articles (2.8%) are from *Anchorage Daily News*; eight articles are from *NewsDay* (11.4%). National newspapers in different political spectrum are also sampled, which include *The New York Times* (N=4, 5.7% of the sample) and *The Christian Science Monitor* (N=3, 4.3% of the sample). Unlike traditional framing research of climate change (Jang & Sol Hart, 2015; Stecula & Merkley, 2019), we did not solely rely on national (or supposedly influential) news outlets (such as *the New York Times, Wall Street Journal, The Washington Post*). Most American readers are likely to receive news about climate change from their local newspapers instead. What they think about the importance of climate change still plays a significant role in the democratic process that will results in policy changes and government actions (Stecula & Merkley, 2019).

We followed the data cleaning procedures in excluding unimportant words or characters, lowercase conversion, stop word removal, text segmentation, and word stemming (Kobayashi et al., 2018). Some examples include the removal of words such as "Percent" (case frequency=75), "Year" (case frequency=47), and "Mr." (case frequency=39).

Findings and Discussion

To answer our research questions, several commonly used text mining procedures were employed to provide empirical data about the salience of various keywords and phrases before and after Trump's Presidency (RQ1 and RQ2). The extraction of keywords and phrases is "a concise representation of the article's content" (Vivek, 2018). Aggregately, these keywords and phrases can help researchers to identify major concepts in the media corpus. In addition, we also examine the frequency statistics, called Term-Frequency (TF) or TF-IDF (Term-Frequency-Inverse document Frequency) among extracted keywords, phrases, or terms to estimate their relative importance within the collected media documents (Tesoa, Olmedillab, Martínez-Torresc, & Toral, 2018). TF-IDF statistics calculates the occurrence of a word after adjusting for the rarity of its usage (*UC Business Analytics R Programming Guide*, n.d.). The statistics will help researchers to identify important content words, relevant to their research topics, by decreasing the weight of words such as "the", "a", or "an" commonly appearing in a document (*UC Business Analytics R Programming Guide*, n.d.).

In addition, we also employed the data visualization procedure, word cloud analysis, in the text mining methods to represent graphically the frequency of keywords, phrases, and terms (Srivastava, 2014). The word cloud analysis shows repetitive words such as "Global" (N=110, TF-IDF=21.1), "National" (N=95, TF-IDF=36.4), "Science" (N=92, TF-IDF=32.9), "Policy" (N=84, TF-IDF=27.6), "Government" (N=74, TF-IDF=24.2), "Adaptation" (N=69, TF-IDF=30.9), and "Carbon" (N=66, TF-IDF=27.9) (refer to Fig. 23.1 and Table 23.1 below).

Although previous framing research on climate change has criticized the biased news coverage among the elite media (such as *The New York Times, The Los Angeles Times, The Washington Post*) (Boykoff & Boykoff, 2004), the extracted keywords do not demonstrate a strong tendency to distort what causes climate change, what remedies should be taken, and by whom. The repetitive occurrence of the keywords, "Policy" and "Government", point to the role of political intervention to address climate change problems at both national and global levels. Furthermore, the causes of climate change have been identified as "carbon (dioxide)". The emergence of "Science" as an important keyword in the database also concurs with the role of scientists and science consensus on what causes global warming (Marlon et al., 2019).

Fig. 23.1 Word cloud. NOTE: on the basis of word frequency. Source: The authors

Table 23.1 Keyword extraction

	Frequency	% Total	No. cases	% Cases	TF • IDF
Global	112	0.25%	47	67.14%	19.4
National	95	0.21%	29	41.43%	36.4
Science	93	0.21%	31	44.29%	32.9
State	93	0.21%	25	35.71%	41.6
Policy	88	0.19%	34	48.57%	27.6
Percent	77	0.17%	20	28.57%	41.9
Government	74	0.16%	33	47.14%	24.2
Public	74	0.16%	28	40.00%	29.4
Adaptation	69	0.15%	25	35.71%	30.9
Scientists	69	0.15%	28	40.00%	27.5
Environmental	68	0.15%	35	50.00%	20.5
Carbon	66	0.15%	27	38.57%	27.3
Trump	66	0.15%	10	14.29%	55.8
Country	64	0.14%	32	45.71%	21.8
Environment	64	0.14%	29	41.43%	24.5
Issues	64	0.14%	35	50.00%	19.3
Impacts	62	0.14%	27	38.57%	25.7
Warming	60	0.13%	29	41.43%	23.0
Energy	58	0.13%	22	31.43%	29.2
Issue	58	0.13%	37	52.86%	16.1
Effects	57	0.13%	34	48.57%	17.9
Department	55	0.12%	18	25.71%	32.4
Human	54	0.12%	24	34.29%	25.1
Research	54	0.12%	28	40.00%	21.5
Report	52	0.12%	21	30.00%	27.2
Security	51	0.11%	21	30.00%	26.7
Threat	49	0.11%	19	27.14%	27.8
Weather	49	0.11%	24	34.29%	22.8

Source: The authors

Key Phrase Extraction

QDA Miner and *WordStat* also offer an easy-to-use tool to extra key phrases in the unstructured texts from our media corpus. This text mining procedure enables researchers to extract the most salient phrases in the documents and is useful for "document categorization, clustering, indexing, search, and summarization" (DeWilde, 2014, n.p.). As seen Fig. 23.2 and Table 23.2 below, the key phrases, "global warming" is the most conspicuous phrase when the newspaper media in the United States frame climate change topics. The term has appeared 44 times (39.29%) (TF-IDF=20.5). Another noteworthy key phrase in our corpus is "Carbon Dioxide" (N=22, 11.43%, TF-IDF=20.7). "National Security" is also a significant key phrase in our media corpus (N=22, 12.86%, TF-IDF=19.6), as well as "Weather Events" (N=15, 10%, TF-IDF=15.0), "Weather Patterns" (N=14, 10% TF-IDF=14.0), "Clean Energy" (N=13, 8.57% TF-IDF=13.9).

DISASTER MANAGEMENT PROVINCIAL GOVERNMENTS
LONG TERM   CAUSED BY HUMANS
WEATHER PATTERNS   DEFENSE DEPARTMENT
DONALD TRUMP WEATHER EVENTS
CARBON DIOXIDE EARTH HOUR
GLOBAL WARMING
FOOD SECURITY NATIONAL SECURITY
HUMAN ACTIVITY
UNITED NATIONS OPINION LEADERS
CARBON EMISSIONS FOSSIL FUEL CLEAN ENERGY
ADAPTATION AND MITIGATION SEA LEVELS

Fig. 23.2 Key phrase extraction. NOTE: minimum=10. Source: The authors

Table 23.2 Extracted key phrases (Minimum frequency=10)

	Frequency	No. cases	% Cases	TF-IDF
Global warming	44	24	34.29%	20.5
Carbon dioxide	22	8	11.43%	20.7
National security	22	9	12.86%	19.6
Opinion leaders	20	1	1.43%	36.9
Donald Trump	16	6	8.57%	17.1
Weather events	15	7	10.00%	15.0
Defense Department	14	5	7.14%	16.0
United Nations	14	12	17.14%	10.7
Weather patterns	14	7	10.00%	14.0
Clean energy	13	6	8.57%	13.9
Earth hour	13	1	1.43%	24.0
Fossil fuel	13	6	8.57%	13.9
Carbon emissions	12	7	10.00%	12.0
Adaptation and mitigation	11	7	10.00%	11.0
Caused by humans	11	6	8.57%	11.7
Food security	11	7	10.00%	11.0
Human activity	11	5	7.14%	12.6
Long term	11	5	7.14%	12.6
Sea levels	11	8	11.43%	10.4
Disaster management	10	5	7.14%	11.5

Source: The authors

Similar to what traditional framing research has reported about climate change, the extracted key phrases below concur with the focus on causes of climate change in recent literature. Emerging key phrases that are related to climate change are observed in terms of "Fossil Fuels" (N=13, 8.57% TF-IDF=13.9), "Carbon Emissions" (N=12, 10% TF-IDF=12.0), "Caused by Humans" (N=11, 8.57% TF-IDF=11.7), and "Human Activity" (N=11, 7.14%

TF-IDF=12.6). The TF-IDF statistics suggest how these key phrases are used in the media corpus to describe (frame) climate change in the United States (Silge & Robinson, 2019).

These most important frames as emerged in our media corpus are mainly the causality frame, meaning what causes climate change and global warming to occur. These findings are consistent with the large-scale national Yale survey that most U.S. adults agree that global warming is caused by human activities (52%) and CO_2 as a main source of pollutant that needs to be regulated (72%) (Marlon et al., 2019). The discussion of bio-fuel, though important, does not appear to be the most important frame (Kim et al., 2014).

Variations Before and After Trump's Presidency in 2017

Our second research question aims to compare whether climate change narratives have changed in response to Trump's Presidency as a result of frame building by media organizations. Several key phrases (frames) related to the representations of climate change in the U.S. newspaper media are identified to examine whether Trump's Presidency accounts for how different frames are used before and after his election. For example, in terms of "Global Warming", the frame appears 37 times before Trump's Presidency, but only appears 7 times afterwards (refer to Fig. 23.3 below).

Scepticism is often associated with claims about the climate change effects (Jang & Sol Hart, 2015). This mentality persists among many sceptics regardless when Trump was elected. For example, before Trump's Presidency, media have voiced their disbelief by saying, "Why would some people always want to believe that global warming is wholly man-made?" (Article #199). While the percent of people who deny the cause of human activities is decreasing from 37% in March 2012 to 23% in December 2018, the longitudinal data suggest the group of climate change deniers often account for 1/3 of the U.S. population, reflecting their existence in the U.S. society (Marlon et al., 2019).

However, Trump's Presidency seems to worsen the already existing political partisan division among climate change supporters and non-believers (Jang & Sol Hart, 2015). Jang and Sol Hart (2015) observe that Republicans tend to

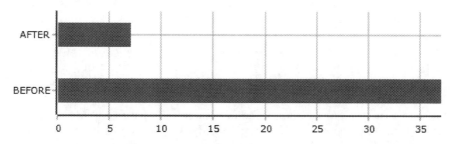

Fig. 23.3 "Global Warming" before and after Trump's Presidency. Source: The authors

take a passive stance and often use a hoax frame when referring to climate change. Gustafson et al. (2020) used a national survey of representative Americans and confirmed that, while Republicans support the use of renewal energy for economic benefits, Democrats are motivated by global warming concerns. President Trump's positions on climate change and global warming issues have led 70% of Democrats to believe that environmentalists will lose influence under his administration (Statista, 2017). While Trump's overall job approval rating is high at 45% on December 15, 2019 (Gallup, 2019), only 36% approve, yet 55% disapprove, his handling of environmental issues (Statista, 2019c). President Trump has been accused of "swapping scientists for sycophants" and "puppeteering the climate change narrative" (Menarndt & Menard, 2018, n.p.).

Furthermore, the Trump Administration has also been said to remove the mentioning of climate change and global warming from several government websites or even the access to documents related to these two topics (*ibid.*). According to a report by *The Guardian* (2017), Bianca Moebius-Clune, the Director of Soil Health, under the Department of Agriculture, was reported to replace phrases such as "climate change" and "climate change adaptation" with "weather extremes" and "resilience to weather extremes" in her internal emails (Milman, 2017). This suggests the Trump Administration attempts to frame climate change and global warming issues differently to shape public perceptions of these issues. On Earth Day 2020, President Trump claimed, after planting a tree outside the White House, that the United States has "the cleanest air and cleanest water than anywhere else on Earth"—a statement Obama criticizes to be a lie (Woodward, 2020).

In one of his press releases in front the White House, President Trump openly criticized the negative impacts of environmental regulations on American economy and his campaign promises (Zurcher, 2018, n.p.):

> For many decades, an ever-growing maze of regulations, rules, restrictions has cost our country trillions and trillions of dollars, millions of jobs, countless American factories, and devastated many industries. But all that changed the day I took the oath of office.

Another frame of climate change causes, "Carbon Dioxide", also shows variations before and after Trump's Presidency (before=14 times, after=8 times) (refer to Fig. 23.4 below). The framing of carbon dioxide (emissions) as the cause of climate change is also linked to human activities. For example, in Article #96, human activity is considered to be "at the core of the controversy. … carbon dioxide generated by human activity is the overwhelming cause of current warming." Another article (#91) also confirms that "Carbon dioxide is still the cause. But now, human activity, not nature, is generating it." Furthermore, the emission of carbon dioxide is associated with terms such as "a greenhouse gas and black carbon or soot as a sunlight-absorbing warming agent" which all lead to "human-caused climate change" (Article #647). These

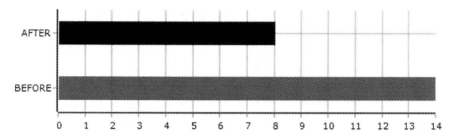

Fig. 23.4 "Carbon Dioxide" before and after Trump's Presidency. Source: The authors

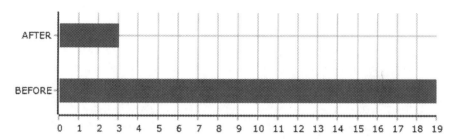

Fig. 23.5 "National Security" before and after Trump's Presidency. Source: The authors

newspaper articles also support the majority of scientific consensus that agree climate change and global warming are due to the use of non-renewable sources of energy (such as coal, fracking, gas, oil, and nuclear plants) to meet the needs for energy (Greenpeace, n.d.-a, n.d.-b). As a result of the emissions of greenhouse gases and carbon dioxide, climate change and global warming have led to the rise of extreme weather events, increasing global temperature, the melting of polar ice (Greenpeace, n.d.-a, n.d.-b), and even human health (Maibach et al., 2015).

"National Security" also stands out as one of the noticeable frames before (N=19) and after (N=3) Trump's Presidency (refer to Fig. 23.5). Previous literature (Jang & Sol Hart, 2015; Stecula & Merkley, 2019) had not identified this aspect of climate change as an important frame. Existing research on the framing of climate change often examine its economic benefit and consequence, ideological division that causes bipartisan perception of climate change, and scepticism about scientific facts supporting its existence and impacts (Stecula & Merkley, 2019), but rarely tie it with national security concerns. Interestingly, this frame emerges even before Trump Presidency, as seen in the following newspaper article (#327) about the Democrats' primary election among several presidential contestants:

> The suggestion of a link between climate change and terrorism sends Republicans into new rounds of apoplexy. During the Nov. 14 Democratic presidential debate

in Iowa, the day after the terrorist attacks in Paris, U.S. Sen. Bernie Sanders reaffirmed his assertion that climate change is a greater national security threat than terrorism, saying, In fact, climate change is directly related to the growth of terrorism.

Interestingly, while the "Weather Events" frame appears 15 times before Trump's Presidency, none has appeared afterwards (refer to Fig. 23.6 below). Similarly, "Carbon Emissions" frame appears 12 times before Trump's Presidency, while zero occurrence has been observed afterwards (refer to Fig. 23.7 below).

Before Trump's Presidency, the media outlets had emphasized on the negative effects of climate changes by providing a vivid description of these extreme weather events:

> The map comes two weeks after the publication of a massive report that also analyzed climate change for anthropogenic contributions. In that report, the scientists plumbed 12 extreme weather events from 2012 for the degree to which human factors contributed to the disasters, finding that about half the events had anthropogenic underpinnings. Among the events in which humans were contributing factors was Hurricane Sandy, which in part derived its unusual force from high sea levels that sent tides ballooning over the US's East Coast, the researchers said. (Article #134)

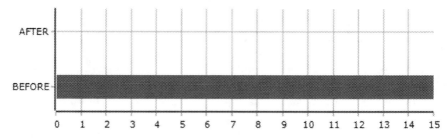

Fig. 23.6 "Weather Events" before and after Trump's Presidency. Source: The authors

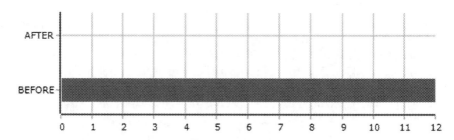

Fig. 23.7 "Carbon Emissions" before and after Trump's Presidency. Source: The authors

Echoing Jang and Sol Hart's (2015) observation on the framing practice of climate change is linked with the risk, climate change is often framed as "uncertainty and risk" as reported by Stecula and Merkley (2019). This type of framing building of climate change issues often associate climate change and its consequence with negative effects of greenhouse gas emissions, fossil fuel consumption, and global warming (Stecula & Merkley, 2019) as seen in the article below:

> Rising global temperatures, changing precipitation patterns, climbing sea levels, and more extreme weather events will intensify the challenges of global instability, hunger, poverty, and conflict. (Article #327)

Interestingly, as noted in Milman (2017) about the censorship of climate change terms by the Trump Administration, it seems that Trump has rather tried to dissociated climate change as a human-caused event, and attributed any extreme weather patterns to God's will, as seen below:

> Trump has made it clear that he is a climate change conspiracy theorist. He does not accept that the phenomenon is man-made nor that it even exists. Instead, Trump states that all the shown effects of climate change are actually weather events (Article #224)

One of the frames related to climate change focuses on its remedies and solutions (Jang & Sol Hart, 2015). In our findings, we note that, "Carbon Emissions" is often associated with potential solutions such as green technology as seen in two articles below:

> Event organizers say that this year's Earth Hour is particularly important because of the recent Paris agreement on climate change, which includes worldwide efforts to reduce carbon emissions and spread green technology. (Article #86)

> Sanders' plan includes the following goals: create a clean-energy workforce of 10 million jobs, a 100 percent clean energy system, ban nuclear energy, cut carbon emissions by 40 percent with a tax, and return billions of dollars to consumers affected by climate change. (Article #228)

Framing climate change as the consequence of human activities is common among environmental communication researchers (Jang & Sol Hart, 2015). In the text mining data, we also note that, before Trump's Presidency, there are ten occurrences of this key phrase, while afterwards, there is only one instance (refer to Fig. 23.8). To remedy any negative consequences of climate change, policies, regulations, technological innovations, and even consumer behaviours are required to adapt and mitigate these effects. Before Trump's Presidency, there are 11 occurrences of this phrase, while none appears afterwards (refer to Figs. 23.8 and 23.9 below).

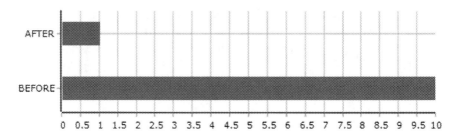

Fig. 23.8 "Caused by Humans" before and after Trump's Presidency. Source: The authors

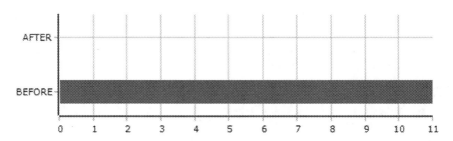

Fig. 23.9 "Adaption and Mitigation" before and after Trump's Presidency. Source: The authors

The "Caused by humans" frame is considered one type of ideological frame (Stecula & Merkley, 2019) and commonly associate with political bipartisanship in the United States. Echoing Jang and Sol Hart's (2015) observation on how Republicans and Democrats view climate change, whether climate change is caused by human activities depends on how journalists and political elites use this type of frames to emphasize "the ideological threat of climate action, in the form of larger government, reduced American sovereignty, and sizable restrictions on free market competition" (Stecula & Merkley, 2019).

In the Republican primary, presidential candidates have also viewed climate change issues differently below:

> Kasich's views on climate change differ considerably from the other GOP candidates' views. Kasich said he accepts that climate change is a reality and serious problem caused by humans. ... Both Trump and Cruz said they believe climate-change is in some way pseudo-scientific and that weather is the primary source to blame, while Kasich finds climate change to be an issue that is being caused by humans. (Article #228)

Conclusion

This text mining study confirms the consistency of framing climate change across different media platforms (Jang & Sol Hart, 2015). Our study confirms the close relationship between climate change and global warming as framed in the newspaper articles in the United States. Jang and Sol Hart (2015) argue that sceptics of climate change favour "global warming" over more neutral term, "climate change". Jang and Sol Hart (2015) also reports that "global warming" is preferred over "climate change" when referring to any negative effects of greenhouse gas emissions. Unfortunately, the methodological limitations of this text mining study do not allow us to investigate Jang and Sol Hart's (2015) assessment further.

Several research limitations should be cautioned to interpret our findings. First, text mining methods are limited by the type and the number of articles entered into the database. Second, methodological considerations of text mining methods also include (1) the decision to choose frames at different levels of analysis (e.g., words, phrases, sentences, paragraphs, articles); (2) how big/comprehensive should our corpus be?; (3) how to create and interpret Frames?; and (4) transparency and clarity in the data analysis (Lin et al., 2016). This study mainly focuses on newspaper articles from the United States. Future research may explore a comparative approach of analysing newspaper corpus from two or multiple countries (Aykut et al., 2012). In addition, scholars have also examined the framing of climate change and global warming issues on Twitter (Jang & Sol Hart, 2015) and at various geographical locations (Zhang, van der Linden, Marlon, Howe, & Leiserowitz, 2018). Further research may explore frame building practices among different media platforms (Olteanu et al., 2015) and at different geographical locations. Third, we used Trump's Presidency in 2017 as a major historical event to compare our pre- and post-Trump framing building practices Future research that employs multiple historical events (such as 2020 Presidential Election) will help assess the rigour and usefulness of text mining methods as a viable research technique.

One of the contributions of this study is to employ text mining techniques to help analyse media discourses about climate change in the United States. This book chapter has identified recurrent keywords and key phrases about climate change on the basis of a large set of mass media discourses in the United States. The study has provided evidence to demonstrate the emerging frames related to climate change before and after Trump's Presidency. As demonstrated in the empirical data, Trump's Presidency has affected how mass media such as newspapers in the United States represent climate change issues. Furthermore, this study has explored the relationships between media's framing practices and Trump's Presidency. However, increasingly, some scholars have begun to explore how individual journalists influence the framing of a news story (Vossen, van Gorp, & Schulpen, 2018). Lastly, unlike previous environmental communication research (Jang & Sol Hart, 2015; Stecula & Merkley, 2019), this study also offers an initial attempt to apply the text mining method to study the framing of climate change.

References

Alemany, Jacqueline. (2017, March 28). Trump executive order will dismantle Obama environmental regulations. *CBS New*: Retrieved April 22, 2020, from https://www.cbsnews.com/news/trump-executive-order-will-dismantle-obama-environmental-regulations/.

Anderson, Ashley A. (2017, March). Effects of Social Media Use on Climate Change Opinion, Knowledge, and Behavior. *Oxford Research Encyclopedia of Climate Science*: 1-20. https://doi.org/10.1093/acrefore/9780190228620.013.369.

Aykut, S. C., Comby, J.-B., & Guillemo, H. (2012). Climate Change Controversies in French Mass Media 1990-2010. *Journalism Studies, 13*(2), 157–174. https://doi.org/10.1080/1461670X.2011.646395

BBC News. 2018, November 26. Trump on Climate Change Report: 'I Don't Believe It'. *BBC News*: Retrieved December 28, 2019 from https://www.bbc.com/news/world-us-canada-46351940.

Boykoff, M. T., & Boykoff, J. M. (2004). Balance of Bias: Global Warming and the US Prestige Press. *Global Environmental Change, 14*, 125–136.

Bradsher, Keith, & Lisa Friedman. (2017, December 19). China Unveils an Ambitious Plan to Curb Climate Change Emissions. *The New York Times*: Retrieved December 29, 2019 from https://www.nytimes.com/2017/12/19/climate/china-carbon-market-climate-change-emissions.html.

Brewster, Jack. (2020, March 30). Trump, In Latest Blow to Obama's Environmental Legacy, To Announce Loosening of Vehicle Fuel Economy Standards. *Forbes*. Retrieved April 22, 2020, from https://www.forbes.com/sites/jackbrewster/2020/03/30/trump-in-latest-blow-to-obamas-environmental-legacy-to-announce-loosening-of-vehicle-fuel-economy-standards/#8bf85f43688b.

Cook, J. (2019). Understanding and Countering Misinformation About Climate Change. In I. Chiluwa & S. Samoilenko (Eds.), *Handbook of Research on Deception, Fake News, and Misinformation Online* (pp. 281–306). Hershey, PA: IGI-Global.

D'Angelo, P., & Kuypers, J. A. (2010). Introduction: Doing News Framing Analysis. In P. D'Angelo & J. A. Kuypers (Eds.), *Doing News Framing Analysis: Empirical and Theoretical Perspectives* (pp. 1–14). New York, NY: Routledge.

Davis, J. J. (1995). The Effects of Message Framing on Response to Environmental Communication. *Journal of Journalism and Mass Communication Quarterly, 72*(2), 285–299.

DeWilde, Burton. (2014, September 23). Intro to Automatic Keyphrase Extraction. *Burton DeWilde Website*: Retrieved April 25, 2019 from http://bdewilde.github.io/blog/2014/09/23/intro-to-automatic-keyphrase-extraction/.

Diakopoulos, N., Zhang, A., & Salway, A. (2013). Visual Analytics of Media Frames in Online News and Blogs. IEEE InfoVis Workshop on Text Visualization, Atlanta, Georgia, USA, October 13-18.

Donald J. Trump for President, Inc. (n.d.). Energy and Environment: President Donald J. Trump Achievements. *Donald J. Trump for President, Inc.*: Retrieved April 22, 2020 from https://www.promiseskept.com/achievement/overview/energy-and-environment/.

Ellis, Katherine K. (2019, September 26). How Social Media Is Driving the Climate Change Conversation. *Newship*. Retrieved April 24, 2020 from https://www.newswhip.com/2019/09/social-media-is-driving-the-climate-change-conversation/.

Entman, R. M. (1993). Framing: Toward Clarification of a Fractured Paradigm. *Journal of Communication, 43*(4), 51–58.

Entman, R. M. (2010). Framing Media Power. In P. D'Angelo & J. A. Kuypers (Eds.), *Doing News Framing Analysis: Empirical and Theoretical Perspectives* (pp. 331–355). New York, NY: Routledge.

Gallup. (2019). *Trump Job Approval.* Washington, DC: Gallup.

Greenpeace. (n.d.-a). "Global Warming Issues & Threats." *Greenpeace*: Retrieved on April 22, 2020 from https://www.greenpeace.org/usa/global-warming/issues/.

Greenpeace. (n.d.-b). "Climate Change Impacts." *Greenpeace*: Retrieved on April 22, 2020 from https://www.greenpeace.org/usa/issues/climate-change-impacts/.

Gustafson, A., Goldberg, M., Kotcher, J., Rosenthal, S., Maibach, E., Ballew, M., et al. (2020). Republicans and Democrats Differ In Their Primary Reasons For Supporting Renewable Energy. *Energy Policy, 141*, 11448.

Harrington, Rebecca. (2016, November 9). President-elect Donald Trump Doesn't Believe in Climate Change. Here's His Platform on the Environment. *Business Insider.* Retrieved September 9, 2018 from https://www.businessinsider.com/donald-trump-climate-change-global-warming-environment-policies-plans-platforms-2016-10.

Hase, V., Engelke, K. M., & Kieslich, K. (2020). The Things We Fear. Combining Automated and Manual Content Analysis to Uncover Themes, Topics and Threats in Fear-Related News. *Journalism Studies, 21*(6), 1–19. https://doi.org/10.1080/1461670X.2020.1753092

He, W., Zha, S., & Li, L. (2013). Social Media Competitive Analysis and Text Mining: A Case Study in the Pizza Industry. *International Journal of Information Management, 33*(3), 464–472.

Irfan, Umair. (2019, June 25). "Why the Democratic Party Doesn't Want a Presidential Debate About Climate Change." *Vox*: Retrieved December 29, 2019 from https://www.vox.com/policy-and-politics/2019/6/14/18662697/climate-change-2019-democratic-debates.

Jang, S. M., & Sol Hart, P. (2015). Polarized Frames on "Climate Change" and "Global Warming" Across Countries and States: Evidence from Twitter Big Data. *Global Environmental Change, 25*(3), 11–17.

Johnson, Carrie. (2017, January 20). "In Inaugural Address, Trump Decries 'Carnage' and Promises 'America First'." *National Public Radio (NPR)*: Retrieved December 28, 2019 from https://www.npr.org/2017/01/20/510746700/donald-trump-sworn-in-as-the-45th-president-of-the-united-states.

Kaufman, Alexander C. (2017, June 1). "Donald Trump Pulls U.S. Out of Paris Accord in Crushing Blow to Climate Fight." *HuffPost*, 2017, June 1. Retrieved September 9, 2018 from https://www.huffingtonpost.com/entry/donald-trump-paris-agreement-global-warming_us_593030dae4b07572bdbf9a33.

Kim, S.-H., Besley, J. C., Sang-Hwa, O., & Kim, S. Y. (2014). Talking About bio-Fuel in the News. *Journalism Studies, 15*(2), 218–234. https://doi.org/10.1080/1461670X.2013.809193

Kobayashi, Vladimer B., Mol, Stefan T., Berkers, Hannah A., Kismihók, Gábor, & Den Hartog, Deanne N. (2018). Text Mining in Organizational Research. *Organizational Research Methods, 21*(3), 733–765.

Lashof, Daniel. (2004, May 24). "Global Warming and 'The Day After Tomorrow'." *Gotham Gazette*: Retrieved December 29, 2019 from https://www.gothamgazette.com/environment/2430-global-warming-and-the-day-after-tomorrow.

Lin, Fu-Ren, Ha, De, & Liao, Dachi. (2016). "Automatic Content Analysis of Media Framing by Text Mining Techniques." 49th Hawaii International Conference on System Sciences, January 5-8.

Liptak, Kevin, & Acosta, Jim. (2017, June 2). "Trump on Paris accord: 'We're getting out'." *CNN Politics*, 2017, June 2, Retrieved September 9, 2018 from https://www.cnn.com/2017/06/01/politics/trump-paris-climate-decision/index.html.

Lorenz, Jonna. (2014, November 19). "Global Warming Movies: The 8 Most Influential Climate Change Movies." *Newsmax*: Retrieved December 29, 2019 from https://www.newsmax.com/FastFeatures/global-warming-movies-influential/2014/11/19/id/607971/.

Maibach, E. W., Kreslake, J. M., Roser-Renouf, C., Rosenthal, S., Feinberg, G., & Leiserowitz, A. A. (2015). Do Americans Understand That Global Warming Is Harmful to Human Health? Evidence from a National Survey. *Annals of Global Health, 81*(3), 396–409.

Marlon, Jennifer, Howe, Peter, Mildenberger, Matto, Leiserowitz, Anthony, & Wang, Xinran. (2019, September 17). "Yale Climate Opinion Maps 2019." *Yale Program on Climate Change*: Retrieved April 23, 2020 from https://climatecommunication.yale.edu/visualizations-data/ycom-us/.

Mathiesen, Karl. (2017, May 31). "Trump: Paris Agreement Decision Will Make America Great Again." *Climate Home News*: Retrieved December 29, 2019 from https://www.climatechangenews.com/2017/05/31/trump-withdraw-paris-agreement-reports/.

McConnell, Scott. (2016, June 27). "Why Trump Wins." *The American Conservative*: Retrieved April 23, 2020 from https://www.theamericanconservative.com/articles/why-trump-wins/.

McKewon, E. (2012). Talking Points AMMO: The Use of Neoliberal Think Tank Fantasy Themes to Delegitimise Scientific Knowledge of Climate Change in Australian. *Journalism Studies, 13*(2), 277–297. https://doi.org/10.1080/1461670X.2011.646403

Menarndt, Aubrey, & Menard, Luke. (2018, February 6). "Evaluating the environmental impacts of Trump's Presidency." *Pacific Standard*: Retrieved January 2, 2020 from https://psmag.com/environment/trumps-impact-on-the-environment.

Meyerowitz, Beth E., & Chaiken, Shelly. (1987). The Effect of Message Framing on Breast Self-Examination Attitudes, Intentions and Behavior. *Journal of Personality and Social Psychology, 52*, 500–510.

Milman, Oliver. (2017, August 7). "US Federal Department Is Censoring Use of Term 'Climate Change', Emails Reveal." *The Guardian*: Retrieved January 3, 2020 from https://www.theguardian.com/environment/2017/aug/07/usda-climate-change-language-censorship-emails.

Newburger, Emma. (2019, December 26). "5 Major Environmental Regulation Changes Made by Trump Admin. in 2019." *NBC New York*: Retrieved December 28, 2019 from https://www.nbcnewyork.com/news/national-international/5-major-environmental-regulation-changes-made-trump-admin-2019/2250415/.

Nisbet, M. C. (2010). Knowledge into Action: Framing the Debates Over Climate Change and Poverty. In P. D'Angelo & J. A. Kuypers (Eds.), *Doing News Framing Analysis: Empirical and Theoretical Perspectives* (pp. 43–83). New York, NY: Routledge.

Novak, Jake. (2017, May 31). "Trump's Paris Accord Exit Will Save the Environmental Movement from Itself." *CNBC*, 2017, May 31, Retrieved September 9, 2018 from https://www.cnbc.com/2017/05/31/trump-paris-accord-exit-is-good-for-the-environment-commentary.html.

Odijk, D., Burscher, B., Vliegenthart, R., & de Rijke, M. (2013). Automatic Thematic Content Analysis: Finding Frames in News. In A. Jatowt et al. (Eds.), *Social Informatics. SocInfo 2013. Lecture Notes in Computer Science (Vol. 8238)*. Cham, Switzerland: Springer.

Olausson, U. (2014). The Diversified Nature of 'Domesticated' News Discourse: The Case of Climate Change in National News Media. *Journalism Studies, 15*(6), 711–725. https://doi.org/10.1080/1461670X.2013.837253

Olteanu, Alexandra, Castillo, Carlos, Diakopoulos, Nicholas, & Aberer, Karl. (2015, May 26-29). "Comparing Events Coverage in Online News and Social Media: The Case of Climate Change." Proceedings of the Ninth International AAAI Conference on Web and Social Media, Oxford, UK.

Perez, Matt. (2020, March 31). In Rare Knock on Trump, Obama Compares Coronavirus Response to Climate Change Denials. *Forbes*. Retrieved April 23, 2020 from https://www.forbes.com/sites/mattperez/2020/2003/2031/in-rare-knock-on-trump-obama-compares-coronavirus-response-to-climate-changedenials/#c64059379150.

Pew Research Center. (2016, October 4). "The Politics of Climate." *Pew Research Center*. Retrieved April 23, 2020 from https://www.pewresearch.org/science/2016/10/04/the-politics-of-climate/.

Plumer, Brad, & Davenport, Coral. (2019, December 28). "Science Under Attack: How Trump Is Sidelining Researchers and Their Work." *The New York Times/MSN*: Retrieved December 28, 2019 from https://www.msn.com/en-us/news/us/science-under-attack-how-trump-is-sidelining-researchers-and-their-work/ar-BBYqouK?li=BBnbklE.

Qiu, Linda. (2016, July 15). "Donald Trump's top 10 campaign promises." *PolitiFact*: Retrieved April 22, 2020 from https://www.politifact.com/article/2016/jul/15/donald-trumps-top-10-campaign-promises/.

Rathore, A. S., & Roy, D. (2014). Performance of LDA and DCT models. *Journal of Information Science, 40*(3), 281–292.

Revkin, Andrew. (2019, January 23). "Most Americans Now Worry About Climate Change and Want to Fix It." *National Geographic*: Retrieved April 22, 2020 from https://www.nationalgeographic.com/environment/2019/01/climate-change-awareness-polls-show-rising-concern-for-global-warming/#close.

Shehata, A., & Hopmann, D. N. (2012). Framing Climate Change. *Journalism Studies, 13*(2), 175–192. https://doi.org/10.1080/1461670X.2011.646396

Silge, J., & Robinson, D. (2019, March 23). *Text Mining with R: A Tidy Approach*. Sebastopol, California: O'Reilly.

Srivastava, Tavish. (2014). "Build a Word Cloud using Text Mining Tools of R." *Analytics Vidhya*, May 7. Retrieved April 25, 2019, from https://www.analyticsvidhya.com/blog/2014/05/build-word-cloud-text-mining-tools/.

Statista. (2017). "Opinion on Who Will Gain/Lose Influence Under a Trump Presidency as of January 2017." *Statista*. Retrieved April 22, 2020 from https://www.statista.com/statistics/661111/gainers-and-losers-under-president-trump/.

Statista. (2018). *Climate Change Sources Considered Most Trustworthy Among U.S. Adults in 2017 and 2018*. New York, NY: Statista, Inc.

Statista. (2019a). *Global Climate Change*. New York, NY: Statista, Inc.

Statista. (2019b). *Opinions of Climate Change in the U.S*. New York, NY: Statista, Inc.

Statista. (2019c). *Do You Approve or Disapprove of the Way Donald Trump Is Handling the Following Issues?* New York, NY: Statista, Inc.

Stecula, Dominik A., & Merkley, Eric. (2019). "Framing Climate Change: Economics, Ideology, and Uncertainty in American News Media Content From 1988 to 2014." *Frontier in Communication*: Retrieved January 5, 2020 from https://www.frontiersin.org/articles/10.3389/fcomm.2019.00006/full. doi:https://doi.org/10.3389/fcomm.2019.00006.

Tesoa, E., Olmedillab, M., Martínez-Torresc, M. R., & Toral, S. L. (2018). Application of Text Mining Techniques to the Analysis of Discourse in eWOM communications from a Gender Perspective. *Technological Forecasting and Social Change*, 129, 131–142.

The White House President Obama. (2013, June 25). "Cutting Carbon Pollution in America." *The White House President Obama*: Retrieved April 23, 2020 from https://obamawhitehouse.archives.gov/energy/climate-change.

Trilling, D., & Jonkman, J. G. F. (2018). Scaling up Content Analysis. *Communication Methods and Measures*, 12(2-3), 158–174.

UC Business Analytics R Programming Guide. (n.d.) "Text Mining: Term vs. Document Frequency." *Text Mining: Term vs. Document Frequency*: Retrieved January 4, 2020 from https://uc-r.github.io/tf-idf_analysis.

UNESCO. (n.d.). "Addressing Climate Change." *UNESCO*: Retrieved April 23, 2020 from https://en.unesco.org/themes/addressing-climate-change.

Vivek, Sowmya. (2018, December 17). "Automated Keyword Extraction from Articles using NLP." *Analytics Vidhya*: Retrieved April 24, 2020 from https://medium.com/analytics-vidhya/automated-keyword-extraction-from-articles-using-nlp-bfd864f41b34.

Vossen, M., van Gorp, B., & Schulpen, L. (2018). Thinking and Writing About Global Poverty. *Journalism Studies*, 19(14), 2088–2107. https://doi.org/10.1080/1461670X.2017.1316682

Woodward, Alex. (2020, April 20). "Demand More: Obama Calls for People to Stand Against Climate Change as Trump Lies About Air and Water Quality." *The Independent*: Retrieved April 23, 2020 from https://news.yahoo.com/demand-more-obama-calls-people-230724087.html.

Wozniak, A., Wessler, H., & Lück, J. (2017). Who Prevails in the Visual Framing Contest about the United Nations Climate Change Conferences? *Journalism Studies*, 18(11), 1433–1452. https://doi.org/10.1080/1461670X.2015.1131129

Xu, D. Y., Kang, X. W., Zhuang, D. F., & Pan, J. J. (2010, April). Multi-scale Quantitative Assessment of the Relative Roles of Climate Change and Human Activities in Desertification: A Case Study of the Ordos Plateau, China. *Journal of Arid Environments*, 74(4), 498–507.

Yang, Kenneth C. C., & Kang, Y. W. (2018). "A Text Mining Exploration of Mainstream and Social Media Discourses on Internet Censorship and Privacy-Invasive Information-Communication Technologies (ICTs) in China: A Cultural Ecological Analysis." The New Paradigms Communication Education Stream, The Asian Congress for Media and Communication (ACMC) 2018 International Conference, National Chengchi University, Taipei, Taiwan, October 27-29.

Yardley, William. (2016, November 10). "Will Paris Climate Accord and Other Environmental Pacts Survive a Trump Presidency?" *Los Angeles Times*, 2016, November 10, Retrieved September 9, 2018 from http://www.latimes.com/nation/la-na-trump-environment-20161109-story.html.

Zezima, Katie, & Callahan, Matthew. (2016, September 23). "Donald Trump vs. Hillary Clinton on the issues." *The Washington Post*. Retrieved April 22, 2020 from https://www.washingtonpost.com/graphics/politics/political-issues/.

Zhang, Baobao, Linden, Sander van der, Marlon, Jennifer, Howe, Peter, & Leiserowitz, Anthony. (2018, April 16). Experimental Effects of Climate Nessages Vary Geographically. *Nature Climate Change, 8*, 370–374.

Zurcher, Anthony. (2018, January 12). "Ten Ways Trump Has Changed America." *BBC News*. Retrieved April 22, 2020 from https://www.bbc.com/news/world-us-canada-42653793.

CHAPTER 24

Communicating Development: News Coverage of the SDGs in the Nigerian Press

Habeeb Idris Pindiga and Bashir Sa'ad Abdullahi

Introduction

The adoption of the SDGs by the United Nations in September 2015 was characterized by hype on the prospects of the new global agenda in solving the world's most pressing development challenges (Rios, 2015). Comprising 17 goals covering a broad range of development issues, the agenda is anchored on the earlier Millennium Development Goals (MDGs) declared in 2000 as a global reference for development policies. The media has a crucial role to play in the success of the SDGs: in raising awareness about the goals, facilitating communication dialogue among stakeholders and tracking of implementation progress. As Servaes (2008, p. 15) notes, "development programmes cannot produce change without an ongoing, culturally and socially relevant communication dialogue among development providers and clientele, and within the recipient group itself". It is therefore instructive to attempt to make sense of the media coverage of the SDGs.

Despite the centrality of communication in global development, academic studies have not adequately investigated the media coverage of the SDGs. For example, studies have not fully explored answers to these questions: what is the

---

H. I. Pindiga (✉)
University of Leicester, Leicester, UK
e-mail: hip2@leicester.ac.uk

B. Sa'ad Abdullahi
University of Westminster, London, UK
e-mail: bashir.abdullahi@my.westminster.ac.uk

© The Author(s), under exclusive license to Springer Nature Switzerland AG 2021
M. J. Yusha'u, J. Servaes (eds.), *The Palgrave Handbook of International Communication and Sustainable Development*,
https://doi.org/10.1007/978-3-030-69770-9_24

overall nature of the SDGs coverage, what goals received most attention and why, what challenges do journalists face in reporting the SDGs, and what lessons can we learn from the media coverage? This chapter seeks to address this gap, by examining the coverage of the SDGs in the Nigerian press and the challenges journalists face in reporting the SDGs. The Nigerian press was not left far behind in the MDGs-SDGs hype, much in line with the global press (McArthur & Zhang, 2018). But studies on the Nigerian press coverage of SDGs issues mostly singled out only a few of the goals and analysed their coverage (see, e.g. Abana, 2017; Bello, 2015; Onyeizu & Binta, 2014). The narrow nature of the studies means that they have not provided a full understanding of the overall reporting of the SDGs as a whole and the implication of the coverage on the success of the global agenda.

This chapter uses a combination of content analysis, framing analysis and semi-structured interviews to examine the reporting of the SDGs in Nigerian newspapers and the challenges Nigerian journalists face in covering the SDGs. The chapter seeks to determine the dominant news frames used in representing the SDGs; the SDGs targets receiving the most attention and why; and the key issues journalists grapple with in covering the SDGs. News coverage of SDGs in two Nigerian national dailies, namely *Daily Trust* and *Vanguard*, is analysed, covering the period from September 2014, a year to the date when the UN adopted the SDGs in 2015, to March 2019 when this study started. Analysis of the news coverage is followed by semi-structured interviews with a selection of Nigerian journalists, to gain further understanding of the nature of the coverage and the challenges of reporting the SDGs in the Nigerian context.

The chapter finds that the two newspapers constructed the SDGs within four news frames, namely problem frame, solution frame, action frame and responsibility frame. This framing narrowed the scope of understanding of the SDGs as a global agenda for sustainable development, with possible implications for journalists, academics, policymakers, civil society and multilaterals. Furthermore, the chapter finds that the newspapers paid more attention to some of the goals than to others, indicating what the press considers as the most important or most urgent development targets. Findings from the interviews show that journalists face certain constraints in reporting the SDGs. These include the journalists' lack of adequate understanding of the SDGs and poor working conditions. Moreover, the so-called brown envelopes[1] syndrome affected the SDGs coverage, particularly in terms of news sourcing and framing, further narrowing the understanding of the SDGs. The chapter concludes that the Nigerian press has a crucial role to play in the country's journey towards achieving the SDGs. However, there is need for sensitization of journalists and ensuring better working conditions for them.

---

[1] 'Brown envelopes' are favours often given to journalists by news sources to influence their reporting decisions. The 'brown envelope' syndrome is caused by, among other factors, poor remuneration which makes journalists vulnerable to influence from politicians, businesses and individuals (Ciboh, 2017; Idowu, 2018; Yusha'u, 2018a).

Following the introduction section, a contextual background is provided through a discussion on the media, communication and SDGs, as well as a historical overview of the SDGs at the global level and in the Nigerian context. The chapter then turns its attention to a review of the previous literature on reporting SDGs in the Nigerian press, followed by the methodology, key findings of the study, and finally a conclusion section that summarizes the chapter and considers the wider implications of our findings.

Perspectives on Media, Communication and SDGs

Media studies on the role of effective communications in the development of Third World countries could be traced back to the 1960s when the theories, objectives and methods of the communications sub-discipline were debated and developed by researchers. As narrated by Huesca (2003), theories on development communication were initially introduced by researchers in North American universities as an offshoot of existing social sciences disciplines like sociology, political science and economics.

There were a lot of debates about what constitutes development and underdevelopment, what are the traits of development and what role do the press and other media play in the mix (Servaes, 1986). Rist (2014) delves extensively on the definition of development, its history from the ancient Greece, to the colonial period, to the coining of the 'underdevelopment' phrase by U.S. President Truman, to the development of the dependency school, the new international economic order, the setting in of debt problem in the 'underdeveloped world', and the advent of MDGs at the turn of the century and its successor programme, the SDGs.

Early researchers ascribed 'too much' power to the media in the development process, stressing that having an effective media in a society, especially in Third World countries, will lead to its development (Bourgault, 1995; Servaes & Malikhao, 2007). However, according to McCall (2011:2), "by the late 1970s, it was abundantly clear that members of the public were not passive recipients of information, and that media alone could not change people's mindsets and behaviours".

Some researchers later developed the diffusion theory. This theory denotes that the role of the media in influencing the adoption of a new development in a society is much more complex than earlier defined. These researchers stressed that personal influence has more role, than does the mass media, in determining whether a new development will gain acceptance in a society (Servaes, 2007). A more modern model of development communication prescribed the involvement of the members of the society themselves in drawing up communication plans for the development projects to be situated in their communities, and this was dubbed participatory model. This led to coming up with what could be termed as indigenous/local understanding of what the role of media in development is or should be (Huesca, 2003). As Servaes (2002) notes, communication and people's involvement are central to the success or otherwise of any development project, making participatory communication policies imperative in the planning and execution of development projects.

A review of the literature on development communication will be incomplete without highlighting the discourse on modernization and dependency theories, as advanced by two divergent schools of thoughts on development communication. The birth of the UN in 1945, its subsequent role in encouraging relations between countries, and the competition between the then two superpowers (the US and former Soviet Union) during the Cold War period gave birth to the modernization and growth theory, which views development more in the purview of economic development (Servaes & Malikaho, 2002). However, this perspective was challenged by scholars from Latin America, and their criticism then gave birth to the dependency and underdevelopment theory, which posits that "development and underdevelopment must be understood in the context of the world system" (Servaes, 2002: 6).

Another theory worth mentioning in this context is McQuail's development media theory, which, according to Nwosu (1994:104), theorizes that the "Media should support the development effort in line with the established policy". He added that the theory "seems to be the most dominant in the developing countries today and is therefore most likely to shape or affect the role of the newspaper in the developing of the developing nation".

Having given this overview on development theories, we now turn our attention to exploring how the SDGs came about, what they are intended to achieve and the role of communication therein.

SDGs: Background and Context

The history of the SDGs can be traced to the early 1980s when the UN General Assembly mandated the setting up of a 'World Commission on Environment and Development', chaired by Mrs. Gro Harlem Brundlant, the then Prime Minister of Norway (Rist, 2014). The Brundlant commission developed the concept of 'sustainable development' in its report of 1987 which states that "Humanity has the ability to make development sustainable to ensure that it meets the needs of the present without compromising the ability of future generations to meet their own needs" (WCED, 1987, p. 16).

Years after, in September 2000, the UN General Assembly proclaimed the eight-goal MDGs Declaration (Timothy & Robin, 2003). As the MDGs neared the end date of 2015, a UN General Assembly working group in July 2014 proposed new set of goals that came to be known as the SDGs, setting the stage for an ambitious global development agenda (UN, 2014). In September 2015, all UN member states adopted the 2030 Agenda for Sustainable Development, at the heart of which are the 17 SDGs with 169 targets that aim to address issues related to poverty, food security, health, education, inequality, economic growth and environment.

The UN system acknowledges the central role of communication in achieving development programmes. This led to its hosting of World Congress on

Communication for Development in Rome in 2006, which eventually produced "the working definition of C4D (Communication for Development) articulated in the Rome Consensus" (McCall, 2011:13). Furthermore, in 2018 the UN put together an SDG Media Compact to encourage more media coverage for SDGs (UN, 2018). The acknowledgement by the UN system reinforces the notion that the media play a central role in communicating development policies to the citizens and helping them in forming public opinion that make governments to be more responsive to the yearnings of the citizens (McArthur & Zhang, 2018).

This chapter will focus on reviewing the newspaper coverage of development stories as one of the key mediums highlighting the achievement of the desired change or otherwise by the SDGs. In reviewing the history and role of newspapers in communicating development messages, Nwosu (1994:118) notes that the newspaper "is quite effective in helping to raise awareness and provide the information and education which must be acquired by individuals and groups before development can occur at any level". Hence our decision to appraise the coverage of the SDGs in the Nigerian newspapers.

SDGs in Nigeria: Implementation and Studies on Media Coverage

In Nigeria, the SDGs aim to build on the successes recorded by the predecessor MDGs programme. Nigeria's implementation of the SDGs is coordinated through the Office of the Senior Special Assistant to the President on SDGs (UNDP, 2015). The government has also established a multi-sectoral institutional framework at national and sub-national levels to improve coordination in achieving the SDGs targets. This has resulted in the national government, along with some state governments, aligning their development policies with the SDGs (FRN, 2017).

In a review report on the progress towards attaining the SDGs in the country, the government identified the media as one of the key stakeholders in the realization of the goals. The report indicated the deepening of advocacy and communication involving various national structures as a key priority in the next phase of SDGs implementation (FRN, 2017). Furthermore, a UNDP report on Nigeria's transition to SDGs from MDGs stressed that the SDGs implementation in the country will witness intensified role of the media in raising awareness about the goals (UNDP, 2015). However, the journalists interviewed for this chapter indicated that this expectation is yet to be met. Also, a check on the UN Media Compact website, developed by the UN to encourage effective SDGs coverage by the media, shows that only four media organizations in Nigeria are part of the compact as of April 2019 (UN, 2018). The shortcomings identified above suggest that those in charge of communicating the SDGs in the country may not be doing enough in engaging the media.

It is perhaps not surprising, therefore, that studies picked holes in the effectiveness of the reporting of the MDGs, the transition to the SDGs and the SDGs journey so far in Nigeria (Abana, 2017; Kayode & Adeniran, 2012;

Nkereuwem & Ralph, 2014; Nwabueze & Egbra, 2016; Onyeizu & Binta, 2014; Titus, 2017). Many of the media studies on the MDGs-SDGs in Nigeria examined press coverage of singled out development targets rather than taking a holistic look at the coverage of all the goals as one global agenda. For example, Kayode and Adeniran (2012:1) looked at the Nigerian newspaper coverage of the MDGs and concluded that:

> The Nigerian media did not give equal coverage to the development issues they covered. They reported some issues frequently, while other equally pressing developmental challenges in the country were neglected. Furthermore, the Nigerian media did not do much to educate, enlighten or motivate the public towards the need to achieve the developmental issues reported.

This finding is reinforced by Lugo-Ocando and Nguyen (2019). In contrast, McArthur and Zhang (2018) concluded that newspapers in Nigeria (especially *Vanguard*, one of the newspapers studied by this chapter) and elsewhere had significant coverage of the SDGs.

Some of the studies looked at the press coverage of development issues that fall within the scope of SDGs, but they studied them as standalone issues without necessarily linking them to the SDGs (see, e.g., Nelson & Oyedepo, 2011; Nwabueze & Egbra, 2016; Oronje, Undie, Zulu, & Crichton, 2011). In their study, Nwabueze and Egbra (2016) investigated the newspaper framing of climate change in Nigeria and Ghana. They found that newspapers did not give adequate attention to climate change, despite the dangers posed by climate change globally. In a sample of 844 editions of four newspapers in Nigeria and Ghana, they found that only 37 stories were on climate change.

Elsewhere, in their content analysis of newspaper coverage of SDGs campaign which focused on the angle and pattern of the SDGs reporting by Nigerian newspapers, Talabi et al. (2019) concluded that the newspapers portrayed the SDGs in a positive tone. However, the study did not highlight the factors that might have influenced the reporting, which is one of the gaps that this chapter fills. Other studies examined the SDGs from other perspectives unrelated to media coverage, like security implications and politics of the SDGs (see Akanni, 2017; Nwamaka & Stephen, 2018).

In view of the foregoing, it is safe to conclude that most research into SDGs coverage in Nigeria has mostly focused on specific aspects, like environmental, education and health matters (Abana, 2017; Bello, 2015; Nwabueze & Egbra, 2016). While these studies have provided useful insights on the media coverage of these topics as standalone development issues, they have not provided a full understanding of the overall reporting of the SDGs as a global consensus on development. This shortcoming has been addressed by this chapter in an attempt to fill the existing literature gap.

Methodological Considerations

In order to achieve the objectives of this study, we employed a mixed methods design that combines content analysis, framing analysis and semi-structured interviews. Mixed methods design is used in studies where, as in the case of this work, a full understanding of a phenomenon is considered unachievable by using one method alone (Berger, 2011; Bryman, 2012). We used a sequential explanatory mixed methods design, by first conducting the content analysis and framing analysis, followed by the semi-structured interviews to further explain and enhance the findings (Creswell, 2014; Ivankova, Creswell, & Stick, 2006). The value of using this design is that the results of the content analysis and framing analysis helped to inform the design of questionnaire for the semi-structured interviews.

The advantages of content analysis as an efficient method for identifying patterns in large quantities of data have been well documented (Bryman, 2012; Riffe, Lacy, & Fico, 2005). Given the substantial global attention on the SDGs and the high expectations in developing countries like Nigeria, the newspaper data to be collected is expected to be large, underscoring the value of content analysis for this study. We further employed semi-structured interviews to explain more the results from the content analysis and framing analysis. Ten journalists were purposively selected and interviewed, and the data was thematically analysed. Specific steps in the content analysis and framing analysis as well as in the semi-structured interviews are explained in the subsequent sections.

Content Analysis

The challenge in a content analysis in which lots of data is expected to be generated is to have an efficient sample. We therefore decided to sample two Nigerian national dailies. Given that the Nigerian press is polarized along the country's historical north-south regional divide (Campbell & Page, 2018; Yusha'u, 2018b), we selected one newspaper from northern Nigeria (*Daily Trust*) and one from southern Nigeria (*Vanguard*). *Daily Trust* is considered to be the most widely read newspaper in northern Nigeria and the mouthpiece of the region (Musa & Ferguson, 2013; Mustapha-Koiki, 2019). *Vanguard* is one of the leading independent newspapers, with an avowed aim to "serve the people through unflinching commitment to free enterprise, the rule of law and good governance" (Vanguard Online, n.d.). Both are commercial newspapers largely independent of political control (Yusha'u, 2018b). The research covers the period from September 2014, a year to the date when the UN adopted the SDGs, to March 2019 when this study started. This sampling allows us to trace the reporting of the SDGs from the MDGs-SDGs transition to the most recent period.

In order to collect the data from the two newspapers, a search was conducted on Nexis database using the search terms 'SDGs' and 'Sustainable

Development Goals'. The result is a large number of articles in different genres of newspaper content. Since our focus is on news coverage, we screened out articles that are not pure news articles, like full question-and-answer interviews, editorials and feature articles. The search result also included one article that contains the acronym 'SDG' which stands for the name of a political group in Nigeria and not the UN development agenda, so we dropped it. We further dropped articles appearing more than once in the search results and stories with only tangential mention of SDGs. This resulted in 147 articles in *Daily Trust* and 159 in *Vanguard*, making a total of 306 news articles.

News Framing

A traditional content analysis that focuses on frequencies has been criticized for merely producing numbers without according them much meaning (Hansen & Machin, 2013). This is where we employed framing analysis to attempt to make sense of the content. Framing refers to the way the media select, present and emphasize issues and events (Entman, 2004; McQuail, 2010). News framing typically involves the media "selecting and highlighting some aspects of perceived reality, and enhancing the salience and interpretation of that reality" (Entman, 2004: 26). In reporting of issues and events, journalists write the news by choosing what to put in and what to leave out, what to emphasize or downplay, "much as a painter chooses what to put in the frame of a painting" (Straubhaar & LaRose, 2008: 48). Sources also play a key role in news framing, as the way they present the information in their possession to the journalists also help in determining how the journalists report those facts. Key facts of stories often arrive at the reporter's or the editor's desk "with a built-in frame that suits the purpose of the source" (McQuail, 2010).

This chapter uses framing analysis to analyse the newspapers' coverage of the SDGs to unpack the dominant perspectives from which newspapers reported the goals. The choice of framing analysis is because it helps to identify underlying assumptions and meanings in a text (Hansen & Machin, 2013; McQuail, 2010). Although different newspapers may share "same set of news priorities" (McQuail, 2010), they tend to frame such news items in different ways. Several factors such as ownership, political leanings, elite influence and geographical locations (Yusha'u, 2018b) influence why a reporter or editor will select, emphasize, downplay or frame a story or set of facts in a particular way.

We used the inductive approach, in which frames emerge during the course of analysis of the text itself (De Vreese, 2005). Thus, we identified four dominant frames in the sampled SDGs coverage by the two newspapers. These are:

- **Problem frame**: Here the story focuses on the impediments to attaining the SDGs (e.g., financial resources required, management of resources for SDGs).

- **Solution frame**: This frame prescribes solutions in terms of what needs to be done in order to achieve the SDGs, or how meeting the targets could solve the development challenges confronting the society.
- **Action frame**: The frame focuses on the steps or actions taken by government, organization or individual to support realizing SDGs targets. This frame also highlights the progress of implementation in a way that shows something is being done to achieve the targets.
- **Responsibility frame**: This frame attributes responsibility or blame to one or more parties for the issues at hand in the journey towards attaining the SDGs.

These are explained and discussed in the findings sections.

Semi-Structured Interviews

We interviewed ten journalists and editors who specialize in reporting on all or some of the areas related to the SDGs, to further validate the results of the content analysis. Ayress (2008, p. 2) defines semi-structured interview as "a qualitative data collection strategy in which the researcher asks informants a series of predetermined but open-ended questions". It was difficult to hold face-to-face interviews with the respondents due to distance, geographical location and time constraints. We therefore conducted the interviews virtually using the WhatsApp messenger and email as 'asynchronous' communication tools. The advantage of using asynchronous methods in qualitative research, as noted by Egan (2008) and Burns (2010), is that asynchronicity enables convenience for both researchers and interview respondents, and may also produce data of richer quality.

To select the respondents for the interviews, we used purposive sampling method in which respondents are selected based on a specific purpose (Teddlie & Yu, 2007). This sampling method is particularly relevant for this chapter because it helps in ensuring representativeness and comparability. Three journalists were selected from each of the two newspapers (*Daily Trust* and *Vanguard*). In addition, four other journalists specializing in the coverage of SDGs were selected from other Nigerian newspapers based in both the southern and northern parts of the country.

The chapter adopted name anonymity for the interviewed journalists to encourage openness, objectivity and frankness in their answers. However, the study used identifiable titles, occupations, geographical locations and other attributes "to preserve the richness of the interview material wherever possible while also protecting participants" (Saunders, Kitzinger, & Kitzinger, 2015, p. 1). The interviewed journalists were each asked the same set of questions. The questions are on whether the SDGs get prominent and adequate coverage in the Nigerian press and why; why does the press give more attention to some SDGs over others in their coverage; whether region of location of Nigerian newspapers affect their coverage of SDGs; what are the main challenges

Nigerian journalists face in the coverage of SDGs; and what role can the Nigerian press play towards achieving the SDGs.

Findings and Analysis: Content Analysis

As mentioned earlier, a total of 306 news articles were analysed, made up of 147 news articles from *Daily Trust* and 159 from *Vanguard*. Table 24.1 shows the total number of references to each of the 17 SDGs in the articles analysed, with a column also for articles in which the SDGs in general are referred to with no focus on any particular goal. The data in the table shows the SDGs that received most attention from the newspapers and those that seemed to be relegated.

As shown in Table 24.1, the SDG with the most mentions or references is Goal 3 (Good Health and Well-being). This goal took the centre stage with 14 per cent of the total SDGs coverage by both newspapers. This is perhaps not

Table 24.1 The SDGs and the number of references to them in the analysed content

SDGs	No. of references (Daily Trust)	No. of references (Vanguard)	Total	Percentage
GOAL 1: No poverty	17	21	38	6
GOAL 2: Zero hunger	4	25	29	5
GOAL 3: Good health and well-being	37	44	81	14
GOAL 4: Quality education	27	31	58	10
GOAL 5: Gender equality	20	27	47	8
GOAL 6: Clean water and sanitation	20	17	37	6
GOAL 7: Affordable and clean energy	4	4	8	1
GOAL 8: Decent work and economic growth	14	19	33	6
GOAL 9: Industry, innovation and infrastructure	9	19	28	5
GOAL 10: Reduced inequality	22	18	40	7
GOAL 11: Sustainable cities and communities	1	5	6	1
GOAL 12: Responsible consumption and production	3	2	5	1
GOAL 13: Climate action	11	9	20	3
GOAL 14: Life below water	3	0	3	1
GOAL 15: Life on land	11	9	20	3
GOAL 16: Peace, justice & strong institutions	30	37	67	11
GOAL 17: Partnerships to achieve the goals	20	22	42	7
No particular goal	14	13	27	5
TOTAL	267	322	589	

surprising as health is a major issue of concern globally. Goal 3 is followed closely by Goals 16 (Peace, Justice & Strong Institutions), 4 (Quality Education) and 5 (Gender Equality) in terms of gaining the attention of the newspapers. Reduced Inequality (Goal 10) received 7 per cent of the coverage, while Goal 8 (Decent Jobs) received 6 per cent. The biggest surprise is that Goal 1 (No Poverty) and Goal 2 (Zero Hunger) received relatively lower coverage despite these two being core issues in Nigeria. At least half of Nigeria's population of about 190 million people live in extreme poverty (World Data Lab, n.d.). Nigeria is also among 41 countries in need of external food assistance (FAO, 2019).

Overall, the SDGs coverage had a total of 589 references in the two newspapers. In each of the two newspapers, Goal 3 was dominant, followed by Goal 16. However, in the coverage of a number of other SDGs, the two newspapers had different priorities. *Daily Trust* had few references to Zero Hunger, despite the northern part of Nigeria, the newspaper's base, being the hardest hit by food shortages (FAO, 2019). For its part, *Vanguard* gave this goal relatively much higher coverage. Reduced Inequality is among the targets with high mentions in *Daily Trust*, while it is among the least covered in *Vanguard*. *Vanguard* also paid more attention to Gender Equality than did *Daily Trust*, which is in front in covering Life on Water and Climate Change matters.

Analysing the Frames

Having established the volume of coverage of SDGs, and the relative importance accorded the goals by the newspapers, this section will dwell on the dominant frames used by the newspapers in their reporting of the SDGs. As mentioned earlier, the four dominant frames in the coverage are problem frame, solution frame, action frame and responsibility frame. Table 24.2 shows the relative presence of each frame across the two newspapers.

Problem Frame

The problem frame presents the story with a focus on the impediments to attaining the SDGs, including issues like the financial resources required, management of resources for SDGs, scale of the problems to tackle under the SDGs and lamentation on slow progress towards meeting the targets. This is the

Table 24.2 Number of appearances of news frames, by newspaper

	Problem	Solution	Action	Responsibility
Daily Trust	68	55	68	28
Percentage	31	25	31	13
Vanguard	62	63	76	24
Percentage	27	28	34	11
TOTAL	130	118	144	52
Percentage	29	27	32	12

second most dominant frame in all the coverage by the two newspapers. Some examples can be cited. One story in *Daily Trust* reported the lamentation that Nigeria is left behind in the efforts to eradicate poverty. "Nigeria seems to be retrogressing in terms of the global push for eradication of extreme poverty which is what the sustainable development goals have said it would eradicate", the *Daily Trust* quoted a charity official as saying.[2]

In another example, *Vanguard* headlined a story thus: "Trillions of dollars needed in fresh bid to end poverty by 2030".[3] The newspaper reports, "World leaders have drawn up ambitious goals to end extreme poverty by 2030 and promote development over the next 15 years, but now they have to figure out how to pay the bill". This story framed the issues in terms of the problem of the scale of financial resources needed to achieve the SDGs.

The problem frame was frequently used in the months following the announcement of the SDGs agenda in September 2014, through to the adoption by the UN of the SDGs in September 2015. The newspapers reported the legacy problems of MDGs as constituting an obstacle to SDGs.

Many reports spread out statistics to highlight the scale of developmental challenges coming within the scope of the SDGs. Like this report in *Daily Trust* titled, "Pneumonia kills 210,557 kids in 2015", which says: "An estimated 210,557 children in Nigeria have died from pneumonia and diarrhoea this year. ... That's 28 percent of the 750,000 children aged under five who died this year alone."[4]

Solution Frame
This frame presents the SDGs issue in terms of what needs to be done in order to achieve the goals, or how meeting the targets could solve the development challenges confronting the society, or in the perspective of how to find the resources and other things needed to attain the SDGs. The solution frame is the third most dominant in the coverage by the two newspapers. Many news reports that use the problem frame tend to also use the solution frame, such that following the diagnosis of the problem in attaining the SDGs, the news stories highlight possible solutions. For example, education-related news stories often state the huge numbers of out-of-school children as a potential impediment to achieving SDG 4, and then bring solution(s) to the fore like provision of higher budget allocation and building of more schools. A story in *Vanguard* reported the sacking of 21,780 teachers in a Nigerian state for failing a competency test. The paper constructed the story in a problem-solution frame by giving salience to the teachers' mass failure of the test and the proposed solution of firing the teachers.[5]

---

[2] 'Nigeria not on path to eradicate poverty', *Daily Trust*, 17/7/2018.
[3] 'Trillions of dollars needed in fresh bid to end poverty by 2030', *Vanguard*, 19/4/2015.
[4] 'Pneumonia Kills 210,557 Kids in 2015', *Daily Trust*, 12/11/2015.
[5] 'Buhari backs plan to fire 21,780 teachers ...', *Vanguard*, 14/11/2017.

In another example, a *Daily Trust* news report says over 700 million people live in extreme or moderate poverty globally, quoting figures from the International Labor Organization (ILO) top official. The news story then highlights a solution suggested by ILO: that government and other employers of labour should provide decent jobs as a way out of poverty.[6]

Action Frame
This is the most dominant issue in the analysed content, although its level of presence in the two newspapers varied remarkably. News stories reported using this frame focused on the steps or actions taken by government, organization or individual towards realizing the SDGs targets or highlighting the progress of implementation in a way that shows something is being done to address the challenges that the SDGs are meant to tackle. For example, stories emphasize the amount of budget allocation made to address one or more SDGs, or policy decisions to spur SDGs implementation. Stories about provision of healthcare services highlight actions like budget provision, building of hospitals and provision of maternal care services.

Here are some examples from the two newspapers. *Vanguard* reported that the Nigerian government planned to outlaw open defecation by 2025 as step towards realizing the SDG on water and sanitation.[7] This signals that policy action was being taken to achieve Goal 6 (Clean Water and Sanitation). *Daily Trust* similarly reported about a government agency providing free medical care to displaced people in the federal capital territory. The emphasis is placed on the action being taken to achieve the health targets of the SDGs. Another story in *Vanguard*, headlined, "Bill Gates Foundation moves to boost rice, yam production in Nigeria",[8] reports on the action taken by the Foundation to ensure food sufficiency to help meet SDG 2 (Zero Hunger).

Overall, *Daily Trust* used the action frame fewer times than the *Vanguard*, although this frame is still the most used in both newspapers (Fig. 24.1). Given the dominance of the action frame, it can be deduced that newspapers focused more on what is being done to achieve the SDGs. The predominance of the action frame can also be linked to the dominance of government and other official sources in the coverage. This point will be discussed further under the subsection on news sources.

Responsibility Frame
In the context of this chapter, the responsibility frame refers to highlighting where the responsibility or blame lies in the journey towards attaining the SDGs. This frame is the least dominant frame in the analysed coverage. It is often used in reports that also use the problem frame, where the blame is apportioned to one party or another, usually government, for the lack of

---

[6] 'ILO harps on decent jobs', *Daily Trust*, 4/3/2019.
[7] 'Govt to outlaw open defecation by 2025', *Vanguard*, 20/3/2019.
[8] 'Bill Gates Foundation moves to boost rice, yam production in Nigeria', *Vanguard*, 13/9/2016.

Fig. 24.1 The dominant frames as percentages

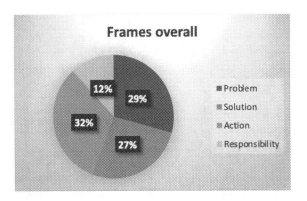

progress in achieving the SDGs. This frame was used frequently in the transitional period from the MDGs era to that of the SDGs. Officials attribute responsibility for failure to achieve the MDGs to others, and also use this as an excuse to portray the coming difficulties to be faced in implementing the SDGs. The relative low numbers for the responsibility frame can be interpreted to mean that the newspapers did not find it necessary to focus on the blame game, but instead on what needs to be done and what is being done to achieve the SDGs.

Some examples are relevant here. *Daily Trust* reported the ruling APC party blaming the opposition PDP party for stealing public funds such that there were no adequate funds left to implement the SDGs. The report quoted a public anti-corruption official saying the misappropriation of billions of dollars under the previous PDP government "showed that the corruption onslaught was devastating, unrelenting and driving Nigeria further from sustainable development goals".[9] *Vanguard* reported the attribution of blame to the previous administration, by the minister of water resources, regarding the poor irrigation system. The minister is reported saying that the government "inherited 116 ongoing and abandoned irrigation and water projects from the immediate past government in 2015".[10]

Primary Sources

In studying the nature of news coverage, an analysis of sources used in the news is important given the significant role sources play in shaping the news. Sources usually provide the raw materials from which the news is made, which means their level of appearance in the news signifies the depth of the opportunity they have to air their views on issues (Hansen & Machin, 2013). By using certain sources instead of others, the journalist emphasizes the perspective of one

---

[9] 'Govt—How trillions were squandered under PDP', *Daily Trust*, 6/62017.
[10] 'FG inherits 11 abandoned irrigation, water projects', *Vanguard*, 23/12/2018.

source over another's (Reese, 2007). Thus, it is safe to say that the level of dominance of sources helps in determining the frames used in the news.

Based on the analysis of the data collected from the two newspapers, the main sources in the coverage are categorized into four main groups, plus an 'Other' category, as follows: (i) Nigerian government and official; (ii) international organization and foreign official; (iii) CSO and NGO and (iv) private sector. The 'Other' category is added to include sources that do not fit into the four most dominant categories, and these include journalist's investigations, experts, ordinary citizens and former government officials. Only the primary source of the news is counted. This is defined as the predominant or most prominent source of the story; the first source to be mentioned as the source of the story in the headline or intro, or the source of the action that is reported as the main thrust of the story.

The data in Table 24.3 shows that government officials dominate as sources of news coverage on SDGs in both newspapers, followed by international organizations and foreign officials. The analysis shows a large presence of what can be categorized as 'official sources'. The first and second categories (Nigerian and foreign officials) are both public official sources, and they command 70 per cent of the total sources used (Fig. 24.2). Even the other two categories (CSO/NGO and corporate organization) can be considered official if the meaning is broadened to include officials of non-governmental and private sector organizations. The dominance of official sources reflects the tendency in which Nigerian journalists rely on 'information subsidies' from elite sources (Ciboh, 2017). One significant point is that there is paucity of investigative stories in the news coverage. This can also be linked to the reliance of journalists on government and other official sources for SDGs information. The dominance of official sources also explains why the action frame is the most used frame of the four. Government officials and officials of private sector organizations tend to amplify what they are doing to achieve the SDGs. In some cases, they apportion blames to other groups or individuals.

Findings and Analysis: Semi-Structured Interviews

As mentioned earlier, we conducted semi-structured interviews to further explain the results from the content analysis and framing analysis. Ten journalists were interviewed (see Table 24.4) and the data was thematically analysed. Thematic analysis is "a data reduction and analysis strategy by which qualitative data are segmented, categorized, summarized, and reconstructed in a way that captures the important concepts within the data set" (Ayres, 2008, p. 1). Analysis of the interviews produced some interesting results regarding the SDGs coverage in Nigerian newspapers, the key issues journalists grapple with in reporting the SDGs and the way forward.

The themes that emerged from the interview data are as follows:

Table 24.3 Main news sources

	Nigerian government/official	International organization/foreign official	CSO/NGO	Private sector/corporate organization	Others
Daily Trust	66	35	30	3	13
Vanguard	64	51	24	6	14
TOTAL	130	86	54	9	27
PERCENTAGE	**42**	**28**	**18**	**3**	**9**

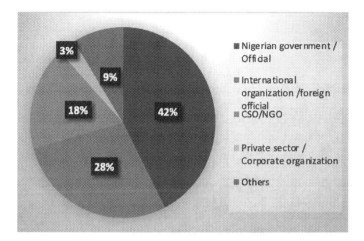

Fig. 24.2 The use sources by percentage in the two newspapers

Table 24.4 The journalists interviewed and their newspaper organizations

Newspaper	Region of location	Respondents
Daily Trust	North	Editor (1)
		Reporter covering SDGs-related issues (1)
		Reporter covering SDGs-related issues (1)
Vanguard	South	Editor (1)
		Reporter covering SDGs-related issues (1)
		Reporter covering SDGs-related issues (1)
Tribune	South	Reporter covering SDGs-related issues (1)
Leadership	North	Reporter covering SDGs-related issues (1)
Punch	South	Reporter covering SDGs-related issues (1)
Blueprint	North	Reporter covering SDGs-related issues (1)

- **Theme 1**: The SDGs do not get adequate coverage in Nigerian newspapers due to some factors determining the news agenda.
- **Theme 2**: There was uneven coverage of the SDGs between north-based and south-based newspapers in Nigeria.
- **Theme 3**: Many Nigerian journalists are not adequately informed about the SDGs.
- **Theme 4**: Many Nigerian journalists are poorly remunerated, and this influences the type of issues they focus on in their reporting, with the SDGs receiving relatively less coverage.

The next section of this chapter discusses and analyses the responses of the interviewees. The discussion will consider the circumstances surrounding or influencing the SDGs coverage which could not be deduced from the news stories themselves.

Inadequate Coverage for SDGs Due to Factors Determining the News Agenda

One of the key issues explored in the interviews was on the level of attention given to the SDGs by Nigerian newspapers. Journalists were asked whether they think the coverage was adequate, given the significance of the SDGs for Nigeria as a developing country. Most of the interviewees concluded that the SDGs are not receiving adequate coverage in the Nigerian press. They attributed this to the inability of journalists to drive the messages/significance of the SDGs home for the average Nigerians, as this reporter from *Punch* newspaper noted:

> I do not think they (the SDGs) get enough coverage. I feel it's because journalists have not been able to break them down and relate them to our society. As such, they cannot see the numerous issues that abound.

Other reasons adduced for lack of enough coverage of the SDGs include the elitist nature of the newspaper readers, who are not necessarily interested in news coverage of some of the SDGs issues. This position is stressed by an editor of *Daily Trust*: "This is because the elite form the majority of readers of Nigerian newspapers, and they are more interested in political and business stories." Some previous studies agree with this assertion about this orientation of the Nigerian press (see Idowu, 2018; Jimoh, 2011; Owolabi, 2014).

Other interview respondents are of the opinion that both the government and journalists have not been able to articulate facts about the SDGs, stressing that the governments and especially the UN agencies responsible for the SDGs are not doing enough to promote the SDGs in the public domain.

Some of the interview respondents were, however, of the opinion that the SDGs have received enough coverage in the Nigerian newspapers, with a varying degree from one goal to another as we could see from the response of this editor:

> Some SDGs get covered better than others and this is not unique to Nigeria. It has to do with the fact that nations or media tend to focus more on things they consider more relevant or are prevalent in their market. So, I think it's fair to say some are covered well while others aren't.

This line of thinking agrees with the conclusion by McArthur and Zhang (2018, p. 323), who note that "major newspapers from India and Nigeria […] had high frequency of SDG coverage in 2016". The findings of Talabi et al. (2019) similarly show that there is enough coverage of SDGs in the Nigerian newspapers. These divergent conclusions reflect the pattern we highlighted in the earlier sections of this chapter that depicted contradictory findings by previous studies on adequacy of coverage of development issues in Nigeria.

Differences in Coverage Between North-Based and South-Based Newspapers

Here again most of the respondents agree that there is a clear influence of the regional peculiarities in the newspaper reporting of the SDGs in Nigeria. As mentioned in the earlier sections of the chapter, findings of previous research indicate that region of location influences the journalistic practices of Nigerian newspapers (Yusha'u, 2018b). This editor from northern Nigeria sums up various points and opinions expressed by different respondents with regards to uneven differences in the SDGs coverage between newspapers based in the southern and northern Nigeria:

> Papers have their biases and invest in areas that meet these biases. [Newspapers] tend to provide regional news that cater to their audiences. For instance, there are more reports on child marriage, out of school children in northern Nigeria than in the south or west or east. In the south there are reports of environmental degradation as a result of oil spills dying aquatic life and the impacts on communities there.

This reporter from *Vanguard* newspaper offered his own understanding of the reasons behind the contrasting coverage based on the newspapers' region of location:

> The regional location of the newspapers has direct bearing to the needs and aspirations of that region. It tends to focus more on the immediate and important needs of that environment. In northern Nigeria for example, education is a key factor to be considered unlike the south where it is mostly about economic development.

Other interviewees interpret the differences in the coverage as a deliberate attempt by the newspapers to cater to the preferences of their audiences, and not necessarily because of the papers' geographical locations. One respondent, however, seems to adopt a middle way in the debate. The reporter agrees that in general differences do exist in how the newspapers cover issues based on their region of location.

Journalists Not Adequately Informed About SDGs

One of the major themes that emerged from responses obtained from the journalists is that many journalists are not knowledgeable enough or adequately informed about the SDGs, as is evident from the following response by one of the journalists interviewed:

> Lack of knowledge amongst some journalists is also a key factor in less coverage of some SDGs. Some journalists don't even know them, or they don't see stories in them because they don't generate catchy headlines.

A similar position was espoused by a journalist from *Vanguard*: "The newspapers (journalists/reporters) are not sufficiently informed about the goals of the SDGs and how they will affect the people."

Poor Remuneration for Journalists

In discussing the possible reasons for lack of adequate coverage for SDGs in the Nigerian newspapers, some respondents stressed that many journalists are poorly remunerated in the country and this contributes to their lack of attention for stories about SDGs. As one of the respondents puts it, "writing about SDGs doesn't bring steady brown envelopes". One reporter from *Punch* newspaper agrees with this point, thus:

> I feel it's because journalists have not been able to break them (SDGs) down and relate them to our society. As such, they cannot see the numerous issues that abound. However, their being able to see the issues could also be affected by stomach and pocket infrastructure.[11]

This reporter from *Punch* newspaper sums up the economic landscape in which Nigerian newspaper reporters operate:

> Poor remuneration so much so that there are no finances to maintain a family not to talk of sourcing for data or doing research to source for data, all for free. Hence, motivation is low in every sense of the word. Even the media houses that pay well, their staff are sometimes overworked so much so that any issues related to the SDGs or other topical human-interest issues, take months to be published.

Constraints highlighted by the journalists above corroborate some of the findings of Lugo-Ocando and Nguyen (2019).

Conclusion

In this chapter, we explored the nature of the reporting of the SDGs in the Nigerian press and the challenges journalists face in reporting the SDGs. Our starting premise was that development programmes like the SDGs need to be backed by effective communication dialogue among stakeholders, in order for these programmes to succeed. Using a combination of content analysis, framing analysis and semi-structured interviews, the chapter identified the dominant news frames and the relative attention given to the SDGs targets in two selected Nigerian newspapers (*Daily Trust* and *Vanguard*); and also explored the key issues Nigerian journalists struggle with in the SDGs coverage.

---

[11] Stomach infrastructure is used in the context of especially Nigerian elections where voters elect a leader because of gifts (especially food items) and not his promised policies or physical infrastructures to be built. Ayeni et al. (2020, p. 1) define it as "an act of sharing money, material resources and other benefits for immediate satisfaction of the non-elite". See also Aborisade (2016).

In their news coverage, *Daily Trust* and *Vanguard* constructed the SDGs within four news frames, namely problem frame, solution frame, action frame and responsibility frame. It is argued that the use of these frames has narrowed the scope of understanding of the SDGs as a global agenda for sustainable development. Understandably, some of the SDGs targets received more attention over others. However, it was a surprise that the newspapers gave relatively little attention to the twin goals of ending poverty and zero hunger, given the critical poverty levels and food shortages in Nigeria.

The chapter further finds that Nigerian journalists lack adequate understanding of the SDGs, and therefore this affected their manner of reporting. Other challenges identified include poor working conditions of journalists and 'brown envelopes' offered to journalists. These factors affected the coverage, both in terms of sourcing and framing. Journalists predominantly relied on official sources, thereby limiting the communication dialogue that is crucial for the success of the SDGs.

In the final analysis, the Nigerian press has a crucial role to play in the country's journey towards achieving the SDGs. The press can help facilitate dialogue among development experts, politicians, the civil society and the general public. However, Nigerian journalists need to be sensitized to ensure they understand the SDGs. Journalists must first have adequate understanding of the SDGs before they can effectively report on the subject. Working conditions of journalists also need to be improved, so that they would be able to do their jobs properly.

Future studies can focus on audience research to understand how news audiences consume and perceive the SDGs. The audience perception of SDGs is needed in order to make a definitive judgement on whether the news coverage influenced public policies and public response as it relates to the SDGs implementation. As more and more people now consume their news via online and social media platforms, it will also be imperative to conduct further studies on the coverage of the SDGs in the new media/social media to understand how effective these new platforms are in communicating the SDGs.

This chapter will serve as a valuable reference material for media, communication and development courses in universities and for those working in the intersection of communication and development.

Recommendations

- The journalists' lack of adequate understanding of the SDGs highlights the need for SDGs implementers in Nigeria to engage more with journalists and media practitioners, to further enlighten them about the SDGs and the significant role the media should play in achieving the goals. In this regard, the government agencies responsible for the SDGs and civil society groups should organize workshops and refresher courses for journalists to ensure that they have better grasp of the SDGs.

- There is need to ensure better working conditions for Nigerian journalists. Journalists' unions, like the Nigerian Union of Journalists and the Nigerian Guild of Editors, should engage with the country's newspaper proprietors to improve the working conditions of journalists.
- There is also the need to re-orient and upskill the media/communication officers of the government agencies responsible for the SDGs on media engagement and effective communication. This can be done through workshops and training courses for these officers.
- Government agencies responsible for the SDGs should embrace the use of online and social media platforms in their communication design and implementations, as more and more Nigerians now consume their news and information from the social media and the wider internet.

References

Abana, A. (2017). Press Coverage of Maternal Health Issues in Selected Nigerian Newspapers. *Media and Communication Currents*, 1(1), 1–18.

Aborisade, P. O. (2016). Stomach Infrastructure' and the Reconceptualization of Political Communication in Nigeria. In A. Durotoye (Ed.), *Elections in Nigeria: A Contemporary Analysis* (pp. 75–90). Saarbrucken: VAP Lambert Academic Publishing.

Akanni, E. C. (2017). Sustainable Development Goals (SDGs) and the Politics of Development. *Journal of Emerging Trends in Educational Research and Policy Studies*, 8(3), 182–189.

Ayeni, E., Sani, K., Idris, I., & Ozoigwe, M. (2020). Stomach Infrastructure and Politics of Redistribution in Africa: A Study of Nigeria (2014–2019). *Ilorin Journal of Administration and Development*, 5(2), 54–61.

Ayres, L. (2008). Thematic Coding and Analysis. In M. G. Lisa (Ed.), *The SAGE Encyclopedia of Qualitative Research Methods*. Thousand Oaks, CA: Sage.

Bello, S. M. (2015). *Newspaper Coverage of Health Issues in Nigeria: The Frequency of Reporting Malaria, HIV/AIDS and Polio and the Effect of Seeking Health Information on the Health Behaviours of Newspaper Readers*. PhD Thesis, University of Canterbury, New Zealand.

Berger, A. A. (2011). *Media and Communication Research Methods: An Introduction to Qualitative and Quantitative Approaches* (2nd ed.). Thousand Oaks, CA: Sage.

Bourgault, L. M. (1995). *Mass Media in Sub-Saharan Africa*. Bloomington: Indiana University Press.

Bryman, A. (2012). *Social Research Methods* (4th ed.). Oxford University Press.

Burns, E. (2010). Developing Email Interview Practices in Qualitative Research. *Sociological Research Online*, 15(4), 1–12.

Campbell, J., & Page, M. T. (2018). *Nigeria: What Everyone Needs to Know*. Oxford: Oxford University Press.

Ciboh, R. (2017). Journalists and Political Sources in Nigeria. *The International Journal of Press/Politics*, 22(2), 185–201.

Creswell, J. (2014). *Research Design: Qualitative, Quantitative and Mixed Methods Approaches* (4th ed.). Thousand Oaks, CA: Sage.

De Vreese, C. H. (2005). News Framing: Theory and Typology. *Information Design Journal & Document Design*, 13(1), 51–62.

Egan, J. (2008). Email Interview. In M. G. Lisa (Ed.), *The SAGE Encyclopedia of Qualitative Research Methods*. Thousand Oaks, CA: Sage.

Entman, R. M. (2004). *Projections of Power: Framing News, Public Opinion, and U.S. Foreign Policy*. Chicago: University of Chicago Press.

FAO. (2019). FAO Report Cites 41 Countries Needing External Assistance for Food. Retrieved December 21, 2019, from http://www.fao.org/news/story/en/item/1208508/icode/

FRN (Federal Republic of Nigeria). (2017). Implementation of the SDGs: A National Voluntary Review. Retrieved May 1, 2020, from https://sustainabledevelopment.un.org/content/documents/16029Nigeria.pdf

Hansen, A., & Machin, D. (2013). *Media & Communication Research Methods*. Hampshire: Palgrave Macmillan.

Huesca, R. (2003). From Modernization to Participation: The Past and Future of Development Communication in Media Studies. In A. N. Valdivia (Ed.), *A Companion to Media Studies*. Oxford: Blackwell Publishing Ltd.

Idowu, L. (2018). Corruption in the Nigerian Media: The Brown Envelope Syndrome. In A. Olutokun (Ed.), *Watchdogs or Captured Media? A Study of The Role of the Media in Nigeria's Emergent Democracy 1999–2016* (pp. 93–136). Diamond Publications Ltd: Lagos.

Ivankova, N. V., Creswell, J. W., & Stick, S. L. (2006). Using Mixed-Methods Sequential Explanatory Design: From Theory to Practice. *Field Methods, 18*(1), 3–20.

Jimoh, J. (2011). Commercialism, Mass Media and the Imperative of Health Communication. In U. Pate & L. Oso (Eds.), *Mass Media and Society in Nigeria*. Lagos: Malthouse Press.

Kayode, J., & Adeniran, R. (2012). Nigerian Newspaper Coverage of the Millennium Development Goals: The Role of the Media. *Itupale Online Journal of African Studies, IV*, 1–17.

Lugo-Ocando, J., & Nguyen, A. (2019). *Developing News, Global Journalism and the Coverage of 'Third World' Development*. New York: Routledge.

McArthur, J. W., & Zhang, C. (2018) Measuring the diffusion of the Millennium Development Goals across major print media and academic outlets. Retrieved May 5, 2019, from https://onlinelibrary.wiley.com/doi/epdf/10.1111/1758-5899.12553

McCall, E. (2011). *Communication for Development: Strengthening the Effectiveness of the United Nations*. New York: UNDP.

McQuail, D. (2010). *McQuail's Mass Communication Theory* (6th ed.). London: Sage.

Musa, A. O., & Ferguson, N. (2013). Enemy Framing and the Politics of Reporting Religious Conflicts in the Nigerian Press. *Media, War & Conflict, 6*(1), 7–20.

Mustapha-Koiki, A. R. (2019). *Journalism and Risk: The Impact of Boko Haram Attacks on News Content and Journalists' Patterns of News Gathering and Reporting in Nigeria (2011–2012)*. PhD thesis, University of Canterbury, New Zealand.

Nelson, O., & Oyedepo, T. (2011). Newspaper Reportage and Its Effect Towards Promoting Agricultural Development in Nigeria. *Journal of Media and Communication Studies, 3*(2), 27–32.

Nkereuwem, U., & Ralph, N. (2014). MDGs in Nigeria, Communication and the Media. *Journal of African Media Studies, 6*(2), 139–156.

Nwabueze, C., & Egbra, S. (2016). Newspaper Framing of Climate Change in Nigeria and Ghana. *Applied Environmental Education and Communication, 15*(2), 111–124.

Nwamaka, O. J., & Stephen, D. (2018). Insecurity and Sustainable Development in Nigeria (in Context of Terrorism). *Asian Journal of Economics, Business and Accounting, 7*(2), 1–10.

Nwosu, I. E. (1994). The Newspapers in the Development of Developing Nations. In A. Moemeka (Ed.), *Communication for Development: A New Pan-disciplinary Perspective*. New York: State University of New York Press.

Onyeizu, O. U., & Binta, D. O. (2014). Newspaper Coverage of Health Issues in Nigeria (A Study of the Guardian and the Punch Newspapers, January 2010 to December 2011). *New Media and Mass Communication, 23*, 16–24.

Oronje, R., Undie, C., Zulu, E., & Crichton, J. (2011). Engaging Media in Communicating Research on Sexual and Reproductive Health and Rights in Sub-Saharan Africa: Experiences and Lessons Learned. *Health Research Policy and Systems, 9*, 2–10.

Owolabi, T. (2014). Implications of the Media Coverage of SMEs for National Development in Nigeria. *International Journal of Development and Economic Sustainability, 2*(3), 45–57.

Reese, S. (2007). The Framing Project: A Bridging Model for Media Research Revisited. *Journal of Communication, 57*, 148–154.

Riffe, D., Lacy, S., & Fico, F. G. (2005). *Analyzing Media Messages: Using Quantitative Content Analysis in Research* (2nd ed.). Mahwah, New Jersey: Lawrence Erlbaum Associates.

Rios, M. (2015). What Does Media Coverage of the SDGs Tell Us? *World Economic Forum*. Retrieved June 10, 2019, from https://www.weforum.org/agenda/2015/10/what-does-media-coverage-of-the-sdgs-tell-us/

Rist, G. (2014). *The History of Development*. London: Zed Books Ltd.

Saunders, B., Kitzinger, J., & Kitzinger, C. (2015). Anonymising Interview Data: Challenges and Compromise in Practice. *Qualitative Research, 15*(5), 616–632.

Servaes, J. (1986). Development Theory and Communication Policy: Power to the People! *European Journal of Communication, 1*(2), 203–229.

Servaes, J. (2002). By Way of Introduction. In J. Servaes (Ed.), *Approaches to Development Communications*. Paris: UNESCO.

Servaes, J. (2007). Development Communication – For Whom and For What? *South African Journal for Communication Theory and Research, 21*(1), 39–49.

Servaes, J. (2008). Introduction. In J. Servaes (Ed.), *Communication for Development and Social Change* (pp. 14–28). New Delhi: Sage.

Servaes, J., & Malikaho, P. (2002). Development Communication Approaches in an International Perspective. In J. Servaes (Ed.), *Approaches to Development Communications*. Paris: UNESCO.

Servaes, J., & Malikhao, P. (2007) *Communication and Sustainable Development*. Selected Papers from the 9th UN Roundtable on Communication for Development. Retrieved April 2, 2019, from http://www.fao.org/3/a1476e/a1476e01.pdf

Straubhaar, J., & LaRose, R. (2008). *Media Now: Understanding Media, Culture, and Technology*. Belmont, CA: Thomson Wadsworth.

Talabi, F., Tokunbo, A. A., & Sanusi, B. (2019). A Content Analysis of Newspaper Coverage of Sustainable Development Goals (SDGs) Campaign. *University of Nigeria Interdisciplinary Journal of Communication Studies, 24*(1), 21–34.

Teddlie, C., & Yu, F. (2007). Mixed Methods Sampling: A Typology with Examples. *Journal of Mixed Methods Research, 1*(1), 77–100.

Timothy, B., & Robin, S. (2003) Halving Global Poverty. Retrieved May 2, 2019, from http://econ.lse.ac.uk/staff/rburgess/wp/jep11.pdf

Titus, Z. (2017). The Role of the Media Since the Adoption of the Sustainable Development Goals. Retrieved May 2, 2019, from https://www.nmt.africa/uploads/5a2e5d9c4a234/TheroleofAfricanmediainpromotingandentrenchingtheethosoftheSDGs.pdf

UN. (2014). UN General Assembly's Open Working Group Proposes Sustainable Development Goals. Retrieved April 5, 2019, from https://sustainabledevelopment.un.org/content/documents/4538pressowg13.pdf

UN. (2018). SDG Media Compact. Retrieved April 4, 2019, from https://www.un.org/sustainabledevelopment/sdg-media-compact-about/

UNDP. (2015). Nigeria's Road to SDGs: Country Transition Strategy. Retrieved September 18, 2019, from https://www.undp.org/content/dam/nigeria/docs/IclusiveGrwth/Nigeria%20transition%20strategy%20to%20SDGs.pdf

Vanguard Online. (n.d.). About Us. Retrieved May 6, 2019, from https://www.vanguardngr.com/about/

WCED. (1987). Our Common Future. Retrieved May 10, 2019, from https://sustainabledevelopment.un.org/content/documents/5987our-common-future.pdf

World Data Lab. (n.d.). World Poverty Clock. Retrieved January 10, 2020, from https://worldpoverty.io/

Yusha'u, M. J. (2018a). Poor Capitalisation and Corruption Within the Nigerian Press. In H. M. Mabweazara (Ed.), *Newsmaking Cultures in Africa: Normative Trends in the Dynamics of Socio- Political & Economic Struggles* (pp. 185–205). London: Palgrave Macmillan.

Yusha'u, M. J. (2018b). *Regional Parallelism and Corruption Scandals in Nigeria: Intranational Approaches to African Media Systems.* Cham: Palgrave Macmillan.

CHAPTER 25

Selected Journalists' Role Perception Towards Achieving *Agenda 2030* in Nigeria

Taye C. Obateru

INTRODUCTION

Already grappling with the challenges of underdevelopment, many countries face other problems which exacerbate the living condition of their people, making the achievement of the United Nations' Sustainable Development Goals (Agenda 2030) more arduous. Sustainable Development Goals (SDGs) are a wide range of global sustainable development targets for the environment, society and economy which were launched by the United Nations (UN) in 2015. The agenda aims at shifting the world to a sustainable, resilient path. However, based on their failure to meet previous targets and goals, fears are being expressed in certain quarters on the ability of developing countries like Nigeria to deliver on Agenda 2030. Oleribe and Taylor-Robinson (2016) for instance, noted that Nigeria failed to achieve the Millennium Development Goals (MDGs) targeted to have been achieved by 2015 for various reasons. This underscores the importance of research that might contribute to averting a similar result in Agenda 2030 among developing countries especially in Sub-Saharan Africa.

The role of communication in the success of various development agenda, though acknowledged, does not appear sufficiently appreciated in the implementation process. Okoro (2018, p. 163) notes past difficulty in examining and analysing development communication, media role and politics in Africa

---

T. C. Obateru (✉)
Department of Mass Communication, University of Jos, Jos, Nigeria
e-mail: obaterut@unijos.edu.ng

© The Author(s), under exclusive license to Springer Nature Switzerland AG 2021
M. J. Yusha'u, J. Servaes (eds.), *The Palgrave Handbook of International Communication and Sustainable Development*,
https://doi.org/10.1007/978-3-030-69770-9_25

because of what he described as the "adversarial relationship existing between the media and governance over the years". His argument buttresses findings from previous studies (e.g. Nwokeafor & Okunoye, 2013) on the herculean nature of analysing development communication in African countries because governance and the media have not cooperated to bring this about.

In many developing countries such as Nigeria, the news media do not seem to be paying sufficient attention to issues relating to the SDGs beyond their routine coverage of issues as they arise. Interactions with journalists also reveal a limited knowledge of the agenda and its 169 targets. Since communication is a key factor towards achieving the targets and the news media, as agents of information dissemination, enlightenment and agenda setting, are important aspects of the process, the need to explore the level of awareness of the Sustainable Development Goals and how journalists perceive their role in the process became necessary. This is more so that current trends in Africa's development efforts in the twenty-first century underscore the critical role of the news media in achieving and sustaining democratic transformation (Okoro, 2018).

Development-geared communication is well acknowledged to have contributed to the success of various development programmes (see Bessette, 2004; Servaes, 2006), therefore making the potential role the news media in propagating the ideals of Agenda 2030 obvious. Scholars appear unanimous that it was not until recently that attention began to be paid to communication as a deliberate strategy (e.g. Brown, Budd, Bell, & Rendel, 2011; Jimada, 2006; Mefalopulous & Grenna, 2004; Sosale, 2008). The realisation of the importance of communication in achieving sustainable development made the United Nations to identify Communication for Development as an important component of its development agenda (UNESCO, 2007). Despite this, there is little in the literature on the level of awareness of the SDGs among journalists in Nigeria and their understanding of their role in the development process. This is the gap this chapter seeks to fill.

Given the above, coupled with the fact that many of the factors blamed for Nigeria's inability to meet most of the initial Millennium Development Goals (MDGs), the precursor to the SDGs, such as bureaucracy, poor resource management, corruption and insecurity, among others still subsist (Oleribe & Taylor-Robinson, 2016), the following questions agitated this study:

- Do Nigerian journalists have sufficient understanding of Agenda 2030 to be able to communicate it effectively to Nigerians?
- What is the level of professional commitment by journalists to promoting the realisation of the SDGs in line with the postulation of the Development Journalism Theory?
- To what extent can the online and mobile platforms of the news media, which are largely interactive, be deployed to enhance participatory communication for achieving the agenda?

- What policies can promote the achievement of development communication in sub-Saharan Africa?

A study of journalists' understanding of the Sustainable Development Goals (SDGs) is germane in view of arguments that the news media did not accord previous development targets sufficient coverage. For example, *GTZ* (2006) in an analysis of the media treatment of Poverty Reduction Strategic Papers (PRSPs) under the Millennium Development Goals (MDGs) reported a low level of awareness of PRSP processes within the media and cited possible reasons for this to include: lack of technical skills within journalism to report on economic development and sectorial specific issues such as health, education or agriculture; poor relationship between government and journalists, hindering investigative and strong coverage of PRSP related issues; lack of interaction between non-governmental organisations (NGOs) and media which could lead to greater understanding and engagement by media, as well as, that media outlets increasingly demand payment for coverage of development-related issues (*GTZ*, 2006, pp. 9–10).

The findings above underscore the importance of engaging the news media more in propagating development agenda considering their acknowledged importance in the process (Servaes, 2006). As Jimada (2006) observes, the news media constitute a social instrument used in moulding society consciously or unconsciously and are "powerful and influential" (p. 3).

Literature Review

Major Communication Paradigms in the Development Context

Mefalopulous and Grenna (2004) identified the Modernization Paradigm and Dependency Theory as the origin of debates on development. According to them, the modernization paradigm as a concept developed in 1949 and propounds that the "rich countries" of the world should work together to address underdevelopment in economically weak countries. It "entails a worldwide program to support local economies, while at the same time promoting the spread of democratic values and institutions" (Mefalopulous & Grenna, 2004, p. 25). President Truman of the United States who was given credit for this paradigm believed that peace and prosperity would be achieved worldwide if the paradigm was implemented and encouraged the underdeveloped parts of the world to achieve greater productivity through the application of technological knowledge and scientific methods. In other words, by emulating the economic and development strategies of the richer countries, the poorer countries would become richer (Mefalopulous & Grenna, 2004). The paradigm recognised the role of communication as a major tool for diffusing the innovations through the mass media in a one-way, top-down process (Melkote, 1991, cited in Mefalopulous & Grenna, 2004).

However, the paradigm was criticised for neglecting the place of local, social, cultural and political contexts and tended to blame the poorer countries for their conditions. Soola (2003) observes that the failure of this dominant paradigm of development which was the popular thinking in the 1950s and 1960s necessitated new thoughts on the concept of development. He explains that the old paradigm assumed that "injecting western socioeconomic and political theories and practices in the development process" would address the backwardness of underdeveloped countries (Soola, 2003, p. 11).

Arising from the criticism of the Modernisation Paradigm which was faulted for ignoring the historical circumstance that resulted in the dependence of poorer countries on the richer ones and tending to blame the developing countries for their condition, came the Dependency Theory. The theory advocates the use of communication through the mass media to educate the people and encourage cooperation for their growth. It postulated that the mass media be placed under the control of the state which it believes, would advance the best interest of citizens (Servaes, 1991, cited in Mefalopulous & Grenna, 2004). Again, contrary to the assumptions of the paradigm, the situation in many developing countries especially in Africa did not make the theory workable. Over time, communication scholars began to explore other models that would accommodate the peculiarities of developing countries. Many African scholars have been part of the debate and the next section examines some of their perspectives.

Development Communication in Africa

Notwithstanding the views of different scholars (e.g. Nwokeafor & Okunoye, 2013; Okoro, 2018) on the difficulty in situating the impact of development communication in Africa, current trends in the continent's political development efforts in the twenty-first century emphasise the critical role of the media in achieving and sustaining democratic transformation (Okoro, 2018). In this regard, many African scholars have their perspectives on the role of development communication in promoting sustainable growth. There tends to be unanimity that communication has a vital role to play in promoting development with some of them prescribing different approaches. Olise (2011, p. 131) for instance, sees development communication as the utilisation of different news media for the dissemination of development-oriented messages "so as to better the life of the people in rural and urban areas as well as create a balance in the flow of information globally". He asserts that development journalism strives to bridge the information gap between the developed and developing countries, as well as, between the rural and urban populace.

This is similar to the position of Anaeto (2008) who views communication for development as using the media to disseminate information that would promote change and progress in the lives of the people. Globally, people need to be well informed about development issues by the news media. Similarly, development communication attempts to bridge the information gap between the developed and developing countries with the understanding that development cannot be said to have been achieved without evident transformation in the lives of the people. It is concerned with the exchange of ideas for achieving development objectives (Salawu, 2008).

To Anaeto (2008), communication for development is the use of the news media to disseminate information that would promote change and progress in the lives of the people. He advocates what he called "localism in media channel" which he defined as using media to communicate development-oriented information and agrees with Soola (2003) that development should be of the people, by the people and for the people. He argues that development countries should focus on their peculiar challenges such as poverty, illiteracy, poor health and where necessary, employ community and traditional media for disseminating communication information.

> Even in a globalized world, development communication appropriately seeks to localize communication efforts in finding solutions to problems. This simply means that localized problems are given localized communication treatment in consideration of the peculiar local factors, regardless of the globalized communication system. (Anaeto, 2008, p. 71)

Communication and Sustainable Development

As pointed out earlier, the positive role communication plays in promoting development is well established in the literature. Brown et al. (2011) for instance, report that newspapers in the United Kingdom shape understanding of climate change a great deal. Sosale (2008, p. 85) notes that communication and development are intertwined and "one is believed to guarantee the other". Development-oriented communication is also adjudged to have made significant impact in various development programmes (Servaes, 2006). This is particularly evident in the "Third World" where communication and the media are rated as having made significant contributions to development (Bessette, 2004).

The United Nations (UN) Roundtable on Communication for Development listed three major approaches to communication for development. While Behavioural Change Communication (BCC) approach focuses on empowering individuals to, as members of communities, make informed choices on their well-being and act accordingly, the Communication for Social Change (CFSC) approach targets emphasising strategies to bring about collective community change and long-term social change through dialogue. The third approach, Advocacy Communication, stresses organised efforts through coalitions and networking to influence among others, policy and programming decisions, the political climate, public perceptions of social norms (UNESCO, 2007). Hence, that communication plays a key role in achieving sustainable development and that the news media are important in the process of keeping the people informed or educated on development programmes is a settled fact. The question as Jimada (2006, p. 3) posed is, "are journalists doing enough towards the development of society?"

Development Journalism and Sustainable Development

Development Journalism scholarship illuminates the role of the news media in promoting development. Development Journalism Theory advocates a journalism model that fits the need of developing countries especially in Africa and Asia (Hanusch & Uppal, 2015). It is a concept that arose from calls that the news media in Africa should partner with their governments in promoting development (Anaeto & Solo-Anaeto, 2010). It prescribes a self-assigned task to be taken up by the news media to focus on issues that can fast-track development. Ramirez (1989) views development journalism as the resolve of a country's news media to deliberately seek solutions to development challenges with the aim of engendering a better or improved quality of life for the people. On their part, Obijiofor and Hanusch (2011, p. 11) defined it as journalism which promotes the belief that "journalists should serve as agents of social change and development in the societies in which they operate".

The prescriptions of Development Journalism Theory tallies substantially with those of the Development Media Theory which seeks to explain "the normative behaviour of the press in countries conventionally classified together as developing countries" (Olise, 2011, p. 137). It advocates the positive uses of the press for national development, among others. Olise believes that development journalism should pursue reaching the people with the right messages that would transform their minds towards development. This suggests that development communication messages rooted in the political, social and cultural nuances of a people would make greater impact. Also, Akinfeleye (2017) posits that the mass media are potent tools for national development through the promotion of understanding of the political, social and cultural systems of the society. He asserts that the mass media in Nigeria must reach the people with development-oriented messages that can drive human and material development. The author adds that for the mass media to be seen as playing a pivotal role in raising the quality of life and development of the people "developmental information on important issues such as economic, agricultural, social and political development should be played up in our mass media system than other items" (Akinfeleye, 2017, pp. 143–144).

Olusola and Areoye (2008) take the argument further asserting that education and orientation of the people on development objectives by the mass media are crucial to the achievement of the objectives. They opine that the news media as agents in the promotion of good governance, peace and human rights, as well as, in combating poverty and crime, should be involved in defining development strategies and "help in obtaining widespread support for such strategies" (p. 48). Soola in Mojaye (2008) also contends that development must be people-oriented and participatory to be effective and that social change and economic transformation must be grounded in effective communication.

Also looking at the importance of communication in achieving development agenda, Mojaye (2008) observes that communication has been used to achieve major changes in individual and social behaviour of the people in many countries, especially in health and agricultural sectors. He regrets, however, that Nigeria and many developing countries are yet to inculcate communication concerns into their development programmes. He submits that a needs-based development communication approach would be more effective for promoting people-centred development programmes. Mojaye adds that the needs-based development model "operates on the fundamental principle that development programmes must be based on the needs of the people and that the people must in turn, be involved in deciding what these needs are—right from the design stage of such projects" (Mojaye, 2008, p. 61).

Okoro (2018) and Ekeanyanwu (2008) in different studies acknowledge the potential of development communication to promote growth in Africa even as they acknowledge the dismal standing of the continent on the global development index. On his part, Ekeanyanwu (2008) identifies the challenges inhibiting development in Africa as hunger and poverty, disputes, wars and disarmament, underdevelopment and unemployment. He laments that Africa is almost two centuries behind Europe and America on the development ladder despite abundant natural resources. He notes further that "God has endowed the African continent with rich mineral deposits and sufficient human resources. Her soil is also fertile and the climate very mild and susceptible to all year round cultivation and exploitation" (p. 85). The author therefore recommends what he tags as Integrated Development Communication (IDC) which he defines as a community-based, participatory and decentralised multi-cultural approach in the use of communication structures for development.

In his study, Okoro (2018) highlights the importance of strategic development communication for accelerating growth. He notes that development communication has begun to take new directions since the beginning of the twenty-first century resulting in reconceptualisation of issues associated with development among mass media scholars. He states that issues such as the interdependence between media and politics, the role of the news media in disseminating development-focused news and so on have attracted the attention of scholars, thereby buttressing the importance of strategic communication. However, he contends that the minimal role of the mass media in educating citizens and encouraging effective participation in the political process has undermined the efforts of some African governments committed to political and economic development.

The above perspectives from African scholars on development communication concretise the position of the Development Journalism Paradigm on the need for journalism to deliberately advance the cause of development in developing countries. Journalistic activities that support development would obviously contribute to the realisation of the 17 SDGs and the 169 targets of Agenda 2030. The emphasis of the Development Journalism paradigm on the participation of citizens in development planning and using the news media to galvanise government and the people towards addressing development problems also agrees with the three approaches identified by the United Nations (UN) Roundtable on Communication for Development, cited earlier (UNESCO, 2007). Juxtaposed with the postulations of the Development Journalism Theory, there is no doubt that the pursuit of development journalism would assist in promoting the achievement of Agenda 2030 in Nigeria and other developing countries. This is amplified by their peculiarities. As Jimada (2006, p. 3) notes, "most news media in developing countries have the added social responsibility of character nourishment and the promotion of social, political and economic philosophies that influence the individual, family or community".

This study believes that the news media in developing countries like Nigeria can, apart from stimulating development internally, over time, change the negative narratives that scare away potential investors if they devote more attention to positive development issues, especially those that highlight the economic potentials of their countries. This is particularly so in this era of media convergence and global presence of most news media facilitated by the internet. In line with this, Kalyango (2011) observes that coverage of Africa's positive economic trends and good governance can accelerate its integration into the global economy as an attractive destination for trade and investment. He asserts:

> Much of Africa has a favourable economic climate, indicators of consistent—albeit slow—growth and sound economic and regulatory frameworks. The media can play a crucial role in disseminating such economic information, which can effectively guide international public opinion about Africa's potential. (Kalyango, 2011, p. 185)

METHODOLOGY

The qualitative research method is adopted for this study, using focus group as instrument. Qualitative research is hinged on the social constructivist worldview and is utilised to explore and understand how individuals or groups perceive a social or human problem. Focus group is a type of interview to elicit the views of people on a specific topic or issue (Bryman, 2004). According to Creswell (2014, p. 4), qualitative research "involves emerging questions and procedures, data typically collected in the participant's setting, data analysed inductively building from particulars to general themes, and the researcher making interpretations of meaning of the data".

Bryman (2004), while noting the tendency to use them interchangeably, distinguishes between group interviews (which could cover various issues and are carried out to save the researcher time and money), and focus groups which also involves groups but "typically emphasize a specific theme or topic that is explored in depth" (p. 346). The focus group researcher is more interested in how individuals discuss the issue at hand as members of a group rather than as individuals. Being mostly qualitative in nature, focus group studies are out to get the views and perspectives of the participants on the issues that produce a joint construction of meaning. The researcher looks out for such things as how people respond to each other's views and build up a view out of the interaction among group members (Gray, 2014; May, 2011). The focus group is usually held in a fairly unstructured setting where the moderator or facilitator guides the session without being obstructive.

Focus group had been in use for market research for many years but gained recent popularity in social science research. Bryman (2004) identifies the interactive nature of focus groups which affords participants to challenge each other's views and modify their initial responses based on perspectives introduced by others in the group. According to him, "this process of arguing means that the researcher may stand the chance of ending up with a more realistic account of what people think because they are forced to think about and possibly revise their views" (p. 348). As in all qualitative studies, the researcher is interested in not just what people say, but how they say it.

Creswell and Creswell (2018), while acknowledging the advantages of focus group as a method of eliciting the perspectives of participants on issues, however, noted the possibility of biased responses from participants as a result of the researcher's presence. They also note that not all people are equally articulate and perceptive, which might result in some group members dominating discussion and influencing the perspectives of others.

To address the issue of the possibility of some members dominating the groups, three focus group sessions were held with different groups of journalists totalling 20. The sessions were arranged at the venue of a National Delegates Conference of the Nigeria Union of Journalists (NUJ) where journalists from the 36 states of the country and those from the Federal Capital Territory (FCT) converged. The first two sessions had seven participants each while the last session had six. The researcher served as the moderator for the sessions raising questions relating to the issues of interest to the study. The questions revolved around whether Nigerian journalists have sufficient awareness or understanding of Agenda 2030 to be able to communicate it effectively to Nigerians, the level of professional commitment by journalists to promoting the realisation of the SDGs in line with the postulation of the development journalism theory and the extent to which the online and mobile platforms of the news media can be deployed to enhance participatory communication for achieving Agenda 2030.

The study opted for focus group because it has been recognised as a valuable tool for investigation by allowing a researcher to explore group norms and dynamics in relation to the matter being studied (May, 2011). Focus group according to Gray (2014, p. 468) is "an organised discussion among a selected group of individuals with the aim of eliciting information about their views". It is used to gain insights into particular subjects or situations by generating interactions and discussions among groups. Focus group also assists to shed light on issues through follow-up questions and affords observation of non-verbal responses such as frowns, gestures or smiles (Stewart, Shamdasani, & Rook, 2007).

In focus groups, participants enrich the views of other members of the group by adding to the points made. This makes it possible to distinguish similarities and differences in the opinions and values held by participants (Freeman, 2006). To reap the benefits inherent in focus groups, the moderator posed the same questions to the three sets of participants and encouraged them to discuss the issues freely. Conscious of the possibility of the sessions getting out of control, which is one of the identified limitations of focus groups (Morgan, 1997), the moderator ensured that none of the participants dominated the discussion unduly, by inviting other participants to air their views on the issues being discussed.

Despite the other limitations of focus group such as, the absence of confidentiality of participants' views (Kitzinger, 1995, cited in Morgan 1997) and the non-generalisability of the results being based on convenience samples (Stewart et al., 2007), the sessions generated rich data sets. A grid was developed for the conglomeration and analysis of the transcripts of the sessions which enabled the study to identify the collective perspectives of the selected Nigerian journalists on the issues raised. It also made possible the validation of related ideas and concepts resulting in a richer data. Table 25.1 shows the news organisations represented by the participants and the states of the country in which they practice as journalists:

Table 25.1 Media organisations

S/No.	Media organisation	State of posting
1.	Plateau Radio Television Corporation PRTVC	Plateau State
2.	Blue Print Newspaper	Imo State
3.	Ondo Broadcasting Corporation	Ondo State
4.	National Pilot Newspaper	Niger State
5.	Vanguard Newspaper	Federal Capital Territory (FCT)
6.	Radio Nigeria	Kaduna
7.	Nigerian Television Authority	Kano
8.	The Guardian Newspaper	Lagos
9.	Nasarawa Broadcasting Corporation	Nasarawa
10.	The Sun Newspaper	Gombe
11.	Vanguard Newspaper	Lagos
12.	Channels Television	Federal Capital Territory (FCT)
13.	The Punch Newspaper	Enugu
14.	Daily Trust Newspaper	Federal Capital Territory
15.	Federal Radio Corporation of Nigeria	Sokoto
16.	The Sun Newspaper	Enugu
17.	Radio Benue	Benue State
18.	TVC	Kwara
19.	Radio Kaduna	Kaduna
20.	News Agency of Nigeria	Katsina

The choice of participants was random and based on the willingness of participants. While some of those approached readily agreed, some declined. The researcher ensured that two women participated in each of the three focus group sessions to ensure gender representation.

Findings

Five key findings emerged from the data:

1. Most of the participants have a general awareness of Agenda 2030 but only some of them have detailed knowledge of the 17 Sustainable Development Goals (SDGs).
2. Some of the discussants do not think they have any special obligation to take interest in or promote SDGs beyond their regular line of journalistic duties except if commissioned to do so through advertisements or special projects.
3. The journalists subscribe to the prescriptions of the Development Journalism Theory and believe that by playing their constitutionally assigned watchdog role through drawing attention to anomalies within society, holding government accountable and promoting the well-being of the people, among others, they are contributing to meeting the objectives of Agenda 2030.
4. There is a consensus among the participants that the online and mobile platforms of news media could serve as platforms for participatory communication for the promotion of the SDGs. They note, however, that this would require implementing agencies and other stakeholders initiating such collaboration with the news media.
5. Participants believe that governments in sub-Saharan Africa should introduce policies to promote the tenets of development communication to accelerate sustainable development on the continent.

Discussion of Findings

As reported above, five major findings emerged from the data based on the questions this study sought answers to. The first question interrogated the level of awareness among participants of the United Nations 2030 Development Agenda otherwise known as Agenda 2030 and the 17 new Sustainable Development Goals adopted in 2015. Discussions during the three focus group sessions revealed that while most of the journalists know about Agenda 2030, only some of them, particularly those covering beats related to the SDGs, had a deep knowledge of the goals. Some of them excused their little knowledge on the fact that their journalistic responsibilities did not fall directly under issues related to the SDGs to warrant a deeper knowledge. These views illustrate the point:

> I have heard and read about Agenda 2030 and some of the targets, but I cannot claim to know them in details. I am not covering the health or environmental beats which are usually related to programmes like this, hence what I have is a kind of general knowledge of the programme. As a journalist, I support anything that would promote development and I believe that the goals and targets are laudable even if I do not know them in details. And I know I can get it on the internet if I need it, so why bother to know them in details? The Internet has made one kind of lazy because of the consciousness that one can always get what one needs online. (Focus Group 1 Participant)

> I am familiar with many but not all of the SDGs. I cover the environmental beat for my medium and I have done a number of reports on the SDGs. The targets are many so one can only be conversant with those that relate to one's beat. This is not to say that I'm not interested in them. As a journalist, I am committed to promoting development and would always do what I can in my capacity as a journalist to support development goals. But unless one is doing a news story or a feature on the SDGs, it will be difficult to remember them off hand. We're talking about almost 170 goals. Thank God, we are in the internet era and one can search for information on the go; so if I need details of the agenda and goals, Google is there to help me out. (Focus Group 3 Participant)

However, one would have expected that since the 17 SDGs and the 169 targets appear all-embracing covering environmental, social and economic issues like climate change, water, peace and economic growth, security and the like journalists would be knowledgeable about them. If journalists who are supposed to educate and inform the people on the SDGs have insufficient knowledge of the goals, how would they educate the people or take actions to promote them? Nevertheless, as some of the participants observed, not knowing the SDGs by heart does not signify ignorance. It is also possible that, just as one of them noted, the ease of accessing information online made possible by new digital technologies have tended to make people "lazy" in keeping information in memory. This equally suggests that agencies responsible for the implementation of the SDGs might need to consider sensitisation programmes for journalists so that they can become effective partners in promoting the goals. This will be in line with Okoro's (2018) suggestion that the mass media should be blended in the national agenda of countries to promote and sustain development efforts.

In the same vein, the second finding affirms that some of the participants do not feel obligated to promote the SDGs beyond their normal line of duty even though they believe that journalists should take interest in development issues as proposed by the Development Journalism model. One of the participants stated:

> I hope you are not suggesting that it is an obligation for journalists to be conversant with the SDGs or to promote them. Yes, I know of the so-called Agenda 2030 and I have read about some of the targets, but I don't think it is compulsory for me to know

them in details. Journalists cannot know everything, but where the need arises or one needs to write on any of the issues, one would conduct research to understand them. Also, even if I know them, promoting the achievement of the agenda is limited by the specific journalistic duties I'm saddled with at a given period. So for instance, if I am not covering any of the beats that relates to the goals, there is little I can do because I cannot intrude into another person's beat except in special circumstances. I agree with you that the goals are wide-spread and cover almost every aspects of life but for now, there is no special interest in promoting the SDGs beyond my normal duty as a journalist. (Focus Group 1 Participant)

Another added:

As journalists we are interested in promoting development. It is a duty we owe our society and our people, but is it really an obligation in the sense you are suggesting? I can declare that I support anything that would enhance development and raising the standard of life of the people. I have written several stories to draw attention to development problems and challenges faced by people in different places and if some of them fall within the SDGs, all well and good. However, it will be difficult for me to say categorically that this is what I have done to promote the SDGs or Agenda 2030. (Focus Group 2 Participant)

Another responded thus:

I am sure some of us here who are covering ministries, agencies and other beats related to the SDGs must have written stories on them, so such people can refer to what they have done to promote the SDGs. But I think that is where it ends. We are journalists and we write stories based on what comes up, but we may not be able to go out of our way to specifically identify with the SDGs. As one of us already said, as journalists, we are committed to the development of our country and people and we do whatever we can as professionals to promote development. This, I think is one of our core normative duties as journalists; I mean working for the betterment of our society If I see an important story on the SDGs in the course of my professional duty, I go for it and write the story, but where I have to go out of my way to try and promote the SDG-related issues, it may look like I'm doing it for some benefit. One can be easily misunderstood. My advice will be that the ministries or agencies in charge of Agenda 2030 should place periodic adverts or supplements in the media to propagate their activities. (Focus Group 3 Participant)

The responses above could indicate that while journalists would take interest in anything that is development related, they have no special interest nor feel any sense of attachment to the SDGs. This tends to authenticate the finding of an earlier study by Olusola and Areoye (2008, p. 48) which blamed the reluctance of the news media to report economic development reform programmes on "lack of understanding of the issue, lack of interest in a topic that is still not very visible, and lack of recognition by the media of its own role and responsibility". That some of the participants feel promotional information on the SDGs should come as paid-for adverts or supplements corroborates the earlier cited report by *GTZ* (2006, pp. 9–10) that media outlets demand payment for coverage of development-related issues. Notwithstanding, the fact that the participants aligned with the postulation of the Development Journalism Theory which urges them to support development ideals (Obijiofor & Hanusch, 2011) gives hope that they would not hesitate to promote the SDGs whenever they have the opportunity.

Nevertheless, the absence of a sense of obligation to promote the SDGs underscore the need for government and other development partners to mobilise the news media to support the SDGs by involving them in their activities. If as Nwabueze and Ebeze (2013) argue, the mass media are crucial to nation building and that no nation can survive without effective use of the media, it stands to reason that deliberate steps should be taken to make effective use of journalists towards the achievement of Agenda 2030 in Nigeria and elsewhere. This stand is buttressed by Esan (2016, p. 1) who notes, "whereas media institutions in Nigeria remain as adjuncts to the political, they have always been viewed as important to the business of nation building".

Equally, that participants were unanimous in the potential of deploying the online and mobile platforms of news media to facilitate two-way and other forms of interactive communication among stakeholders in the push for the achievement of the SDGs is instructive. Since internet penetration in Nigeria continues to improve and people in many remote parts of the country now have access to internet services, more people can be reached with messages that promote the achievement of Agenda 2030. The participants agreed that with the interactive nature of the platforms, citizens can express their views on the SDGs as it affects them thereby serving as a feedback mechanism which policy formulators and implementers could use to make adjustments where necessary. This would be an example of participatory communication which has been identified as an important component towards the achievement of the SDGs. It would also substantiate the position by Wu, Guo, Huang, Liu, and Xiang (2018) that Information and Communication Technologies (ICTs) could be key catalysts to promoting the SDGs. They note that ICTs can accelerate substantially the development process of human beings and "would have great potentials in playing important and key roles to support global economical, social and environmental sustainability, which wait for the relevant discovery based on global and multi-disciplinary efforts" (p. 13).

Also, the participants observed that governments in sub-Saharan Africa should introduce policies to promote the tenets of development communication to accelerate sustainable development on the continent. They agreed that the adversarial relationship between governments in most African countries and journalists do not make for a unanimity of purpose to pursue the development agenda:

> *The tensions between journalists and those in government in African countries whereby government functionaries see journalists as irritants cannot make for the kind of cooperation that would accelerate development. Probably because of the fear*

that journalists would expose their misdeeds, a lot of governments keep journalists at arm's length. Majority of the times, critical information is denied journalists and they have to rely on unofficial sources to get them. How then can there be a unity of purpose to pursue the development agenda? Unless and until governments in Africa shed their corrupt tendencies which make them hostile towards journalists for fear of being exposed, it would be difficult for journalists to see government as a partner in promoting development. (Focus Group 3 Participant)

A second member of the same group had this to say:

There is a lack of sincerity on the part of those in government. Most of them do not see themselves as servants of the people and lack any commitment to the development of their people. They subscribe to international instruments and programmes on development, but they are not committed to them. They say something but act differently. In fact, I will not be wrong to say that even for these SDGs that we are discussing, they are merely paying lip service; they are neither interested nor committed to their success. This Agenda 2030 was launched since 2015, but how many African leaders have demonstrated commitment to them in terms of budget allocation and other steps? So you can see why it is difficult for them to work with journalists. They will rather keep them far from them (government) so that they (journalists) will not pry into what they are doing. I'm sure you are aware of situations here in Nigeria where funds meant for specific programmes have been diverted by those is government. This tendency makes it difficult for them to want to work with journalists. But this must change if we want our country and our continent to develop. Our leaders should be more patriotic and work for the development of the continent and they need journalists as partners to achieve this.

If as Ekeanyanwu (2008, p. 91) noted, the media can contribute to addressing hunger and poverty through the building up of a spirit of solidarity "in a common effort towards societal re-engineering and development", it is important for governments in Africa to accept this reality and see journalists as partners in progress and not adversaries. Equally, Akinfeleye (2017), who also sees the mass media as potent tools for national development, advocates a communication policy for Nigeria that would accelerate society's aspirations especially in the area of good governance in all ramification.

Conclusion

This paper sought primarily to investigate the perception of selected journalists in Nigeria of their roles towards achieving the Sustainable Development Goals under Agenda 2030. The study was anchored on the Development Journalism Theory which proposed that journalists should be partners with government and others in promoting development. It is clear from the findings of this study that journalists need to be sensitised more to key into the agenda. It should be a thing of concern that a lot of journalists who are supposed to be purveyors of information are not abreast of a lot of the SDGs to be in position to educate citizens about them. Based on the findings, this study submits that journalists have a duty to promote development ideals as postulated by the Development Journalism Theory, but they need the enabling environment to deploy their journalistic duties to the promotion of development. Towards achieving this, the adversarial relationship between governance and journalism should be addressed by giving journalists more freedom to perform their professional duties especially in promoting development communication. Similarly, the role the news media can play in using their online and mobile platforms to engender participatory communication should be appreciated better for the success of Agenda 2030 in Nigeria. What is important as Odogu (2018) opines, is for the right attitude and strategy to be deployed by both bureaucrats and political leaders in implementing the SDGs. It is imperative for African leaders to see Agenda 2030 as an opportunity to accelerate development in their respective countries and reverse the perception of the continent as backward, risky and unsafe for investment (Kalyango, 2011). Only then will the right atmosphere for African countries to tap their rich endowments for sustainable development be feasible.

References

Akinfeleye, R. A. (2017). Nigeria's National Communication Policy and Strategy: Approaches, Policy and Possible Options. In H. S. Gladima & A. M. Adeyanju (Eds.), *Towards Nigeria's National Communication Policy and Strategy: Challenges and Prospects* (pp. 99–157). Kuru: The National Institute.

Anaeto, G. S., & Solo-Anaeto, M. (2010). *Rural/Community Newspaper: Principles and Practice*. Ibadan: Stirling-Horden Publishers Ltd.

Anaeto, S. G. (2008). Localism in Communication for Development in a Globalized World. In E. M. Mojaye, O. O. Oyewo, R. M'Bayo, & I. A. Sobowale (Eds.), *Globalization and Development Communication in Africa* (pp. 67–82). Ibadan: Ibadan University Press.

Bessette, G. (2004). *Involving the Community: A Guide to Participatory Development Communication*. Ottawa: Southbound and International Development Research Centre.

Brown, T., Budd, L., Bell, M., & Rendel, H. (2011). The Local Impact of Global Climate Change: Reporting on Landscape Transformation and Threatened Identity in the English Regional Newspaper Press. *Public Understanding Science*, 20(5), 658–673.

Bryman, A. (2004). *Social Research Methods* (2nd ed.). Oxford: Oxford University Press.

Creswell, J. (2014). *Research Design: Qualitative, Quantitative and Mixed Methods Approaches* (4th ed.). Los Angeles: Sage.

Creswell, J. W., & Creswell, J. D. (2018). *Research Design: Qualitative, Quantitative and Mixed Methods Approaches* (5th ed.). Los Angeles: Sage.

Ekeanyanwu, T. N. (2008). Africa and Global Challenges: The Need for Integrated Development Communication. In E. M. Mojaye, O. O. Oyewo, R. M'Bayo, & I. A. Sobowale (Eds.), *Globalization and Development Communication in Africa* (pp. 83–99). Ibadan: Ibadan University Press.

Esan, O. (2016). Introduction: Media Practices and National Challenges. In O. Esan (Ed.), *Taking Stock: Nigerian Media and National Challenges* (ACSPN Book Series) (pp. 1–9). Ontario: Canada University Press.

Freeman, T. (2006). 'Best Practice' in Focus Group Research: Making Sense of Different Views. *Journal of Advanced Nursing*, 56(6), 491–497.

Gray, E. D. (2014). *Doing Research in the Real World* (3rd ed.). Los Angeles: Sage.

GTZ. (2006). *Strategic Communication for Sustainable Development: A Conceptual Overview*. Bonn, Germany: Schneller Druck.

Hanusch, F., & Uppal, C. (2015). Combining Detached Watchdog Journalism with Development Ideals: An Exploration of Fijian Journalism Culture. *The International Communication Gazette*, 77(6), 557–576. https://doi.org/10.1177/1748048515597873

Jimada, U. (2006). *Essentials of Development News Reporting*. Ibadan: Evans Brothers (Nigeria Publishers) Limited.

Kalyango, Y. (2011). *African Media and Democratization: Public Opinion, Ownership and Rule of Law*. New York: Peter Lang Publishing Inc.

May, T. (2011). *Social Research: Issues, Methods and Process* (4th ed.). Berkshire: Open University Press.

Mefalopulous, P., & Grenna, P. (2004). Promoting Sustainable Development Through Strategic Communication. In D. Hami, E. Anochincloss, & W. Goldstein (Eds.), *Communicating Protected Areas* (pp. 24–31). Cambridge, UK: IUCN.

Mojaye, E. M. (2008). Needs-Based Communication for People-Oriented Development of Nigeria's Niger Delta. In E. M. Mojaye, O. O. Oyewo, R. M'Bayo, & I. A. Sobowale (Eds.), *Globalization and Development Communication in Africa* (pp. 55–82). Ibadan: Ibadan University Press.

Morgan, D. L. (1997). *Focus Groups as Qualitative Research* (2nd ed.). Thousand Oaks, CA: Sage.

Nwabueze, C., & Ebeze, E. (2013). Mass Media Relevance in Combating Insecurity in Nigeria. *International Journal of Development and Sustainability*, 2(2), 861–870.

Nwokeafor, C. U., & Okunoye, A. (2013). Media Power in Elections: Evidence of the Role of Agenda-Setting Theory in Political Communication in Nigeria Evolving Democracy. *International Conference on ICT for Africa 2013, Harare, Zimbabwe*.

Obijiofor, L., & Hanusch, F. (2011). *Journalism Across Cultures: An Introduction*. Basingstoke: Palgrave Macmillan.

Odogu, G. (2018, July 5). *Assessing SDGs Implementation in Nigeria*. Retrieved from https://punch.ng.com

Okoro, E. (2018). Development Communication and Politics in Sub-Saharan Africa: Analysing Media's Impact on Governance and Political Participation. *International Journal of Language and Literature*, 6(2), 63–67. https://doi.org/10.15640/ijll.v6n2Q19

Oleribe, O. O., & Taylor-Robinson, S. D. (2016). Before Sustainable Development Goals (SDG): Why Nigeria Failed to Achieve the Millennium Development Goals (MDG). *The Pan African Medical Journal*. https://doi.org/10.11604/pamj.22/06/2016.24.156.8447

Olise, F. P. (2011). The Utilisation of New Media for Development Journalism Practice in Delta State Nigeria. *The Journal of the African Council for Communication Education (ACCE). Nig. Chapter*, 9(1), 129–152.

Olusola, S. O., & Areoye, M. O. (2008). Communication and Economic Development: An Assessment of the Impact of the Nigerian Press on NEEDS. In E. M. Mojaye, O. O. Oyewo, R. M'Bayo, & I. A. Sobowale (Eds.), *Globalization and Development Communication in Africa* (pp. 43–53). Ibadan: Ibadan University Press.

Ramirez, T. B. (1989). *Philippines Journalism Handbook* (3rd ed.). Manila: National Bookstore Inc.

Salawu, A. (2008). Development Communication: The Preliminaries. In E. M. Mojaye, O. O. Oyewo, R. M'Bayo, & I. A. Sobowale (Eds.), *Globalization and Development Communication in Africa* (pp. 13–22). Ibadan: Ibadan University Press.

Servaes, J. (2006, October 25–27). Communication for Development: Making a Difference. *Mainstreaming Paper for the World Congress on Communication for Development (WCCD), Rome.* Washington, DC: World Bank.

Soola, E. O. (Ed.). (2003). *Communicating for Development Purposes.* Ibadan: Kraft Books Ltd.

Sosale, S. (2008). The Panoptic View: A Discourse Approach to Communication and Development. In J. Savaes (Ed.), *Communication for Development and Social Change* (pp. 85–95). London: Sage.

Stewart, D. W., Shamdasani, P. N., & Rook, D. W. (2007). *Focus Groups: Theory and Practice* (2nd ed.). Thousand Oaks, CA: Sage.

UNESCO. (2007). *Towards a Common System Approach: Harnessing Communication to Achieve the Millennium Development Goals.* A Background Paper for the 10th UN Inter-Agency Communication for Development Round Table, Addis Ababa, Ethiopia, pp. 12–14.

Wu, J., Guo, S., Huang H., Liu, W., & Xiang, Y. (2018). Information and Communications Technologies for Sustainable Development Goals: State-of-the-art, Needs and Perspectives. arXiv:1802.09arXiv.1802.09345v2(cs.345cs.345cs.CY).

PART IV

Conclusion

CHAPTER 26

Beyond the SDGs: From 2030 to 2050 Agenda for Development

Muhammad Jameel Yusha'u and Jan Servaes

Introduction

If there is one thing that is uncertain about the future, it is the uncertainty of the future itself. Yet, we remain optimistic about the future despite the challenges of achieving the dream of a world that is sustainable, fair and equitable. When we started editing this book, there was nothing like COVID-19 in sight. Our focus was mainly on the SDGs and the role of communication for development and social change in achieving this noble but arduous objective by the year 2030.

COVID-19 was a major setback in the attempt to achieve the 2030 agenda for development. Some of the progress being recorded has been delayed due to the COVID-19 pandemic. As we write this concluding chapter, more than 113 million people have been infected with COVID-19 globally and more than 2.5 million have passed away (Coronavirus Resource Centre, 2020). It also shows that the future belongs to those who work for it. Despite being the largest economy and a hub for technological innovation, the United States has been hit hardest by the COVID-19 pandemic due to the way it grappled with it. The contrast on how COVID-19 was handled between the strongest

M. J. Yusha'u (✉)
Islamic Development Bank, Jeddah, Saudi Arabia

J. Servaes
KU Leuven, Leuven, Belgium

economy in the world, the United States, and the expected strongest economy of the future, China says a lot about the debate on the future of development. Sachs (2020a, para 3) summarized this succinctly:

> The profound crisis of US politics has been starkly demonstrated in two ways this year. First, the federal government failed utterly to suppress the COVID-19 pandemic—or even to try. As 2020 draws to a close, the daily rate of new cases is approaching 200,000, far exceeding the previous peaks in April and July. During the week of November 15–21, the US had nearly 1.2 million newly confirmed cases, while China, America's putative Great Power rival, had just 86 newly confirmed cases, despite having more than four times the US population.

If there is one major lesson to be drawn from the challenges of COVID-19 as discussed in this book, is that Communication for Development and Social Change has become more pertinent than ever. COVID-19 is both a health and an economic crisis. But as public health experts have shown, it is impossible to tackle the pandemic without effective communication aimed at changing behaviour. Managing COVID-19 means people need to make more lasting adjustments in their daily lives. Staying more at home, washing hands regularly, maintaining social distance, staying away from large gatherings such as weddings, sporting activities, family events and more are some of the areas where major adjustments are needed. This may not be as easy as it sounds. People differ in the way they receive and respond to the need for behavioural changes depending on culture, faith, capacity, location and environment. These changes can't happen overnight as we have seen with many countries struggling to adapt to new changes. The difficulty of some world leaders like the former US President Donald Trump, UK's Prime Minister Boris Johnson and Brazilian President Jair Bolsonaro are some of the examples of how difficult it is to adjust to new ways of life. Whether the behaviour of these three leaders calling the COVID-19 "China Virus", or "Little Flu", was politically motivated or not, it shows why changing behaviour is a difficult task. It doesn't matter what influenced the behaviour of these leaders, the impact of their actions resonates with their supporters which makes managing the pandemic even more difficult. At the end of the day, these three leaders ended up testing positive for the virus due to their inability to adjust to the requirements for containing the pandemic as advocated by public health experts.

A more complicated phenomenon that emerged during the COVID-19 pandemic is managing fake news. Disinformation was a critical factor, thereby adding to the challenges that communication for development and social change needs to tackle. In the words of Sachs (2020a, para 17) "the new social media have led to the disintegration of a single national discourse and the pervasive misrepresentation of reality. With as many 'truths' as Facebook groups, agreement on basic facts, much less a consensus about what they mean, has collapsed."

From the economic and developmental point of view, another major lesson that we have learned from this book is the impact of COVID-19 on the wellbeing of ordinary people. As described by Savio (2020, para 10) "the impact of the Covid-19 virus is stronger than expected, and it will bring about a global social imbalance that will have a lasting impact on several millions of people—in fact, about 300 million people". Savio went on to explain that "According to the World Bank, 720 million people will be living in extreme poverty (less than 1.90 dollars a day). Of those, 114 million are the direct result of Covid-19: that is 9.4% of the world's population. According to the UN World Food Programme, more than 265 million are already starving, and many will die. And according to the International Labor Organization 200 million will lose their job" (Savio, 2020, para 11).

The COVID-19 pandemic also struck when the United Nations Population Fund (UNFPA) aims to achieve three world-changing results by 2030, the deadline for achieving the Sustainable Development Goals. These are: end unmet need for family planning; end gender-based violence, including harmful practices such as female genital mutilation and child marriage; and end all preventable maternal deaths. The COVID-19 pandemic could critically undermine the progress made in achieving these goals. In conjunction with migratory movements partly influenced by climate change, managing our already overcrowded planet must be a priority concern of policymakers and politicians.

The impact of climate change has also made conditions more favourable for the spread of certain infectious diseases. Future risks are not easy to predict, but climate change is hitting hard on several fronts relevant to where and when pathogens appear, including temperature and precipitation patterns. To help reduce the risk of infectious diseases, we must do everything we can to massively reduce greenhouse gas emissions and limit global warming to 1.5 degrees. As the planet warms, animals large and small, on land and in the sea, are moving to the poles to get out of the heat. That means animals come into contact with other animals that they normally wouldn't, and that creates an opportunity for pathogens to get into new hosts. Many of the underlying causes of climate change also increase the risk of pandemics. Deforestation, mainly for agricultural purposes, is the largest cause of habitat loss worldwide. Loss of habitat forces animals to migrate and potentially come into contact with other animals or humans and share germs. Large livestock farms can also serve as a source of overflow of infections from animals to humans. Less demand for animal meat and more sustainable livestock farming could reduce the risk of emerging infectious diseases and greenhouse gas emissions.

There are several conclusions that we can draw from the various chapters in this book. These conclusions can be summarized as follows:

- Embracing the tenets of communication for development is key to achieving the SDGs. It was a major oversight from the part of the UN to miss a goal for communication in the SDGs. The UN should seriously review the SDGs and include SDG18 (Communication for all) among the global goals. There are several movements for including SDG18 such as life with artificials, love and joy, animal health and rights, and more (Kelman, 2020). But none stands out like the need for a standalone goal for communication.

- The COVID-19 pandemic has shown to the world why communication is important in tackling development challenges. Following a review of communication strategies by development organizations such as the World Bank, WHO, UNICEF, IFRC, a communication strategy for tackling pandemics was proposed.
- The missing role of communication and culture in both MDGs and SDGs is a major oversight. There are various perspectives on the SDGs ranging from optimists to sceptics. Some of the SDGs and their targets are not properly quantified and lack clear timeline.
- The need to tackle environmental change, preserve oceans, forests and develop a strategy for a blue growth economy.
- Also religion has a role to play in development communication. Therefore, we have been looking at the Buddhist approach to participatory communication.
- The role of globalization, media regulation, media diversity, journalistic practices in achieving sustainability is crucial.
- The contribution of non-traditional sources in financing the SDGs shouldn't be overlooked. The role of Islamic finance in bridging the financing gap in the SDGs by addressing poverty through institutions like Zakat was an example of that.
- A general overview of each of the 17 SDGs and their targets highlights the needed investment on each of the SDGs and the progress made so far.
- Television stations and how they frame the debate on SDGs in countries like Egypt contributes to awareness about the SDGs.
- Advertising campaigns are relevant in communicating SDG3, health for all, as exemplified in German-speaking countries.
- The role of community learning centres in achieving quality education should be studied more thoroughly.
- The media contributes in literacy campaigns to achieve sustainable development and there are lessons to be learned in higher education, with specific recommendations for universities following the COVID-19 pandemic.
- The role of gender equality in achieving sustainable development and how community radio in countries like India contributes to achieving SDG5 on gender equality signifies the importance of communication in the empowerment of women.
- Communication for development and social change plays a vital role in promoting responsible consumption through poultry farming in Northern Ireland.
- In the age of misinformation and infodemics, fake news can temper with the effort to achieve SDG16.

- That language frames used by media organizations play a role in describing how food sovereignty movements frame the discourses on food security in Ecuador.
- Lessons drawn from the relationship between media and the environment through the coverage of Rio Olympic Games were key moments in the evolution of the SDGs.
- How media organizations provide coverage on climate change at the time of intense competition between the United States and China. An empirical analysis of news coverage in the two countries illustrated that.
- How the position of Donald Trump as US president influences media coverage of climate change issues in the United States.
- How micro-philanthropy is contributing to achieving the SDGs in China.
- News coverage of SDGs in Nigeria and how Nigerian journalists perceive their role in covering stories related to the SDGs.
- The challenges of communicating sustainability issues through the pollinator crisis with the possibility of two thirds of the world population living in cities by 2050.
- The Indian experience and approaches to the 2030 agenda for development.
- Looking at the enormity of the 2030 agenda, it is difficult to achieve the global goals by 2030. A reconsideration of the timeline should be on the cards.
- For some, technology can make it easy to facilitate the delivery of some of the SDGs.

Based on the conclusions drawn from various chapters, we can deduce at least four major lessons that should be taken seriously. First, is that funding the SDGs remains a huge challenge. Second, there is hunger to promote journalism for sustainable development, and mainstream communication for development and social change at various societal levels. Third, is the role of technology in development and; fourth, a clarion call to reconsider the timeline for delivering the SDGs from 2030 to a more realistic and achievable timeline. The next sections will focus on explaining these four lessons.

Funding the SDGs: An Unlikely But Not Impossible Feat

Whatever the debates about the SDGs, delivering the 2030 agenda might be achieved based on three factors. The first is financing. The critical question being asked in several fora on the SDGs ends with this question, who will finance the SDGs? Where will the money come from? How can low- and middle-income countries generate enough resources to fund the 2030 agenda for development. Remember that we are talking about 17 gigantic goals and 169 targets. Although each country has its own priorities, paying the bills for the SDGs remains a headache. According to the Asia-Europe Foundation (2020, p. 6):

Based on sectoral assessments, the total investment cost of achieving the SDGs by 2030 ranges between USD 5 and USD 7 trillion per year at the global level and between a total of USD 3.3 and USD 4.5 trillion per year in developing countries. This implies a mid-range USD 2.5 trillion yearly SDG investment need in the latter. To have an improved understanding of the real financial demands of the SDGs, countries should prepare their own assessments at least for their priority targets.

Mobilizing an average of US $2.5 trillion per annum up to 2030 is not an easy feat. But as the optimists for achieving the SDGs would argue, it is not impossible to do so. Perhaps when you look at the size of the global economy, and if the 193 UN member states that signed off to be part of the SDGs would see themselves as a single family, working collectively to deliver the 2030 agenda, the future of the SDGs might look brighter. The prospects of achieving the 2030 agenda would look more likely. The global economy is estimated to be worth US $133 trillion in 2019 compared to US $120 trillion dollars two years earlier, though the global economy is expected to shrink due to the impact of COVID-19 by the time the report on the global economy for 2021 is out (Hamadeh, Yamanaka, & Purdie, 2020).

The second important factor that would help achieve the SDGs is political will. There are several beautiful plans that have been produced whether at the global, regional or national levels. What makes the difference is the political will to deliver them. Many countries have produced ambitious national development plans that look amazing on paper. How many of them end up being achieved? Where you see success in changing the fortunes of a country through effective implementation of national plans, you cannot divorce such achievements from the strong political will of the leaders. The example of China and how it transformed its economy is a case in point.

To illustrate the importance of political will in achieving the SDGs, Sachs (2020b, para 1) explains what is expected in what he describes as mission sustainable development:

> Sixty years ago next May, President John F. Kennedy put the United States on a mission to the future. "I believe that this nation should commit itself to achieving the goal, before this decade is out, of landing a man on the moon and returning him safely to the earth. No single space project in this period will be more impressive to mankind, or more important for the long-range exploration of space; and none will be so difficult or expensive to accomplish." Our generation's moonshot is sustainable development on Earth.

Sachs went on to state that "we have already set the goals, but not yet embraced the challenges in full. In two pivotal moments in late 2015, all of the world's governments unanimously adopted the 17 Sustainable Development Goals (SDGs) and the Paris climate agreement. The world pledged to end extreme poverty, ensure universal health care, and provide education for all children by 2030", and in his usual optimism about the possibility of achieving the SDGs, Sachs concludes that "these bold goals are no less achievable than the moonshot, which the US accomplished on Kennedy's original timeline, in July 1969. The US moonshot in fact illuminates how to achieve bold goals such as the 17 SDGs and the needed energy transformation" (Sachs, 2020b, para 1–3).

The UN Secretary General, Antonio Guterres too expressed the need for political will if the SDGs are ever to be realized. In a speech delivered at the Sustainable Development Goals moment in New York, he stated that "we can make tremendous progress over the coming decade, especially for the most vulnerable and the poorest of the poor. When the public appetite for change is matched with political will and smart policy choices, rapid progress is unstoppable" (UN, 2020, para 3).

The critical question to ask is whether this political will exists. The UN Secretary General provided the answer in the same speech, "but, there is no escaping the fact that one critical ingredient is still missing. Political will. Without it, neither public appetite nor stakeholder action will be sufficient" (UN, 2020, para 13). Here lies the challenge of achieving the SDGs. Even if enough financing is provided, the SDGs cannot execute themselves, they must be matched by a vociferous political will. Throwing money at problems will not solve them. It wasn't money that made the mission to the moon possible. It was the unquestionable political will behind it.

The third factor, of course, is why we compiled this book. A robust communication for development and social change so that the political will can be transmitted to all stakeholders. Leaders who inspire change, do so using the tools of communication available in their age. Several studies have discussed the efficacy and challenges of applying communication for development paradigm in addressing development challenges. These studies have shown how communication for development, if applied properly whether at community or national levels, can serve as a driver for social change. Communication for development has served and continues to serve as a means of community empowerment, promoting social inclusion, diversity, reducing inequality and generating behavioural change. Such studies in one form or the other include Rogers (1976), Servaes (1986), Epskamp and Swart (1991), Kennedy (1993), Melkote (1993), Pratt (1993), Moemeka (1997), Otsyina and Rosenberg (1997) and Servaes (2020).

An area that needs significant effort in financing the SDGs is through the private sector and engaging philanthropists. While governments and ordinary people have been hit hard by the health and economic severity of COVID-19, it might in a way be good news to billionaires, many of whom have witnessed an astronomical increase in their wealth. A report by the Washington-based Institute of Policy Studies indicated that American billionaires have increased their wealth by US $1 trillion between March and November 2020. The report shows that Jeff Bezos, the owner of Amazon and the richest person in the world today has increased his wealth by 61 per cent from March to November 2020. His wealth increased from US $113 billion to US $182.4 billion within this period. The report of the Institute of Policy Studies added that just three years ago, there was no single centi-billionaire, that is a person with net worth of over US $100 billion. By November 2020, at the peak of COVID-19 pandemic, there are now at least 5 centi-billionaires, namely, Jeff Bezos of Amazon; Bernard Arnault, chairman of Louis Vuitton; Bill Gates, founder of Microsoft; Mark Zuckerberg of Facebook; and Elon Musk of Tesla (Huffington Post, 2020).

These billionaires along with the more than two thousand billionaires all over the world are rich enough to help make substantial progress in some of the SDGs. They can do that by dedicating a portion of their wealth to help address the development challenges being faced by humanity.

Journalism for Sustainable Development

One of the lessons that emerged from the chapters that focused on media coverage of the SDGs is the need for more focus on the idea of sustainable journalism. Journalism in the twenty-first century is still heavily influenced by excessive commercialism and the liberal model of journalism. As assessed by Hallin and Mancini (2004), this form of commercial journalism is based on the American and to some extent UK's commercial journalism culture, and it is having sway on journalism today.

To achieve the SDGs, there has to be a shift in focus to journalism that is based on the idea of sustainability. Berglez, Olausson, and Ots (2017) have explored the concept of sustainable journalism which focuses on the integration of environmental, social and economic challenges in journalism. To avoid mixing sustainable journalism with the recent challenges of dwindling revenues affecting media organizations, which is also called sustainable journalism, we choose to refer to journalism for sustainable development. This is a type of journalism that focuses on reporting and analysing issues related to sustainable development in all its forms.

Building a community of informed journalists and media organizations that understand the SDGs, and the challenges of achieving the global goals will be needed if meaningful progress is to be achieved in the implementation of the 2030 agenda for development. Three things will be required to achieve this type of journalism:

- **Capacity building for journalists**: Journalists need more training to appreciate the SDGs. The United Nations and its relevant agencies such as UNESCO and UNDP should dedicate more resources to train journalists and media proprietors to understand the urgency of enhancing the fecundity and quality of reporting on the SDGs. Partnership with unions for journalists, associations of media proprietors, philanthropic organizations, research institutes, NGOs and civil societies would be key. Part of the activities on World Press Freedom Day could be utilized for this purpose. Media organizations built on the idea of public service such as the

BBC, ABC, SABC, NTA, KBC and more have a role to play in achieving this objective.
- **The role of Universities**: Universities have a major role to play through their media, communication and journalism departments. The universities produce future journalists. Communication schools should integrate the SDGs into their syllabuses in terms of the why and how to report the SDGs for maximum impact. The teaching of communication for development should be mainstreamed in all universities, to be taught as a general studies course. This should include lower levels as well as was done in the Netherlands where the SDGs were integrated into school curricula. With this approach, future policy makers will be produced with a better understanding of the role of communication in addressing development challenges.
- **Research and publications on media coverage of the SDGs**: More research is needed on how the SDGs are covered by the traditional and social media. These researches should not be confined to journals and books. A forum for academics and media professionals needs to be created where the outcome of these researches will be shared with professional journalists. More collaboration between media and communication research organizations such as IAMCR, ICA, ECREA with professional journalism unions, broadcasting organizations and professional public relations arms will be needed for brainstorming and drafting policies that could enhance the coverage of the SDGs in traditional and social media. In essence, a community that grows with the SDGs should be built.

Technology for All

The decade of action from 2020 to 2030 comes amidst the sporadic development of technology. The era described as the fourth industrial revolution. To achieve the SDGs, the global community must embrace and use appropriate technology. If there is a short cut, especially for low- and middle-income countries, it is through this kind of technology. In Servaes (2014) the role of technology and culture in social change is being questioned. The contributors challenge us to reconsider and rethink the impact of new information and communication technologies on civil society contributions. Access to information and communication technologies is a necessity, and the importance of access should not be trivialized, but a plea for digital literacy implies recognizing that access is the beginning of ICT policies and not the end of it. Digital literacy requires using the Internet and social media in socially and culturally useful ways aimed at the inclusion of everybody in the emerging information/knowledge society. Technology matters, but people matter more. Advancement in research and innovation has made it possible to use technology in ways that were few years ago unthinkable. We have seen that being demonstrated during the COVID-19 pandemic. Imagine the set back that will ensue in the education sector if technology was not available to make remote learning possible (see Chap. 7 for more discussion on SDG4).

Therefore, according to Herweijer and Waughray (2019), one way of fast-tracking the implementation of the SDGs is by embracing technology. They argued that "an estimated 70% of new value created in the economy over the next decade will be based on digitally enabled platforms—and leading innovators are re-imagining how we innovate, create, distribute and capture value in the new systems that are emerging. Taking AI alone, estimates at PwC are that AI could increase global GDP by US$15.7 trillion by 2030" (Herweijer & Waughray, 2019, para 7).

Most of the SDGs can be achieved by embracing appropriate technology. For instance, Christensen, Ojomo, and Dillion (2019) have in their classic book, *Prosperity Paradox: How Innovations Can Lift Nations Out of Poverty*, discussed at length how innovation spurs the emergence of new technologies that led to economic prosperity in many countries, which leads to massive reduction in extreme poverty. This shows how appropriate technology can aid the realization of SDG1. Though the book was promoting the ideals of free market economy to a fault, at least it provides enough evidence to show how technology can contribute in reducing poverty.

If you take each of the 17 SDGs, you could find a role for technology. The latest example was during the COVID-19 pandemic when most international meetings took place virtually. The Convention of the Democratic Party during the 2020 election campaign, which was organized completely virtually, highlights how technology could contribute even in strengthening political institutions.

However, the picture is not as rosy as it sounds. Technology has also created a monster called misinformation, fake news or infodemic. For instance, Wilson and Wiysonge (2020) found that the use of social media to organize offline action is strongly associated with the perception that vaccinations are unsafe. The creation of doubt is particularly harmful when it comes to vaccination, because uncertainty causes vaccine hesitancy. Vaccine hesitancy has resulted in many of the measles outbreaks in Europe and North America from 2018 to 2020. This perception escalates as more organization occurs on social media. In addition, foreign disinformation online is strongly associated with both an increase in negative discussion of vaccines on social media and a decline in vaccination coverage over time. As discussed in Chaps. 1 and 16, tackling misinformation is one of the key challenges in achieving the SDGs. How could misinformation be tackled? West (2017) has prepared a comprehensive report for the Brookings Institution on the causes of fake news and how to tackle it. But for the purpose of this book, we would like to propose the following on the implementation of the SDGs:

- **Developing SDGs fake news tracker**: The UN should develop a dashboard for fake news: the dashboard should have a section for each of the

SDGs and highlight the potential fake news about the SDG using available technological monitoring tools.
- **Coalition of champions against fake news on SDGs**: The UN should mobilize a coalition of journalists, academics, faith leaders, celebrities and influencers against misinformation on the SDGs. Some of the Advocates on the SDGs appointed by the UN Secretary General should have "war against misinformation" as one of their advocacy roles.
- **Public education and media literacy**: More public education is needed on fake news and this should be the responsibility of all. There is need for more diligence and caution in spreading unverified information.
- **Hold social media companies accountable**: However, the study by Wilson and Wiysonge (2020) demonstrates that public outreach and public education about the importance of vaccination will not be enough to ensure optimal uptake of COVID-19 vaccines. Governments should hold social media companies accountable by mandating them to remove false anti-vaccination content, regardless of its source. The key to countering online misinformation is its removal by social media platforms. Presentation of arguments against blatant misinformation paradoxically reinforces the misinformation, because arguing against it gives it legitimacy.

AGENDA 2050: REVIEWING THE TIMELINE FOR THE 2030 AGENDA FOR DEVELOPMENT

Now comes the reality about the SDGs. How realistic is it to achieve the SDGs by 2030? This debate started right from 2015, the year the SDGs were adopted as the successor to the MDGs. The Overseas Development Institute (ODI) tried to answer this question in a report published in 2015 called *Projecting Progress: Reaching the SDGs by 2030*. In an in-depth analysis of the report, Hoy (2015, para 2) states:

> Using projections from leading international organisations, including the World Bank, the OECD, and the World Health Organization, the report quantifies how much the world would need to accelerate current trends in order to achieve the SDGs by 2030. To make the task more manageable, only one key target is examined for each of the 17 goals. Goals are "graded", based upon how close they would come to being achieved if the current progress toward the goals were to continue to 2030. An "A" grade implies that current progress is sufficient to meet the target, while "B", "C", "D" and "E" grades represent a continuum of how much faster progress would need to be. An "F" grade indicates that the world is currently heading in the wrong direction—there may actually be a regression in progress toward the goal by 2030.

By looking at the scorecard of ODI, answering the question about the likelihood of achieving the SDGs becomes easier. None of the 17 SDGs got an A grade in the scorecard, which means it is impossible to achieve any of the SDGs adequately by 2030. But the picture is even clearer when you analyse the rest of the scorecard. Only three SDGs, SDG1 (no poverty), SDG8 (economic growth and decent jobs) and SDG15 (biodiversity) received B grade. SDGs 3 (health for all), 4 (quality education), 16 (peace, justice and strong institutions), 17 (partnerships for the goals), 2 (zero hunger), 6 (water & sanitation), 7 (energy), 5 (gender) and 9 (industrialization) all got an average C grade. SDGs 10 (inequality), 11 (cities), 12 (waste), 13 (climate change) and 14 (oceans) all got an F grade.

Based on the ODI scorecard, only 3 out of the 17 SDGs were on track to achieve a reasonably acceptable result by 2030. This scored was developed in 2015, before COVID-19 struck (Table 26.1).

Table 26.1 SDGs scorecard

SDG SCORECARD 2030

Goal	Target	Grade
1. POVERTY	1.1 End extreme poverty	B
8. GROWTH	8.1 Economic Growth in LDCs	B
15. BIODIVERSITY	15.2 Halt Deforestation	B
3. HEALTH	3.1 Reduce Maternal Mortality	C
4. EDUCATION	4.1 Universal Secondary Education	C
16. PEACE	16.1 Reduce Violent Deaths	C
17. PARTNERSHIPS	17.1 Mobilise Domestic Resources	C
2. HUNGER	2.1 End Hunger	D
6. WATER & SANITATION	6.2 Universal Access to Sanitation	D
7. ENERGY	7.1 Universal Access to Energy	D
5. GENDER	5.3 End Child Marriage	E
9. INDUSTRIALISATION	9.2 Industrialisation in LDCs	E
10. INEQUALITY	10.1 Reduce Income Inequality	F
11. CITIES	11.1 Reduce Slum Populations	F
12. WASTE	12.5 Reduce Waste	F
13. CLIMATE CHANGE	13.2 Combat Climate Change	F
14. OCEANS	14.2 Protect Marine Environments	F

Source: Overseas Development Institute (2015)

With the devastating effect of COVID-19 in almost every sector of the global economy, and the outcry by the UN Secretary General Antonio Guterres that the SDGs are off-track, it is clear that achieving the SDGs by 2030 is next to impossible. In fact, a critical look at the progress made globally, even before the MDGs, suggests that addressing development objectives by nation states is more difficult than acknowledged by the framers of the 2030 agenda for development. A study by Lin and Monga (2017) on how to successfully build the economy of developing countries, reduce poverty and achieve prosperity makes it clear how arduous this task is. In their analysis, from 1950 to 2008 only 28 countries managed to reduce their gaps with the United States by 10 per cent or more. That is a period of 58 years, and the 2030 agenda is expected to be achieved within 15 years. Out of the 28 countries mentioned by Lin and Monga, only 12 of them were not European or non-oil economies.

According to Lin and Monga, the challenge of revamping the economy of developing countries is not unconnected with some of the intellectual and policy mistakes imposed by the Washington consensus during the 1970s to 1990s, the years described as the lost decade for developing countries. In fact, Banerjee and Duflo (2019), who shared the 2019 Nobel Prize in economics for their work on poverty alleviation, highlighted how the economists who design development policies are out of touch with the reality of ordinary people.

What is the way forward? We propose the following:

- The UN and the rest of the international community should be realistic and review the 2030 agenda for development by revising the timeline from 2030 to 2050. Some regional organizations such as the African Union have set the date for delivering their development objectives to 2063. The SDGs should be prioritized with SDG1 on ending extreme poverty as the most important target for the next ten years. Ending extreme poverty would likely have an impact on other SDGs, especially SDGs 2, 3, 4, 5 and 6. The effort to eradicate extreme poverty should not be based on slogans, but rather governments, financing institutions, donors and philanthropists should see it as the best chance to save humanity. The intellectual mistakes and policy prescriptions imposed on low- and middle-income countries that plunge them further into the abyss of underdevelopment should be avoided. Setting the timeline for delivering the SDGs by 2050 will provide sufficient time to reassess the progress made so far, fill the missing goals such as SDG18 on communication for all, and regain the lost ground from the devastating impact of COVID-19 on the SDGs. It will also afford the global community sufficient time to strategize on how to handle the potential emergence of right wing and nationalist governments such as those of Donald Trump, who may put constrains on the SDGs due to their disdain for multilateralism. Plans can also be made in advance to mitigate against the next disasters that could harm the realization of the SDGs.

- The UN should immediately begin the review process and convene a stakeholder conference to agree on the revised timeline for agenda 2050.
- Build a new coalition of statesmen, government representatives, development institutions, media professionals, private sector, academics and philanthropists to oversee the development of a robust and unprecedented resource mobilization plan aimed at financing the SDGs. This coalition should be permanent rather than produce a report and disappear. This could complement the political dimension of the SDGs and give a chance to the billionaires and financing institutions to do more for humanity. In other words: no more time to waste, action please!

REFERENCES

Asia-Europe Foundation. (2020). *Who Will Pay for the Sustainable Development Goals?* Retrieved December 5, 2020, from https://www.asef.org/images/docs/ASEF%20-%20Who%20Will%20Pay%20for%20the%20Sustainable%20Development%20Goals_9Dec_v7%20HIGHRES.pdf

Banerjee, A. V., & Duflo, E. (2019). *Good Economics for Hard Times.* New York: Public Affairs.

Berglez, P., Olausson, U., & Ots, M. (2017). *What Is Sustainable Journalism?* USA: Peter Lang.

Christensen, C. N., Ojomo, E., & Dillion, K. (2019). *Prosperity Paradox: How Innovation Can Lift Nations out of Poverty.* USA: Harper Collins Publishers.

Coronavirus Resource Centre. (2020). *COVID-19 Dashboard by the Centre for Systems Science and Engineering (CSSE) at Johns Hopkins.* Retrieved March 1, 2021, from https://coronavirus.jhu.edu/map.html

Epskamp, K. P., & Swart, J. R. (1991). Popular Theatre and the Media: The Empowerment of Culture in Development Communication. *International Communication Gazette, 48,* 177–192.

Hallin, D. C., & Mancini, P. (2004). *Comparing Media Systems. Three Models of Media and Politics.* Cambridge: Cambridge University Press.

Hamadeh, H., Yamanaka, Y., & Purdie, E. (2020). *The Size of the World Economy in 2019: A Baseline from Which to Measure the Impact of COVID-19 and Track Economic Recovery.* Retrieved December 5, 2020, from https://blogs.worldbank.org/opendata/size-world-economy-2019-baseline-which-measure-impact-covid-19-and-track-economic-recovery

Herweijer, C., & Waughray, D. K. N. (2019). *How Technology Can Fast-Track the Global Goals.* Retrieved December 5, 2020, from https://www.weforum.org/agenda/2019/09/technology-global-goals-sustainable-development-sdgs/

Hoy, C. (2015). *Can the SDGs Be Achieved by 2030?* Retrieved December 6, 2020, from https://devpolicy.org/can-the-sdgs-be-achieved-by-2030-20150924/

Huffington Post. (2020). *US Billionaires Grow Wealth by Over $1 Trillion Since Pandemic Began: Report.* Retrieved December 5, 2020, from https://www.huffpost.com/entry/billionaires-wealth-grows-coronavirus-pandemic_n_5fbeb24dc5b61d04bfa69373?guccounter=1&guce_referrer=aHR0cHM6Ly93d3cuZ29vZ2xlLmNvbS8&guce_referrer_sig=AQAAAIu1QrngitY9ff8f0yLccB_X9UKi1PuB-iMSrAUNnOkbl5tXOoTdsu6YJMSye5VOaDRaxI5RorAa6WteIHNF

DqF109axsyh33RAaDQ112WsJ3YyrN39n-ekP5Sdb-BEffr_zH2a1d7PES4NJALL-ZEbIIoYrr1BYGbisPzIvI7OiC

Kelman, I. (2020). *Sustainable Development Goal 18. Do Proposals for Expanding the Global Goals Stand up to Scrutiny.* Retrieved December 6, 2020, from https://www.psychologytoday.com/intl/blog/disaster-choice/202007/sustainable-development-goal-18

Kennedy, L. B. (1993). Communication Development in Vietnam: The Politics of Planning. *International Communication Gazette, 51,* 219–235.

Lin, J. Y., & Monga, C. (2017). *Beating the Odds: Jump-Starting Developing Countries.* New Jersey: Princeton University Press.

Melkote, S. R. (1993). From Third World to First World: New Roles and Challenges for Development Communication. *International Communication Gazette, 52,* 145–158.

Moemeka, A. A. (1997). Development Communication for Developing Societies: Facing the Realities. *International Communication Gazette, 59*(4–5), 379–393.

Otsyina, J. A., & Rosenberg, D. B. (1997). Participation and the Communication of Development Information: A Review and Reappraisal. *Information Development, 13*(2), 89–93.

Overseas Development Institute. (2015). *Projecting Progress: Reaching the SDGs by 2030.* Retrieved December 6, 2020, from http://developmentprogress.odi.org/sdgs-scorecard/

Pratt, C. B. (1993). Fallacies and Failures of Communication for Development: A Commentary on Africa South of the Sahara. *International Communication Gazette, 52,* 93–107.

Rogers, E. M. (1976). New Perspectives on Communication and Development: Overview. *Communication Research, 3*(2), 99–106.

Sachs, J. (2020a). *America's Political Crises and the Way Forward.* Retrieved December 1, 2020, from https://www.project-syndicate.org/onpoint/america-political-crisis-and-global-cooperation-by-jeffrey-d-sachs-2020-11?h=pH%2foOwgQpqUg9Qc9qjwOa8YBZwEijS%2bwcrkIr0NEdNU%3d&

Sachs, J. (2020b). *Mission Sustainable Development.* Retrieved December 5, 2020, from https://www.project-syndicate.org/commentary/mission-sustainable-development-by-jeffrey-d-sachs-2020-12

Savio, R. (2020). *Millions of New Poor Are on the Way. Who Cares?* Retrieved December 2, 2020, from http://www.ipsnews.net/2020/11/millions-new-poor-way-cares/?utm_source=English+-+SDGs&utm_campaign=0a9e85c2e3-EMAIL_CAMPAIGN_2020_11_30_10_14&utm_medium=email&utm_term=0_08b3cf317b-0a9e85c2e3-4622673

Servaes, J. (1986). Development Theory and Communication Policy: Power to the People. *European Journal of Communication, 1,* 203–229.

Servaes, J. (Ed.). (2014). *Technological Determinism and Social Change. Communication in a Tech-Mad World.* Lanham: Lexington, 330pp.

Servaes, J. (2020). *Handbook of Communication for Development and Social Change I & II.* Singapore: Springer.

UN. (2020). *With Political Will, Smart Policy Choices, 'Tremendous' Gains Possible over Coming Decade, Secretary-General Says, Pointing to Transformative Moment for Change.* Retrieved December 5, 2020, from https://www.un.org/pressTechnological

West, D. M. (2017). *How to Combat Fake News and Disinformation*. Retrieved December 6, 2020, from https://www.brookings.edu/research/how-to-combat-fake-news-and-disinformation/

Wilson, S. L., & Wiysonge, C. S. (2020, December 3). Misinformation on Social Media Fuels Vaccine Hesitancy: A Global Study Shows the Link. *The Conversation*. Retrieved from https://theconversation.com/misinformation-on-social-media-fuels-vaccine-hesitancy-a-global-study-shows-the-link-150652

Index[1]

NUMBERS AND SYMBOLS

2015, 24, 27, 31, 37, 55, 56, 60, 62, 63, 79, 81, 140, 143, 149, 151, 160, 161n9, 171, 174, 179, 206, 216, 247, 260, 269, 280, 306, 310, 314, 326, 347, 349, 375, 377, 379, 381, 393, 427, 456, 507, 509, 517, 518, 520, 521, 559, 560, 562, 570, 570n3, 570n4, 572, 585, 595, 599, 610, 615, 616

2030 Agenda, 10, 26, 27, 31, 44, 47, 81, 86, 87, 96, 138, 149, 150, 171, 216, 237, 238, 244, 247, 292, 293, 305, 346, 351, 366, 371–386, 393–395, 397, 404, 416, 451, 508, 562, 609, 610

2030 agenda for development, 4, 9, 10, 20, 23, 24, 27, 53–70, 605, 609, 612, 615–618

A

Action frame, 560, 567, 569, 571, 573, 579
Adern, Jacinda, 60
Adult education, 24, 172, 175–178, 182, 188, 217, 218, 224, 230

Affordable, 18, 43, 61, 64, 70, 151, 157, 219, 534
Africa, 14, 17, 45, 46, 57, 64, 153, 185, 236, 325, 326, 329, 336, 340, 372n1, 381, 385, 585, 588–592, 599
African Union, 53, 617
Age groups, 337–339
Agenda for development communication, 327–328
Agriculture, 15, 57, 67, 80, 176, 177, 262, 272, 305, 311, 315, 348–351, 353, 355, 359, 360, 362–364, 393, 394, 396, 397, 435, 490, 587
AIDS, 26, 113, 132, 449–477
Akhbar al Youm, 442–443, 445
Al Ahram, 442, 444, 497, 498
Alibaba, 376
Aljazeera, 18, 19
Amazon, 128, 498, 500, 611
Ambitious, 12, 33–35, 44, 53, 55–57, 61, 174, 247–249, 285, 350, 372n1, 517, 562, 570, 610
Americans, 141, 535, 546
Architects, 32–33, 37, 66
Asia, 14, 17, 152, 185, 497, 519, 522, 590

---

[1] Note: Page numbers followed by 'n' refer to notes.

A

Audiences, 17, 84, 86, 90, 91, 130, 135, 138–140, 195, 297, 337, 338, 354, 356, 394, 399, 402–406, 412, 452, 454, 458, 477, 490, 491, 501, 510–512, 524, 525, 577, 579
Audience segment, 456–458, 466, 468
Austria, 450, 459–464, 473, 475

B

Badan Wakaf Indonesia (BWI), 159
Baidu, 376, 377
Behaviour, 201–203, 207, 262, 450, 452–454, 457, 458, 469, 473, 474, 519, 525, 526, 539
Beijing declaration, 246
Beyond cherry-picking, 39–40
Biodiversity, 26, 66, 67, 77, 79, 87n1, 127–131, 138, 139, 143, 315, 353, 393–395, 397, 401–403, 409–414, 499, 536, 616
Blue economy, 79–83, 85, 86, 91
Blue growth, 23, 24, 77–96, 608
Brazil, 4, 66, 350, 492, 497–500
British Broadcasting Corporation (BBC), 18, 491, 534, 613
Broadcasting, 18, 19, 272, 440, 613
Brundtland, 79, 507
Brundtland Commission, 507
Buddhism, 101–104, 106–107, 110, 113, 119, 122, 158
Buddhist, 120–122, 608
Bureaucratic, 33–35, 45, 94
Burkina Faso, 45
BWI, *see* Badan Wakaf Indonesia

C

Capacity building, 91, 297, 299–300, 302, 325, 340, 341, 612
Capitalism, 63, 137, 141, 142, 246, 269, 307, 310, 316, 511
Carbon emission, 17, 61, 66, 525, 544, 548, 549
CARE, 495
CCTV, 18
Chinese media, 517, 520, 525
Chinese philanthropy, 372, 373, 381, 383–386
Chinese President, 382
Civil Society Mechanism (CSM), 346, 352, 354, 360–362, 364, 365
CLC, *see* Community Learning Centre
Climate action, 65–66, 141, 151, 237, 550
Climate change, 17, 24, 27, 55, 58, 61, 65, 80–82, 127–143, 199, 292, 310, 311, 314, 374, 378, 400, 412, 416, 491, 494, 498, 499, 501, 507–527, 533–551, 564, 589, 596, 607, 609, 616
Climate change communication, 65, 134
Climate change denialism, 24, 128, 136
Cloud, 132, 338, 542
CNN, 17, 18, 21, 490
Commission, 12, 13, 488, 562
Committee on World Food Security (CFS), 26, 346–349, 349n3, 354, 360–367
Communicating development, 200, 559–580
Communicating health, 449–477, 608
Communication, 3–27, 35, 42–43, 53, 69–70, 77–96, 101–122, 127–143, 150, 154–156, 172, 176–178, 193, 199–201, 218, 238, 268–270, 283–285, 289, 295–296, 306, 309–310, 325, 327–328, 346, 374, 393–416, 438, 450, 452–454, 487–501, 510, 536, 559, 585, 587–590, 605
Communication for all, 23, 40, 43, 55, 63, 69–70, 607, 617
Communication for development and social change (CDSC), 8, 12–15, 18, 20, 24, 54, 78, 83–86, 92, 94, 96, 194, 261, 328, 374, 394, 399, 400, 402, 404, 405, 501, 605, 606, 608, 609, 611
Communication for Sustainable Social Change (CSSC), 26, 42, 345–367
Communication landscapes, 128
Communication principle, 395, 398, 402–415
Communication response, 8, 9
Communication strategy, 4, 5, 7, 9, 20, 23, 24, 84–86, 92, 96, 173,

262–263, 265, 285, 312, 412, 414, 451, 452, 608
Communist Party, 499, 517
Community, 4, 34, 54, 64, 78, 104–107, 130, 150, 171, 179–183, 185–188, 200, 217, 235, 263, 289, 295–296, 318, 328, 351, 379, 394, 428, 450, 488, 510, 535, 577, 592, 608
Community Learning Centre (CLC), 24, 58, 171–189
Community radio (CR), 25, 264, 289–302
Community Resource Persons (CRP), 279
Comparative analysis, 65, 507–527
Compassionate leadership, 108, 120, 121
Concepts, 9, 40, 41, 79–80, 82, 86, 87, 92, 94, 96, 102, 104, 110, 113, 116, 118, 120, 130, 132, 157, 171–175, 182–184, 186, 187, 220, 222, 238, 239, 242, 263, 265, 268, 274, 284, 295, 302, 308, 352, 358, 400, 402, 413, 428, 436, 438, 440, 447, 452, 455, 458, 462, 474, 488, 499, 507, 511, 541, 562, 573, 587, 588, 590, 594, 612
Conclusion, 10, 12, 27, 33, 40, 58, 60, 140, 150, 203, 346, 450, 561, 576, 607, 609
Conference of Parties (COP), 509, 517, 518, 520
Congo, 8, 45
Consumerism, 141
Content, 23, 26, 27, 131, 133, 138, 177, 178, 197, 199, 206, 215, 221–223, 226, 228, 229, 290, 291, 296, 298, 301–302, 329, 331, 332, 337, 341, 364, 428, 431, 434, 437, 438, 440, 447, 450, 454, 462, 465, 469, 472, 474, 476, 477, 497, 512, 514, 516, 525, 527, 533–551, 560, 564–573, 578, 615
Content analysis, 27, 223, 364, 450, 473, 477, 496, 514, 516, 527, 539, 540, 560, 564–573, 578
Contrasting discourses, 81–83
Coronavirus, 4, 8, 10, 18, 54, 226
Corporate Social Responsibility (CSR), 309, 310, 318, 373, 376–378, 385
Cost of transactions, 156

COVID-19, 3–27, 40, 44–47, 54, 55, 57–60, 62n1, 63, 64, 68, 69, 154, 156, 206, 207, 220, 226, 227, 230, 237, 539, 605–608, 610–617
Creating awareness, 452–458, 467, 474
Criminologists, 307–309
CRP, *see* Community Resource Persons
CR, see Community radio
Cultural diversity, 128–130, 139, 142, 143, 194, 247, 266, 410
Culture, 14, 35, 40, 42–43, 47, 70, 94, 95, 101, 102, 104, 106, 118, 128, 138, 178, 183, 194, 223, 224, 246, 261, 328, 385, 399, 401, 402, 410, 440, 497, 511, 513, 514, 606, 608, 612, 613
Curricula, 69, 187, 195–199, 201, 203–207, 613

D

Daily Trust, 27, 560, 565–572, 576, 578, 579
Dashboard, 17, 69, 70, 614
Data, 34, 43, 45, 59, 64, 66–67, 70, 87, 91, 92, 94, 131, 141, 151, 160, 162, 166, 185, 195, 220, 226, 325, 335, 346, 352–354, 357, 365, 384, 401, 404, 413, 428, 458, 467, 518, 535, 539–542, 545, 549, 551, 565, 567, 568, 573, 578, 592, 594, 595
Decent work, 10, 58, 61–63, 151, 311
Democracy, 35, 43, 47, 141, 174, 176, 187, 188, 224, 269, 340, 366, 517
Demographics, 219, 228, 334, 337, 338, 340, 341, 373, 477
Dependency, 14, 365, 561, 562
Desertification, 66, 67
DevCom, *see* Development communication
Development, 3–27, 31, 40–42, 53–70, 77–96, 101–122, 127–143, 149, 171–173, 193–208, 215–230, 236, 245–251, 259, 261–266, 268–270, 283–285, 290, 294–295, 325, 327–328, 345, 371–386, 394, 398–400, 428–431, 449, 487–501, 507–510, 559–580, 585, 587–592, 605–618

Development communication
(DevCom), 4, 9, 13, 14, 63, 65, 84,
112, 115, 142, 156, 261, 262, 266,
269, 295, 327–328, 447, 476,
488–489, 561, 562, 585–591, 595,
598, 600, 608
Development practice, 104–107, 366
Diffusion, 14, 84, 85, 92, 261,
262, 329, 332–334, 357, 364,
411, 561
Digital communication
strategies, 262–263
Digital divide, 43, 54, 60, 300, 384, 487
Digital inclusion, 40, 43, 217
Digital solution, 371–386
Digitization, 278, 334
Dignity, 70, 129, 130, 236, 239, 240,
247, 294, 298, 301
Distance learning, 220

E
Earth, 47, 63, 129, 307, 348, 395, 397,
439, 488, 546, 610
Earth Summit, 26, 350, 487–501
Eastern, 41
Eco-narratives, 137–140
Economic growth, 10, 12, 35, 56, 59,
61–63, 77, 80, 81, 84, 87, 94, 136,
141, 151, 160, 172, 174, 179, 194,
228, 245, 307, 309, 311, 313, 315,
317, 347, 374, 382, 446, 507, 562,
596, 616
Economy, 10, 11, 13, 23, 24, 41, 54, 63,
66, 69, 79–83, 85, 87, 87n1, 91,
94, 102, 127, 136–137, 141, 151,
154, 155, 159, 173, 181, 184, 194,
206, 228, 249, 261, 263, 266, 267,
269, 271–274, 284–286, 305, 307,
312, 313, 317, 337, 382, 427, 429,
432, 433, 441, 446, 493, 494, 509,
514, 534, 535, 546, 585, 587, 592,
605, 606, 608, 610, 614, 617
Ecuadorian, 353–359, 364, 365, 498
Education, 9, 35, 54, 58–59, 81, 105,
151, 171, 176–178, 183–184,
193–208, 215–230, 246, 268, 292,
311, 326, 353, 372, 400, 433, 452,
562, 587, 608

Education for all (EFA), 58–59, 174,
175, 179, 217, 224, 230, 610
EFA, *see* Education for all
Effects, 10, 17, 24, 27, 81, 102, 103,
130–134, 140, 152, 172, 187, 201,
205, 239, 250, 261–263, 292,
306–308, 312, 317, 325, 327–329,
333, 357, 398, 406, 409, 439, 445,
452, 456, 464–466, 475, 476, 492,
494, 513, 517, 534, 538, 539, 545,
548, 549, 551, 617
Efficiency, 56, 65, 68, 153–155, 199,
201, 312–315, 329, 375, 491, 511,
526, 534, 535, 539
Egypt, 26, 64, 69, 158, 237, 349,
427–447, 608
Egyptian, 427–447, 497, 498
Emotional appeals, 249, 454, 455, 464,
466, 467, 470–475
Empowerment, 14, 15, 33, 44, 59,
60, 62, 70, 84, 85, 105, 114,
118–120, 218, 220, 228, 229,
235–254, 266, 268, 269, 290–297,
608, 611
Energy, 13, 42, 56, 61, 64, 65, 67, 77,
79–81, 87, 87n1, 135, 136, 151,
173, 199, 201, 249, 260, 282, 311,
313, 314, 316, 363, 383, 410, 433,
435, 436, 491, 495, 499, 501, 509,
514, 534, 537, 546, 547, 549,
611, 616
Engagement, 13, 34, 43, 56, 70, 83, 87,
92, 96, 102, 112, 116, 138, 201,
223, 229, 249, 251, 252, 291,
293, 297, 298, 309, 310, 318, 328,
329, 364, 374, 383, 385, 397, 404,
405, 408, 453, 460, 462, 469,
580, 587
Environment, 11, 13, 24, 26, 41, 42, 44,
64, 78, 80, 82, 85, 94, 102–104,
106, 112, 113, 115, 116, 139, 141,
151, 157, 173, 185, 187, 194, 199,
206, 221, 229, 266, 282, 293,
298–300, 306, 308, 309, 315–317,
336, 340, 366, 372, 374, 375, 378,
399–403, 409, 411, 412, 414, 415,
427, 451, 488–495, 498–500, 507,
511, 518, 534, 535, 562, 577, 585,
600, 606, 609

INDEX   625

Environmental communication, 307, 309–310, 318, 346, 491, 496, 537, 540, 549, 551
Environmental consciousness, 106–107, 114
Eradicating poverty, 31, 38, 56, 57, 384
Europe, 17, 24, 69, 77, 79, 85–87, 91, 142, 152, 216, 329, 340, 341, 381, 460, 490, 491, 497, 591, 614
European Commission, 8, 80, 83, 85–87, 91, 96, 216, 217
European Union (EU), 8, 10, 19, 24, 53, 78, 80, 83, 85–87, 92–94, 96, 361, 364, 491
Evaluation, 35, 40, 85, 107, 119, 165, 185, 193–208, 222–224, 299, 305, 384, 404, 406, 436, 441, 460–462, 464–475, 512

F
Fabrication, 330, 331
Fake news, 7, 9, 26, 225, 226, 325–341, 606, 608, 614, 615
Fake news Ghana, 26, 325–341
FAO, *see* Food and Agriculture Organisation
Fear appeals, 406, 454–456, 475
Filter, 134, 135, 215, 337, 510, 511, 526, 541
Five tracks, 166
Food and Agriculture Organisation (FAO), 26, 46, 58, 65, 80, 305, 306, 311, 312, 346–348, 349n3, 353, 354, 360, 363, 364, 395, 397, 569
Food security, 57, 79–82, 106, 121, 174, 311, 346, 347, 349, 351, 356, 357, 360–367, 393, 494, 562, 609
Food sovereignty, 26, 345–367, 609
Food systems, 318, 345–351, 353, 354, 356–359, 361, 365–367
Forests, 66, 67, 77, 81, 106, 115, 121, 277, 278, 413, 496, 499, 608
Framers of SDGs, 9, 56–60, 62–64, 66, 68
Frames, 27, 82, 133, 134, 260, 291, 345–367, 398, 402, 407, 415, 450, 455, 456, 462, 464, 471, 472, 474–477, 491, 508, 511–515, 518, 519, 521, 524, 525, 527, 535–540, 543, 545–551, 560, 566, 567, 569–573, 578, 579, 608, 609
Framework, 5, 9, 20, 21, 23, 34, 37, 40, 42, 44, 47, 55, 56, 60, 78, 84, 87, 91–95, 111, 112, 114, 139, 151, 157, 166, 172, 173, 175, 197, 205, 217, 235–254, 265, 284, 291, 294, 307, 308, 311, 346, 347, 349, 350, 361, 373–376, 394, 399, 441, 525, 537–540, 563, 592
Framing, 24, 26, 27, 133–135, 345–351, 355–359, 362, 364, 366, 367, 394, 476, 508, 510, 511, 513–516, 527, 535–542, 544, 546, 547, 549, 551, 560, 564–567, 573, 578, 579
Framing building, 27, 535, 549, 551
Framing climate change, 510, 536–540, 549, 551
Framing research, 539–542, 544
Free Lunch for Children (FLC), 373, 375, 378–381, 383–385
Funding, 34, 57, 61, 86–91, 149, 156, 185, 280, 283, 302, 354, 356, 376, 509, 534, 609–612
Fundraising, 374, 376, 379–381, 383, 413

G
Gaps and omissions, 32, 40–46
GCC, 152, 153
Gender, 15, 25, 32–35, 39, 56, 59–60, 87n1, 96, 151, 194, 228, 229, 235–254, 264, 266, 289–302, 311, 337–339, 347, 349, 595, 608, 616
Gender balance, 299–300
Gender equality, 151, 228, 229, 235–254, 290–292, 294–295, 297–301, 311, 347, 349, 608
Gender-sensitive, 60, 289–302
Germany, 4, 8, 18, 237, 375, 396, 450, 459, 465–469, 473, 475
GHG, *see* Greenhouse gas
Girl-child, 179
Global communication, 487–501
Global Education Monitoring Report, 59

Global goals, 23, 24, 53, 55–56, 59, 62–64, 68–70, 607–609, 612
Global health coverage, 449
Globalism, 141–142
Global media system, 487
Global north, 12, 16, 18, 19, 93, 172, 175, 350, 489, 497
Global Report, 216
Global south, 12, 16–19, 45, 79, 82, 172, 173, 175, 489, 491, 497
Global warming, 65, 131, 134, 135, 137, 307, 491, 492, 496, 497, 517, 534–539, 542, 543, 545–547, 549, 551, 607
Goal 4, 25, 171–189, 228, 378
Goals, 11, 12, 17, 23, 25, 26, 31–38, 42, 43, 45, 47, 53–56, 58, 60–65, 68–70, 82, 87n1, 91, 104, 110, 116, 118, 121, 132, 138, 150, 151, 171, 174, 176, 186, 189, 218, 228–230, 237, 239, 247, 249–251, 254, 260, 267, 269, 274, 280, 283, 285, 286, 292, 294, 297, 300, 309, 311, 312, 317, 318, 325, 326, 345, 350, 367, 378, 393, 398–402, 405, 406, 428–434, 436–441, 447, 449, 450, 453, 460, 473, 475, 501, 509, 549, 559, 560, 562–564, 566, 568–570, 576, 578, 579, 585, 595–597, 607–611, 615–617
Green criminology, 307–309
Greenhouse gas (GHG), 311, 314, 409, 499, 509, 517, 521, 525, 537, 546, 547, 549, 551, 607
The Guardian, 20, 106n1, 494–498, 546

H

Hazardous, 451
Health, 4, 31, 56, 58, 78, 132, 151, 176, 198, 218, 246, 262, 292, 307, 326, 351, 372, 394, 433, 449–477, 493, 514, 534, 562, 587, 606
Health campaigns, 26, 450, 452–454, 458, 474, 476
Health for all, 26, 449–477, 608, 616
Health theory, 450, 456–458, 464, 466, 471, 472
Hegemony, 176, 509–514

High-Level Political Forum (HLPF), 24, 58, 60
HIV/AIDS, 26, 113, 449–477
HLPF, *see* High-Level Political Forum
Human capital, 59, 158
Human rights, 33, 35, 43, 44, 47, 55, 82, 85, 130, 143, 188, 194, 217, 224, 227, 245, 247, 292, 360, 361, 374, 399, 451, 462, 590
Hunger, 33, 36, 38, 39, 46, 57, 58, 60, 64, 65, 141, 249, 272, 278, 281, 310, 311, 347, 348, 351, 360, 365, 366, 381, 384, 393–395, 397, 493, 507, 549, 591, 599, 609

I

Ideas, 8, 14, 21, 42, 63, 70, 78, 86–91, 108, 110, 112, 114, 115, 119, 127, 132, 133, 157, 194, 196, 197, 199, 202, 238, 242–245, 247, 254, 265, 271, 291, 294, 299, 307, 318, 333, 346, 359, 363, 383, 397–399, 401, 402, 406, 414, 433, 434, 437–440, 447, 487–490, 492, 496–498, 500, 501, 511, 512, 519, 589, 594, 612
Ideological polarization, 128, 133–136
Ideology, 24, 35, 40, 94, 128, 133, 136, 141, 142, 250, 271, 272, 294, 338, 346, 347, 364–366, 511–515, 524, 525
IFSI, *see* Islamic financial services industry
Illiteracy, 172, 175, 182, 188, 189, 216, 493, 589
ILO, *see* International Labour Organisation
IMF, 10, 46, 58
Impact of COVID-19, 9–12, 607, 610, 617
India, 3, 4, 12, 18, 25, 56, 69, 199, 236, 237, 259–264, 266, 267, 269, 271, 272, 274, 280–283, 289–302, 360, 497, 498, 514, 576, 608
Indigenous rights, 40, 43–44
Indonesia, 69, 150, 157, 160, 167, 372, 497, 498, 518
Industrialization, 63, 156, 249, 616

Inequality/inequalities, 32, 36, 38, 39, 47, 54–56, 59, 63–64, 81, 85, 87n1, 149, 151, 162–165, 206, 219, 220, 238–240, 245–247, 249–251, 253, 271, 290, 292, 293, 311, 382, 395, 416, 489, 495, 562, 611, 616

Infodemic, 7–9, 608, 614

Information, 4n1, 6, 8, 9, 15, 21, 36, 37, 42, 54, 59, 62, 63, 65, 69, 70, 78, 84–86, 91, 92, 94, 95, 105, 110–112, 115, 119, 120, 129, 131, 133–137, 140, 143, 178, 182, 200, 207, 218, 219, 221, 224–226, 228, 252, 260, 262–266, 291, 292, 295, 296, 301, 307, 310, 317, 325–334, 336–338, 374, 379, 380, 398, 400, 402–404, 408, 411, 428, 437, 438, 440, 443, 446, 447, 452–454, 456–458, 460, 467, 471–474, 510, 512, 516, 519, 524, 526, 538, 561, 563, 566, 573, 580, 586, 588–590, 592, 593, 596, 597, 599, 613, 615

Information dominance, 136–137

Information influencers, 108, 111–112, 121

Infrastructure, 23, 37, 47, 54, 58, 59, 62–63, 65, 68, 70, 87n1, 166, 175, 188, 227, 229, 267, 268, 271, 274, 283, 284, 311, 372n1, 373, 384, 395, 396, 534, 537, 578, 578n11

Innovation, 14, 43, 55, 62–63, 68, 77, 78, 91, 92, 142, 151, 159, 198, 261, 262, 311, 312, 359, 363, 371, 374, 383, 549, 587, 605, 613, 614

Instagram, 92, 138, 139, 329

Integrated Community-Based Adult Education (ICBAE), 181–182, 185, 187, 188

Integrated Model of Communication for Social Change (IMCFSC) model, 102, 109, 121

Integrity, 174, 176, 333, 440

Intercoder reliability, 519–520

Internal stimulus, 107–110

International climate, 509, 525

International Labour Organisation (ILO), 10, 32, 61, 571, 571n6

Internet, 4, 19, 62, 63, 181, 218, 220, 225, 227, 229, 263, 278, 327, 329, 336, 337, 341, 373–377, 379, 381–384, 492, 592, 596, 598, 613

Internet giants, 376, 377

Internet philanthropy, 26, 371–386

Interviews, 27, 137, 223, 225, 227, 300, 352–359, 365, 379, 430, 431n6, 431n7, 432, 438, 439, 519, 560, 565–568, 573–578, 592

Investigative journalism, 310

iSDGs, 260, 266, 270, 272, 280–285

Islamic banking, 152, 153, 160

Islamic finance, 24, 149–167, 608

Islamic financial services industry (IFSI), 24, 150–156, 160, 165

Islamic funds, 153

Islamic monetary policies, 157

Islamic social financial instruments, 150

J

Jakarta Post, 497, 498

Japan Times, 497, 498

Journalism, 26, 132, 133, 310, 318, 332, 333, 336, 340, 399, 437, 440, 489–491, 500, 510, 511, 514, 587, 588, 590–592, 600, 609, 612–613

Journalism theory, 593

Journalistic, 130, 132–134, 262, 301, 340, 591, 595, 597, 600

Journalistic practice, 24, 127, 128, 130–133, 577, 608

Journalists, 15, 17, 20, 27, 132–134, 140, 225, 227, 296, 337, 340, 379, 492, 495, 501, 510–512, 517, 526, 538, 550, 551, 560, 560n1, 563, 565–568, 572, 573, 575–580, 585–600, 609, 612, 613, 615

Jurisdictions, 152, 153, 157, 358, 443

K

Kyoto protocol, 509, 517, 520

L

Land, 44, 66–67, 70, 115, 151, 162, 278, 282, 305, 316, 348, 359, 362, 395–397, 403, 446, 498, 534, 607
Land degradation, 66, 67
Language framing, 26, 346–351, 355, 364, 366
Lao PDR, 24, 101–122
Latin America, 14, 17, 45, 46, 59, 69, 194, 519, 522, 524, 526, 562
La Vía Campesina, 348–351, 361–367
Learning approaches, 172, 175–178, 181
Le Devoir, 497, 499
Letters for life, 25, 217, 218, 220–228, 230
Life below water, 66, 77, 151
Life in Water, 81, 82
Lifelong learning, 24, 58–59, 171–189, 205, 206, 216, 224, 228
Life on Water, 569
LinkedIn, 15, 92
Literacy, 25, 77, 81, 127, 142, 178–181, 184, 186, 188, 207, 215–230, 266, 293, 334, 335, 340, 341, 402, 608, 613, 615
Local, 6, 7, 19–22, 25, 34, 44, 57, 69, 78, 81–83, 91, 92, 94–96, 101, 105–107, 106n1, 110, 115, 116, 118, 121, 122, 171, 175, 177, 178, 182–184, 186–188, 199–201, 206, 222, 225, 226, 229, 230, 235, 236, 243, 246, 251, 263, 282, 289, 294, 296, 300, 302, 313, 318, 357–359, 362, 363, 365–367, 386, 397, 399, 408, 410, 413, 428, 430, 431, 440, 441, 460, 487, 488, 534, 541, 561, 587–589
Location, 18, 92, 106, 162, 181, 242, 281, 329, 335, 352, 403, 404, 451, 551, 566, 567, 577, 606
Lockdown, 4, 10, 11, 16, 17, 54, 59
Low-income, 10, 69, 111, 157, 395

M

Malaria, 36, 58, 449, 451
Malikhao, P., 13, 14, 40, 41, 54, 70, 78, 79, 105, 172, 173, 177, 189, 312, 362, 398, 451, 474, 476, 561, 562
Manual strategies, 264–265
Maqasid, 150, 151
Maqasid al-sharīʿah, 154, 155
Maracana, 499, 500
Market competition, 18, 141, 550
Market economy, 141, 181, 273–274, 382, 427, 614
Measurement models, 157
Media, 4, 42, 54, 83, 112, 128, 172, 193, 215, 236, 262, 290, 308, 326, 373, 398, 428, 453, 508, 535, 559, 585, 606
Media and communications, 20, 63, 70, 224, 259, 374, 375, 613
Media logic, 24, 128, 130–133
Media messages, 127, 135, 430, 431, 436, 439
Media reactions, 492–496
Media regulation, 130, 142–143, 608
Media representation, 137–140
Media studies, 218, 227–228, 561, 564
Mediatization, 24, 128, 130–133, 449
Merkel, Angela, 60
MESA, *see* Middle East and South Asia
Methodology, 221, 222, 266, 334–335, 346, 352, 353, 400, 515, 516, 561, 592–595
Methods, 13, 107, 111, 113, 176, 185, 195–196, 266, 352–354, 399, 516–520, 539–541, 551, 565, 567, 592, 593
Micro-philanthropy, 26, 378–381, 384, 609
Middle East, 59, 446, 497, 519, 522, 526
Middle East and South Asia (MESA), 152, 153
Millennium Development Goals (MDGs), 4, 9, 12, 23, 31–39, 44, 45, 47, 55, 56, 62–64, 79, 166, 174, 238, 246–247, 249, 250, 259, 260, 262, 266, 267, 269, 270, 272, 274–280, 283–285, 326, 347, 559, 561–564, 570, 572, 585–587, 608, 615, 617
Miscommunication, 25, 130, 305–318
Misinformation, 5, 7–9, 21, 70, 129, 329, 332, 334, 336, 338, 340, 608, 614, 615

INDEX 629

The missing goal, 63, 69–70, 617
Missing ventilator, 23, 53–70
Mitigation, 157, 508, 525, 536
Mobile phones, 218, 329, 336, 380
Modernization, 13, 14, 82, 84, 101, 194, 244–246, 260, 262, 265, 268, 269, 365, 562, 587
Moral and ethical norms, 117–118, 121
Moy Park, 25, 306, 307, 313–317
MPI, *see* Multidimensional Poverty Index
Multidimensional Poverty Index (MPI), 57

N

National Health Service (NHS), 18, 19
National security, 385, 543, 547, 548
New capital, 280, 443
News agenda, 134, 575, 576
News frames, 27, 512, 560, 569, 578, 579
News framing, 511, 513, 514, 538, 566–567
Newspaper content, 27, 533–551, 566
Newspapers, 15, 27, 131, 188, 221, 225, 226, 335, 398, 400, 434n17, 442–444, 489, 490, 496–501, 513–515, 535, 536, 538–541, 543, 545, 547, 551, 560, 562–573, 575–580, 589
Newsworthiness, 132
New York Times, 18, 495–497, 541, 542
New Zealand, 60, 202
NGOs, *see* Non-governmental organisations
Nigeria, 19, 27, 138, 237, 340, 497, 498, 563–566, 569–572, 570n2, 571n8, 575–577, 579, 585–600, 609
Nigerian journalists, 27, 560, 568, 573, 575, 578–580, 586, 593, 594, 609
Nigerian media, 564
Nigerian press, 27, 559–580
Non-fear appeals, 454–456
Non-governmental organisations (NGOs), 6, 15, 21–23, 25, 34, 65, 80, 95, 133, 139, 178, 187, 198, 289, 290, 293, 348, 349, 360, 365, 373, 374, 378, 381, 383–385, 406, 411, 412, 495, 573, 587
Northern Ireland, 25, 305–318, 608

O

Olympic Games, 26, 487–501
Open and Distance Learning (ODL), 180, 181, 188
Organisation for Economic Co-operation and Development (OECD), 63, 87, 87n1, 183, 453, 615
Organisation of Islamic Cooperation (OIC), 150, 158
Orientation, 25, 193–208, 301, 428, 475, 538, 539, 576, 590
Our Common Future, 172, 488
Out-of-school children, 59, 61, 175, 178, 181, 182, 184, 570

P

Pandemic, 3–5, 7–12, 15–20, 23, 44, 46, 54, 55, 57–61, 64, 68, 156, 220, 226, 227, 230, 236, 237, 264, 605, 606
Paradigm, 14, 39, 79, 84, 92, 140, 194, 245, 246, 260, 262, 266, 269, 293, 313, 318, 357, 358, 361, 362, 365, 367, 402, 489, 587, 588, 591, 611
Paris Agreement, 372, 549
Parody, 330, 331
Participatory communication, 14, 24, 85, 96, 101–122, 172, 173, 175–178
Partners, 9, 204, 215–230, 236, 245, 295, 296, 299, 373, 430, 467, 472, 596, 598, 599
Partnerships, 46, 68–69, 91, 151, 183, 265, 378, 436, 441, 616
Peace, justice and strong institutions, 62, 151, 326, 616
Perception, 27, 40, 101, 104, 203, 225, 338, 355, 356, 410, 411, 439, 500, 510, 547, 579, 599, 600, 614
Philanthropy, 161, 371–386
Philosophical, 41, 173, 176, 186, 239
Philosophy, 113, 175, 176, 184, 188, 301, 312, 382
Photo manipulation, 331, 332

Pillars, 13, 16, 20, 21, 41, 85, 151, 166, 173, 526
Planning management, 297–298
Plastic consumption, 131
Policy makers, 9, 10, 20, 23, 24, 151, 271, 450, 613
Policy/policies, 8, 32, 60, 78, 115, 130, 149, 157, 171, 183–184, 194, 196–199, 215, 238, 262, 290, 308, 325, 345, 371–386, 396, 428, 450, 492, 508, 534, 559, 587, 611
Political, 8, 18, 24, 26, 27, 32, 36, 37, 40, 42, 43, 46, 55, 62, 65, 68, 83, 101, 103, 105, 106, 111, 115, 129, 135–137, 140–142, 151, 174, 179–183, 193, 199, 223–225, 236–240, 242–244, 248–252, 254, 259, 262, 269, 278, 283–285, 292, 293, 301, 302, 307, 312, 317, 328–331, 333, 336, 337, 341, 350, 351, 355, 357, 359, 363, 365, 372n1, 374, 375, 383, 385, 404, 408, 429, 431, 439, 489, 490, 493–497, 499, 508, 510, 511, 513–518, 525, 526, 533–539, 541, 542, 545, 550, 561, 565, 566, 576, 588–592, 598, 600, 610, 611, 614, 618
Political leadership, 431, 439, 515
Pollinator crisis, 397–398, 609
Pollinators, 394–398, 402, 403, 405, 407, 409, 411, 413, 414
Poor, 31, 33–36, 47, 56, 57, 63, 65–67, 70, 84, 150, 162–165, 175, 179, 183, 188, 218, 219, 237, 250, 264, 271, 272, 274, 278, 279, 282–284, 295, 374, 394, 404, 407, 491, 494, 560, 572, 578, 579, 586, 587, 589, 611
Portrayal, 298, 301, 456, 460, 510, 512
Portugal, 79, 197, 215–219, 224, 228, 230, 497
Poverty, vii, 17, 24, 25, 31, 33, 36–39, 42, 46, 54–57, 60, 61, 64, 65, 70, 79–83, 85, 87n1, 149–151, 160, 162–165, 167, 179, 180, 219, 237, 247, 249, 250, 264, 266, 270–272, 277–279, 281, 283, 286, 292, 294, 296, 301, 310, 311, 326, 327, 347, 361, 377–379, 384, 395, 400, 488, 492, 507, 549, 562, 569–571, 570n2, 570n3, 579, 589–591, 599, 607, 608, 610, 614, 616, 617
PPE, 45
Practices, 24, 26, 46, 65, 78, 81, 82, 85, 86, 91, 92, 94, 96, 106–121, 127, 128, 130–133, 172, 178–187, 189, 195, 196, 198, 201, 220, 221, 224, 248, 265, 266, 279, 289–302, 308, 311–315, 317, 337, 346, 350, 351, 353, 355–357, 359, 366, 371–386, 394, 396, 398, 405, 406, 410–412, 415, 447, 453, 534, 535, 537–540, 551, 577, 588
Primary sources, 151, 572–575
Private sector mechanism (PSM), 361
Privatization, 137, 266, 271, 272, 284
Problem frame, 560, 566, 569–571
Production, 26, 42, 64–65, 67, 82, 87n1, 138, 151, 154, 177, 198, 225, 245, 297, 298, 300, 305–318, 328, 350, 358, 361, 363, 394, 395, 397, 401, 409, 414, 427, 435, 510, 512
Progress, 4, 10, 25, 34, 36–38, 45, 47, 58, 60, 65, 68, 86, 129, 156, 198, 201, 224, 228, 230, 240, 244–247, 250, 280, 285, 290, 292, 301, 302, 360–363, 428, 449, 451, 507, 509, 559, 563, 567, 569, 571, 572, 588, 589, 599, 605, 607, 608, 611, 612, 615, 617
Projects, 24, 37, 40, 44, 78, 80, 85–86, 90–94, 96, 176, 177, 184, 187, 196, 202, 225, 262, 267, 274, 277, 283–285, 309, 313, 317, 373, 375, 377, 378, 383, 384, 433–437, 439, 441–444, 450, 561, 562, 572, 591, 595
Propaganda model, 508–511, 513, 515, 524–526

Public communication, 86, 455
Public health, 8, 15, 17, 45, 46, 58, 206, 226, 356, 514, 534, 606
Punch, 576, 578
Pushing the boundaries, 294–295

Q
Quality education, 608, 616

R
Radical shift, 37–39
Recommendations, 6, 23, 24, 27, 79, 140, 195, 196, 216, 226, 340–341, 367, 457, 476, 579–580, 608
Regional, 6, 7, 12, 22, 55, 83, 91, 94, 152, 202, 204, 221, 225, 226, 252, 264, 266, 277, 308, 357–360, 362, 429, 431, 435, 493, 516, 565, 577, 610, 617
Regulatory framework, 157, 166, 373–376, 592
Religions, 6, 24, 101, 151, 329, 336, 608
Reports, 7, 10, 12, 13, 15, 42, 45, 57–60, 62–64, 70, 79, 80, 83, 95, 164, 172, 173, 179, 219, 224, 226, 237, 247, 259n1, 270, 280, 283, 316, 326, 364, 373, 375, 376, 382, 429, 499, 507, 511, 518, 525, 534, 535, 546, 548, 562, 563, 566, 570–572, 579, 587, 589, 597, 598, 610–615, 618
Research questions, 515–516, 522, 536, 540, 541, 545
Resilience, 40, 44, 47, 110, 116, 151, 364, 537, 546
Responses, 6–9, 15, 18, 46, 47, 80, 83, 114, 135, 140, 155, 157, 172, 216, 224, 226, 229, 251, 335, 356, 357, 359, 396, 453, 457, 476, 477, 514, 534, 539, 545, 575–577, 579, 593, 594, 597
Responsibility frame, 560, 567, 569, 571–572, 579
Responsible consumption, 65, 608
Responsible consumption and production, 25, 64–65, 138, 151, 305–318
Rio 1992, 26, 487–501
Rio 2016, 26, 487–501
Risk, 5, 43, 66, 67, 78, 80, 81, 83, 132, 134, 135, 140–141, 153, 157, 179, 189, 196, 219, 225, 226, 230, 266, 334, 335, 383, 384, 400, 402, 406, 442, 452, 453, 457, 469–474, 516, 539, 549, 607
Risk management, 157
Russia, 4, 513, 519, 522

S
Sampling, 335, 352, 353, 540–541, 565, 567
Sangha, 101–108, 110–113, 116, 117, 119–122
Satire, 330, 331
Satu Data Initiative, 69
Scholar, 13–16, 54, 55, 61, 70, 81, 84, 85, 96, 151, 155, 156, 244, 261, 262, 269, 271, 284, 294, 295, 349, 350, 353, 361, 362, 374, 394, 399, 401, 411, 501, 508, 510–514, 516, 518, 525, 535, 539, 551, 562, 586, 588, 591
Science, 9, 68, 79, 91, 94, 104, 132, 134, 135, 137, 138, 140, 180, 183, 266, 398, 400–404, 488–490, 525, 542, 561, 593
SDS, *see* Sustainable development strategy
Security, 34, 57, 70, 77, 79–82, 106, 121, 174, 219, 222, 224–226, 279, 299, 326, 327, 346, 347, 349, 351, 356, 357, 360–367, 385, 393, 494, 547, 548, 562, 564, 596, 609
Servaes, J., 13–15, 23, 27, 34–36, 39–41, 44, 46, 54, 55, 70, 78, 79, 83, 85, 105, 156n4, 172, 173, 177, 189, 194, 195, 261, 262, 265, 269, 293, 309, 310, 312, 327, 328, 348, 357, 362, 365, 374, 398, 399, 451, 474, 488, 507, 559, 561, 562, 588, 611, 613

Sharī'ah, 150, 151, 155–157, 161
Sharm El-Sheikh, 427, 434
SIWAK, 162
Smart Cities, 281–283
Social change, 8, 12–15, 18, 20, 24, 40, 44, 54, 60, 78, 79, 82, 83, 85, 86, 91, 96, 102–107, 110, 112, 114–118, 120, 122, 138, 165–167, 172, 173, 176, 185, 187, 188, 194, 197, 198, 215, 230, 236, 238, 241, 242, 245–248, 250, 261, 262, 293, 294, 299, 301–302, 312, 316, 318, 328, 352, 367, 371, 374, 379, 398, 399, 438, 492, 501, 589, 590, 605, 606, 608, 609, 611, 613
Social change paradigm, 398–400
Social housing, 442
Social innovation, 78, 82, 83, 86, 92, 96
Social media, 8, 92, 131, 138, 139, 178, 200, 326, 327, 329, 331–334, 336–338, 340, 341, 373, 377–380, 399, 402, 407, 408, 415, 441, 476, 492, 539, 579, 580, 606, 613–615
Social mobilization, 384, 451
Society, 11–16, 23, 26, 33–35, 39–45, 47, 58–60, 65, 68, 70, 79, 81–83, 91, 95, 101–104, 112, 116–120, 128, 135, 138, 140, 151, 155, 157, 162, 173, 174, 176, 177, 180, 182, 185, 186, 188, 193, 194, 198, 200, 202, 207, 215–220, 222, 224, 227, 228, 230, 236, 240, 241, 243, 245, 248–250, 259, 260, 262, 268, 269, 277, 278, 291, 293, 295, 301, 306, 308, 310, 317, 325, 328, 329, 332, 345n1, 348, 349, 353, 357, 359–361, 366, 374, 382, 383, 394, 398, 399, 402, 404, 416, 427, 429–432, 435, 437–440, 446, 447, 456, 462, 487, 488, 492, 501, 511, 545, 560, 561, 567, 570, 576, 578, 579, 585, 587, 590, 595, 597, 599, 612, 613
Solution frame, 560, 567, 569–571, 579
South East Asia, 153
South Korea, 18, 514
Spanish Flu, 3, 4, 17
Stakeholder engagement, 13, 56, 328

Stakeholders, 13, 37, 46, 54, 56, 68, 78, 86–91, 96, 106, 114–116, 119, 150, 154–157, 166, 173, 177, 186, 193, 224, 247, 266, 291, 295, 306, 314, 315, 317, 328, 346, 348–350, 354, 360, 361, 363–365, 367, 373, 383, 394, 398, 402, 407, 427, 431, 449, 451, 474, 535, 539, 559, 563, 578, 595, 598, 611, 618
Strategic communication, 200, 206, 400–402, 408, 453, 591
Strategies, 4, 5, 7, 9, 15, 20, 23–26, 31, 32, 35, 41, 44–46, 69, 77–81, 84–87, 90, 92, 96, 121, 133, 136, 172, 173, 185, 188, 194, 195, 197–201, 204, 206, 207, 215, 222, 224, 244, 246, 253, 262–265, 296, 306, 309, 312, 313, 315, 318, 335, 348, 362, 366, 372n1, 375, 380, 402, 409, 412, 414, 416, 427–432, 434, 434n14, 435n17, 436–438, 440, 447, 452, 468, 493, 517, 525, 567, 586, 587, 590, 600, 608
Students, 9, 113, 139, 176, 179, 183, 184, 195–204, 207, 218, 220, 221, 224–228, 353, 519
Sub-Saharan Africa, 45, 58, 69, 152, 519, 522, 526, 585, 587, 595, 598
The Successes of MDGs, 23, 36–37, 56
Suez Canal, 445
Ṣukūk, 151–153
Summer Olympic, 487, 492, 496, 501
Sustainability, 12, 26, 36, 39–41, 43, 44, 80, 93–95, 106, 118, 128, 129, 131, 132, 139–143, 159, 171, 173–175, 185–188, 193, 195–207, 267, 283–286, 306–310, 312–315, 317, 318, 350, 351, 394, 398, 400, 405, 406, 408, 409, 411, 412, 414, 415
Sustainable Cities and communities, 64, 151
Sustainable development, 3–27, 32, 55, 77–96, 101–122, 127–143, 149, 171, 193–208, 215–230, 237, 292, 307, 325, 346, 371–386, 394, 428–431, 449, 487–501, 507, 560, 585, 608
Sustainable development conference, 200

Sustainable Development Goals (SDGs), 4, 9–12, 31–47, 53, 55–56, 77, 105, 129, 149–151, 160, 171–189, 193, 215, 237, 259–286, 291, 305, 325, 346, 371, 376–378, 393, 397–398, 433, 449–477, 494, 508, 559–580, 585, 605–618
   SDG1, 46, 56–58, 60, 61, 64, 150, 160, 162–167, 237, 311, 614, 616, 617
   SDG2, 57–58, 60, 61, 64, 237, 311, 346–351, 366, 393, 397, 571, 617
   SDG3, 10, 16, 26, 58, 60, 61, 237, 311, 608, 616, 617
   SDG4, 10, 24, 25, 58–61, 62n1, 105, 171, 172, 174–175, 178–184, 188, 189, 194, 206, 237, 311, 570, 614, 617
   SDG5, 25, 59–61, 237, 248, 250, 292, 311, 608, 617
   SDG6, 60–61, 311, 617
   SDG7, 61, 64, 311
   SDG8, 10, 58, 61–64, 105, 311, 616
   SDG9, 62–64, 311
   SDG10, 54, 63–64, 150, 160, 162–167, 311, 616
   SDG11, 58, 64, 393
   SDG12, 25, 64–65, 305–318
   SDG13, 58, 65–66, 237, 311
   SDG14, 66, 77, 81, 82, 378
   SDG16, 25, 26, 68, 291, 292, 325–341, 608
   SDG17, 55–56, 68–69, 83, 149, 171, 174, 175, 237, 249, 292, 310, 311, 326, 372, 384, 397, 416, 562, 568, 591, 596, 608, 611, 614–616
   SDG18, 23, 40, 43, 53–70, 607, 608, 617
Sustainable development strategy (SDS), 26, 427–447
Sustainable social change, 172, 188, 238, 242, 245, 248, 250
Sustainable society, 185, 200
Switzerland, 16, 237, 450, 459, 469–473, 475, 497

T
Taiwan, 60, 514
Takāful, 151–153
Tanzania, 24, 172, 177, 179–182, 185–189, 381
Target groups, 21, 87–92, 281, 458, 471, 474
Targets, 5–7, 11, 21, 23, 25, 31–40, 53–55, 57, 58, 61–65, 62n1, 70, 86, 90, 91, 94, 139, 151, 174, 175, 194, 195, 208, 216, 237, 239, 247–249, 259, 260, 265–267, 274, 277, 278, 280, 283–286, 291, 292, 306, 307, 310–312, 315, 318, 331, 333, 360, 372, 397, 409, 429, 430, 435, 436, 447, 449, 451, 453, 456, 458, 460, 464, 466–469, 471, 474–476, 491, 509, 560, 562–564, 567, 569–571, 578, 579, 585–587, 589, 591, 596, 608–610, 615, 617
Teachers, 176, 177, 185, 188, 189, 193–208, 218, 221, 277, 570
Technology, 4, 15, 17, 20, 31, 62, 68, 69, 94, 102, 104, 153, 155, 156, 159, 180, 219, 228, 248, 278, 291, 293, 298, 300, 311, 316, 317, 329, 331, 351, 359, 384, 385, 399, 400, 490, 549, 609, 613, 614
Text mining, 27, 533–551
Thailand, 24, 172, 177, 182–186, 188, 189, 499
Theory, 260, 261, 266, 269, 271, 326, 333, 450, 456–458, 495, 514, 537, 561, 562, 586, 588, 593
Tourism, 77, 78, 80, 81, 85, 92, 94, 96
Town Hall, 398
Tradition, 118, 121, 161, 176, 188, 227, 246, 266, 294, 372, 401
Trump, Donald (President), 8, 10, 17, 18, 66, 141, 331, 533–535, 537, 545–547, 549, 550, 606, 609
Truth, 47, 132, 315, 437, 462
Tsai Ing-Wen, 60
TV channels, 434, 435n17, 437, 439, 440
TV talk shows, 428, 437
Twitter, 15, 92, 263, 329, 332, 336, 375, 398, 400, 551
Types of fake news, 330–332

U

Uncertainty, 41, 43, 110, 114, 134, 135, 140–141, 152, 513, 539, 549, 605, 614
Uncritical pluralism, 141–142
UNECA, 36
UN Environmental Program (UNEP), 61, 80, 139
UN General Assembly, 12, 31, 33, 105, 141, 247, 372, 562
Unidirectional communication, 398
United Kingdom (UK), 18, 19, 198, 200, 237, 271, 306, 313, 349, 396, 494, 499, 515, 589, 606, 612
United Nations Development Programme (UNDP), 15, 32, 33, 55, 56, 60, 65, 80, 248, 292, 351, 372, 373, 449, 563, 612
United Nations Educational, Scientific and Cultural Organization (UNESCO), 42, 59, 143, 171, 174, 175, 183–185, 189, 193–195, 216, 218, 261, 291, 292, 298, 299, 329, 536, 586, 589, 592, 612
United Nations Framework Convention on Climate Change (UNFCCC), 509, 518, 521
United Nations International Children's Emergency Fund (UNICEF), 5, 7–9, 32, 56, 179, 181, 182, 189, 259, 608
United Nations (UN), 4, 8, 10, 13n2, 16–18, 23, 24, 26, 32, 34, 35, 38, 40, 45, 46, 53, 54, 56–58, 60, 62, 64, 68, 69, 77–81, 96, 129, 138, 139, 142, 150, 171, 174, 194, 196, 206, 215, 216, 227, 228, 244, 246–250, 270, 291–293, 310, 311, 326, 346–348, 349n3, 353, 354, 356, 360–362, 393–395, 416, 428, 449–451, 460, 462, 495, 514, 559, 560, 562, 563, 565, 566, 570, 576, 585, 586, 589, 592, 595, 607, 610–612, 614, 615, 617, 618
United States (US)/United States of America (USA), 4, 7–10, 15, 17, 18, 20, 24, 27, 37, 45, 57–59, 63, 65, 66, 79, 131, 133, 137, 141, 152, 201, 269, 272, 281, 309, 326, 328, 330, 331, 349, 350, 361, 364, 373–375, 377, 379–381, 396, 403, 404, 406, 409, 413, 490, 491, 494, 497, 508–511, 513–515, 517, 520, 521, 524–526, 561, 562, 587, 605, 606, 609–612, 617
University, 9, 54, 91, 194–208, 265, 283, 519, 561, 579, 608, 613
UN system, 249, 493, 562, 563

V

Vandemoortele, Jan, 32–35, 38, 39, 47
Vanguard, 27, 560, 564–572, 577–579
Venezuela, 45, 346, 349, 365, 497
Vision 2030, 26, 326, 427–447
Volunteer community, 103–107, 116, 117, 299
Vulnerabilities, 166, 219, 236, 334, 338–341, 457

W

Water, 36, 39, 57, 60–61, 66, 78, 81, 87, 92, 151, 179, 227, 277, 278, 282, 305, 307, 311, 314, 315, 357, 362, 409, 443, 499, 534, 546, 571, 572, 596, 616
Water and sanitation, 57, 60–61, 151, 451, 571, 616
WeChat, 377, 378, 380
Welfare state, 268–272
Western, 17, 18, 40, 41, 47, 59, 141, 142, 245, 261, 269, 284, 379, 385, 496, 517, 519, 522, 524, 588
Western nations, 513
WhatsApp, 226, 377, 567
Women empowerment, 60, 228, 238, 244, 246, 278, 293–295, 297
Women in communities, 293, 295–296
Workshops, 92, 217–223, 225–229, 291, 353, 401, 579, 580
World Bank, 4, 5, 7, 9, 15, 21, 32, 57, 62, 69, 80, 179, 188, 259, 278, 364, 607, 608, 615
World Economic Forum, 62, 64

World Education Forum (WEF), 62, 64, 175
World Health Organization (WHO), 5, 7–10, 15, 16, 21, 34, 58, 140, 236, 451, 452, 474, 477, 608, 615
World philanthropy forum, 372
World Social Report, 63

X
Xi Jinping (President), 382

Y
Yale researchers, 135
YouTube, 19, 92, 137, 263

Z
Zakat, 161–167, 608
Zero hunger, 57–58, 60, 64, 151, 237, 326, 345–367, 397, 569, 571, 579, 616
Zimbabwe, 45